PATTERNS
OF
EXPOSITION

PATTERNS

OF

EXPOSITION

16th Edition

Robert A. Schwegler
University of Rhode Island

Longman

New York   San Francisco   Boston
London   Toronto   Sydney   Tokyo   Singapore   Madrid
Mexico City   Munich   Paris   Capetown   Hong Kong   Montreal

Editor-in-Chief: Joseph Terry
Acquisitions Editor: Lynn M. Huddon
Marketing Manager: Carlise Paulson
Supplements Editor: Donna Campion
Production Manager: Denise Phillip
Project Coordination, Text Design, and Electronic Page Makeup: WestWords, Inc.
Cover Designer/Manager: Nancy Danahy
Cover Photo: © PhotoDisc, Inc.
Senior Manufacturing Buyer: Dennis J. Para
Printer and Binder: R. R. Donnelley and Sons
Cover Printer: Coral Graphics Services, Inc.

For permission to use copyrighted material, grateful acknowledgment is made to the copyright holders on pp. 691, which are hereby made part of this copyright page.

Library of Congress Cataloging-in-Publication Data

Patterns of exposition 16 / [edited by] Robert A. Schwegler.
    p. cm.
  Rev. ed. of: Decker's patterns of exposition 15. 1997.
  Includes bibliographical references and index.
  ISBN 0-321-07242-1
    1. College readers.   2. Exposition (Rhetoric)   3. English language—
  Rhetoric. I. Schwegler, Robert A.   II. Decker's patterns of exposition 15.
  PE1417 .P3954 2000
  808'.0427—dc21   00-026107

Please visit our website at http://www.awl.com/schwegler

ISBN 0–321–07242–1

1 2 3 4 5 6 7 8 9 10—DOH—03 02 01 00

Contents

1 Reading as a Writer / 1

Brent Staples, *Just Walk on By* / 6
A black man looks at some of the frightened and frightening ways people have reacted to his presence.

2 Ways of Writing / 21

3 Illustrating Ideas by Use of *Example* / 45

Student Essay: Adrian Boykin, *Overcoming an Impediment: A Rite of Passage* / 50

Andy Rooney, *In and of Ourselves We Trust* / 58
This columnist decides that stopping for red lights is part of a contract Americans have with each other—and we trust each other to honor the contract.

William F. Buckley, Jr., *Why Don't We Complain?* / 61
The dean of conservative writers believes that we've become so numb to mistakes and injustices that we no longer have the spunk to complain about anything and that this apathy could have grave consequences.

13 Using Patterns for *Argument* / 577

Thematic Contents

Politics and Leaders

Personality and Behavior

Nature and the Environment

Society and Social Change

Media

Essay Pairs

Among the selections in *Patterns of Exposition,* 16th Edition are a number of essay pairs whose similarities in topic or theme and contrasts in perspective or style offer interesting insights. These relationships show that the strategies a writer chooses can affect the way readers come to view the subject matter of an essay. The following list identifies some sets of essays that are particularly well suited for study and discussion; there are, of course, many other interesting and revealing ways of pairing the selections in the text.

A few of the pairs illustrate different ways of using the same pattern, such as example or definition. In other sets, the patterns offer contrasting strategies for expression or alternate ways of viewing a subject.

Andy Rooney, In and of Ourselves We Trust, 58
Peter Hillary, Everest Is Mighty, We Are Fragile, 345

William F. Buckley, Jr., Why Don't We Complain?, 61
Michael Ventura, Don't Even Think About It, 113

Mary Karr, Dysfunctional Nation, 69
Michael Dorris, Father's Day, 409

Alan Buczynski, Iron Bonding, 82
Brenda Peterson, Life Is a Musical, 134

Judith Stone, Personal Beast, 105
Alice Walker, Am I Blue?, 170

Henry Han Xi Lau, I Was a Member of the Kung Fu Crew, 78
Renee Tajima, Lotus Blossoms Don't Bleed: Images of Asian
    American Women, 125

Mark Twain, Two Ways of Seeing a River, 154
E.B. White, Once More to the Lake, 468

Bruce Catton, Grant and Lee: A Study in Contrasts, 158
Wayne Worcester, Arms and the Man, 524

To the Instructor

Instructors familiar with *Patterns of Exposition* will notice in this edition substantially expanded discussions of rhetorical patterns, student essay examples, extensively revised chapters on reading and writing, and many new ad interesting readings—but the same overall design, basic principles, and apparatus that have been so useful in preceding editions. Both new and previous users of the book will notice how the focus on patterns of exposition and argument and on essays illustrating these strategies have been supplemented and extended to demonstrate the ways rhetorical patterns enable writers and readers to explore, understand, and take a stand on questions of culture, identity, and value in college communities, in the workplace, and in society at large.

Chapter 1, "Reading as a Writer," introduces students to reading strategies especially useful for the essays in this text, for academic reading in general, and for turning reading into writing. Brent Staples's essay, "Just Walk on By," appears early in the chapter and introduces students to the kinds of readings they will encounter in the text and to ways they can use reading as a springboard to writing. The chapter pays particular attention to critical reading and reading for technique as well as reading for understanding. It introduces students to concrete reading strategies for use in composition courses, in other college courses, and beyond.

Chapter 2, "Ways of Writing," introduces students to the composing process and to a variety of useful techniques for discovering ideas and information, planning an essay, developing a thesis, drafting, and revising. The chapter also provides numerous student examples, including a student essay in draft and revised form. Our emphasis here and elsewhere in the text is on the practical: concrete writing strategies, specific suggestions, and concise illustrations.

As in previous editions, each chapter covering a pattern of exposition (or argument) begins with a discussion of the roles the particular pattern can play for writers and readers. In this edition, however, the discussions have been expanded to provide a definition of the pattern; a paragraph example taken from the work of an accomplished, professional writer; a discussion of the various uses of the pattern ("Why Use. . . ?"); suggestions for designing essays that employ the pattern ("Choosing a Strategy"); and techniques for developing the content of an essay as well as individual paragraphs and sentences ("Developing. . .").

The first few essay selections in each chapter illustrate some of the many roles a pattern can play in organizing thought and expression within an essay or the roles a pattern can play working with other rhetorical patterns to create an organized, purposeful, effective exposition (or argument).

Each chapter concludes with a cluster of essays focusing on "Issues and Ideas" of contemporary and (perhaps) enduring significance. The primary goal of these clusters is not simply to encourage students to think and write about the specific themes and issues, but to help students develop an awareness of rhetorical strategies as a critical tool for understanding differing perspectives and to demonstrate the variety of purposes a strategy can serve. It is precisely the broad similarity in subject matter and strategy among the essays in a cluster that serves to highlight for students the important differences and the varied models for expression the selections provide.

The questions at the end of each selection highlight important issues of meaning, technique, and style that help develop students' abilities as readers and the range of options available to them as they write. The "Read to Write" activities following the questions have been extensively revised for this new edition. The first activity in each set, labeled "Collaborating," offers students a chance to work with their classmates to develop ideas, essay plans, brief essays, and, occasionally, a collaboratively written essay. The second activity, labeled "Considering Audience," directs students' attention to readers' expectations and audience constraints. Some of the activities ask them to consider the likely reactions of readers to the essay presented in the text; other activities call for speculation about readers' reactions to different writing strategies. The third activity, "Developing an Essay," helps students view the sample essay in the text as a broad model for their own work—a model which they are encouraged to alter and develop in a fashion appropriate to their own perspectives and purposes. These activities provide practice, linking reading to writing—one of the primary focuses of the book as a whole. The "Writing Suggestions" at the end of each section have been expanded to include collaborative activities and offer further avenues for students to follow from reading into writing.

In choosing new essays and retaining those from previous editions, I have looked first for selections that are well-written and insightful and that reward careful (re-)reading and then for selections that can serve as useful models for thought, organization, and expression. I have also drawn on suggestions from the text's instructor-users and have reviewed the responses of students. Although obviously I am unable to comply with all requests, I have seriously considered and fully appreciated all of them, and I have incorporated many suggestions into this new edition. I have responded, as well, to requests for added essays in some of the most heavily used chapters of the book.

The wealth of excellent and recent nonfiction writing reflecting the perspective of many different cultural and social groups has made it possible for me to choose selections reflecting the intellectual ferment and challenge of our times. In drawing on this diversity, I have not tried to represent every identity in an unimaginative and rigid fashion but have instead tried to use it to create an exciting mixture of perspectives and backgrounds designed to encourage varied, engaged responses from students.

Because so many instructors find it useful, I continue to retain the table of contents listing pairs of essays. Each pair provides contrasts (or similarities) in theme, approach, and style that are worth study. The essay pairs can form the focus of class discussion or writing assignments.

The "Further Readings: Combining Patterns" chapter provides contemporary selections to provoke discussion. The pieces also suggest some intriguing combinations of patterns and goals for writing essays that can be pursued in the hands of skilled and daring writers. The essays in this section can be used on their own or with the other chapters of the book.

Throughout *Patterns of Exposition,* 16th Edition I have tried to make possible the convenient use of all materials in whatever ways instructors think best for their own classes. With a few exceptions, only complete essays or freestanding units of larger works have been included. With their inevitable overlap of patterns, they are more complicated than excerpts illustrating single principles, but they are also more realistic examples of exposition and more useful for other classroom purposes. Versatility has been an important criterion in choosing materials.

Forty-seven of the selections best liked in previous editions have been retained. Twenty-four selections are new, and all but a few of these are anthologized for the first time.

The arrangement of essays is but one of the many workable orders; instructors can easily develop another if they so desire. The

Thematic Contents and the table of Essay Pairs also suggest a variety of arrangements.

I have tried to vary the study questions—and undoubtedly have included far more than any one teacher will want—from the purely objective to those calling for some serious self-examination by students. (The Instructor's Manual supplements these materials.)

"A Guide to Terms," at the end of the book, briefly discusses matters from *Abstract* to *Unity* and refers whenever possible to the essays themselves for illustrations. Its location is designed to permit unity and easy access, but there are cross-references to it in the study questions following each selection.

In all respects—size, content, arrangement, format—I have tried to keep *Patterns of Exposition* uncluttered and easy to use.

ACKNOWLEDGMENTS

This edition of *Patterns of Exposition* is the first that has not had Randall Decker as coeditor. I wish to acknowledge his work on all the prior editions and to thank him very much for sharing this book with me over the years.

This edition of *Patterns of Exposition* is a truly collaborative effort, and I want to acknowledge and thank my collaborators: Nancy Newman Schwegler and Robin Schutt. I have benefitted immensely from their insights and efforts. Working with them has been a pleasure as well as a learning experience for me. In addition, Nancy Newman Schwegler has contributed to prior editions of the text, but I have not had a chance to acknowledge her contributions in a way they certainly deserve, and I would like to do so now.

I would also like to thank Brian and Tara Schwegler for their advice on current social developments and cultural trends; Christopher Schwegler for tolerating this all; and Ashley Marie Schwegler for putting up with two authors in the house and making our lives a lot sunnier. And I want to thank Nancy Newman Schwegler for her love and support.

In addition, special thanks are due to the many users of this text and to the reviewers for this revision:

- Dr. Mary McAleer Balkun (Seton Hall University)
- Dr. Billye Givens (Eastern Oklahoma State College)
- Richard Greenwood (Montgomery County Community College)
- Mary Hurst (Cuyahoga Community College)
- Steve Katz (State Technical Institute)

- William Kimbrel (East Georgia College)
- Michael Love (Community College Southern Nevada)
- Jeanne Mauzy (Valencia Community College-West)
- Dr. Nellie McCrory (Gaston College)
- Mary J. Milam (Central Christian College)
- Taryn Rice (Johnston Community College)
- Jesse Swan (Eastern New Mexico University)
- Mary Ann Tighe (Troy State University)
- Victor Uszerowicz (Miami Dade Community College)

Robert A. Schwegler

1

Reading as a Writer

Reading and writing work together. Good writers understand and rely on this relationship. They draw ideas and information from reading and use it to help understand an audience's likely reactions. They read critically to discover techniques of expression and as a springboard for their own writing. As a writer, you can read for all of these purposes—for understanding, for critical response, and for technique—or for only a few, depending on your needs and your purpose(s) for writing. This book, assumes that much of your time and thought will be devoted to two important purposes for writing, **exposition** and **argument.** The book provides the kind of reading experiences that will contribute to your development as a writer of expository and argumentative prose.

You encounter **expository writing** every day in one of its many forms, including essays, magazine articles, reports, memos, newspaper reports, and nonfiction books. Expository writing brings you facts and insights—it helps writers and readers share experiences and build understanding.

You also encounter **argumentative writing** in many places: editorials and opinion essays, reports and proposals, policy statements and investigative reporting, and academic or professional writing. Argumentative writing focuses on differences and helps build agreement; it provides reasons for readers to agree with writers or at least come to an understanding of another's perspective.

To develop your skills as a reader of expository and argumentative texts and to draw on your reading as you write, you need to pay attention to three ways of approaching a text—reading for understanding, critical reading, and reading for technique. First, however, you have some important work to do before you begin reading.

PREVIEWING

If your way of reading is to plunge right into the task and put the article, essay, or book aside quickly once you have finished, then you are missing important opportunities for understanding, interpreting, and responding critically. Effective readers (and writers) treat reading as a process consisting of **previewing, reading,** and **reviewing.** They have also developed techniques for each stage of the process.

You can develop your ability to read critically and actively by paying attention to each stage of the reading process and by employing strategies like those outlined in the following pages. You will find the strategies particularly helpful for the essays contained in this book and for other occasions when you are reading in order to write. After you have looked over the discussion of "Previewing Techniques" (below), you can apply them to Brent Staples's essay, "Just Walk on By" (pp. 6–9). Staples's essay will also give you a chance to practice reading and reviewing techniques.

PREVIEWING TECHNIQUES

People who are able to turn their reading into writing know how important it is to **preview,** or "read before you start reading." They also know where to look for help in accomplishing this task. Newspapers provide headlines to tell you what to expect in an article; authors create titles; book writers and editors often provide brief summaries at the beginning of a chapter or in a table of contents, just as we do at the beginning of this text; and magazine editors often take key statements from an article and reprint them in large type within boxes where you can see them as you flip through an article prior to reading it.

The knowledge and expectations you bring to a piece of writing can determine how well you understand it and what you are able to draw from it. For example, reading an expository or argumentative essay without an idea of where it is going or what the author plans to do is like following a complicated set of directions without any idea of what you are building or where you are going.

Likewise, when you already know something about a topic or issue, you can more readily understand and evaluate the complex information presented in an essay, or the author's arguments, or a specific point of view.

Previewing is the process of bringing to mind what you already know about a subject before you begin to move sentence by sentence through an essay, and of developing reasonable expectations about the directions that the explanation or argument will take. It can also involve learning something new about the subject, the author, or the kind of writing.

LOOK FOR HELP FROM THE WRITER OR EDITOR

Writers and editors recognize the importance of previewing, and they often provide you with considerable guidance. Titles are a good place to start. Some may be imaginative and intriguing and not particularly helpful. Others may tell you as much about a work's contents and organization as Don Aslett's *How Do I Clean the Moosehead? And 99 More Tough Questions about Housecleaning.*

Look at the table of contents in a book or collection of essays for detailed information about the contents and purpose of the work and perhaps even for a summary of chapters and selections. The table of contents for this book, for example, offers brief summaries of the essays it contains identifying the general topic and the writer's perspective. Here, for instance, is the entry for William F. Buckley, Jr.'s essay,"Why Don't We Complain?"

> The dean of conservative writers believes that we've become so numb to mistakes and injustices that we no longer have the spunk to complain about anything. And this apathy could have grave consequences.

Once you know that Buckley writes from the perspective of the political right, you can read his essay (pp. 61–66) with a greater appreciation of the origin and consequences of his ideas.

When an article or a book does not have a table of contents, skim through the text looking for headings and subheadings that reveal the writer's plan and the topics being covered. If the editor highlights important passages, pay attention to them. Here are three passages from Randall Rothenberg's essay "What Makes Sammy Walk?" (p. 332–342) that the editor of the magazine in which it first appeared chose to reprint in large type in the middle of a page.

> Less than 70 percent of U. S. men are now full-time year-round workers.
>
> "You don't have a social life," Dave's daughter says, "and you don't do anything."
>
> "I just put in a proposal to cut my hours to thirty-two a week and take a 20 percent pay cut," says a woman. "It's been accepted. I'm so happy."

These brief quotes help you begin reading with expectations about both the essay's subject and the author's attitude toward it.

LOOK FOR HELP FROM THE CONTEXT

Pay attention to the kind of magazine, journal, or newspaper in which an essay appears. Some have a reputation for publishing articles with a particular point of view. Look for any statements of the periodical's editorial outlook; pay attention to the magazine's title and to the titles of the other articles it contains. The dust jacket of a book often provides a brief summary of its contents and perspective or quotations from reviewers that highlight its main points.

The date when a work was published can help you interpret and evaluate its facts and ideas. Any information you can gather from the book jacket or a "Writer's Profile" page in a magazine can also prove helpful.

The headnotes to essays in this collection provide background information on the author and the selection that can help you in previewing. Here is one headnote from the text.

CULLEN MURPHY

CULLEN MURPHY grew up in Greenwich, Connecticut and attended school in both Greenwich and Dublin, Ireland. He received a B.A. from Amherst College in 1974 and soon after began working in the production department of *Change* magazine. In 1977, he was named editor of *The Wilson Quarterly,* and he has been managing editor of *The Atlantic Monthly* since 1985. In his parallel career, he has written the comic strip *Prince Valiant* since the middle 1970s (a comic strip which his father draws). Murphy is an essayist and non-fiction writer as well. His essays on different topics, many with a humorous or satirical view of contemporary society and behavior, have appeared in *The Atlantic Monthly* and other magazines, including *Harper's.* His first book, *Rubbish!* (with William Rathje), appeared in 1992, and a collection of his essays, *Just Curious,* was published in 1995.

A reader looking over this headnote might be prepared for an essay taking a critical and humorous look at contemporary habits or tastes and might expect writing that reflects the writer's wide range of interests. (Such expectations would be quite accurate, as the essay on pp. 308–311 demonstrates.)

Use some or all of these techniques to preview Brent Staples's essay, "Just Walk on By," below, on pp. 6–9.

READING FOR UNDERSTANDING

When you read for understanding, you pay attention to ideas and information, you try to identify the main idea (thesis) and the line of reasoning that supports it, and you explore meanings and values. To do these things, you should keep four questions in mind as you read.

- What is it about?
- What does it mean?
- What is its purpose?
- How is the main idea developed or supported?

As you read the following essay, think of these questions. When you are finished with the essay, write down a brief answer for each question as a way to think about what we do when we read for understanding.

BRENT STAPLES

Brent Staples was born in 1951 in Chester, Pennsylvania. He received his B.A. in 1973 from Widener University and his Ph.D. (in psychology) in 1982 from the University of Chicago. He is a member of *The New York Times* editorial board, writing on matters of culture and society. He was formerly a reporter for *The Chicago Sun Times* and an editor of *The New York Times Book Review*. Staples is the author of *Parallel Time* (1994), a memoir.

Just Walk on By

The power of examples to enable a reader to see through someone else's eyes is evident in this selection. Though many of the examples in the essay draw on a reader's sympathy, their main purpose appears to be explanatory; hence, the author accompanies them with detailed discussions. The result is a piece that is both enlightening and moving.

My first victim was a woman—white, well dressed, probably in her early twenties. I came upon her late one evening on a deserted street in Hyde Park, a relatively affluent neighborhood in an otherwise mean, impoverished section of Chicago. As I swung onto the avenue behind her, there seemed to be a discreet, uninflammatory distance between us. Not so. She cast back a worried glance. To her, the youngish black man—a broad six feet two inches with a beard and billowing hair, both hands shoved into the pockets of a bulky military jacket—seemed menacingly close. After a few more quick glimpses, she picked up her pace and was soon running in earnest. Within seconds she disappeared into a cross street. 1

That was more than a decade ago. I was 22 years old, a graduate student newly arrived at the University of Chicago. It was in the echo of that terrified woman's footfalls that I first began to know the unwieldy inheritance I'd come into—the ability to alter public space in ugly ways. It was clear that she thought herself the quarry of a mugger, a rapist, or worse. Suffering a bout of insomnia, however, I was stalking sleep, not defenseless wayfarers. As a softy who is scarcely able to take a knife to a raw chicken—let alone hold it to a person's throat—I was surprised, embarrassed, and dismayed all at once. Her flight made me feel like an accomplice in tyranny. It also made it clear that I was indistinguishable from the muggers who occasionally seeped into the area from the surrounding ghetto. That 2 first encounter, and those that followed, signified that a vast, un-nerving gulf lay between nighttime pedestrians—particularly women—and me. And I soon gathered that being perceived as dangerous is a hazard in itself. I only needed to turn a corner into a dicey situation, or crowd some frightened, armed person in a foyer somewhere, or make an errant move after being pulled over by a policeman. Where fear and weapons meet—and they often do in urban America—there is always the possibility of death.

In the first year, my first away from my hometown, I was to become thoroughly familiar with the language of fear. At dark, shadowy intersections in Chicago, I could cross in front of a car stopped at a traffic light and elicit the *thunk, thunk, thunk, thunk* of the driver—black, white, male, or female—hammering down the door locks. On less traveled streets after dark, I grew accustomed to but never comfortable with people who crossed to the other side of the street rather than pass me. Then there were the standard unpleasantries with police, doormen, bouncers, cab drivers, and others whose business it is to screen out troublesome individuals *before* there is any nastiness.

I moved to New York nearly two years ago and I have remained an avid night walker. In central Manhattan, the near-constant crowd cover minimized tense one-on-one street encounters. Elsewhere—visiting friends in SoHo, where sidewalks are narrow and tightly spaced buildings shut out the sky—things can get very taut indeed.

Black men have a firm place in New York mugging literature. Norman Podhoretz in his famed (or infamous) 1963 essay, "My Negro Problem—And Ours," recalls growing up in terror of black males; they "were tougher than we were, more ruthless," he writes—and as an adult on the Upper West Side of Manhattan, he continues, he cannot constrain his nervousness when he meets black men on certain streets. Similarly, a decade later, the essayist and novelist Edward Hoagland extols a New York where once "Negro bitterness bore down mainly on other Negroes." Where some see mere panhandlers, Hoagland sees "a mugger who is clearly screwing up his nerve to do more than just *ask* for money." But Hoagland has "the New Yorker's quick-hunch posture for broken-field maneuvering," and the bad guy swerves away.

I often witness that "hunch posture," from women after dark on the warrenlike streets of Brooklyn where I live. They seem to set their faces on neutral and, with their purse straps strung across their chests bandolier style, they forge ahead as though bracing themselves against being tackled. I understand, of course, that the danger they perceive is not a hallucination. Women are particularly vulnerable to street violence, and young black males are drastically over-represented among the perpetrators of that violence. Yet these truths are no solace against the kind of alienation that comes of being ever the suspect, against being set apart, a fearsome entity with whom pedestrians avoid making eye contact.

It is not altogether clear to me how I reached the ripe old age of 22   7
without being conscious of the lethality nighttime pedestrians attributed to me. Perhaps it was because in Chester, Pennsylvania, the small, angry industrial town where I came of age in the 1960s, I was scarcely noticeable against a backdrop of gang warfare, street knifings, and murders. I grew up one of the good boys, had perhaps a half-dozen fist fights. In retrospect, my shyness of combat has clear sources.

Many things go into the making of a young thug. One of those   8
things is the consummation of the male romance with the power to intimidate. An infant discovers that random flailings send the baby bottle flying out of the crib and crashing to the floor. Delighted, the joyful babe repeats those motions again and again, seeking to duplicate the feat. Just so, I recall the points at which some of my boyhood friends were finally seduced by the perception of themselves as tough guys. When a mark cowered and surrendered his money without resistance, myth and reality merged—and paid off. It is, after all, only manly to embrace the power to frighten and intimidate. We, as men, are not supposed to give an inch of our lane on the highway; we are to seize the fighter's edge in work and in play and even in love; we are to be valiant in the face of hostile forces.

Unfortunately, poor and powerless young men seem to take all   9
this nonsense literally. As a boy, I saw countless tough guys locked away; I have since buried several. They were babies, really—a teenage cousin, a brother of 22, a childhood friend in his mid-twenties—all gone down in episodes of bravado played out in the streets. I came to doubt the virtues of intimidation early on. I chose, perhaps even unconsciously, to remain a shadow—timid, but a survivor.

The fearsomeness mistakenly attributed to me in public places   10
often has a perilous flavor. The most frightening of these confusions occurred in the late 1970s and early 1980s when I worked as a journalist in Chicago. One day, rushing into the office of a magazine I was writing for, with a deadline story in hand, I was mistaken for a burglar. The office manager called security and, with an ad hoc posse, pursued me through the labyrinthine halls, nearly to my editor's door. I had no way of proving who I was. I could only move briskly toward the company of someone who knew me.

Another time I was on assignment for a local paper and killing   11
time before an interview. I entered a jewelry store on the city's affluent

Near North Side. The proprietor excused herself and returned with an enormous red Doberman pinscher straining at the end of a leash. She stood, the dog extended toward me, silent to my questions, her eyes bulging nearly out of her head. I took a cursory look around, nodded, and bade her good night. Relatively speaking, however, I never fared as badly as another black male journalist. He went to nearby Waukegan, Illinois, a couple of summers ago to work on a story about a murderer who was born there. Mistaking the reporter for the killer, police hauled him from his car at gunpoint and but for his press credentials would probably have tried to book him. Such episodes are not uncommon. Black men trade tales like this all the time.

In "My Negro Problem—And Ours," Podhoretz writes that the hatred he feels for blacks makes itself known to him through a variety of avenues—one being his discomfort with that "special brand of paranoid touchiness" to which he says blacks are prone. No doubt he is speaking here of black men. In time, I learned to smother the rage I felt at so often being taken for a criminal. Not to do so would surely have led to madness—via that special "paranoid touchiness" that so annoyed Podhoretz at the time he wrote the essay.   12

I began to take precautions to make myself less threatening. I move about with care, particularly late in the evening. I give a wide berth to nervous people on subway platforms during the wee hours, particularly when I have exchanged business clothes for jeans. If I happen to be entering a building behind some people who appear skittish, I may walk by, letting them clear the lobby before I return, so as not to seem to be following them. I have been calm and extremely congenial on those rare occasions when I've been pulled over by the police.   13

And on late-evening constitutionals along streets less traveled by, I employ what has proved to be an excellent tension-reducing measure: I whistle melodies from Beethoven and Vivaldi and the more popular classical composers. Even steely New Yorkers hunching toward nighttime destinations seem to relax, and occasionally they even join in the tune. Virtually everybody seems to sense that a mugger wouldn't be warbling bright, sunny selections from Vivaldi's *Four Seasons*. It is my equivalent of the cowbell that hikers wear when they know they are in bear country.   14

WHAT IS IT ABOUT?

Some essays focus on one topic throughout. Other essays, equally good and effective, discuss several related topics, such as the effect of television on attitudes toward violence as well as its consequences for family life. Brent Staples's essay, "Just Walk on By," presents a variety of examples and brief incidents, but they are all illustrations of how people reacted to the author's presence. As a reader, you need to be able to identify the topic or related topics around which an essay is constructed and avoid the temptation to pay attention only to ideas and information that interest you and thereby risk mis-understanding the real focus of an essay.

To make sure you understand the primary topic or focus of an essay, use one or more of these strategies when you pause during reading or when you take a few minutes for review after you have finished reading.

Look for Cues

Writers frequently use a title, headings in the text, or direct state-ments as cues identifying an essay's topic or focus.

> **Title:** "Women, Men, and the Media"
> **Heading:** "Stereotypical Portrayals of Men and Women"
> **Direct Statements:** "But in what ways are our behaviors, espe-cially those of children, shaped by the inaccurate and over-simplified portraits of men and women that populate the mass media?"

Make a List of Topics

Review what you have read and make a list of the topics or impor-tant ideas discussed in the essay. If the elements in your list fit clearly within a broader topic, state it; or if they do not, try stating their relationship in a way that identifies the essay's focus.

> local restaurants replaced by fast food
> small shops replaced by malls
> family farms turn into agribusinesses
> hardware stores replaced by home building centers
> small towns replaced by sprawling suburbs
> **Overall Topic:** change from small,individualized social organi-zations to large, more impersonal ones.

Look for Repetition

Identify words, ideas, or subjects that appear repeatedly in the text. Such repetitions provide evidence of an essay's focus and may even be intentional signals provided by the writer. In "Just Walk on By," for example, Brent Staples uses words like "softy," "embarrassed," and "frightening" to refer to himself, his feelings, and his reaction to the incidents he describes. He uses a contrasting set of words like "fearsomeness," "dangerous," and "terror" to describe people's (mistaken) reactions to him and to other young black men like him.

WHAT DOES IT MEAN?

Expository writing offers conclusions and insights. Argumentative writing offers opinions or proposes a course of action. Much of the value of these kinds of writing lies in the insights, ideas, and opinions conveyed: What the writing means. Sometimes direct statements announce the meaning(s) of an essay, as when Brent Staples in "Just Walk on By" says that "The fearsomeness mistakenly attributed to me in public places often has a perilous flavor." Often, however, conclusions are presented less directly or even implied, requiring you to provide an answer to the question, "What does it mean?" Good writing generally offers more than one insight or conclusion, typically a main point and several related points. Identifying the main point is an important step for any reader trying to understand an essay.

*Mis*understanding is always possible, however. Some of an essay's conclusions may be relatively difficult to understand; some may be implied rather than stated directly; some may seem very important to you because you find them particularly interesting, even though their role in the essay may not be that significant. The following strategies can help you identify and interpret the key conclusions or opinions in an essay.

Highlight Direct Statements

While you read or when you have finished reading an essay, try highlighting, underlining, or otherwise making note of conclusions, generalizations, or opinions stated directly to readers. This can include statements (or re-statements) of an essay's main idea or *thesis* like the following:

> "Taboos, big or small, are always about having to respect somebody's (often irrational) boundary—or else."
>
> —Michael Ventura, "Don't Even Think About it" (p.113)

> "I am a peace-loving woman. But several events in the past 10 years have convinced me I'm safer when I carry a pistol."
>
> —Linda Hasselstrom, "A Peaceful Woman Explains
> Why She Carries a Pistol" (p. 314)

It can also include headings in the text, topic sentences in paragraphs, or other statements that receive special emphasis.

For many essays, a list of such statements would provide a rough but revealing outline of the writer's exploration of a subject or of the chain of argument supporting a thesis. Here is the list Shauna Benoit compiled from her reading of Cullen Murphy's essay, "Hello, Darkness" (pp. 308–311). Note how the list clarifies the way the writer has arranged the essay.

> "... the average American a hundred years ago was able to sleep 20 percent longer than the average American today."
> "Other evidence seems to indicate that the rate of sleep loss is in fact accelerating."
> "... we are laboring under a large and increasingly burdensome 'sleep deficit' ...."
> "Many commentators would blame it on what might be called the AWOL factor—that is, the American Way of Life. We are by nature a busy and ambitious people whom tectonic social forces ... have turned into a race of laboratory rats on a treadmill going nowhere ever faster."
> "Yet electricity's ubiquitous and seemingly most innocuous use—to power the common light bulb—could not help exacting a price in sleep."
> "Whatever it is that we wish or are made to do—pursue leisure, earn a living—there are simply far more usable hours now in which to do it."

Look For Repetition And Emphasis

Look for words, phrases, details, and ideas that the writer repeats throughout a text. They are cues to ideas or issues that receive special emphasis within the text—even if not all the repetition was consciously intended by the writer. Such repetitions can help you interpret the meanings and values around which an essay has been constructed and can also act as evidence for your conclusions about the essay.

Pause And Summarize

As you read an essay you will likely pause at a number of "resting places," between sections or paragraphs, for example. When you pause, take a moment to summarize what the essay has already said and to predict what it will say next. Glance back over the essay for evidence to support your interpretation, then read ahead to test the accuracy of your predictions as well as your understanding of the essay's meanings and values.

WHAT IS ITS PURPOSE?

Expository and argumentative writing each have general purposes: expository—to explain and explore; argumentative—to convince and persuade. To understand an individual essay, you need to recognize its more specific purpose(s), however. By taking purpose into account as you read, you can more easily grasp an essay's meaning and evaluate its likely effect on readers. Sometimes, writers state their purpose directly; at other times, you will need to pay attention to repeated phrases and ideas in a text to understand its purpose. Remember, too, that essays often have secondary purposes as well as primary ones.

HOW IS THE MAIN IDEA DEVELOPED OR SUPPORTED?

Once you have identified the main idea (thesis) and related ideas in an essay, you can pay attention to the distinction between them and the examples, information, and discussions that develop or support them. To do so, try keeping two questions in mind as you read: How is the main idea developed or supported? How adequate is the development/support?

Writers will often make your job easier by using familiar words or phrases to signal supporting details, discussions, or examples. Here are a few of the most familiar.

for example	supports	in the case of
for instance	explains	sheds light on
contribute to	because	illustrates
justifies	as a consequence	explains

In "Just Walk on By," for example, Brent Staples uses phrases like "In my first year," "that was more than a decade ago," "I often witness," and "Another time," to emphasize that the examples he presents show an enduring pattern of mistaken reactions to him—simply because of his age and race.

READING CRITICALLY

You read critically when you question and challenge a text. Critical reading treats a text simply as a starting point. Its aim is to help you develop your own ideas and conclusions or to evaluate the ideas and information you encounter in a text, often with an eye toward drawing on this material for your own work. In short, critical reading is closely related to writing. Developing a habit of critical reading is an important part of developing your ability as a writer.

Critical reading is, above all, active reading. This means it involves some activity on your part—jotting down ideas and responses, evaluating the conclusions and information in a text, speculating about the consequences of a concept, or making notes for an essay of your own, to mention just a few possibilities. At times, of course, you may wish to read simply to gather ideas and information, not to interact. But even when you do, critical reading habits can come to your aid by prompting you to consider just how reliable a text's information is.

RESPONDING AS YOU READ

Critical, active reading takes place with a pen, pencil, or keyboard close by—or sometimes with an exceptionally sharp memory. You can use reading journals, marginal notes, and question sets to help you read and respond with critical attention.

A **reading journal** is a notebook, folder, or computer file in which you keep your responses to reading: notes, questions, ideas, criticisms, and the like. Turning the fleeting ideas, questions, and responses that occur to you as you read into sentences in a journal helps you remember them, gives you a chance to consider them at greater length, and makes them available for later use, perhaps in an essay of your own.

You can organize entries in a reading journal according to the particular selection, allotting a few pages to each article, chapter, or book, for example. Or you can organize the journal by categories, such as "Responses (and Objections) to Readings about New Roles for Men and Women" or "Quotations and Information for Use in My 'Dangers of Dieting' Paper."

The organization you choose and the notes you make should reflect your purposes as a reader and writer. Are you looking for topics and issues to address in your own writing? Make notes about interesting or controversial topics you encounter in reading, particularly those about which you have strong feelings or a distinct point of view or those which the author treats superficially, leaving you an opportunity to provide a detailed treatment of your own. Are you looking for conclusions or perspectives that differ from yours? Summarize or quote any that you encounter and explore them in writing along with your own point of view so you can discover ways to incorporate both in an essay of your own.

Marginal Notes

Marginal notes are the scribbles, jottings, abbreviations, and other annotations you make in the margins of a book or magazine. Typically, you make such annotations when something you read prompts a strong response that you can record in brief form. You may wish to use marginal notes to record agreements or disagreements with what the writer says, to highlight passages or techniques you admire, or to note important ideas and information.

Your marginal notes are most likely to be of use to you when they indicate ways to turn the text or your response to it into material for your own writing, as with the following.

> No! Putting attractive people in an ad is not necessarily a way of using sex to sell.
> People can be attractive without being sexy, for example.
> And the people belong in the ad because they show how the product works. (They wear safety goggles, for example.)
> Would it be better to have ugly people? Or just plain looking people? I bet audiences would be critical of that approach, too.

To make your marginal annotations as useful as possible, try to give some variety to your responses. Consider making comments like these.

> Interpretations of what the author is trying to say
> Questions you wish the author had answered
> Objections to the author's conclusions
> Counter arguments the writer fails to mention
> Notes on passages you find confusing
> Evaluations of the writer's conclusions or techniques of expression

Evaluating

Evaluating the trustworthiness of a source and identifying its strengths and limitations are important parts of critical reading. Their aims are to identify opportunities (topics, issues) for your own writing and to help judge the reliability of concepts and information you may wish to draw on as you write.

Opportunities for Writing

To identify opportunities for your own writing, respond to your reading with questions like the following.

1. What topics or issues does the writer address satisfactorily and completely? What questions are left unanswered, problems left unsolved, or issues left unresolved?

2. Does the writer present a balanced perspective in offering conclusions or are important explanations and points of view left unconsidered?

3. Does the writer reason fairly and provide adequate support for conclusions? Or is the writing clearly biased, omitting evidence or misrepresenting facts and distorting other's positions?

4. Are there other kinds of information and experiences or different ideas and approaches that might lead to conclusions differing from those offered by the writer?

Evaluating a Source's Reliability and Usefulness

To help evaluate the reliability and usefulness of a source of concepts and information, respond to your reading with questions like these.

1. What conclusions or generalizations does the source offer? Are they supported adequately or do they go beyond the facts presented in the text? Are they consistent with your knowledge of the topic?

2. Consider the reputation of the author, of the publisher, or the publication in which the text appeared. Is the reputation one of thoroughness and balance or of bias and carelessness? How does this piece of writing compare with others on the topic?

3. Are there any obvious errors? Which parts of the discussion are detailed and well documented?

4. Does the text acknowledge and document its own sources? Does it appear to treat others' opinions fairly, presenting them in clear summaries or through quotations?

Evaluating Electronic Sources

Electronic sources such as web pages and listservs or discussion groups pose some special problems. While they can be rich and provocative sources of ideas and details, electronic sites are often produced by individuals or organizations whose trustworthiness or bias are difficult to determine—unlike those for sources in scholarly journals, well-known magazines, or books from reputable publishers. Use these questions to help you evaluate electronic sources.

1. Who is responsible for the site? Are there any obvious signs of bias or distortion, such as highly selective information or exaggerated language and points of view? In what ways does the site serve the interests of the person or organization that produced it, and how might this affect its reliability?

2. Are sources for information indicated clearly, or are details, examples, and ideas presented without attribution or documentation? Is information presented clearly and carefully? Are ideas and opinions explained thoroughly? Are alternate points of view acknowledged and discussed?

Reading for Technique

When you read for technique, you look for writing strategies you can adapt for your own work: patterns of organization, ways to explore ideas and present supporting details, and ways to use words and sentences. The questions following each selection in this text draw your attention to technique, especially those following the headings "Expository (or Argumentative) Techniques" and "Diction and Vocabulary." By working with these questions, you can develop your ability to analyze the techniques writers employ. Here are two other ways to read for technique.

Pay Attention to Patterns

Writers make use of expository and argumentative patterns in a variety of ways, for whole essays or parts, alone or in combination. The introductions to chapters 3–13 in this book discuss the patterns and their uses. The following questions can also help you identify patterns and the roles they play in an essay.

Questions	Pattern
Does the essay use examples and illustrations to illustrate a generality? Does the writer use examples to help readers understand the topic and his/her conclusions? Does the essay use examples to illustrate and support a thesis?	Example (Chapter 3)

Does the essay present ideas or information in categories? Are the categories arranged to explain or support the writer's conclusions?	Classification (Chapter 4)
Does the essay discuss differences or similarities among concepts, activities, outlooks, situations, or subjects? Are contrasts or similarities used to make a point or support a thesis?	Comparison and Contrast (Chapter 5)
Does the essay highlight surprising similarities between one subject and another, seemingly very different subjects? Does it use the similarities to illustrate or explain issues, processes, objects, or concepts?	Analogy (Chapter 6)
Does the essay explain how something works or how it can be done? Does it use the explanation to support conclusions or a thesis?	Process Analysis (Chapter 7)
Does the essay tell why something happened and what is likely to happen in the future? Is the discussion of causes and effects organized to explain or to support the author's opinion?	Cause and Effect (Chapter 8)
Does the writer offer an extended definition or a number of definitions? Are they arranged to support or lead up to the writer's conclusions? Does the writer use definitions to present an issue and develop reasons for agreeing with his/her opinion?	Definition (Chapter 9)
Does the essay discuss the features (physical, emotional, etc.) of the subject? Is this discussion arranged to support the essay's conclusions or to develop support for the writer's stand on an issue?	Description (Chapter 10)
Does the essay explain what happened? To whom? When? Where? Is the story	Narration (Chapter 11)

arranged to make a point or provide an
explanation? To support an opinion?

Does the writer reason from facts or   Induction and Deduction
events to arrive at a generalization or   (Chapter 12)
move from a generalization to interpret
facts and events?

Does the writer offer an opinion (an   Argument (Chapter 13)
argumentative thesis or proposition)?
Does the writer provide evidence to
support the opinion and persuade
readers to agree with it?

Turn to "A Guide to Terms"

"A Guide to Terms" at the end of this book contains entries for important writing techniques, from subjects such as essay "Introductions" and "Closings" to creating "Emphasis" and choice of words
("Diction") or sentence structure ("Syntax"). Before reading a selection in this book or elsewhere, turn to the "Guide," choose an entry
that interests you, and then read with attention to the technique described in the entry.

REVIEWING

The questions you ask while reading, your pauses to summarize
and understand, your marginal notes and journal entries, your evaluations and responses—all these should come to mind when you
have finished reading an essay and begin to review it. You may find
the following framework helpful for review: Meanings and Values,
Expository (or Argumentative) Techniques, Diction and Vocabulary,
and Reading to Write. Questions and activities to lead you through
these areas of review follow the selections in the text.

When you focus on meanings and values, you look back at the
different topics covered in a text and the writer's conclusions about
them. You ask if the topics are linked by a focus on a primary concern and if the various conclusions or interpretations are unified by
a single perspective or thesis. You also consider the values and value
judgments advanced in the essay.

When you focus on expository or argumentative techniques,
you pay attention to overall patterns of organization and development (see pp. 17–19), to opening and closing strategies, to paragraph

and sentence techniques, to the use of detail and kinds of support—
in short, to the many different strategies a writer employs, except for
those dealing primarily with words and groups of words.

In focusing on diction and vocabulary, you look at the words an
author has chosen, the patterns of word choice (or diction), the way
the diction supports the writer's purposes, and any words you need
to look up in order to understand the text.

Finally, when you focus on reading to write, you look at the
ways you can use the essay as a springboard for collaborating with
other writers, for considering possible audiences, and for developing an essay of your own.

2

Ways of Writing

Confident writers know they need to do more than string loosely related ideas and information together in order to create a worthwhile and effective essay or report. Their confidence comes in part from their understanding of the importance of each of the stages of the composing process: discovering, drafting, revising, and editing and proofreading. They also know there is no single formula for all writing tasks, so they try to develop a variety of techniques, remaining flexible enough as they write to try several strategies until they find an appropriate one. Making choices among strategies for these writers means paying attention to the needs of their potential readers and the demands of their particular writing task, as well as their subject matter and their purposes for writing.

Viewed from a distance, as they apply to writing in general, the stages of the writing process look regular and orderly: discovering, planning, drafting, revising, proofreading and editing. Viewed from close up, however, as part of an actual writing task, the lines between these activities often blur: Writers often discover worthwhile new ideas as they draft and revise or amend an essay's plan in response to further insight or reader's responses. In your own writing, therefore, you need to maintain an awareness of the stages of the writing process and of the importance of activities like planning and revising while remaining flexible in responding to the demands of a particular writing task, the needs of your audience, and your purposes for writing.

GETTING STARTED

Most writing begins with an assignment or invitation: an essay for a college course, a report at work, or a call for submissions to a local newspaper, for example. Your success or lack of success as a writer depends to a great extent on your ability to analyze and respond. At the same time, good writing is frequently self-sponsored, growing from a writer's experiences and feelings and taking initial shape in the writer's journal or personal writing. Some of the best writers are those able to blend an understanding of task and audience with the impulse toward personal expression.

Look for the Assignment's Focus and Purpose

When your writing begins with an assignment, as is often the case in college settings, make sure you have the exact wording—along with any explanatory comments from the person making the assignment.

Sometimes an assignment will announce a topic clearly. Often, however, assignments use nouns and noun phrases to introduce the various elements of the topic. Consider underlining any direct statements and associated nouns and noun phrases in your assignment. Then, draw on them as you write out the topic focus of the assignment. Rachel Baez underlined terms in the following assignment, then summarized it for herself.

> Many of the <u>studies</u> we have read about <u>violent behavior among teens</u> point to the influence of <u>violent scenes on television and in movies.</u> In the <u>interviews</u> we read, however, teenagers themselves point to <u>different causes:</u> social pressures, the personalities of individuals, drug and alcohol use, or a "desire for excitement and adventure." Analyze the differences among these explanations, tell which you find most convincing, and support your conclusions.

What do I see as the focus of this assignment? Two sets of explanations, one set in the studies and one set in the interviews.

Look for Purposes and Patterns in an Assignment

The verbs and verb phrases in an assignment set goals (purposes) for your writing and may even suggest patterns for organizing and developing an essay. Verbs like *inform, explain, analyze, discuss,* and *show* suggest that your purpose will be *expository;* helping readers understand ideas, events, and information and offering carefully reasoned and supported conclusions about a subject. Words like *argue, persuade,* and *evaluate* suggest that your purpose will be argumentative: presenting reasoned arguments and supporting evidence designed to convince readers to share your opinion on an issue. Underline such words in your assignment and write a purpose statement for your task, including information about the topic. When she went back to her assignment, here are the action words Rachel Baez underlined and the purpose statement she prepared.

> Many of the studies we have read about violent behavior among teens point to the influence of violent scenes on television and in movies. In the interviews we read, however, teenagers themselves point to different causes: social pressures, the personalities of individuals, drug and alcohol use, or a "desire for excitement and adventure." <u>Analyze</u> the differences among these explanations, <u>tell</u> which you find most convincing, and <u>support</u> your conclusions.

What are my purposes for this assignment? To give specific information about the differences, to offer my conclusion about the causes, and to give reasons and information that will help readers understand why my conclusions are reasonable.

Verbs and other words in the assignment may suggest (or require) patterns of exposition (or argument) for you to employ in all or part of an essay, alone or in combination with other patterns. Look for words like the following (or their synonyms) and consult the appropriate chapters in this book for ideas on using these patterns:

> *illustrate* or provide *examples* (Chapter 3)
> *classify* or *classification* (Chapter 4)
> *compare* and *contrast* (Chapter 5)
> create an *analogy* (Chapter 6)
> analyze or explain a *process* or *process analysis* (Chapter 7)
> analyze *cause* and *effect* (Chapter 8)
> *define* or provide a *definition* (Chapter 9)
> *describe* or create a *description* (Chapter 10)
> *narrate* or use *narration* (Chapter 11)
> reason *inductively* and *deductively* or use *induction* and *deduction* (Chapter 12)
> *argue* or present an *argument* (Chapter 13)

Use these words, combined with information about your topic and purpose, to create a *design statement* for your writing, as did Rachel Baez.

> **I plan to begin with a section contrasting the sets of explanations for violent behavior among teens and indicating the specific differences. Then I will state clearly those I find convincing: media influence, social pressures, and the personalities of individuals. Finally, I will present examples and reasons why I think these are probably the most important causes for violent behavior.**

KEEP A WRITING JOURNAL

A *writing journal* (or *academic journal*) is a place (often a notebook or a computer file) in which you jot down ideas and discoveries, try out different perspectives on a topic, prepare rough drafts of paragraphs or essays, and note responses to reading or observations. Journals are not diaries: journals are starting places for public writing while diaries are places to record and keep your private observations.

This passage from Scott Giglio's journal, made in response to an article in his local newspaper, illustrates some of the ways journals can provide an imaginative start for the essay-writing process while at the same time being hard for anyone but the author to read.

> Article in PrJo 6/10/00 "Hispanics losing ground in strong economy" hadn't thought about this. Why? I figured unemployment was down etc. and that most people were either doing well or things getting better for them so what abt. Hispanics? Article claims—uh, where is it—Census Bureau claims Hispanic families income down 5.1% rest up 2.7 (can get rest of stats from article if impt. cut it out of paper) Ok Ok why happening and why important is this something to argue about or can I use it as part of paper on how people just seem to be same but lead diff. lives?? A campaign issue or do people vote on personality rather than how things are going?

Questioning

Once you have a topic in mind, you can begin envisioning how to develop it into an essay. Many writers use groups of questions to identify aspects of a subject likely to interest readers, to develop perspectives and insights worth sharing, or to clarify their purposes for writing. Questions can also suggest possible designs for an essay.

Focusing questions help you identify goals or main ideas for your writing and may suggest general ways to divide a topic into parts and organize an essay around key points. They may even point toward a thesis around which you can build an essay (see pp. 27-28).

Here are some focusing questions that ask you to consider both your perspective on a topic and your readers' likely responses.

- What parts of this subject or ways of looking at it interest me the most? Is the subject as a whole interesting or does some part of it or specific way of looking at it seem more intriguing?
- What aspect of the subject is most likely to interest readers?
- What would I most like to learn about this subject? Would readers like to learn the same thing?
- What feelings about the subject do I want to share with readers? What knowledge, opinions, or insights do I want to share?
- How is my perspective different from the ones readers will likely bring with them?
- What are two (three? four?) fresh, unusual, unsettling, or controversial insights I have to share? Why may some readers have trouble understanding or accepting them?

PLANNING

Planning before you draft an essay does not mean deciding ahead of time the exact order in which you will present each detail or idea and the precise conclusions you will offer and support in each paragraph. For most writers, writing is itself a form of discovery. The very act of putting sentences and paragraphs together brings ideas and information into often unanticipated relationships that create fresh perspectives worth sharing with readers.

But a lack of planning can be harmful to the quality of an essay or report and frustrating to you as the writer. If you begin writing without a plan, you are probably dooming yourself to false starts and long periods of inactivity when you try to decide what to say next—or whether to scrap the whole draft and start over.

How can you know when to begin planning? Sometimes your exploration of a topic suggests a clear pattern and direction for your writing. Sometimes your **discovering** activities (pp. 22-25) suggest a point or **thesis** as a focus. And still other times, you have gathered so many ideas, opinions, and details that you need to move ahead before you are overwhelmed. All these are good times to begin planning.

Clustering and Diagramming

Both clustering and diagramming (creating tree diagrams) lead to conceptual maps that group ideas to help you see relationships and develop focal points for your writing.

In **clustering** you develop ideas related to a central topic and link the ideas with lines to display how they are associated. Clustering encourages the interconnection of ideas. You may begin by developing a single idea into several seemingly unconnected nodes, but on further reflection recognize some connections you hadn't yet considered.

Begin by writing a concept, idea, or topic in the center of a page, and circle it. Then randomly jot down associations with the central idea, circling them and connecting them with lines to the center, like the spokes of a wheel. As you continue to generate ideas around the central focus, think about the interconnections among subsidiary ideas, and draw lines to show those.

You can also create clusters in cycles, each subsidiary idea becoming the central focus on a new page. You'll soon find that some clusters begin petering out once you've exhausted your fund of knowledge. Stand back and assess what you have. Is there enough to go on, without further consideration? If so, you may be ready to start some harder, more critical consideration of your paper's direction. If not, perhaps further strategies will open up additional ideas.

Tree diagrams resemble clusters, but their branches tend to be a little more linear, with few interconnections. Tree diagrams rely on the notion of subordination: each larger branch can lead to smaller and smaller branches. For this reason, tree diagramming can provide a useful way to visualize the components of your paper. You can even revise a tree diagram into a sort of preliminary outline (see p. 29) to use when deciding what to place in each paragraph of your paper.

Using Patterns of Exposition (and Argument)

As you become familiar with the patterns of exposition (and argument) discussed in the text, you can use them to develop a plan for an essay, using them either alone or in combination. One way to do this is to treat the patterns like questions. Can I develop my essay through examples that illustrate a generality or by examining the categories into which the ideas and information fall (Example, ch. 3; Classification, ch. 4)? Can I look at similarities and differences or at the surprising similarities between seemingly very different subjects (Comparison and Contrast, ch. 5; Analogy, ch. 6)? Should I write about how my subject works or can be done, or about how it happened and what is likely to occur in the future (Process Analysis, ch. 7; Cause and Effect, ch. 8)? Should I define my subject, or describe it in detail (Definition, ch. 9; Description, ch. 10)? Should I talk about what happened, or should I reason from facts a conclusion and use the conclusion to arrive at further interpretations (Narration, ch. 11; Induction and Deduction, ch. 12)? Should I argue for a proposition and provide evidence to convince readers (Argument, ch. 13)?

Developing a Thesis

Perhaps the most important and useful planning technique involves focusing on what you want to say and do. In a finished essay, a thesis statement creates focus by announcing your main idea(s) to readers and helping organize supporting ideas, evidence, and discussions. An effective thesis statement is specific and limited; it announces and highlights the main idea without getting bogged down in details.

> **Specific:** A good community exercise program makes provisions for four kinds of exercisers: people dedicated to fitness, people wanting to become fit, people struggling with health problems, and children building a base for a healthy lifestyle.
>
> **Vague:** A community exercise program is good when it has room for people who want to exercise for all sorts of different reasons.
>
> **Limited:** Extensive use of fossil fuels and widespread changes in agriculture have had significant effects on our climate in the last 75 years.
>
> **Too Broad:** The last several centuries have seen massive changes in industrial production, in the use of fossil fuels, in transportation, in the development of cities, in agriculture, and in many other areas which have had an impact on our climate.
>
> **Direct:** Despite all their protests to the contrary, people tend to value appearance, likelihood of success, and similarity of background in choosing a mate.
>
> **Bogged:** People may say they look for spiritual qualities rather than looks in choosing a mate, yet research points out that

they are more likely to be influenced by some traditional factors, and these are likely to include how a person looks, whether or not a person is likely to succeed financially or in social terms, and the extent to which the people's families, experiences, and social class are similar.

But effective thesis statements seldom start out specific, limited, and direct. They begin as **tentative thesis statements** that provide a focus for planning. As you draft and revise, they become clearer and more sharply focused, eventually taking final form in a finished essay.

Here are some techniques for developing a tentative thesis statement as part of your planning.

List Your Conclusions and Evidence

Create a list of possible conclusions and evidence you wish to offer in an essay. Then sum them up in generalization which highlights the main idea linking them all.

> **Support:** Fashions in children's toys change quickly—sometimes several times a year.
>
> **Support:** Toy manufacturers must make product decisions a year before the toys appear in stores, so they need to predict trends a year ahead.
>
> **Support:** Bringing a new toy to market can cost millions of dollars.
>
> **Support:** Most new toys are not successes; many make very little money.
>
> **Support:** There are many well-managed and imaginative companies competing for business in the toy market.
>
> **Tentative Thesis:** Manufacturing children's toys is a risky business.

Create a Tentative Purpose Statement

Try writing yourself a note stating your potential topic along with your conclusions and possible goals for writing. To remain flexible and open to new ideas, you might begin your statement with a phrase like "I'd like to . . ." or "I'm planning to . . . ."

> I'm planning to explain the reasons why many college students lose their motivation to work hard at their studies.
>
> —Bippin Kumar

I'd like to tell what it felt like to be forced to leave my homeland, Haiti, so that my readers can understand why to leave something you love is to die a little.

—Fredza Léger

Create a Rough Purpose/Thesis Outline

When you have in mind the various ideas and details you wish to present in an essay, create a purpose/thesis outline arranging the ideas and details in groups by clustering the details and summing up your conclusions and purpose for each section of an essay.

Here is Bippin Kumar's purpose outline for a paper exploring the reasons why college students may lose the motivation necessary to succeed at their studies.

1. Get readers' attention by mentioning the *bad habits* most of us have and that we may be able to correct on our own. (minor causes of the problem)
> lack of sleep
> disorganization
> distractions (television, etc.)
2. Show how we are often responsible because of the choices we make and explain that we need to make wiser choices. (more serious causes)
> sports and other extracurricular activities
> friends and socializing
> Greek life
> letting ourselves get frustrated and angry over daily hassles (bookstores, commuting)
3. Conclude with problems that we can't avoid and that may require special planning or counseling to overcome. (more serious causes)
> work
> financial stresses
> family demands or problems
> lack of necessary skills

DRAFTING

Drafting involves a good deal more than setting pen to paper or fingers to keyboard and letting the words flow according to your plan. It means paying attention to the way each section of an essay relates to the other sections and to the central theme. It means making sure you begin and end the essay in ways that are clear, helpful, and interesting to readers. And it means making sure each section and each paragraph present sufficient, detailed information so that readers can understand your subject and have reasons to agree with your explanations and conclusions.

Drafting does not mean getting everything right the first time. Such a goal is likely to prove both exhausting and impossible to achieve. A much better goal is to draft with the most important features of an essay in mind and to work quickly enough so that you have sufficient time to revise later and then pay attention to details.

As you draft, therefore, make sure that you introduce readers to your topic, indicate its importance, generate interest in it, and suggest the direction your essay will take. The essays in this collection can provide you with models of successful strategies for the beginnings of essays, and the *Introductions* entry in the "Guide to Terms" (at the back of the text) offers a detailed list of opening strategies. The "Guide" also provides advice about another important feature that should be a focus during drafting—your essay's conclusion.

Keep in mind the various sections you have planned for your essay, or keep at hand a copy of any planning strategies you have used, especially those that identify the planned parts of your essay, their general content, and their purposes.

Most likely, you will also alter, revise, or change the main point (theme or thesis) of your essay as you write, and such changes often make for a better essay. By the time your essay is complete, moreover, you will also have to decide whether to announce your main point directly to readers in a concise thesis statement (see below), to present it less directly in a series of statements in the body of the essay, or to imply it through the details and arrangement of the paper. No matter which strategy you choose, you should have a relatively clear idea of your thesis before you begin drafting. Try stating your thesis to yourself in a tentative form. You can do this in several ways:

- Start with a phrase like "I want my readers to understand . . ." or "The point of the whole essay is . . ."
- Make up a title that embodies your main idea.
- Send an imaginary note to your readers: "By the time you are finished with this essay, I hope you will see (or agree with me) that . . ."

If you want to share your knowledge of bicycling as a sport, for instance, you might try one or more of these thesis-building strategies, as in the following examples.

    1. The point of the whole essay is that people can choose what kind of bicycle riders they want to be—recreational, competitive, or cross-country.

2. What Kind of Bicycle Rider Do You Want to Be?
3. By the time you finish this essay, I hope you will be able to choose the kind of bicycle riding—recreational, competitive, or cross-country—that is best for you.

A **tentative thesis statement** can guide your drafting by reminding you of your essay's main point. You can create a tentative thesis statement by summing up in a sentence or two your main point, the conclusion you plan to draw from the information and ideas you will present, or the proposition for which you plan to argue. You may eventually use a revised form of the tentative thesis statement in your completed essay as a way of announcing clearly to readers the main idea behind your writing.

For example, when Kin Chin was preparing a paper on different meanings of the phrase "recent immigrant," he used the following tentative thesis statement: "For some people, *recent immigrant* means a threat to their jobs or more strain on the resources of schools and social service agencies. For others it means fresh ideas and a broadening of our culture and outlook." In his final paper he used this thesis statement: "For some, *recent immigrant* means *cheap labor* or *higher taxes;* for others, it means *fresh ideas* and *a richer, more diverse culture.*"

As you write, include statements that alert readers to the various sections, along with transitions marking the movement from one section to the next (or from paragraph to paragraph). Make sure, too, that in making shifts in time, place, ideas, and content you do not confuse readers, but instead give them adequate indication of the shifts. Remember to provide readers with concrete, specific details and evidence that will give them the information they need about your topic, or the support necessary to make your explanations or arguments convincing.

Pay attention to the arrangement of your essay, especially to the patterns of exposition or argument you are employing. In any essay that classifies, for example, don't provide a detailed treatment of one category in the classification but skimpy treatment of the others—unless you have a special reason for doing so. Let your readers know, directly or indirectly, whatever pattern(s) you are employing. This will make them aware of your essay's design and will help to guide their attention to the key points you cover. Make every effort to stick to your main idea (perhaps using your tentative thesis statement as a guide), and check to see that the parts of the essay are clearly related to and support the main idea. If you have trouble developing a section because you need more information, or because you can't express ideas as clearly as you want, make a note of the things that need to be done and then move on.

REVISING

When you shift your focus to revising, you pay special attention to the success with which your draft essay embodies your intentions and meets your readers' likely expectations. You examine the draft to see if it does a good job presenting insights, reasoning, and details. You look at the draft from a reader's perspective to see if the discussions are clear and informative, the reasoning is logical, and the examples and supporting details are related to the central theme.

Reading for Revision

Revision starts with rereading—looking over your draft with a dual perspective: as an author and as a member of your potential audience. As you read for revision, keep track of the places that need more work and make note of the directions your rewriting might take. Most writers find it hard to read for revision directly from a computer screen, and they print a hard copy of their drafts for this purpose.

Whether you are working with a handwritten text, a typed copy, or a print from a word processor, you may find reading for revision most effective if you do it with a pencil or pen in hand to record your reactions and plans for revision.

Reading for revision can be even more effective when another writer does it for you (and you return the favor). Remember, collaborative readings of this sort are best done in a cooperative, rather than harshly critical atmosphere. Your job and that of your reader(s) is to identify strengths as well as weaknesses and to suggest (if possible) ways to turn weaknesses into strong points. (For more about collaborative revising and editing, see pp. 38–39.)

Whether you are reading your own work or someone else's, you may find these symbols useful shortcuts for making marginal comments to guide revision.

Reader Response Symbols

?	Could you explain this a bit more? I can't really understand this.
Add?	I would like to know more about this. I think you could use more detail here.
Leave out?	This information or this passage may not be necessary. You have already said this.

Missing?	Did you leave something out? I think there is a gap in the information, explanation, or argument here.
Confusing?	I have trouble following this explanation/argument. The information here is presented in a confusing manner.
Reorganize?	I think this section (or paper) would be more effective if you presented it in a different order.
Interesting, Good, Effective, etc.	Your writing really works here. I like it.

You may be tempted to revise as you read, and for sentences or paragraphs that need a quick fix, this approach is often adequate. In most cases, however, your revisions need to go beyond tinkering with words and sentences if they are to lead to real improvement. You will need to pay attention to the overall focus, to the need for additional paragraphs presenting detailed evidence, and to the arrangement of the steps in an explanation or argument. To see the need for such large-scale changes you need to read the draft paying attention to the essay as a whole, something you cannot do if you stop frequently to rework the parts. In addition, it makes little sense to correct the flaws in a sentence if you realize later on that the entire paragraph ought to be dropped.

Questioning Reading

One good way to read for revision is to prepare questions that will focus your attention as you read—questions appropriate for your topic, your purposes, your pattern(s) of exposition or argument, and your intended readers. You may wish to direct attention to those features you worked on while drafting (introductions, or transitions for example). You may wish to use questions that reflect the specific topic or purposes of your essay or that reflect the probable outlook of your intended readers. Make notes in the margins of your draft or on a separate sheet of paper (or computer file). Don't keep too many questions in mind as you read; instead, reread as many times as necessary, each time with a different set of questions. Following are some possible questions to help you evaluate your draft.

Questions for Revision

General
>Does my essay have a clear topic and focus?
>Does it stick to the topic and focus throughout?
>How have I signaled the topic and focus to readers?
>Is the essay divided into parts? What are they?
>Are the parts clearly identified for readers?

Thesis and theme
>Does the essay have a thesis statement? Is it clearly stated?
>Is the thesis statement in the best possible location?
>Should the thesis statement be more (or less) specific?
>Are all the different parts of the essay clearly related to the thesis statement or the central theme?
>In what ways have I reminded readers of the thesis or theme in the course of the essay? Do I need to remind them more often or in other ways?

Introductions and conclusions
>Does my introduction make the topic clear? Does it interest readers in what I will have to say?
>Does my introduction give readers some indication of the arrangement of the essay and its purpose(s)?
>Does the conclusion help tie together the main points of the essay or remind readers of the significance of the information and ideas I have presented?
>Does my conclusion have a clear purpose or have I ended the essay without any clear strategy?

Information and ideas
>Have I presented enough information and enough details so that readers will feel they have learned something worthwhile about the topic?
>At what specific places would the essay be improved if I added more information?
>What information can be cut because it is repetitive, uninteresting, or unrelated to the topic or theme of the essay?
>Is my information fresh and worth sharing? Do I need to do more thinking or research so that the content of my essay is worth sharing?
>Do the examples and details I present support my conclusions in a convincing way? Do I need to explain them more fully?

Would more research or thinking enable me to offer better support? What kinds of support would readers find helpful?

Have I learned something new or worthwhile about my topic and communicated it to readers?

Sentences and paragraphs

Have I divided the essay into paragraphs that help readers identify shifts in topic, stages in an explanation, steps in a line of reasoning, key ideas, or important segments of information?

Does each paragraph make its topic or purpose clear to readers?

Which short paragraphs need greater development through the addition of details or explanations?

Which long paragraphs could be trimmed or divided?

Do the sentences reflect what I want to say? Which sentences could be clearer?

Are the sentences varied in length? Do they provide appropriate emphasis to key ideas?

Can I word the explanations or arguments more clearly?

Can I use more vivid and concrete language?

Would the paper benefit from more complicated or imaginative language? From simpler, more direct wording?

Readers' perspective

In what ways are my readers likely to view this topic or argument? Have I taken their perspectives into account?

What do I want my readers to learn from this essay? What opinion do I want them to share? What do I want them to do?

Have I considered what my readers are likely to know or believe and how this will shape their response to my purpose(s) for writing?

Sample Student Essay

Here is the draft of an essay Sarah Lake produced in response to an assignment asking her to write about a community of some sort, taking the perspective of an outsider trying to understand how the community works and what kinds of relationships people in the community form. The marginal comments on the paper are notes she has addressed to the classmates (peer readers) who will be responding to her paper with revision suggestions.

Welcome to the Gym!

As I stepped up to the door to the field house I saw myself in the reflection from the door. I had chosen mesh shorts, a white v-neck T-shirt, and tattered old sneakers in hope to "fit in" with the crowd. Luckily, I still possess the Ram sticker on the back of my I.D. I was all set. I was in. A cheery eyed student asked for my I.D., and pointed me towards the training room. So far, so good, I thought. My only hopes were that the gym was going to be a great place.

The smell was rather distinct; one part sweat, one part machine oil, and one part cleaner, or maybe it was the chorine coming from the pool. Surprisingly, it was a rather welcoming smell. The kind of smell that says "Come on in, have fun, workout, sweat, be hot and sticky and smelly, it's O.K." I liked what it had to say, so I continued on, farther into the training room. As I stepped inside to the training room, heavy breathing and strenuous shouts of "One!, Two!, Three!" could be heard. The shouting seemed common, and went unnoticed by regulars. Weightlifters, mostly men, would grunt, scream, moan, and sometimes yell in agony as they tried to lift weights two, three times the weight they could handle. Their heads turned a tomato red and looked as if they were about to explode. Their veins, like thick rope, popped through the skin on their necks, arms, and legs. Due to the fact that I'm not a weightlifter or a man, I surely don't understand the meaning behind this behavior. It looked rather painful and it

I've tried to make this interesting. Is it?

This is the community I studied. Is my purpose clear?

I added a lot of detail. Does it work?

wasn't very flattering to them, but it was entertaining.

I squirmed my way through the machines, and people, and found myself a spot on one of the stair masters. I curiously stared at the screen in front of me. Blinking letters zoomed across the screen reading enter your weight and then press enter. Enter my weight? That's a lot to ask of a girl. I thought about it, and even considered lying to the machine, but reality set in, I realized it was just a machine. Why lie to a machine? I punched in my weight, and continued to answer the questions the screen produced.

As I started my workout, I began to gaze around and inspect everyone's interaction with each other. "Rules of the Gym" were listed on the wall and were followed by everyone. Everyone respected everyone and everything. On the other hand rules for socializing weren't posted, but underlying rules seemed to be understood. Socializing while working out or better yet, while in motion was not encouraged. Talking only took place while one was motionless or waiting for a machine. It seemed as if it took so much concentration to work out that no one could even talk while doing so. I, on the other hand, couldn't wait to talk when I got finished. I felt like I had gone through withdrawal. I needed some sort of outlet to make the time go by and my workout faster so I turned from people behavior watching to people's attire watching.

Gym attire was rather diverse. Some wore the typical workout uniform, which

I think my punctuation and grammar got a bit out of control at times in this draft. Help!

Are my sentences clear?

consisted of tight spandex. It included
tops, tops over tops, bottoms, bottoms
over bottoms, etc., etc. Others wore outfits very similar to my own which was very
comforting. My favorite outfit (I'm being
sarcastic) was on a young woman, about 21,
who turned more heads in twenty minutes
than Cindy Crawford has in her whole career. It consisted of, from top to bottom:
a bright pink scrunchie (one of those
cloth elastics), a black headband, a
Is this too   bright pink jog bra, black lycra spandex,
much detail?   covered by a workout g-string, also bright
pink in color. As I worked my eyes down to
her legs and then to her feet I noticed
she had boxing sneakers on. The ones NIKE
made in the eighties with the high laces.
Smashing, was the only word to describe
her ensemble.

Peer Response

Before you revise (or in between successive drafts), getting a look at
your work through another's eyes can help you spot strengths and
weaknesses and identify steps you can take to improve your essay.
To do this, ask a person or a group of people to read and comment
on the strengths and weaknesses of your draft essay. Ask them, too,
to suggest ways the writing might be improved. Their comments are
most likely to be useful if you ask them to respond to specific questions (like those in the list on pp. 34-35) and to make concrete suggestions for improvement.

Here are some comments Tonya Williams and Dave Cisneros
made on Sarah Lake's essay.

Does this essay have a clear and interesting thesis statement or generalization?

TONYA: I don't see any thesis statement. The assignment asked us
to make a generalization about the community. What is
yours?

DAVE: In the planning materials you shared with us, you talked about the reasons people were exercising. Could you add a generalization about the motivations of people in this community?

Does this essay provide detailed examples that support or explain the essay's thesis statement or generalization?

TONYA: I like some of the pictures of gym life that you provide, but I don't see how they fit with any kind of generalization. The last example probably talks too much about clothes.

DAVE: I suggest cutting the last paragraph. It doesn't fit with the rest of the paper.

Are the sentences clear and effective? How might they be improved?

TONYA: A lot of the sentences begin with I, so the paper seems to focus on you rather than the community you are exploring.

DAVE: I like the way you write. I think your sentences are easy to read in general. At times, though, the paper seems a bit informal. I'm not sure whether the writing is too informal in style or whether you are focusing more on your personal feelings than on the kinds of observations and conclusions you are trying to explain.

Are there any places the grammar and spelling might be improved?

TONYA: I think you have some grammar problems, especially fragments and run-ons. I put a question mark next to these on the paper.

DAVE: I noticed a few spelling problems and other small errors. I tried to mark them, but I may have missed a few.

EDITING AND FINAL REVISION

After you have carefully rewritten your essay at least one time and perhaps several, you can focus on editing and final revision. In creating your finished paper, pay special attention to matters such as the style and clarity of sentences and paragraphs as well as correctness in grammar and usage. Before you hand in your final draft, carefully correct any typographical errors along with any mistakes in spelling or expression that remain.

Here is the final version of Sarah Lake's paper, including some revision that she made during a last reading and some editing before she typed the final copy. In revising, Sarah took into account the comments of her classmates and those her instructor wrote on a copy of her draft. In addition, she went back to her planning document for ideas she left out of the draft, and she developed these ideas at some length in the revised version of the paper. The comments in the margin of the paper below have been added to highlight features of the essay.

Welcome to the Gym:

A Community of Worriers

As I stepped up to the door of the field house, I saw my reflection in the glass, and I started worrying. I had chosen mesh shorts, a white v-neck T-shirt, and tattered old sneakers in hopes of fitting in

Moves from personal experience to the conclusion that will be explored in the essay.

with the community I planned to observe: people exercising for fitness inside the gym. I was worrying about how well I would fit in. After my visit, I realized I fit in quite well. Not only had I dressed appropriately, but I was also worried, and worrying about appearance seemed to be one trait everybody at the gym shared. *It*

Thesis statement

seems to be the attribute that defines this community and ties its members together.

As I stepped inside the training room I heard heavy breathing and strenuous shouts of "One! Two! Three!" Weightlifters,

Paragraph presents observations

mostly men, were grunting, screaming, moaning, and yelling in agony as they tried to lift weights two, three times more than they could handle. Their heads turned tomato red, and they looked as if they were about to explode. I'm neither a

man nor a weightlifter, and I had no idea
why they were trying to overexert themselves, or so it seemed to me.

**Evidence
supports
overall thesis**

When I spoke with several of the
weightlifters, they admitted that for many
people who spend time lifting weights, appearance is a primary concern. They
claimed that many male weightlifters begin
exercising because they feel inferior
about their physical appearance or because
they want to get that "He-man" or
"Caveman" look that they consider an ideal
for men. Though the men I talked to said
that they, personally, weren't that anxious about the way they looked, they also
admitted that they felt that potential
dates pay more attention to a man who has
"bulked up." I asked why they felt it was
important to have a muscular and masculine
appearance in today's society, especially
when a lot of people (women especially)

**Observations
likely to
surprise and
intrigue
reader**

talk about the need for men to be "sensitive." I was surprised by the answers because they seemed to reveal worry and
insecurity—which was surprising coming
from a group of very well muscled college
men. The weightlifters said they thought
sensitivity was a good thing, and they
claimed to work towards it in their relationships. They also said that sensitivity
grows out of self-confidence, and that for
men self-confidence often comes through
physical fitness and athletic ability.

**Transition to
second set of
observations**

Though the weightlifters seemed sincere,
as a woman I felt rather awed by their appearance and kept waiting for one of them
to knock one of the female exercisers over
the head and drag her back to his cave.
This thought made me shift my attention to

the women, most of whom were working on machines like Stair Masters, stationary bicy-
cles, or Nautilus. To enter into the
women's part of this community, I squirmed
my way through the machines and people, and
I found a spot on one of the Stair Masters.
I stared curiously at the screen in front
of me. Blinking letters zoomed across the
screen asking me to enter my weight. "Enter
my weight," I thought, "That's a lot to ask
of a girl." I even thought about lying, but
then I got embarrassed about lying to a machine. Later, when I shared this worry with
some of the women at the gym, I realized
they shared my apprehension and a lot of my
other worries.

Like the men, the women shared many concerns about their appearance, especially
about their attractiveness and about the
relationship of appearance to self-
confidence. They spoke of how the
"Baywatch" girls are the ideals of appearance for women in our society, and of how
they felt a need to compete with the
"Barbies" of this world, even though such
an appearance is unrealistic for the average woman. They also talked about having a
kind of balance scale in their heads. As
their weight increases, they feel less
attractive, and as their weight decreases,
they feel more attractive. They pointed
out how magazines, TV programs, and movies
seem to equate thinness with attractiveness and link attractiveness to self-
confidence. Though they admitted that
working women with responsibilities as
wives and mothers might not have time or
energy to work out in a gym, they worried
about how their self-confidence might suf-

Side notes:

Personal experience supports thesis

Observations act as evidence for thesis

Summarizes interviews

fer if they didn't have the opportunity to exercise to control their weight.

After my time on the Stair Master came to an end and I had finished talking to the members of the gym community, I left, feeling as though I fit in. I was a worrier and I had dressed like many of the women. On my way out, however, I passed a woman dressed in a daring pink and black outfit who began turning heads as soon as she walked in the door. I started worrying again, and I knew the people in the gym were now worrying even more about their looks.

Conclusion echoes main point

3

Illustrating Ideas by Use of *Example*

The use of examples to illustrate an idea under discussion is the most common, and frequently the most efficient, pattern of exposition. It is a method we use almost instinctively; for instance, instead of talking in generalities about the qualities of a good city manager, we cite Angela Lopes as an example. We may go further and illustrate her virtues as a manager by a specific account of her handling a crucial situation during the last power shortage or hurricane. In this way, we put our abstract ideas into concrete form—making them clearer and more convincing. As readers, we look for examples as well, often responding to general statements with a silently voiced question, "for instance?" and expecting the writer to provide us with appropriate specifics.

Examples can be short or long: a brief illustration within a sentence or a fully developed instance filling a paragraph or more. They can appear singly, or they can work together in clusters, as in the following paragraph where brief examples serve to make a generalization vivid and convincing.

Generality	*There were many superstitions regarding food.* Dropping a
Example 1	fork meant that company would be coming. If we were
Example 2	to take a second helping of potatoes while we still had
	some left on our plate, someone always predicted that
	a person more hungry than we were would drop in
Example 3	during the day. Every housewife believed that food
	from a tin can had to be removed immediately after
	opening, or it would become deadly poison within a
Example 4	few seconds. My mother always ran across the room to
	dump the contents immediately.

—Lewis Hill, "Black Cats and Horse Hairs"

45

Whether making an explanation clear, a generality more convincing, or an argument more persuasive, examples work in the same way. They make the general more specific, the abstract more concrete, and in so doing they illustrate a sound principle of writing.

WHY USE EXAMPLES?

Examples clarify by showing readers what a general statement means in terms of individual events, people, or ideas. By pointing out students who use "lucky" pens to take a test, lawyers who wear "special" ties or shoes to a big day in court, and engineers who begin a new project with a special breakfast, a writer can aid understanding of the statement, "Even educated people often make superstition part of their everyday lives." On the other hand, lack of clear illustrations may leave readers with only a hazy conception of the points the writer has tried to make. Even worse, readers may try to supply examples from their own knowledge or experience, leading them to an impression different from that intended by the author. Since writers are the ones trying to communicate, clarity is primarily their responsibility.

Not only do good examples put into clear form what otherwise might remain vague and abstract, they serve to make generalizations and conclusions convincing. Not every generality requires supporting examples, of course. An audience with even a passing familiarity with films probably does not need extended examples to understand and accept the statement, "Action films are characterized by physical violence, explosions, chase scenes, and broadly-drawn characters." Conclusions about unfamiliar or complicated subjects, technical discussions, and perspectives that may be difficult for readers to share initially usually call for examples. College instructors, for instance, will usually look for examples to render an interpretation convincing; business and public audiences will search reports and memorandums for examples that make the writer's judgments plausible.

With something specific for readers to visualize, a statement becomes more convincing—but convincing within certain limitations. If you use the Volvo as an example of Swedish manufacturing, the readers is probably aware that this car may not be entirely typical. For ordinary purposes of explanation, the Volvo example could make its point convincingly enough. In supporting an argument, however, you need either to choose an example that is clearly typical or to present several examples to show that you have represented the situation fairly.

CHOOSING A STRATEGY

As a writer, you need to recognize not only places where individual examples can aid your writing but also occasions when your ideas might be most effectively presented through the use of examples as the primary strategy for an essay. If you have a fresh, unusual, or surprising conclusion to offer readers, consider using examples in a **thesis-and-support** strategy. Announce your thesis (perspective, interpretation) to readers, then offer evidence of its reasonableness in the form of varied, carefully developed examples, as illustrated in the following plan for an essay.

Tentative Thesis	Modern technology offers many new creative outlets for writers, musicians, and artists.
Supporting Point	Cable television has multiplied the opportunities for creative work by increasing greatly the number of television programs.
	Example: More work for scriptwriters of all kinds: dramatic, documentary, news, sports, and comedy.
	Example: More opportunities for actors, cinematographers, and directors.
	Example: More programs calling for original music, art, and graphics.
Supporting Point	Software development calls for creative artists as well as software engineers.
	Example: Games require scriptwriters, artistic designers, graphic artists, and composers (for music to accompany the action).
	Example: Office programs require graphic design; home and landscape design programs involve artistic and graphic design; educational software calls for writers and designers (sometimes even music).
Supporting Point	Personal computers and the Internet provide the means to create and distribute works of art without significant financial resources.
	Example: Composers and performers can create musical works without hiring performers

> or renting a studio and distribute their work on the World Wide Web.
>
> **Example:** Desktop publishing allows writers to create printed copies of their novels, essays, and other writing without the expense or difficulty of working with publishers and printers.
>
> **Example:** Design programs and drawing/painting programs let visual artists create without having to maintain a studio or buy expensive materials, and the World Wide Web gives them a way to advertise and distribute their work.

If an extended, especially detailed example covers all aspects of your topic that need explaining or provides a particularly appropriate instance of your main idea, consider using a **representative example** strategy. A representative example needs to be interesting in itself because it will serve as the main focus of the writing, preceded or followed (or both) by the main idea it illustrates. In this chapter, Andy Rooney's "In and of Ourselves We Trust" provides a particularly successful instance of a representative example (stopping at a red light when no one is around) followed by the writer's conclusion that "the whole structure of our society depends on mutual trust, not distrust." William F. Buckley's "Why Don't We Complain?" shows yet another alternative: several extended examples building on each other to explore the author's thesis about the ways modern society and politics have undermined our assertiveness.

CHOOSING EXAMPLES

Successful writers select and use example cautiously, keeping in mind their readers and their own specific purposes for communicating. To be effective, an example must be pertinent to the chief qualities of the generality it illustrates. In writing about horror films, for instance, you might offer this interpretation: "The films generally have contemporary settings, yet most reinforce traditional, even old-fashioned roles for both men and women." To be pertinent, examples would need to address the various elements of this thesis, including the contrast between the contemporary setting and the old-fashioned values, the roles of both men and women, and exceptions to the conclusion ("most" horror films, but not all).

Examples should be representative as well, presenting in a fair manner the range of situations, people, or ideas to which a generality applies. In discussing a new approach to education, you should be ready to consider it in terms of urban and rural as well as suburban communities. Your interpretation of a play, film, novel, or recording should take into account the work as a whole, not simply those parts corresponding most directly to your thesis. If you wish readers to adopt your perspective, you should choose examples that represent any important differences among their outlooks, often the product of differences in background, gender, ethnicity, or education.

It is possible to provide too many examples and make them too long, but for most writers, the opposite is usually the problem. We frequently underestimate the number of examples needed because we pay attention only to those that come to mind most readily. Almost any part of a subject can provide potential examples, however. With your generality or thesis in mind, look for representative events, situations, quotations, or people; typical attitudes, opinions or ideas; and characteristic physical and emotional details. Make a conscious effort to draw examples from a variety of sources.

- *Your Experiences:* Draw on your involvement with the topic. For an essay on work, draw on jobs you have held. For an essay on sports, think of your experiences (pleasant and unpleasant) as an athlete or spectator. For a report on health care, begin with your own broken bones, doctor's appointments, sessions in the dentist's chair, and trips to the hospital either as patient or visitor.
- *Your Reading:* Add to your knowledge of a topic by searching a library catalog or using an Internet browser. Choose articles and reports that expand your understanding and suggest the ways others may respond to your conclusions. Draw examples (including statistics) from your reading, being careful to acknowledge your sources.
- *Other People:* Think about other people whose experiences are consistent with your conclusions: the neighbor whose job history reflects a changing view of loyalty to an employer or your cousin whose reliance on the Internet for shopping illustrates changing patterns of consumption.
- *One from a Group:* When your thesis or generalization applies to a wide variety of people, situations, organization, or experiences, you may be tempted to provide numerous examples as a way of representing the group as a whole but instead end up with a cluster of indistinct, ineffective illustrations. Instead, consider focusing on one or two members of the group and presenting them in

extended detail that explains and supports your conclusions. To illustrate the features of science fiction movies, for example, turn to one or two films likely to be familiar to your readers.

There is no set length for effective examples; they can be as short as a few words or several paragraphs in length, depending on the purpose they serve. For a thesis-and-support essay, however, a paragraph of four to six sentences provides a good measure. Each paragraph supporting your main idea should provide several brief examples (as in the sample paragraph on p. 45) or several sentences presenting the example and discussing it in detail. Writers often overestimate how much their readers know about a subject and offer examples lacking in important ideas and information, as in the following student example from a paper for a course on public health policy.

> Nonprescription drugs are still drugs and can be dangerous if misused. Many people make themselves ill by doubling or tripling the dosage of nonprescription drugs in order to get a greater effect.

When her instructor and fellow students pointed out the lack of information in this paragraph, the writer realized that she could have included examples of the toxic effects of high dosages of aspirin and other painkillers, of allergic reactions to excessive intake of vitamin and mineral supplements, and of physical damage that can result from overuse of digestive remedies—examples her readers would have found informative and useful.

Remember, a good example must be either instantly obvious to readers or fully developed so that they learn exactly what it illustrates, and how. Sometimes, however, illustration may be provided best by something other than a real-life example—a fictional anecdote, an analogy, or perhaps a parable that demonstrates the general idea. Here even greater care is needed to be sure these examples are both precise and clear.

Student Essay

If you looked back over the events in your life, how would you interpret them? Would you be able to state the perspective or idea that ties them together? The generality that runs through them? How would you select and present examples to illustrate the generality and help readers understand and share your perspective?

Adrian Boykin's experiences as a stutterer and his struggles to deal with the impediment shaped many of the events in his life, and he is able to share an understanding of his experiences and his perspective through carefully selected examples in the essay that follows.

Overcoming an Impediment: A Rite of
Passage

Adrian Boykin

Dramatic Opening

"Sp, sp, sp, sp spit it out already Adrian!" These were among the insults I received from classmates throughout elementary and junior high school. Inheriting the stuttering, dominantly linked phenotype from my father's side of my family has affected my speech, and in turn my relationships since I first began to speak.

Thesis Statement

Short examples of how his family has been affected

Starting when I was only eight years old and in the third grade, I took speech lessons at school in an attempt to overcome a speech impediment. The trait dates back to my great grandfather. In the last four generations, many Boykin men have expressed a stutter, while others, such as my younger brother, have not. Throughout childhood I often encountered a block in my speech at the first word of each sentence when beginning to speak. From third grade through my freshman year in high school, I participated in monthly, one-on-one speech classes. Through my working diligently with a speech specialist, I have, for the most part, been able to overcome this genetic defect successfully and speak without impediment.

Background explanation of stuttering

As a stutterer, it is difficult to explain to a non-stutterer why we sometimes just can't get the words out. Speaking in a casual one-on-one situation has never been a problem for me. Only in stressful situations where a large group of people were gathered, or in a setting where

Uses an analogy to explain—see Chapter 4

everyone is attempting to speak, did my speech impediment become evident. At these times I would compare the first word of my sentence to ice cream which has been in the freezer for a month on the coldest setting. No matter how hard you try to get a full scoop out of the container, only small tastes of the ice cream will come out. Unfortunately, for the stutterer, that small, unfulfilling taste of ice cream is the first syllable of the stutterer's first word. Repeatedly.

Examples of how his father's life was affected

The problems I encountered with speech never rivaled what my dad experienced growing up. Unable to answer the telephone, speak in class, or even speak without incessant stuttering at the dinner table, my father attended a summer camp in Michigan for three months each summer, four summers in a row, with the hopes of correcting his impediment. Today, though he still often stutters momentarily at the beginning of his sentences, he is a successful custom furniture designer and businessman. About ten years ago, still having difficulty speaking in front of groups, dad completed the Toastmasters speaking course. Because his speech impediment hindered his social development for so many years and in so many ways, he was determined to never let my impediment hold me back socially.

Short examples of how stuttering made him feel in elementary school and junior high school

Because children are often cruel, I was picked on many times by my peers in elementary and junior high school for stuttering. Friends often made fun of me by imitating the stutter I had at the beginning of my sentences. Furthermore, I grew up watching television shows such as *In*

Living Color and movies such as *Harlem Nights* and *Billy Madison*, which depict people with speech impediments as being stupid outcasts or class clowns. Looking back at these television shows and movies, I sometimes ask myself why dehumanization of stutterers is tolerated by the public. Racist stabs at minorities are viewed as disgusting and intolerable by the masses, but attacks and mockery aimed at stutterers are seen as hilarious.

Extended Example

Fortunately, my speech impediment was never something which hindered me from experiencing all the things that other students with normal speech experienced. Because my father knew first-hand what it was like to have a speech impediment, he made sure that I was given therapy to correct my stutter. My father first sent me to a speech therapist affiliated with my elementary school in Denver. Only eight years old, I saw speech therapy as a fun way to get out of class and meet another boy, Michael, who also had a "block in his throat." Attending therapy with another child helped me get away from the feeling that I was alone in my speech problem. During speech class though, I really never concentrated on Michael. What I remember is my therapist, Mrs. Rainart. "Wow," I always thought, "she is the nicest lady, and pretty too!" This was better than playing with G. I. Joe's! By fifth grade, the main reason I liked going to therapy was because I liked seeing her.

Elementary school— relationships with another stutterer and with therapist

Extended Example

Fifth grade was a time of physical change and of change in how I looked at the girls. Mrs. Rainart's milky white teeth and spiral, burgundy colored hair

Begins to develop new kinds of relationships— successfully

made speech therapy more than tolerable for me. You know how elementary school children all have a crush on a teacher at one time or another? I guess that teacher was Mrs. Rainart for me.

My mother got a job in Boulder with Celestial Seasonings Tea Company when I was eleven. As a result we moved to a house in a suburb called Broomfield, wherein my father promptly found me another speech therapist in Boulder. The change in scenery made me nervous. Entering Birch Elementary School, I had to make all new friends. Fortunately, everyone at Birch was really nice. My confidence was soaring, and I was convinced that I no longer needed to go to some stupid speech class.

Extended Example

Then came my worst ever stuttering experience. For my seventh grade birthday, my parents let me have a party for both my boyfriends and my girlfriends. The night started well, with my friends and I boogying down to the latest Michael Jackson album. I was wearing my nicest polyester shirt to go with my loafers and tight Wrangler's. My parents interrupted our disco party for cake, ice cream and presents.

Junior High school stuttering undermines relationships

With the speech impediment seemingly gone, I started socializing with the group while I was opening my gifts. My girlfriend, Emily, gave me the coolest Michael Jordan poster. I began to tell Emily how much I appreciated her gift, when out of nowhere, a heavy encompassing piece of cake got stuck in my throat, and I could only stutter to Emily. I ran to the sink to get water when I realized it wasn't the cake that wasn't letting me speak, but that frickin' stutter. Trying to regain my composure, I went back into the family room and said to Emily, "Th, th, th, th." Once more, I tried to thank Emily, "Th, th, th, th."

Embarrassed, I could not speak, but only hear the laughter of ten wild seventh graders reverberating throughout the room. My good friend Shawn, always quick-witted, decided to slash open my wound a little further and promptly pour a tablespoon of salt on it. He said clearly and loudly, "Dang, Adrian speaks about as well as a cat barks."

High School stuttering pushes him to excel

More than anything, my stuttering as a child pushed me to aspire to excel so-cially. Throughout high school, I strug-gled to become a class leader whom others admired as someone who would express the concerns and wants of the school and group.

Extended Example

Meets and overcomes challenges

At the end of my junior year, my speech impediment was rarely noticeable. Furthermore, I wanted to prove to myself that I could speak in the most pressure-packed situations without a problem. Thus, I decided to run for senior class Vice President. I gave my election speech in front of my senior class of about 300 and Broomfield High School's faculty. Appr-

Develops new relationships and self-confidence

oaching the podium, I was nervous, but confident in my speech. Usually having difficulties with my first word, I concen-trated on my therapy tactics. "Keep it slow in the first word," I reminded my-self. "Breathe deeply and imagine being in a one-on-one conversation." The sweat flowing in large beads down my back, I delivered a strong, stutter-free, three minute speech. The crowd could not concentrate on my impediment because there was none. My classmates were forced to concentrate on the content of my speech. The next day I was given word of my election as class vice president.

No longer needs speech therapy

During my senior year I realized that I was no longer getting any comments about my speech. I also started using my techniques learned from seven years of speech therapy without thinking about them. I had not been in a dusty brown, eight-by-twelve cubicle for three years. Even better, there was no reason for me to ever foresee going back. My father and I sat down and discussed our impediment from time to time, but his assistance was all I would need.

Extended Example

On his own— biggest challenge

By the time I graduated from high school, I had overcome the biggest fear of my speech impediment. Speaking in front of large groups was no longer a time where my speech impediment would reveal itself. As the senior class Vice President, I was responsible for giving the closing address at graduation, probably the most high-pressure speech of all. For three weeks I rehearsed my graduation speech.

The biggest speech of my life was delivered on June 3, 1995, in front of two thousand friends, classmates, faculty and family. The football stadium stands were packed like a Mexican piñata for a Cinco De Mayo celebration. Over two thousand were in attendance, all to hear my closing address. Walking into the stadium I looked at the happy, but tightly squeezed crowd and realized that this was going to be a special moment in my eighteen-year-old life. More than the high school graduation that the class of 1995 was celebrating, I was celebrating my ability to speak in front of crowds.

For the following two hours I tried listening intently to all of the other speeches. I found myself getting very nervous, but my stutter did not once come to my mind as being a problem. I was only nervous because I was soon going to be on the biggest stage I had ever been on before. Principal Martin gave a short address after we received our diplomas. He then said, "Ladies and gentlemen, the closing address will be given by Class of 1995 Vice President Adrian Boykin."

Builds to climax emphasizing his victory over the impediment and the barriers it creates

I looked to the crowd, started slowly and let my voice flow continuously and smoothly, similar to an eagle soaring through the sky. As I concluded, I looked into the dots of faces in the crowd and my eyes met my father's.

Throwing my graduation cap into the still, windless sky, I celebrated a rite of passage.

ANDY ROONEY

Andrew A. Rooney was born in 1920 in Albany, New York. Drafted into the army while still a student at Colgate University, he served in the European theater of operations as a Stars and Stripes reporter. After the war Rooney began what has been a prolific and illustrious career as a writer-producer for various television networks—chiefly for CBS—and has won numerous awards, including the Writers Guild Award for Best Script of the Year (six times—more than any other writer in the history of the medium) and three National Academy Emmy awards. The author of a number of magazine articles in publications like *Esquire, Harper's,* and *Playboy,* Rooney is nonetheless probably most familiar for his regular appearances as a commentator on the television program *"60 Minutes."* Rooney also writes a syndicated column, which appears in more than 250 newspapers, and has lectured on documentary writing at various universities. His most recent books are *Pieces of My Mind* (1984), *Word for Word* (1986), *Not That you Asked* . . . (1989) *Sweet and Sour* (1992), and *My War* (1995). He now lives in Rowayton, Connecticut.

In and of Ourselves We Trust

"In and of Ourselves We Trust" was one of Rooney's syndicated columns. Rooney's piece uses one simple example to illustrate a generality. He draws from it a far-reaching set of conclusions: that we have a "contract" with each other to stop for red lights—and further, that our whole system of trust depends on everyone doing the right thing.

Last night I was driving from Harrisburg to Lewisburg, Pa., a dis-   1
tance of about 80 miles. It was late, I was late, and if anyone asked me how fast I was driving, I'd have to plead the Fifth Amendment to avoid self-incrimination.

At one point along an open highway, I came to a crossroads   2
with a traffic light. I was alone on the road by now, but as I approached the light, it turned red, and I braked to a halt. I looked left, right, and behind me. Nothing. Not a car, no suggestion of head-

lights, but there I sat, waiting for the light to change, the only human being, for at least a mile in any direction.

I started wondering why I refused to run the light. I was not 3 afraid of being arrested, because there was obviously no cop anywhere around and there certainly would have been no danger in going through it.

Much later that night, after I'd met with a group in Lewisburg 4 and had climbed into bed near midnight, the question of why I'd stopped for that light came back to me. I think I stopped because it's part of a contract we all have with each other. It's not only the law, but it's an agreement we have, and we trust each other to honor it: We don't go through red lights. Like most of us, I'm more apt to be restrained from doing something bad by the social convention that disapproves of it than by any law against it.

It's amazing that we ever trust each other to do the right thing, 5 isn't it? And we do, too. Trust is our first inclination. We have to make a deliberate decision to mistrust someone or to be suspicious or skeptical.

It's a darn good thing, too, because the whole structure of our 6 society depends on mutual trust, not distrust. This whole thing we have going for us would fall apart if we didn't trust each other most of the time. In Italy they have an awful time getting any money for the government because many people just plain don't pay their income tax. Here, the Internal Revenue Service makes some gestures toward enforcing the law, but mostly they just have to trust that we'll pay what we owe. There has often been talk of a tax revolt in this country, most recently among unemployed auto workers in Michigan, and our government pretty much admits that if there were a widespread tax revolt here, they wouldn't be able to do any thing about it.

We do what we say we'll do. We show up when we say we'll 7 show up.

I was so proud of myself for stopping for that red light. And 8 inasmuch as no one would ever have known what a good person I was on the road from Harrisburg to Lewisburg, I had to tell someone.

MEANINGS AND VALUES

1. Explain the concept of a "contract we all have with each other" (par. 4). How is the "agreement" achieved (par. 4)?

2.   Why do you suppose exceeding the speed limit (par. 1) would not also be included in the "contract"? Or is there some other reason for Rooney's apparent inconsistency?

3.   Explain the significance of the title of this selection.

EXPOSITORY TECHNIQUES

1.   How does the example of the red light "work" for readers? How does an analysis of this example help us better understand each other?

2.   What other uses of example do you find in the selection?

3.   What, if anything, do the brief examples in paragraph 6 add to this piece? (See "Guide to Terms": *Evaluation*.)

DICTION AND VOCABULARY

1.   Does it seem to you that the diction and vocabulary levels of this selection are appropriate for the purpose intended? Why or why not? (Guide: *Diction*.)

2.   Could this be classified as a formal essay? Why or why not? (Guide: *Essay*.)

3.   Rooney uses the word "trust" six times in paragraphs 4–6. How effective is the repetition of such a word? Why might Rooney have chosen this strategy?

READ TO WRITE

1.   **Collaborating:** Working in groups of three, list several examples that could help convey a main idea similar to the generality Rooney advances in his essay. Then, together, write a brief essay using these examples and employing a casual tone of voice similar to Rooney's.

2.   **Considering Audience:** Andy Rooney often appears on television as an oral commentator on events and social behavior. The style of this essay is more similar in some ways to spoken language than written language. How effective is this style for the essay's audience? Why is it/isn't it effective? Rewrite Rooney's essay in a more formal style and analyze the effectiveness of your new version.

3.   **Developing an Essay:** Choose an experience that revealed to you something about your personal characteristics, the traits of family or friends, or the "character" of a larger cultural or social group to which you belong. Using Rooney's essay as a model, use this experience as an example to illustrate a generality about your subject, and draw also on briefer examples in the course of your essay.

(NOTE: Suggestions for topics requiring development by use of EXAMPLE are on pp. 86-87 at the end of this chapter.)

WILLIAM F. BUCKLEY, JR.

WILLIAM F. BUCKLEY, Jr., was born in 1925 in New York, where he now lives. He graduated from Yale University and holds honorary degrees from a number of universities, including Seton Hall, Syracuse University, Notre Dame, and Lafayette College. He was editor in chief of *National Review* from 1955 to 1990. In addition, he has been a syndicated columnist since 1962, and host of public television's *Firing Line* since 1966. Generally considered one of the most articulate conservative writers, Buckley has published in various general circulation magazines and has received numerous honors and awards. He lectures widely and is the author of many novels and nonfiction books, among them *God and Man at Yale: The Superstitions of "Academic Freedom"* (1951), *Saving the Queen* (1976), *Stained Glass* (1978), *Marco Polo, If You Can* (1982), *Atlantic High* (1982), *Overdrive: A Personal Documentary* (1983), *The Story of Henri Tod* (1984), *The Tall Ships* (1986), *Mongoose R.I.P.* (1988), *On the Firing Line: The Public Life of Our Public Figures* (1989), *Happy Days Were Here again* (1993), *Brothers No More* (1996), and *McCarthy and His Enemies* (1995).

Why Don't We Complain?

First published in *Esquire*, "Why Don't We Complain?" is a good illustration of the grace and wit that characterize most of Buckley's writing. For students of composition, it can also provide another demonstration of the use of varied examples—some well developed, others scarcely at all—to make a single generality more specific. And the generality itself, as we can see toward the end, is of considerably broader significance than it appears at first.

It was the very last coach and the only empty seat on the entire train, so there was no turning back. The problem was to breathe. Outside, the temperature was below freezing. Inside the railroad car the temperature must have been about 85 degrees. I took off my overcoat, and few minutes later my jacket, and noticed that the car was flecked with the white shirts of the passengers. I soon found my hand moving to loosen my tie. From one end of the car to the other, as we rattled through Westchester County, we sweated; but we did not moan.

I watched the train conductor appear at the head of the car. "Tickets, all tickets, please!" In a more virile age, I thought, the passengers would seize the conductor and strap him down on a seat over the radiator to share the fate of his patrons. He shuffled down the aisle, picking up tickets, punching commutation cards. *No one addressed a word to him.* He approached my seat, and I drew a deep breath of resolution. "Conductor," I began with a considerable edge to my voice. . . . Instantly the doleful eyes of my seatmate turned tiredly from his newspaper to fix me with a resentful stare: what question could be so important as to justify my sibilant intrusion into his stupor? I was shaken by those eyes. I am incapable of making a discreet fuss, so I mumbled a question about what time were we due in Stamford (I didn't even ask whether it would be before or after dehydration could be expected to set in), got my reply, and went back to my newspaper and to wiping my brow.

The conductor had nonchalantly walked down the gauntlet of eighty sweating American freemen, and not one of them had asked him to explain why the passengers in that car had been consigned to suffer. There is nothing to be done when the temperature *outdoors* is 85 degrees, and indoors the air conditioner has broken down; obviously when that happens there is nothing to do, except perhaps curse the day that one was born. But when the temperature outdoors is below freezing, it takes a positive act of will on somebody's part to set the temperature *indoors* at 85. Somewhere a valve was turned too far, a furnace overstocked, a thermostat maladjusted: something that could easily be remedied by turning off the heat and allowing the great outdoors to come indoors. All this is so obvious. What is not obvious is what has happened to the American people.

It isn't just the commuters, whom we have come to visualize as a supine breed who have got on to the trick of suspending their sensory faculties twice a day while they submit to the creeping dissolution of the railroad industry. It isn't just they who have given up trying to rectify irrational vexations. It is the American people everywhere.

A few weeks ago at a large movie theater I turned to my wife and said, "The picture is out of focus." "Be quiet," she answered. I obeyed. But a few minutes later I raised the point again, with mounting impatience. "It will be all right in a minute," she said apprehensively. (She would rather lose her eyesight than be around when I make one of my infrequent scenes.) I waited. It was *just* out of focus—not glaringly out, but out. My vision is 20–20, and I assume that is the vision, adjusted, of most people in the movie house. So, after hectoring my wife throughout the first reel, I finally prevailed upon her to admit that it *was* off, and very annoying. We then settled down, coming to rest on the presumption that: (a) someone connected with the management of the theater must soon notice the blur and make the correction; or (b) that someone seated near the rear of the house would make the complaint in behalf of those of us up front; or (c) that—any minute now—the entire house would explode into catcalls and foot stamping, calling dramatic attention to the irksome distortion.

What happened was nothing. The movie ended, as it had begun,   6
just out of focus, and as we trooped out, we stretched our faces in a variety of contortions to accustom the eye to the shock of normal focus.

I think it is safe to say that everybody suffered on that occasion.   7
And I think it is safe to assume that everyone was expecting someone else to take the initiative in going back to speak to the manager. And it is probably true even that if we had supposed the movie would run right through the blurred image, someone surely would have summoned up the purposive indignation to get up out of his seat and file his complaint.

But notice that no one did. And the reason no one did is because   8
we are all increasingly anxious in America to be unobtrusive, we are reluctant to make our voices heard, hesitant about claiming our rights; we are afraid that our cause is unjust, or that if it is not unjust, that it is ambiguous; or if not even that, that it is too trivial to justify the horrors of a confrontation with Authority; we still sit in an oven or endure a racking headache before undertaking a head-on, I'm-here-to-tell-you complaint. That tendency to passive compliance, to a heedless endurance, is something to keep one's eyes on—in sharp focus.

I myself can occasionally summon the courage to complain, but   9
I cannot, as I have intimated, complain softly. My own instinct is so strong to let the thing ride, to forget about it—to expect that someone will take the matter up, when the grievance is collective, in my behalf—that it is only when the provocation is at a very special key, whose vibrations touch simultaneously a complexus of nerves, allergies, and passions, that I catch fire and find the reserves of courage and assertiveness to speak up. When that happens, I get quite carried away. My blood gets hot, my brow wet, I become unbearably and unconscionably sarcastic and bellicose; I am girded for a total showdown.

Why should that be? Why could not I (or anyone else) on that   10
railroad coach have said simply to the conductor, "Sir"—I take that

back: that sounds sarcastic—"Conductor, would you be good enough to turn down the heat? I am extremely hot. In fact, I tend to get hot every time the temperature reaches 85 degr—" Strike that last sentence. Just end it with the simple statement that you are extremely hot, and let the conductor infer the cause.

Every New Year's Eve I resolve to do something about the   11
Milquetoast in me and vow to speak up, calmly, for my rights, and for the betterment of our society, on every appropriate occasion. Entering last New Year's Eve, I was fortified in my resolve because that morning at breakfast I had had to ask the waitress three times for a glass of milk. She finally brought it—after I had finished my eggs, which is when I don't want it any more. I did not have the manliness to order her to take the milk back, but settled instead for a cowardly sulk, and ostentatiously refused to drink the milk— though I later paid for it—rather than state plainly to the hostess, as I should have, why I had not drunk it, and would not pay for it.

So by the time the New Year ushered out the Old, riding in on   12
my morning's indignation and stimulated by the gastric juices of resolution that flow so faithfully on New Year's Eve, I rendered my vow. Henceforward I would conquer my shyness, my despicable disposition to supineness. I would speak out like a man against the unnecessary annoyances of our time.

Forty-eight hours later, I was standing in line at the ski repair   13
store in Pico Peak, Vermont. All I needed, to get on with my skiing, was the loan, for one minute, of a small screwdriver, to tighten a loose binding. Behind the counter in the workshop were two men. One was industriously engaged in servicing the complicated requirements of a young lady at the head of the line, and obviously he would be tied up for quite a while. The other—"Jiggs," his workmate called him—was a middle-aged man, who sat in a chair puffing a pipe, exchanging small talk with his working partner. My pulse began its telltale acceleration. The minutes ticked on. I stared at the idle shopkeeper, hoping to shame him into action, but he was impervious to my telepathic reproof and continued his small talk with his friend, brazenly insensitive to the nervous demands of six good men who were raring to ski.

Suddenly my New Year's Eve resolution struck me. It was now   14
or never. I broke from my place in line and marched to the counter. I was going to control myself. I dug my nails into my palms. My effort was only partially successful:

"If you are not too busy," I said icily, "would you mind handing   15
me a screwdriver?"

Work stopped and everyone turned his eyes on me, and I expe-   16
rienced that mortification I always feel when I am the center of centripetal shafts of curiosity, resentment, perplexity.

But the worst was yet to come. "I am sorry, sir," said Jiggs def-   17
erentially, moving the pipe from his mouth. "I am not supposed to
move. I have just had a heart attack." That was the signal for a great
whirring noise that descended from heaven. We looked, stricken,
out the window, and it appeared as though a cyclone had suddenly
focused on the snowy courtyard between the shop and the ski lift.
Suddenly a gigantic army helicopter materialized, and hovered
down to a landing. Two men jumped out of the plane carrying a
stretcher, tore into the ski shop, and lifted the shopkeeper onto the
stretcher. Jiggs bade his companion good-by, was whisked out the
door, into the plane, up to the heavens, down—we learned—to a
nearby army hospital. I looked up manfully—into a score of man-
eating eyes. I put the experience down as a reversal.

As I write this, on an airplane, I have run out of paper and need   18
to reach into my briefcase under my legs for more. I cannot do this
until my empty lunch tray is removed from my lap. I arrested the
stewardess as she passed empty-handed down the aisle on the way
to the kitchen to fetch the lunch trays for the passengers up forward
who haven't been served yet. "Would you please take my tray?"
"Just a *moment*, sir!" she said, and marched on sternly. Shall I tell her
that since she is headed for the kitchen anyway, it could not delay the
feeding of the other passengers by more than two seconds necessary
to stash away my empty tray? Or remind her that not fifteen minutes
ago she spoke unctuously into the loudspeaker the words undoubtedly devised by the airline's highly paid public relations counselor:
"If there is anything I or Miss French can do for you to make your
trip more enjoyable, *please* let us—" I have run out of paper.

I think the observable reluctance of the majority of Americans   19
to assert themselves in minor matters is related to our increased
sense of helplessness in an age of technology and centralized political and economic power. For generations, Americans who were too
hot, or too cold, got up and did something about it. Now we call the
plumber, or the electrician, or the furnace man. The habit of looking
after our own needs obviously had something to do with the assertiveness that characterized the American family familiar to readers of American literature. With the technification of life goes our
direct responsibility for our material environment, and we are conditioned to adopt a position of helplessness not only as regards the
broken air conditioner, but as regards the overheated train. It takes

an expert to fix the former, but not the latter; yet these distinctions, as we withdraw into helplessness, tend to fade away.

Our notorious political apathy is a related phenomenon. Every year, whether the Republican or the Democratic Party is in office, more and more power drains away from the individual to feed vast reservoirs in far-off places; and we have less and less say about the shape of events which shape our future. From this alienation of personal power comes the sense of resignation with which we accept the political dispensations of a powerful government whose hold upon us continues to increase.   20

An editor of a national weekly news magazine told me a few years ago that as few as a dozen letters of protest against an editorial stance of his magazine was enough to convene a plenipotentiary meeting of the board of editors to review policy. "So few people complain, or make their voices heard," he explained to me, "that we assume a dozen letters represent the inarticulated views of thousands of readers." In the past ten years, he said, the volume of mail has noticeably decreased, even though the circulation of his magazine has risen.   21

When our voices are finally mute, when we have finally suppressed the natural instinct to complain, whether the vexation is trivial or grave, we shall have become automatons, incapable of feeling. When Premier Khrushchev first came to this country late in 1959, he was primed, we are informed, to experience the bitter resentment of the American people against his tyranny, against his persecutions, against the movement which is responsible for the great number of American deaths in Korea, for billions in taxes every year, and for life everlasting on the brink of disaster; but Khrushchev was pleasantly surprised, and reported back to the Russian people that he had been met with overwhelming cordiality (read: apathy), except, to be sure, for "a few fascists who followed me around with their wretched posters, and should be horse-whipped."   22

I may be crazy, but I say there would have been lots more posters in a society where train temperatures in the dead of winter are not allowed to climb to 85 degrees without complaint.   23

MEANINGS AND VALUES

1.   Restate completely what you believe to be the meaning of the last sentence of paragraph 8. How close does Buckley's sentence, or your

version of it, come to stating the central theme of the selection? (See "Guide to Terms": *Unity*.)

2. Why do you think the author said to "strike that last sentence" of the quoted matter in paragraph 10?

3. Explain the connection between anti-Khrushchev posters and complaining about the heat in a train (par. 23).

EXPOSITORY TECHNIQUES

1. What generality do Buckley's examples illustrate?

2. Does the use of examples seem to you the best way for the writer to have developed his theme? If not, what might have been a better way?

3. Which of the standard methods of introduction does the first paragraph demonstrate? How successful is its use? (Guide: *Introductions; Evaluation*.)

4. How effective is the example of the elderly man (pars. 13–17)? Why does Buckley immediately follow this with the airline example?

5. Why do you think the Khrushchev example is kept until last? (Guide: *Emphasis*.)

DICTION AND VOCABULARY

1. Explain the allusion to Milquetoast in paragraph 11. (Guide: *Figures of Speech*.)

2. Explain the meaning (in par. 22) of Khrushchev's being "met with overwhelming cordiality (read: apathy)."

3. To what extent, if at all, were you annoyed by Buckley's liberal use of "dictionary-type" words? Is the use of such terms a matter of personal style alone or does it serve other purposes? What might those other purposes be?

4. Use a dictionary as needed to understand the meanings of the following words: virile, doleful, sibilant, discreet (par. 2); gauntlet, consigned (3); supine, faculties, dissolution, rectify (4); hectoring (5); purposive (7); unobtrusive, ambiguous (8); provocation, complexus, unconscionably, bellicose, girded (9); infer (10); ostentatiously (11); impervious, reproof (13); centripetal (16); deferentially (17); unctuously (18); technification (19); apathy, phenomenon, dispensations (20); stance, plenipotentiary, inarticulated (21); automatons (22).

READ TO WRITE

1. **Collaborating:** Much like Rooney's essay, Buckey's piece places personal commentary paragraphs between the examples. Identify such paragraphs and, working in a group, assign each person one of the

paragraphs. Have each person then write an analysis of how effective is the relationship of the commentary paragraph to the examples on which it comments or to the essay as a whole.

2.   **Considering Audience:** Buckley seems to suggest that if we assert ourselves in small matters, we will be willing to do so in important ones as well. Write a brief description of three situations (relatively unimportant, somewhat important, and very important) in which people might have the opportunity to assert themselves. Poll some of your friends or fellow students to find out whether or not they would speak up in each situation, and then ask them to explain the reasoning behind their choices. Report the responses and reasons in a short paper, indicating also whether you believe Buckley has correctly judged the attitudes and likely actions of his readers.

3.   **Developing an Essay:** Follow Buckey's lead in using a series of examples to explain a generality about ways we commonly behave and to suggest what we might do to "improve" our behavior. Consider including some examples from your own behavior, including ones in which you poke fun at yourself or criticize your own actions.

(NOTE: Suggestions for topics requiring development by use of EXAMPLE are on pp. 86-87 at the end of this chapter.)

MARY KARR

MARY KARR's highly-praised memoir of her Texas childhood and unusual family, *The Liar's Club,* was first published in 1995. It won a
PEN Prize and is frequently cited as among the best of the many
moving and insightful accounts of growing up that have appeared
in recent years. Karr, who teaches creative writing at Syracuse
University, has also published several volumes of poetry: *Abacus*
(1987) and *The Devil's Tour* (1993).

Dysfunctional Nation

To make the point that her dysfunctional family was far from
unique, Karr draws examples from the many stories of other families she heard on a tour to promote her memoir. She suggests, in
addition, that growing up in such a setting may not prevent a person from achieving a healthy identity and sense of self as an adult.

When I set out on a book tour to promote the memoir about my   1
less-than-perfect Texas clan, I did so with soul-sucking dread.
Surely we'd be held up as grotesques, my beloveds and I. Instead, I
shoved into bookstores where sometimes hundreds of people stood
claiming to identify with my story, which fact stunned me.

For one thing, my artist mother had been married seven times,   2
twice to my Texas oil-worker daddy, who was Nos. 5 and 7. Both of
my parents drank hard enough to hit some jackpots. Both were well
armed. (The tile man who came to redo my mother's kitchen last
spring pried more than one .22 slug from the wall.)

Yet in towns across this country I sat at various bookstore tables   3
till near closing and heard people posit that reading about my tribe
brought not slack-jawed horror, but recognition. Maybe these peoples' family lives differed from mine in terms of surface pyrotechnics—houses set afire and fortunes squandered. But the feelings
didn't. After eight weeks of travel, I ginned up this working definition
for a dysfunctional family: any family with more than one person in it.

Even the most perfect-looking clan seemed to suffer a rough   4
patch. "I'm from one of these Donna Reed households you always
wanted to belong to," said the elegant woman in Chicago. But her

doctor daddy got saddled with a wicked malpractice suit, a few more martinis than usual got poured from his silver shaker every night. Rumor was he took up with his nurse.

What happened? "We worked it out. It passed." But not before   5 his Cadillac plowed over her bicycle one drunken night and her mother threatened divorce. Like me, she'd lain awake listening to her parents storm around in the masks of monsters and felt the metaphorical foundations of her house tremble, hopeless to prop it all up.

Not all folks reported such rough times as mere blips on the fam-   6 ily time line. In fact, I met dozens of people from way more chaotic households than mine. One guy's drug-dealer parents allegedly dragged him across several borders with bags of heroin taped under his Doctor Denton sleeper. Another woman had, at age 5, watched her alcoholic mother stick her head in a noose and step off a kitchen stool while the girl fought to shield her toddler brother's eyes. Surely many don't survive such childhoods intact (or they don't go to book signings because they're too busy being serial killers). But the myth that such a childhood condemns you to a life curled up in the back ward of a mental institution dissolved for me. On the surface, people seemed to have got over their troubled upbringings.

The female therapist in a Portland bookstore talked specifically   7 about the power of narrative in her life. She'd been raised by a chronic schizophrenic. On a given day, her school clothes were selected by God himself talking to her mother through scalp implants. The girl got good at worming her way into the homes of neighbors and any halfway decent teacher. In college, she fought depression with counseling she continued for nearly 10 years.

At 50, happily married, she wore a Burberry raincoat and toted   8 a briefcase of fine leather. She showed no visible signs of trauma. The real miracle? She was in fairly close touch with her mother, whose psychosis had diminished with new medications.

In part, this woman claimed to have survived through stories.   9 Traditional therapy, of course, starts with retelling family dramas. Talk about it, in the old wisdom, and the hurt eventually recedes. From narratives about her childhood, a self eventually emerged. Her tendency otherwise would have been to lop herself off from her own past, to make a false self for navigating the world. But false selves rarely withstand the real blows life delivers, hence, her need for stories, her own and other peoples'.

In our longing for some assurance that we're behaving O.K. in-   10 side fairly isolated families, personal experience has assumed some new power. Just as the novel form once took up experiences of urban, industrialized society that weren't being handled in epic poems or epistles, so memoir—with its single, intensely personal voice—wrestles subjects in a way readers of late find compelling. The good ones I've read confirm my experience in a flawed family. They reassure the same way belonging to a community reassures.

My bookstore chats did the same. On the road, I came to believe   11
that our families are working, albeit in new forms. People go on birthing babies and burying dead and loving those with whom they've shared deeply wretched patches of history. We do this partly by telling stories, in voices that seek neither to deny family struggles nor to make demons of our beloveds.

MEANINGS AND VALUES

1. What conclusion about families does Karr offer in paragraph 3? What examples does she provide to illustrate and support this generality?

2. Does Karr believe our identities and well being are primarily determined by our family backgrounds? If so, where in the essay does she make this point? If not, what else does she believe shapes who we are?

EXPOSITORY TECHNIQUES

1. Explain how the statement, "On the surface, people seemed to have got over their troubled upbringings" (par. 6), serves both to separate the two halves of the essay and to link them (see "Guide to Terms": *Transition*.) In what ways does the second half of the essay answer questions suggested by the statement?

2. In what specific ways does the example in the second half of the essay (pars. 7–9) and the way it is presented differ from the examples in the first half? How much space does the writer devote to presenting the later example and how much to commenting on and interpreting it?

3. What strategy does the writer employ to conclude the essay? (Guide: *Closings*.)

DICTION AND VOCABULARY

1. Karr uses a number of vivid phrases in the course of the essay: "soul-sucking dread" (par. 1); "drank hard enough to hit some jackpots" (2), "in the masks of monsters" and "the metaphorical foundations of her house" (5). Tell what each of these phrases means and what it contributes to the essay's effectiveness.

2.   If you do not know the meaning of any of the following words, look them up in a dictionary: memoir, grotesques (par. 1); pyrotechnics, squandered, ginned, dysfunctional (3); trauma, psychosis (8); epistles (10); albeit (11).

READ TO WRITE

1.   **Collaborating:** Karr's essay touches on a variety of subjects, including storytelling, alcoholism, and family relationships. Make a list of all the subjects she mentions, and then choose two that you find most interesting. Then for each subject, make a list of topics or issues you might wish to explore in an essay of your own. Share your list with a group of classmates, asking them to identify topics they find most intriguing. Do the same for their lists, and, as a group, decide which topics are the most compelling and why.

2.   **Considering Audience:** Other than the ones Karr discusses, what situations, relationships, or social forces make it hard for people to establish healthy identities? How many of these is the average person likely to encounter in his or her life? How many are they likely to know about from other people's experiences? How do people learn about such matters if not from their own experiences? Prepare a short essay discussing why readers in general would be likely to be comfortable or uncomfortable with an essay that presents examples of each type of negative situation, relationship, or social force. Include an explanation of why different groups of readers might react in different ways.

3.   **Developing an Essay:** Karr begins her essay by describing a situation that surprised her by turning out to be the opposite of what she expected. Use this strategy to begin an essay of your own, and then go on to explore what you learned through the experience (just as Karr does).

(NOTE: Suggestions for topics requiring development by use of EXAMPLE are on pp. 86-87 at the end of this chapter.)

Issues and Ideas:

Identities

- Will Haygood, *Underground Dads*
- Henry Han Xi Lau, *I Was a Member of the Kung Fu Crew*
- Alan Buczynski, *Iron Bonding*

Discovering (or constructing) our identities—the attitudes, feelings, and ways of behaving that make us individuals—is an ongoing job for most people. Personal identity is a favorite topic for writers, too, because it plays an important role in determining what we believe and how we act.

Though they may agree on its importance, writers are just as likely to disagree about the meaning of "identity" and to argue over whether each of us has one true identity or many different ones. For some, identity is the sum of what we are as individuals, the product of our unique experiences and personal outlooks. For others, it is part of the "character" we share with people who are shaped by similar social and cultural forces. For still others, an identity is a role we construct for ourselves and play in specific settings or for particular purposes, and we are likely to have more than one identity.

The first three essays in this chapter (by Andy Rooney, William F. Buckley, Jr., and Mary Karr) alert readers to some of the perspectives that shape our lives. The three essays that follow (by Wil Haygood, Henry Han Xi Lau, and Alan Buczynski) offer generalities and examples that focus more specifically on the various ways we discover, construct, use, and struggle with our various identities.

WIL HAYGOOD

WIL HAYGOOD is the author of *The Heygoods of Columbus*, a memoir of his family.

Underground Dads

Parents generally play key roles in shaping our identities, but what happens to someone who has not one parent or two, but a number of people who fill the role? Using as examples the men who acted as "underground fathers" for him, Haygood explains how unconventional parenting of the kind he experienced as a boy can be loving, supportive, and successful. This essay first appeared in the *New York Times Magazine*.

For years, while growing up, I shamelessly told my playmates   1
that I didn't have a father. In my neighborhood, where men went to work with lunch pails, my friends thought there was a gaping hole in my household. My father never came to the park with me to toss a softball, never came to see me in any of my school plays. I'd explain to friends, with the simplicity of explaining to someone that there are, in some woods, no deer, that I just had no father. My friends looked at me and squinted. My mother and father had divorced shortly after my birth. As the years rolled by, however, I did not have the chance to turn into the pitiful little black boy who had been abandoned by his father. There was a reason: other men showed up. They were warm, honest (at least as far as my eyes could see) and big-hearted. They were the good black men in the shadows, the men who taught me right from wrong, who taught me how to behave, who told me, by their very actions, that they expected me to do good things in life.

There are heartbreaking statistics tossed about regarding single-   2
parent black households these days, about children growing up fatherless. Those statistics must be considered. But how do you count the other men, the ones who show up—with perfect timing, with a kind of soft-stepping loveliness—to give a hand, to take a boy to watch airplanes lift off, to show a young boy the beauty of planting tomatoes in the ground and to tell a child that all of life is not misery?

In my life, there was Jerry, who hauled junk. He had a lean   3
body and a sweet smile. He walked like a cowboy, all bowlegged,

swinging his shoulders. It was almost a strut. The sound of his pickup truck rumbling down our alley in Columbus, Ohio, could raise me from sleep.

When he wasn't hauling junk, Jerry fixed things. More than once, he fixed my red bicycle. The gears were always slipping; the chain could turn into a tangled mess. Hearing pain in my voice, Jerry would instruct me to leave my bike on our front porch. In our neighborhood, in the 60's, no one would steal your bike from your porch. Jerry promised me he'd pick it up, and he always did. He never lied to me, and he cautioned me not to tell lies. He was, off and on, my mother's boyfriend. At raucous family gatherings, he'd pull me aside and explain to me the importance of honesty, of doing what one promised to do.

And there was Jimmy, my grandfather, who all his life paid his bills the day they arrived: that was a mighty lesson in itself—it taught me a work ethic. He held two jobs, and there were times when he allowed me to accompany him on his night job, when he cleaned a Greek restaurant on the north side of Columbus. Often he'd mop the place twice, as if trying to win some award. He frightened me too. It was not because he was mean. It was because he had exacting standards, and there were times when I didn't measure up to those standards. He didn't like shortcutters. His instructions, on anything, were to be carried out to the letter. He believed in independence, doing as much for yourself as you possibly could. It should not have surprised me when, one morning while having stomach pains, he chose not to wait for a taxi and instead walked the mile to the local hospital, where he died a week later of stomach cancer.

My uncles provided plenty of good background music when I was coming of age. Uncle Henry took me fishing. He'd phone the night before. "Be ready. Seven o'clock." I'd trail him through woods—as a son does a father—until we found our fishing hole. We'd sit for hours. He taught me patience and an appreciation of the outdoors, of nature. He talked, incessantly, of family—his family, my family, the family of friends. The man had a reverence for family. I knew to listen.

I think these underground fathers simply appear, decade to decade, flowing through the generations. Hardly everywhere, and hardly, to be sure, in enough places, but there. As mystical, sometimes, as fate when fate is sweet.

Sometimes I think that all these men who have swept in and out of my life still couldn't replace a good, warm father. But inasmuch as I've never known a good, warm father, the men who entered my life, who taught me right from wrong, who did things they were not asked to do, have become unforgettable. I know of the cold statistics out there. And yet, the mountain of father-son literature does not haunt me. I've known good black men.

Meanings and Values

1. What are some of the important things that fathers are supposed to teach their sons? Why in paragraph 1 does Haygood compare a boy without a father to woods without a deer?

2. Twice in the essay Haygood mentions "good black men." Why do you think he makes race an issue with this reference?

3. In the beginning of paragraph 2, Haygood speaks of "heartbreaking statistics tossed about regarding single-parent households . . . . " He says that these figures must be considered, yet he goes on to talk about households such as his, where "good black men" have helped raise children. Why does he mention such statistics if he does not plan to focus on them in the essay?

Expository Techniques

1. What examples does the author present of fatherly acts he experienced while growing up?

2. Would the examples of fatherly acts be sufficient to convince most readers that the writer should not be pitied for the lack of a father in his home? (See "Guide to Terms": *Evaluation*.)

3. Why does Haygood list several men who had an effect on his life and attitudes? Would his essay have been more effective if he had built it around one representative example of an influential man?

Diction and Vocabulary

1. Why does the writer use the words "gaping hole" to describe his friends' image of his household? Is this a figure of speech? (Guide: *Figures of Speech*.)

2. How does the word "shamelessly" (par. 1) help define the image of himself the writer presents to readers? What other words and phrases does he employ to shape his audience's responses to himself?

Read to Write

1. **Collaborating:** Prepare a list of men (not including your biological or adoptive father) who have had a profound impact on your life. Note

also their relationship to you. Share your list with two other students in your class. Compare the roles that these men have had in shaping you into an adult. Write a two-page essay analyzing the similarities and differences between the adult males in your life and those in the lives of your classmates.

2. **Considering Audience:** Haygood's essay may strike chords in readers who have been raised without a father at home. However, even readers who have had fathers in their daily lives are likely to respond strongly to this essay. Why would both groups of readers understand the points Haygood makes? What similarities exist between children raised with fathers as a daily presence and those without? What are important differences, if any? Consider the varied ways in which readers might react to this essay based on their upbringing. Prepare a short essay explaining the different reactions readers might have to Haygood's essay.

3. **Developing an Essay:** Haygood mentions his mother briefly in paragraph 1 of his essay; however, he does not discuss her effect on his life or the expectations he held for her. Make a list of the traditional "teaching" responsibilities of mothers and of fathers. Using these responsibilities as examples, prepare an essay supporting or refuting the notion that one person can take on the roles of both parents.

(NOTE: Suggestions for topics requiring development by use of EXAMPLE are on pp. 86-87 at the end of this chapter.)

HENRY HAN XI LAU

Henry Han Xi Lau is a student at Yale University.

I Was a Member of the Kung Fu Crew

Do clothes and actions simply communicate our identities or do they help create them? Do identities come naturally or do we have to work at establishing them? What if we take on different identities for different parts of our lives? These are some of the questions the author addresses using vivid examples drawn from his experience as part of the "Kung Fu Crew." The essay first appeared in the *New York Times Magazine*.

Chinatown is ghetto, my friends are ghetto, I am ghetto. I went   1
away to college last year, but I still have a long strand of hair that reaches past my chin. I need it when I go back home to hang with the K.F.C.—for Kung Fu Crew, not Kentucky Fried Chicken. We all met in a Northern Shaolin kung fu class years ago. Our *si-fu* was Rocky. He told us: "In the early 1900's in China, your grand master was walking in the streets when a foreigner riding on a horse disrespected him. So then he felt the belly of the horse with his palms and left. Shortly thereafter, the horse buckled and died because our grand master had used *qi-gong* to mess up the horse's internal organs." Everyone said, "Cool, I would like to do that." Rocky emphasized, "You've got to practice really hard for a long time to reach that level."

By the time my friends and I were in the eighth grade, we were   2
able to do 20-plus push-ups on our knuckles and fingers. When we practiced our crescent, roundhouse and tornado kicks, we had 10-pound weights strapped to our legs. Someone once remarked, "Goddamn—that's a freaking mountain!" when he saw my thigh muscles in gym class.

Most Chinatown kids fall into a few general categories. There   3
are pale-faced nerds who study all the time to get into the Ivies. There are the recent immigrants with uncombed hair and crooked teeth who sing karaoke in bars. There are the punks with highlighted hair who cut school, and the gangsters, whom everyone else avoids.

Then there is the K.F.C. We work hard like the nerds, but we   4
identify with the punks. Now we are reunited, and just as in the old

days we amble onto Canal Street, where we stick out above the older folks, elderly women bearing leaden bags of bok choy and oranges. As an opposing crew nears us, I assess them to determine whether to grill them or not. Grilling is the fine art of staring others down and trying to emerge victorious.

How the hair is worn is important in determining one's order   5 on the streets. In the 80's the dominant style was the mushroom cut, combed neatly or left wild in the front so that a person can appear menacing as he peers through his bangs. To gain an edge in grilling now, some kids have asymmetrical cuts, with long random strands sprouting in the front, sides or back. Some dye their hair blue or green, while blood red is usually reserved for gang members.

Only a few years ago, examination of the hair was sufficient.   6 But now there is a second step: assessing pants. A couple of years ago, wide legs first appeared in New York City, and my friends and I switched from baggy pants. In the good old days, Merry-Go-Round in the Village sold wide legs for only $15 a pair. When Merry-Go-Round went bankrupt, Chinatown kids despaired. Wide-leg prices at other stores increased drastically as they became more popular. There are different ways of wearing wide legs. Some fold their pant legs inward and staple them at the hem. Some clip the back ends of their pants to their shoes with safety pins. Others simply cut the bottoms so that fuzzy strings hang out.

We grill the opposing punks. I untuck my long strand of hair so   7 that it swings in front of my face. Nel used to have a strand, but he chewed it off one day in class by accident. Chu and Tom cut their strands off because it scared people at college. Jack has a patch of blond hair, while Tone's head is a ball of orange flame. Chi has gelled short hair, while Ken's head is a black mop. As a group, we have better hair than our rivals. But they beat us with their wide legs. In our year away at college, wide legs have gone beyond our 24-inch leg openings. Twenty-six- to 30-inch jeans are becoming the norm. If wide legs get any bigger, they will start flying up like a skirt in an updraft.

We have better accessories, though. Chi sports a red North Face   8 that gives him a rugged mountain-climber look because of the jungle of straps sprouting in the back. Someone once asked Chi, "Why is the school bag so important to one's cool?" He responded, "Cuz it's the last thing others see when you walk away from them or when they turn back to look at you after you walk past them." But the other crew has female members, which augments their points. The encounter between us ends in a stalemate. But at least the K.F.C. members are in college and are not true punks.

In the afternoon, we decide to eat at the Chinatown   9
McDonald's for a change instead of the Chinese bakery Maria's, our
dear old hangout spot. "Mickey D's is a good sit," Nel says. I answer: "But the Whopper gots more fat and meat. It's even got more
bun." Nel agrees. "True that," he says. I want the Big Mac, but I buy
the two-cheeseburger meal because it has the same amount of meat
but costs less.

We sit and talk about ghettoness again. We can never exactly ar-   10
ticulate what being ghetto entails, but we know the spirit of it. In
Chinatown toilet facilities we sometimes find footprints on the seats
because F.O.B.'s (Fresh off the boats) squat on them as they do over
the holes in China. We see alternative brand names in stores like
Dolo instead of Polo, and Mike instead of Nike.

We live by ghettoness. My friends and I walk from 80-something   11
Street in Manhattan to the tip of the island to save a token. We gorge
ourselves at Gray's Papaya because the hot dogs are 50 cents each.
But one cannot be stingy all the time. We leave good tips at Chinese
restaurants because our parents are waiters and waitresses, too.

We sit for a long time in the McDonald's, making sure that there   12
is at least a half-inch of soda in our cups so that when the staff wants
to kick us out, we can claim that we are not finished yet. Jack positions a mouse bite of cheeseburger in the center of a wrapper to support our claim.

After a few hours, the K.F.C. prepares to disband. I get in one of   13
the no-license commuter vans on Canal Street that will take me to
Sunset Park in Brooklyn, where my family lives now. All of my
friends will leave Chinatown, for the Upper East Side and the Lower
East Side, Forest Hills in Queens and Bensonhurst in Brooklyn. We
live far apart, but we always come back together in Chinatown. For
most of us, our homes used to be here and our world was here.

Meanings and Values

1. According to the author of this essay, what are the two tests to determine a person's order in the streets? Why are these two so important?

2. In paragraph 10, the writer says, "We sit and talk about ghettoness
   again. We can never exactly articulate what being ghetto entails, but
   we know the spirit of it." What examples of the spirit does he give?
   What is he trying to get his readers to understand through these
   examples?

EXPOSITORY TECHNIQUES

1.   According to the author, what four types of people are representative of the population in the ghetto? Are these examples exclusive to the ghetto? What role does this classification play in the overall development of the exposition? (See the introduction to Chapter 4.)

2.   What distinguishes the Kung Fu Crew from other groups? How does this distinction affect their image?

3.   What use does the author make of an anecdote in paragraph 1?

DICTION AND VOCABULARY

1.   Why does the writer say "I am the ghetto" in paragraph 1? Why does he follow this statement with a sentence informing the reader that he is in college?

2.   What is "grilling" (par. 4)? How successful at "grilling" is the Kung Fu Crew on this occasion?

READ TO WRITE

1.   **Collaborating:** Consider the things you and your friends did in high school for fun. Prepare a list of these events and compare your lists with those of several classmates. Are there similarities? Do some experiences seem to cross social and economic boundaries to become universal to teens in North America? Write a short essay on the topic of growing up in America, drawing on the experiences you share with your classmates, or write an essay exploring the contrasts you discovered among your experiences and those of your classmates.

2.   **Considering Audience:** Think about the different groups of people that might read this essay. How do you think teens would react to it? Would they identify with the examples? Would their responses vary according to the neighborhoods where they lived? Would the examples in this piece be effective for a sixty-year-old reader? Why, or why not? Are the experiences of such a reader in any way similar to those described in the essay? Put yourself in the role of various readers by writing four one-paragraph responses to the essay: one from the perspective of an eighteen-year-old who grew up in an inner city; one from the perspective of an eighteen-year-old from a rural community; one from the perspective of a fifty-year-old raised in the suburbs; and one from the perspective of a fifty-year-old living and raised in a large city.

3.   **Developing an Essay:** Write an essay describing the culture of your neighborhood. Be sure to provide examples of the different types of people you knew and the different groups of friends that lived there. What did you need to "fit in" the neighborhood? Were there different "requirements" for each group?

(NOTE: Suggestions for topics requiring development by use of EXAMPLE are on pp. 86-87 at the end of this chapter.)

ALAN BUCZYNSKI

ALAN BUCZYNSKI is a construction worker and a writer who lives in the Detroit area.

Iron Bonding

Newspaper columns, magazine articles, and everyday conversations are often filled with generalities about the different ways men and women behave. This essay looks at the emotional life of men, offering a working person's perspective rather than that of the intellectuals and professional people often associated with the "men's movement." The essay first appeared in *The New York Times Magazine*.

"I just don't get it." We were up on the iron, about 120 feet, waiting for the gang below to swing up another beam. Sweat from under Ron's hard hat dripped on the beam we were sitting on and evaporated immediately, like water thrown on a sauna stove. We were talking about the "men's movement" and "wildman weekends." 1

"I mean," he continued, "if they want to get dirty and sweat and cuss and pound on things, why don't they just get real jobs and get paid for it?" Below, the crane growled, the next piece lifting skyward. 2

I replied: "Nah, Ron, that isn't the point. They don't want to sweat every day, just sometimes." 3

He said: "Man, if you only sweat when you want to, I don't call that real sweatin." 4

Although my degree is in English, I am an ironworker by trade; my girlfriend, Patti, is a graduate student in English literature. Like a tennis ball volleyed by two players with distinctly different styles, I am bounced between blue-collar maulers and precise academicians. My conversations range from fishing to Foucault, derricks to deconstruction. There is very little overlap, but when it does occur it is generally the academics who are curious about the working life. 5

Patti and I were at a dinner party. The question of communication between men had arisen. Becky, the host, is a persistent interrogator: "What do you and Ron talk about?" 6

I said, "Well, we talk about work, drinking, ah, women."   7

Becky asked, "Do you guys ever say, 'I love you' to each other?"   8
This smelled mightily of Robert Bly and the men's movement.

I replied: "Certainly. All the time."   9

I am still dissatisfied with this answer. Not because it was a lie,   10
but because it was perceived as one.

The notion prevails that men's emotional communication skills   11
are less advanced than that of chimpanzees, that we can no more
communicate with one another than can earthworms.

Ironworkers as a group may well validate this theory. We are   12
not a very articulate bunch. Most of us have only a basic education.
Construction sites are extremely noisy, and much of our communication takes place via hand signals. There is little premium placed
on words that don't stem from our own jargon. Conversations can
be blunt.

Bly's approach, of adapting a fable for instruction, may instinc-   13
tively mimic the way men communicate. Ironworkers are otherwise
very direct, yet when emotional issues arise we speak to one another
in allegory and parable. One of my co-workers, Cliff, is a good storyteller, with an understated delivery: "The old man got home one
night, drunk, real messed up and got to roughhousing with the cat.
Old Smoke, well she laid into him, scratched him good. Out comes
the shotgun. The old man loads up, chases Smoke into the front yard
and blam! Off goes the gun. My Mom and my sisters and me we're
all screamin'. Smoke comes walkin' in the side door. Seems the old
man blew away the wrong cat, the neighbor's Siamese. Red lights
were flashin' against the house, fur was splattered all over the lawn,
the cops cuffed my old man and he's hollerin' and man, I'll tell you,
I was cryin'."

Now, we didn't all get up from our beers and go over and hug   14
him. This was a story, not therapy. Cliff is amiable, but tough, more
inclined to solving any perceived injustices with his fists than verbal
banter, but I don't need to see him cry to know that he can. He has
before, and he can tell a story about it without shame, without any
disclaimers about being "just a kid," and that's enough for me.

Ron and I have worked together for nine years and are as close as   15
29 is to 30. We have worked through heat and cold and seen each
other injured in the stupidest of accidents. One February we were
working inside a plant, erecting steel with a little crane; it was near
the end of the day, and I was tired. I hooked onto a piece and, while
still holding the load cable, signaled the operator "up." My thumb
was promptly sucked into the sheave of the crane. I screamed, and the

operator came down on the load, releasing my thumb. It hurt. A lot. Water started leaking from my eyes. The gang gathered around while Ron tugged gently at my work glove, everyone curious whether my thumb would come off with the glove or stay on my hand.

"O.K., man, relax, just relax," Ron said. "See if you can move   16
it." Ron held my hand. The thumb had a neat crease right down the center, lengthwise. All the capillaries on one side had burst and were turning remarkable colors. My new thumbnail was on back order and would arrive in about five months. I wiggled the thumb, an eighth of an inch, a quarter, a half.

"You're O.K., man, it's still yours and it ain't broke. Let's go   17
back to work."

Afterwards, in the bar, while I wrapped my hand around a cold   18
beer to keep the swelling and pain down, Ron hoisted his bottle in a toast: "That," he said, "was the best scream I ever heard, real authentic, like you were in actual pain, like you were really *scared.*"

If this wasn't exactly Wind in His Hair howling eternal friend-   19
ship for Dances With Wolves, I still understood what Ron was saying. It's more like a 7-year-old boy putting a frog down the back of a little girl's dress because he has a crush on her. It's a backward way of showing affection, of saying "I love you," but it's the only way we know. We should have outgrown it, and hordes of men are now paying thousands of dollars to sweat and stink and pound and grieve together to try and do just that. Maybe it works, maybe it doesn't. But no matter how cryptic, how Byzantine, how weird and weary the way it travels, the message still manages to get through.

Meanings and Values

1.   According to the writer, how do men communicate with each other on emotional matters?

2.   Buczynski concludes that "no matter how cryptic, how Byzantine, how weird and weary the way it travels, the message still manages to get through" (par. 19). Does he convince you that this generality is well-founded? Why or why not?

Expository Techniques

1.   Identify those places in the essay where the generality being illustrated is stated more or less directly. Would presenting the generality as a thesis statement in the opening paragraphs make the essay more effective? (See "Guide to Terms": *Thesis; Evaluation.*)

2.   What strategy does the writer use in paragraphs 1–10 to open the essay? (Guide: *Introduction.*)

3.   Identify the main examples Buczynski uses and then discuss the effectiveness of each. (Guide: *Evaluation.*)

DICTION AND VOCABULARY

1.   Discuss how the simile in the third sentence of the opening paragraph, "like water thrown on a sauna stove," heightens the contrast between iron workers and people involved in the "men's movement." (Guide: *Figures of Speech.*)

2.   Explain how the word choice in paragraph 5 emphasizes contrasts between academics and blue-collar workers. (Guide: *Diction; Emphasis.*)

3.   If you do not know the meaning of any of the following words, look them up in a dictionary: maulers (par. 5); interrogator (6); articulate (12); allegory, parable (13); disclaimers (14).

READ TO WRITE

1.   **Collaborating:** Working in a small group, discuss the roles of stories, especially allegories or parables, in communicating emotions within your college environment. How do you, as college students, share emotions? Can you think of particular stories that helped you share such feelings? Has there been a significant event on campus that has generated such stories? Write a list of such events and stories that might be good examples for use in an expository essay about communicating.

2.   **Considering Audience:** How do the communication and self-disclosure examples help this writer to establish an identity? Does the reader need some prior understanding of "blue-collar" workers to understand Buczynski's piece? With what other examples of male camaraderie and emotion sharing are Americans familiar? How about examples of female identity building and emotional sharing?

3.   **Developing an Essay:** Using "Iron Bonding" as a model, use examples to create an essay explaining the communication strategies of a particular group of people with which you are familiar.

(NOTE: Suggestions for topics requring development by use of EXAMPLE follow.)

Writing Suggestions for Chapter 3

EXAMPLE

Use one of the following statements or another suggested by them as your central theme. Develop it into a unified composition, using examples from history, current events, or personal experience to illustrate your ideas. Be sure to have your reader-audience clearly in mind, as well as your specific purpose for the communication.

1. Successful businesses keep employees at their highest level of competence.

2. In an age of working mothers, fathers spend considerable time and effort helping raise the children.

3. Family life can create considerable stress.

4. Laws holding parents responsible for their children's crimes would (or would not) result in serious injustices.

5. Letting people decide for themselves which laws to obey and which to ignore would result in anarchy.

6. Many people find horror movies entertaining.

7. Service professions are often personally rewarding.

8. Religion in the United States is not dying.

9. Democracy is not always the best form of government.

10. A successful career is worth the sacrifices it requires.

11. "An ounce of prevention is worth a pound of cure."

12. The general quality of television commercials may be improving (or deteriorating).

13. An expensive car can be a poor investment.

14. "Some books are to be tasted; others swallowed; and some few to be chewed *and* digested." (Francis Bacon, English scientist-author, 1561–1626).

15. Most people are superstitious in one way or another.

16. Relationships within the family are much more important than relationships outside the family.

COLLABORATIVE EXERCISE

Working in a group, begin with the statement "Many people find horror movies entertaining," and ask each person to identify two examples to illustrate and support the generality advanced in the statement. (This task will probably require each group member to do some research.) After the examples have been collected, group members should present them, and the group as a whole should vote for those that best illustrate the generality. Each group member should then create a short essay using the examples to explain and support the statement. (Statements 7, 10, 12, and 13 also lend themselves well to this activity.)

4

Analyzing a Subject by *Classification*

People naturally like to sort and classify things. A young child, moving into a new dresser of her own, will put handkerchiefs together, socks and underwear in separate stacks, and hair clips in a pretty holder for the dresser top. Another young child may classify animals as those with legs, those with wings, and those with neither. As they get older, they may find schoolteachers have ways of classifying *them*, not only into reading or math groups, but periodically on the basis of "A," "B," or "C" papers. On errands to the grocery store, they discover macaroni in the same department as spaghetti, pork chops somewhere near the ham, and apples just down from the miniature carrots (themselves part of larger groups like "carrots" and "root vegetables"). In reading the local newspaper, they observe that its staff has done some classifying for them, putting most of the comics together and seldom mixing sports stories with news of social affairs and marriage announcements (classifications based in turn on traditional categories of behavior). Eventually, they find courses neatly classified in college catalogs, and they know enough not to look for biology courses under "Social Science" or "Arts and Letters."

Classification also helps writers and readers sort through and understand detailed information or ideas. It groups people, ideas, objects, experiences, or concepts according to shared qualities and helps point out patterns of relationships among them. For example, if you were writing an article to help people understand their personal characteristics, you might draw on the ancient Indian concept of "ayurveda," as does the author of the following paragraph.

> The three ayurvedic types (or doshas) are vata, pitta, and kapha.
> Vatas (space and air) are creative, thin people with light bones and

dark hair and eyes who are light sleepers, dislike routine, and tend toward fear and anxiety when they're under stress. Pittas (fire and water) are medium built, light-eyed, oily-skinned people who enjoy routine, make good leaders and initiators, are opinionated, and tend toward anger and frustration when they're under stress. Kaphas (water and earth) are amply built, thick-skinned and thick-haired people who are good at running projects, love leisure, sleep soundly, and tend to avoid difficult situations.

—Lynette Lamb, "Living the Ayurvedic Way"

WHY USE CLASSIFICATION?

A classification creates groups on the basis of shared characteristics. It is a useful strategy when you are dealing with facts, events, or ideas whose differences are worth detailed examination. Many subjects which you may need to write and think about will remain a hodgepodge of facts and opinions unless you can find some system of analyzing the material, dividing the subject into categories, and classifying individual elements into those categories. The two patterns, **division** and **classification**, or *dividing* and *grouping*, move in different directions, at least to begin with. But when put in use for analysis and understanding, the two processes become inevitable companions that lead to a system of classification you can employ in your writing.

Expository writing both explains and informs, and classification is a pattern that enables writers to bring clarity to discussions of complicated subjects.. Exercise programs, undergraduate majors, investment strategies, personal computers, ways to prepare for tests, even used cars—all these come in various types that are worth understanding. So, too, do other possible subjects for writing: behavior patterns; literary or anthropological theories; careers in engineering, business, or communications; management techniques; or environmental policies.

When readers encounter a classification, however, they expect more than a simple identification of categories. They look for an explanation of the qualities that distinguish each category and an explanation of the overall arrangement of the categories. In short, they expect the writer to provide a conclusion—a thesis—about the categories themselves, perhaps an explanation of why the subject falls into a particular set of categories or what implications the pattern of sorting has. A conclusion helps readers decide what to do with the information being presented; it helps them choose among alternatives, understand the specific uses of each set of policies or products; or grasp the implications of different psychological perspectives and social groupings.

CHOOSING A STRATEGY

If you choose to employ classification as a strategy for sharing information and ideas, your readers will expect you to take them into account from the beginning. They will want to know what information you are going to present and why it is important to them. They will expect you to make clear the purpose for your classification and the main idea or thesis tying it together.

From the start, therefore, you need to focus clearly on a **principle of classification,** that is, the quality members of each group share and what distinguishes them from the members of other groups. The simplest classifications form two groups, those with a particular quality and those without it: vegetarians and meat-eaters, closed-end mutual funds and open-ended funds, introverts and extroverts, environmentally sensitive policies and environmentally destructive policies. But such simple classifications often break down, usually because the differences among groups are matters of degree or level (varying levels of environmental sensitivity; different degrees of strictness in adhering to a vegetarian diet) and not absolute.

In creating a classification, then, you should choose a strategy that reflects your purpose for writing while allowing you to maintain clear and logical distinctions among the categories. If your purpose is to help people understand the dietary options available to them—vegan, ovo-lacto-vegetarian, avoidance of all meat except fish, and meat eating, for example—then your categories should be built around the kinds of food that people choose to include or avoid in their diet. In addition, the principle of classification should be consistent throughout the categories and complete with respect to the subject being investigated.

It would not be logical to divide movies into categories such as action films, science fiction films, romantic films, political films, serious films, and entertaining films because the principles of classification are not consistent and the categories therefore overlap: romantic films can be serious, entertaining, or both, for example. Likewise, it would not make sense to limit discussion of religious practices in North America to those of Christians, Jews, and Moslems because to do so would exclude, for example, the many people who identify themselves as Buddhists and Hindus. A more limited system might be appropriate, however, when discussing the religious backgrounds of residents in a particular region (southwest Louisiana, rural Mexico) or from a particular cultural or ethnic group (Hungarians, Native Americans in Alaska or northern Canada). While your classification system need not be exhaustive, it should at the same time not omit significant numbers of whatever behaviors, people, or ideas you are planning to discuss.

In many cases, the pattern of classification you choose will also serve to organize your writing, as the following tentative plan for an essay illustrates.

Tentative Thesis	People who love sports but have only limited athletic talent need not give up their dreams of a career in professional sports because being a player is only one of many career paths.
Category	Name: administrators. Definition: people involved in management of sports teams. Members: managers, coaches, public relations specialists, personnel managers.
Category	Name: medical staff. Definition: people concerned with physical and mental health of athletes. Members: trainers, team doctors, sports psychologists.
Category	Name: facilities staff. Definition: people who create and maintain sports facilities. Members: sports architects and designers, engineers, groundskeepers, facilities managers.
Category	Name: equipment specialists. Definition: people who design, manufacture, and sell sports equipment. Members: designers, testers, advertisers, manufacturing engineers, sales representatives.

A plan like this could logically include player's agents and legal representatives, people who work in financing sports, and people who arrange travel for sports teams. But while this would be a logical classification it would be far too detailed for most readers. You should therefore limit the number of categories you present in an essay to avoid overwhelming and confusing your readers, but make sure you do not leave out any that are essential to the subject. Four categories of sports-related jobs should be enough to support and explain the writer's thesis (though some mention of sports broadcasting might be appropriate because most readers will expect discussion of the category). A brief mention of the other kinds of jobs, perhaps near the essay's conclusion, would help complete the classification without overburdening readers with detail.

Any plan like this seems almost absurdly obvious, of course—*after* the planning is done. It appears less obvious, however, to inexperienced writers who are dealing with a jumble of information they must explain to someone else. This is when writers should be aware of the patterns at their disposal, and one of the most useful of these, alone or combined with others, is classification.

DEVELOPING CATEGORIES

At the center of any essay employing classification are the paragraphs that present, explain, and illustrate categories. There is no single strategy for presenting categories, and the way you approach the task should vary according to your subject and purpose for writing. Nonetheless, many writers find the following techniques useful for alerting readers to the structure of an essay, structuring the presentation of categories, and making sure they present each category with enough explanatory detail.

- *Use transitions:* You can make effective use of transitional terms to signal the beginning of a new category.

type	sort	trait	segment
category	kind	species	characteristic
class	aspect	element	component
part	subcategory	subset	group

- *Name the categories:* To help identify categories and also help readers remember them, try giving each a name when you explain it. The names can be purely descriptive ("supporters of the policy/opponents/compromisers") or they can be somewhat imaginative ("lookers/browsers/testers/buyers").
- *Provide detailed examples:* To help readers visualize and understand each category, consider providing at least one extended example or a cluster of shorter ones. By making the examples detailed and specific, you help explain the categories while making them more memorable.
- *Explain:* Remind readers of the principle of classification, of the qualities that characterize a category, and of the ways it differs from other categories. Let them know, too, how the categories are

related: Do they represent differing or contradictory approaches to a problem? Are they different products with similar functions? Will readers be faced with sharply differing options or a gradual range of choices?

Here is how one student, Hung Bui, put these techniques to work in a paragraph.

> Cigarettes play an even larger role in the lives of the next group, habitual smokers. They cannot quit as readily as the casual smoker can because of one key factor: habit. When the phone rings, they quickly grab an ashtray and cigarettes and chat. When having a cup of coffee in the morning, they simply must have a cigarette because "The coffee won't taste as good without it." And always, without fail, a good meal is followed by a good cigarette. Habitual smokers also smoke on an regular basis—a pack or two a day, never more, never less. They become irritated when they discover they are down to their last cigarette and rush to buy another pack. They also play games by buying only packs instead of cartons, rationalizing that because cigarettes aren't always on hand, they can't be smoking too much. They are constantly trying to cut down and tell everyone so, but never actually do, because in reality, smoking is an essential part of their lives.

Student Essay

Whenever you are learning, you do so in stages, from beginner, to novice, to (perhaps) expert. Heather Farnum applied these stages to a task she knew well (playing the piano) and came up with a system of classification that readers can apply to musicians in general and extend to other learners as well.

Piano Recitals

by Heather Farnum

Begins with anecdote introducing the topic and creating interest

Last night while I was sitting at the piano and relaxing by playing some old recital pieces, memories of playing in piano recitals as a child and high school student came flooding back to me. I remember looking at each pianist intently, watching how she or he presented a piece, and imagining myself sitting at the piano and playing in a similar way. I watched how each presented a selection—whether or not the person gave feeling to the music and was comfortable with playing it. Most of all, I watched how the pianist interpreted a piece, for there are several quite different ways to interpret the same selection for an audience.

Thesis statement

Novice pianists, intermediate pianists, and top class pianists all approach the job of interpretation in different and characteristic ways. You can help me explain these differences if you will imagine a stage in a brightly-lit church hall or school auditorium. Stretched across the stage is a grand piano, set up so the audience of parents, friends, and fellow students can see the recitalist.

Category 1 Example

The first person to walk tentatively across the stage to polite applause is a novice pianist. Like all novices, this one either rushes through the piece or plays much too slowly. He bobs his head up and down trying to maintain the tempo, messes up notes, and plays too loudly or too softly, but seldom in between.

Another example (detailed)

The best example of a novice pianist I can recall is Stephany Cody, a girl of about seven. For her first recital, Stephany played "Twinkle, Twinkle, Little Star" as loudly as she could, bobbing her head throughout the familiar piece. Every time she reached the "twinkle, twinkle, little star" she speeded up because she knew that part best. However, when she reached "up above the sky so gray," she slowed way down as she struggled through the less familiar notes.

Category 2 Example

Next across the stage is an intermediate pianist. Sitting down, she strives for a professional look in form and stature.

Unlike the novice pianist, she has control over dynamics, yet she is more tense because she is more aware of the things she needs to do and the things that can go wrong.

Another example (detailed)

John Cody (Stephany's ten-year-old brother) comes to my mind as an image of the intermediate pianist. For one of his recitals, John played a piece called "Festival of Arragon." He sat down at the piano with a serious disposition, like a professional. When he began playing, however, his form fell apart. His shoulders sagged and he held his head at an awkward angle because he was paying more attention to the correct tempo and the correct shade of loudness or softness than to the image he was presenting of himself and the music.

Category 3 Example

Last across the stage is an advanced pianist. She (or he) sits in a relaxed yet formal manner at the piano. When she plays, the dynamics and shades of sound are balanced and put the piece on display rather than the pianist. The tempo is even and steady, and the audience senses a performer in control with a strong stage presence.

Another example (detailed)

My piano teacher, Ann Fitch, remains in my mind as an image of the advanced pianist. Whenever she sits at the piano, she is calm and relaxed; her disposition alone makes the audience feel relaxed and at ease—ready for the piece to begin. She plays with tempos and rhythms that are steady and gradual. Most of all, however, she makes the audience members feel they are living the music.

Example continues

An advanced pianist like Ann goes even further with her performance. She plays

with a mood and a stage presence that enables listeners to share the pianist's
emotions. A top flight pianist can convey
feelings of love, romance, anger, sadness,
depression, and excitement and arrange
them in ways that guide listeners to the
heart of the music without overwhelming
them. Finally, if advanced pianists have a
secret, it is that they keep four questions always in mind:

In place of a conventional conclusion-a list of things all pianists should keep in mind.

1. What is the tempo I want to follow for this piece?
2. What mood do I wish to present?
3. What emotions do I want to convey?
4. How can I play so that the audience can live the piece of music at the same time I do?

JUDITH VIORST

JUDITH VIORST was born in Newark, New Jersey, and attended Rutgers University. Formerly a contributing editor of Redbook magazine, for which she wrote a monthly column, she has also been a newspaper columnist, and in 1970 she received an Emmy award for her contributions to a CBS television special. She has written numerous fiction and nonfiction books for children, including *Alexander and the Terrible, Horrible, No Good, Very Bad Day* (1982). Among her various books of verse and prose for adults are *It's Hard to Be Hip Over Thirty and Other Tragedies of Married Life* (1968) (a collection of poems), *Yes, Married: A Saga of Love and Complaint* (1972) (prose pieces), and, more recently, *If I Were in Charge of the World and Other Worries* (1981), *Love and Guilt and the Meaning of Life* (1984), *Necessary Losses* (1986), and *Murdering Mr. Monti* (1995) (a novel).

What, Me? Showing Off?

In "What, Me? Showing Off?" first published in *Redbook*, Viorst uses classification to explore a behavior that most of us notice readily enough in other people but may be reluctant to acknowledge in our own actions—showing off. Though its tone is breezy and it contains frequent touches of humor, this essay is carefully organized and serious in purpose. Besides classification, Viorst makes good use of examples, definition, brief narratives, and even a short dramatic episode.

We're at the Biedermans' annual blast, and over at the far end of   1
the living room an intense young woman with blazing eyes and a throbbing voice is decrying poverty, war, injustice and human suffering. Indeed, she expresses such anguish at the anguish of mankind that attention quickly shifts from the moral issues she is expounding to how very, very, very deeply she cares about them.

She's showing off.   2

Down at the other end of the room an insistently scholarly fel-   3
low has just used *angst, hubris,* Kierkegaard and *epistemology* in the same sentence. Meanwhile our resident expert in wine meditatively sips, then pushes away, a glass of unacceptable Beaujolais.

They're showing off.   4

And then there's us, complaining about how tired we are today   5
because we went to work, rushed back to see our son's school play,
shopped at the market and hurried home in order to cook gourmet,
and then needlepointed another dining-room chair.

And what we also are doing is showing off.   6

Indeed everyone, I would like to propose, has some sort of need   7
to show off. No one's completely immune. Not you. And not I. And
although we've been taught that it's bad to boast, that it's trashy to
toot our own horn, that nice people don't strut their stuff, seek attention or name-drop, there are times when showing off may be forgivable and maybe even acceptable.

But first let's take a look at showing off that is obnoxious, that's   8
not acceptable, that's never nice. Like showoffs motivated by a
fierce, I'm-gonna-blow-you-away competitiveness. And like narcissistic showoffs who are willing to do anything to be—and stay—the
center of attention.

Competitive showoffs want to be the best of every bunch.   9
Competitive showoffs must outshine all others. Whatever is being
discussed, they have more—expertise or money or even aggrava-
tion— and better—periodontists or children or marriages or recipes
for pesto—and deeper—love of animals or concern for human suffering or orgasms. Competitive showoffs are people who reside in a
permanent state of sibling rivalry, insisting on playing Hertz to
everyone else's Avis.

(You're finishing a story, for instance, about the sweet little   10
card that your five-year-old recently made for your birthday when
the CSO interrupts to relate how her daughter not only made her a
sweet little card, but also brought her breakfast in bed and saved
her allowance for months and months in order to buy her—obviously much more beloved—mother a beautiful scarf for her birthday. *Grrr.*)

Narcissistic showoffs, however, don't bother to compete be-   11
cause they don't even notice there's anyone there to compete with.
They talk nonstop, they brag, they dance, they sometimes quote
Homer in Greek, and they'll even go stand on their head if attention
should flag. Narcissistic showoffs want to be the star while everyone
else is the audience. And yes, they are often adorable and charming
and amusing—but only until around the age of six.

(I've actually seen an NSO get up and leave the room when the   12
conversation shifted from his accomplishments. "What's the matter?" I asked when I found him standing on the terrace, brooding

darkly. "Oh, I don't know," he replied, "but all of a sudden the talk started getting so superficial." *Aagh!*)

Another group of showoffs—much more sympathetic types—   13
are showoffs who are basically insecure. And while there is no easy way to distinguish the insecure from the narcissists and competitors, you may figure out which are which by whether you have the urge to reassure or to strangle them.

Insecure showoffs show off because, as one close friend ex-   14
plained, "How will they know that I'm good unless I tell them about it?" And whatever the message—I'm smart, I'm a fine human being, I'm this incredibly passionate lover—showoffs have many different techniques for telling about it.

Take smart, for example.   15

A person can show off explicitly by using flashy words, like the   16
hubris-Kierkegaard fellow I mentioned before.

Or a person can show off implicitly, by saying not a word and   17
just wearing a low-cut dress with her Phi Beta Kappa key gleaming softly in the cleavage.

A person can show off satirically, by mocking showing off: "My   18
name is Bill Sawyer," one young man announces to every new acquaintance, "and I'm bright bright bright bright bright."

Or a person can show off complainingly: "I'm sorry my daugh-   19
ter takes after me. Men are just so frightened of smart women."

Another way showoffs show off about smart is to drop a Very   20
Smart Name—if this brain is my friend, goes the message, I must be a brain too. And indeed, a popular showing-off ploy—whether you're showing off smartness or anything else—is to name-drop a glittery name in the hope of acquiring some gilt by association.

The theory seems to be that Presidents, movie stars, Walter   21
Cronkite and Princess Di could be friends, if they chose, with anyone in the world, and that if these luminaries have selected plain old Stanley Stone to be friends with, Stanley Stone must be one hell of a guy. (Needless to say, old Stanley Stone might also be a very dreary fellow, but if Walt and Di don't mind him, why should I?)

Though no one that I know hangs out with Presidents and   22
movie stars, they do (I too!) sometimes drop famous names.

As in: "I go to John Travolta's dermatologist."   23

Or: "I own the exact same sweater that Jackie Onassis wore in a   24
newspaper photograph last week."

Or: "My uncle once repaired a roof for Sandra Day O'Connor."   25

Or: "My cousin's neighbor's sister-in-law has a child who is   26
Robert Redford's son's best friend."

We're claiming we've got gilt—though by a very indirect asso- 27
ciation. And I think that when we do, we're showing off.

Sometimes showoffs ask for cheers to which they're not enti- 28
tled. Sometimes showoffs earn the praise they seek. And sometimes
folks achieve great things and nonetheless do not show off about it.

Now *that's* impressive. 29

Indeed, when we discover that the quiet mother of four with 30
whom we've been talking intimately all evening has recently been
elected to the state senate—*and she never even mentioned it!*—we are
filled with admiration, with astonishment, with awe.

What self-restraint! 31

For we know damn well—I certainly know—that if we'd been 32
that lucky lady, we'd have worked our triumph into the conversation. As a matter of fact, I'll lay my cards right on the table and confess that the first time some poems of mine were published, I not
only worked my triumph into every conversation for months and
months, but I also called almost every human being I'd ever known
to proclaim the glad tidings both local and long distance.
Furthermore—let me really confess—if a stranger happened to stop
me on the street and all he wanted to know was the time or directions, I tried to detain him long enough to enlighten him with the
news that the person to whom he was speaking was a Real Live
Genuine Honest-to-God Published Poet.

Fortunately for everyone, I eventually—it took me awhile— 33
calmed down.

Now, I don't intend to defend myself—I was showing off, I was 34
bragging and I wasn't the slightest bit shy or self-restrained, but a
golden, glowing, glorious thing had happened in my life and I had
an overwhelming need to exult. Exulting, however (as I intend to argue farther on), may be a permissible form of showing off.

Exulting is what my child does when he comes home with an A 35
on his history paper ("Julius Caesar was 50," it began, "and his good
looks was pretty much demolished") and wants to read me the entire masterpiece while I murmur appreciative comments at frequent
intervals.

Exulting is what my husband does when he cooks me one of his 36
cheese-and-scallion omelets and practically does a tap dance as he
carries it from the kitchen stove to the table, setting it before me with
the purely objective assessment that this may be the greatest omelet
ever created.

Exulting is what my mother did when she took her first grand- 37
son to visit all her friends, and announced as she walked into the

room, "Is he gorgeous? Is that a gorgeous baby? Is that the most gorgeous baby you ever saw?"

And exulting is what that mother of four would have done if   38
she'd smiled and said, "Don't call me 'Marge' any more. Call me
'Senator.'"

Exulting is shamelessly shouting our talents or triumphs to the   39
world. It's saying: I'm taking a bow and I'd like to hear clapping.
And I think if we don't overdo it (stopping strangers to say you've
been published is overdoing it), and I think if we know when to quit
("Enough about me. Let's talk about you. So what do you think about
me?" does not count as quitting), and I think if we don't get addicted
(i.e., crave a praise-fix for every poem or A or omelet), and I think if
we're able to walk off the stage (and clap and cheer while others take
their bows), then I think we're allowed, from time to time, to exult.

Though showing off can range from very gross to very subtle,   40
and though the point of showing off is sometimes nasty, sometimes
needy, sometimes nice, showoffs always run the risk of being
thought immodest, of being harshly viewed as ... well ...
showoffs. And so for folks who want applause without relinquishing their sense of modesty, the trick is keeping quiet and allowing
someone else to show off *for* you.

And I've seen a lot of marriages where wives show off for hus-   41
bands and where husbands, in return, show off for wives. Where
Joan, for instance, mentions Dick's promotion and his running time
in the marathon. And where Dick, for instance, mentions all the
paintings Joanie sold at her last art show. And where both of them
lean back with self-effacing shrugs and smiles and never once show
off about themselves.

Friends also may show off for friends, and parents for their chil-   42
dren, though letting parents toot our horns is risky. Consider, for example, this sad tale of Elliott, who was a fearless and feisty
public-interest lawyer:

"My son," his proud mother explained to his friends, "has al-   43
ways been independent." (Her son blushed modestly.)

"My son," his proud mother continued, "was the kind of person   44
who always knew his own mind." (Her son blushed modestly.)

"My son," his proud mother went on, "was never afraid. He   45
never kowtowed to those in authority." (Her son blushed modestly.)

"My son," his proud mother concluded, "was so independent   46
and stubborn and unafraid of authority that we couldn't get him toilet-trained—he wet his pants till he was past four." (Her son ...)

But showing off is always a risk, whether we do it ourselves or   47
whether somebody else is doing it for us. And perhaps we ought to

consider the words Lord Chesterfield wrote to his sons: "Modesty is   48
the only sure bait when you angle for praise."

And yes, of course he's right, we know he's right, he must be right. But sometimes it's so hard to be restrained. For no matter what we do, we always have a lapse or two. So let's try to forgive each other for showing off.

MEANINGS AND VALUES

1. Name the categories into which Viorst divides showoffs (and non-showoffs). Which of the categories does Viorst divide into subcategories? What are the subcategories? Where, if anywhere, do the categories in this essay overlap? If the categories overlap, is the result confusing and misleading, or is some overlap inevitable in any classification that attempts to explain human behavior?

2. According to the examples in paragraphs 36 and 37, exulting may sometimes mean exaggerating or stretching the truth. Do you agree with Viorst that exulting should be permissible even if it means inflating one's accomplishments? Be ready to defend your answer.

3. What does Viorst imply about the personalities of narcissistic showoffs when she says, "they are often adorable and charming and amusing—but only until around the age of six" (par. 11)? What message is the woman with the Phi Beta Kappa key conveying (par. 17)?

EXPOSITORY TECHNIQUES

1. In what order are the categories arranged? Worst to best? Most forgivable to least forgivable? Some other order? Where and how is this arrangement announced to the reader?

2. The introduction to this essay is relatively long (pars. 1–8). What does Viorst do to get readers interested in the subject? Where in the introduction does she announce the central theme (thesis)? Where else in the essay does she speak directly about it? Where in the introduction does she indicate the plan of organization? (See "Guide to Terms": *Introductions.*)

3. At several places in the essay Viorst comments on its organization and summarizes the categories. Identify these places.

4. For some of the categories the discussion consists of a general definition followed by examples. Which discussions follow this arrangement? Describe briefly the organization of the remaining discussions.

5. Identify a section of the essay where Viorst uses parallel paragraphs and discuss their effect. Do the same with parallel sentences and parallel sentence parts. (Guide: Parallel Structure.)

DICTION AND VOCABULARY

1. What words or kinds of words does Viorst repeat frequently in the course of the essay? What purposes does the repetition serve?

2. To what does the phrase "gilt by association" allude? (Guide: *Figures of Speech.*) Identify as many as you can of the direct references and allusions to people, ideas, or events in the following paragraphs: pars. 3, 9, 11, 21, and 23–26. What purposes do these references serve?

3. How is irony (understatement) used in paragraph 36? (Guide: *Irony.*) How is exaggeration used in paragraph 32?

4. Viorst uses some devices that in many essays would seem excessively informal or careless: unusual or made-up words ("*Grrr,*" par. 10; "*Aagh,*" 12); informal phrases ("strut their stuff," 7); exclamation points; and parentheses surrounding an entire paragraph, among other things. In what ways do such devices contribute to the humor of the essay? To its overall tone? (Guide: *Style/Tone.*)

5. If you are unfamiliar with any of the following words, consult your dictionary as necessary: decrying, expounding (par. 1); *angst, hubris, epistemology* (3); narcissistic (8); periodontists, sibling (9); brooding (12); cleavage (17); dermatologist (23); enlighten (32); exult (34); appreciative (35); assessment (36); shamelessly, crave (39); gross, immodest, relinquishing (40); feisty (42); kowtowed (45).

READ TO WRITE

1. **Collaborating:** With a group of classmates (and fellow writers), go to a social gathering and, following Viorst's lead, use the social event as the basis for an essay you write collaboratively. In the essay, classify the human behaviors you observe at the event.

2. **Considering Audience:** How might readers of various kinds react to Viorst's essay? Is she trying to get her readers to place themselves within the categories as they read? If so, is she successful at this? Do you see yourself as a particular kind of showoff? Prepare a short essay explaining why you, your friends, or your relatives fit into the categories Viorst presents.

3. **Developing an Essay:** Showing off is not the only irritating but understandable behavior you are likely to encounter in everyday life. In the morning, make a list of all such irritating behaviors that come to mind. Then spend the rest of the day on the lookout for these and other behaviors. In the evening, use your observations to expand the list; include notes about examples of behaviors you observed. Use this list to help develop an essay of your own classifying typical kinds of behavior.

(NOTE: Suggestions for topics requiring development by use of CLASSIFICATION are on pp. 141–142 at the end of this chapter.)

JUDITH STONE

JUDITH STONE has been a regular contributor to a number of magazines, including *Discover.* Her writings have been collected in *Light Matters: Essays in Science from Gravity to Levity* (1991). As the title suggests, Stone writes about science and scientific matters with both wit and detailed knowledge.

Personal Beast

From the play on words in its title through the rest of its many puns and humorous images, this essay looks critically and understandingly at our often exaggerated and absurd affection for pets—and the status they can confer on their owners. The essay first appeared as a column in *Discover* magazine.

For the past several millennia, dogs have pretty much had the 1 Man's Best Friend market cornered. Lately, however, thanks to a sort of demographic Darwinism, several strong contenders for the title are nipping at the heels of the chosen species.

The dog emerged as protopet in Mesopotamia, where our no- 2 madic ancestors first began living in villages about 12,000 to 14,000 years ago. (And if you think it's hard to paper-train a puppy, imagine having to use stone tablets.)

"Domestication was an urban event," explains Alan Beck, 3 Ph.D., Director of the University of Pennsylvania's Center for the Interaction of Animals and Society. "The garbage generated by these new high-density human communities probably attracted wolf packs; villagers may have bred the pups into pets with the idea of making peace with the pack. These domesticated creatures could bark a warning when nondomestic animals came around, and also help with trash control. And perhaps one of the earliest reasons for breeding pets was for companionship; the desire to nurture is part of human culture." (Those days, when Hector was a pup, probably marked the first time in history that a human being uttered the words, "Aw, Ma, can't I keep it?")

Now a new kind of urbanization is creating a new kind of pet. 4 People are choosing animals that better fit a busier life and a smaller dwelling. Is there room for Fido in Mondo Condo, a world of two-income families with less time but more discretionary income? Folks want pets that are small and independent, pets that offer them a way to announce their individuality in a crowded, standardized world. Miniaturization, convenience, chic—the pet of the nineties has many of the same fine qualities as an under-the-counter microwave or a car phone. Here, hot off the Ark Nouveau, are the exotic animals that busy Americans simply must have.

Some of you may be seeking a companion that's low-maintenance, affectionate, cute (though swaybacked and paunchy), and perfectly content curled up in front of the TV, pigging out on junk food. (Yeah, yeah, I know—you're already married to it. You're a scream, honestly.) I mean the Vietnamese pot-bellied pig, the nation's top-selling Asian import. A black, beagle-sized porker that's also called a Chinese house pig, it looks like a cross between a hog, a honey bear, and a hand puppet.   5

"If you can keep a poodle, you can keep one of these pigs," says Fredericka Wagner, co-owner, with husband Bob, of Flying W Farms in Piketon, Ohio, which sends more of the little piggies to market than anyone in the country. "They're very appealing. Full grown, they weigh up to 45 or 50 pounds and stand about 12 to 13 inches high. They graze instead of root. Ordinary pigs have a long, straight snout; this one has a short, pushed-in, wrinkly nose. Its little ears stick straight up like a bat's and it has a straight tail that it wags like a dog's. It barks, too, and it can learn tricks—to come when it's called, sit up and beg, or roll over and play dead hog instead of dead dog." And it's easier to housebreak than a cat, Wagner says. Her three little pigs, Choo-Choo, Matilda, and Hamlet; like to sit around with the family and watch movies on TV (presumably *Porky's I* through *III*), and they enjoy supplementing their diet of Purina Pig Chow with candy, brownies, peanuts, and potato chips.   6

When the pigs arrived two years ago from Vietnam (by way of Sweden and Canada, after three years of red tape), the Wagners already ran a midget menagerie, selling impossibly cute 18-inch miniature sheep (perfect for baby sweaters, easy to count for insomniacs), pygmy goats, miniature donkeys, and championship miniature Arabian horses. (Apparently there are no bonsai bovines, or the Wagners would have them.) "Miniature horses are bred down from larger horses—anything from huge Belgian draft horses to Shetland ponies—a process that can take a century," Wagner says. "In our experience, to reduce a horse from 48 inches to 34 inches takes six generations—about twenty years. You can do it in only three gener-   7 ations if you have a 30-inch stallion, but you'd have to dig a hole to put the mare in."

Wagner first heard about the pigs from a friend in California; reportedly they'd been imported by Vietnam veterans who recalled the friendly critters from their tours of duty. Though Wagner was instantly attracted to them, she wasn't sure she'd get the business off the ground. But the swine flew. "We can't keep up with the demand," she says. "In the first eighteen months we sold a hundred pigs." Wagner is boarish on pot-bellied pigs as an investment. "Not even the stock market will pay you back as fast as these pigs will. I've had several retired people buy them to supplement their income. They breed at six months [the pigs, not the retirees] and it takes three weeks, three months, and three days for them to have babies. By the time your gilt is a year old—a gilt is a pregnant sow— she's given you her first litter of pigs and you have your investment back three times over." Since you can only have gilt by association, those who want to breed pigs must buy an unrelated pair for $2,500. "We expect that to go up to $3,000, because the demand is so great," says Wagner, in hog heaven. "We've sold them to everyone from poets to princes—we shipped some overseas to a Saudi Arabian prince. Stephanie Zimbalist, the actress, has one." 8

Stephanie Zimbalist! A recommendation, indeed. But what about having the same pet as *Michael Jackson?* For part of his personal zoo (boa, deer, chimp/valet, glove, and, nearly, the Elephant Man), Jackson has chosen a taller order of hip creature, the llama. His is one of about 15,000 in the country. "But in years to come, we'll see more and more of them in the average home," says Florence Dicks, owner of the Llonesome Llama Ranch in Sumner, Washington. "They're great hiking companions, their wool is increasingly in demand, and they make wonderful pets. They've been part of domestic life in South America for centuries. I think of them as one of life's necessities." 9

Dicks, who runs Llama Lluvs Unltd., the world's only Llamagram delivery service, notes that the recent lifting of a government ban on imports will increase the llama population; most American-born llamas are descended from a single herd owned by William Randolph Hearst. 10

"They're very gentle," Dicks says. "Many of my fifteen llamas lived in the house for their first year. They're easier to house-train than a cat." (You know how all weird meat is described as "sort of like chicken"? Apparently all weird pets are easier to housebreak than a cat.) Dicks explains, in more detail than necessary, that llamas 11 are what's called communal voiders—a great name for a rock band. Spread some llama droppings where you want them to go, and, in the comradely way of communal voiders everywhere, they will use that spot forever after. "We've shared our bathroom with llamas for five years, and they've never had an accident," Dicks says. Okay, they squeeze the toothpaste from the top, but nobody's perfect.

"I train my llamas to hum—that's the noise they make—when   12
they want to go outside," Dicks reports. "They communicate by tone variance. If they're relaxed, there's a musical quality to the hum. If they're stressed, you can hear the anxiety. I have a llama who hums with a rising inflection when he's curious."

Full-grown llamas can stand over six feet tall and weigh up to   13
500 pounds. A male costs between $1,500 and $15,000. (And at a recent auction, a male said to have outstanding stud qualities—he always sends a thank-you note—fetched $100,000). A gelded male will set you back $700 or $800, a female about $8,000. The only bad thing about llamas, Dicks says, is that you have to clip their toenails every three or four months. Which doesn't sound like a big deal if you're already sharing a bathroom.

But more and more of us have life-styles and living spaces—to   14
use a pair of expressions even more nauseating than the word *pus*— that can't accommodate a dog, let alone a llama. I know I barely have room in my apartment for a pet peeve. Hence the proliferation among city dwellers of ferrets, dwarf rabbits, and birds. According to the American Veterinary Medical Association, birds are the fastest growing pet category. Their numbers increased 24 percent between 1983 and 1987, from 10.3 million to 12.8 million. Talking birds, like Amazon parrots, are especially sought after, reports veterinarian Katherine Quesenberry, head of the exotic pet service of the Animal Medical Center of New York. (And I guess if you crossed these South American birds with llamas, you'd get Fernando Llamas six-foot communal voiders that squawk, "You look *mah*velous." Cheep gag.)

The ferret, a more personable cousin of the weasel, has been   15
bred in captivity for a century, mostly for lab research. But its popularity as a pet has steadily risen over the last decade. Says Tina Ellenbogen, a Seattle veterinarian and information services director for the Delta Society, a national organization dedicated to the study of human-animal bonding, "People become attached to ferrets because they have a lot of personality. They're small, clean, and amusing." (It's sometimes hard to tell when people are talking about ferrets and when they're talking about Dudley Moore.) You can

walk them on a harness or let them play on a ferrets wheel. They're easily litter-trained, says Ellenbogen—easier than a cat, I imagine— and statistically less likely to bite than a dog is. Males are unpleasant if you don't remove their stink glands, and females are sexually insatiable until you have them fixed, but hey.

Maybe you're a person who doesn't understand all the sound and   16 furry over mammals. Maybe you'd rather see something in cold blood.

The reptile of the hour is the African Old World chameleon.   17 "Having one is like owning a dinosaur!" says Gary Bagnall, head of California Zoological Supplies, one of the five largest reptile distributors in the country. "They look truly prehistoric. Their eyes move independently and they have 10-inch tongues with stickum at the end for catching insects. The base color is green, but they can blend into their surroundings by changing to yellow, orange, white, black, brown, and sometimes blue." The 6- to 10-inch chameleons start at $35; a foot-long variety, called Miller's chameleon, goes for $1,000. "We get only about four of them a year," Bagnall says. "There's a waiting list."

The nation's most sought-after amphibian, according to   18 Bagnall, is the poison arrow frog, a tiny (less than an inch long), jewel-like native of South America that comes in orange and black, yellow and black, or blue. The really great thing about the poison arrow frog is that if you boil up about fifty of them, you get enough of the toxin they secrete to brew a dandy blowdart dip guaranteed to make hunting small jungle mammals a breeze.

Alive, the frogs, which cost from $35 to $200, require a lot of at-   19 tention, Bagnall warns. "They can't take extremes in temperature or dryness, and their diet is restricted to very small insects. In fact, you have to raise fruit flies for them." Most of us don't have time to raise fruit flies for our families, let alone for a pet. But, paradoxically, though exotic pet owners are getting busier, they're also getting savvier and more dedicated.

"The whole pet industry has changed," says Bagnall. "Exotic   20 pet owners can't afford to be ignorant, because they're paying more." Making a fatal mistake with a $3,500 miniature ram and ewe is a whole different thing from accidentally offing a twenty-five-cent baby turtle. (I'd like to take this opportunity to make a public confession. I'm sorry, Shelly. I was only seven, and I didn't know that painting your back with nail polish would kill you. Forgive me, too, for digging you up two weeks after the funeral, but I was curious to see if the rumors I'd heard about deterioration were true. You didn't disappoint.) Continues Bagnall, "I can't speak for birds and mammals, but the prices of even standard, bread-and-butter reptiles—boas, garter snakes, pythons—have tripled over the last three years because of government regulation of imports." But the high prices seem to add to the mystique, he says. "Reptiles attract people who want something not everybody has. Also, if you're allergic to fur, they're a nice alternative." (And probably a certain percentage of newly minted MBAs are even now saying to their mentors, "Rep *ties?* I thought you said 'invest in some rep*tiles!'"*) Bagnall adds that poison arrow frogs and Old World chameleons are especially popular now because they've only recently appeared in zoos. "And if a reptile shows up in a movie, its popularity increases tenfold, like the Burmese python in *Raiders of the Lost Ark.*"

Yes, it's a cachet as cachet can world. Perhaps all human   21
progress stems from the tension between two basic drives: to have just what everyone else has and to have what no one has. Covet your neighbor's ass? Get yourself a miniature one and watch him mewl with envy. But be careful: Once an odd animal enters the mainstream, those on the cutting edge of the pet thing have to push for a new personal beast. "Pygmy goats used to be really rare," Fredericka Wagner says with a sigh. "Now everyone has them." (Haven't you noticed that the first question you're asked at the best restaurants these days is "May I check your goat?")

The proliferation of peculiar pets may necessitate a revamping   22
of terminology, says veterinarian Quesenberry. "The term *exotics* is no longer valid. We're talking about animals that haven't historically been domesticated, but they're not wild anymore, either, because they're being bred in captivity and exposed to humans from an early age. Somebody has suggested using the term *special species* for these animals, and reserving the term exotics for the zoo stuff."

If you're not ready to pay big bucks for little pigs, you'll be   23
happy to know that the classic exotic pet, the simple yet eloquent sea monkey, retails for just $3.99. Remember sea monkeys? When some of us were kids, during what scientists call the Late Cleaver-Brady Epoch, sea monkeys were advertised in the backs of magazines, usually between the Mark Eden Bust Developer and the Can You Draw This Elf School of Art. A smiling, bikini-clad creature with the head of a monkey and the body of a seahorse promised the requisite hours of fun for kids from eight to—if I recall the stats correctly—eighty. Remember your disappointment when the "monkeys" turned out to be brine shrimp, so infinitesimal that they could only be clearly seen with the enclosed magnifying glass? Remember how not one of them wore a bathing suit? Well, for the same low price, a

new generation of kids can learn a powerful lesson about the true nature of existence (sometimes when you expect a bikini-clad aquatic primate, you get a bunch of stupid, skinny-dipping germs). And sea monkeys are easier to house-train than cats.

MEANINGS AND VALUES

1. In your own words, tell what Stone considers the main qualities of the pet of the 90s. Explain the differences she sees between contemporary pets (and owners) and those of the past.

2. Identify the categories Stone presents in this essay. Are there any subcategories? If so, what are they? Do any of the categories overlap? If so, is the overlap confusing?

3. If you believe this essay has a serious purpose, tell what it is.

EXPOSITORY TECHNIQUES

1. Can the second sentence in this essay be considered a thesis statement? If so, why? (See "Guide to Terms": *Thesis*.) Are there any other sentences that might be considered additional thesis statements or repetitions and developments of the second sentence? Identify any such sentences and discuss their role in the essay.

2. Why does the author choose to begin the essay by discussing dogs? Would the essay have been more effective had she begun with a discussion of cats or of some other familiar kind of pet? (Guide: *Evaluation*.)

3. Discuss the role of the comments within the parentheses in paragraph 20. Explain the ways these comments are similar to or different from other parenthetical comments in the essay.

DICTION AND VOCABULARY

1. What does "Mondo Condo" (par. 4) mean, and for what purpose does the writer use the phrase?

2. Identify the source of each of the following allusions, and discuss what each means: Hector (par. 3); Ark Nouveau (4); swine flew (8); in cold blood (16). (Guide: *Figures of Speech*.)

3. How does the word choice in the last sentence of paragraph 5 emphasize the meaning and create a pattern of sound? (Guide: *Emphasis; Diction*.)

4. If you do not know the meaning of some of the following words, look them up in the dictionary; nomadic (par. 2); discretionary (4); voiders (11); variance (12); gelded (13); insatiable (15); cachet (21).

READ TO WRITE

1. **Collaborating:** Working with a group of fellow students, list several categories of dogs (or some other animal). Subdivide these categories if you can. Then as a group, write down what you consider the stereotypical characteristics of people who own the different kinds of animals you classified. Develop all or most of these categories of people and animals into a short essay of your own, and compare your essay with those written by the others in your group.

2. **Considering Audience:** Are readers who do not own pets likely to find much in this essay to interest them? What other subjects can be sorted into categories that a wide range of readers are likely to find interesting? Make a list of such subjects, and be ready to explain what kinds of readers are likely to find each subject interesting or uninteresting? To what extent does the presentation rather than the subject determine readers' interest? Why?

3. **Developing an Essay:** Taking Stone's essay as a model, classify the contemporary versions of some activity or object (other than pet owning and pets) that has been around in different forms for a long time. Following Stone's lead, show how the modern versions reflect changes in attitude and fashion.

(NOTE: Suggestions for topics requiring development by use of CLASSIFICATION are on pp. 141–142 at the end of this chapter.)

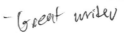

MICHAEL VENTURA — *great writer*

MICHAEL VENTURA worked as an editor for the *Austin Sun* and the *Los Angeles Weekly* (which he co-founded). He has been a columnist for the *Austin Chronicle* and the *Los Angeles Village View*. His books include *The Mollyhawk Poems* (1977), *Night Time, Losing Time* (1989), and *The Zoo Where You're Fed to God* (1994). His most recent book is a novel, *The Death of Frank Sinatra*.

Don't Even Think About It!

In this essay, Michael Ventura explains how taboos, which many readers might associate with primitive societies or superstitions, help shape the things we do in our daily lives. By showing how many different kinds of taboos we routinely observe (more categories than readers usually encounter in an essay), Ventura demonstrates their prevalence and importance. The concrete examples that Ventura provides help keep the numerous categories from seeming overwhelming and abstract. The illustrations also help readers recognize taboos in their own behavior.

Taboos come in all sizes. Big taboos: when I was a kid in the Italian neighborhoods of Brooklyn, to insult someone's mother meant a brutal fight—the kind of fight no one interferes with until one of the combatants goes down and stays down. Little taboos: until the sixties, it was an insult to use someone's first name without asking or being offered permission. Personal taboos: Cyrano de Bergerac would not tolerate the mention of his enormous nose. Taboos peculiar to one city: in Brooklyn (again), when the Dodgers were still at Ebbets Field, if you rooted for the Yankees you kept it to yourself unless you wanted a brawl. Taboos, big or small, are always about having to respect somebody's (often irrational) boundary—or else.

There are taboos shared within one family: my father did not feel free to speak to us of his grandmother's suicide until his father died. Taboos within intellectual elites: try putting a serious metaphysical or spiritual slant on a "think-piece" (as we call them in the trade) written for the *New York Times*, the *Washington Post*, or most big name magazines—it won't be printed. Taboos in the corporate and legal worlds: if you're male, you had best wear suits of somber colors, or you're not likely to be taken seriously; if you're female, you have to strike a very uneasy balance between the attractive and the prim, and even then you might not be taken seriously. Cultural taboos: in the Jim Crow days in the South, a black man who spoke with familiarity to a white woman might be beaten, driven out of town, or (as was not uncommon) lynched.

Unclassifiable taboos: in Afghanistan, as I write this, it is a sin—   3
punishable by beatings and imprisonment—to fly a kite. Sexual taboos: there are few communities on this planet where two men can walk down a street holding hands without being harassed or even arrested; in Afghanistan (a great place for taboos these days) the Taliban would stone them to death. Gender taboos: how many American corporations (or institutions of any kind) promote women to power? National taboos: until the seventies, a divorced person could not run for major public office in America (it wasn't until 1981 that our first and only divorced president, Ronald Reagan, took office); today, no professed atheist would dare try for the presidency. And most readers of this article probably approve, as I do, of this comparatively recent taboo: even the most rabid bigot must avoid saying "nigger," "spic," or "kike" during, say, a job interview—and the most macho sexist must avoid words like "broad."

Notice that nearly all of our taboos, big and small, public and in-   4
timate, involve silence—keeping one's silence, or paying a price for not keeping it. Yet keeping silent has its own price: for then silence begins to fill the heart, until silence becomes the heart—a heart swelling with restraint until it bursts in frustration, anger, even madness.

The taboos hardest on the soul are those which fester in our inti-   5
macies—taboos known only to the people involved, taboos that can make us feel alone even with those to whom we're closest. One of the deep pains of marriage—one that also plagues brothers and sisters, parents and children, even close friends—is that as we grow more intimate, certain silences often become more necessary. We discover taboo areas, both in ourselves and in the other, that cannot be transgressed without paying an awful price. If we speak of them, we may endanger the relationship; but if we do not speak, if we do not violate the taboo, the relationship may become static and tense, until the silence takes on a life of its own. Such silences are corrosive. They eat at the innards of intimacy until, often, the silence itself causes the very rupture or break-up that we've tried to avoid by keeping silent.

The Cannibal in Us All

You may measure how many taboos constrict you, how many   6
taboos you've surrendered to—at home, at parties, at work, with your lover or your family—by how much of yourself you must sup-

press. You may measure your life, in these realms, by what you cannot say, do, admit—cannot and must not, and for no better reason than that your actions or words would disrupt your established order. By this measure, most of us are living within as complex and strictured a system of taboos as the aborigines who gave us the word in the first place. You can see how fitting it is that the word "taboo" comes from a part of the world where cannibalism is said to be practiced to this day: the islands off eastern Australia—Polynesia, New Zealand, Melanesia. Until 1777, when Captain James Cook published an account of his first world voyage, Europe and colonial America had many taboos but no word that precisely meant taboo. Cook introduced this useful word to the West. Its instant popularity, quick assimilation into most European languages, and constant usage since, are testimony to how much of our lives the word describes. Before the word came to us, we'd ostracized, coerced, exiled, tormented, and murdered each other for myriad infractions (as we still do), but we never had a satisfying, precise word for our reasons.

We needed cannibals to give us a word to describe our behavior, so how "civilized" are we, really? We do things differently from those cannibals, on the surface, but is the nature of what we do all that different? We don't cook each other for ceremonial dinners, at least not physically (though therapists can testify that our ceremonial seasons, like Christmas and Thanksgiving, draw lots of business—something's cooking). But we stockpile weapons that can cook the entire world, and we organize our national priorities around their "necessity," and it's a national political taboo to seriously cut spending for those planet-cookers. If that's "progress," it's lost on me. In China it's taboo to be a Christian, in Israel it's taboo to be a Moslem, in Syria it's taboo to be a Jew, in much of the United States it's still taboo to be an atheist, while in American academia it's taboo to be deeply religious. Our headlines are full of this stuff. So it's hardly surprising that a cannibal's word still describes much of our behavior. 7

I'm not denying the necessity of every society to set limits and invent taboos (some rational, some not) simply in order to get on with the day—and to try to contain the constant, crazy, never-to-be-escaped longings that blossom in our sleep and distract or compel us while awake. Such longings are why even a comparatively tiny desert tribe like the ancient Hebrews needed commandments and laws against coveting each other's wives, stealing, killing, committing incest. That the tribe hadn't seen violent, sexy movies, hadn't listened to rock 'n' roll, hadn't been bombarded with ads featuring half-naked models, and hadn't watched too much TV. They didn't 8 need to. Like us, they had their hearts, desires, and dreams to instruct them how to be very, very naughty. The taboo underlying all others is that we must not live by the dictates of our irrational hearts—as though we haven't forgiven each other, or ourselves, for having hearts.

If there's a taboo against something, it's usually because a considerable number of people desire to do it. The very taboos that we employ to protect us from each other and ourselves, are a map of our secret natures. When you know a culture's taboos (or an individual's, or a family's) you know its secrets—you know what it really wants.   9

Favorite Taboos

It's hard to keep a human being from his or her desire, taboo or not.   10
We've always been very clever, very resourceful, when it comes to sneaking around our taboos. The Aztecs killed virgins and called it religion. The Europeans enslaved blacks and called it economics. Americans tease each other sexually and call it fashion.

If we can't kill and screw and steal and betray to our heart's de-   11
sire, and, in general, violate every taboo in sight—well, we can at least watch other people do it. Or read about it. Or listen to it. As we have done, since ancient times, through every form of religion and entertainment. The appeal of taboos and our inability to escape our longing for transgression (whether or not we ourselves transgress) are why so many people who call themselves honest and law-abiding spend so much time with movies, operas, soaps, garish trials, novels, songs, Biblical tales, tribal myths, folk stories, and Shakespeare—virtually all of which, both the great and the trivial, are about those who dare to violate taboos. It's a little unsettling when you think about it: the very stuff we say we most object to is the fundamental material of what we call culture.

That's one reason that fundamentalists of all religions are so   12
hostile to the arts. But fundamentalists partake of taboos in the sneakiest fashion of all. Senator Jesse Helms led the fight against the National Endowment for the Arts because he couldn't get the (vastly overrated) homosexual art of Robert Mapplethorpe or the most extreme performance artists out of his mind—he didn't and doesn't want to. He, like all fundamentalists, will vigorously oppose such art and all it stands for until he dies, because his very opposition gives him permission to concentrate on taboo acts. The Taliban of Afghanistan will ride around in jeeps toting guns, searching out any woman who dares show an inch of facial skin or wear white socks

(Taliban boys consider white socks provocative), and when they find such a woman they'll jail and beat her—because their so-called righteousness gives them permission to obsess on their taboos. Pat Robertson and his ilk will fuss and rage about any moral "deviation," any taboo violation they can find, because that's the only way they can give themselves permission to entertain the taboos. They get to not have their taboo cake, yet eat it too.

We are all guilty of this to some extent. Why else have outlaws   13
from Antigone to Robin Hood to Jesse James to John Gotti become folk heroes? Oedipus killed his father and slept with his mother, and we've been performing that play for 2500 years because he is the ultimate violator of our deepest taboos. Aristotle said we watch such plays for "cartharsis," to purge our desires and fears in a moment of revelation. Baloney. Ideas like "catharsis" are an intellectual game, to glossy-up our sins. What's closer to the truth is that we need Oedipus to stand in for us. We can't have changed much in 2500 years, if we still keep him alive in our hearts to enact our darkest taboos for us. Clearly, the very survival of Oedipus as an instantly recognizable name tells us that we still want to kill our fathers and screw our mothers (or vice versa).

A Country of Broken Taboos

Taboos are a special paradox for Americans. However much we   14
may long for tradition and order, our longings are subverted by the inescapable fact that our country was founded upon a break with tradition and a challenge to order—which is to say, the United States was founded upon the violation of taboos. Specifically, this country was founded upon the violation of Europe's most suffocating taboo: its feudal suppression (still enforced in 1776, when America declared its independence) of the voices of the common people. We were the first nation on earth to write into law that any human being has the right to say anything, and that even the government is (theoretically) not allowed to silence you.

At the time, Europe was a continent of state-enforced religions,   15
where royalty's word was law and all other words could be crushed by law. (Again: taboo was a matter of enforced silence.) We were the first nation to postulate verbal freedom for everyone. All our other freedoms depend upon verbal freedom; no matter how badly and how often we've failed that ideal, it still remains our ideal.

Once we broke Europe's verbal taboos, it was only a matter of   16
time before other traditional taboos fell too. As the writer Albert

Murray has put it, Americans could not afford piety in their new homeland: "You can't be over respectful of established forms; you're trying to get through the wilderness of Kentucky." Thus, from the moment the Pilgrims landed, our famous puritanism faced an inherent contradiction. How could we domesticate the wilderness of this continent; how could peasants and rejects and "commoners" form a strong and viable nation; how could we develop all the new social forms and technologies necessary to blend all the disparate peoples who came here—without violating those same Puritan taboos which are so ingrained, to this day, in our national character?

It can't be over-emphasized that America's fundamental stance   17
against both the taboos of Europe and the taboos of our own Puritans, was our insistence upon freedom of speech. America led the attack against silence. And it is through that freedom, the freedom to break the silence, that we've destroyed so many other taboos. Especially during the last 40 years, we've broken the silence that surrounded ancient taboos of enormous significance. Incest, child abuse, wife-battering, homosexuality, and some (by no means all) forms of racial and gender oppression, are not merely spoken of, and spoken against, they're shouted about from the rooftops. Many breathe easier because of this inevitable result of free speech. In certain sections of our large cities, for the first time in modern history, gay people can live openly and without fear. The feminist movement has made previously forbidden or hidden behaviors both speakable and doable. The National Organization of Women can rail against the Promise Keepers all they want (and they have some good reasons), but when you get a million working-class guys crying and hugging in public, the stoic mask of the American male has definitely cracked. And I'm old enough to remember when it was shocking for women to speak about wanting a career. Now virtually all affluent young women are expected to want a career.

Fifty years ago, not one important world or national leader was   18
black. Now there are more people of color in positions of influence than ever. Bad marriages can be dissolved without social stigma. Children born out of wedlock are not damned as "bastards" for something that wasn't their fault. And those of us who've experienced incest and abuse have finally found a voice, and through our voices we've achieved a certain amount of liberation from shame and pain.

These boons are rooted in our decidedly un-Puritan freedom of   19
speech. But we left those Puritans behind a long time ago—for the

breaking of silence is the fundamental political basis of our nation, and no taboo is safe when people have the right to speak.

Keeper of Your Silence

In the process, though, we've lost the sanctity of silence. We've lost 20 the sense of dark but sacred power inherent in sex, in nature, even in crime. Perhaps that is the price of our new freedoms.

It's also true that by breaking the silence we've thrown our- 21 selves into a state of society's structure. Without them, that structure has undeniably weakened. We are faced with shoring up the weakened parts, inventing new ways of being together that have pattern and order—for we cannot live without some pattern and order—but aren't so restrictive. Without sexual taboos, for instance, what are the social boundaries between men and women? When are they breached? What is offensive? Nobody's sure. Everybody's making mistakes. This is so excruciating that many are nostalgic for some of the old taboos. But once a taboo is broken, then for good or ill it's very hard, perhaps impossible, to reinstate it.

But there is another, subtler confusion: yes, enormous taboos 22 have fallen, but many taboos, equally important, remain. And, both as individuals and as a society, we're strained enough, confused enough, by the results of doing away with so many taboos in so short a time, that maybe we're not terribly eager for our remaining taboos to fall. We may sincerely desire that, but maybe we're tired, fed up, scared. Many people would rather our taboos remain intact for a couple of generations while we get our act together again, and perhaps they have a point. But the price of taboos remains what it's always been: silence and constriction.

What do we see, when we pass each other on the street, but many 23 faces molded by the price paid for keeping the silences of the taboos that remain—spirits confined within their own, and their society's, silences? Even this brief essay on our public and intimate strictures is enough to demonstrate that we are still a primitive race, bounded by fear and prejudice, with taboos looming in every direction—no matter how much we like to brag and/or bitch that modern life is liberating us from all the old boundaries. The word taboo still says much more about us than most prefer to admit.

What is the keeper of your silence? The answer to that question 24 is your own guide to your personal taboos. How must you confine yourself in order to get through your day at the job, or to be acceptable in your social circle? The answer to that is your map of your society's taboos. What makes you most afraid to speak? What desire, what word, what possibility, freezes and fevers you at the same time, making any sincere communication out of the question? What makes you vanish into your secret? That's your taboo, baby. You're still in the room, maybe even still smiling, still talking, but not really—what's really happened is that you've vanished down some hole in yourself, and you'll stay there until you're sure the threat to your taboo is gone and it's safe to come out again. If, that is, you've ever come out in the first place. Some never have.

What utterance, what hint, what insinuation, can quiet a room   25
of family or friends? What makes people change the subject? What makes those at a dinner party dismiss a remark as though it wasn't said, or dismiss a person as though he or she wasn't really there? We've all seen conversations suddenly go dead, and just as suddenly divert around a particular person or subject, leaving them behind in the dead space, because something has been said or implied that skirts a silently shared taboo. If that happens to you often, don't kid yourself that you're living in a "free" society. Because you're only as free as your freedom from taboos—not on some grand abstract level, but in your day-to-day life.

It is probably inherent in the human condition that there are no   26
"last" taboos. Or perhaps it just feels that way because we have such a long way to go. But at least we can know where to look; right in front of our eyes, in the recesses of our speechlessness, in the depths of our silences. And there is nothing for it but to confront the keepers of our silence. Either that, or to submit to being lost, as most of us silently are, without admitting it to each other or to ourselves—lost in a maze of taboos.

MEANINGS AND VALUES

1.   Ventura says that "Taboos, big or small are always about having to respect somebody's (often irrational) boundary—or else" (par. 1). Do you agree with this definition of the word "taboo"? Why, or why not? Why do you think that we must honor other people's boundaries? What does "or else" mean?

2.   Explain the connection that Ventura makes in paragraph 5 between silence and taboos. How does silence impact us personally and in relationships?

3. Why does much of our popular culture violate many societal taboos? How do the media encourage this?

EXPOSITORY TECHNIQUES

1. Ventura places taboos into many categories. Some are broad (e.g. "big taboos" and "little taboos") while others are very specific (i.e. "corporate taboos" and "language taboos"). Does he deliberately give equal standing to specific taboos? If so, why?

2. Beginning in paragraph 14, Ventura explains how enforced silence led to a whole series of taboos. What are some of the subcategories of taboos that disappeared with the American practice of free speech, and what connection does Ventura make between these subcategories and Americans' willingness to talk?

DICTION AND VOCABULARY

1. Ventura uses the expression "social stigma" in paragraph 18 in conjunction with dissolved marriages. He uses the words "shame" and "pain" connected to incest and abuse. Why does he use such words when he is comparing American society before its willingness to speak openly with contemporary, more open American society? (See "Guide to Terms": *Diction*.)

2. Why does Ventura provide us with the etymology (history) of the word "taboo" and an explanation of its assimilation into languages (par. 6)?

3. If you do not know the meaning of some of the following words, look them up in a dictionary: assimilation, ostracized, coerced (par 6); garish (10); catharsis (13); piety, disparate (16); stoic (17).

READ TO WRITE

1. **Collaborating:** Ventura makes clear his opinion that taboos, though a reflection of human nature, are dangerous to society because they cause us to be silent about many horrible things that may be happening in our lives. Can you think of cases where silence and taboos might be positive? In a small group, create a list of such instances, and as a team prepare a short essay classifying and explaining these taboos.

2. **Considering Audience:** Society's taboos about premarital and extramarital sex are less strong now than they were in the first half of the twentieth century. Other taboos have changed as well. Consider an audience reading this essay in the 1960s. What parts of the discussion and examples might have worked well for most readers at the time. What taboos were probably no longer as forceful for these readers as they might have been for readers earlier in the century? Prepare an

essay examining how one or more taboos changed during the course of the century.

3.   **Developing an Essay:** Look over one or more editions of a local newspaper. Identify and list some issues or behaviors that the articles treat as taboos. Separate the items in the list into categories. Adding further examples from your experience and knowledge, develop the list into an essay on the way newspapers and similar media such as magazines reinforce or undermine taboos. You might also examine the various kinds of news programs on television (both "hard" and "soft" news) and write about the way they treat taboos.

(NOTE: Suggestions for topics requiring development by use of CLASSIFICATION are on pp. 141–142 at the end of this chapter.)

Issues and Ideas:

Images of Sound & Sight

- Rene Tajima, *Lotus Blossoms Don't Bleed: Images of Asian American Women*
- Brenda Peterson, *Life Is a Musical*

Every day on television, in films, through songs, in magazine articles, and in countless other places we encounter images of people like us and also images of people whose lives are unfamiliar to us except as we encounter them through these images. Because images have the power to shape perceptions, relationships, and values, we need to recognize they can sometimes represent accurately and yet sometimes simplify and distort.

But what is an image? This is an easy question to answer for visual media like films, television, advertisements, and posters. It is a representation of a person's actions, attitudes, character traits, and relationships. The image can represent the person as an individual or as a typical member of a group. When the image is constructed simply from the traits of a group (often negative traits) we can refer to it as a stereotype. Negative (and often hurtful) stereotypes are quite familiar: the bimbo, the less-than-intelligent "jock," the absent-minded professor, or the violent gang member.

People frequently share traits with other members of a group, of course, but a stereotype erases individual differences. When all we know about a group comes from stereotypic images, especially negative ones, we need to be aware of the limitations of our understanding and look for more accurate images. Renee Tajima's goal in "Lotus Blossoms Don't Bleed: Images of Asian American Women" is in part to alert us to the need for more realistic images and to the unfortunate effects of inaccurate ones, both of individuals and of the society at large.

The images we receive through music, literature, and other forms of reading can be a bit harder to describe. In representing relationships, feelings, and values, these media present us with definitions of appropriate (or inappropriate) behavior and attitudes. These, in turn, can shape our perceptions, self-understanding, values, and relationships. Many of the images we receive through music can be positive and useful, as Brenda Peterson points out in "Life Is a Musical." Renee Tajima also emphasizes the role of positive, realistic images in her discussion of recent films by independent directors.

Images are not simply given to us by others. We can create them as well, especially in this age of recorders, cameras, and computers. Brenda Peterson's discussion of the way her family uses music to create and maintain its identity and the ways she integrates collections of songs into her own life are particularly interesting illustrations of how we can create images of ourselves (and others)—images that may act as creative responses to those thrust upon us every day.

RENEE TAJIMA

RENEE E. TAJIMA is a filmmaker and writer. She produced a documentary for public television entitled "Adopted Son: The Death of Vincent Chin." Currently she is associate editor of *The Independent Film and Video Monthly* as well as a freelance writer. With Christine Choy she runs the Film News Now Foundation. Formerly editor of *Bridge: Asian American Perspectives,* Tajima has also edited *Journey Across Three Continents: Black and African Films, Asian American Film and Video,* and *Reel Change: Guide to Social Issue Media* (2d ed.).

Lotus Blossoms Don't Bleed: Images of Asian American Women

Categories are an important tool for thinking, but unless created with care, they can become unrepresentative stereotypes. Tajima's essay reminds us of the need to be aware of how the categories presented by film and television can shape our perceptions. And she demonstrates how restrictive and harmful stereotypes can be. The classification system here is somewhat complex, consisting of two different kinds of characters, "Lotus Blossoms" and "Dragon Ladies," that appear in several different types of movie roles.

In recent years the media have undergone spectacular technical innovations. But whereas form has leaped toward the year 2000, it seems that content still straddles the turn of the last century. A reigning example of the industry's stagnation is its portrayal of Asian women. And the only real signs of life are stirring far away from Hollywood in the cutting rooms owned and operated by Asian America's independent producers.   1

The commercial media are, in general, populated by stereotyped characterizations that range in complexity, accuracy, and persistence over time. There is the hooker with a heart of gold and the   2 steely tough yet honorable mobster. Most of these characters are white, and may be as one-dimensional as Conan the Barbarian or as complex as R. P. McMurphy in *One Flew Over the Cuckoo's Nest.*

Images of Asian women, however, have remained consistently   3
simplistic and inaccurate during the sixty years of largely forget-table screen appearances. There are two basic types: the Lotus Blossom Baby (a.k.a. China Doll, Geisha Girl, shy Polynesian beauty), and the Dragon Lady (Fu Manchu's various female rela-tions, prostitutes, devious madames). There is little in between, al-though experts may differ as to whether Suzie Wong belongs to the race-blind "hooker with a heart of gold" category, or deserves one all of her own.

Asian women in American cinema are interchangeable in ap-   4
pearance and name, and are joined together by the common lan-guage of non-language—that is, uninterpretable chattering, pidgin English, giggling, or silence. They may be specifically identified by nationality—particularly in war films—but that's where screen ac-curacy ends. The dozens of populations of Asian and Pacific Island groups are lumped into one homogeneous mass of Mama-sans.

Passive Love Interests

Asian women in film are, for the most part, passive figures who ex-   5
ist to serve men, especially as love interests for white men (Lotus Blossoms) or as partners in crime with men of their own kind (Dragon Ladies). One of the first Dragon Lady types was played by Anna May Wong. In the 1924 spectacular *Thief of Bagdad* she uses treachery to help an evil Mongol prince attempt to win the Princess of Bagdad from Douglas Fairbanks.

The Lotus Blossom Baby, a sexual-romantic object, has been the   6
prominent type throughout the years. These "Oriental flowers" are utterly feminine, delicate, and welcome respites from their often loud, independent American counterparts. Many of them are the spoils of the last three wars fought in Asia. One recent television ex-ample is Sergeant Klinger's Korean wife in the short-lived series "AfterMash."

In the real world, this view of Asian women has spawned an   7
entire marriage industry. Today the Filipino wife is particularly in vogue for American men who order Asian brides from picture cata-logues, just as you might buy an imported cheese slicer from Spiegel's. (I moderated a community program on Asian American women recently. A rather bewildered young saleswoman showed

up with a stack of brochuers to promote the Cherry Blossom companion service, or some such enterprise.) Behind the brisk sales of Asian mail-order brides is a growing number of American men who are seeking old-fashioned, compliant wives, women they feel are no longer available in the United States.

Feudal Asian customs do not change for the made-for-movie   8
women. Picture brides, geisha girls, concubines, and hara-kari are all mixed together and reintroduced into any number of settings. Take for example these two versions of Asian and American cultural exchange:

1. It's Toko Riki on Japan's Okinawa Island during the late   9
1940s in the film Teahouse of the August Moon. American occupation forces nice guy Captain Fisby (Glenn Ford) gets a visit from Japanese yenta Sakini (Marlon Brando).

Enter Brando: "Hey Boss, I Sonoda has a present for you."   10
Enter the gift: Japanese actress Machiko Kyo as a geisha, giggling.   11
Ford: "Who's she?"   12
Brando: "Souvenir . . . introducing Lotus Blossom geisha girl   13
first class."

Ford protests the gift. Kyo giggles.   14
Brando sneaks away with a smile: "Goodnight, Boss." Kyo,   15
chattering away in Japanese, tries to pamper a bewildered Ford who holds up an instructive finger to her and repeats slowly, "Me . . . me . . . no." Kyo looks confused.

2. It's San Francisco, circa 1981, in the television series "The   16
Incredible Hulk." Nice guy David Banner (Bill Bixby a.k.a. The Hulk) gets a present from Chinese yenta Hyung (Beulah Quo).

Enter Quo: "David, I have something for you."   17
Enter Irene Sun as Tam, a Chinese refugee, bowing her head   18
shyly.

Quo: "The Floating Lotus Company hopes you will be very   19
happy. This is Tam, your mail-order bride."

Bixby protests the gift. Sun, speaking only Chinese, tries to   20
pamper a bewildered Bixby who repeats slowly in an instructive tone, "you . . . must . . . go!" Sun looks confused.

Illicit Interracial Love

On film Asian women are often assigned the role of expendability   21
in situations of illicit Asian-white love. In these cases the most expedient way of resolving the problems of miscegenation has been to get rid of the Asian partner. Thus, some numbers of hyphenated

(made-for-television, wartime, wives-away-from-home) Asian women have expired for the convenience of their home-bound soldier lovers. More progressive-minded GI's of the Vietnam era have returned to Vietnam years later to search for the offspring of these love matches.

In 1985 the General Foods Gold Showcase proudly presented a   22 post-Vietnam version of the wilting Lotus Blossom on network television. "A forgotten passion, a child he never knew. . . . All his tomorrows forever changed by *The Lady from Yesterday*." He is Vietnam vet Craig Weston (Wayne Rogers), official father of two, and husband to Janet (Bonnie Bedelia). She is Lien Van Huyen (Tina Chen), whom Weston hasn't seen since the fall of Saigon. She brings the child, the unexpected consequence of that wartime love match, to the United States. But Janet doesn't lose her husband, she gains a son. As *New York Times* critic John J. O'Connor points out, Lien has "the good manners to be suffering from a fatal disease that will conveniently remove her from the scene."

The geographic parallel to the objectification of Asian women is   23 the rendering of Asia as only a big set for the white leading actors. What would "Shogun" be without Richard Chamberlain? The most notable exception is the 1937 movie version of Pearl Buck's novel *The Good Earth*. The story is about Chinese in China and depicted with some complexity and emotion. Nevertheless the lead parts played by Louise Rainer and Paul Muni follow the pattern of choosing white stars for Asian roles, a problem which continues to plague Asian actors.

One film that stands out as an exception because it was cast   24 with Asian people for Asian characters is *Flower Drum Song* (1961), set in San Francisco's Chinatown. Unfortunately the film did little more than temporarily take a number of talented Asian American actresses and actors off the unemployment lines. It also gave birth for a while to a new generation of stereotypes—gum-chewing Little Leaguers, enterprising businessmen, and all-American tomboys— variations on the then new model minority myth. *Flower Drum Song* hinted that the assimilated, hyphenated Asian American might be much more successful in American society than the Japanese of the 1940s and the Chinese and Koreans of the 1950s, granted they keep to the task of being white American first.

The women of *Flower Drum Song* maintain their earlier image   25 with few modernizations. Miyoshi Umeki is still a picture bride. And in *Suzie Wong* actress Nancy Kwan is a hipper, Americanized version of the Hong Kong bar girl without the pidgin English. But updated clothes and setting do not change the essence of these images.

In 1985 director Michael Cimino cloned Suzie Wong to TV news   26
anchor Connie Chung and created another anchor, Tracy Tzu
(Ariane), in the disastrous exploitation film *Year of the Dragon*. In it
Tzu is ostensibly the only positive Asian American character in a
film that vilifies the people of New York's Chinatown. The Tzu character is a success in spite of her ethnicity. Just as she would rather eat
Italian than Chinese, she'd rather sleep with white men than
Chinese men. (She is ultimately raped by three "Chinese boys.")
Neither does she bat an eye at the barrage of racial slurs fired off by
her lover, lead Stanley White, the Vietnam vet and New York City
cop played by Mickey Rourke.

At the outset Tzu is the picture of professionalism and sophisti-   27
cation, engaged in classic screen love/hate banter with White. The
turning point comes early in the picture when their flirtatious sparring in a Chinese restaurant is interrupted by a gangland slaughter.
While White pursues the culprits, Tzu totters on her high heels into
a phone booth where she cowers, sobbing, until White comes to the
rescue.

The standard of beauty for Asian women that is set in the   28
movies deserves mention. Caucasian women are often used for
Asian roles, which contributes to a case of aesthetic imperialism for
Asian women. When Asian actresses are chosen they invariably have
large eyes, high cheekbones, and other Caucasian-like characteristics
when they appear on the silver screen. As Judy Chu of the University
of California, Los Angeles, has pointed out, much of Anna May
Wong's appeal was due to her Western looks. Chu unearthed this
passage from the June 1924 Photoplay which refers to actress Wong,
but sounds a lot like a description of Eurasian model/actress Ariane:
"Her deep brown eyes, while the slant is not pronounced, are typically oriental. But her Manchu mother has given her a height and
poise of figure that Chinese maidens seldom have."

Invisibility

There is yet another important and pervasive characteristic of Asian   29
women on the screen, invisibility. The number of roles in the
Oriental flower and Dragon Lady categories have been few, and
generally only supporting parts. But otherwise Asian women are absent. Asian women do not appear in films as union organizers, or divorced mothers fighting for the custody of their children, or fading
movie stars, or spunky trial lawyers, or farm women fighting bank
foreclosures; Asian women are not portrayed as ordinary people.

Then there is the kind of invisibility that occurs when individ-   30
ual personalities and separate identities become indistinguishable
from one another. Some memorable Asian masses are the islanders
fleeing exploding volcanoes in *Krakatoa: East of Java* (1969) and the
Vietnamese villagers fleeing Coppola's airborne weaponry in various scenes from *Apocalypse Now* (1979). Asian women populate
these hordes or have groupings of their own, usually in some type of
harem situation. In *Cry for Happy* (1961), Glenn Ford is cast as an
American GI who stumbles into what turns out to be the best little
geisha house in Japan.

Network television has given Asian women even more oppor-   31
tunities to paper the walls, so to speak. They are background characters in "Hawaii 5-0," "Magnum PI," and other series that transverse
the Pacific. I've seen a cheongsam-clad maid in the soap "One Life to
Live," and assorted Chinatown types surface whenever the cops
and robbers shows revive scripts about the Chinatown Tong wars.

The most stunning exceptions to television's abuse of Asian im-   32
ages is the phenomenon of news anchors: Connie Chung (CBS) and
Sasha Foo (CNN) have national spots, and Tritia Toyota (Los
Angeles), Wendy Tokuda (San Francisco), Kaity Tong (New York),
Sandra Yep (Sacramento), and others are reporters in large cities. All
of them cover hard news, long the province of middle-aged white
men with authoritative voices. Toyota and Yep have been able to
parlay their positions so that there is more coverage of Asian
American stories at their stations. Because of their presence on
screen—and ironically, perhaps because of the celebrity status of today's newscasters—these anchors wield much power in rectifying
Asian women's intellectual integrity in the media. (One hopes *Year
of the Dragon's* Tracy Tzu hasn't canceled their positive effect.)

Undoubtedly the influence of these visible reporters is fortified   33
by the existence of highly organized Asian American journalists.
The West Coast-based Asian American Journalists Association has
lobbied for affirmative action in the print and broadcast media. In
film and video, the same types of political initiatives have spurred a
new movement of independently produced works made by and
about Asian Americans.

Small Gems from Independents

The independent film movement emerged during the 1960s as an al-   34
ternative to the Hollywood mill. In a broad sense it has had little direct impact in reversing the distorted images of Asian women,

although some gems have been produced.... But now Asian American independents, many of whom are women, have consciously set out to bury sixty years of Lotus Blossoms who do not bleed and Mama-sans who do not struggle. These women filmmakers—most of whom began their careers only since the 1970s—often draw from deeply personal perspectives in their work: Virginia Hashii's *Jenny* portrays a young Japanese American girl who explores her own Nikkei heritage for the first time; Christine Choy's *From Spikes to Spindles* (1976) documents the lives of women in New York's Chinatown; Felcia Lowe's *China: Land of My Father* (1979) is a film diary of the filmmaker's own first reunion with her grandmother in China; Renee Cho's *The New Wife* (1978) dramatizes the arrival of an immigrant bride to America; and Lana Pih Jokel's *Chiang Ching: A Dance Journey* traces the life of dancer-actress-teacher Chiang. All these films were produced during the 1970s and together account for only a little more than two hours of screen time. Most are first works with the same rough-edged quality that characterized early Asian American film efforts.

Women producers have maintained a strong presence during the 1980s, although their work does not always focus on women's issues.... Also in this decade veteran filmmakers Emiko Omori and Christine Choy have produced their first dramatic efforts. Omori's *The Departure* is the story of a Japanese girl who must give up her beloved traditional dolls in pre-World War II California.... In *Fei Tien: Goddess in Flight,* Choy tries to adapt a nonlinear cinematic structure to Genny Lim's play *Pigeons*, which explores the relationship between a Chinese American yuppie and a Chinatown "bird lady." 36

Perhaps the strongest work made thus far has been directed by a male filmmaker, Arthur Dong. *Sewing Woman* is a small, but beautifully crafted portrait of Dong's mother, Zem Ping. It chronicles her life from war-torn China to San Francisco's garment factories. Other films and tapes by Asian men include Michael Uno's *Emi* (1978), a portrait of the Japanese American writer and former concentration camp internee Emi Tonooka; the Yonemoto brothers' neonarrative *Green Card*, a soap-style saga of a Japanese immigrant artist seeking truth, love, and permanent residency in Southern California; and Steve Okazaki's *Survivors,* a documentary focusing on the women survivors of the atomic blasts over Hiroshima and Nagasaki. All these filmmakers are American-born Japanese. *Orientations*, by Asian Canadian Richard Fung, is the first work I've seen that provides an in-depth look at the Asian gay community, and it devotes a good amount of time to Asian Canadian lesbians.

Our Own Image

These film and videomakers, women and men, face a challenge far   37
beyond creating entertainment and art. Several generations of Asian
women have been raised with racist and sexist celluloid images. The
models for passivity and servility in these films and television programs fit neatly into the myths imposed on us, and contrast sharply
with the more liberating ideals of independence and activism.
Generations of other Americans have also grown up with these images. And their acceptance of the dehumanization implicit in the
stereotypes of expendability and invisibility is frightening.

Old images of Asian women in the mainstream media will   38
likely remain stagnant for a while. After sixty years, there have been
few signs of progress. However, there is hope because of the growing number of filmmakers emerging from our own communities.
Wayne Wang in 1985 completed *Dim Sum,* a beautifully crafted feature film about the relationship between a mother and daughter in
San Francisco's Chinatown. *Dim Sum,* released through a commercial distributor, could be the first truly sensitive film portrayal of
Asian American women to reach a substantial national audience. In
quality and numbers, Asian American filmmakers may soon constitute a critical mass out of which we will see a body of work that
gives us a new image, our own image.

MEANINGS AND VALUES

1. What are the two main images of Asian women in Hollywood films
   (par. 3)? What are the three main roles Asian women have played in
   Hollywood films? (Note: See paragraphs 5, 21, and 29.)

2. How do the roles Asian women play in recent independent productions differ from those generally created for them in Hollywood productions?

3. How would you characterize the overall tone of this essay? (See
   "Guide to Terms": *Style/Tone.*) Identify any sections of the essay
   where the tone varies noticeably. Point out any passages in the essay
   that offer clear instances of irony, especially sarcasm or understatement. (Guide: *Irony.*)

EXPOSITORY TECHNIQUES

1. Does Tajima offer a clear definition of each category? If not, how
   might the categories be introduced and defined more clearly?

2.   Are the categories in this essay distinct or is there some overlapping? If the categories overlap, does the author acknowledge this? Where?

3.   Would this essay be more effective if it had fewer examples? A greater number? Explain. (Guide: Evaluation.) Evaluate the examples in the following paragraphs for clarity and effectiveness: 8–20, 22, and 26–27.

4.   Discuss whether the examples of work by independent filmmakers provide convincing evidence that these films go beyond the stereotypes.

DICTION AND VOCABULARY

1.   The names used to identify many of the standard character types are clichés. Point out the clichés used in this way in paragraphs 2 and 3.

2.   Explain the meaning of the following terms: "cutting rooms" (par. 1); "Mama-sans" (4); "a cheongsam-clad maid" (31).

3.   If you do not know the meanings of some of the following words, look them up in a dictionary: simplistic (par. 3); homogeneous (4); Mongol (5); compliant (7); yenta (9); objectification (23); vilifies (26); pervasive (29).

READ TO WRITE

1.   **Collaborating:** Films and television programs frequently follow stereotypes in their treatment of various ethnic and social groups (such as African Americans or people in their twenties) or in the representation of groups united by beliefs or behaviors (religious conservatives or athletes, for example). Working with a group of classmates, list groups of people you often encounter that are represented by stereotypical characters on film or television. Then, in an essay of your own, arrange and discuss the different groups based on the way they are represented.

2.   **Considering Audience:** Readers today might be familiar with a newer image of Asian women—that of a character in a "martial arts" video game who often battles aggressively with men. Prepare a short discussion of this image that could be added to Tajima's essay as an update.

3.   **Developing an Essay:** As Tajima's essay explains, immigrant groups are often subject to negative stereotyping. Draw on your own knowledge or experience for examples of this practice or on research into immigrant groups that were once treated as outsiders though they are now considered part of mainstream society. Using the information you have gathered, write an essay of your own, classifying the ways immigrants are or have been treated.

(NOTE: Suggestions for topics requiring development by use of CLASSIFICATION are on pp. 141–142 at the end of this section.)

BRENDA PETERSON

> BRENDA PETERSON, a novelist and essayist, was born in 1950 on a forest ranger station in the Sierra Nevada Mountains. As a child she lived in many different places, especially in the Southeast. Currently, she lives in Seattle. Peterson received a B.A. in 1972 from the University of California-Davis. From 1972 to 1976 she worked as an editorial assistant at *The New Yorker* magazine. She has taught creative writing at Arizona State University and now works as an environmental writer. Her novels include *River of Light* (1978), *Becoming the Enemy* (1988), and *Duck and Cover* (1991). Her essays have been collected in *Living by Water: Essays on Life, Land and Spirit* (1990), *Nature and Other Mothers* (1992), and *Sister Stories: Taking the Journey Together* (1996).

Life Is a Musical

In this essay, Peterson offers several closely related classifications as a way of exploring the ways music can (and ought to) enrich and heal our emotional lives. This essay was first published in *Nature and Other Mothers*.

When the day is too gray, when the typewriter is too loud, after 1 a lovers' quarrel, when a sister calls with another family horror story, when the phone never stops and those unanswered messages blink on my machine like angry, red eyes—I tune out my life and turn up the music. Not my favorite public radio station but my own personal frequency—I have my own soul's station. It is somewhere on the dial between Mozart's *Magic Flute,* the gospel-stomping tiger growl of Miss Aretha Franklin, Motown's deep dance 'n' strut, and the singing story of Broadway musicals.

Whether it's Katie Webster's Swamp Boogie Queen singing 2 "Try a Little Tenderness," or a South American samba, whether it's the Persuasions crooning "Let It Be" or that throbbing baritone solo "Other Pleasures" from *Aspects of Love,* my musical solace is so complete it surrounds me in a mellifluous bubble like a placenta of sound. To paraphrase the visionary Stevie Wonder, I have learned to survive by making sound tracks in my own particular key of life.

For years now I've made what I call "tapes against terror" to   3
hide me away from the noisy yak and call of the outside world.
These homemade productions are dubbed Mermaid Music; sometimes I send them to friends for birthdays and feel the pleasure of
playing personal disc jockey to accompany their lives too. Among
my siblings, we now exchange music tapes instead of letters. It is
particularly gratifying to hear my nieces and nephews singing along
to my tapes, as another generation inherits our family frequency.

I trace making my musical escapes to a childhood of mov-   4
ing around. As we packed the cardboard boxes with our every
belonging—sometimes we hadn't even bothered to unpack our
dresses from those convenient hanging garment containers provided by the last moving company—the singing began. From every
corner of the emptying house, we'd hear the harmonies: my father a
walking bass as he heaved-ho in the basement; my mother's soprano sometimes shrill and sharp as the breaking glass in the
kitchen; my little brother between pure falsetto and a tenor so perfect we knew he'd stopped packing his room simply to sing; my sisters and I weaving between soprano and first and second alto from
our bedrooms as we traded and swapped possessions for our next
life. At last gathered in the clean, white space that was once our
house, we'd hold hands and sing "Auld Lang Syne." Piling into the
station wagon, with the cat in a wooden box with slats for air holes,
Mother would shift into a rousing hymn, "We'll Leave It All
Behind," or sometimes, if she was mutinously happy to hightail it
out of some small "burg" as she called them, she'd lead us into
"Shuffle Off to Buffalo," substituting wherever we were moving for
the last word. "Chattanooga Choo Choo" and "California, Here We
Come" were her standard favorites for leave-taking. If, as we drove
past our schools and our friends' houses for the last time, the harmonies in the backseat faltered, Mother might remind us that choirs
of angels never stayed long in one place singing because the whole
world needed music. Father might suggest some slower songs, as
long as they weren't sad.

In all the shifting landscapes and faces of my childhood, what   5
stays the same is the music. First, there was my mother's music,
which seems now to have entered effortlessly into her children's
minds as if we were tiny tape recorders: the mild, sweetly suave
Mills Brothers, Mitch Miller's upbeat swing, the close sibling harmonies of the Andrews Sisters, and always the church music, the
heartfelt Sunday singing, which is the only thing I ever miss since
leaving that tight fellowship of Southern Baptist believers.

Ever since I can remember—certainly I have flashes of being   6
bounced around in the floating dark of my mother's womb as she
tap-danced on the church organ pedals, sang at the top of her voice,
and boogied across the keys—there has been this music. It is the
only counterpoint to, the only salvation from a sermon that para-
lyzes the soul into submitting to a jealous God. From the beginning,
music was an alternative to that hellfire terror. I can still hear it: a
preacher's voice, first a boom, then a purr that raises into a hiss and
howl to summon that holy hurricane of fire and brimstone. But after
enduring the scourge of sins, there came the choir. Cooing and
shushing, mercy at last fell upon those of us left on an Earth that this
God had long ago abandoned. Listening to the full-bodied harmonies, I could close my eyes and heretically wonder, Wasn't
Heaven still here?

Yessss, hallelujah, still here . . . Hush, can't you hear? the choir   7
murmured like so many mammies' lullabies. Then silence as a small
woman stepped forward, her rapt vibrato shimmering like humid
heat lightning right before rain. Or a baritone dropping his woes
and his dulcet voice low as a cello, caressing a whole congregation.
If we were blessed that Sunday, there might be a shorter sermon and
a "songfest" with harmonies we could hear in our heads, syncopat-
ing, counterpointing in a lovely braid of bright sound that beckoned
us. *Sing now, brothers and sisters.* And we were many voices making
one song. The fundamental fear was gone; weren't we already angels in Heaven?

Now that I am forty and have been what my family pityingly   8
refers to as "settled-down" for ten years, now that I am so far back-
slid from the fellowship of the Southern Baptist believers, now that I
no longer even make top ten on my mother's prayer list, now that
the terror of Hell has been replaced by the terror of living, I still find
myself calling upon my homemade choirs to accompany me in my
car, to surround my study or kitchen and sing back the demons of
daily life. Sometimes I've even caught myself slipping another tape
against terror into the stereo and singing a distracted riff of my
mother's favorite, "We'll Leave It All Behind."

During the recent holy war between the United States and Iraq,   9
with the apocalyptic rhetoric about "Satan" and "infidels" eerily
reminiscent of southern revivals—Mermaid Music was working
long hours to meet my own and my friends' wartime demands. To
offset NPR's daily interviews with military experts commenting on
the allied video-war air strikes with the zealous aplomb of sports-
casters, I'd surrender to the tender tenor of Aaron Neville singing

"With God on Our Side" or "Will the Circle Be Unbroken?" As I drove along freeways where phosphorescent orange bumper stickers shouted USA KICKS BUTT! or OPERATION DESERT STORM, as if it were a souvenir banner of a hot vacation spot, I wondered that there was no music for the Gulf War. Where were the songs like "My Buddy" or "It's a Long Way to Tipperary"?

During the last days of the war, I relied upon Bach's Violin Concerto in D Minor, the fierce longing of Jacqueline DePres's cello, Fauré's Requiem and, as always, Mozart. On a particularly bad day, between the Pentagon press conferences—men with pointers, target maps, smart-bomb videos, and a doublespeak war doggerel that called bombing "servicing a target"—I made a beeline to my public library and checked out every musical from *Oklahoma* to *Miss Saigon.* I made a tape entitled "Life Is a Musical" and divided it into three sections: (1) Love Found in Strange Places, (2) Love Lost Everywhere, and (3) Love Returns. It was astonishing how songs from vastly different time periods and places segued together. My favorite storyline riff is "Empty Chairs at Empty Tables," from *Les Misérables* to "The American Dream" from *Miss Saigon* to "Carefully Taught" from *South Pacific* to "Don't Cry for Me, Argentina," from *Evita* to "Bring Him Home" from *Les Misérables.* When I sent copies out to a select group of musicals-loving friends, it was as if we were all together at a candlelight mass or cross-continent communion, trying to imagine a war where no bombs fell.

Playing my own tapes against terror is a way to document and summon back the necessities that mothered them. For example, "My Funny Valentine," with its Billie Holiday/Sarah Vaughan/Ella Fitzgerald/Alberta Hunter blues and ebullience is still a favorite, long after that lover has gone. Upon hearing that an old friend had bone cancer, I made him a tape called "Music to Heal By," which included the Delta Rhythm Boys' version of "Dry Bones." My friend wrote to say it was the first time he'd laughed in a long time. Now he's making his own tapes. After a writer friend of mine drank herself to death, I felt so bereft—since, after all, we'd planned to retire to the Black Hole Nursing Home for Wayward Writers together—that I made a tape called "The Ten Commandments of Love, or Southern Baptists Beware!" It's every song I ever slow-danced to or memorized in the sweaty backseat of a borrowed car as my date and I broke Sunday school rules on Saturday night. Declared by my siblings and southern pals to have gone into "metal" (their word for platinum or gold), it includes Etta James's soaring "At Last," Sam Cooke's silky "Wonderful World," and a steamy duet of

10

11

"634–5789" with Robert Cray and Tina Turner. It's a great tape for getting in the mood.

Since ancient times, the Chinese have believed that certain   12
sounds can balance and heal. In acupressure, for example, each organ has a sound. Listening to a healthy heart, an astute healer can hear laughter or, if there is disease, wind. The gallbladder shouts; the stomach speaks in a singsong, sometimes overly sympathetic voice; and the kidney, ever the perfectionist, groans. Sighs can be a sign of liver ailments, and the pitch of a person's voice can tell a story of that body's health just as well as a tongue. In some Taoist practices to enhance longevity, re-creating the sounds of certain organs can strengthen and tone them. For example, the *whuuuh whuuuh* sound of the kidney can revitalize the adrenals, fortifying the immune system. If one cannot take time to sing in the key of every organ, I'd suggest Chinese wind chimes like the ones that grace my back porch. When a strong salt wind blows off the beach, my chimes, which are perfectly pitched to a five-element Chinese scale, play an impromptu arpeggio—a momentary transport to some monastic garden, a Shangri-la of sound. Scientific studies report that the actual sound of nature resonates at the level of eight hertz; by comparison, a refrigerator reverberates at eighty hertz. Is it any wonder some of us need to return to a musical womb to retreat from such technological onslaughts to our nervous systems?

In fact, our time in the womb is not at all quiet; it is a noisy sym-   13
phony of voices, lower-tract rumbles, whirrings like waterfalls, and white noise. One of my friends found that if she played a tape of the roar of her sturdy Kirby vacuum cleaner, the sound immediately put her boisterous newborn twins to sleep. I have another friend whose entire house is wall-to-wall egg cartons, which absorb sound as well as enhance his audiophilic tendencies. I've visited houses that sound like living inside an aquarium, where pleasant underwater burbles from elaborate tropical fish tanks drown out the world. I've also entered homes where cuckoo clocks, grandfather chimes, and deep gongs count the hours so that I felt I was inside a ticking time bomb. Consciously or unconsciously we all make sound tracks to underscore our lives.

Mermaid Music has allowed me to enter a reverie of song, a   14
backstage "smaller-than-life" sojourn away from all the stresses. Right now I'm at work on two dance tapes for a summer roll-up-the-rug party. Entitled "Bop till You Drop" and "Bad Girls," the tapes defy all hearers not to kick up their heels with such all-time hits as "Heat Wave" and "I Heard It Through the Grapevine," as well as the ever-popular "R-E-S-P-E-C-T." Of course, I've had request for

sequels and am at work on "Life Is a Musical II" divided into (1) "Falling," (2) "Feeling," and (3) "Forever Ruined/Recovery." It flows from "People Will Say We're in Love" to "Happy Talk" to "Just You Wait, Henry Higgins!"

My siblings say I should sell my tapes against terror on late- 15
night TV in the company of such classics as Veg-O-Matics and "Elvis Lives" medleys. The idea fills me with horror. After all, there are copyright violations cops who come like revenuers in the dark of the night to bust local moonshiners and music makers. I'd rather stay strictly small-time and nonprofit, like that long-ago lullaby service I had in college, a trio of nannies against nightmares. But if anyone out there in music land is making his or her own tapes against terror, I'd be open to an exchange. After all, it's better than bombs through the mail or collecting baseball cards.

So tune in, and maybe we'll find ourselves on the same fre- 16
quency. On this lifelong Freeway of Love, I just want to be an Earth Angel with my Magic Flute. Because after all, Everybody Plays the Fool and Ain't Nobody's Business If I Do.

MEANINGS AND VALUES

1. In a paragraph of your own, summarize what this essay has to say about music, human emotions, and the relationship between them.

2. What subject or subjects is Peterson classifying in this essay?

3. Explain what the writer means by the phrase "my soul's station" (par. 1).

EXPOSITORY TECHNIQUES

1. Which paragraph announces the purpose and theme of the essay? (See "Guide to Terms": *Purpose; Unity.*) Can this essay be said to have a thesis statement? If so, where is it? (Guide: *Thesis.*)

2. What pattern other than classification does the writer employ in paragraph 4? (Hint: see Chapter 8.)

3. What different subjects does Peterson classify in this essay? How, if at all, does the writer keep these different classifications from over-lapping in a confusing manner? Would this essay be more effective if the writer had concentrated on only one or two of the classifications? Explain. (Guide: *Evaluation.*)

4. What is the function of the clauses that open the first sentence in the essay? (Guide: *Syntax; Introductions.*)

Diction and Vocabulary

1. Identify the extended comparison in paragraph 12 and explain its relation to the central theme of the essay. (Guide: *Figures of Speech; Unity.*)

2. Identify those paragraphs in the essay that begin with transition words indicating that they will further develop the topic or ideas of the preceding paragraph. Discuss whether the transition words serve effectively to link paragraphs and ideas within the essay. (Guide: *Transition.*)

3. If you do not know the meaning of some of the following words, look them up in the dictionary: solace, mellifluous, placenta (par. 2); falsetto (4); suave (5); heretically (6); dulcet (7); riff (8); eerily, zealous, aplomb (9); segued (10); ebullience (11); astute (12); audiophilic (13).

Read to Write

1. **Collaborating:** Working in a group, list several types or categories of music. Then list the types of experiences, moods, or activities each group member associates with the different types of music. Note any similarities or patterns the group observes in the relationship between the kinds of music and the responses or uses of the music. Collectively plan an essay explaining the kinds of music and the typical responses to them. Consider drawing on this plan for an essay of your own.

2. **Considering Audience:** How effective are Peterson's examples for a young adult audience today? For an audience in some other age group? Write an essay on a plan similar to Peterson's but using musical examples directed at a particular age or cultural group with which you are familiar.

3. **Developing an Essay:** Drawing strategies from Peterson's essay, prepare an essay of your own, classifying tastes in art, movies, sports, or some other area of cultural or social activity. Try to explain why differences in people's tastes can be understood on the basis of differences in character, background, or some other factor.

(Note: Suggestions for topics requiring development by use of classification follow.)

Writing Suggestions for Chapter 4

CLASSIFICATION

Use division and classification (into at least three categories) as your basic method of analyzing one of the following subjects from an interesting point of view. (Your instructor may have good reason to place limitations on your choice of subject.) Narrow the topic as necessary to enable you to do a thorough job.

1. College students.
2. College teachers.
3. Athletes.
4. Coaches.
5. Salespeople.
6. Hunters (or fishers).
7. Parents.
8. Drug users.
9. Police officers.
10. Summer (or part-time) jobs.
11. Sailing vessels.
12. Game show hosts.
13. Friends.
14. Careers.
15. Horses (or other animals).
16. Television programs.
17. Motivations for study.
18. Methods of studying for exams.
19. Lies.
20. Selling techniques.
21. Tastes in clothes.
22. Contemporary music or films.
23. Love.
24. Ways to spend money.
25. Attitudes toward life.
26. Fast foods (or junk foods).

27. Smokers.

28. Investments.

29. Actors.

30. Books or magazines.

COLLABORATIVE EXERCISES

1. Working in a group, prepare a classification essay on college life using numbers 1–4 in the preceding exercise as the major sections for your classification. Assign group members to divide each of the four sections into two or three further categories and to prepare a section of an essay explaining these categories. Then prepare a collaboratively written essay linking each section with clear transitions and unifying the whole with a central idea on which all members of the group agree. (See "Guide to Terms": *Unity*.)

2. As a group, create three or more categories from the subject "careers" (see number 14). Have each member of the group research one of the types of careers and then create a collaboratively written essay with an appropriate introduction, conclusion, thesis, and transitions.

5

Explaining by Means of *Comparison* and *Contrast*

One of the first expository methods we used as children was *comparison*, noticing similarities of objects, qualities, and actions, or *contrast*, noticing their differences. We compared the color of the new puppies with that of their mother, contrasted a parent's height with our own. Then the process became more complicated. Now we employ it frequently in college essay examinations or term papers when we compare or contrast forms of government, reproductive systems of animals, or ethical philosophies of humans. In the business or professional world, we prepare important reports based on comparison and contrast—between kinds of equipment for purchase, the personnel policies of different departments, or precedents in legal matters. Nearly all people use the process of comparison (meaning both *comparing* and *contrasting*) many times a day—in choosing a head of lettuce, in deciding what to wear to school, in selecting a house, or a friend, or a religion.

In expository writing, brief comparisons—a sentence or two—may serve to alert readers to similarities or highlight differences. Longer comparisons need to do more; they need to explore the subject and convey the writer's perspective. For a longer comparison or contrast that explains or explores ideas, you need an ordered plan to avoid having a mere list of characteristics or a frustrating jumble of similarities and differences. You also need to give attention to all the important points of similarity (or difference). The following paragraph accomplishes all these things.

> We really are terribly confused about our relationship with nature.
> On the one hand, we like to live in houses that are tidy and clean, and if
> nature should be rude enough to enter—in the form of a bat in the attic,

or a mouse in the kitchen, or a cockroach crawling along the skirting boards—we stalk it with the blood-lust of a tabby cat; we resort to chemical warfare. In fact, we judge people harshly if their house is full of dust and dirt. And yet, on the other hand, we just as obsessively bring nature indoors. We touch a switch and light floods the room. We turn a dial and suddenly it feels like summer or winter. We live in a perpetual breeze or bake of our devising. We buy posters and calendars with photographs of nature. We hang paintings of landscapes on our walls. We scent everything that touches our lives. We fill our houses with flowers and pets. We try hard to remove ourselves from all the dramas and sensations of nature, and yet without them we feel lost and disconnected. So, subconsciously, we bring them right back indoors again. Then we obsessively visit nature—we go swimming, jogging, or cross-country skiing, we take strolls in a park. Confusing, isn't it?

—Diane Ackerman, *Deep Play*

WHY USE COMPARISON?

Highlighting similarities and differences is the most obvious use for comparison, but merely a starting point for effective writing. Whenever you employ the pattern, therefore, make sure you give it a worthwhile purpose. You can contrast llamas with potbellied pigs, for example, but your efforts will likely seem silly or trivial unless tied to some larger goal, as in the case of Judith Stone's essay, "Personal Beast" (Ch. 4), in which she contrasts their relatively suitability as pets.

The question of purpose is especially important in a formal, full-scale analysis by comparison and contrast where the pattern lends shape to an entire essay. Sometimes the purpose may be merely to reveal *surprising or frequently overlooked likenesses and differences*, with the goal of adding to readers' knowledge, satisfying curiosity, or developing our self-awareness. For example, an essay on generational differences over responsibility for housework might explain that younger people are more likely to share the work of cooking and cleaning, but that all generations seem to be maintaining traditional gender differences in the responsibility of home maintenance. Mark Twain, in the selection "Two Ways of Seeing a River" (pp. 154–155) contrasts his view of the Mississippi as a young man with his perspective as an experienced river pilot. In doing so, he helps readers understand how radically experience and changes in attitude can affect our perceptions of the external world—even making the same stretch of scenery appear a different place.

The aim may be to show *the superiority* of one thing over another. Or it may be to *explain* and *evaluate*, as in a discussion of alternatives or of differing points of view on an issue. For instance, you might examine competing proposals for an anti-smoking campaign, one designed by teenagers and the other by advertising professionals, evaluating the strengths and limitations of each.

The purpose could be to explain the *unfamiliar* (wedding customs in Ethiopia) by comparing it to the *familiar* (wedding customs in Kansas). Or it could be to support and explore a thesis, as is the case with several of the essays in this chapter. Alice Walker ("Am I Blue?"), for example, uses comparison to advance the thesis that animals have emotional lives similar to those of humans; Scott Russell Sanders ("The Men We Carry in Our Minds") shows how some of the differences we readily assume between the lives of men and women may not hold true when we consider the struggles of poor, hardworking men like his father.

CHOOSING A STRATEGY

To take a comparison beyond the obvious and develop knowledge and insight worth sharing with readers, you need to begin by identifying **points of comparison** (or contrast), both major and minor. Some important points of comparison will be apparent to you (and your readers) from the outset, and therefore, should be part of your analysis. Others will be less apparent, though not necessarily less important. Including them will enable you to provide a fresh or more thorough perspective, adding to your reader's understanding. Consider using the following questions to identify and explore points of comparison, adapted, of course, to the particular demands of your subjects.

What are the similar (or different) **physical aspects** (shape, color, size, texture, movement) of the subjects you are analyzing?

Parts and Processes (elements and their relationships, methods of operation, instructions)?
Benefits (individual, social, political, environmental)?
Problems (dangers, difficulties, limitations)?
Costs (financial, emotional, political)?
Uses (personal, social, environmental; to provide benefits, to create relationships, to accomplish a particular goal)?

As you develop responses to questions like these, keep in mind that you are trying to develop fresh insights both for yourself and your readers. Consider using questions like these to help you develop such a perspective.

What similarities (or differences) are readers likely to consider . . .

Intriguing or surprising?

Useful or worth learning about?

Quite different from what they expected before they began reading?

Significant enough to make them more likely to consider different opinions on an issue or approaches to a problem?

Important enough to guide their choice among alternative policies, products, or conclusions?

The points of comparison you choose, along with your tentative thesis, your purpose for writing, and the complexity of your materials, will usually suggest an arrangement for your writing. The number of subjects making up any comparison (two or more) and the likelihood that you will be exploring multiple points of comparison along with their supporting details means that you should plan the organization of an essay carefully and remember to make this arrangement clear to readers.

One of the two basic methods of comparison is to present all the information on the two (or more) subjects, one at a time, and to summarize by combining their most important similarities and differences. Here is a subject-by-subject plan for an essay.

Subject-by-Subject Pattern

Introduction

    Subjects: Bella Costa Medical Center (curing illness) and Foothills Regional Health Complex (creating wellness)

    Tentative Thesis: Today's healthcare dilemmas have gone beyond choices among insurance plans to choices between two very different kinds of medical treatment, one focused on curing illness (represented by Bella Costa M.C.), the other focused on creating wellness (represented by Foothills R.H.C.)

    Subject 1: Bella Costa Medical Center

        Feature 1: Traditional medicine—curing illness

        Feature 2: Large hospital, newest equipment

        Feature 3: Large staff of physicians

        Feature 4: Emphasis on drugs, surgery, physical therapy

    Subject 2: Foothills Regional Medical Center

        Feature 1: Preventive medicine—creating wellness

        Feature 2: Small hospital, limited facilities, local clinics

        Feature 3: Some physicians, other staff including nutritionists, exercise specialists, alternative therapists

        Feature 4: Emphasis on diet, exercise, alternative therapies (acupuncture, holistic medicine), healthy lifestyle

Conclusion (summary): Summarize reasons for choosing either one and suggest that personal preferences may play an important role.

This method may be desirable if there are few points to compare, or if the individual points are less important than the overall picture they present.

However, if there are several points of comparison to be considered, or if the points are of individual importance, alternation of the material would be a better arrangement.

Point-by-Point Pattern

Subjects: *The Mummy* (1932) starring Boris Karloff
The Mummy (1999) starring Brendan Fraser

Tentative Thesis: The original version of *The Mummy* (1932) takes itself and horror movie form seriously and provides an often scary portrait of evil. The remake (1999) takes itself only half seriously and gently pokes fun at the conventions of the horror movie, so it is only occasionally scary and conveys no sense of evil.

Subject 1: Original version of *The Mummy*

Feature 1 Acting: Boris Karloff, serious acting style, dramatic scenes and speeches

Feature 2 Script: provides motivation for characters, emphasizes force of evil desires

Feature 3 Special effects: support story line, emphasize unnatural desires and presence of evil

Subject 2: Remake of *The Mummy*

Feature 1 Acting: Brendan Fraser, comic or ironic acting style, action scenes and physical comedy

Feature 2 Script: little motivation for characters, highlights stereotypes and conventions of horror movies

Feature 3 Special effects: call attention to themselves, emphasize unreal, exaggerated elements of horror stories

Conclusion (summary)

Original and remake show changing attitudes toward the horror movie as a portrait of evil

Often the subject matter or the purpose itself will suggest a more casual treatment, or some combination or variation of the two basic methods. We might present the complete information on the first subject, then summarize it point by point within the complete information on the second. And although expository comparisons and contrasts are frequently handled together, it is sometimes best to present all similarities first, then all differences—or vice versa, depending on the emphasis desired. In any basic use of comparison, the important thing is to have a plan that suits the purpose and material, thoughtfully worked out in advance.

DEVELOPING COMPARISONS

In writing an essay using comparison as a primary pattern of exposition, keep these two important tasks in mind: 1) take care that your comparisons are logical and arranged in a manner that will be clear to your readers; 2) provide detailed explanations of the similarities and differences in order to support your conclusions.

Above all, your comparison needs to be *logical.* A logical comparison or contrast can be made only between subjects of the same general type. (Analogy, a special form of comparison used for another purpose, is discussed in the next chapter.) For example, contrasting modern medicine (prescription drugs, surgery) and traditional medicine (herbal remedies, acupuncture) could be useful or meaningful, but little would be gained by contrasting surgery and carpentry.

Transition words and phrases are a big help with both logic and the arrangement of an essay, reminding you of an essay's plan as you write and signaling the arrangement to readers. Some transition words identify the elements of a subject; some indicate logical realtionships or highlight the place of a paragraph in the overall organization, and some identify conclusions and supporting detail.

Elements of a Subject: trait, characteristic, element, part, segment, unit, feature

Logical Relationships and Arrangement: in comparison, in contrast, on the other side, on the other hand, likewise, moreover, similarly, in the same (different) manner, in addition, then, further, yet, but, however, nonetheless, first, second, third, although, still

Conclusions and Supporting Detail: in conclusion, to sum up, finally, for example, for instance

Paragraphs are especially important in writing that compares or contrasts. Typically, they are devoted to one of the major steps in the exposition, often to one of the main points of comparison. In focusing on points of similarity or dissimilarity, be thorough. Provide facts, concrete details, and examples. Consider those that support your conclusions or recommendations as well as those that provide contrary evidence. Remember, too, that effective comparisons serve a purpose, so include details that support your overall thesis and further the purpose for which you are writing.

Student Essay

In the following essay, Amy Bell uses comparison as a pattern of thinking: a way to raise questions about and explore her topic. She inquires into the "truthfulness" of two pieces of writing that claim to be portrayals of events that really happened and in so doing raises questions about what really constitutes "truth" in writing. Amy uses comparison effectively in her own writing both as a way of representing her thinking and as a way of helping readers understand the many detailed similarities and differences she analyzes.

Perception of Truth

by Amy Bell

    "The following motion picture is based on a true story." How many times have you seen this on the movie screen and thought, "Yeah, right, 'true' story my foot"? We all know that the movie producers/directors take huge liberties with the facts and portray events differently from the way they

Focuses on general topic/issue to be explored

actually occurred. The same is true in nonfiction writing. Each author chooses what information to give to the reader and what information to withhold. In doing this the "truth" is blurred and the author's personal bias emerges. Truman Capote and Norman Mailer are both hailed as authors who succeeded in writing "true-story" nov-

Focuses on specific topic of essay

els. In describing Norman Mailer's *The Executioner's Song*, critics have said he is "our greatest chronicler" and "the best journalist in the country." (Mailer cover). Critics have described Truman Capote's *In Cold Blood* as a "superbly written 'true account'" and "the best documentary of an

American crime" (Capote cover). All of
these book reviews imply that Mailer and
Capote gave only the truth in their books.
However this is not possible. Mailer's and
Capote's personal opinions also must be in

Purpose of
essay—to be
accomplished
by comparing
and
contrasting

these novels. So which novel is more truthful? This question cannot be answered. How
can we ever know what information these authors changed or what information they left
out completely? However, it is possible to
show which novel creates a greater impres-

Thesis
statement

sion of truth. Truman Capote's novel, *In
Cold Blood,* seems more truthful than
Mailer's *The Executioner's Song.* The im-

General plan
for essay—
compare the
works

pression of truth in these novels was
partly created by the way in which each author portrayed the murderer in his story.

   Norman Mailer and Truman Capote both had
unlimited access to the facts about the

Background—
both Mailer
and Capote

murderers, Gary Gilmore and Perry Smith
[respectively]. In researching Gilmore,
Mailer collected interview manuscripts,
court records and documents. He also conducted nearly 300 interviews, which added
up to a manuscript of 15,000 pages (Mailer
1020). Capote also collected numerous official records and conducted interviews
(Capote acknowledgements page). Capote and
Mailer used carefully selected bits of
truth from this multitude of information
to portray their murderers differently.

Feature 1:
Quotations

   One obvious way in which Mailer and
Capote described the murderers was to di-

Discussion of
Mailer

rectly quote them. Norman Mailer put a numerous amount of quotations from Gilmore
in his novel. Nearly forty letters written
by Gilmore to his girlfriend Nicole were
printed in the book. Mailer also included
a great deal of interviews between Gilmore

Supporting details

and his two lawyers. A lot of "truth" is divulged because so much personal information about Gilmore is given. However, for the reader this truth becomes blurred because of Gilmore's contradicting feelings and intense emotions. For instance, in one letter Gilmore writes to Nicole he says, "I saw a simple, quiet Truth, a profound, deep, and personal Truth of beauty and love" (qtd. in Mailer 345). It would seem that through these words the reader might see who the "true" Gary is. However, in the next letter the reader is bombarded with ". . . these chickens—t pricks. Give a motherf—er a little authority and they think they have to start taking privileges away from people . . . bunch of slack-jawed . . . gurgling . . . punks" (Mailer 348). Gilmore's variety of raving emotions weaves in and out of the letters in the book, leaving the reader wary of believing anything Gilmore says. Norman Mailer gives

Interpretation of details

us too much information from an unreliable Gilmore, and in doing so there seems to be less truth.

Feature 1: Quotations

Discussion of Capote

Capote also quotes his murderer, Perry Smith; however, he uses fewer, carefully selected quotations. Capote only uses enough quotations to give an ample description of Smith. This creates less confusion for the reader about Smith. Smith could have been just as confusing to understand

Supporting details

as Gilmore was; after all, Smith did kill four people without knowing why he did it. For example, Capote includes a few carefully selected quotations to describe Smith's childhood. Smith is describing the brutality of the nuns in an orphanage he lived in as a child: "She woke me up. She had a flashlight, and she hit me with it. Hit me and hit me. And when the flashlight broke, she went on hitting me in the dark" (qtd. in Capote 93). This well-chosen quotation gives the reader an understanding of Smith's childhood and gives a glimpse into the mind of Smith. Capote tells the reader who Smith is, instead of the reader having to figure out who Smith is by sorting through hundreds of Smith's thoughts. **Interpretation of details** Capote gives us what he thinks the truth about Smith is, and he does it in such a way that the reader is compelled to believe it.

Feature 2: Equal weight in presentation

Discussion of Mailer

One way to make a story more believable and truthful is to give equal weight to everyone's side of the story. Mailer thoroughly gives Gilmore's side of the story, however the stories of the victims are hardly mentioned. In chapters twelve and fifteen of part four, Mailer gives a basic description of the lives of the Bushnells and the Jensens. He only devotes about twenty pages out of 1000 pages to these people. Also, Mailer's description of these people is not an intimate one. He gives an overview of their lives in a distant, journalistic style. Mailer writes, "It was at Utah State that Colleen was introduced to her future husband, Max Jensen" (Mailer 212). This is simply a description, and the voices and feelings of Max and Colleen are not seen.

Conclusion followed by supporting details

Capote on the other hand gives an equal amount of time to everyone's side of the story. In the first chapter, "Last to See **Feature 2: Equal weight in presentation** Them Alive," Capote describes the Clutter family while also describing Dick [Smith's accomplice] and Perry [Smith]. Capote shows each member of the Clutter family,

Discussion of Capote

Conclusion followed by supporting details

their relationships with each other and with the community. Capote includes a lot of dialogue between members of the family, so that the reader can see the murder victims as real people. The following is a conversation between Nancy Clutter and her brother, Kenyon. [Nancy speaks first.]

"I keep smelling cigarette smoke."

"On your breath?" inquired Kenyon.

"No funny one. Yours." (Capote 19)

In this interplay between brother and sister the reader can relate to the Clutters as human beings and not just as murder victims. Capote gives an in-depth, intimate description of every person's

Interpretation of details

side of the story. For the reader this is creates a perception that Capote was less biased, and therefore the story seems truthful.

Summary Conclusion: Capote seems more truthful

Using basic logic, it would seem that Mailer probably wrote down more "truth" in a 1,000-page book than Capote wrote in a meager 350-page book. However, the amount of truth and the perception of truth are two very different things. Truman Capote's *In Cold Blood* gives a greater perception of truth than Norman Mailer's *The Executioner's Song*. Then again this statement is merely my opinion. As the author of this essay I selected only the "appropriate" bits of information from these two novels to give my reader(s) my perception of what "truth" is.

Works Cited

Mailer, Norman. *The Executioner's Song*. New York: Warner, 1979.

Capote, Truman. *In Cold Blood*. 1965. New York: Vintage, Random, 1993.

MARK TWAIN

MARK TWAIN was the pen name of Samuel Clemens (1835–1910). He was born in Missouri and became the first author of importance to emerge from "beyond the Mississippi." Although best known for bringing humor, realism, and Western local color to American fiction, Mark Twain wanted to be remembered as a philosopher and social critic. Still widely read, in most languages and in all parts of the world, are his numerous short stories (his "tall tales," in particular), autobiographical accounts, and novels, especially *Adventures of Huckleberry Finn* (1884). Ernest Hemingway called the last "the best book we've had," an appraisal with which many critics agree.

Two Ways of Seeing a River

"Two Ways of Seeing a River" (editors' title) is from Mark Twain's "Old Times on the Mississippi," which was later expanded and published in book form as *Life on the Mississippi* (1883). It is autobiographical. The prose of this selection is vivid, as is all of Mark Twain's writing, but considerably more reflective in tone than most.

Now when I had mastered the language of this water and had come to know every trifling feature that bordered the great river as familiarly as I knew the letters of the alphabet, I had made a valuable acquisition. But I had lost something, too. I had lost something which could never be restored to me while I lived. All the grace, the beauty, the poetry, had gone out of the majestic river! I still kept in mind a certain wonderful sunset which I witnessed when steamboating was new to me. A broad expanse of the river was turned to blood; in the middle distance the red hue brightened into gold, through which a solitary log came floating, black and conspicuous; in one place a long, slanting mark lay sparkling upon the water; in another the surface was broken by boiling, tumbling rings that were as many-tinted as an opal; where the ruddy flush was faintest was a smooth spot that was covered with graceful circles and radiating lines, ever so delicately traced; the shore on our left was densely wooded, and the somber shadow that fell from this forest was broken in one place by a long, ruffled trail that shone like silver; and high above the forest wall a clean-stemmed dead tree waved a single leafy bough that glowed like a flame in the unobstructed splendor that was flowing from the sun. There were graceful curves, reflected images, woody heights, soft distances, and over the whole scene, far and near, the dissolving lights drifted steadily, enriching it every passing moment with new marvels of coloring.

I stood like one bewitched. I drank it in, in a speechless rapture. The world was new to me and I had never seen anything like this at home. But as I have said, a day came when I began to cease from noting the glories and the charms which the moon and the sun and the twilight wrought upon the river's face; another day came when I ceased altogether to note them. Then, if that sunset scene had been repeated, I should have looked upon it without rapture and should have commented upon it inwardly after this fashion: "This sun means that we are going to have wind tomorrow; that floating log means that the river is rising, small thanks to it; that slanting mark on the water refers to a bluff reef which is going to kill somebody's steamboat one of these nights, if it keeps on stretching out like that; those tumbling 'boils' show a dissolving bar and a changing channel there; the lines and circles in the slick water over yonder are a warning that that troublesome place is shoaling up dangerously; that silver streak in the shadow of the forest is the 'break' from a new snag and he has located himself in the very best place he could have found to fish for steamboats; that tall dead tree, with a single living branch, is not going to last long, and then how is a body ever going to get through this blind place at night without the friendly old landmark?"

No, the romance and beauty were all gone from the river. All the value any feature of it had for me now was the amount of usefulness it could furnish toward compassing the safe piloting of a steamboat. Since those days, I have pitied doctors from my heart. What does the lovely flush in a beauty's cheek mean to a doctor but a "break" that ripples above some deadly disease? Are not all her visible charms sown thick with what are to him the signs and symbols of hidden decay? Does he ever see her beauty at all, or doesn't he simply view her professionally and comment upon her unwholesome condition all to himself? And doesn't he sometimes wonder whether he has gained most or lost most by learning his trade?

MEANINGS AND VALUES

1.   What is the point of view in paragraph 1? (See "Guide to Terms": *Point of View.*) Where, and how, does it change in paragraph 2? Why is the shift important to the author's contrast?

2. Show how the noticeable change of tone between paragraphs 1 and 2 is related to the change in point of view. (Guide: Style/Tone.) Specifically, what changes in style accompany the shift in tone and attitude? How effectively do they all relate to the central theme itself? (Remember that such effects seldom just "happen"; the writer *makes* them happen.)

3. Is the first paragraph primarily objective or subjective? (Guide: *Objective/Subjective.* How about the latter part of paragraph 2? Are your answers related to point of view? If so, how?

4. Do you think the last sentence refers only to doctors? Why, or why not?

EXPOSITORY TECHNIQUES

1. Where do you find a second comparison or contrast? Which is it? Is the comparison/contrast made within itself, with something external, or both? Explain.

2. Is the second comparison/contrast closely enough related to the major contrast to justify its use? Why, or why not?

3. In developing the numerous points of the major contrast, would an alternating, point-to-point system have been better? Why, or why not? Show how the author uses organization within the groups to assist in the overall contrast.

4. What is the most noteworthy feature of syntax in paragraphs 1 and 2? (Guide: *Syntax.*) How effectively does it perform the function intended?

5. What is gained by the apparently deliberate decision to use rhetorical questions only toward the end? (Guide: *Rhetorical Questions.*)

DICTION AND VOCABULARY

1. In what ways do the word choices in paragraph 1 differ from those in paragraph 2? (Guide: *Diction.*)

2. Compare the quality of metaphors in the quotation of paragraph 2 with the quality of those preceding it. (Guide: *Figures of Speech.*) Is the difference justified? Why, or why not?

READ TO WRITE

1. **Collaborate:** We spend much of our lives preparing for work, working, and thinking about work. As Twain's essay points out, moreover, work shapes the way we perceive things and respond to them. Work can therefore be an excellent source of writing topics that are interesting to both writers and readers. Working in a group, add five more questions about work to the following list, and then use it to help generate possible topics for an essay: How do specific kinds of work shape perceptions and values? Are people's outlooks likely to vary according to the kinds of jobs they hold (or want to hold)? How

do my work habits, preferences, or experiences set me apart from others (or bring me closer)?

2. **Considering Audience:** Would readers of Twain's era, used to traveling by steamboat, horse-drawn carriage, steam-powered trains, and horseback, respond differently than readers of today to this essay? Write a brief essay of your own (1–3 paragraphs) explaining why readers might or might not respond differently. In doing so, consider the ways in which modern means of transportation affect our perceptions and values.

3. **Developing an Essay:** Twain's essay not only describes two scenes but also explains what changes in outlook and experience make them seem different. Prepare an essay of your own with a similar purpose. Choose a scene or event that you have observed more than once and from differing perspectives. Explain to readers the ways in which the scene appeared different and what it was about your perceptions that accounted for the difference.

(NOTE: Suggestions for topics requiring development by use of COMPARISON and CONTRAST are on pp. 193–194, at the end of this chapter.)

BRUCE CATTON

Bruce Catton (1899–1978) was a Civil War specialist whose early career included reporting for various newspapers. In 1954 he received both the Pulitzer Prize for historical work and the National Book Award. He served as director of information for the United States Department of Commerce and wrote many books, including *Mr. Lincoln's Army* (1951), *Glory Road* (1952), *A Stillness at Appomattox* (1953), *The Hallowed Ground* (1956), *America Goes to War* (1958), *The Coming Fury* (1961), *Terrible Swift Sword* (1963), *Never Call Retreat* (1966), *Waiting for the Morning Train: An American Boyhood* (1972), and *Gettysburg: The Final Fury* (1974). For five years, Catton edited *American Heritage*.

Grant and Lee: A Study in Contrasts

"Grant and Lee: A Study in Contrasts" was written as a chapter of *The American Story,* a collection of essays by noted historians. In this study, as in most of his other writing, Catton does more than recount the facts of history: he shows the significance within them. It is a carefully constructed essay, using contrast and comparison as the entire framework for his explanation.

When Ulysses S. Grant and Robert E. Lee met in the parlor of a   1
modest house at Appomattox Court House, Virginia, on April 9, 1865, to work out the terms for the surrender of Lee's Army of Northern Virginia, a great chapter in American life came to a close, and a great new chapter began.

These men were bringing the Civil War to its virtual finish. To be   2
sure, other armies had yet to surrender, and for a few days the fugitive Confederate government would struggle desperately and vainly, trying to find some way to go on living now that its chief support was gone. But in effect it was all over when Grant and Lee signed the papers. And the little room where they wrote out the terms was the scene of one of the most poignant, dramatic contrasts in American history.

They were two strong men these oddly different generals, and   3
they represented the strengths of two conflicting currents that,
through them, had come into final collision.

Back of Robert E. Lee was the notion that the old aristocratic   4
concept might somehow survive and be dominant in American life.

Lee was tidewater Virginia, and in his background were family,   5
culture, and tradition . . . the age of chivalry transplanted to a New
World which was making its own legends and its own myths. He
embodied a way of life that had come down through the age of
knighthood and the English country squire. America was a land that
was beginning all over again, dedicated to nothing much more complicated than the rather hazy belief that all men had equal rights and
should have an equal chance in the world. In such a land Lee stood
for the feeling that it was somehow of advantage to human society
to have a pronounced inequality in the social structure. There
should be a leisure class, backed by ownership of land; in turn, society itself should be keyed to the land as the chief source of wealth
and influence. It would bring forth (according to this ideal) a class of
men with a strong sense of obligation to the community; men who
lived not to gain advantage for themselves, but to meet the solemn
obligations which had been laid on them by the very fact that they
were privileged. From them the country would get its leadership; to
them it could look for the higher values—of thought, of conduct, or
personal deportment—to give it strength and virtue.

Lee embodied the noblest element of this aristocratic ideal.   6
Through him, the landed nobility justified itself. For four years, the
Southern states had fought a desperate war to uphold the ideals for
which Lee stood. In the end, it almost seemed as if the Confederacy
fought for Lee; as if he himself was the Confederacy . . . the best thing
that the way of life for which the Confederacy stood could ever have
to offer. He had passed into legend before Appomattox. Thousands
of tired, underfed, poorly clothed Confederate soldiers, long since
past the simple enthusiasm of the early days of the struggle, somehow considered Lee the symbol of everything for which they had
been willing to die. But they could not quite put this feeling into
words. If the Lost Cause, sanctified by so much heroism and so many
deaths, had a living justification, its justification was General Lee.

Grant, the son of a tanner on the Western frontier, was every-   7
thing Lee was not. He had come up the hard way and embodied
nothing in particular except the eternal toughness and sinewy fiber
of the men who grew up beyond the mountains. He was one of a
body of men who owed reverence and obeisance to no one, who

were self-reliant to a fault, who cared hardly anything for the past but who had a sharp eye for the future.

These frontier men were the precise opposites of the tidewater aristocrats. Back of them, in the great surge that had taken people over the Alleghenies and into the opening Western country, there was a deep, implicit dissatisfaction with a past that had settled into grooves. They stood for democracy, not from any reasoned conclusion about the proper ordering of human society, but simply because they had grown up in the middle of democracy and knew how it worked. Their society might have privileges, but they would be privileges each man had won for himself. Forms and patterns meant nothing. No man was born to anything, except perhaps to a chance to show how far he could rise. Life was competition.   8

Yet along with this feeling had come a deep sense of belonging to a national community. The Westerner who developed a farm, opened a shop, or set up in business as a trader could hope to prosper only as his own community prospered—and his community ran from the Atlantic to the Pacific and from Canada down to Mexico. If the land was settled, with towns and highways and accessible markets, he could better himself. He saw his fate in terms of the nation's own destiny. As its horizons expanded, so did his. He had, in other words, an acute dollars-and-cents stake in the continued growth and development of his country.   9

And that, perhaps, is where the contrast between Grant and Lee becomes most striking. The Virginia aristocrat, inevitably, saw himself in relation to his own region. He lived in a static society which could endure almost anything except change. Instinctively, his first loyalty would go to the locality in which that society existed. He would fight to the limit of endurance to defend it, because in defending it he was defending everything that gave his own life its deepest meaning.   10

The Westerner, on the other hand, would fight with an equal tenacity for the broader concept of society. He fought so because everything he lived by was tied to growth, expansion, and a constantly widening horizon. What he lived by would survive or fall with the nation itself. He could not possibly stand by unmoved in the face of an attempt to destroy the Union. He would combat it with everything he had, because he could only see it as an effort to cut the ground out from under his feet.   11

So Grant and Lee were in complete contrast, representing two diametrically opposed elements in American life. Grant was the modern man emerging; beyond him, ready to come on the stage, was the great age of steel and machinery, of crowded cities and a restless burgeoning vitality. Lee might have ridden down from the   12 old age of chivalry, lance in hand, silken banner fluttering over his head. Each man was the perfect champion of his cause, drawing both his strengths and his weaknesses from the people he led.

Yet it was not all contrast, after all. Different as they were—in background, in personality, in underlying aspiration—these two great soldiers had much in common. Under everything else, they were marvelous fighters. Furthermore, their fighting qualities were really very much alike. 13

Each man had, to begin with, the great virtue of utter tenacity and fidelity. Grant fought his way down the Mississippi Valley in spite of acute personal discouragement and profound military handicaps. Lee hung on in the trenches at Petersburg after hope itself had died. In each man there was an indomitable quality . . . the born fighter's refusal to give up as long as he can still remain on his feet and lift his two fists. 14

Daring and resourcefulness they had, too: the ability to think faster and move faster than the enemy. These were the qualities which gave Lee the dazzling campaigns of Second Manassas and Chancellorsville and won Vicksburg for Grant. 15

Lastly, and perhaps greatest of all, there was the ability, at the end, to turn quickly from war to peace once the fighting was over. Out of the way these two men behaved at Appomattox came the possibility of a peace of reconciliation. It was a possibility not wholly realized, in the years to come, but which did, in the end, help the two sections to become one nation again . . . after a war whose bitterness might have seemed to make such a reunion wholly impossible. No part of either man's life became him more than the part he played in their brief meeting in the McLean house at Appomattox. Their behavior there put all succeeding generations of Americans in their debt. Two great Americans, Grant and Lee—very different, yet under everything very much alike. Their encounter at Appomattox was one of the great moments of American history. 16

MEANINGS AND VALUES

1. Clarify the assertions that through Lee "the landed nobility justified itself" and that "if the Lost Cause . . . had a living justification," it was General Lee (par. 6.) Why are these assertions pertinent to the central theme?

2. Does it seem reasonable that "thousands of tired, underfed, poorly clothed Confederate soldiers" (par. 6) had been willing to fight for the aristocratic system in which they would never have had even a

chance to be aristocrats? Why or why not? Can you think of more likely reasons why they were willing to fight?

3. What countries of the world have recently been so torn by internal war and bitterness that reunion has seemed, or still seems, impossible? Do you see any basic differences between the trouble in those countries and that in America at the time of the Civil War?

4. The author calls Lee a symbol (par. 6). Was Grant also a symbol? If so, of what? (See "Guide to Terms": *Symbol*.) How would you classify this kind of symbolism?

EXPOSITORY TECHNIQUES

1. Make an informal list of paragraph numbers from 3 to 16, and note by each number whether the paragraph is devoted primarily to Lee, to Grant, or to direct comparison or contrast of the two. This chart will show you Catton's basic pattern of development. (Notice, for instance, how the broad information of paragraphs 4–6 and 7–9 seems almost to "funnel" down through the narrower summaries in paragraphs 10 and 11 into paragraph 12, where the converging elements meet and the contrast is made specific.)

2. What new technique of development is started in paragraph 13?

3. What is gained, or lost, by using one sentence for paragraph 3? For paragraph 4?

4. How many paragraphs does the introduction comprise? How successfully does it fulfill the three basic requirements of a good introduction? (Guide: *Introductions*.)

5. Show how Catton has constructed the beginning of each paragraph so that there is a smooth transition from the one preceding it. (Guide: *Transition*.)

6. What seems to be the author's attitude toward Grant and Lee? Show how his tone reflects this attitude. (Guide: *Style/Tone*.)

DICTION AND VOCABULARY

1. Why would a use of colloquialisms have been inconsistent with the tone of this writing?

2. List or mark all metaphors in paragraphs 1, 3, 5, 7–11, and 16. (Guide: *Figures of Speech*.) Comment on their general effectiveness.

3. If you are not already familiar with the following words, study their meanings as given in the dictionary and as used in this essay: virtual, poignant (par. 2); concept (4); sinewy, obeisance (7); implicit (8); tenacity (11); diametrically, burgeoning (12); aspiration (13); fidelity, profound, indomitable (14); succeeding (16).

READ TO WRITE

1. **Collaborating:** Catton focuses on a dramatic moment in history and explains its long-range significance. Drawing on his approach, list some dramatic moments in history. In a group, compare your lists. Does your definition of "dramatic moment" match those of other group members? Decide as a group on one moment you all agree is dramatic and, in a short essay, explain its long-range significance.

2. **Considering Audience:** Ask yourself how much you knew about the topic of "Grant and Lee" before you began reading the essay, then go through the text and highlight sections that present information that was new to you. To what extent do you think that your initial knowledge of the topic was similar to that of most readers? Why? Study the ways Catton introduces information that most readers are likely to be unfamiliar with, and identify techniques you could use to present new information in your own writing.

3. **Developing an Essay:** One special achievement of Catton's "Grant and Lee: A Study in Contrasts" is its portrait of the two generals as embodiments of contrasting societies and cultures. Consider using this strategy in an essay offering a contrast between ideas, values, or cultures by means of a contrast between people who embody the differences. The strategy can be applied to a wide variety of subjects, not simply to public or political ones. You might use it to talk about different parenting strategies, for example, or about various religious beliefs or value systems.

(NOTE: Suggestions for topics requiring development by means of COMPARISON and CONTRAST are on pp. 193–194 at the end of this chapter.)

PHILLIP LOPATE

PHILLIP LOPATE was born in 1943 in New York City. He attended
Columbia University and received a B.A. in 1964. He has taught cre-
ative writing in the Teachers and Writers Collaborative program in
New York City and is currently on the faculty of Hofstra. His publi-
cations include *The Eyes Don't Always Want to Stay Open* (1972) and
The Daily Round (1976) (poems); *Confessions of Summer* (1979),
Bachelorhood: Tales of the Metropolis (1981), and *The Rug Merchant*
(1988) (fiction); *Being with Children* (1975) (nonfiction); and *Against
Joie de Vivre: Personal Essays* (1989), *Portrait of My Body* (1996), and
Totally, Tenderly, and Tragically (1998) (collections of essays). His es-
says have appeared in a variety of publications, including *New Age
Journal, Texas Monthly, The New York Times Book Review, Columbia,
House and Garden, Vogue, Esquire,* and *Interview.*

A Nonsmoker with a Smoker

In this essay, which first appeared in *New Age Journal,* Lopate uses
comparison and contrast to explore his own ambiguous feelings
about smoking—and about his relationship with a smoker. In the
course of the essay, he touches on many aspects of the smoking/
nonsmoking conflict, yet he offers a personal perspective often lost
in the public controversy.

L ast Saturday night my girlfriend, Helen, and I went to a dinner   1
party in the Houston suburbs. We did not know our hosts, but
were invited on account of Helen's chum Barry, whose birthday
party it was. We had barely stepped into the house and met the
other guests, seated on a U-shaped couch under an A-framed ceiling, when Helen lit a cigarette. The hostess froze. "Uh, could you
please not smoke in here? If you have to, we'd appreciate your using
the terrace. We're both sort of allergic."

Helen smiled understandingly and moved toward the glass   2
doors leading to the backyard in a typically ladylike way, as though
merely wanting to get a better look at the garden. But I knew from
that gracious "Southern" smile of hers that she was miffed.

As soon as Helen had stepped outside, the hostess explained that they had just moved into this house, and that it had taken weeks to air out because of the previous owner's tenacious cigar smoke. A paradigmatically awkward conversation about tobacco ensued: like testifying sinners, two people came forward with confessions about kicking the nasty weed; our scientist-host cited a recent study of indoor air pollution levels; a woman lawyer brought up the latest California legislation protecting nonsmokers; a roly-poly real estate agent admitted that, though he had given up smokes, he still sat in the smoking section of airplanes because "you meet a more interesting type of person there"—a remark his wife did not find amusing. Helen's friend Barry gallantly joined her outside. I did not, as I should have; I felt paralyzed. 3

For one thing, I wasn't sure which side I was on. I have never been a smoker. My parents both chain-smoked, so I grew up accustomed to cloudy interiors and ever since have been tolerant of other people's nicotine urges. To be perfectly honest, I'm not crazy about inhaling smoke, particularly when I've got a cold, but that irritating inconvenience pales beside the damage that would be done to my pluralistic worldview if I did not defend smokers' rights. 4

On the other hand, a part of me wished Helen *would* stop smoking. That part seemed to get a satisfaction out of the group's "banishing" her: they were doing the dirty work of expressing my disapproval. 5

As soon as I realized this, I joined her in the garden. Presently a second guest strolled out to share a forbidden toke, then a third. Our hostess ultimately had to collect the mutineers with an announcement that dinner was served. 6

At the table, Helen appeared to be having such a good time, joking with our hosts and everyone else, that I was unprepared for the change that came over her as soon as we were alone in the car afterward. "I will never go back to that house!" she declared. "Those people have no concept of manners or hospitality, humiliating me the moment I stepped in the door. And that phony line about 'sort of allergic'!" 7

Normally, Helen is forbearance personified. Say anything that touches her about smoking, however, and you touch the rawest of nerves. I remembered the last time I foolishly suggested that she "think seriously" about stopping. I had just read one of those newspaper articles about the increased possibility of heart attacks, lung cancer, and birth deformities among women smokers, and I was worried for her. My concern must have been maladroitly expressed, because she burst into tears. 8

"Can't we even talk about this without your getting so sensi- 9
tive?" I had asked.

"You don't understand. Nonsmokers never understand that it 10
is a real addiction. I've tried quitting, and it was hell. Do you want
me to go around for months mean and cranky outside and angry inside. You're right, I'm sensitive, because I'm threatened with having
taken away from me the thing that gives me the most pleasure in
life, day in, day out," she said. I shot her a look: careful, now. "Well,
practically the most pleasure. You know what I mean." I didn't. But
I knew enough to drop it.

I love Helen, and if she wants to smoke, knowing the risks in- 11
volved, that remains her choice. Besides, she wouldn't quit just because I wanted her to; she's not that docile, and that's part of what I
love about her. Sometimes I wonder why I even keep thinking about
her quitting. What's it to me personally? Certainly I feel protective of
her health, but I also have selfish motives. I don't like the way her
lips taste when she's smoked a lot. I associate her smoking with nervousness, and when she lights up several cigarettes in a row, I get jit-
tery watching her. Crazy as this may sound, I also find myself
becoming jealous of her cigarettes. Occasionally, when I go to her
house and we're sitting on the couch together, if I see Helen eyeing
the pack I make her kiss me first, so that my lips can engage hers
(still fresh) before the competition's. It's almost as though there were
another lover in the room—a lover who was around long before I entered the picture, and who pleases her in mysterious ways I cannot.

A lit cigarette puts a distance between us: it's like a weapon in 12
her hand, awakening in me a primitive fear of being burnt. The
memory is not so primitive, actually. My father used to smoke ab-
sentmindedly, letting the ash grow like a caterpillar eating every leaf
in its path, until gravity finally toppled it. Once, when I was about
nine, my father and I were standing in line at a bakery, and he accidentally dropped a lit ash down my back. Ever since, I've inwardly
winced and been on guard around these little waving torches, which
epitomize to me the dangers of intimacy.

I've worked hard to understand from the outside the satisfaction 13
of smoking. I've even smoked "sympathetic" cigarettes, just to see
what the other person was experiencing. But it's not the same as being
hooked. How can I really empathize with the frightened but stubborn
look Helen gets in her eyes when, despite the fact we're a little late going somewhere, she turns to me in the car and says, "I need to buy a
pack of cigarettes first"? I feel a wave of pity for her. We are both embarrassed by this forced recognition of her frailty—the "indignity," as
she herself puts it, of being controlled by something outside her will.

I try to imagine myself in that position, but a certain smugness   14
keeps getting in the way (I don't have that problem and *am I glad*).
We pay a price for our smugness. So often it flip-flops into envy: the
outsiders wish to be included in the sufferings and highs of others,
as if to say that only by relinquishing control and surrendering to
some dangerous habit, some vice or dependency, would one be able
to experience "real life."

Over the years I have become a sucker for cigarette romanti-   15
cism. Few Hollywood gestures move me as much as the one in *Now
Voyager,* when Paul Henreid lights two cigarettes, one for himself,
the other for Bette Davis: these form a beautiful fatalistic bridge between them, a complicitous understanding like the realization that
their love is based on the inevitability of separation. I am all the
more admiring of this worldly cigarette gallantry because its experi-
ential basis escapes me.

The same sort of fascination occurs when I come across a literary   16
description of nicotine addiction, like this passage in Mailer's *Tough
Guys Don't Dance:* "Over and over again I gave them up, a hundred
times over the years, but I always went back. For in my dreams,
sooner or later, I struck a match, brought flame to the tip, then took in
all my hunger for existence with the first puff. I felt impaled on desire
itself—those fiends trapped in my chest and screaming for one drag."

"Impaled on desire itself"! Such writing evokes a longing in me   17
for the centering of self that tobacco seems to bestow on its faithful.
Clearly, there is something attractive about having this umbilical relation to the universe—this curling pillar, this spiral staircase, this
prayer of smoke that mediates between the smoker's inner substance and the alien ether. Inwardness of the nicotine trance, sad
wisdom ("every pleasure has its price"), beauty of ritual, squandered health—all those romantic meanings we read into the famous
photographic icons of fifties saints, Albert Camus or James Agee or
James Dean or Carson McCullers puffing away, in a sense they're
true. Like all people who return from a brush with death, smokers
have gained a certain power. They know their "coffin nails." With
Helen, each cigarette is a measuring of the perishable, an enactment
of her mortality, from filter to end-tip in fewer than five minutes. I
could not stand to be reminded of my own death so often.

MEANINGS AND VALUES

1. Tell why you think the writer made the title say *with* rather than *and*.

2. Does the writer's portrayal of the party (pars. 1–6) make Helen's anger (7) seem justified? Why or why not?

3. To what parts of this essay might smokers and nonsmokers react in different ways? How might their reactions differ? Be specific in answering this question.

4. What conclusion about smoking, if any, does the writer reach in the last paragraph of the essay?

EXPOSITORY TECHNIQUES

1. The focus of the essay shifts at the end of paragraph 3. What role does the last sentence in the paragraph play, and in what way does the focus shift?

2. How would you characterize the tone and style in paragraph 1? In paragraph 3? (See "Guide to Terms": *Style/Tone.*) What contrast does the writer emphasize through the differences in tone and style?

3. To what extent does the focus of paragraphs 7–11 lie on the question of smoking versus not smoking, and to what extent does it focus on the relationship between the writer and Helen? Be ready to defend your answer with specific evidence from the text.

4. What is being compared in paragraph 11? How is this comparison related to the overall pattern of comparison in the essay?

5. In what ways do paragraphs 13 and 14 contrast with 15 and 16?

6. State in your own words the contrast the author makes in the last two sentences of the essay. Do these sentences make an effective conclusion? (Guide: *Closings; Evaluation.*)

DICTION AND VOCABULARY

1. Identify the informal diction in paragraph 1 and the formal diction in paragraph 3. (Guide: *Diction.*) Why has the writer created these contrasts in diction? (Hint: see "Expository Techniques.")

2. Identify the similes in paragraph 12, and tell what they suggest about the effect of smoking on personal relationships. (Guide: *Figures of Speech.*)

3. Explain how cigarettes act as symbols in paragraph 15. (Guide: *Symbol.*)

4. Identify the metaphors in paragraph 15. Discuss their meaning and their effect, both as individual metaphors and as a cluster. (Guide: *Figures of Speech.*)

5. If you do not know the meaning of some of the following words, look them up in a dictionary: tenacious, paradigmatically, ensued (par. 3); pluralistic (4); toke (6); forbearance, maladroitly (8); epitomize (12); fatalistic, complicitious (15).

READ TO WRITE

1. **Collaborating:** In his essay, Lopate views behaviors and attitudes not so much as matters of choice but as outgrowths of our experiences, personalities, and interactions with others. Follow Lopate's approach and explore in freewriting (see pp. 00–00) a pattern of behavior (perhaps one you disapprove of) by looking at the motivations of someone who engages in it and by exploring your own reactions to the behavior. Then turn your freewriting into two lists, one of motivations, one of reactions, and share your lists with a partner. Then write a short response to your partner's lists, indicating the extent to which you agree or disagree with the items on them.

2. **Considering Audience:** Compare and contrast how smokers and non-smokers might react to this essay. Will they think Lopate is fair to both groups? Write notes for a short essay outlining the differing perspectives of two people on a similar conflict or issue such as wearing helmets while driving motorcycles or using seatbelts in cars and trucks.

3. **Developing an Essay:** Even familiar issues and controversies can be a source of new understanding for you and your readers when you take a personal approach to them and write with an expository purpose. Explore some potential subjects by asking questions like these: If smoking, wearing a fur coat, or some other activity or belief offends you, should you let the person doing the activity know about your feelings? What steps can you take to communicate your feelings without offending the other person? Should you worry about upsetting the other person?

(NOTE: Suggestions for topics requiring development by use of COMPARISON and CONTRAST are on pp. 193–194 at the end of this chapter.)

ALICE WALKER

ALICE WALKER was born in Georgia in 1944, the youngest in a family of eight. Her parents were sharecroppers, and she attended rural schools as a child, going on eventually to attend Spelman College and Sarah Lawrence College, from which she graduated. She worked as an editor of *Ms.* magazine and taught at several colleges. At present she teaches at the University of California—Berkeley and lives in northern California. Her work as a poet, novelist, and essayist has been highly acclaimed, and one of her novels, *The Color Purple* (1982), received both a Pulitzer Prize and the American Book Award for fiction. Some of her other works are *Revolutionary Petunias and Other Poems* (1973) *Her Blue Body Everything We Know: Earthling Poems 1989–1990* (1991); *In Love and Trouble* (1973), short stories; *Meridian* (1976), *The Temple of My Familiar* (1989), *Possessing the Secret of Joy* (1992), and *By the Light of My Father's Smile* (1998), novels; and *In Search of Our Mothers' Gardens* (1983), *Living by the Word* (1988), and *The Same River Twice: Honoring the Difficult* (1996), essays.

Am I Blue?

Humans and horses might seem at first so different that any comparison would have to take the form of an analogy—a pairing of essentially unlike subjects whose limited similarities can be used for explanatory purposes (see Chapter 4). Walker's strategy in this essay from *Living by the Word* is just the opposite, however. She explains that despite their obvious differences, humans and animals are essentially alike, at least in important matters such as the capacity to love and to communicate.

"Ain't these tears in these eyes tellin' you?"   1

For about three years my companion and I rented a small house   2
in the country that stood on the edge of a large meadow that appeared to run from the end of our deck straight into the mountains.

The mountains, however, were quite far away, and between us and them there was, in fact, a town. It was one of the many pleasant aspects of the house that you never really were aware of this.

It was a house of many windows, low, wide, nearly floor to ceiling in the living room, which faced the meadow, and it was from one of these that I first saw our closest neighbor, a large white horse, cropping grass, flipping its mane, and ambling about—not over the entire meadow, which stretched well out of sight of the house, but over the five or so fenced-in acres that were next to the twenty-odd that we had rented. I soon learned that the horse, whose name was Blue, belonged to a man who lived in another town, but was boarded by our neighbors next door. Occasionally, one of the children, usually a stocky teenager, but sometimes a much younger girl or boy, could be seen riding Blue. They would appear in the meadow, climb up on his back, ride furiously for ten or fifteen minutes, then get off, slap Blue on the flanks, and not be seen again for a month or more. 3

There were many apple trees in our yard, and one by the fence that Blue could almost reach. We were soon in the habit of feeding him apples, which he relished, especially because by the middle of summer the meadow grasses—so green and succulent since January—had dried out from lack of rain, and Blue stumbled about munching the dried stalks half-heartedly. Sometimes he would stand very still just by the apple tree, and when one of us came out he would whinny, snort loudly, or stamp the ground. This meant, of course: I want an apple. 4

It was quite wonderful to pick a few apples, or collect those that had fallen to the ground overnight, and patiently hold them, one by one, up to his large, toothy mouth. I remained as thrilled as a child by his flexible dark lips, huge, cubelike teeth that crunched the apples, core and all, with such finality, and his high, broad-breasted *enormity*; beside which, I felt small indeed. When I was a child, I used to ride horses, and was especially friendly with one named Nan until the day I was riding and my brother deliberately spooked her and I was thrown, head first, against the trunk of a tree. When I came to, I was in bed and my mother was bending worriedly over me; we silently agreed that perhaps horseback riding was not the safest sport for me. Since then I have walked, and prefer walking to horseback riding—but I had forgotten the depth of feeling one could see in horses' eyes. 5

I was therefore unprepared for the expression in Blue's. Blue was lonely. Blue was horribly lonely and bored. I was not shocked that this should be the case; five acres to tramp by yourself, endlessly, even in the most beautiful of meadows—and his was—cannot pro- 6 vide many interesting events, and once rainy season turned to dry that was about it. No, I was shocked that I had forgotten that human animals and nonhuman animals can communicate quite well; if we are brought up around animals as children we take this for granted. By the time we are adults we no longer remember. However, the animals have not changed. They are in fact *completed* creations (at least they seem to be, so much more than we) who are not likely to change; it is their nature to express themselves. What else are they going to express? And they do. And, generally speaking, they are ignored.

After giving Blue the apples, I would wander back to the house, aware that he was observing me. Were more apples not forthcoming then? Was that to be his sole entertainment for the day? My partner's small son had decided he wanted to learn how to piece a quilt; we worked in silence on our respective squares as I thought   7

Well, about slavery: about white children, who were raised by black people, who knew their first all-accepting love from black women, and then, when they were twelve or so, were told they must "forget" the deep levels of communication between themselves and "mammy" that they knew. Later they would be able to relate quite calmly, "My old mammy was sold to another good family." "My old mammy was_____ _____." Fill in the blank. Many more years later a white woman would say: "I can't understand these Negroes, these blacks. What do they want? They're so different from us."   8

And about the Indians, considered to be "like animals" by the "settlers" (a very benign euphemism for what they actually were), who did not understand their description as a compliment.   9

And about the thousands of American men who marry Japanese, Korean, Filipina, and other non-English-speaking women and of how happy they report they are, *"blissfully,"* until their brides learn to speak English, at which point the marriages tend to fall apart. What then did the men see, when they looked into the eyes of the women they married, before they could speak English? Apparently only their own reflections.   10

I thought of society's impatience with the young. "Why are they playing the music so loud?" Perhaps the children have listened to much of the music of oppressed people their parents danced to before they were born, with its passionate but soft cries for acceptance and love, and they have wondered why their parents failed to hear.   11

I do not know how long Blue had inhabited his five beautiful, boring acres before we moved into our house; a year after we had arrived—and had also traveled to other valleys, other cities, other worlds—he was still there.   12

But then, in our second year at the house, something happened   13
in Blue's life. One morning, looking out the window at the fog that
lay like a ribbon over the meadow, I saw another horse, a brown
one, at the other end of Blue's field. Blue appeared to be afraid of it,
and for several days made no attempt to go near. We went away for
a week. When we returned, Blue had decided to make friends and
the two horses ambled or galloped along together, and Blue did not
come nearly as often to the fence underneath the apple tree.

When he did, bringing his new friend with him, there was a dif-   14
ferent look in his eyes. A look of independence, of self-possession, of
inalienable *horse*ness. His friend eventually became pregnant. For
months and months there was, it seemed to me, a mutual feeling between me and the horses of justice, of peace. I fed apples to them
both. The look in Blue's eyes was one of unabashed "this is *it*ness."

It did not, however, last forever. One day, after a visit to the   15
city, I went out to give Blue some apples. He stood waiting, or so I
thought, though not beneath the tree. When I shook the tree and
jumped back from the shower of apples, he made no move. I carried
some over to him. He managed to half-crunch one. The rest he let
fall to the ground. I dreaded looking into his eyes—because I had of
course noticed that Brown, his partner, had gone—but I did look. If
I had been born into slavery, and my partner had been sold or killed,
my eyes would have looked like that. The children next door explained that Blue's partner had been "put with him" (the same expression that old people used, I had noticed, when speaking of an
ancestor during slavery who had been impregnated by her owner)
so that they could mate and she conceive. Since that was accomplished, she had been taken back by her owner, who lived somewhere else.

Will she be back? I asked.   16

They didn't know.   17

Blue was like a crazed person. Blue *was*, to me, a crazed person.   18
He galloped furiously, as if he were being ridden, around and around
his five beautiful acres. He whinnied until he couldn't. He tore at the
ground with his hooves. He butted himself against his single shade
tree. He looked always and always toward the road down which his
partner had gone. And then, occasionally, when he came up for apples, or I took apples to him, he looked at me. It was a look so piercing,
so full of grief, a look so *human*, I almost laughed (I felt too sad to cry)
to think there are people who do not know that animals suffer. People
like me who have forgotten, and daily forget, all that animals try to tell
us. "Everything you do to us will happen to you; we are your teachers,

as you are ours. We are one lesson" is essentially it, I think. There are those who never once have even considered animals' rights: those who have been taught that animals actually want to be used and abused by us, as small children "love" to be frightened, or women "love" to be mutilated and raped.... They are the great-grandchildren of those who honestly thought, because someone taught them this: "Women can't think," And "niggers can't faint." But most disturbing of all, in Blue's large brown eyes was a new look, more painful than the look of despair: the look of disgust with human beings, with life; the look of hatred. And it was odd what the look of hatred did. It gave him, for the first time, the look of a beast. And what that meant was that he had put up a barrier within to protect himself from further violence; all the apples in the world wouldn't change that fact.

And so Blue remained, a beautiful part of our landscape, very   19
peaceful to look at from the window, white against the grass. Once a friend came to visit and said, looking out on the soothing view: "And it *would* have to be a white horse; the very image of freedom." And I thought, yes, the animals are forced to become for us merely "images" of what they once so beautifully expressed. And we are used to drinking milk from containers showing "contented" cows, whose real lives we want to hear nothing about, eating eggs and drumsticks from "happy" hens, and munching hamburgers advertised by bulls of integrity who seem to command their fate.

As we talked of freedom and justice one day for all, we sat   20
down to steaks. I am eating misery, I thought, as I took the first bite. And spit it out.

Meanings and Values

1. In which paragraphs does Walker describe what she believes to be Blue's thoughts and feelings?

2. According to Walker, in what ways is Blue similar to a human? In what ways is he different? To what other groups does the author compare Blue and his relationships with humans in paragraphs 8–11?

3. What thematic purposes are served by the following phrases:

   a. "human animals and nonhuman animals" (par. 6)

   b. "who did not understand their description as a compliment" (par. 9)

   c. "Am I Blue?" (title)

   d. "If I had been born into slavery, and my partner had been sold or killed, my eyes would have looked like that." (par. 15)

e. "It gave him, for the first time, the look of a beast." (par. 18)

EXPOSITORY TECHNIQUES

1. Why do you think Walker chose to wait until near the end of the essay (paragraph 18) for a detailed discussion of its theme? ("Guide to Terms": *Unity*.) To what extent does the placement of this discussion give the essay an expository rather than an argumentative purpose? (Guide: *Argument*.)

2. Discuss how the "'images'" presented in paragraph 19 can be regarded as ironic symbols. (Guide: *Symbol; Irony*.)

3. Describe the way Walker alters the tempo of the sentences and builds to a climax in the concluding paragraph of the essay. (Guide: *Closings*.)

4. Some readers might consider the ending effective. Others might consider it overly dramatic or distasteful. Explain which reaction you consider most appropriate. (Guide: *Evaluation*.)

DICTION AND VOCABULARY

1. Describe the ways in which Walker uses syntax and figurative language (simile) for thematic purposes in this passage: "Blue was like a crazed person. Blue *was*, to me, a crazed person" (par. 18). (Guide: *Syntax; Figures of Speech*.)

2. In speaking of the "'settlers,'" Walker says that this term is "a very benign euphemism for what they actually were" (par. 9). What does she mean by this comment? What other terms might be applied to them (from Walker's point of view)? Why might she have chosen not to use such terms?

3. The title of this essay is taken from a song of the same name. In terms of the content of the essay, to what ideas or themes does it refer? Can it be considered a paradox? (Guide: *Paradox*.) The quotation from the song that opens the essay points to some of the ideas discussed in the essay. What are they?

READ TO WRITE

1. **Collaborating:** Working in groups of four, discuss different animals that you have known. What have you learned from these animals? Can you apply what you have learned to your human relationships? To your understanding of human nature? How would you contrast the behavior of animals in specific situations with typical human behavior in such situations? As a group, plan an essay comparing and contrasting likely animal and human behavior in a set of situations you have chosen.

2. **Considering Audience:** Walker repeatedly refers to expressions and feelings seemingly conveyed through Blue's eyes. How might read-

ers who have their own pets react to Walker's descriptions of the animal's eyes? How might readers without pets react? Will readers who have pets understand Walker's comparison of animal owners and slave owners better than non-pet owners? Will most pet owners be offended by such a comparison? Who, if anyone, might be offended by the conclusions Walker draws about Blue's and other animals' feelings and intelligence? In two to three paragraphs, offer your answers to some or all of these questions as a way of describing readers' likely reactions to Walker's essay.

3. **Developing an Essay:** Walker's essay moves from obvious differences to surprising similarities, getting there through careful observation and comparison of horses and humans. Apply this pattern to a topic of your own choosing, using it to express hidden similarities you have already noticed or to reveal similarities as you write.

(NOTE: Suggestions for topics requiring development by means of COMPARISON and CONTRAST are on pp. 193–194 at the end of this chapter.)

Issues and Ideas

Gender Differences

- Scott Russell Sanders, *The Men We Carry in Our Minds*
- Nicholas Wade, *Method and Madness: How Men and Women Think*
- Rene Denfield, *Lady of the Ring*

We understand our world by differences: wealthy, less wealthy, and a lot less wealthy; black, white, and brown; educated and uneducated; female and male. We come to understand who and what we are by learning who and what we are not.

One way we understand and deal with the world is through the difference between male and female, a distinction grounded in biological differences but extended to issues of emotion, intellectual ability, relationships, values, and social rules. These differences are maintained in various ways: through clothing styles, social organizations, sports teams, men's/women's publications, names (Kate/Carl), and kinship systems (aunt/uncle).

But how many of these differences are "real" and how many "imagined" or constructed by social custom? Just how different are men and women, and are their differences significant ones with important consequences?

As an expository pattern, comparison and contrast parallels the identification of gender differences and similarities. Scott Russell Sanders, Nicholas Wade, and Rene Denfield make good use of the pattern to explore surprising similarities that complicate, or even call into question, differences that many readers may consider obvious and unchanging. For Sanders, class differences complicate easy conclusions about male privilege. The comparisons he offers suggest the need to refuse to consider gender alone but to treat it as part of a larger set of social relationships governing the distribution of hardships and rewards in our culture.

Nicholas Wade looks to science, specifically brain research, for hard evidence of gender contrasts. He finds evidence of real contrasts, but not simple ones. And the implications for behavior and social organization are even more complex and sometimes contradictory. Rene Denfield draws on her own journey into what used to be the most masculine of worlds—boxing. She tells of encountering and overturning some familiar assumptions and discovering some important bonds between men and women in values and emotions.

SCOTT RUSSELL SANDERS

SCOTT RUSSELL SANDERS was born in 1945 in Memphis, Tennessee. He studied at Brown University (B.A., 1967) and Cambridge University (Ph.D., 1971). Since 1971, he has been teaching in the English Department at Indiana University. Sanders has published a wide variety of books, including a scholarly study of the British novelist D. H. Lawrence; several children's books including *Aurora Means Dawn* (1989) and *Bad Man Ballad* (1986); and a collection of short stories, *Invisible Company* (1989). His essays have appeared in a number of collections, among them, *The Paradise of Bombs* (1987), *In Limestone Country* (1991), and *Writing From the Center* (1995). In 1995, Sanders won the Lanna Literary Award, thereby joining the ranks of some of the finest essayists of recent decades.

The Men We Carry in Our Minds

In this essay, originally published in 1984 in the journal *Milkweed Chronicle,* Sanders questions the assumption that differences come in simple pairs: men and women, rich and poor, oppressed and op-pressor, and the like. In place of such oppositions, he offers a more complex view of the differences that help construct each of us. He also expresses a hope that these very differences might develop into grounds for mutual understanding.

"This must be a hard time for women," I say to my friend   1
Anneke. "They have so many paths to choose from, and so many voices calling them."

"I think it's a lot harder for men," she replies.   2

"How do you figure that?"   3

"The women I know feel excited, innocent, like crusaders in a   4
just cause. The men I know are eaten up with guilt."

"Women feel such pressure to be everything, do everything," I   5
say. "Career, kids, art, politics. Have their babies and get back to the office a week later. It's as if they're trying to overcome a million years' worth of evolution in one lifetime."

"But we help one another. And we have this deep-down sense   6
that we're in the *right*—we've been held back, passed over, used—

while men feel they're in the wrong. Men are the ones who've been discredited, who have to search their souls."

I search my soul. I discover guilt feelings aplenty—toward the poor, the Vietnamese, Native Americans, the whales, an endless list of debts. But toward women I feel something more confused, a snarl of shame, envy, wary tenderness, and amazement. This muddle troubles me. To hide my unease I say, "You're right, it's tough being a man these days." 7

"Don't laugh," Anneke frowns at me. "I wouldn't be a man for anything. It's much easier being the victim. All the victim has to do is break free. The persecutor has to live with his past." 8

How deep is that past? I find myself wondering. How much of an inheritance do I have to throw off? 9

When I was a boy growing up on the back roads of Tennessee and Ohio, the men I knew labored with their bodies. They were marginal farmers, just scraping by, or welders, steelworkers, carpenters; they swept floors, dug ditches, mined coal, or drove trucks, their forearms ropy with muscle; they trained horses, stoked furnaces, made tires, stood on assembly lines wrestling parts onto cars and refrigerators. They got up before light, worked all day long whatever the weather, and when they came home at night they looked as though somebody had been whipping them. In the evenings and on weekends they worked on their own places, tilling gardens that were lumpy with clay, fixing broken-down cars, hammering on houses that were always too drafty, too leaky, too small. 10

The bodies of the men I knew were twisted and maimed in ways visible and invisible. The nails of their hands were black and split, the hands tattooed with scars. Some had lost fingers. Heavy lifting had given many of them finicky backs and guts weak from hernias. Racing against conveyor belts had given them ulcers. Their ankles and knees ached from years of standing on concrete. Anyone who had worked for long around machines was hard of hearing. They squinted, and the skin of their faces was creased like the leather of old work gloves. There were times, studying them, when I dreaded growing up. Most of them coughed, from dust or cigarettes, and most of them drank cheap wine or whiskey, so their eyes looked bloodshot and bruised. The fathers of my friends always seemed older than the mothers. Men wore out sooner. Only women lived into old age. 11

As a boy I also knew another sort of men, who did not sweat and break down like mules. They were soldiers, and so far as I could tell they scarcely worked at all. But when the shooting started, many 12 of them would die. This was what soldiers were *for*, just as a hammer was for driving nails.

Warriors and toilers: those seemed, in my boyhood vision, to be   13
the chief destinies for men. They weren't the only destinies, as I
learned from having a few male teachers, from reading books, and
from watching television. But the men on television—the politicians,
the astronauts, the generals, the savvy lawyers, the philosophical
doctors, the bosses who gave orders to both soldiers and laborers—
seemed as remote and unreal to me as the figures in Renaissance ta-
pestries. I could no more imagine growing up to become one of
these cool, potent creatures than I could imagine becoming a prince.

A nearer and more hopeful example was that of my father, who   14
had escaped from a red-dirt farm to a tire factory, and from the assembly line to the front office. Eventually he dressed in a white shirt
and tie. He carried himself as if he had been born to work with his
mind. But his body, remembering the earlier years of slogging work,
began to give out on him in his fifties, and it quit on him entirely before he turned 65.

A scholarship enabled me not only to attend college, a rare   15
enough feat in my circle, but even to study in a university meant for
the children of the rich. Here I met for the first time young men who
had assumed from birth that they would lead lives of comfort and
power. And for the first time I met women who told me that men
were guilty of having kept all the joys and privileges of the earth for
themselves. I was baffled. What privileges? What joys? I thought
about the maimed, dismal lives of most of the men back home. What
had they stolen from their wives and daughters? The right to go five
days a week, 12 months a year, for 30 to 40 years to a steel mill or a
coal mine? The right to drop bombs and die in war? The right to feel
every leak in the roof, every gap in the fence, every cough in the engine as a wound they must mend? The right to feel, when the layoff
comes or the plant shuts down, not only afraid but ashamed?

I was slow to understand the deep grievances of women. This was   16
because, as a boy, I had envied them. Before college, the only people I
had ever known who were interested in art or music or literature, the
only ones who read books, the only ones who ever seemed to enjoy a
sense of ease and grace were the mothers and daughters. Like the men-
folk, they fretted about money, they scrimped and made do. But, when
the pay stopped coming in, they were not the ones who had failed.
Nor did they have to go to war, and that seemed to me a blessed fact.
By comparison with the narrow, ironclad days of fathers, there was an
expansiveness, I thought, in the days of mothers. They went to see

neighbors, to shop in town, to run errands at school, at the library, at church. No doubt, had I looked harder at their lives, I would have envied them less. It was not my fate to become a woman, so it was easier for me to see the graces. I didn't see, then, what a prison a house could be, since houses seemed to me brighter, handsomer places than any factory. I did not realize—because such things were never spoken of— how often women suffered from men's bullying. Even then I could see how exhausting it was for a mother to cater all day to the needs of young children. But if I had been asked, as a boy, to choose between tending a baby and tending a machine, I think I would have chosen the baby. (Having now tended both, I know I would choose the baby.)

So I was baffled when the women at college accused me and my 17 sex of having cornered the world's pleasures. I think something like my bafflement has been felt by other boys (and by girls as well) who grew up in dirt-poor farm country, in mining country, in black ghettos, in Hispanic barrios, in the shadows of factories, in third World nations—any place where the fate of men is just as grim and bleak as the fate of women.

When the women I met at college thought about the joys and 18 privileges of men, they did not carry in their minds the sort of men I had known in my childhood. They thought of their fathers, who were bankers, physicians, architects, stockbrokers, the big wheels of the big cities. They were never laid off, never short of cash at month's end, never lined up for welfare. These fathers made decisions that mattered. They ran the world.

The daughters of such men wanted to share in this power, this 19 glory. So did I. They yearned for a say over their future, for jobs worthy of their abilities, for the right to live at peace, unmolested, whole. Yes, I thought, yes yes. The difference between me and these daughters was that they saw me, because of my sex, as destined from birth to become like their fathers, and therefore as an enemy to their desires. But I knew better. I wasn't an enemy, in fact or in feeling. I was an ally. If I had known, then, how to tell them so, would they have believed me? Would they now?

MEANINGS AND VALUES

1. Identify the differences that Sanders discusses in this essay. Does he treat some as more important than others? If so, which ones? Why does he consider them more important?

2. How do you think readers are likely to react to Sanders's essay? Do you think that some groups of readers are likely to find his essay reasonably convincing and others less so? Which groups, and why?

3. To what extent does this essay have an expository purpose and to what extent is its purpose argumentative? Which purpose predominates? Be ready to defend your answer with references to the text. (See "Guide to Terms": *Argument; Purpose.*)

EXPOSITORY TECHNIQUES

1. Does this essay have a thesis statement? If so, what is it? (Guide: *Thesis.*) If not, state the central theme in your own words.

2. What strategy does Sanders use to introduce this essay? (Guide: *Introductions.*) Do you consider the opening effective? Why or why not? (Guide: *Evaluation.*)

3. Explain the use of transition words to highlight contrasts and relationships among ideas in paragraph 16. (Guide: *Transition.*) Tell how Sanders uses parallelism in paragraphs 15 and 17 to emphasize ideas. (Guide: *Parallel Structure.*) How else does he create emphasis in these paragraphs?

4. Where in the essay does the writer use rhetorical questions, and for what reasons does he employ them? (Guide: *Rhetorical Questions.*)

DICTION AND VOCABULARY

1. Tell how the diction in paragraphs 10 and 11 contributes to their overall effectiveness (Guide: *Diction.*)

2. How does the writer qualify his statements in paragraph 16? Why do you think he decided to qualify his ideas and generalizations in this part of the essay? (Guide: *Qualification.*)

READ TO WRITE

1. **Collaborating:** The differences we notice among people are often an inheritance from the behaviors we observed as we were growing up and from the attitudes of parents and friends. Working in a group, consider possible topics for an essay. Think about the attitudes you encountered when you were a child. Were they consistent or contradictory? Have you accepted them or modified them? Does preserving such an inheritance help build continuity and community or is it a way of holding up necessary progress?

2. **Considering Audience:** Insights into the way people differ often arise in conversation—something the opening of "The Men We Carry in Our Minds" seems to acknowledge. Consider opening an essay of your own with part of a conversation (recollected or invented) that touches on ideas you wish to explain and explore.

3. **Developing an Essay:** Sanders begins with an "opposition" many people take for granted and modifies it by showing that it is not simple and does not apply to everyone in the same way. He also suggests that people who appear to be opposites may actually share many traits and attitudes. Using Sanders's essay as a model, challenge another set of differences that people routinely accept (perhaps distinctions of race, class, intelligence, or taste) in a way that shows they are neither simple nor universal.

(NOTE: Suggestions for topics requiring development by use of COMPARISON and CONTRAST are on pp. 193–194 at the end of this chapter.)

NICHOLAS WADE

> NICHOLAS WADE is a journalist who writes about science and scientific discoveries. His books include *A World Beyond Healing* (1987), *Noble Dues* (1981), and *The Ultimate Experiment* (1977). He has also edited a series of books for young people on nature and science.

Method and Madness:
How Men and Women Think

> We often look to science for firm answers to hard questions but get responses that are complex and raise as many questions as they answer. Looking over current research, the author of this essay reports that while there are clearly differences between men's and women's brains, what the differences mean is not that apparent. At times the research confirms stereotypes, but just as often it challenges them. What is clear in this essay is the writer's effective use of comparison and contrast as strategies for explaining the complicated relationships among biology, behavior, and gender.

The human brain, according to an emerging new body of scientific research, comes in two different varieties, maybe as different as the accompanying physique. Men, when they are lost, instinctually fall back on their in-built navigational skills, honed from far-off days of tracking large prey miles from home. Women, by contrast, tend to find their way by the simpler methods of remembering local landmarks or even asking help from strangers. 1

Men excel on psychological tests that require the imaginary twisting in space of a three-dimensional object. The skill seems to help with higher math, where the topmost ranks are thronged with male minds like Andrew Wiles of Princeton, who proclaimed almost a year ago that he had proved Fermat's Last Theorem and will surely get around to publishing the proof almost any day now. 2

Some feminist ideologues assert that all minds are created equal and women would be just as good at math if they weren't discouraged in school. But Camilla Benbow, a psychologist at Iowa State University, has spent years assessing biases like male math teachers or parents who favor boys. She concludes that boys' superiority at math is mostly innate. 3

But women, the new studies assert, have the edge in most other ways, like perceptual speed, verbal fluency and communications skills. They also have sharper hearing than men, and excel in taste, 4 smell and touch, and in fine coordination of hand and eye. If Martians arrived and gave job interviews, it seems likely they would direct men to competitive sports and manual labor and staff most professions, diplomacy and government with women.

The measurement of intellectual differences is a field with a long and mostly disgraceful past. I.Q. tests have been regularly misused, sometimes even concocted, in support of prevailing prejudices. Distinguished male anatomists used to argue that women were less intelligent because their brains weighed less, neglecting to correct for the strong influence of body weight on brain weight.   5

The present studies of sex differences are venturing on ground where self-deception and prejudice are constant dangers. The science is difficult and the results prone to misinterpretation. Still, the budding science seems free so far of obvious error. For one thing, many of the field's leading practitioners happen to be women, perhaps because male academics in this controversial field have had their lives made miserable by militant feminists.   6

For another, the study of brain sex differences does not depend on just one kind of subvertible measure but draws on several different disciplines, including biology and anatomy. As is described in a new book, 'Eve's Rib,' by Robert Pool, and the earlier 'Brain Sex,' by Anne Moir and David Jessel, the foundations of the field have been carefully laid in animal research. Experiments with rats show that exposure in the womb to testosterone indelibly imprints a male pattern of behavior; without testosterone, the rat's brain is female.   7

In human fetuses, too, the sex hormones seem to mold a male and female version of the brain, each subtly different in organization and behavior. The best evidence comes from girls with a rare genetic anomaly who are exposed in the womb to more testosterone than normal; they grow up doing better than their unaffected sisters on the tests that boys are typically good at. There's also some evidence, not yet confirmed, that male and female brains may be somewhat differently structured, with the two cerebral hemispheres being more specialized and less well interconnected in men than in women.   8

If the human brain exists in male and female versions, as modulated in the womb, that would explain what every parent knows, that boys and girls prefer different patterns of play regardless of well-meaning efforts to impose unisex toys on both.   9

The human mind being very versatile, however, any genetic propensities are far from decisive. In math, for example, the average girl is pretty much as good as the average boy. Only among the few students at the peak of math ability do boys predominate. Within the loose framework set by the genes, education makes an enormous   10 difference. In Japan, boys exceed girls on the mental rotation tests, just as in America. But the Japanese girls outscore American boys. Maybe Japanese kids are just smarter or, more likely, just better taught, Japan being a country where education is taken seriously and parents and teachers consistently push children to excel.

There are some obvious cautions to draw about the social and political implications that might one day flow from brain sex research. One is that differences between individuals of the same sex often far exceed the slight differences between the sexes as two population groups: 'If I were going into combat, I would prefer to have Martina Navratilova at my side than Robert Reich,' says Patricia Ireland, president of the National Organization for Women. Even if men in general excel in math, an individual woman could still be better than most men.   11

On the other hand, if the brains of men and women really are organized differently, it's possible the sexes both prefer and excel at different occupations, perhaps those with more or less competition or social interaction. 'In a world of scrupulous gender equality, equal numbers of girls and boys would be educated and trained for . . . all the professions. . . . [Hiring would proceed] until half of every workplace was made up of men and half, women,' says Judith Lorber in 'Paradoxes of Gender,' a new work of feminist theory. That premise does not hold if there are real intellectual differences between the sexes; the test of equal opportunity, when all unfair barriers to women have fallen, will not necessarily be equal outcomes.   12

Greek mythology tells that Tiresias, having lived both as a man and a woman for some complicated reason, was asked to settle a dispute between Zeus and Hera as to which gender enjoyed sex more. He replied there was no contest—it was 10 times better for women. Whereupon Hera struck him blind for his insolence and Zeus in compensation gave him the gift of foresight. Like Tiresias, the brain sex researchers are uncovering some impolitic truths, potent enough to shake Mount Olympus some day.   13

MEANINGS AND VALUES

1. Paragraph 6 addresses current studies of sex difference as well as Wade's belief that much of the scientific research on the subject has been misinterpreted. Wade goes on to say that "... Many of the field's leading practitioners happen to be women, perhaps because male academics in this controversial field have had their lives made

miserable by militant feminists." What point is Wade trying to make here? In what ways is the comment related to his statements about the misinterpretation of the data? Is his comment about feminists a conscious exaggeration? Why, or why not?

2. Why is Tiresias (par. 13) a good choice for Wade's essay? (See "Guide to Terms": *Figures of Speech, Allusion.*)

3. Does Wade imply that one sex has a better way of thinking? Why, or why not? Is he neutral in his choice of evidence? Explain. What are the attributes people traditionally value in each of the sexes? In which paragraphs does Wade address these attributes?

EXPOSITORY TECHNIQUES

1. Wade's first five paragraphs include several comparison/contrast examples. Why might he have begun his essay this way? Is this an effective introduction for the piece? (Guide: *Introductions, Evaluation.*)

2. In paragraph 10, the writer uses a comparison within a comparison when he addresses the differences between Japanese boys and girls as well as American boys and girls, and then continues by comparing Japanese students overall to American students overall. Why might he have chosen this technique? What point is he trying to make through this use of "dual" comparison?

DICTION AND VOCABULARY

1. How would you classify Wade's style and tone in this selection? (Guide: *Tone, Style.*) Are his word choices effective tools for communicating a message and a mood? (Guide: *Diction.*) Do you consider his use of phrases like "militant feminists" appropriate? Why, or why not?

2. This article first appeared in the *New York Times* in 1994. Was the level of difficulty of the vocabulary appropriate for the audience? Why, or why not?

3. If you do not know the meaning of some of the following words, look them up in a dictionary: ideologue (par. 3); indelibly (7); modulated (9); propensities (10).

READ TO WRITE

1. **Collaborating:** Working in a group, make a list of what most people consider the major differences between men and women. As a group, decide how justified these generalizations are. Then choose three items from the list that all group members feel are reasonably justified and plan a comparison/contrast paper analyzing and explaining these differences. Make sure you include supporting details and examples in your plan.

2.   **Considering Audience:** Are Wade's choices of comparison/contrast examples accessible for male and female readers of a variety of ages? Why, or why not? Is his concluding story of Tiresias effective? Rewrite the conclusion of the essay (par. 13) using a different story or example that might be more accessible for modern readers.

3.   **Developing an Essay:** Wade discusses how we identify ourselves based on gender as well as how we compare ourselves to the opposite gender. He says that "The present studies of sex differences are venturing on ground where self-deception and prejudice are constant dangers" (par. 6). What does he mean by this sentence? Prepare an essay discussing the kind of self-deception to which Wade refers. Consider how men and women typically see their gender in relation to the other gender. Think also about some clichés we often use in discussing gender differences.

(NOTE: Suggestions for topics requiring development by use of COMPARISON and CONTRAST are on pp. 193–194 at the end of this chapter.)

RENE DENFIELD

RENE DENFIELD is the author of two books: *The New Victorians: A Young Woman's Challenge to the Old Feminist Order* (1995) and *Kill the Body, the Head Will Follow: A Closer Look at Women, Violence, and Aggression* (1998).

Lady of the Ring

Boxing used to be an all-male sport. What happens when a woman takes up boxing? How do male boxers react to her? How does she view herself? Who changes the most? These are just some of the questions about gender expectations and gender roles that Rene Denfield addresses in this essay, that first appeared in the *New York Times Magazine*.

I started boxing as a lark, a fantasy. I saw myself becoming glistening, fit and tough—a woman fighter. I saw myself rising from the canvas and fighting back, delivering amazing combinations until my opponent fell among the ropes, vanquished.   1

My first week in the gym in a run-down neighborhood in Portland, Ore., squashed my fantasy as I began to understand the long, difficult training regimen ahead of me. But I fell in love with the sport: the sound of the timer and the guys talking; the flying, hissing jump ropes; the punishment of the heavy bags, and, above all, the relationships between the fighters and our trainer, Jess Sandoval.   2

When I first went into the gym, Jess was in his 70's and increasingly infirm. He had lost his own professional career when he shipped out during World War II, but taught the sport afterward. He was shy around me, his only female fighter. We were all drawn close to Jess, though, an uneasy group, grieving in advance for the frail, titular head of our family.   3

Most of the other fighters were Mexican immigrants like Jess. Sometimes, when they were away for a while, Jess would make sad remarks about prison. Still, their lives were not the easy, cheap simplifications about laziness and crime that many Americans believe about immigrants and illegal aliens. The younger ones seemed touchingly self-conscious despite their macho baggy pants and careful gang attire. Alberto worked at McDonald's and attended school. Bob supported his family by working as a janitor, while his wife sewed satin trunks for the fighters—$25 a pair.   4

Immigration got Ernesto, Jess told us grimly. But one day 5
Ernesto was back. He snuck in, Jess said, triumphant. I still think
about how hard it must be for these young men, who are torn between a love for their native country (he changed flags, they said
contemptuously of one Mexican fighter who trains under a gringo
coach) and a longing to be wanted and appreciated right here.

I understand. As a woman in a boxing gym, I had changed 6
flags, too. I'm sure Jess never imagined training a woman, and I'm
sure the other fighters never imagined having to spar with one.
Ernesto would hit me as hard as he would a man—hard enough to
bruise my ribs, water my eyes, cut my lips and make my nose
bleed. He had to, you see: if he didn't hit back, I would beat him.
This is the dilemma I forced on these men. Hitting a woman? They
think that only a bully, a wife beater, does that. But the prospect of
being beaten by a woman? Only a sissy, a punk. And yet we found
a way to manage. There in that safe place, we had an unspoken
truce.

Sparring with men, I felt liberated from generations of fear, self- 7
doubt, finger-waving and genteel restrictions: men aren't so tough, I
found, once you get close enough. Perhaps women's fear has been
misplaced, conferring a malignant power on those who neither deserve nor desire it.

In entering this world, I lost more than superficial fantasy and 8
gained more than physical self-confidence. My perceptions of the
sexes have been altered, and this has affected nearly every aspect of
my life. I feel differently when I walk down the street alone—
stronger, less fearful. No longer do I assume that I am less capable of
handling anger and conflict.

But the greatest challenge was to the male fighters. I imagined 9
their worries: What will she think of us when she realizes we are
not as tough, as cold or as mean as women everywhere have been
led to believe? Will she breathe a sigh of relief, or laugh in
contempt?

A boxing gym is only one of many places where the myth of 10
male superiority in strength and aggressiveness remains unques-
tioned. But it is also a place where the myth can begin to unravel.
Just as I have always been strong, and never realized it, men have always been vulnerable and complicated.

Now the fighter of my dreams is replaced by myself, in honest 11
memory, leaning over the ropes at the Golden Gloves after having
won the title. My opponent was already receding, like a vapor be-

hind me, while the men from the gym cheered in the audience. But there was only me, and Jess, and I was kissing his face, in thanks.

Not long ago, Jess passed away. When I heard the news, I put down the phone and cried, thinking, with surprise, I've lost my father. I had gone into a boxing gym to learn how to be tough. But I also found affection, sincerity and caring—and the deep bond between athlete and coach. Boxing has, in the end, left me softer.

MEANINGS AND VALUES

1. To what is Denfield referring when she says, "I had changed flags, too" (par. 6)? What do flags typically represent? How does this help her argument?

2. In paragraph 8, Denfield says, ". . . I lost more than superficial fantasy and gained more than physical self-confidence." Why was her fantasy superficial? What has changed her view?

3. In the closing line of the essay, the writer says, "Boxing has, in the end, left me softer." What makes that line ironic? (See "Guide to Terms": *Irony*.) How does this fit with the point that she is trying to make in the essay?

EXPOSITORY TECHNIQUES

1. The writer uses several comparison/contrast examples. One is in paragraph five where she compares her plight to that of the immigrants who are her fellow boxers. Explain the significance of the comparison.

2. What are the major similarities and differences between male and female boxers? Do these reflect stereotypical similarities and differences? Explain your response.

3. Why does Denfield use "Lady" in the title and "woman" throughout the rest of the essay?

DICTION AND VOCABULARY

1. What does Denfield mean in paragraph 7 when she says, "Perhaps women's fear has been misplaced, conferring a malignant power on those who neither deserve nor desire it"? Why do you think she chose the word "malignant" to express her point? (Guide: *Diction*.)

2. Define the following words and use them each in a sentence: vanquished, inform, and contemptuously.

READ TO WRITE

1. **Collaborating:** In a group, discuss formerly all-male sports besides boxing that are now coed or have equal-level teams for men and women. Prepare a list of the changes in attitudes toward sports that group members believe have been the result of the increased participation of women. Then extend your list to include any controversies that are still unresolved concerning gender and sports. Choose three that would make a good topic for an expository essay and come up with at least two tentative thesis statements for each topic.

2. **Considering Audience:** Are most readers likely to view Denfield's participation in boxing sympathetically? Why, or why not? Make a list of different kinds of readers who might be sympathetic and those who might be unsympathetic. Which groups does Denfield seem to address in this essay? Write out a brief plan for revising her essay to increase its appeal to groups that might be unsympathetic.

3. **Developing an Essay:** Using Denfield's essay as a model, prepare an essay of your own describing your participation (or that of someone you know) in an activity where your gender, personality, ethnicity, or social identity initially made you an unlikely participant. Explain any changes you or others involved underwent as a result of your participation.

(NOTE: Suggestions for essays requiring development by COMPARISON and CONTRAST follow.)

Writing Suggestions for Chapter 5

COMPARISON AND CONTRAST

Base your central theme on one of the following, and develop your composition primarily by use of comparison and/or contrast. Use examples liberally for clarity and concreteness, chosen always with your purpose and reader-audience in mind.

1. Two kinds of families.
2. Two web browsers.
3. The innate qualities needed for success in two different careers.
4. Dog people vs. cat people.
5. Two musicians.
6. Two radio personalities.
7. Two methods of parental handling of teenage problems.
8. Two family attitudes toward the practice of religion.
9. Two "moods" of the same town at different times.
10. The personalities (or atmospheres) of two cities or towns of similar size.
11. Two politicians with different leadership styles.
12. Careers vs. jobs.
13. Two different attitudes toward the same thing or activity: one "practical," the other romantic or aesthetic.
14. The beliefs and practices of two religions or denominations concerning one aspect of religion.
15. Two courses on the same subject: one in high school and one in college.
16. The differing styles of two players of some sport or game.
17. The hazards of frontier life and those of life today.
18. Two companies with very different styles or business philosophies.
19. Two recent movies or rock videos.
20. Two magazines focusing on similar subjects but directed at different audiences.
21. The "rewards" of two different kinds of jobs.

COLLABORATIVE EXERCISES

1. Choose a partner, and using topic number 19 above, write an essay comparing and contrasting two movies or rock videos. Each member

of the team should be responsible for researching one of the movies or videos.

2. Working with a partner, choose a topic on which you have differing perspectives, and prepare an essay, each writing a section of the essay reflecting his or her own perspective. Combine the sections into a draft, then revise each other's section so that the essay reads as a smooth, consistent, and logical whole.

6

Using *Analogy* as an Expository Device

Analogy is a special form of comparison that you can use for a specific purpose to explain something abstract or difficult to understand by showing its similarity to something concrete or easy to understand. A much less commonly used technique than comparison (and contrast), analogy is, nonetheless, a highly efficient means of explaining some difficult concepts or of giving added force to the explanations.

When you use comparison as an explanatory strategy, you need to make sure both subjects belong to the same general class of things, and you assume that readers will be more or less equally interested in both subjects. This is not the case with analogy. In analogy you and your readers are really concerned only with one of the subjects; the second serves just to help explain the first. The two subjects, which may have little in common, also do not belong to the same class of things. The few elements they do share, however, are what gives analogy the power to explain—and even to speculate about how things *might* be.

Certainly, for example, the universe is nothing like raisin bread—or so any reasonable person would think. But an analogy between the two can help explain a very difficult concept, as the following paragraph illustrates.

If distant galaxies are really receding from the earth, and if more distant galaxies are receding faster than nearby ones, a remarkable picture of the universe emerges. Imagine that the galaxies were raisins scattered through a rising lump of bread dough. As the dough expanded, the raisins would be carried farther and farther apart from each other. If you were standing on one of the raisins, how would things look? You wouldn't feel any motion yourself, of course, just as

195

you don't feel the effects of the earth's motion around the sun, but you would notice that your nearest neighbor was moving away from you. This motion would be due to the fact that the dough between you and your nearest neighbor would be expanding, pushing the two of you apart.

—James Trefil, *The Dark Side of the Universe*

WHY USE ANALOGY?

In an analogy, you compare two things that are similar in some specifics but otherwise unlike. You can use this strategy to explain a complex, abstract, or unusual subject in familiar and easy-to-understand terms. Or you can use it to speculate about possible interpretations and consequences. For example, to explain how an electromagnetic field transmits radio signals from a station's transmitter to the radio in a listener's home or car, the physicist Richard Feynman asked his readers to imagine two corks floating in a pool of water. If we jiggle one cork, he pointed out, the waves in the water transmit the influence of our action and the second cork begins to jiggle, too. Like the water, an electromagnetic field transmits energy from sender to receiver in the form of waves—electromagnetic waves—conveying radio signals, a television picture, a radar image, or even plain light.

Analogy is not limited to scientific subjects, however. You can use it to explain and support your conclusions about other kinds of topics as well. For instance, a music critic, trying to explain her conclusion that jazz has and will continue to influence modern music of all kinds, compares the jazz tradition to a tune that plays in the back of your mind all day, affecting your mood, the rhythm of your way, and your tone of voice. Jazz, she explains, is a presence in the minds of composers and performers that shapes their choice of harmonies and rhythms, influences the tone of their compositions and the choice of instruments, and makes "hipness" (a mixture of sophistication, intensity, and emotional distancing) an attitude to which many of them aspire.

CHOOSING A STRATEGY

For a writer, the choice between using a brief analogy or an extended analogy is a significant one. A brief analogy, a sentence or two in length, can serve as an illustration or explanation of a difficult point or concept. To explain the need for a wide selection of college courses and the need for balance in a course of study, you might draw an analogy to a cafeteria, which serves desserts as well as meat, vegetables, and potatoes, allowing for various combinations adding up to balanced, full-course meals. If you wanted to extend this analogy to explain issues of curriculum and course choice in depth, however, you might run into problems with logic and with the adequacy of the particular analogy as an explanatory tool. Which courses, for example, should be classified as "desserts," and would all teachers and students agree on the classification? Does the concept of a well-balanced meal offer an adequate framework for understanding the specific kinds of balance appropriate for course choices?

An extended analogy, if carefully chosen for its logic and the points of comparison it offers, can serve as a framework for detailed explanation. In addition, it can offer a way to gain a fresh perspective on a problem, a controversy, or a puzzling phenomenon. For example, we often unconsciously draw on what we learn about relationships through family life in order to develop relationships within social organizations. Thus while businesses and other organizations are certainly different from families in many ways, there are still enough similarities to make an analogy worthwhile. Such an analogy asks readers to adopt a creative, "as if" perspective: Let us examine the conflicts within an organization *as if* they were arguments among various members of a family to see whether the conflicts might be resolved in ways similar to those that work successfully in families. An analogy like this can be extended logically and consistently to explore a relatively broad topic, and it provides reasons for considering seriously the conclusions or interpretations the writer offers.

Analogies can take many different forms, and this flexibility is one of their appeals for both writers and readers. When you use an extended analogy to structure an essay, however, consider adopting a point-by-point arrangement to avoid confusing readers with too many comparisons at once. This is the approach taken in the following plan for an essay.

> Tentative Thesis: We can better understand corporations by viewing them as if they were large, extended families.
>
> Point 1: Employee ranks are similar to family roles (CEOs, board members = grandparents; VPs = parents, and so on)
>
> Point 2: Different parts of the company are similar to different parts of an extended family (main office = nuclear family; branch offices = families of uncles, aunts, and cousins, and so forth)
>
> Point 3: Conflicts over resources within a company are similar to rivalry among cousins or struggles over a will

Point 4: Struggles over advancement within a company is similar to sibling rivalry

Point 5: Training programs aim to help employees work together for the good of the company while family therapy tries to help maintain healthy relationships that preserve the family

Point 6, 7, 8 . . . [if necessary]

DEVELOPING ANALOGIES

Simply stating an analogy and the specific grounds of similarity is seldom enough to make it an effective strategy, especially in the case of an extended analogy. The analogy needs to be clear to readers and developed in enough detail so that it provides convincing explanations and support for the writer's conclusions.

For an analogy to be effective, readers need to be familiar enough with the easier subject so that it really helps explain the more difficult one. Or the easier subject must be one which readers can understand with minimal discussion. An explanation of the human circulatory system, including the heart and arteries, in terms of a pump forcing water through the pipes of a plumbing system would be easily apprehended by readers. The analogy could be carried further to liken the effect of cholesterol deposits on the inner walls of the arteries to that of mineral deposits that accumulate inside water pipes and eventually close them entirely.

It is not enough for you as a writer simply to state an analogy, leaving for readers the job of understanding its significance. You need to explain both the analogy itself and its implications so that readers view it in the same way you do. To say that the world is like an overcrowded lifeboat will mean little in itself. You need also to explain that the lifeboat is in danger of sinking unless the number of passengers is reduced or the craft gains extra flotation power. And then you need to point out the implications: the world is overpopulated, and we must either limit population growth or increase our ability to sustain and feed people—without destroying the environment and, in effect, sinking the boat in which we are traveling.

Student Essay

People often use sports analogies to explain relationships and events in their lives. Kevin Nomura heard such analogies when he was growing up, especially comparisons between life and baseball. His essay draws on baseball for an extended analogy, but he uses it for a surprising purpose: to show how the analogy *fails* to explain much about life. Nonetheless, his essay makes effective use of analogy as a pattern and develops each element of the comparison in interesting, effective, and humorous detail.

Life Isn't Like Baseball
by Kevin Nomura

My father loves baseball. So does my mom. My sister was a star softball player in high school, and she is the regular shortstop on her college team. When my father tried to sign me up for little league, however, I let him know that I would rather be playing soccer or tennis.

Introduces the analogy It was about this time that he started trying to convince me that "Life is like

Thesis statement baseball." I wasn't convinced the first time he told me and I'm still not. Let me explain why.

First element of the analogy *Striking Out*. People who think life is like baseball often talk about "striking out," "staying ahead on the count," or "taking a big swing." When you are up to bat in baseball, you get a lot of chances— not just three strikes but also four balls and any number of fouled off pitches. I

Why the comparison is illogical have made some serious mistakes at work, at school, and in my love life, but while I have been lucky enough to get an occa-

An inaccurate example sional second chance, I have never gotten any more. When I have failed at something, I have never failed as completely, as obviously, and as publicly as a baseball player does striking out. I suppose that getting booed off the stage is like striking out, but when I sang off tune in my high school's production of "Bye, Bye Birdie," no one yelled at me or called me

back to the dugout (woops, dressing room).
Instead my parents told me they were proud
of me no matter what, and the director
told me ways to get through my part of the
song fast.

Second element of the analogy

Hitting a Home Run. People seldom strike
out in real life, and they do not hit home
runs either. When baseball fans talk about
"hitting a home run" at work or in some
other activity, they mean accomplishing
something dramatic whose success and importance no one can deny. Who has a job

Questions pointing out why the analogy is faulty

that is big enough or important enough to
allow for a home run? Can the manager of a
MacDonald's hit a home run? Can a clerk in
a department store or a steelworker do it?
Who has a job that allows for dramatic and
significant achievement? Can a teacher
create brilliant students overnight or an
artist become famous for one drawing
rather than a lifetime of careful, patient
effort? I don't think so, or only so seldom that such an achievement is unrealistic for us mortals.

Third element of the analogy

Like a Spitball. People who believe that
life is like baseball often ignore those
parts of the game that don't fit very well
with everyday experience or that are not

Questions and examples that highlight the usefulness of the analogy

very pleasant. Is life like a spitball?
Are successful people the ones who load
things up with petroleum jelly or scuff
them with emery boards, then lie when confronted with evidence—and boast about
their deception afterwards? And if some
do, should we pretend their actions are
good sport and hold them up as examples
for the kids? Should we praise people for
"stealing" and put the biggest thieves in
the record books? Should we treat every

botched move—every balk—as a serious error and a public humiliation? Would you
like it if a slight slip on your part automatically allowed your competitors to
advance a base and maybe even bring home
the winning run?

Conclusion-maintains humorous tone of the essay

    I realize that I probably haven't con-
vinced any real baseball fans to stop seeing life in terms of their game. I also
realize that people will go on talking
about "taking a good cut" or "winding up
too long before the pitch." My younger
brother says he agrees with me, but then
he thinks life is a slap shot.

BRET ANTHONY JOHNSTON

BRET ANTHONY JOHNSTON is a freelance writer who lives in Oxford, Ohio.

My Mother, the Catwoman

The people Johnston writes about (including himself) understand themselves and each other through the twenty-six cats (more or less) they live with—projecting their emotions onto the cats and speaking to each other by talking about their cats. In effect, they construct an analogy between themselves and their cats as a way of dealing with emotions and experiences they cannot confront directly. In explaining this relationship, the author also draws on analogy—as an expository strategy. This essay first appeared in *Glamour* magazine.

She lives on the corner, the house with the overgrown lawn. The neighbors see her once a day, at feeding time. They call her "catwoman," and laugh because she looks nothing like Michelle Pfeiffer, who wore that tight suit in *Batman Returns.* This catwoman looks more like Aunt Bee from Andy Griffith's Mayberry. And she's my mom. 1

I remember when 26 cats lived with my parents and me. They gathered in our yard, ate off paper plates and killed birds. Some of the cats were young, some old; some roamed constantly, while others never left the porch. Almost all of them were black. 2

My father referred to them as "your mother's cats." He much preferred canines and growled at the money my mother spent on cat food. Still, he listened attentively when she told him about new kittens or about how she finally managed to pet a skittish one. 3

Sometimes when I helped my father in his garage, slipping wrenches to him under our car, he would say, "I cleaned up one of your mother's cats today." 4

Secretly, we called the busy street where we most often found their bodies Population Control. Whenever a cat died, my father would drop it in a garbage bag and tie a knot strong enough to contain the stench. No matter which cat it was, my mother cried. 5

Luther was the feline I remember most vividly. If Luther had been human, he'd have been the type to sing the blues, eat dynamite and sleep with your wife while you washed his Cadillac. Luther fathered most of my mother's kittens and won fights with dogs the 6 size of pigs. Unlike the other cats, who got dry food, he ate canned food off his own plate. His preferential treatment, I believe, stemmed from the fact that even my father liked him.

Once my mother and I caught my dad sneaking chicken bones   7
to Luther. Another time, I saw him holding the cat close, whispering, "Stay away from Population Control, OK?"

And Luther, to our surprise, obliged. Sometimes he disap-   8
peared for weeks, but just when we began to worry he might be dead, he would stroll onto our porch, demanding dinner.

Everything was going great for our family, including the cats,   9
when my father died suddenly. My mother was devastated. She quit her job and rarely left the house. She continued feeding the cats, but their numbers declined. Luther was relegated to eating dry food with the others. Although my mother stopped weeping for the cats, I, at 21, started tearing up like a little boy whenever I lifted one off the pavement. I tried tying knots like my father, but even with the cat in a garbage can on the curb, our house reeked of the odor of death.

The spring after she found my father dead in our yard, my   10
mother found Luther on our porch looking as if a tank rather than a car had hit him. Blood dripped from his whiskers, and his tail was mangled. Any reputable vet would have put him to sleep on sight. I considered shooting him with my father's pistol. I would dig a hole, I thought, and bury Luther behind the garage to save both of us the embarrassment of plastic bags and awkward knots. But my mother didn't give me the chance.

That day, something changed. Or maybe things just returned to   11
normal. She converted the garage into an intensive care unit. She fed Luther cream from a bottle, splinted his legs and smothered him with affection. Sometimes as she tended to him, I stood behind her, handing her brushes and damp rags, the way I used too hand my father his tools.

Time passed, and when I was 24, I moved away. By then,   12
Luther had fathered another litter, and my mother had found a new job. Things had pretty much reverted back to the way they had been.

These days, my mother and I call each other often. Every time   13
we talk, I hear about her cats. The count still hasn't reached the old high of 26, but there are enough cats to draw scowls from the neighbors. She's confessed that Luther now lives inside and eats three cans of food per day. Population Control, she said recently, has been quiet. I considered asking her when my father clued her in to our secret term, but instead I told her about my new cat.

I first saw him stalking around my apartment complex's trash   14
bin. Now, I feed him every night. He won't let me touch him, I said,
and my mother assured me that it just takes time.

I told her how, earlier that night, I'd brought the bones from my   15
chicken dinner outside for my pet. I relayed this story without thinking, but in the silence that immediately fell between Ohio and Texas,
we both called up the picture of a man who disliked cats inviting
one to eat from his hand. For a moment, it seemed as if we might
discuss my dad.

But the silence passed, as it always will until we're ready to dis-   16
cuss my father's death. We stayed on the phone for the rest of the
evening, talking about love, hope, sadness and healing, all—I realize
now—disguised as stories about our cats.

MEANINGS AND VALUES

1. Why does Johnston describe his mother as a woman who looks " . . .
    like Aunt Bee from Andy Griffith's Mayberry . . . (Par. 1)? What im-
    ages does Aunt Bee evoke in a reader's mind?

2. Why do Johnston and his father refer to the busy street as "Population
    Control" (par. 5)? How does Johnston react years later when his
    mother refers to that street with the same expression (par. 14)?

3. How does Luther's injury affect Johnston's mother? Why might her
    deep concern about the cats have been rekindled?

4. In paragraph 15 Johnston talks about his new cat. Why does the cat's
    chicken bone diet lead to silence between Johnston and his mother?
    Explain.

EXPOSITORY TECHNIQUES

1. The subtitle of this essay clearly shows the use of analogy. To what
    does Johnston compare his family's methods of communication?
    How effective is this analogy as a subtitle of an essay?

2. Point to specific sentences where Johnston's parents relate to each
    other through cat discussions. What tone does Johnston use when he
    shares these stories? (See "Guide to Terms": *Tone*.)

3. Why does Johnston's mother put so much effort into saving Luther?
    Why might she have converted the garage into an "intensive care
    unit" (par 13)? Consider the circumstances of the death of Johnston's
    father. How might this have led to his mother's insistence on caring
    for Luther?

DICTION AND VOCABULARY

1. As early as in the title the reader is introduced to the analogy of Johnston's mother as a "catwoman." In what way does he describe her as a catwoman? How is she different from the initial interpretation of that word that many readers might have?

2. What level of vocabulary does Johnston use for this essay? Is it appropriate for the type of reader who might read this magazine? Would you classify the writing as formal or informal? Explain.

READ TO WRITE

1. **Collaborating:** Johnston identifies his family relationships with the cats in his mother's life. Working in groups of three, list the ways that each of you identifies with and relates to your families. Is there a particular interest or activity that has unified your family? Discuss your list with the other group members. Are there similarities in the things or events that have held all of your individual families together? Each of you should then write a short analysis comparing and contrasting the types of events and experiences people have and that represent some large part of family relations.

2. **Considering Audience:** What emotions does this essay evoke from the reader? Consider who might be reading this piece in the "His" section of *Glamour* magazine. Is Johnston searching for a certain reaction from these readers? Why might he have chosen to focus on his mother to explain his relationship with his father? How might a female writer have written a similar piece for a "Her" section in the same magazine? Would Johnston have written this differently if he were writing it for *Gentlemen's Quarterly*? How might a female writer have written this for a "Her" section in *G.Q.*? Write a similar essay to Johnston's for a magazine geared toward the opposite sex. Use some family method of communicating or maintaining relationships from your own experience as a basis for the analogy.

3. **Developing an Essay:** Animals often connect people who have otherwise very little in common. Pet owners often bring their four-legged companions with them to nursing homes for emotional and physical therapy. Some juvenile disciplinary programs incorporate animal care into their reform schedule. What are the implementers of these programs hoping will result from such interactions with animals? To what might being involved with animal care be analogous? Write a short essay about the roles animals play in connecting people or in improving their lives.

(NOTE: Suggestions for topics requiring development by use of ANALOGY are on pp. 234-235 at the end of this chapter.)

PATRICIA RAYBON

PATRICIA RAYBON was born in 1949. She attended Ohio State University (B.A. 1971) and the University of Colorado (M.A. 1977). For a number of years she was a newspaper reporter, writer, and editor. Currently she is an associate professor at the University of Colorado School of Journalism and Mass Communication. Her work has been published in a wide variety of magazines and newspapers, including *The New York Times Magazine* and *USA Today*. Raybon's book, *My First White Friend: Confessions on Race, Love, and Forgiveness* appeared in 1996.

Letting in Light

The analogy around which this essay is built is a subtle but particularly effective one. To observe it at work, consider the following relationships as you read: washing windows *equals* women's work *equals* letting in light. By the end of the essay, Raybon may have changed your mind about activities that many people no longer consider particularly important or valuable. This essay first appeared in *The New York Times Magazine*.

The windows were a gift or maybe a bribe—or maybe a bonus—   1
for falling in love with such a dotty old house. The place was a wreck. A showoff, too. So it tried real hard to be more. But it lacked so much—good heat, stable floors, solid walls, enough space. A low interest rate.

But it had windows. More glass and bays and bows than people   2
on a budget had a right to expect. And in unlikely places—like the window inside a bedroom closet, its only view a strawberry patch planted by the children next door.

None of it made sense. So we bought the place. We saved up   3
and put some money down, then toasted the original builder—no doubt some brave and gentle carpenter, blessed with a flair for the grand gesture. A romantic with a T-square.

We were young then and struggling. Also, we are black. We   4
looked with irony and awe at the task now before us. But we did not faint.

The time had come to wash windows.   5

Yes, I do windows. Like an amateur and a dabbler, perhaps, but   6
the old-fashioned way—one pane at a time. It is the best way to pay
back something so plain for its clear and silent gifts—the light of
day, the glow of moon, hard rain, soft snow, dawn's early light.

The Romans called them *specularia*. They glazed their windows   7
with translucent marble and shells. And thus the ancients let some
light into their world.

In my own family, my maternal grandmother washed win-   8
dows—and floors and laundry and dishes and a lot of other things
that needed cleaning—while doing day work for a rich, stylish red-
head in her Southern hometown.

To feed her five children and keep them clothed and happy, to   9
help them walk proudly and go to church and sing hymns and have
some change in their pockets—and to warm and furnish the house
her dead husband had built and added onto with his own hands—
my grandmother went to work.

She and her third daughter, my mother, put on maids' uniforms   10
and cooked and sewed and served a family that employed my grandmother until she was nearly 80. She called them Mister and Missus—
yes, ma'am and yes, sir—although she was by many years their
elder. They called her Laura. Her surname never crossed their lips.

But her daughter, my mother, took her earnings from the cook-   11
ing and serving and window washing and clothes ironing and went
to college, forging a life with a young husband—my father—that
granted me, their daughter, a lifetime of relative comfort.

I owe these women everything.   12

They taught me hope and kindness and how to say thank you.   13

They taught me how to brew tea and pour it. They taught me   14
how to iron creases and whiten linen and cut hair ribbon on the bias
so it doesn't unravel. They taught me to carve fowl, make butter
molds and cook a good cream sauce. They taught me "women's
work"—secrets of home, they said, that now are looked on mostly
with disdain: how to sweep, dust, polish and wax. How to mow,
prune, scrub, scour and purify.

They taught me how to wash windows.   15

Not many women do anymore, of course. There's no time. Life   16
has us all on the run. It's easier to call a "window man," quicker to
pay and, in the bargain, forget about the secret that my mother and
her mother learned many years before they finally taught it to me:

Washing windows clears the cobwebs from the corners. It's   17
plain people's therapy, good for troubles and muddles and other

consternations. It's real work, I venture—honest work—and it's a sound thing to pass on. Mother to daughter. Daughter to child. Woman to woman.

This is heresy, of course. Teaching a girl to wash windows is now an act of bravery—or else defiance. If she's black, it's an act of denial, a gesture that dares history and heritage to make something of it. 18

But when my youngest was 5 or 6, I tempted fate and ancestry and I handed her a wooden bucket. Together we would wash the outdoor panes. The moment sits in my mind: 19

She works a low row. I work the top. Silently we toil, soaping and polishing, each at her own pace—the only sounds the squeak of glass, some noisy birds, our own breathing. 20

Then, quietly at first, this little girl begins to hum. It's a nonsense melody, created for the moment. Soft at first, soon it gets louder. And louder. Then a recognizable tune emerges. Then she is really singing. With every swish of the towel, she croons louder and higher in her little-girl voice with her little-girl song. "This little light of mine—I'm gonna let it shine! Oh, this little light of mine—I'm gonna let it shine!" So, of course, I join in. And the two of us serenade the glass and the sparrows and mostly each other. And too soon our work is done. 21

"That was fun," she says. She is innocent, of course, and does this work by choice, not by necessity. But she's not too young to look at truth and understand it. And her heart, if not her arm, is resolute and strong. 22

Those years have passed. And other houses and newer windows—and other "women's jobs"—have moved through my life. I have chopped and puréed and polished and glazed. Bleached and folded and stirred. I have sung lullabies. 23

I have also marched and fought and prayed and taught and testified. Women's work covers many bases. 24

But the tradition of one simple chore remains. I do it without apology. 25

Last week, I dipped the sponge into the pail and began the gentle bath—easing off the trace of wintry snows, of dust storms and dead, brown leaves, of too much sticky tape used to steady paper pumpkins and Christmas lights and crepe-paper bows from holidays now past. While I worked, the little girl—now 12—found her way to the bucket, proving that her will and her voice are still up to the task, but mostly, I believe, to have some fun. 26

We are out of step, the two of us. She may not even know it. But   27
we can carry a tune. The work is never done. The song is two-part
harmony.

MEANINGS AND VALUES

1. Why do windows make the house attractive (pars. 1–2)? What do
   they seem to symbolize in paragraphs 1–4? 26? (See "Guide to
   Terms": *Symbol.*) Do they take on symbolic meaning anywhere else in
   the essay? If so, what are these other meanings?

2. According to the essay, why might people view window washing as
   a negative, unnecessary, or demeaning act? Be specific in your answer and point to passages that support your conclusions. What positive reasons for washing windows does the author give? Be specific.

3. Where in the essay does the author equate washing windows with
   "women's work"?

4. Raybon points out that washing windows means letting in light. Are
   we to take the idea of letting in light simply and literally, or might it
   have deeper meanings? If it has deeper meanings, point to passages
   that suggest them, and summarize in your own words the ideas being conveyed.

EXPOSITORY TECHNIQUES

1. How does Raybon call attention to a particular subject in the opening
   sentences of paragraphs 1 and 2? (Guide: *Emphasis.*)

2. Explain the role paragraph 5 plays as a transition. Is it effective?
   (Guide: *Transition; Evaluation.*)

3. Point out the parallel sentence structures in paragraphs 13–15 and
   tell what the writer achieves with this use of parallelism. (Guide:
   Parallel Structure.)

4. Identify the transitions in paragraphs 16 and 23 and discuss their
   function within the essay as a whole.

DICTION AND VOCABULARY

1. To what extent should the phrase "clears the cobwebs from the corners" (par. 17) be taken literally? To what extent can it be regarded as
   a metaphor? Explain. (Guide: *Figures of Speech.*)

2. Explain how the phrase "A romantic with a T-Square" might be applied to the author, the "we" of paragraphs 3–4, and the house itself.

Discuss how the phrase might be regarded as presenting a paradox. (Guide: *Paradox.*)

3. The song quoted in paragraph 21 is an allusion (Guide: *Figures of Speech.*) To what does it allude? What does the allusion suggest about the meaning of light for the writer?

4. Are we to take the last sentences of the essay literally as a statement about singing? If not, what figurative or metaphoric meaning might they carry? Explain. (Guide: *Figures of Speech.*)

5. Raybon uses the phrase "dawn's early light" when she discusses what the windows allow her to see (par. 6). Why might she have chosen the exact words from "The Star Spangled Banner" in her description? What points about the United States does this attempt to make?

READ TO WRITE

1. **Collaborating:** Break into groups of four. Discuss the parent-child relationships and experiences similar to what Raybon describes that you and your classmates have had. Plan an essay using representative experiences from each member of the group. Be sure to choose the experiences carefully so that the analogy that develops from each can be connected through transitions to develop a coherent essay.

2. **Considering Audience:** Much of this essay discusses "women's work" from a very traditional standpoint. How might readers describe "men's work" for a similar type of essay? Prepare an essay similar in style and use of analogy to Raybon's that might appeal to a male audience.

3. **Developing an Audience:** As the basis for her analogy, Raybon uses an object (windows) that comes to symbolize and embody ideas and values in the essay. Use a similar strategy in an essay of your own. Chose an object or place, develop an analogy from it, letting it stand for values and concepts.

(NOTE: Suggestions for topics requiring development by use of ANALOGY are, at the end of this chapter.)

Issues and Ideas

Human and Animals

- Tom Wolfe, *O Rotten Gotham—Sliding Down into the Behavioral Sink*
- Barbra Kingsolver, *High Tide in Tuscon*

Like most people, you have probably spent considerable time and effort trying to understand how people behave and how they maintain (or fail to maintain) relationships with each other. One way to do this is through careful observation of social interaction. Yet the complexity of human behavior often makes it difficult to isolate the patterns that can explain our relationships or predict our actions.

For this reason, scientists and other students of human behavior often look for explanatory patterns in studies of plants, animals, or natural processes. Historians sometimes discuss a civilization in terms of its germination, growth, flowering, and decay, for example. A sociologist may use a concept like "entropy" (from physics) to explain a society's decline into chaos, and an anthropologist may turn to biology and natural history to explain our reluctance to abandon settings that once held meaning for us.

To borrow such explanatory patterns is to make use of analogy: explaining complex behaviors by those behaviors that seem simpler and easier to understand (though they may, in truth, be just as difficult and complicated). The risk in borrowing explanatory patterns is that they may oversimplify relationships (bees can represent hardworking groups, but bee societies are certainly less complex than human ones) or that they may be mostly inappropriate (we can talk of a friendship "blossoming" while we know that it has few other similarities to plants or plant life).

In reading the discussions of human behavior in Tom Wolfe's "O Rotten Gotham" and Barbara Kingsolver's "High Tide in Tucson," therefore, pay attention to how the writers use analogy as an effective expository strategy, and also to the ways they use it as a tool for understanding. Bear in mind that an explanation that is rhetorically successful may still take unfounded logical leaps or leave important questions unanswered.

TOM WOLFE

TOM WOLFE was born in 1931 and grew up in Richmond, Virginia, graduated from Washington and Lee University, and took his doctorate at Yale. After working for several years as a reporter for *The Washington Post,* he joined the staff of the *New York Herald Tribune* in 1962. He has won two Washington Newspaper Guild Awards, one for humor and the other for foreign news. Wolfe has been a regular contributor to *New York, Esquire,* and other magazines. His books include *The Kandy-Kolored Tangerine-Flake Streamline Baby* (1965), *The Electric Kool-Aid Acid Test* (1968), *The Pump House Gang* (1968), *Radical Chic and Mau-Mauing the Flak Catchers* (1970), *The New Journalism* (1973), *The Painted Word* (1975), *The Right Stuff* (1977), *In Our Time* (1980), *Underneath the I-Beams: Inside the Compound* (1981), *From Bauhaus to Our House* (1981), *The Purple Decades: A Reader* (1984), *The Bonfire of the Vanities* (1986), and *A Man in Full* (1999).

O Rotten Gotham—Sliding Down into the Behavioral Sink

"O Rotten Gotham—Sliding Down into the Behavioral Sink," as used here, is excerpted from a longer selection by that title in Wolfe's book *The Pump House Gang* (1968). Here, as he frequently does, the author investigates an important aspect of modern life— seriously, but in his characteristic and seemingly freewheeling style. It is a style that is sometimes ridiculed by scholars but is far more often admired. (Wolfe, as the serious student will discover, is always in complete control of his materials and methods, using them to create certain effects, to reinforce his ideas.) In this piece his analogy is particularly noteworthy for the extensive usage he is able to get from it.

Ijust spent two days with Edward T. Hall, an anthropologist,   1
watching thousands of my fellow New Yorkers short-circuiting themselves into hot little twitching death balls with jolts of their own adrenalin. Dr. Hall says it is overcrowding that does it.

Overcrowding gets the adrenalin going, and the adrenalin gets them hyped up. And here they are, hyped up, turning bilious, nephritic, a queer, autistic, sadistic, barren, batty, sloppy, hot-in-the-pants, chancred-on-the-flankers, leering, puling, numb—the usual in New York, in other words, and God knows what else. Dr. Hall has the theory that overcrowding has already thrown New York into a state of behavioral sink. Behavioral sink is a term from ethology, which is the study of how animals relate to their environment. Among animals, the sink winds up with a "population collapse" or "massive die-off." O Rotten Gotham.

It got to be easy to look at New Yorkers as animals, especially   2
looking down from some place like a balcony at Grand Central at the rush hour Friday afternoon. The floor was filled with the poor white humans, running around, dodging, blinking their eyes, making a sound like a pen full of starlings or rats or something.

"Listen to them skid," says Dr. Hall.   3

He was right. The poor old etiolate animals were out there skid-   4
ding on their rubber soles. You could hear it once he pointed it out. They stop short to keep from hitting somebody or because they are disoriented and they suddenly stop and look around, and they skid on their rubber-soled shoes, and a screech goes up. They pour out onto the floor down the escalators from the Pan-Am Building, from 42nd Street, from Lexington Avenue, up out of subways, down into subways, railroad trains, up into helicopters—

"You can also hear the helicopters all the way down here," says   5
Dr. Hall. The sound of the helicopters using the roof of the Pan-Am Building nearly fifty stories up beats right through. "If it weren't for this ceiling"—he is referring to the very high ceiling in Grand Central—"this place would be unbearable with this kind of crowding. And yet they'll probably never 'waste' space like this again."

"They screech! And the adrenal glands in all those poor white   6
animals enlarge, micrometer by micrometer, to the size of cantaloupes. Dr. Hall pulls a Minox camera out of a holster he has on his belt and starts shooting away at the human scurry. The Sink!

Dr. Hall has the Minox up to his eye—he is a slender man, calm,   7
52 years old, young-looking, an anthropologist who has worked with Navajos, Hopis, Spanish-Americans, Negroes, Trukese. He was the most important anthropologist in the government during the crucial years of the foreign aid program, the 1950s. He directed both the Point Four training program and the Human Relations Area Files. He wrote *The Silent Language* and *The Hidden Dimension*, two books that are picking up the kind of "underground" following his

friend Marshall McLuhan started picking up about five years ago. He teaches at the Illinois Institute of Technology, lives with his wife, Mildred, in a high-ceilinged town house on one of the last great residential streets in downtown Chicago, Astor Street; he has a grown son and daughter, loves good food, good wine, the relaxed, civilized life—but comes to New York with a Minox at his eye to record!—perfect—The Sink.

We really got down in there by walking down into the   8
Lexington Avenue line subway stop under Grand Central. We inhaled those nice big fluffy fumes of human sweat, urine, effluvia, and sebaceous secretions. One old female human was already stroked out on the upper level, on a stretcher, with two policemen standing by. The other humans barely looked at her. They rushed into line. They bellied each other, haunch to paunch, down the stairs. Human heads shone through the gratings. The species North European tried to create bubbles of space around themselves, about a foot and a half in diameter—

"See, he's reacting against the line," says Dr. Hall.   9

—but the species Mediterranean presses on in. The hell with   10
bubbles of space. The species North European resents that, this male human behind him presses forward toward the booth . . . breathing on him, he's disgusted, he pulls out of the line entirely, the species Mediterranean resents him for resenting it, and neither of them realizes what the hell they are getting irritable about exactly. And in all of them the old adrenals grow another micrometer.

Dr. Hall whips out the Minox. Too perfect! The bottom of The   11
Sink.

It is the sheer overcrowding, such as occurs in the business sec-   12
tions of Manhattan five days a week and in Harlem, Bedford-Stuyvesant, southeast Bronx every day—sheer overcrowding is converting New Yorkers into animals in a sink pen. Dr. Hall's argument runs as follows: all animals, including birds, seem to have a built-in inherited requirement to have a certain amount of territory, space, to lead their lives in. Even if they have all the food they need, and there are no predatory animals threatening them, they cannot tolerate crowding beyond a certain point. No more than two hundred wild Norway rats can survive on a quarter acre of ground, for example, even when they are given all the food they can eat. They just die off.

But why? To find out, ethologists have run experiments on all   13
sorts of animals, from stickleback crabs to Sika deer. In one major experiment, an ethologist named John Calhoun put some domesti-

cated white Norway rats in a pen with four sections to it, connected by ramps. Calhoun knew from previous experiments that the rats tend to split up into groups of ten to twelve and that the pen, therefore, would hold forty to forty-eight rats comfortably, assuming they formed four equal groups. He allowed them to reproduce until there were eighty rats, balanced between male and female, but did not let it get any more crowded. He kept them supplied with plenty of food, water, and nesting materials. In other words, all their more obvious needs were taken care of. A less obvious need—space—was not. To the human eye, the pen did not even look especially crowded. But to the rats, it was crowded beyond endurance.

The entire colony was soon plunged into a profound behavioral   14
sink. "The sink," said Calhoun, "is the outcome of any behavioral process that collects animals together in unusually great numbers. The unhealthy connotations of the term are not accidental: a behavioral sink does act to aggravate all forms of pathology that can be found within a group."

For a start, long before the rat population reached eighty, a sta-   15
tus hierarchy had developed in the pen. Two dominant male rats took over the two end sections, acquired harems of eight to ten females each, and forced the rest of the rats into the two middle pens. All the overcrowding took place in the middle pens. That was where the "sink" hit. The aristocrat rats at the end grew bigger, sleeker, healthier, and more secure the whole time.

In The Sink, meanwhile, nest building, courting, sex behavior,   16
reproduction, social organization, health—all of it went to pieces. Normally, Norway rats have a mating ritual in which the male chases the female, the female ducks down into a burrow and sticks her head up to watch the male. He performs a little dance outside the burrow, then she comes out, and he mounts her, usually for a few seconds. When The Sink set in, however, no more than three males—the dominant males in the middle sections—kept up the old customs. The rest tried everything from satyrism to homosexuality or else gave up on sex altogether. Some of the subordinate males spent all their time chasing females. Three or four might chase one female at the same time, and instead of stopping at the burrow entrance for the ritual, they would charge right in. Once mounted, they would hold on for minutes instead of the usual seconds.

Homosexuality rose sharply. So did bisexuality. Some males   17
would mount anything—males, females, babies, senescent rats, anything. Still other males dropped sexual activity altogether, wouldn't fight and, in fact, would hardly move except when the other rats

slept. Occasionally, a female from the aristocrat rats' harems would come over the ramps and into the middle sections to sample life in The Sink. When she had had enough, she would run back up the ramp. Sink males would give chase up to the top of the ramp, which is to say, to the very edge of the aristocratic preserve. But one glance from one of the king rats would stop them cold and they would return to The Sink.

The slumming females from the harems had their adventures 18 and then returned to a placid, healthy life. Females in The Sink, however, were ravaged, physically and psychologically. Pregnant rats had trouble continuing pregnancy. The rate of miscarriages increased significantly, and females started dying from tumors and other disorders of the mammary glands, sex organs, uterus, ovaries, and Fallopian tubes. Typically, their kidneys, livers, and adrenals were also enlarged or diseased or showed other signs associated with stress.

Child-rearing became totally disorganized. The females lost the 19 interest or the stamina to build nests and did not keep them up if they did build them. In the general filth and confusion, they would not put themselves out to save offspring they were momentarily separated from. Frantic, even sadistic competition among the males was going on all around them and rendering their lives chaotic. The males began unprovoked and senseless assaults upon one another, often in the form of tail-biting. Ordinarily, rats will suppress this kind of behavior when it crops up. In The Sink, male rats gave up all policing and just looked out for themselves. The "pecking order" among males in The Sink was never stable. Normally, male rats set up a three-class structure. Under the pressure of overcrowding, however, they broke up into all sorts of unstable subclasses, cliques, packs—and constantly pushed, probed, explored, tested one another's power. Anyone was fair game, except for the aristocrats in the end pens.

Calhoun kept the population down to eighty, so that the next 20 stage, "population collapse" or "massive die-off," did not occur. But the autopsies showed that the pattern—as in the diseases among the female rats—was already there.

The classic study of die-off was John J. Christian's study of Sika 21 deer on James Island in the Chesapeake Bay, west of Cambridge, Maryland. Four or five of the deer had been released on the island, which was 280 acres and uninhabited, in 1916. By 1955 they had bred freely into a herd of 280 to 300. The population density was only about one deer per acre at this point, but Christian knew that this was already too high for the Sikas' inborn space requirements, and something would give before long. For two years the number of deer remained 280 to 300. But suddenly, in 1958, over half the deer died; 161 carcasses were recovered. In 1959 more deer died and the population steadied at about 80.

In two years, two-thirds of the herd had died. Why? It was not starvation. In fact, all the deer collected were in excellent condition, with well-developed muscles, shining coats, and fat deposits between the muscles. In practically all the deer, however, the adrenal glands had enlarged by 50 percent. Christian concluded that the die-off was due to "shock following severe metabolic disturbance, probably as a result of prolonged adrenocortical hyperactivity. . . . There was no evidence of infection, starvation, or other obvious cause to explain the mass mortality." In other words, the constant stress of overpopulation, plus the normal stress of the cold of the winter, had kept the adrenalin flowing so constantly in the deer that their systems were depleted of blood sugar and they died of shock.   22

Well, the white humans are still skidding and darting across the floor of Grand Central. Dr. Hall listens a moment longer to the skidding and the darting noises, and then says, "You know, I've been on commuter trains here after everyone has been through one of these rushes, and I'll tell you, there is enough acid flowing in the stomachs in every car to dissolve the rails underneath."   23

Just a little invisible acid bath for the linings to round off the day. The ulcers the acids cause, of course, are the one disease people have already been taught to associate with the stress of city life. But over-crowding, as Dr. Hall sees it, raises a lot more hell with the body than just ulcers. In everyday life in New York—just the usual, getting to work, working in massively congested areas like 42nd Street between Fifth Avenue and Lexington, especially now that the Pam-Am Building is set in there, working in cubicles such as those in the editorial offices at Time-Life, Inc., which Dr. Hall cites as typical of New York's poor handling of space, working in cubicles with low ceilings and, often, no access to a window, while construction crews all over Manhattan drive everybody up the Masonite wall with air-pressure generators with noises up to the boil-a-brain decibel level, than rushing to get home, piling into subways and trains, fighting for time and for space, the usual day in New York—the whole now-normal thing keeps shooting jolts of adrenalin into the body, breaking down the body's defenses and winding up with the work-a-daddy human animal stroked out at the breakfast table with his head apoplexed like a cauliflower out of his $6.95 semi-spread Pima-cotton shirt, and nosed   24 over into a plate of No-Kolresto egg substitute, signing off with the black thrombosis, cancer, kidney, liver, or stomach failure, and the adrenals ooze to a halt, the size of eggplants in July.

One of the people whose work Dr. Hall is interested in on this   25
score is Rene Dubos at the Rockefeller Institute. Dubos's work indicates that specific organisms, such as the tuberculosis bacillus or a pneumonia virus, can seldom be considered "the cause" of a disease. The germ or virus, apparently, has to work in combination with other things that have already broken the body down in some way—such as the old adrenal hyperactivity. Dr. Hall would like to see some autopsy studies made to record the size of adrenal glands in New York, especially of people crowded into slums and people who go through the full rush-hour-work-rush-hour cycle every day. He is afraid that until there is some clinical, statistical data on how overcrowding actually ravages the human body, no one will be willing to do anything about it. Even in so obvious a thing as air pollution, the pattern is familiar. Until people can actually see the smoke or smell the sulphur or feel the sting in their eyes, politicians will not get excited about it, even though it is well known that many of the lethal substances polluting the air are invisible and odorless. For one thing, most politicians are like the aristocrat rats. They are insulated from The Sink by practically sultanic buffers—limousines, chauffeurs, secretaries, aides-de-camp, doormen, shuttered houses, high-floor apartments. They almost never ride subways, fight rush hours, much less live in the slums or work in the Pam-Am Building.

MEANINGS AND VALUES

1. Who are members of the "species Mediterranean"? The "species North European"? What could account for their differences in space requirements (pars. 8–10)?

2. Is this writing primarily objective or subjective? (See "Guide to Terms": *Objective/Subjective*.) Why?

3. Do you get the impression that the author is being unkind,"making fun"of the harried New Yorkers? How, if at all, does he prevent such an impression?

EXPOSITORY TECHNIQUES

1. Is this analogy a success, or does the author work it too hard? Be prepared to defend your answer. (Guide: *Evaluation*.)

2. What are the benefits of the frequent return to what Dr. Hall is doing or saying (e.g., in pars. 3, 5, 7, 9, 11, and 23)?

3. Paragraph 12 has a useful function beyond the simple information it provides—a sort of organic relation to the coming development. Explain how this is accomplished.

4. The preceding two questions highlight the ways Wolfe deals with problems of transition in this essay. (Guide: Transition.) How are such issues also matters of coherence? (Guide: *Coherence.*)

5. Analyze stylistic differences, with resulting effects, between the following sections of the essay (Guide: *Style/Tone*):

   a. the description of chaos at Grand Central and the information about Dr. Hall in paragraph 7

   b. the Grand Central scene and the account of the laboratory experiment with rats in paragraphs 8–20

   c. the Grand Central scene and the final paragraph.

6. What is gained or lost by the unusual length and design of the last sentence of paragraph 24? (We can be sure that it did not "just happen" to Wolfe—and equally sure that a sentence of such length would be disastrous in most writing.) (Guide: *Syntax.*)

DICTION AND VOCABULARY

1. What is the significance of the word "Gotham"?

2. Why do you think the author refers to "my fellow New Yorkers" in the first sentence? What would have been the effect had he not taken such a step?

3. Why does he consistently, after paragraph 2, refer to the people as "poor white humans," "poor human animals," etc.?

4. In paragraph 14 he refers to the connotations of the word "sink." What are its possible connotations? (Guide: *Connotations/Denotation.*)

5. Cite examples of verbal irony to be found in paragraphs 5, 8, and 24.

6. Consult your dictionary as needed for full understanding of the following words: autistic, puling (par.1); etiolate (4); effluvia, sebaceous (8); pathology (14); satyrism (16); senescent (17); decibel, thrombosis (24); lethal (25).

READ TO WRITE

1. **Collaborating:** One especially effective technique Wolfe employs in this essay is observation—specifically the overall view afford by a balcony high above the main hall of Grand Central Station. With a team of three other people choose a location that will provide you with a broad overview of human actions and behavior. Go to that spot with notebooks in hand and individually, without discussion,

write your observations. Return to the classroom and compare your notes. What similarities in behavior did you all observe? What different activities and images stood out in your minds? Write a short analysis of your collective observations. Be sure to include an explanation of the behaviors noticeable to all of you and reasons why other behaviors stood out to individual observers.

2. **Considering Audience:** Would this essay have a strong effect on readers raised in a rural area? What aspects of this essay might help someone from a farming environment relate to this? What other behaviors could be addressed to make this more accessible to audiences from rural areas? Choose a particular animal behavior that could be analogous to human activity in rural locations and create a plan for an essay based on the analogy.

3. **Developing an Essay:** Popular magazines can provide good summaries of contemporary research as can specialized encyclopedias and general interest books. Choose a theory or some research you think is insightful and use it to help explain common behaviors, perhaps some that you have observed in the manner described in the "collaborating" question. Prepare an essay built around two or more explanatory theories as Wolfe does in his essay.

(NOTE: Suggestions for topics requiring development by use of ANALOGY are on pp. 234-235 at the end of this chapter.)

BARBARA KINGSOLVER

BARBARA KINGSOLVER was born in 1955 in Annapolis, Maryland, and raised in eastern Kentucky. She studied biology at DePauw University (B.A., 1977) and the University of Arizona (M.S., 1981) and worked as a scientist and scientific writer before beginning her career as a writer of fiction and essays. Her highly acclaimed books include novels *The Bean Trees* (1988), *Animal Dreams* (1990), *Pigs in Heaven* (1993), stories *Homeland and Other Stories* (1989), poetry *Another America* (1992), and essays *High Tide in Tucson: Essays from Now or Never* (1996).

High Tide in Tucson

This essay, from Kingsolver's book with the same title, is built around a surprising and imaginative analogy. It offers a different and more optimistic perspective on modern society and behavior than Tom Wolfe does in the preceding essay ("O Rotten Gotham"), yet, like Wolfe, the author draws heavily on scientific research for her explanations.

A hermit crab lives in my house. Here in the desert he's hiding out from local animal ordinances, at minimum, and maybe even the international laws of native-species transport. For sure, he's an outlaw against nature. So be it.   1

He arrived as a stowaway two Octobers ago. I had spent a week in the Bahamas, and while I was there, wishing my daughter could see those sparkling blue bays and sandy covers, I did exactly what she would have done: I collected shells. Spiky murexes, smooth purple moon shells, ancient-looking whelks sand-blasted by the tide—I tucked them in the pockets of my shirt and shorts until my lumpy, suspect hemlines gave me away, like a refugee smuggling the family fortune. When it was time to go home, I rinsed my loot in the sink and packed it carefully into a plastic carton, then nested it deep in my suitcase for the journey to Arizona.   2

I got home in the middle of the night, but couldn't wait till morning to show my hand. I set the carton on the coffee table for my daughter to open. In the dark living room her face glowed, in the   3

way of antique stories about children and treasure. With perfect del-
icacy she laid the shells out on the table, counting, sorting, designat-
ing scientific categories like yellow-striped pinky, Barnacle Bill's
pocketbook . . . Yeek! She let loose a sudden yelp, dropped her
booty, and ran to the far end of the room. The largest, knottiest
whelk had begun to move around. First it extended one long red
talon of a leg, tap-tap-tapping like a blind man's cane. Then came
half a dozen more red legs, plus a pair of eyes on stalks, and a purple claw that snapped open and shut in a way that could not mean
We come in Friendship.

Who could blame this creature? It had fallen asleep to the sound   4
of the Caribbean tide and awakened on a coffee table in Tucson,
Arizona, where the nearest standing water source of any real account was the municipal sewage-treatment plant.

With red stiletto legs splayed in all directions, it lunged and   5
jerked its huge shell this way and that, reminding me of the scene I
make whenever I'm moved to rearrange the living-room sofa by
myself. Then, while we watched in stunned reverence, the strange
beast found its bearings and began to reveal a determined, crabby
grace. It felt its way to the edge of the table and eased itself over, not
falling bang to the floor but hanging suspended underneath within
the long grasp of its ice-tong legs, lifting any two or three at a time
while many others still held in place. In this remarkable fashion it
scrambled around the underside of the table's rim, swift and sure
and fearless like a rock climber's dream.

If you ask me, when something extraordinary shows up in your   6
life in the middle of the night, you give it a name and make it the
best home you can.

The business of naming involved a grasp of hermit-crab gender   7
that was way out of our league. But our household had a deficit of
males, so my daughter and I chose Buster, for balance. We gave him
a terrarium with clean gravel and a small cactus plant dug out of the
yard and a big cockleshell full of tap water. All this seemed to suit
him fine. To my astonishment our local pet store carried a product
called Vitaminized Hermit Crab Cakes. Tempting enough (till you
read the ingredients) but we passed, since our household leans more
toward the recycling ethic. We give him leftovers. Buster's rapture is
the day I drag the unidentifiable things in cottage cheese containers
out of the back of the fridge.

We've also learned to give him a continually changing assort-   8
ment of seashells, which he tries on and casts off like Cinderella's
stepsisters preening for the ball. He'll sometimes try to squeeze into

ludicrous outfits too small to contain him (who can't relate?). In other moods, he will disappear into a conch the size of my two fists and sit for a day, immobilized by the weight of upward mobility. He is in every way the perfect housemate: quiet, entertaining, and willing to eat up the trash. He went to school for first-grade show-and-tell, and was such a hit the principal called up to congratulate me (I think) for being a broad-minded mother.

It was a long time, though, before we began to understand the content of Buster's character. He required more patient observation than we were in the habit of giving to a small, cold-blooded life. As months went by, we would periodically notice with great disappointment that Buster seemed to be dead. Or not entirely dead, but ill, or maybe suffering the crab equivalent of the blues. He would burrow into a gravelly corner, shrink deep into his shell, and not move, for days and days. We'd take him out to play, dunk him in water, offer him a new frock—nothing. He wanted to be still. 9

Life being what it is, we'd eventually quit prodding our sick friend to cheer up, and would move on to the next stage of a difficult friendship: neglect. We'd ignore him wholesale, only to realize at some point later on the he'd lapsed into hyperactivity. We'd find him ceaselessly patrolling the four corners of his world, turning over rocks, rooting out and dragging around truly disgusting pork-chop bones, digging up his cactus and replanting it on its head. At night when the household fell silent I would lie in bed listening to his methodical pebbly racket from the opposite end of the house. Buster was manic-depressive. 10

I wondered if he might be responding to the moon. I'm partial to lunar cycles, ever since I learned as a teenager that human females in their natural state—which is to say, sleeping outdoors—arrive at menses in synchrony and ovulate with the full moon. My imagination remains captive to that primordial village: the comradely grumpiness of new-moon days, when the entire world at once would go on PMS alert. And the compensation that would turn up two weeks later on a wild wind, under that great round headlamp, driving both men and women to distraction with the overt prospect of conception. The surface of the land literally rises and falls—as much as fifty centimeters!—as the moon passes over, and we clay-footed mortals fall like dominoes before the swell. It's no surprise at all if a full moon inspires lyricists to corny love songs, or inmates to slamming themselves against barred windows. A hermit crab hardly seems this impetuous, but animals are notoriously responsive to the full moon: wolves howl; roosters announce daybreak all 11 night. Luna moths, Arctic loons, and lunatics have a sole inspiration in common. Buster's insomniac restlessness seemed likely to be a part of the worldwide full-moon fellowship.

But it wasn't, exactly. The full moon didn't shine on either end   12
of his cycle, the high or the low. We tried to keep track, but it soon became clear: Buster marched to his own drum. The cyclic force that moved him remained as mysterious to us as his true gender and the workings of his crustacean soul.

Buster's aquarium occupies a spot on our kitchen counter right   13
next to the coffeepot, and so it became my habit to begin mornings with chin in hands, pondering the oceanic mysteries while awaiting percolation. Finally, I remembered something. Years ago when I was a graduate student of animal behavior, I passed my days reading about the likes of animals' internal clocks. Temperature, photoperiod, the rise and fall of hormones—all these influences have been teased apart like so many threads from the rope that pulls every creature to its regulated destiny. But one story takes the cake. F. A. Brown, a researcher who is more or less the grandfather of the biological clock, set about in 1954 to track the cycles of intertidal oysters. He scooped his subjects from the clammy coast of Connecticut and moved them into the basement of a laboratory in landlocked Illinois. For the first fifteen days in their new aquariums, the oysters kept right up with their normal intertidal behavior: they spent time shut away in their shells, and time with their mouths wide open, siphoning their briny bath for the plankton that sustained them, as the tides ebbed and flowed on the distant Connecticut shore. In the next two weeks, they made a mystifying shift. They still carried out their cycles in unison, and were regular as the tides, but their high-tide behavior didn't coincide with high tide in Connecticut, or for that matter California, or any other tidal charts known to science. It dawned on the researchers after some calculations that the oysters were responding to high tide in Chicago. Never mind that the gentle mollusks lived in glass boxes in the basement of a steel-and-cement building. Nor that Chicago has no ocean. In the circumstances, the oysters were doing their best.

When Buster is running around for all he's worth, I can only   14
presume it's high tide in Tucson. With or without evidence, I'm romantic enough to believe it. This is the lesson of Buster, the poetry that camps outside the halls of science: Jump for joy, hallelujah. Even a desert has tides.

When I was twenty-two, I donned the shell of a tiny yellow   15
Renault and drove with all I owned from Kentucky to Tucson. I was

a typical young American, striking out. I had no earthly notion that I was bringing on myself a calamity of the magnitude of the one that befell poor Buster. I am the commonest kind of North American refugee: I believe I like it here, far-flung from my original home. I've come to love the desert that bristles and breathes and sleeps outside my windows. In the course of seventeen years I've embedded myself in a family here—neighbors, colleagues, friends I can't foresee living without, and a child who is native to this ground, with loves of her own. I'm here for good, it seems.

16   And yet I never cease to long in my bones for what I left behind. I open my eyes on every new day expecting that a creek will run through my backyard under broad-leafed maples, and that my mother will be whistling in the kitchen. Behind the howl of coyotes, I'm listening for meadowlarks, I sometimes ache to be rocked in the bosom of the blood relations and busybodies of my childhood. Particularly in my years as a mother without a mate, I have deeply missed the safety net of extended family.

17   In a city of half a million I still really look at every face, anticipating recognition, because I grew up in a town where every face meant something to me. I have trouble remembering to lock the doors. Wariness of strangers I learned the hard way. When I was new to the city, I let a man into my house one hot afternoon because he seemed in dire need of a drink of water; when I turned from the kitchen sink I found sharpened steel shoved against my belly. And so I know, I know. But I cultivate suspicion with as much difficulty as I force tomatoes to grow in the drought-stricken hardpan of my strange backyard. No creek runs here, but I'm still listening to secret tides, living as if I belonged to an earlier place: not Kentucky, necessarily, but a welcoming earth and a human family. A forest. A species.

18   In my life I've had frightening losses and unfathomable gifts: A knife in my stomach. The death of an unborn child. Sunrise in a rain forest. A stupendous column of blue butterflies rising from a Greek monastery. A car that spontaneously caught fire while I was driving it. The end of a marriage, followed by a year in which I could barely understand how to keep living. The discovery, just weeks ago when I rose from my desk and walked into the kitchen, of three strangers industriously relieving my house of its contents.

19   I persuaded the strangers to put down the things they were holding (what a bizarre tableau of anti-Magi they made, these three unwise men, bearing a camera, an electric guitar, and a Singer sewing machine), and to leave my home, pronto. My daughter asked excitedly when she got home from school, "Mom, did you say

bad words?" (I told her this was the very occasion that bad words exist for.) The police said, variously, that I was lucky, foolhardy, and "a brave lady." But it's not good luck to be invaded, and neither foolish nor brave to stand your ground. It's only the way life goes, and I did it, just as years ago I fought off the knife; mourned the lost child; bore witness to the rain forest; claimed the blue butterflies as Holy Spirit in my private pantheon; got out of the burning car; survived the divorce by putting one foot in front of the other and taking good care of my child. On most important occasions, I cannot think how to respond, I simply do. What does it mean, anyway, to be an animal in human clothing? We carry around these big brains of ours like the crown jewels, but mostly I find that millions of years of evolution have prepared me for one thing only: to follow internal rhythms. To walk upright, to protect my loved ones, to cooperate with my family group—however broadly I care to define it—to do whatever will help us thrive. Obviously, some habits that saw us through the millennia are proving hazardous in a modern context: for example, the yen to consume carbohydrates and fat whenever they cross our path, or the proclivity for unchecked reproduction. But it's surely worth forgiving ourselves these tendencies a little, in light of the fact that they are what got us here. Like Buster, we are creatures of inexplicable cravings. Thinking isn't everything. The way I stock my refrigerator would amuse a level-headed interplanetary observer, who would see I'm responding not to real necessity but to the dread of famine honed in the African savannah. I can laugh at my Rhodesian Ridgeback as she furtively sniffs the houseplants for a place to bury bones, and circles to beat down the grass before lying on my kitchen floor. But she and I are exactly the same kind of hairpin.

We humans have to grant the presence of some past adaptations, 20 even in their unforgivable extremes, if only to admit they are permanent rocks in the steam we're obliged to navigate. It's easy to speculate and hard to prove, ever, that genes control our behaviors. Yet we are persistently, excruciatingly adept at many things that seem no more useful to modern life than the tracking of tides in a desert. At recognizing insider/outsider status, for example, starting with white vs. black and grading straight into distinctions so fine as to baffle the bystander—Serb and Bosnian, Hutu and Tutsi, Crip and Blood. We hold that children learn discrimination from their parents, but they learn it fiercely and well, world without end. Recite it by rote like a multiplication table. Take it to heart, though it's neither helpful nor appropriate, anymore than it is to hire the taller of two men applying for a position as bank clerk, though statistically we're likely to do that too. Deference to the physical superlative, a preference for the scent of our own clan: a thousand anachronisms dance down the strands of our DNA from a hidebound tribal past, guiding us toward the glories of survival, and some vainglories as well. If we resent being bound by these ropes, the best hope is to seize them out like snakes, by the throat, look them in the eye and own up to their venom.

But we rarely do, silly egghead of a species that we are. We in-   21
vent the most outlandish intellectual grounds to justify discrimination. We tap our toes to chaste love songs about the silvery moon without recognizing them as hymns to copulation. We can dress up our drives, put them in three-piece suits or ballet slippers, but still they drive us. The wonder of it is that our culture attaches almost unequivocal shame to our animal nature, believing brute urges must be hurtful, violent things. But it's no less an animal instinct that leads us to marry (species that benefit from monogamy tend to practice it); to organize a neighborhood cleanup campaign (rare and doomed is the creature that fouls its nest); to improvise and enforce morality (many primates socialize their young to be cooperative and ostracize adults who won't share food).

It's starting to look as if the most shameful tradition of Western   22
civilization is our need to deny we are animals. In just a few centuries of setting ourselves apart as landlords of the Garden of Eden, exempt from the natural order and entitled to hold dominion, we have managed to behave like so-called animals anyway, and on top of it to wreck most of what took three billion years to assemble. Air, water, earth, and fire—so much of our own element so vastly contaminated, we endanger our own future. Apparently we never owned the place after all. Like every other animal, we're locked into our niche: the mercury in the ocean, the pesticides on the soybean fields, all comes home to our breastfed babies. In the silent spring we are learning it's easier to escape from a chain gang than a food chain. Possibly we will have the sense to begin a new century by renewing our membership in the Animal Kingdom.

Not long ago I went backpacking in the Eagle Tail Mountains.   23
This range is a trackless wilderness in western Arizona that most people would call Godforsaken, taking for granted God's preference for loamy topsoil and regular precipitation. Whoever created the Eagle Tails had dry heat on the agenda, and a thing for volcanic rock. Also cactus, twisted mesquites, and five-alarm sunsets. The hiker's program in a desert like this is dire and blunt: carry in enough water to keep you alive till you can find a water source: then

fill your bottles and head for the next one, or straight back out. Experts warn adventurers in this region, without irony, to drink their water while they're still alive, as it won't help later.

Several canyons looked promising for springs on our topograph-   24
ical map, but turned up dry. Finally, at the top of a narrow, overgrown gorge we found a blessed tinaja, a deep, shaded hollow in the rock about the size of four or five claw-foot tubs, holding water. After we drank our fill, my friends struck out again, but I opted to stay and spend the day in the hospitable place that had slaked our thirst. On either side of the natural water tank, two shallow caves in the canyon wall faced each other, only a few dozen steps apart. By crossing from one to the other at noon, a person could spend the whole day here in shady comfort—or in colder weather, follow the winter sun. Anticipating a morning of reading, I pulled *Angle of Repose* out of my pack and looked for a place to settle on the flat, dusty floor of the west-facing shelter. Instead, my eyes were startled by a smooth corn-grinding stone. It sat in the exact center of its rock bowl, as if the Hohokam woman or man who used this mortar and pestle had walked off and left them there an hour ago. The Hohokam disappeared from the earth in A.D. 1450. It was inconceivable to me that no one had been here since then, but that may have been the case—that is the point of trackless wilderness. I picked up the grinding stone. The size and weight and smooth, balanced perfection of it in my hand filled me at once with a longing to possess it. In its time, this excellent stone was the most treasured thing in a life, a family, maybe the whole neighborhood. To whom it still belonged. I replaced it in the rock depression, which also felt smooth to my touch. Because my eyes now understood how to look at it, the ground under my feet came alive with worked flint chips and pottery shards. I walked across to the other cave and found its floor just as lively with historic debris. Hidden under brittlebush and catclaw I found another grinding stone, this one some distance from the depression in the cave floor that once answered its pressure daily, for the grinding of corn or mesquite beans.

For a whole day I marveled at this place, running my fingers   25
over the knife edges of dark flint chips, trying to fit together thick red pieces of shattered clay jars, biting my lower lip like a child concentrating on a puzzle. I tried to guess the size of whole pots from the curve of the broken pieces: some seemed as small as my two cupped hands, and some maybe as big as a bucket. The sun scorched my neck, reminding me to follow the shade across to the other shelter. Bees hummed at the edge of the water hole, nosing up to the water, their abdomens pulsing like tiny hydraulic pumps; by late afternoon they rimmed the pool completely, a collar of busy lace.

Off and on, the lazy hand of a hot breeze shuffled the white leaves of the brittlebush. Once I looked up to see a screaming pair of red-tailed hawks mating in midair, and once a clatter of hooves warned me to hold still. A bighorn ram emerged through the brush, his head bent low under his hefty cornice, and ambled by me with nothing on his mind so much as a cool drink.

How long can a pestle stone lie still in the center of its mortar? That long ago—that recently—people lived here. Here, exactly, and not one valley over, or two, or twelve, because this place had all a person needs: shelter, food, and permanent water. They organized their lives around a catchment basin in a granite boulder, conforming their desires to the earth's charities; they never expected the opposite. The stories I grew up with lauded Moses for striking the rock and bringing forth the bubbling stream. But the stories of the Hohokam—oh, how they must have praised that good rock.   26

At dusk my friends returned with wonderful tales of the ground they had covered. We camped for the night, refilled our canteens, and hiked back to the land of plumbing and a fair guarantee of longevity. But I treasure my memory of the day I lingered near water and covered no ground. I can't think of a day in my life in which I've had such a clear fix on what it means to be human.   27

Want is a thing that unfurls unbidden like fungus, opening large upon itself, stopless, filling the sky. But *needs,* from one day to the next, are few enough to fit in a bucket, with room enough left to rattle like brittlebush in a dry wind.   28

For each of us—furred, feathered, or skinned alive—the whole earth balances on the single precarious point of our own survival. In the best of times, I hold in mind the need to care for things beyond the self: poetry, humanity, grace. In other times, when it seems difficult merely to survive and be happy about it, the condition of my thought tastes as simple as this: let me be a good animal today. I've spent months at a stretch, even years, with that taste in my mouth, and have found that it serves.   29

But it seems a wide gulf to cross, from the raw, green passion for survival to the dispassionate, considered state of human grace. How does the animal mind construct a poetry for the modern artifice in which we now reside? Often I feel as disoriented as poor Buster, unprepared for the life that zooms headlong past my line of sight. This clutter of human paraphernalia and counterfeit necessities—what does it have to do with the genuine business of life on earth? It feels strange to me to be living in a box, hiding from the steadying influence of the moon; wearing the hide of a cow, which is supposed to be dyed to match God-knows-what, on my feet; making promises over   30 the telephone about things I will do at a precise hour next *year*. (I always feel the urge to add, as my grandmother does, "Lord willing and the creeks don't rise!") I find it impossible to think, with a straight face, about what colors ought not to be worn after Labor Day. I can become hysterical over the fact that someone, somewhere, invented a thing called the mushroom scrubber, and that many other people undoubtedly feel they *need* to possess one. It's completely usual for me to get up in the morning, take a look around, and laugh out loud.

Strangest of all, I am carrying on with all of this in a desert, two   31
thousand miles from my verdant childhood home. I am disembodied. No one here remembers how I was before I grew to my present height. I'm called upon to reinvent my own childhood time and again; in the process, I wonder how I can ever know the truth about who I am. If someone had told me what I was headed for in that little Renault—that I was stowing away in a shell, bound to wake up to an alien life on a persistently foreign shore—I surely would not have done it. But no one warned me. My culture, as I understand it, values independence above all things—in part to ensure a mobile labor force, grease for the machine of a capitalist economy. Our fairy tale commands: Little Pig, go out and seek your fortune! So I did.

Many years ago I read that the Tohono O'odham, who dwell in   32
the deserts near here, traditionally bury the umbilicus of a newborn son or daughter somewhere close to home and plant a tree over it, to hold the child in place. In a sentimental frame of mind, I did the same when my own baby's cord fell off. I'm staring at the tree right now, as I write—a lovely thing grown huge outside my window, home to woodpeckers, its boughs overarching the house, as dissimilar from the sapling I planted seven years ago as my present life is from the tidy future I'd mapped out for us all when my baby was born. She will roam light-years from the base of that tree. I have no doubt of it. I can only hope she's growing as the tree is, absorbing strength and rhythms and a trust in the seasons, so she will always be able to listen for home.

I feel remorse about Buster's monumental relocation; it's a   33
weighty responsibility to have thrown someone else's life into permanent chaos. But as for my own, I can't be sorry I made the trip. Most of what I learned in the old place seems to suffice for the new: if the seasons like Chicago tides come at ridiculous times and I have to plant in September instead of May, and if I have to make up family from scratch, what matters is that I do have sisters and tomato plants, the essential things. Like Buster, I'm inclined to see the material backdrop of my life as mostly immaterial, compared with what

moves inside of me. I hold on to my adopted shore, chanting private vows: wherever I am, let me never forget to distinguish *want* from *need*. Let me be a good animal today. Let me dance in the waves of my private tide, the habits of survival and love.

Every one of us is called upon, probably many times, to start a new life. A frightening diagnosis, a marriage, a move, loss of a job or a limb or a loved one, a graduation, bringing a new baby home: it's impossible to think at first how this all will be possible. Eventually, what moves it all forward is the subterranean ebb and flow of being alive among the living.   34

In my own worst seasons I've come back from the colorless world of despair by forcing myself to look hard, for a long time, at a single glorious thing: a flame of red geranium outside my bedroom window. And then another: my daughter in a yellow dress. And another: the perfect outline of a full, dark sphere behind the crescent moon. Until I learned to be in love with my life again. Like a stroke victim retraining new parts of the brain to grasp lost skills, I have taught myself joy, over and over again.   35

It's not such a wide gulf to cross, then, from survival to poetry. We hold fast to the old passions of endurance that buckle and creak beneath us, dovetailed, tight as a good wooden boat to carry us onward. And onward full tilt we go, pitched and wrecked and absurdly resolute, driven in spite of everything to make good on a new shore. To be hopeful, to embrace one possibility after another—that is surely the basic instinct. Baser even than hate, the thing with teeth, which can be stilled with a tone of voice or stunned by beauty. If the whole world of the living has to turn on the single point of remaining alive, that pointed endurance is the poetry of hope. The thing with feathers.   36

What a stroke of luck. What a singular brute feat of outrageous fortune: to be born to citizenship in the Animal Kingdom. We love and we lose, go back to the start and do it right over again. For every heavy forebrain solemnly cataloging the facts of a harsh landscape, there's a rush of intuition behind it crying out: High tide! Time to move out into the glorious debris. Time to take this life for what it is.   37

MEANINGS AND VALUES

1. In paragraph 22, Kingsolver says, "It's starting to look as if the most shameful tradition of Western civilization is our need to deny we are animals." In what ways, according to the essay, are we like other animals?

2. What are the superficial ways Buster resembles humans (see pars. 5, 8, 9, and 10)? What are the important (even profound) similarities (see pars. 11, 12, 15, 19, 30, and 33)?

3. Paragraphs 15–19 of this essay are devoted to some of the disruptions and problems created by contemporary ways of living. What answers or responses to these problems does the writer offer in paragraph 19? How do the problems and the responses help unify the essay? (See "Guide to Terms": *Unity.*)

EXPOSITORY TECHNIQUES

1. At what point in the essay does Kingsolver first make an analogy between the hermit crab and herself?

2. For what purposes does the author raise, and then dismiss, the comparison of hermit crab behaviors and those of humans and other animals in terms of their correspondence to cycles of the moon? (In answering this question, consider both the scientific reasons and those related to the purpose and design of her essay.)

3. The writer divides this essay into four parts (pars. 1–14, 15–22, 23–28, and 29–37). Explain the content and purpose of each part, and tell why you think she chose to put them in this particular order. (Guide: *Purpose.*)

4. Discuss how the contrast between "wants" and "needs" at the end of paragraph 28 serves as a transition to the next paragraph and those that follow. (Guide: *Transition.*)

5. Discuss how the question "What does it mean, anyway, to be an animal in human clothing?" (par. 19) acts as a transition both within the paragraph and within the essay as a whole. (Guide: *Transition.*) Can the passage be considered a rhetorical question? Why? (Guide: *Rhetorical Questions.*)

6. Kingsolver introduces some briefer analogies in paragraphs 32 and 36. What are they? Do they undermine or add to the effectiveness of the larger analogy around which the essay is constructed? In what ways? (Guide: *Evaluation.*)

DICTION AND VOCABULARY

1. Discuss how the repetition of the word "tide" and related words helps to unify this essay. (Guide: *Unity.*)

2. In many places, Kingsolver mixes styles and kinds of vocabulary (diction) in imaginative ways. Examine paragraph 11 and note the instances in which she has chosen scientific terms and phrases rather than familiar, less formal wording. What seems to be the reason for her word choices. Do the same for instances of notably informal language. (Guide: *Diction; Colloquial Expressions.*) What effect does the mixed diction in the paragraph have on its overall style and tone?

(Guide: *Style/Tone.*) How does the mixture serve, or fail to serve the author's purposes?

3. If you do not know the meaning of any of the following words, look them up in a dictionary: murexes, whelks, (par. 2); deficit, terrarium, cockleshell (7); preening, ludicrous (8); hyperactivity (10); menses, synchrony, ovulate, lyricists, impetuous (11); crustacean (12); siphoning, briny, ebbed (13); tableau, pantheon, yen, proclivity, furtively (19); deference, anachronisms, vainglories (20); copulation, ostracize (21); topographical (24); lauded (26); longevity (27); dispassionate (30); verdant (31); umbilicus (32).

READ TO WRITE

1. **Collaborating:** As mentioned in Question 3 of Expository Techniques Kingsolver divides this essay into four parts (pars. 1–14, 15–22, 23–28, and 29–37). In a group, have each member individually focus on the analogies presented in one of these sections and critique the effectiveness of them. Compare your critiques. Do you all have similar responses to the quality of the analogies as well as the writing overall? Why or why not? Individually, write a short essay answering this question.

2. **Considering Audience:** The theme of this essay is easy to perceive for a reader who has had major life changes. Kingsolver shares her life shifts openly and relates them directly to Buster's environmental changes. Yet this piece is also effective for people who have experienced little changes in their lives. Why? Point to specific paragraphs to explain your response.

3. **Developing an Essay:** Comparing your behavior to that of a pet, as Kingsolver does, can have several advantages for you as a writer. You probably observed a pet's behavior in detail over a long period of time more carefully than you observed the activities of any other animal. You have seen the pet react to the same or similar situations that you have encountered. Follow Kingsolver's lead and prepare an essay on human and animal behavior based on your experiences with a pet.

(NOTE: Suggestions for topics requiring development by use of ANALOGY follow.)

Writing Suggestions for Chapter 6

ANALOGY

In any normal situation, the analogy is chosen to help explain a theme-idea that already exists—such as those in the first group below. But for classroom training, which is bound to be somewhat artificial, it is permissible to work from the other direction, to develop a theme that fits a preselected analogy-symbol.

1. State a central theme about one of the following general topics or a suitable one of your own, and develop it into a composition by use of an analogy of your own choosing.

   a. A well-organized school system.

   b. Starting a new business or other enterprise.

   c. The long-range value of programs for underprivileged children.

   d. Learning a new skill.

   e. The need for cooperation between management and labor.

   f. Today's intense competition for success.

   g. Dealing with stress.

   h. The results of ignorance.

2. Select an analogy-symbol from the list below and fashion a theme that it can illustrate. Develop your composition as instructed.

   a. A freeway at commuting time.

   b. Building a road through a wilderness.

   c. Building a bridge across a river.

   d. A merry-go-round.

   e. A wedding or a divorce.

   f. A car wash.

   g. Flood destruction of a levee.

   h. The tending of a young orchard.

   i. An animal predator stalking prey.

   j. A baseball game.

   k. A juggling act.

   l. An oasis.

   m. A duel.

   n. An airport.

COLLABORATIVE ACTIVITIES

1. Working with a partner, choose a topic from a–h in Exercise 1 on p. 234, and decide on an appropriate analogy. One member of the pair should outline the points that need to be made about the theme. The other member should outline comparative (analogous) details. Combine the two outlines, and write a well-developed essay from the combined plan.

2. In groups of three or more come up with an appropriate analogy for the theme of "adapting to college life in the freshman year." Members should brainstorm to determine the best point of analogy. Once you determine that as a group, each member should provide one point of expansion that fits the analogy, and group members should then write essays of their own drawing on material developed by the group and adding their own ideas and examples.

7

Explaining Through *Process Analysis*

Process analysis focuses on *how* something happens. As an expository pattern, it appears most frequently in *instructions* that tell us how to do something or in *explanations* that explain how something is or was done. Instructions can range from the simple and everyday to the complex and challenging: from the directions for using a new appliance or piece of electronic equipment to a detailed plan showing how to make the United Nations more effective. Effective instructions do more than simply list the steps to be taken. They generally provide detailed justification for individual steps or for the plan as a whole, and they take into account readers' background knowledge and abilities.

Explanations, on the other hand, might explain the stages of a wide variety of operations or actions, of mental or evolutionary process—how stress affects judgment and health, how volcanoes cause earthquakes and mudslides, or how digital telephones work. Effective explanations take into account the things readers want or need to know about, but they can also appeal to curiosity and imagination. You can speculate how space exploration might work or how societies might be better organized.

The following process analysis by L. Rust Hills shows how process analysis can be used in imaginative ways to talk about everyday matters. It takes the form of a set of directions, and though it is short, it is a whole essay in miniature. The second example is an explanation that helps readers understand some of the reasons hurricanes can be so dangerous.

What to Do About Soap Ends
This is admittedly not a problem qualitative on the order of what to do about the proliferation of nuclear weaponry, but quantitatively

it disturbs a great deal of Mankind—all those millions, in fact, who've ever used a bar of soap—except, of course, me. I've solved the problem of what to do about those troublesome, wasteful, messy little soap ends, and I'm ready now to deliver my solution to a grateful world.

The solution depends on a fact not commonly known, which I discovered in the shower. Archimedes made his great discovery about displacement ("Eureka!" and all that) in the bathtub, but I made mine in the shower. It is not commonly known that if, when you soap yourself, you hold *the same side* of the bar of soap cupped in the palm of your hand, that side will, after a few days, become curved and rounded, while the side of the bar you're soaping yourself *with* will become flat. (In between showers or baths, leave the bar curved side down so it won't stick to whatever it's resting on.) When the bar diminishes sufficiently, the flat side can be pressed onto a new bar of soap and will adhere sufficiently overnight to become, with the next day's use, a just slightly oversized new bar, ready to be treated in the same way as the one that came before it, in perpetuity, one bar after another, down through the length of your days on earth, with never a nasty soap end to trouble you ever again. Eureka, and now on to those nuclear weapons. Man is at his best, I feel, when in his problem-solving mode.

—L. Rust Hills

It's not the wind, though, that's the most dangerous part of a hurricane. It's the water, especially when something called the "storm surge" occurs. As the low-pressure eye of the hurricane sits over the ocean, the sea level literally rises into a dome of water. For every inch drop in barometric pressure, the ocean rises a foot higher. Now, out at sea, that means nothing. The rise is not even noticeable. But when that mound of water starts moving toward land, the situation becomes crucial. As the water approaches a shallow beach, the dome of water rises. It may rise ten to fifteen feet in an hour and span fifty miles. Like a marine bulldozer, the surge may rise up twenty feet high, crash onto land, and wash everything away. Then with six- to eight-foot waves riding atop this mound of water, the storm surge destroys buildings, trees, cars, and anything else in its path. It's this storm surge that accounts for 90 percent of the deaths during a hurricane.

—Ira Flatow, "Storm Surge"

WHY USE PROCESS ANALYSIS?

In almost every part of our lives, we rely on **instructions.** They help us cook a meal, repair a car, get to a vacation spot, perform an experiment, and calculate income tax. Essays offering instruction appear in newspapers, magazines, and books on topics from fashion, fitness, and sports to technology, pets, and personal relationships.

We turn to **explanations** not when we want to do things but when we want to understand how things work. Explanations can focus on mechanical or technical subjects (how computer operating systems work), on social matters (how societies create groups of insiders and outsiders), on psychological topics (how stress builds up), or on natural subjects (how cancer cells take over from normal cells).

Process analysis can have imaginative uses as well, helping us speculate about building floating cities, changing our diets for better health, or considering steps that might close the ozone hole over the South Pole. Writers sometimes explain a process in order to amuse or criticize—analyzing with a critical eye some aspects of behavior (as do Kilbourne and Mitford in this chapter) or looking at some surprising natural phenomenon (as does Gup). And process analysis often appears in combination with other expository patterns. You might use it to help readers understand the steps by which a cause (meditating) leads to an effect (reduced physical and mental stress), for example. Or you might explain differences in the processes of forming social relationships as part of an essay contrasting the behaviors of men and women.

Expository writing built around process analysis generally responds to a need for information and understanding. The need may be immediate (how to prepare for an upcoming sales meeting or an exam). It may be practical or helpful (understanding the ways our bodies respond to stress; strategies for incorporating a healthy diet and exercise into a busy schedule). Or it may be a matter of curiosity or a desire for understanding (discovering how puppeteers in Indonesia create hours-long shows that appeal to both children and adults; investigating the ways our brains process information).

CHOOSING A STRATEGY

Having encountered instructions and explanations many times before, your readers will probably expect you to employ some basic strategies. For example, they will expect the opening of a set of instructions to announce its purpose, establish the need for a step-by-step explanation of the process, and indicate any materials needed to accomplish it. The way you choose to accomplish these things should vary from situation to situation and topic to topic, however. If you are addressing a need your readers can readily recognize, such as finding effective ways to take a test, make a speech, or apply for a student loan, you might begin with a brief example of how important such knowledge is. Or you might even state the need directly: "Would you like to know how to give a speech without getting so flustered that you forget half of what you planned to say?" or "Wouldn't you like to know how to get a student loan without all the hassle and paperwork most people encounter?"

In many instances, however, you will have to convince readers that they ought to be interested in the instructions you are offering. This is the situation Heather Kaye faced when she decided to tell readers how to play the game "Bones." In response, she created an opening paragraph reminding her readers how often they get bored and telling them of the simple equipment they will need to pass the time with an amusing game.

> When boredom strikes, what can you do if you are tired of computer games, don't like chess, and don't have the money or time to go to a movie? Just collect a pad of paper, a pen, six dice, and a friend, and you are ready to play a game called "Bones." Bones provides fun and excitement, and you don't have to be Einstein to learn how to play. It is a game of chance and luck, laughter and friendship.

For an explanation, however, you may need to appeal to readers' curiosity or their desire for understanding (practical or otherwise). Emphasizing the mystery, adventure, or even oddity of a process will engage most readers' curiosity: What bodily processes allow pearl divers to stay under water for several minutes when most of us can hold our breaths for only ten or twenty seconds? How do bats produce a kind of "radar" that enables them to fly in the dark and catch minute insects? When you appeal to readers' desire for understanding, you will be most likely to succeed when you suggest a practical dimension for the knowledge. For instance, some readers interested in the natural world may be interested in the complex stages of the honey-making process. Yet to attract the majority of readers you may need to suggest that such knowledge can help them understand honey's virtues as a sweetener or to choose among different kinds of honey as they shop.

Most process analyses are organized into simple, chronological units, either the *steps* involved in accomplishing the task or the *stages* of operation. In planning a set of instructions, begin by breaking it down into steps, approaching the activity as if you were doing it for the first time so that you do not leave out any necessary elements that have become so routine you might easily overlook them. Then create an organization that will help readers keep track of the many steps, perhaps dividing the task into several units, each containing smaller steps. Consider building your plan around a framework like the following.

> Introduction: Need for the information, materials, statement of purpose
> Step 1: Explanations, details
> Substeps 1, 2, 3 . . . (if any)
> Step 2: Explanations, details
> Substeps 1, 2, 3 . . .
> Step 3: Explanations, details
> Substeps 1, 2, 3 . . .
> Summary (if necessary)

In planning an explanation, identify the various stages or components, including any that overlap, and create an organization that presents them in an easy-to-follow, logical order. If the process is complex, divide it into major components and subdivide each in turn, just as the following rough plan does.

> Introduction (tentative thesis identifying need for the information): Because most people do not understand the amount of energy, natural resources, and human effort needed to create paper, they use it wastefully; understanding the process and the resources it requires is an important first step for all of us concerned with preserving our environment.
> Stage 1: Bringing together natural resources
> a. Wood—logging
> b. Water—drawing from rivers or lakes
> c. Fuel for heat and power (oil, gas, or electric)
> Stage 2: Turning logs into pulp
> a. Grinding up logs (uses water and power) *or*
> b. Breaking wood into pulp using chemicals
> Stage 3: Turning pulp into paper
> a. Paper Machine
> 1) Feeding pulp into machine
> 2) Using heated screen to congeal pulp into a mushy sheet of paper
> b. Dryer
> 1) Using heat to further congeal pulp
> 2) Using rollers to stretch and thin the sheet (consumes energy)

Stage 4: Turning paper into paper products (energy and labor intensive)
   a. Creating giant rolls of paper
   b. Cutting and folding rolls of paper into tissues, newsprint, pads, paper towels, and other everyday products.

Maintaining the exact order of a process is sometimes of greatest importance, as in a recipe. But occasionally the organization of an analysis may present problems. You may need to interrupt the step-by-step format for descriptions, definitions, and other explanatory asides. Some processes may even defy a strict chronological treatment because several things occur simultaneously. In explaining the operating process of a gasoline engine, for example, you would be unable to convey at once everything that happens at the same time. Instead, you would need to present the material in *general* stages, each with subdivisions, so your readers could see each stage by itself yet also become aware of interacting relationships.

DEVELOPING A PROCESS ANALYSIS

In developing the paragraphs and sentences that make up an explanation of a process, you also need to pay attention to your readers' expectations. When you are presenting instructions, your readers will expect you to tell them of any necessary materials and will look for frequent summaries to allow them to check if they have followed the steps correctly. They will benefit from warnings of special difficulties they may encounter or any dangers the procedure entails. In addition, they will appreciate words of encouragement ("The procedure may seem strange, but it *will* work.") or reminders of the goal of the process ("No pain, no gain: the only way to a flat tummy is through the hard work of repeating these exercises.").

Effective explanations and instructions alike often have a visual element. Drawings can show how the parts of a mechanism fit together or help readers recognize the differences among the elements of a natural process, such as the growth of an insect or the eruption of a volcano. Pictures can help readers identify ingredients or components and show them what a finished product will look like.

To guide readers through the steps or stages of a process, to remind them of changes that will occur, or to highlight the sequence of events, consider using words that point out relationships among the various elements.

Words identifying different stages—*step, event, element, compo-
nent, phase, state, feature, occurrence*
Words emphasizing relationships in time—*after, next, while,
first, second, third, fourth, concurrently, the next week, later,
preceding, following*
Words indicating changes—*becomes, varies, transforms, causes,
completes, alters, revises, uncovers, synthesizes, cures, builds*

Make sure you include enough details to allow readers to visualize the steps or stages of the process, but not so many that the
details become confusing. Present major steps (or stages) in considerable detail, minor ones in less. If you choose to write in the second
person (*you*) as in a set of directions ("You should then blend the ingredients"), make sure you use this point of view consistently and
do not shift to the first person (*I* or *we*) or the third person (*He, she, it,*
or *they*) without good reason. If you choose *I* or *it* for your perspective, make sure likewise that your presentation is consistent.

Student Essay

Losing weight is not easy for most people, nor is the process a simple one, as Karin Gaffney explains in the essay that follows. As a result, she provided detailed explanations along with her dieting
instructions so that readers can understand not only *how* to diet but
also *why* they should follow certain steps and avoid others.

Losing Weight
by Karin Gaffney

Across the board, regardless of age,
gender, race, or background, most people
spend time trying to lose weight
(Williamson et al.). Some people want to
lose only five or ten pounds while others
worry about getting rid of seventy-five
pounds or more. As a result, weight loss
is both a universal concern and a highly
individualized matter.

Losing weight must mean a lot to
Americans. After all, they spend over
three billion dollars on weight loss

programs each year ("Rating" 353). If you think you need to diet, think again. Many people think they are overweight because they compare themselves to impossibly thin models or imagine themselves in the slimmest of new fashions. So if you think you need to diet, consult a doctor and other reliable sources of health information. Then go to a good weight loss program—if you really need one.

Why should you be careful about going on a diet? A study in 1988 by the Centers for Disease Control concluded that any change of weight either up or down led to a higher rate of heart disease in the people studied ("Losing" 350). This does not necessarily mean that you should forget about dieting, however, because weight loss can also help you avoid other health problems ("Losing" 348, 350).

To lose weight, some people turn to commercial diets and hospital programs, yet the majority rely on self help. For those people who are trying to lose weight on their own, I can offer some general advice along with a simple weight-loss program. The simple advice is no different from what most of us have already heard, but it probably still needs to be repeated: 1) cut down on high fat foods, 2) eat moderate portions of healthy food, and 3) get regular exercise. Above all, consult your doctor not only to determine whether you should diet but to make sure your dietary and exercise programs are appropriate for you (and not for the models and athletes who appear on exercise tapes or talk about their health and muscle power diets in magazines).

A person who is overweight probably has a diet heavy in fat (Beitz 281). A calorie of fat in food becomes part of body fat much more easily than does a calorie of carbohydrate, which is easily burned as energy (Delaney 46). In other words, the body often keeps the fat it takes in but the carbohydrates it uses up. Moreover, a gram of fat has about 2.25 times as many calories as one gram of carbohydrate or protein does (Beitz 281).

The first step in a healthy weight-loss plan is to reduce the fat in your diet. If you eliminate high-fat foods such as ice creams, cheese, hamburgers, and butter from your diet, your body will respond immediately to the change. Low-fat substitutes, such as low-fat milk, can also have a positive effect, as can steps like cutting the fat off meat or taking the skin off poultry ("Losing" 352).

The second step is to eat more foods that are low in fat but high in fiber and carbohydrates. Here are several choices:

1. Potatoes (baked, not fried, and without butter or sour cream)
2. Beans (pinto, kidney, lentils, and so on)
3. Whole grains (cereals, pastas, breads)
4. Fresh fruits
5. Skim milk (and skim milk products).

When you eat foods like these, your blood sugar levels stabilize and you get "filled up," yet you take in only about one-half the number of calories that fatty alternatives provide (Delaney 44–45).

The third step is to snack wisely. Limit your snacks, of course, and choose from foods like the following: string cheese, corn-on-the-cob (without butter), vegetables, angel food cake, pita bread, soft pretzels, fruits, bagels, nonfat yogurt, juice, animal crackers, or fig bars ("30 Low Fat" 3). Food companies have also been adding fat-free items to grocery shelves in recent years, so when you shop, look for low-fat frozen desserts, low-fat cookies, and the like.

The fourth step is to exercise regularly. Exercise can burn up to 200-300 calories per day (Delaney 46). You may also be surprised to learn that exercise can decrease your weight even if you do not radically change your eating habits. Regular exercise increases basal metabolism, the energy needed just to stay alive. One half of the calories in a person's diet, for example, can go to basal metabolism. Exercise can increase the basal metabolism rate so that a person can lose more calories by just living and breathing. The amount of muscle a person has also affects basal metabolism. A person with more muscle has a higher basal metabolism and burns up more of the calories in food through this means ("Losing" 357).

Your exercise routine does not have to be strenuous or exhausting like that of an Olympic trainee. Moderate exercise, such as one-half hour to an hour of good paced walking is beneficial. If you need an incentive to start your exercise program, remember that a person who goes from a non-exerciser to a moderate exerciser will notice the results more than someone going from moderate to advanced. There are other side benefits to exercise as well. For example, people who exercise regularly develop adult diabetes 40 percent less frequently than non-exercisers do ("Losing" 351).

The fifth step is to set reasonable goals for weight loss. Concentrate on losing a pound or two at a time, and try to maintain this small weight loss before continuing ("Losing" 350). This approach will help make you confident of your ability to lose weight and help you avoid the yo-yo effect of losing a lot of weight, then gaining it right back.

The final step is to keep several key points in mind.

1. Make eating right and exercising (not dieting) the focus of your attention and effort.
2. Concentrate on maintaining your healthy lifestyle so that you can make your weight loss permanent and benefit over the long term from good eating and exercise habits.
3. Remember that you are an individual and that the advice offered here may or may not apply to you. Always consult a doctor who knows you and your medical history.

Works Cited

Beitz, Donald C. "Nutrition." *McGraw-Hill Yearbook of Science and Technology.* 1993.

Delaney, Lisa. "The 'No-Hunger' Weight-Loss Plan." *Prevention* Sept. 1993: 43–46.

"Losing Weight: What Works, What Doesn't." *Consumer Reports* June 1993: 347–352.

"Rating the Diets." *Consumer Reports* June 1993: 353–357.

"30 Low Fat Foods to Grab." *Thinline* Sept./Oct. 1993: 3.

Williamson, David F., Mary K. Serdula, Robert F. Auclay, Alan Levy, and Tim Byers. "Weight Loss Attempts in Adults: Goals, Duration, and Rate of Weight Loss." *American Journal of Public Health* Sept. 1992: 82–89.

JOE BUHLER AND RON GRAHAM

Joe Buhler, a professor of mathematics at Reed College, has published many scholarly articles as well as essays for more general audiences. Among the latter are essays on science, juggling, and the game Go. Ron Graham is associated with Bell Labs in Murray Hill, New Jersey, and has had a distinguished career as a mathematician. He has published many articles in his field of research and his work has been honored with membership in the National Academy of Sciences. He is a past president of the International Juggler's Association.

Give Juggling a Hand!

This instructional essay, a particularly compact explanation of an intriguing activity, was first published in *The Sciences*. It reflects the authors' enjoyment of juggling as well as their expertise. By providing some historical background, clear directions, and interesting explanations, the writers make the activity seem as enjoyable to readers as it is to them.

Nothing could be simpler than a game of catch. But just add another ball or two and the game turns magical—the juggled balls take on a life of their own. Suddenly, simple motions and common objects blur into one stunning display after another. 1

In recent years, juggling has experienced a renaissance. Street performers and skilled amateurs are practicing the ancient art in parks, back yards, and on campuses around the globe. Membership in the largely amateur International Jugglers' Association (IJA) has more than doubled since 1979. 2

Juggling is actually 4000 years young. In Egypt, Asia, and the Americas, it was once associated with religious ritual. In medieval Europe, wandering minstrels often juggled; the term derives from these *jongleurs*. 3

Amazing jugglers imported from the Orient—in particular the "East Indian" Ramo Samee, who was said to string beads in his mouth while turning rings with his fingers and toes, and the 4

"Give Juggling a Hand" by Joe Buhler and Ron Graham from *The Sciences,* January/February 1984. Reprinted by permission of THE SCIENCES. Individual Subscriptions are $21 per year in the U.S. Write to: The Sciencies, 2 East 63rd Street, New York, NY 10021.

Japanese artist Takashima, who manipulated a cotton ball with a stick held in his teeth—convinced 19th-century Europeans that juggling could be extraordinary show business.

Perhaps the greatest juggler of all time was variety-show virtuoso Enrico Rastelli. By his death in 1931, he had taught himself to juggle eight clubs, eight plates or ten balls; he could even bounce three balls continuously on his head.   5

Most people assume that a skilled juggler can manage up to 20 objects. In fact, even five-ball juggling is very difficult and requires about a year to master. Only a few jugglers worldwide have perfected seven-ball routines. At the 1986 IJA competition, one entrant separately juggled nine rings, eight balls, and seven clubs.   6

Jugglers use a bewildering variety of objects, including bowling balls, whips, plastic swimming pools, cube puzzles, fruit, flaming torches, and playing cards. Performers trying for the largest number of objects usually choose rings, which allow a tighter traffic pattern and are stable when thrown to great heights. Several jugglers can manage ten or 11 rings, and some are trying for 12 or 13.   7

Clubs are the most visually pleasing objects to juggle. They're especially suited for passing back and forth between performers. Because they take up a lot of space when they rotate and must be caught at one end, juggling even five is tricky. Almost nobody can manage seven, even for a few seconds.   8

Throughout history, all jugglers—from South Sea Islanders to Aztec Indians—have used the same fundamental patterns: 9

The Cascade. Here, each ball travels from one hand to the other and back again, following a looping path that looks like a figure eight lying on its side. The juggler starts with two balls in his right hand, using a scooping motion and releasing a ball when his throwing hand is level with his navel. As the first ball reaches its highest point, the other hand scoops and releases a second ball, and as that one reaches *its* apogee, he throws the third. Skilled jugglers can keep three, five, or even seven balls going in a cascade, but never four or six. With an even number, balls collide at the intersection of the figure eight.   10

The Shower. In this more difficult pattern, the balls follow a circular path as they are thrown upward by the right hand, caught by the left and quickly passed back to the right. Since the right does all the long-distance throwing, the shower is inherently asymmetrical and, therefore, inefficient; it is difficult with more than three objects.   11

The Fountain. This figure allows for a large number of balls. In a four-ball fountain, each hand juggles two balls independently in a   12 circular motion. For symmetry, the number of balls is usually even. If the hands throw alternately and the two patterns interlock, it is surprisingly hard to discern that the fountain is made of two separate components and not one.

Because gravity causes objects to accelerate as they fall, a juggler has only a short time to catch and throw one ball before another drops into his hand—even if he throws high. A juggler who throws a ball eight feet in the air, for example, must catch it 1.4 seconds later, but throwing it four times that high only doubles the flight time.　13

The best way to understand juggling is to learn to do it yourself. Some people get the hang of the three-ball cascade in minutes, although most need at least a few days. Limit your sessions to ten minutes rather than frustrate yourself with a two-hour binge.　14

Step 1: One Ball. Practice throwing a ball from your right hand to your left and back, letting the ball rise to just above your head. Make the ball follow the path of a figure eight lying on its side, by "scooping" the ball and releasing it near the navel. Catch the ball at the side of your body, then repeat the sequence.　15

Step 2: Two Balls. Put one in each hand. Throw the ball in the left hand as in Step 1, and then, just as the ball passes its high point, throw the right-hand ball. Avoid releasing the second throw too early or tossing the balls to unequal heights.　16

At first it may be difficult to catch the balls. Don't worry. Focus instead on the accuracy and height of the throws. Catching will come naturally as soon as the throws are on target. If things seem hectic, try higher throws.　17

Step 3: Two Balls Reversed. Reverse the order of throws so that the sequence is right, then left.　18

Step 4: Three Balls. Now put two balls in your right hand and one in your left. Try to complete Step 2 while simply holding the extra ball. Pause, then do Step 3.　19

The third ball can make it difficult to catch the second throw. To solve this, throw the third ball just after the second reaches its high point. The sequence is thus right, left, right. At first it may be tough to persuade your right hand to make its second throw. Remember: catches are irrelevant in the beginning. Throw high, accurately and slowly. Don't rush the tempo, and don't forget the figure-eight pattern.　20

Once you've mastered the three-ball cascade you'll want to try other patterns. A juggler is never finished: there is always one more ball.　21

Meanings and Values

1. Are readers in general likely to find the topic of this essay interesting? Why or why not? How do the authors encourage readers to consider juggling an amusing or worthwhile activity? Are these reasons presented directly or indirectly?

2. People often think juggling is difficult because it *looks* difficult. What do the writers say about the process to convince readers that they can master it?

3. What purposes are served by the historical background in paragraphs 3, 4, and 5? (See "Guide to Terms": *Purpose*.)

Expository Techniques

1. What technique do Buhler and Graham use to begin the essay? To conclude it? What makes these techniques successful (or unsuccessful) in this particular essay? (Guide: *Introductions; Closings*.)

2. Why do the authors describe different juggling patterns before they provide specific advice on beginning to juggle? Would the selection be more effective or less effective if the order were reversed? (Guide: *Evaluation*.)

3. Which expository patterns, other than process analysis, do the authors use to make juggling readily understandable and to help readers believe that they can master it?

Diction and Vocabulary

1. Tell how the diction and vocabulary choices in paragraphs 10–12 help make juggling seem simple. (Guide: *Diction*.)

2. How does the diction in paragraphs 14–20 contribute to the message that getting started with juggling is not as difficult as most readers might think?

3. If you do not know the meaning of some of the following terms, look them up in a dictionary: renaissance (par 2); virtuoso (5); cascade (10).

Read to Write

1. **Collaborating:** Physical activities can be difficult or challenging, but so can mental, social, or artistic activities. Working in a group, discuss activities you undertake with some success that others might find difficult, and list as many as you can. From the list, choose several that you and other group members are interested in writing or reading about. Note which ones you might be able to explain in ways that will intrigue readers and teach them something useful. Choose

one as the topic for an essay and, as a group, prepare a plan for the essay.

2. **Considering Audience:** In the first seven paragraphs of their essay, Buhler and Graham offer a variety of information about juggling. Looking at each paragraph, describe the kinds of readers who might find the information it presents particularly interesting. Explain why you think these paragraphs are successful or unsuccessful in appealing to a wide range of readers.

3. **Developing an Essay:** Many sports and hobbies can seem difficult or mystifying. Drawing on Buhler and Graham's essay as a model, create a set of instructions to simplify a seemingly challenging, dangerous, or mysterious sport or activity. Make the activity interesting and encourage readers to try it.

(NOTE: Suggestions for topics requiring developing by use of PROCESS ANALYSIS are on p. 294 at the end of this chapter.)

JOHN MCPHEE

Born in 1931 in Princeton, New Jersey, JOHN MCPHEE studied at Princeton University and Cambridge University in England. McPhee wrote for *Time* magazine and is now a regular contributor to the *New Yorker*. McPhee has written twenty-two books on an astonishingly wide range of topics. His subjects include the history and popularity of oranges, in *Oranges* (1967); the pine barrens of central New Jersey, in *The Pine Barrens* (1968), the headmaster of a prep school, in *The Headmaster* (1966); the Scottish Highlands, in *The Crofter and the Laird* (1969); the Swiss army, in *La Place de la Concorde de la Suisse* (1984); and the geology of North America, in *Basin and Range* (1981), *In Suspect Terrain* (1983), *Rising from the Plains* (1986), *The Control of Nature* (1989), and *Assembling California* (1992)—collected in *Annals of the Former World* (1999).

Swimming with Canoes

"Swimming with Canoes," an essay from *New Yorker* magazine, contains several explanations of process which combine explanation with instruction. These explanations serve a larger purpose, however, as part of a story about growing up and learning the importance of practical knowledge and skill in a situation that might be life-threatening for someone who has not learned to swim with canoes.

I grew up in summer camp—Keewaydin—whose specialty was canoes and canoe travel. At the home base, near Middlebury, Vermont, were racks and racks of canoes, at least a hundred canoes—E. M. Whites and Chestnuts, mainly. They were very good wood-and-canvas keeled or keelless canoes, lake or river canoes. We were in them every day wherever we were, in and out of Vermont. We were like some sort of crustaceans with our rib-and-planking exoskeletons, and to this day I do not feel complete or safe unless I am surrounded by the protective shape of a canoe.

Now and again, Keewaydin let us take our canoes not so much onto the water as into it, during swim period. We went swimming with our canoes. We jounced. Jouncing is the art of propelling a canoe without a paddle. You stand up on the gunwales near the stern deck and repeatedly flex and unflex your knees. The canoe rocks, slaps the lake, moves forward. Sooner or later, you lose your balance and fall into the water, because the gunwales are slender rails and the stern deck is somewhat smaller than a pennant. From waters

1

2

deeper than you were tall, you climbed back into your canoe. If you think that's easy, try it.

After three or four splats, and with a belly pink from hauling it   3
over gunwales, you lost interest in jouncing. What next? You sat in your canoe and deliberately overturned it. You leaned hard to one side, grabbed the opposite gunwale, and pulled. Out you went, and into the water. This was, after all, swim period. Now you rolled your canoe—an action it resists far less when it is loaded with water. You could make your canoe spiral like a football inside the lake.

And before long you found the air pocket. Having jounced and   4
spiralled to the far end of your invention span, you ducked beneath the surface and swam in under your upside-down canoe. You rose slowly to miss a thwart—feeling above you, avoiding a bump on the head—and then your eyes, nose, mouth were in air, among chain-link streaks of white and amber light, the shimmers of reflection in a quonset grotto. Its vertical inches were few but enough. Your pals got in there with you and your voices were tympanic in the grotto. Or you just hang out under there by yourself. With a hand on a thwart, and your feet slowly kicking, you could breathe normally, see normally, talk abnormally, and wait indefinitely for a change of mood. You were invisible to the upside, outside world. Even more than when kneeling in a fast current, you were one with your canoe.

Kneeling in a fast current. Once in a while, we went to what is   5
now called Battell Gorge, north of Middlebury, to learn to deal with really fast, pounding, concentrated flow. Otter Creek, there, under-goes an abrupt change in physiolographic character. After meander-ing benignly through the marshes, woodlots, and meadows of the Champlain Valley, it encounters a large limestone outcrop, which it deeply bisects. By a factor of three or four, the stream narrows and the water squeezes into humps, haystacks, souse holes, and stand-ing waves as it drops ten feet in a hundred yards. Then it emerges from the high limestone walls and the darkness of overhanging hemlocks into the light of a pool so wide it seems to be a pond.

Like horse people, we showed up some distance above the head   6
of the gorge with trailers—racked trailers that each carried seven ca-noes. The gorge was a good place to learn how to deal with canoes in white water because it was violent but short. In that narrow, roar-ing flume, you didn't have to choose the best route—didn't have to look for what the *voyageurs* called the *fils d'eau*. There was pretty much one way to go. But you got the sense of a canoe flying in three dimensions; and the more you did it the slower it seemed, the shoot separating itself into distinct parts, as if you were in a balloon rising in sunlight and falling in the shadows of clouds.

One time, when I was about twelve, I went into the gorge in a   7
very old canoe that was missing its stern seat. (We didn't take the better boats there.) Two of us were paddling it. I was kneeling against the
stern thwart, which was so far back it was only eight or ten inches
from gunwale to gunwale, the size of my young butt. My right knee
was on the canoe's ribs, and my right leg extended so far back that my
foot was wedged in the V of the stern when the bucking canoe turned
over. Billy Furey was my partner, and we were doing all we could to
keep things even, but whatever we did wasn't good enough, and we
flipped near the top of the gorge. Billy was ejected. Among the countless wonders of the simple design of the native American canoe is the
fact that it ejects its paddlers when it capsizes.

This one could not eject me, because my foot was stuck. I strug-   8
gled to pull the foot free, but it wouldn't come. Upside down in billows of water, I could not get out. Understand: I have a life-long
tendency to panic. Almost anything will panic me—health, money,
working with words. Almost anything—I'm here to tell you—but an
overturned canoe in a raging gorge. When I was trapped in there, if
panic crossed my mind it went out the other side. I had, after all,
time and time again been swimming with canoes. There was purpose in letting us do that—a thought that had never occurred to me.
After I realized I was caught and was not going to be coming out
from under the canoe, I reached for the stern quarter-thwart, took
hold of it, and pulled my body upward until my eyes, nose, and
mouth were in the grotto. There, in the dancing light, I rode on
through the gorge, and when the water calmed down at the far end
I gave the canoe half a spiral and returned to the open sunlight.

Meanings and Values

1. McPhee describes himself as being like ". . . crustaceans with our rib-
   and-planking exoskeletons . . ." (par. 1). Explain the meaning of this
   simile. (See "Guide to Terms": *Figures of Speech*.) Why might he have
   chosen these particular examples for his comparison?

2. For what reason does McPhee describe himself and his friends as
   "horse people" (par. 6)? Beyond the use of trailers, what other similarities might exist between "horse" and "canoe" people?

3. What is the significance of the title of the essay? McPhee repeats this
   phrase in the last paragraph. In what context does he use it at the end
   of the essay? Does it evoke the same image as it does when used as
   the title? Explain your answer.

Expository Techniques

1.　McPhee explains several processes in his essay. Identify each one. How effective is his approach to analyzing processes? Why? (Guide: *Evaluation.*) How does McPhee connect these various processes to create a unified essay? (Guide: *Unity.*)

2.　McPhee uses much visual description in this essay. Do the descriptions help clarify the processes? If so, in what ways? What other purposes might they serve? (Guide: *Purpose.*)

3.　McPhee uses the second person (you) throughout this essay. Is this an effective technique for the essay? Why, or why not?

Diction and Vocabulary

1.　McPhee uses similes and metaphors in this essay to define and explain words. Identify all of the similes and metaphors that you can find. Which help clarify the meanings McPhee is trying to convey? What other roles do they play? (Guide: *Figures of Speech.*)

2.　Look up the following words in the dictionary: keeled (par. 1), gunwales (par. 2), thwart (par. 3), tympanic (par. 4), souse (par. 5), billows (par. 8). Does McPhee use these words in ways other than the primary definitions given in the dictionary? Which, if any, does he use with meanings that the dictionary does not describe? Can some of these meanings be considered *connotations* rather than *denotations* of the words? If so, which ones? (Guide: *Denotation/connotation.*)

Read to Write

1.　**Collaborating:** In a group, gather information on a local camp or organization that sponsors outdoor activities. Prepare a collaborative paper describing in detail the processes involved in one or more of the activities they sponsor.

2.　**Considering Audience:** Create a list of different kinds of readers who might be especially interested in reading this essay or others like it. Then create a "profile" for each kind of reader containing the kinds of activities or products that might also interest the reader. Drawing on your profiles (taking special note of any overlapping interests), prepare a brief description of what you consider an "ideal" reader for McPhee's essay.

3.　**Developing an Essay:** Choose an activity with which you are very familiar (i.e. dirt biking, surfing, playing a sport, shooting pool, etc.). Using McPhee's essay as a model, analyze and present several different processes associated with the activity.

(NOTE: Suggestions for essays requiring development by PROCESS ANALYSIS are on p. 294 at the end of this chapter.)

TED GUP

> TED GUP is a former writer for the *Washington Post* and *Time* maga-
> zine. His articles have appeared in magazines such as *National
> Geographic, Newsweek, Smithsonian, GQ, Sports Illustrated, The
> Chronicle of Higher Education, Mother Jones,* and the online publica-
> tions *JINN* and *Salon.* He has been William Randolph Hearst Visiting
> Professor at the University of Maryland's College of Journalism and
> currently teaches journalism at Georgetown University.

An Ant's Life Is No Picnic

> In this essay, which first appeared in *Smithsonian* magazine, Gup
> takes a humorous look at the process of setting up an ant farm and
> at the behavior of ants, both captive and wild. At the end of the es-
> say, however, he steps back from the events and draws from them
> an important insight into nature itself.

My wife told me it was a bad idea. I should have listened. The   1
subject was ant farms. Matthew, my 6-year-old, desperately
wanted one. Truth be told, I did, too. I remembered the one I'd had
as a boy. Inside was a miniature plastic farm with a tiny windmill,
silo and barn sitting atop a warren of tunnels teeming with activity.
There were lessons to be learned from ants. They were models of industriousness and teamwork. An ant farm, I argued, would be a
colony of virtues. And so I surprised Matthew one afternoon by
bringing home an ant farm.

This farm came with what it cheerfully called an "Ant   2
Certificate" which for the modest price of $1.50, could be redeemed
for real live ants. All I had to do was send away to some place out
West. A few weeks later, a small yellow envelope arrived. In bold
blue letters, it warned, "Keep from extreme heat & cold! This package contains Western Harvester Ants."

Inside was a narrow plastic vial with a message taped to the   3
side: "CAUTION: ANTS CAN STING!" Then there was this: "CAU-
TION: DO NOT TOUCH ANTS. Their sting may cause swelling and
itching, especially for those allergic to stings. Adult supervision recommended." These ants, the instructions said, were the best to observe because "they were aggressive."

Matthew watched as I gently tapped the vial, sliding the ants   4
into their new abode. One particularly feisty ant climbed out of the

top and tried to make a break for it. I stopped him with the soft pulpy ball of my index finger. I felt a shooting pain as a stinger at the end of the ant's gaster pierced my skin, injecting me with formic acid. After barely smothering a curse, I smiled at Matthew and only later, out of view, dressed my wound. These truly were ants from hell.

For several days, the new ants prospered, excavating tunnels and carting off our offerings of fruit and chocolate Girl Scout cookies. Then, one by one, they began to sicken and die. We offered the survivors more water, pears instead of apples, a few hours of indirect sunlight. And still they died.

I consulted the instructions. "You will be amazed at what these little engineers can do!" But Matthew and I were less than amazed. We sadly eyed the pile of dead bugs and one lone survivor.

About this time, something odd happened. We began to have ants in the kitchen. First just one or two strays, then more. These were not escapees from the farm, but the indigenous species—our own *Marylandis kitchenesis.* They flourished. Across the countertops they formed an endless processional, carrying off crumbs and congregating at spills, especially droplets of soda and maple syrup. Their numbers exploded. We put out ant traps, tiny toxic motels set along their trails. They ignored them. We bombed them with a pesticide and still they came.

Matthew was captivated. We were not living in an ant farm. He utterly forgot about the last remaining harvester ant. Alone, I attempted to nurse the survivor, who staggered across what had become a plastic Boot Hill. Meanwhile, my wife and I were daily grinding the wild ants under heel, or snuffing them out with paper towels, or subjecting them to ever more toxic agents. Rescue and exterminate, rescue and exterminate. It was sheer madness.

On Tuesday, the ant farm went out with the trash. The wild ants continue to plague us, a reminder that nature is rarely compliant and neither to be contained nor managed. Matthew, take note. The lesson may be unintended, but it is no less valuable.

MEANINGS AND VALUES

1. In paragraph 1, the author explains how he came to the decision to bring home an ant farm. He says, "There were lessons to be learned from ants. They were models of industriousness and teamwork. An ant farm, I argued, would be a colony of virtues." Does he believe his

own words? (See "Guide to Terms": *Irony.*) Why might he have made this argument, and to whom might he have made it?

2.   Why does Gup feel so strongly about trying to save the last surviving ant on the farm (par. 8)? How does he describe his attitude towards the ants in his kitchen? Explain his different reactions to the groups of ants.

3.   What is ironic about Gup's references to the captive ants as " . . . ants from hell" (par. 4)? (Guide: *Irony.*)

EXPOSITORY TECHNIQUES

1.   Paragraph 3 shares the warnings posted in an instruction form that accompanied the ant farm. How careful was the writer in following the suggested process? What is the result of his behavior?

2.   What about ants' behavior makes them so suitable for a process analysis? In answering this question, consider how they interact in colonies.

3.   What is the tone of this essay? (Guide: *Tone.*) How does the author feel about the subject that he is discussing? What evidence is there of his feelings in the essay? How does his feeling for the ants help shape the tone?

DICTION AND VOCABULARY

1.   Why does the author use the made-up phrase "Marylandis kitchenesis?" (Guide: *Diction.*) Is he trying in some way to elevate ants or to antagonize scientists? Explain your response.

2.   Use a dictionary to define the following words and use each appropriately in a sentence you create: formic (par. 4), indigenous (par. 7), compliant (par. 9).

READ TO WRITE

1.   **Collaborating:** Ted Gup hopes that young Matthew will learn some lesson from the experience described in the essay (par. 9). In a group, discuss childhood events or projects that had long-term effects on members of the group. Create a plan for an essay presenting these experiences and tying them together with a generalization about their effects. If the events involved learning a particular process, make sure your generalization takes this commonality into account.

2.   **Considering Audience:** This article was first published in *Smithsonian* magazine, a publication that often deals with topics of natural history and nature. Why might this essay be appropriate for *Smithsonian*? Why might it be inappropriate? Create a list of the different kinds of readers that might be interested in the essay. For each

type of reader, indicate which elements of the essay might be particularly appealing.

3.   **Developing an Essay:** Travel to a local zoo and take notes on the behavior of the captive animals that you see. Then research the lives of the same animals in the wild. Use your observations and research to write an essay comparing the daily lives of the animals in the captive setting with those in natural settings.

(NOTE: Suggestions for essays requiring development by PROCESS ANALYSIS are on p. 294, at the end of this chapter.)

JIM HARRISON

JIM HARRISON has written poems, novels, and screenplays. His books include *Legends of the Fall* (1980), *Wolf: A False Memoir* (1989), *Just Before Dark: Collected Nonfiction* (1991), *The Woman Lit by Fireflies* (1991), *The Theory and Practice of Rivers and New Poems* (1989), *After Ikkyu and Other Poems* (1996), *The Shape of the Journey: Collected Poems* (1998), and *Sundog: The Story of an American Foreman, Robert Corvus Strang* (1999).

Going Places

"Going Places" first appeared in *Outside* magazine. In this essay, Harrison presents an unusual set of directions, for drivers "obsessed with going places, pure and simple, for the sake of movement, anywhere and practically anytime." Since the people he claims to be addressing are not the kind likely to follow instructions step by step, he adopts a slightly different approach, offering instead a set of suggestions and precepts. At the same time, however, he speaks to those readers who are less adventurous or independent in their ways, providing a blueprint for adventure and (self-)discovery that he encourages them to follow if only in parts, on short journeys as well as long ones. By the end of the essay, most writers are likely to agree that Harrison's larger purpose is to suggest ways for readers to live richer, freer, and more imaginative lives.

Everyone remembers those kindergarten or first-grade jigsaw puz- 1
zles of the forty-eight states, not including Hawaii and Alaska, which weren't states when I was a child and perhaps for that reason are permanently beyond my sphere of interest. I'm not at all sure at what age a child begins to comprehend the abstraction of maps— Arthur Rimbaud's line about the "child crazed with maps" strikes home. Contiguous states in the puzzle were of different colors, establishing the notion that states are more different from one another than they really are. The world grows larger with the child's mind, but each new step doesn't abolish the previous steps, so it's not much more than a big child who finally gets a driver's license, certainly equivalent to losing your virginity in the list of life's prime events.

It is at this point that pathology enters: Out of a hundred dri- 2
vers the great majority find cars pleasant enough, and some will be obsessed with them in mechanical terms, but two or three out of the hundred will be obsessed with going places, pure and simple, for the sake of movement, anywhere and practically anytime.

"You haven't been anywhere until you've taken Route 2 through   3
the Sand Hills of Nebraska," they're liable to say, late at night.

"Or Route 191 in Montana, 35 in Wisconsin, 90 in West Texas,   4
28 in the Upper Peninsula of Michigan, 120 in Wyoming, 62 in
Arkansas, 83 in Kansas, 14 in Louisiana," I reply, after agreeing that
2 in Nebraska is one of my favorites. To handle Route 2 properly,
you should first give a few hours to the Stuhr Museum in Grand
Island to check on the human and natural history of the Great Plains.
If you don't care all that much about what you're seeing, you should
stay home, or, if you're just trying to get someplace, take a plane.

There is, of course, a hesitation to make any rules for the road;   5
the main reason you're out there is to escape any confinement other
than that of change and motion. But certain precepts and theories
should be kept in mind:

- Don't compute time and distance. Computing time and dis-   6
  tance vitiates the benefits to be gotten from aimlessness.
  Leave that sort of thing to civilians with their specious categories of birthdays, average wage, height and weight, the
  number of steps to second floors. If you get into this acquisi-
  tive mood, make two ninety-degree turns and backtrack for a
  while. Or stop the car and run around in a big circle in a
  field. Climbing a tree or going swimming also helps.
  Remember that habit is a form of gravity that strangulates.
- Leave your reason, your logic, at home. A few years ago I   7
  flew all the way from northern Michigan to Palm Beach,
  Florida, in order to drive to Livingston, Montana, with a
  friend. Earlier in life I hitchhiked 4,000 miles round-trip to
  see the Pacific Ocean. Last year I needed to do some research
  in Nebraska. Good sense and the fact that it was January told
  me to drive south, then west by way of Chicago, spend a few
  days, and drive home. Instead I headed due north into a blizzard and made a three-day backroad circle to La Crosse,
  Wisconsin, one of my favorite hideouts. When I finished in
  Nebraska, I went to Wyoming, pulled a left for Colorado and
  New Mexico, a right for Arizona, headed east across Texas
  and Louisiana to Alabama, then north toward home. My
  spirit was lightened by the thirty-five days and 8,000 or so
  miles. The car was a loaner, and on deserted back roads I
  could drive on cruise control, standing on the seat with
  shoulders and head through the sunroof.
- Spend as little time as possible thinking about the equip-   8
  ment. Assuming you are not a mechanic, and even if you are,

it's better not to think too much about the car over and above minimum service details. I've had a succession of three four-wheel-drive Subaru station wagons, each equipped with a power winch, although recently I've had doubts about this auto. I like to take the car as far as I can go up a two-track, then get out and walk until the road disappears. This is the only solution to the neurotic pang that you might be missing something. High-performance cars don't have the clearance for back roads, and orthodox four-wheel drives are too jouncy for long trips. An ideal car might be a Saab turbo four-wheel-drive station wagon, but it has not as yet been built by that dour land without sunshine and garlic. A Range Rover is a pleasant, albeit expensive, idea, but you could very well find yourself a thousand miles from a spare part.

- A little research during downtime helps. This is the place for   9
the lost art of reading. The sort of driving I'm talking about is a religious impulse, a craving for the unknown. You can, however, add to any trip immeasurably by knowing something about the history of the area or location. For instance, if you're driving through Chadron, Nebraska, on Route 20, it doesn't hurt to know that Crazy Horse, He Dog, American Horse, Little Big Man, and Sitting Bull took the same route when it was still a buffalo path.

- Be careful about who you are with. Whiners aren't appropri-   10
ate. There can be tremendous inconveniences and long stretches of boredom. It takes a specific amount of optimism to be on the road, and anything less means misery. A nominal Buddhist who knows that "the goal is the path" is at an advantage. The essential silence of the highway can allow couples to turn the road into a domestic mud bath by letting their petty grievances preoccupy them. Marriages survive by garden-variety etiquette, and when my wife and I travel together we forget the often suffocating flotsam and jetsam of marriage.

If you're driving solo, another enemy can be the radio or tape   11
deck. This is an eccentric observation, but anyone under fifty in America has likely dissipated a goodly share of his life listening to music. Music frequently draws you out of where you belong. It is hard work to be attentive, but it's the only game in town. D.H. Lawrence said that "the only true aristocracy is consciousness," which doesn't mean you can't listen to music; just don't do it all the

time. Make your own road tapes: Start with cuts of Del Shannon, Merle Haggard, Stravinsky, Aretha Franklin, Bob Seger, Mozart, Buffett, Monteverdi, Woody Guthrie, Jim Reeves, B. B. King, George Jones, Esther Lammandier, Ray Charles, Bob Wills, and Nicholas Thorne. That sort of thing.

If you're lucky, you can find a perfect companion. During a   12
time of mutual stress I drove around Arizona with the grizzly bear expert Douglas Peacock, who knows every piece of flora, fauna, and Native American history in that state. In such company, the most unassertive mesa becomes verdant with possibility.

- Pretend you don't care about good food. This is intensely dif-   13
  ficult if you are a professional pig, gourmand, and trencher-
  man like I am. If you're going to drive around America you
  have to adopt the bliss-ninny notion that less is more. Pack a
  cooler full of disgusting health snacks. I am assuming you
  know enough to stay off the interstates with their sneeze
  shields and rainbox Jell-Os, the dinner specials that include
  the legendary "fried, fried," a substantial meal spun out of
  hot fat by the deep-fry cook. It could be anything from a shoe
  box full of oxygen to a cow plot to a dime-store wig. In honor
  of my own precepts I have given up routing designed to hit
  my favorite restaurants in Escanaba, Duluth, St. Cloud
  (Ivan's in the Park), Mandan, Miles City, and so on. The
  quasi-food revolution hasn't hit the countryside; I've had
  good luck calling disc jockeys for advice. You generally do
  much better in the South, particularly at barbecue places with
  hand-painted road signs. Along with food you might also
  consider amusements: If you stop at local bars or American
  Legion country dances don't offer underage girls hard drugs
  and that sort of thing. But unless you're a total asshole, *Easy
  Rider* paranoia is unwarranted. You are technically safer on
  the road than you are in your own bathroom or eating a dinner of unrecognizable leftovers with your mother.
- Avoid irony, cynicism, and self-judgment. If you were really   14
  smart, you probably wouldn't be doing this. You would be
  in an office or club acting nifty, but you're in a car and no one
  knows you, and no one calls you because they don't know
  where you are. Moving targets are hard to hit. You are doing
  what you want, rather than what someone else wants. This is
  not the time to examine your shortcomings, which will certainly surface when you get home. Your spiritual fathers

range from Marco Polo to Arthur Rimbaud, from Richard Halliburton to Jack Kerouac. Kerouac was the first actual novelist I ever met, back in 1957 or 1958 at the Five Spot, a jazz club in New York City. I saw him several times, and this great soul did not dwell on self-criticism, though, of course, there is an obvious downside to this behavior.

- Do not scorn day trips. You can use them to avoid nervous col-   15
lapse. They are akin to the ardent sailor and his small sailboat. You needn't travel very far unless you live in one of our major urban centers, strewn across the land like immense canker sores. Outside this sort of urban concentration, county maps are available at any courthouse. One summer in Michigan's Upper Peninsula, after a tour in Hollywood had driven me ditzy, I logged more than 5,000 miles in four counties on gravel roads and two-tracks, lifting my sodden spirits and looking for good grouse and woodcock cover (game birds literally prefer to live in their restaurants, their prime feeding areas). This also served to keep me out of bars and away from drinking, because I don't drink while driving.

- Plan a real big one—perhaps hemispheric, or least national.   16
Atrophy is the problem. If you're not expanding, you're growing smaller. As a poet and novelist I have to get out of the study and collect some brand-new memories, and many of our more memorable events are that of the childish, the daffy and irrational. "How do you know but that every bird that cuts the airy wavy is an immense world of delight closed to your senses five?" asked Blake. If you're currently trapped, your best move is to imagine the next road voyage.

I'm planning a trip when I finish my current novel, for which I   17
had to make an intense study of the years 1865 to 1900 in our history, also the history of Native Americans. I intend to check out locations where I sensed a particular magic in the past: certain culverts in western Minnesota, nondescript gullies in Kansas, invisible grave-yards in New Mexico, moonbeam targets in Nebraska, buffalo jumps in Montana, melted ice palaces in the Dakotas, deserted but well-stocked wine warehouses in California. Maybe I'll discover a new bird or animal. Maybe I'll drive up a gravel road that winnows into a two-track that stops at an immense swale, in the center of which is a dense woodlot. I'll wade through the bog into the woods, where I'll find an old, gray farmhouse. In this farmhouse I'll find all my beloved dead dogs and cats in perfect health, tended by the

heroines in my novels. I'll make a map of this trip on thin buckskin that I'll gradually cut up and add to stews. Everyone must find his own places.

MEANINGS AND VALUES

1. Why does Harrison begin this essay with a reflection on experiences learning geography as a child? Is this an appropriate introduction for the remainder of the essay? Explain your response. (See "Guide to Terms": *Introductions, Evaluation.*)

2. Why does Harrison provide readers with statistics (though somewhat unscientific) in paragraph 2? Describe the types of people to whom Harrison refers.

3. Why (in paragraph 11) does Harrison refer to the tape deck and radio as potential enemies? What point might he be trying to make? How successful do you think his alternative is in avoiding the negative aspects of such equipment?

EXPOSITORY TECHNIQUES

1. Harrison's "list" (paragraphs 6–10) is not the same kind of step-by-step that Buhler and Graham present in "Give Juggling a Hand" (pp. 249–251). What type of organization does he use to present the process? How effective is this approach? (Guide: *Evaluation.*)

2. What predominant tone does Harrison use throughout this essay? (Guide: *Tone.*) Where does the essay vary in tone, and why?

3. What type of reality is Harrison attempting to shape or present in his essay? Why does he use quotations in paragraphs 3 and 4? What is the effect of these quotations in shaping reality?

DICTION AND VOCABULARY

1. For what level of reader is Harrison's work written? Make a list of the characteristics you think Harrison assumes his readers will have. What parts of the essay support your conclusions?

2. Highlight any words in the essay that are unfamiliar to you. Look up each of the words in a dictionary and use it appropriately in a sentence.

READ TO WRITE

1. **Collaborating:** From your own perspective, write a list of key elements for a good automobile "travel" experience. Then, working in a group, compare lists. Look for common threads and write out a plan

for an essay similar to Harrison's which expresses your collective thoughts on travel.

2. **Considering Audience:** People who travel frequently by automobile might respond positively to Harrison's essay. Even if they disagree with some of his points, they will likely understand his emphasis on the importance of the process of traveling by car. In writing, describe briefly how you might compose a similar kind of essay for people who generally travel by train, bus, or plane.

3. **Developing an Essay:** The term "rugged individualism" is often applied in a positive way to the character of Americans, particularly those who explored the western frontier. But the trait still shapes the behavior of some Americans today, including people who set out on cross-country drives with no particular destination. Write an essay comparing the concept of "going places" during the exploration and settlement of the western frontier to travel and exploration today. You may need to do some research on the exploration and settlement in nineteenth-century America for your essay.

(NOTE: Suggestions for essays requiring development by PROCESS ANALYSIS are on p. 294, at the end of this chapter.)

Issues and Ideas

Advertising and Appearances

- James B. Twitchell, *We Build Excitement*
- Jessica Mitford, *To Dispel Fears of Live Burial*
- Jean E. Kilbourne, *Beauty . . . And the Beast of Advertising*

Do appearances count? When they come to us on television, in movies, or through advertisements, they do—at least that is what the authors of the essays that follow suggest.

James Twitchell explains how the images and strategies of advertising create and maintain a culture of which we are a part: a culture based on ever-present images and texts encouraging us to buy brand-name products, "adcult," as he refers to it. Adcult makes one product appear better or more desirable and helps shape our tastes, choices, environment, and values, a process Twitchell analyzes in detail.

Jean E. Kilbourne offers a sharply critical analysis of the images of physical appearance and of behavior which dominate various media and have influenced our attitudes toward our bodies, our values, and our behaviors in harmful ways. She focuses especially on the ways women participate in and are affected by this process, but her conclusions also apply to society at large.

Jessica Mitford's treatment of our fascination with appearances has an even harder edge. She offers a bitingly satiric and humorous view of our concern with the appearance of the dead, a form of manipulation that amounts almost to a denial of the reality of death. Though she puts primary blame on the funeral industry for creating and maintaining this obsession with false appearances, she includes in her indictment all of us who willingly tolerate the sham process.

Taken together, these essays demonstrate the importance of media images in contemporary life and suggest ways of interpreting and analyzing these images that can lead to further writing.

JAMES B. TWITCHELL

JAMES B. TWITCHELL was born in Burlington, Vermont, in 1943. He received his B.A. (1962), M.A. (1966), and Ph.D. (1969) from the University of North Carolina—Chapel Hill. He has taught at Duke University, California State University—Bakersfield, and the University of Florida, where he is currently Alumni Professor of English. Though much of Twitchell's writing has appeared in scholarly journals and in books issued by university presses, his work is nonetheless interesting and accessible to a wide audience of readers. Among his books are *Forbidden Partners: The Incest Taboo in Modern Culture* (1986); *Dreadful Pleasures: An Anatomy of Modern Horror* (1987); *Preposterous Violence: Fables of Aggression in Modern Culture* (1989); *Carnival Culture: The Trashing of Taste in America* (1992) (nominated for a National Book Award and a National Book Critics Circle Award); and *Adcult USA: The Triumph of Advertising in American Culture (1996).*

We Build Excitement

In this selection from *Adcult USA* (1996), James Twitchell talks about the process by which advertising became part of our culture and now serves as a primary force in shaping our culture, our perceptions, and our values. The selection is primarily informational and makes use of numerous examples in its analysis of the process. Twitchell is critical, at times, of the work of advertisers, but his criticism is much less harsh than that of many other writers, for, as he admits in the preface to *Adcult USA*, "I have always loved advertising."

The Hatter in the Strand of London, instead of making better felt-hats   1
than another, mounts a huge lath-and-plaster Hat, seven feet high,
upon wheels; sends a man to drive it through the streets; hoping to be
saved *thereby.* He has not attempted to *make* better hats, as he was appointed by the Universe to do, and as with this ingenuity of his he
could very probably have done, but his whole industry is turned to
persuade us that he has made such! He too knows that the Quack has
become God.

—Thomas Carlyle, "Past and Present," 1843

Thomas Carlyle just didn't get it. The Hatter in the Strand of   2
London was not in the business of making hats to make better hats.
He made hats to make money. The Victorians may have commanded the manufacturer to make the best of what he set out to do,

but the culture of capitalism does not care so much about what he makes as about what he can sell. Hence the "best" hat becomes the most profitable hat. Ironically, perhaps he cannot make hats profitably unless he can market what he makes efficiently. The selling determines the making. And once he makes those best hats, especially if he has a machine to help him, heaven help him if he makes too many. If he has to spend some of his productive time acting like a nut in order to sell those hats, so be it.

The ingredients necessary to concoct an Adcult [culture of advertising, eds.] are not complex. The Hatter in the Strand of London is crucial. Because the Hatter probably has enough hats for his own use, he makes something that has exchange value. Assuming that he can control the retail price, the more he manufactures, the more he takes advantage of the economies of mass production and the greater the profit. To control that retail price however, he needs some method to differentiate his hat or he will produce more than he can sell. After all, because the product is partially machine made, it is essentially interchangeable with a competitor's product made with the same machinery.

The process of differentiation, called branding, is the key ingredient in all advertising. Make all the machine-made felt hats, biscuits, shoes, cigarettes, automobiles, or computer chips you want, but you cannot sell effectively until you can call it a Fedora, a Ritz, a Nike, a Marlboro, a Chevrolet, or an Intel 386. If everybody's biscuits are in the same barrel, and if they look pretty much the same, urging people to buy biscuits probably won't do the trick. Chances are, they won't buy your biscuit. As Thomas J. Barratt said at almost the same time that Carlyle was having at the Hatter, "Any fool can make soap. It takes a clever man to sell it."[1] Barratt was a clever man. He made a fortune by the end of the century by calling his soap Pears' Soap and making sure everyone knew about it by defacing miles of Anglo-American wall and newsprint space with "Have you had your Pears' today?" In many ways modern culture has been a battle between Carlyle and Barratt. If you aren't sure who won, look around you.

Adcult also requires purchasers with sufficient disposable income to buy your product. And it doesn't hurt if your audience members have enough curiosity to listen to you tell them your biscuits are different when they know all biscuits are the same. But

3

4

5

---

[1]E. S. Tuner, *The Shocking History of Advertising* (New York: Dutton, 1953).

watch out: this process is not without risk. When money is tight, brands take flight. For reasons no one can understand, from time to time markets fall apart, advertising loses its grip, and the charade has to be reenacted. Procter & Gamble spent billions building its soap brands, Philip Morris did the same with premium cigarettes, as did IBM with the personal computer, only to have the demand for their brands suddenly plummet. Generics appear to eat up what advertising created. Brands can suddenly become just commodities again. The Hatter in the Strand soon responds by dropping his prices and by making a still larger lath-and-plaster hat.

With those ingredients in the pot all an Adcult still needs is a   6
plasma, or conduit, between producer and consumer within which producers can, in the jargon of modern criticism, *inscribe* their message. The ever bigger lath-and-plaster hat is soon subject to diminishing returns. The brand may appear *on* his hat, but its name recognition is created *in* a medium. So along with his sign the Hatter may even decide to hire someone to advertise his product by voice. In the nineteenth century consumers still heard the cries of the costermonger (the coster is a kind of English apple) or other traders announcing their wares:

> *One-a-penny, two-a-penny, hot cross buns!*
> *One-a-penny, two for tup'ence, hot cross buns!*
>
> *Dust, O! Dust O! Bring it out today.*
> *Bring it out today! I shan't be here tomorrow!*
>
> *I sweep your Chimnies clean, O!*
> *I sweep your Chimney clean, O!*
>
> *Buy my Diddle Dumplings, hot! hot!*
> *Diddle, Diddle, Diddle, Dumplings, hot!*
>
> *Maids, I mend old Pans or Kettles,*
> *Mend old Pans or Kettles, O!*
>
> *Muffins, O! Crumpets! Muffins to-day!*
> *Crumpets, O! Muffins, O! Fresh to-day!*

Street cries and moving hats "set upon wheels" are no longer   7
major conduits in modern Adcult. True, the urban bus has become a billboard. And the billboard plastered on a truck is making a comeback in cluttered cities (the sides of such rolling billboards are lit fluorescently and can change panels every ten minutes), and the

human voice can still be heard on street corners.[2] But they are no match for ink and electrons.

With the advent of print and paste, signs moved to walls. From the late seventeenth century to the middle of the nineteenth the great cities of western Europe were nightly plastered over—sometimes twice a night—with what became known as posters. Seventeenth-century London streets were so thick with signs that Charles II proclaimed that "no sign shall be hung across the streets shutting out the air and light of the heavens." Although it was against the law, even Fleet Street Prison was posted. As the "post no bills" regulations took hold, posters became free-standing billboards. The "boards" grew so thick in America that people could barely see Niagara Falls through the forest of Coca-Cola and Mennen's Toilet powder signs. N. W. Ayer Company executives bragged that if all the boards they had erected for Nabisco were painted on a fence, the fence would enclose the Panama Canal on either side, from sea to shining sea.

8

What distinguishes modern advertising is that it has jumped from the human voice and printed posters to anything that can carry it. Almost every physical object now carries advertising, almost every human environment is suffused with advertising, almost every moment of time is calibrated by advertising.

9

Start the day with breakfast. What's on the cereal box but the Ninja Turtles, Batman, or the Addams Family? Characters real or imagined once sold cereal; now they *are* the cereal. Once Wild Bill Hickock, Bob Mathias, Huckleberry Hound, and Yogi Bear touted Sugar Pops or Wheaties. Now the sugar gobs reappear every six months, renamed to cross-promote some event. When the most recent Robin Hood movie was released, a Prince of Thieves Cereal appeared on grocery shelves. Alas, the movie did not show Mr. Hood starting the day with his own brand. But Kellogg has tried for this brass ring of promotion anyway. It has marketed cereals with Jerry Seinfeld and Jay Leno on the boxes and then gone on to buy commercial time on their network, NBC. It is of some comfort that while cereals sporting Barbie

10

---

[2]In a sense, of course, advertising in various media is ancient. Commercial speech starts with the snake's spiel in the Garden of Eden, is heard in the cries of vendors in ancient Persia, is seen on walls of Pompeii as the marks listing prices of various prostitutes, is carried in our surnames (as with Smith, Weaver, Miller, Taylor, Baker . . .), and remains in the coats of arms over European hostelries with names like the Red Crown, the Gold Fox, and the Three Stars as well as in the symbolic images of the barber's pole or the golden balls of a pawn shop.

and Donkey Kong have gone stale on the shelves, the redoubtable Fred Flintstone and his Flintstones cereal survive.

Go to school. The classroom is the Valhalla of place-based media. 11
Better than the doctor's office, the shopping mall, the health club, the hospital, and the airport, here you have the ideal—a captive audience with more disposable income than discretion. Advertising material is all over the place. For home economics classes Chef Boyardee supplies worksheets on how to use pasta; Prego counters with the Prego Science Challenge complete with an "instructional kit" to test the thickness of various spaghetti sauces. General Mills sends out samples of its candy along with a pamphlet, "Gushers: Wonders of the Earth," which encourages the kids to learn about geysers by biting the "fruit snack." Monsanto donates a video suggesting that the world cannot be fed without using pesticides; Union Carbide does the same, saying chemicals "add comfort to your lives." Exxon has an energy awareness game in which nonrenewable natural resources are not losers. K-Swiss sneakers provides shoes for participants in a video creation of an ad for . . . you guessed it. And Kodak, McDonald's, and Coca-Cola plaster a national essay contest about why kids should stay in school with corporate logos and concern. Clearly, one reason to stay in school is to consume more advertising.

Go shopping. The war, as they say, is in the store. Food shoppers 12
make almost two-thirds of their buying decisions when they set foot in the aisle. Capitalizing on these last-minute decisions is why grocers don't alphabetize soup sections, why all the raisin bran cereals are not bunched together, and why high-profit toothbrushes are both nestled with toothpastes and stacked almost at random throughout the store. With more than fifteen hundred new items introduced to supermarkets each month, the need to inform and convince the querulous shopper of the new product is intense. The experience of food buying has become an advertising adventure.

A company called Ad-Tiles puts its ads on the floors in 13
Pathmark stores, charging what amounts to 50 cents per thousand impressions. Flashing coupon dispensers are omnipresent, except near the upright freezers and open dairy case, because shoppers do not like to open doors to compare prices—too cold. They won't even open the door for coupons. The latest hot places for advertising are the checkout line and the shopping cart. The shopping cart, which revolutionized food shopping as much as self-service, because it determined the amount of food a shopper could buy, has come alive. VideOcart is here, almost. This shopping cart has a six-by-nine-inch screen affixed to what used to be the kiddie rumble seat, and in-

frared censors on the ceiling cause it to flash ads, messages, and recipes as you pass various products. The same technology that scans the Universal Product Code on your can of beans now scans the shopper. You are the can.

Go to a sporting event. It's football season. Let's go to a bowl   14 game. Which one? Or which product? The Orange Bowl has become the Federal Express Orange Bowl, the Cotton Bowl has become the Mobil Cotton Bowl, the Sugar Bowl has become the USF&G Sugar Bowl, and the Sun Bowl has become the John Hancock Bowl. Not to mention the Sunkist Fiesta Bowl (now the IBM OS/2 Fiesta Bowl), the Mazda Gator Bowl (now the Outback Steakhouse Gator Bowl), the Sea World Holiday Bowl, the Domino's Pizza Copper Bowl, the California Raisin Bowl, and everyone's favorite, the Poulan/Weed Eater Independence Bowl. For a while even the Heisman Memorial Trophy was up for grabs. Merrill Lynch paid $1.5 million for promotional rights but not for a name change. Not yet. No matter: Merrill Lynch already has a golf tournament.

Take a trip. Get away from Adcult. Weren't we told in the fa-   15 mous Cunard advertisement that getting there is half the fun? Hop in a taxi. Some urban cabs have alphanumeric signs that scroll ten ads per minute across a panel on the back of the front seat. Gannett, the billboard-and-newspaper conglomerate, has been experimenting with installing these "electronic gutters" in subway cars and has contracted with the Transit Authority of New York to put them in six thousand cars. Nothing revolutionary here, just the electrifying of the advertising card, which has been a staple of public transportation since the first trolley. The company has also introduced what it calls the brand train and the brand bus in which a sponsor can buy all the ad space on a particular vehicle that runs a specific route. So Donna Karan's DKNY line has taken over an entire ten-car train that runs under Lexington Avenue on Manhattan's East Side, endlessly running beneath DKNY's superstore at Bloomingdale's. Gannett also installed radio equipment in bus shelters around midtown Manhattan for a news and business station. The New York City Department of Transportation ordered Gannett to pull the plug—too much noise.

No destination is safe. The Russian government has even sold   16 space inside Red Square. For something less than $1 million your message can be part of the May Day celebration. Coca-Cola and Pepsi are already in Pushkin Square. For $100,000 the side of GUM, the largest department store in the world, is yours. Lenin's tomb is off-limits, but above Lenin's tomb is OK. For about $30,000 you can float a blimp. Who's itching to get onto Russian space? The usual suspects: AT&T, Reebok, Sara Lee, and of course the ever-present to-bacco companies.[3]

Finally, no matter where you go in this world or beyond, when   17
you get home, your credit card bill for the trip will eventually ap-pear. When it does, it may have that tear-off tag on the envelope upon which is printed yet another ad.

Almost as interesting as where advertising is, is where it might   18
be. Here are some of the more interesting venues contributed by ad-vertising men and women who make hundreds of thousands of dol-lars thinking up and trying out some of these locations:

- Subway tokens.
- The backs of chairs in commuter trains.
- The Gateway Arch in St. Louis.
- Postage stamps and paper currency.
- In place of the telephone dial tone.
- Polo ponies.
- The bottom of golf holes, to be observed while putting and then while removing the ball.
- Self-serve gasoline pumps. Messages scroll along with the amount of gas pumped.
- Rural mailboxes. Although the Postal Service prohibits ad-vertising on boxes, John Deere has produced a green and yel-low version that retails for about $50.
- Astronauts' uniforms.
- Postcards. Laden with advertising, they are given to patrons by restaurants.
- School buses.
- Slot machines. Why should they come up cherries and or-anges? Why not boxes of Tide?
- Catalogs. This has been done, most notably by *The Sharper Image*, but the reverse is almost as interesting—a recent *Lands' End* catalog included a story by David Mamet.
- Video games. "Cool Spot" is a game like "Pac Man," except it stars "Spot," the 7-Up mascot: "Yo! Noid" is a game centered

---

[3]Nor would you be ad free in outer space. For $500,000 NASA agreed that Columbia Pictures could cover a rocket with an ad for Arnold Schwarzenegger's *Last Action Hero* (the movie bombed before the missile flew). And Joel Babbit, an Atlanta ad exec, almost succeeded in launching a billboard high in the heavens. The space billboard was to be an unfolding screen set in geosynchronous orbit 250 miles above the equa-tor; in the evening it would appear to be about the size of the moon—just right for a logo. The usual suspects were interested, but the U.S. Department of Transportation nixed the idea.

around the Domino's Pizza character. "Mick and Mack: Global Gladiators" has a black hero who battles pollution. To get from level to level the player has to collect golden arches passed out by a gate-tending Ronald McDonald.

It may be of some comfort to critics of this use of the human   19
imagination that a new advertising medium has begun appearing *inside* advertising agencies. Called Media News, it appears on a never ending fifty-four-by-eight-inch alphanumeric display similar to the Dow Jones market ticker. Running across the board is information interspersed with thirty seconds of commercials. Advertisers pay $5,000 for thirteen weeks of ads in a medium described by its creators as "invasive without being aggravating." Poetic justice?

The rise of place-based (as it is known in the trade), in your face   20
(as it is experienced), or new media (as it is presented to the public) follows the principle that where blank space exists, there shall advertising be. The triumph of Adcult is attributable not so much to new products as to new media reaching new audiences. Each new invasion by commercialism is greeted with an outcry, followed by tentative acceptance, assumption, and expectation. And finally, of course, neglect.

MEANINGS AND VALUES

1.   What, according to the writer, did Thomas Carlyle fail to understand (see par. 1)? What key point about business and advertising does the writer make in rejecting Carlyle's point of view?

2.   What are the ingredients of an adcult, and where does the writer discuss them? Is this definition satisfactory? In what ways, if any, might it be improved?

3.   How does modern advertising differ from that of previous centuries? Be specific.

EXPOSITORY TECHNIQUES

1.   In what way are the italicized sentences beginning paragraphs 10, 11, 12, 14, and 15 linked to the second sentence in paragraph 9? Discuss how this linking provides coherence within the second half of the selection. (See "Guide to Terms": *Coherence.*) In what ways does paragraph 9, as a whole, help unify the selection? (Guide: *Unity.*)

2.   In which paragraphs does the writer employ extended examples? In which does he use clusters of brief examples? Which paragraphs

containing brief examples are especially effective? Why? Are any markedly less effective? Explain why.

3. How would you describe the overall tone of this selection? In what ways, if at all, does the tone add to or detract from the informational goals of the piece? Can the tone in paragraphs 10, 11, and 16 be considered either ironic or sarcastic? (Guide: *Irony*.) If so, does this tone undermine the writer's claim that "I have always loved advertising"? Explain. If not, what do you believe is the tone of these paragraphs?

DICTION AND VOCABULARY

1. Would you characterize the diction in paragraphs 11–13 as *specific* or *general*? As *abstract* or *concrete*? (Guide: *Specific/General; Concrete/Abstract*.) Cite examples to support your conclusions. How does the diction contribute to the purpose and effect of these paragraphs? (Guide: *Purpose*.)

2. Compare the diction in paragraphs 5–6 and 15–16. Which makes greater use of formal diction, and why? Which makes greater use of colloquial language, and why? (Guide: *Colloquial Expressions*.) To what extent does the writer use the connotations of terms as well as their denotations to criticize advertisers? (Guide: *Connotation/Denotation*.) Is this criticism harsh or mild, direct or indirect? Explain.

3. If you do not know the meaning of some of the following terms, look them up in a dictionary: lath, quack (par. 1); differentiate (3); charade, plummet (5); conduit, inscribe, costermonger (6); suffused, calibrated (9); redoubtable (10); Valhalla (11); omnipresent (13); invasive (18); attributable, tentative, assumption (19).

READ TO WRITE

1. **Collaborating:** Advertising is a good subject for expository writing. Working with a group make up a set of questions about advertising and then list details, ideas, and possible topics under each. When you are finished, look through the list to see if you can discover possible focuses for essays. Choose the two you find most promising, and develop an essay plan for each. Here are several questions to get you started: Other than manufacturers, who sponsors advertising? What different kinds of advertising do we encounter in a typical day? Do different kinds of advertising achieve their effects through different processes?

2. **Considering Audience:** Twitchell uses many examples in his essay, and in so doing he represents the tastes, values, and interests of many groups of readers. But he does not include all possible readers. Which significant groups (ethnic, occupational, religious, or otherwise) are not represented in the examples? Do any of these omissions seriously weaken the essay? If so, which ones? Suggest several exam-

ples that might be added to the essay to broaden its appeal or make it more effective in some other way.

3.   **Developing an Essay:** Drawing on "We Build Excitement" as a model, create an essay of your own showing how the contemporary form of some activity or process (fishing, basketball, clothing design and manufacture, for example) differs from earlier forms. Also explain the special features of the contemporary process in detail.

(NOTE: Suggestions for topics requiring development by PROCESS ANALYSIS are on p. 294 at the end of this chapter.)

JESSICA MITFORD

JESSICA MITFORD was born in 1917, the daughter of an English peer. Her brother was sent to Eton, but she and her six sisters were educated at home by their mother. At the age of nineteen Mitford left home, eventually making her way to the United States in 1939. She made her home in San Francisco and she became an American citizen in 1944. She did not begin her writing career until she was thirty-eight. Her books are *Lifeitselfmanship* (1956); her autobiography, *Daughters and Rebels* (1960); the bestseller *The American Way of Death* (1963); *The Trial of Dr. Spock* (1969); *Kind and Usual Punishment* (1973), a devastating study of the American penal system; *A Fine Old Conflict* (1977); and *Poison Penmanship* (1979). Mitford's articles have appeared in the *Atlantic, Harper's,* and *McCall's.*

To Dispel Fears of Live Burial

"To Dispel Fears of Live Burial" (editors' title) is a portion of *The American Way of Death,* a book described in *The New York Times* as a "savagely witty and well-documented exposé." The "savagely witty" style, evident in this selection, does not obscure the fact of its being a tightly organized, step-by-step process analysis.

Embalming is indeed a most extraordinary procedure, and one must wonder at the docility of Americans who each year pay hundreds of millions of dollars for its perpetuation, blissfully ignorant of what it is all about, what is done, how it is done. Not one in ten thousand has any idea of what actually takes place. Books on the subject are extremely hard to come by. They are not to be found in most libraries or bookshops. 1

In an era when huge television audiences watch surgical operations in the comfort of their living rooms, when, thanks to the animated cartoon, the geography of the digestive system has become familiar territory even to the nursery school set, in a land where the satisfaction of curiosity about almost all matters is a national pastime, the secrecy surrounding embalming can, surely, hardly be at- 2 tributed to the inherent gruesomeness of the subject. Custom in this regard has within this century suffered a complete reversal. In the early days of American embalming, when it was performed in the home of the deceased, it was almost mandatory for some relative to stay by the embalmer's side and witness the procedure. Today, family members who might wish to be in attendance would certainly be dissuaded by the funeral director. All others, except apprentices, are excluded by law from the preparation room.

A close look at what does actually take place may explain in large measure the undertaker's intractable reticence concerning a procedure that has become his major *raison d'être.* Is it possible he fears that public information about embalming might lead patrons to wonder if they really want this service? If the funeral men are loath to discuss the subject outside the trade, the reader may, understandably, be equally loath to go on reading at this point. For those who have the stomach for it, let us part the formaldehyde curtain 3

The body is first laid out in the undertaker's morgue—or rather, Mr. Jones is reposing in the preparation room—to be readied to bid the world farewell. 4

The preparation room in any of the better funeral establishments has the tiled and sterile look of a surgery, and indeed the embalmer-restorative artist who does his chores there is beginning to adopt the term "dermasurgeon" (appropriately corrupted by some mortician-writers as "demisurgeon") to describe his calling. His equipment, consisting of scalpels, scissors, augers, forceps, clamps, needles, pumps, tubes, bowls and basins, is crudely imitative of the surgeon's as is his technique, acquired in a nine- or twelve-month post-high-school course in an embalming school. He is supplied by an advanced chemical industry with a bewildering array of fluids, sprays, pastes, oils, powders, creams, to fix or soften tissue, shrink or distend it as needed, dry it here, restore the moisture there. There are cosmetics, waxes and paints, to fill and cover features, even plaster of Paris to replace entire limbs. There are ingenious aids to prop and stabilize the cadaver: A Vari-Pose Head Rest, the Edwards Arm and Hand Positioner, the Repose Block (to support the shoulders during the embalming), and the Throop Foot Positioner, which resembles an old-fashioned stocks. 5

Mr. John H. Eckels, president of the Eckels College of Mortuary Science, thus describes the first part of the embalming procedure: "In the hands of a skilled practitioner, this work may be done in a comparatively short time and without mutilating the body other than by slight incision—so slight that it scarcely would cause serious 6 inconvenience if made upon a living person. It is necessary to remove the blood, and doing this not only helps in the disinfecting, but removes the principal cause of disfigurements due to discoloration."

Another textbook discusses the all-important time element: "The earlier this is done, the better, for every hour that elapses between death and embalming will add to the problems and complications encountered . . . ." Just how soon should one get going on the embalming? The author tells us, "On the basis of such scanty information made available to this profession through its rudimentary and haphazard system of technical research, we must conclude that the best results are to be obtained if the subject is embalmed before life is completely extinct—that is, before cellular death has occurred. In the average case, this would mean within an hour after somatic death." For those who feel that there is something a little rudimentary, not to say haphazard, about this advice, a comforting thought is offered by another writer. Speaking of fears entertained in early days of premature burial, he points out, "One of the effects of embalming by chemical injection, however, has been to dispel fears of live burial." How true; once the blood is removed, chances of live burial are indeed remote.

To return to Mr. Jones, the blood is drained out through the veins and replaced by embalming fluid pumped in through the arteries. As noted in *The Principles and Practices of Embalming*, "Every operator has a favorite injection and drainage point—a fact which becomes a handicap only if he fails or refuses to forsake his favorites when conditions demand it." Typical favorites are the carotid artery, femoral artery, jugular vein, subclavian vein. There are various choices of embalming fluid. If Flextone is used, it will produce a "mild, flexible rigidity. The skin retains a velvety softness, the tissues are rubbery and pliable. Ideal for women and children." It may be blended with B. and G. Products Company's Lyf-Lyk tint, which is guaranteed to reproduce "nature's own skin texture . . . the velvety appearance of living tissue." Suntone comes in three separate tints: Suntan; Special Cosmetic Tint, a pink shade "especially indicated for young female subjects"; and Regular Cosmetic Tint, moderately pink.

About three to six gallons of dyed and perfumed solution of formaldehyde, glycerin, borax, phenol, alcohol, and water are soon circulating through Mr. Jones, whose mouth has been sewn together with a "needle directed upward between the upper lip and gum and brought out through the left nostril," with the corners raised slightly "for a more pleasant expression." If he should be bucktoothed, his

7

8

9

teeth are cleaned with Bon Ami and coated with colorless nail polish. His eyes, meanwhile, are closed with flesh-tinted eye caps and eye cement.

The next step is to have at Mr. Jones with a thing called a trocar. 10 This is a long, hollow needle attached to a tube. It is jabbed into the abdomen, poked around the entrails and chest cavity, the contents of which are pumped out and replaced with "cavity fluid." This done, and the hole in the abdomen sewn up, Mr. Jones's face is heavily creamed (to protect the skin from burns which may be caused by leakage of the chemicals), and he is covered with a sheet and left unmolested for a while. But not for long—there is more, much more, in store for him. He has been embalmed, but not yet restored, and the best time to start the restorative work is eight to ten hours after embalming, when the tissues have become firm and dry.

The object of all this attention to the corpse, it must be remem- 11 bered, is to make it presentable for viewing in an attitude of healthy repose. "Our customs require the presentation of our dead in the semblance of normality . . . unmarred by the ravages of illness, disease or mutilation," says Mr. J. Sheridan Mayer in his *Restorative Art.* This is rather a large order since few people die in the full bloom of health, unravaged by illness and unmarked by some disfigurement. The funeral industry is equal to the challenge: "In some cases the gruesome appearance of a mutilated or disease-ridden subject may be quite discouraging. The task of restoration may seem impossible and shake the confidence of the embalmer. This is the time for intestinal fortitude and determination. Once the formative work is begun and affected tissues are cleaned or removed, all doubts of success vanish. It is surprising and gratifying to discover the results which may be obtained."

The embalmer, having allowed an appropriate interval to 12 elapse, returns to the attack, but now he brings into play the skill and equipment of sculptor and cosmetician. Is a hand missing? Casting one in plaster of Paris is a simple matter. "For replacement purposes, only a cast of the back of the hand is necessary; this is within the ability of the average operator and is quite adequate." If a lip or two, a nose or an ear should be missing, the embalmer has at hand a variety of restorative waxes with which to model replacements. Pores and skin texture are simulated by stippling with a little brush, and over this cosmetics are laid on. Head off? Decapitation cases are rather routinely handled. Ragged edges are trimmed, and head joined to torso with a series of splints, wires and sutures. It is a good idea to have a little something at the neck—a scarf or high collar—when time for viewing comes. Swollen mouth? Cut out tissue as needed from inside the lips. If too much is removed, the surface contour can easily be restored by padding with cotton. Swollen necks and cheeks are reduced by removing tissue through vertical incisions made down each side of the neck. "When the deceased is casketed, the pillow will hide the suture incisions . . . as an extra precaution against leakage, the suture may be painted with liquid sealer."

The opposite condition is more likely to present itself—that of   13
emaciation. His hypodermic syringe now loaded with massage cream, the embalmer seeks out and fills the hollowed and sunken areas by injection. In this procedure the backs of the hands and fingers and the under-chin area should not be neglected.

Positioning the lips is a problem that recurrently challenges the   14
ingenuity of the embalmer. Closed too tightly, they tend to give a stern, even disapproving expression. Ideally, embalmers feel, the lips should give the impression of being ever so slightly parted, the upper lip protruding slightly for a more youthful appearance. This takes some engineering, however, as the lips tend to drift apart. Lip drift can sometimes be remedied by pushing one or two straight pins through the inner margin of the lower lip and then inserting them between the two front upper teeth. If Mr. Jones happens to have no teeth, the pins can just as easily be anchored in his Armstrong Face Former and Denture Replacer. Another method to maintain lip closure is to dislocate the lower jaw, which is then held in its new position by a wire run through holes which have been drilled through the upper and lower jaws at the midline. As the French are fond of saying, *il faut souffrir pour être belle.*[1]

If Mr. Jones has died of jaundice, the embalming fluid will very   15
likely turn him green. Does this deter the embalmer? Not if he has intestinal fortitude. Masking pastes and cosmetics are heavily laid on, burial garments and casket interiors are color-correlated with particular care, and Jones is displayed beneath rose-colored lights. Friends will say, "How *well* he looks." Death by carbon monoxide, on the other hand, can be rather a good thing from the embalmer's viewpoint: "One advantage is the fact that this type of discoloration is an exaggerated form of a natural pink coloration." This is nice because the healthy glow is already present and needs but little attention.

The patching and filling completed, Mr. Jones is now shaved,   16
washed and dressed. Cream-based cosmetic, available in pink, flesh, suntan, brunette and blond, is applied to his hands and face, his hair

[1]You have to suffer if you want to be beautiful (Editor's note).

is shampooed and combed (and, in the case of Mrs. Jones, set), his hands manicured. For the horny-handed son of toil special care must be taken; cream should be applied to remove ingrained grime, and the nails cleaned. "If he were not in the habit of having them manicured in life, trimming and shaping is advised for better appearance—never questioned by kin."

Jones is now ready for casketing (this is the present participle of 17 the verb "to casket"). In this operation, his right shoulder should be depressed slightly "to turn the body a bit to the right and soften the appearance of lying flat on the back." Positioning the hands is a matter of importance, and special rubber positioning blocks may be used. The hands should be cupped slightly for a more lifelike, relaxed appearance. Proper placement of the body requires a delicate sense of balance. It should lie as high as possible in the casket, yet not so high that the lid, when lowered, will hit the nose. On the other hand, we are cautioned, placing the body too low "creates the impression that the body is in a box."

Jones is next wheeled into the appointed slumber room where a 18 few last touches may be added—his favorite pipe placed in his hand or, if he was a great reader, a book propped into position. (In the case of little Master Jones a Teddy bear may be clutched.) Here he will hold open house for a few days, visiting hours 10 A.M. to 9 P.M.

MEANINGS AND VALUES

1. What is the author's tone? (See "Guide to Terms": *Style/Tone.*) What does the tone reveal about the writer's attitude towards the intense concern with the appearance of the dead exhibited by embalmers (and other people)?

2. Why was it formerly "almost mandatory" for some relative to witness the embalming procedure (par. 2)?

3. Do you believe that public information about this procedure would cost mortuaries much embalming business (par. 3)? Why, or why not? Why *do* people subject their dead to such a process?

4. Use the three-part system of evaluation found in the "Guide to Terms": *Evaluation* to judge the success of this process analysis.

EXPOSITORY TECHNIQUES

1. What is the central theme? (Guide: *Unity.*) Which parts of the writing, if any, do not contribute to the theme, thus damaging unity? Which contribute to unity?

2. Beginning with paragraph 4, list or mark the transitional devices that help to bridge paragraphs. (Guide: *Transition.*) Briefly explain how coherence is aided by such interparagraph transitions.

3. In this selection, far more than in most, emphasis can best be studied in connection with style. In fact, the two are almost indistinguishable here, and few, if any, of the other methods of achieving emphasis are used at all. (Guide: *Emphasis; Style/Tone.*) Consider each of the following stylistic qualities (some may overlap; others are included in diction) and illustrate, by examples, how each creates emphasis.

    a. Number and selection of details—e.g., the equipment and "aids" (par. 5).

    b. Understatement—e.g., the "chances of live burial" (par. 7).

    c. Special use of quotations—e.g, "that the body is in a box" (par. 17).

    d. Sarcasm and/or other forms of irony—e.g., "How *well* he looks" (par. 15). (Guide: *Irony.*)

DICTION AND VOCABULARY

1. Much of the essay's unique style (with resulting emphasis) comes from qualities of diction. Use examples to illustrate the following. (Some may be identical to those of the preceding answer, but they need not be.)

    a. Choice of common, low-key words to achieve sarcasm through understatement—e.g., "This is nice . . ." (par. 15).

    b. Terms of violence—e.g., "returns to the attack" (par. 12).

    c. Terms of the living—e.g., "will hold open house" (par. 18).

    d. The continuing use of "Mr. Jones."

2. Illustrate the meaning of "connotation" with examples of the quotations from morticians. (Guide: *Connotation/Denotation.*) Are these also examples of "euphemism"?

3. Use the dictionary as needed to understand the meanings of the following words: docility, perpetuation (par. 1); inherent, mandatory (2); intractable, reticence, *raison d'être* (3); ingenious (5); rudimentary, cellular, somatic (7); carotid artery, femoral artery, subclavian vein (8); semblance (11); simulated, stippling, sutures (12); emaciation (13); dispel (7, title).

READ TO WRITE

1. **Collaborating:** Working in a group, think of any other common practices in which we alter appearances to hide reality or create a new reality. Choose one practice and analyze it in detail as the potential subject for an essay.

2.   **Considering Audience:** Many of the processes Mitford describes would be likely to upset or offend many readers, yet she presents them in a way that does not do so except to help readers regard them critically. Choose one such passage and discuss in writing the techniques Mitford employs to present the subject critically but without making it seem distasteful to most readers.

3.   **Developing an Essay:** Mitford presents an unpleasant subject—dead bodies—in such detail that it becomes intriguing (her humor helps here, too). Use a similar strategy in your own writing about a subject that readers might at first consider distasteful or boring.

(NOTE: Suggestions for topics requiring development by PROCESS ANALYSIS are on p. 294 at the end of this chapter.)

JEAN E. KILBOURNE

JEAN E. KILBOURNE is a media critic whose award-winning films *Still Killing Us Softly* and *Calling the Shots* explore the relationships between media and advertising images and our values and behaviors. She lectures regularly on alcohol and cigarette advertising, images of women in advertising, and related issues.

Beauty . . . And the Beast of Advertising

In this essay, first published in *Media & Values* in 1989, Kilbourne analyzes the ways media images shape perceptions and values, particularly those of women. This essay blends a number of patterns, including definition, process analysis, and cause-and-effect analysis.

"You're a Halston woman from the very beginning," the adver- 1 tisement proclaims. The model stares provocatively at the viewer, her long blonde hair waving around her face, her bare chest partially covered by two curved bottles that give the illusion of breasts and a cleavage.

The average American is accustomed to blue-eyed blondes se- 2 ductively touting a variety of products. In this case, however, the blonde is about five years old.

Advertising is an over $100 billion a year industry and affects all 3 of us throughout our lives. We are each exposed to over 2,000 ads a day, constituting perhaps the most powerful educational force in society. The average adult will spend one and one-half years of his/her life watching television commercials. But the ads sell a great deal more than products. They sell values, images and concepts of success and worth, love and sexuality, popularity and normalcy. They tell us who we are and who we should be. Sometimes they sell addictions.

Advertising's foundation and economic lifeblood is the mass 4 media, and the primary purpose of the mass media is to deliver an audience to advertisers, just as the primary purpose of television programs is to deliver an audience for commercials.

Adolescents are particularly vulnerable, however, because they 5 are new and inexperienced consumers and are the prime targets of many advertisements. They are in the process of learning their values and roles and developing their self-concepts. Most teenagers are sensitive to peer pressure and find it difficult to resist or even question the dominant cultural messages perpetuated and reinforced by the media. Mass communication has made possible a kind of nationally distributed peer pressure that erodes private and individual values and standards.

But what does society, and especially teenagers, learn from the 6 advertising messages that proliferate in the mass media? On the most obvious level they learn the stereotypes. Advertising creates a mythical, WASP-oriented world in which no one is ever ugly, overweight, poor, struggling or disabled either physically or mentally (unless you count the housewives who talk to little men in toilet bowls, animated germs in drains or muscle-bound giants clad in white clothing). And it is a world in which people talk only about products.

Housewives or Sex Objects

The aspect of advertising most in need of analysis and change is the 7 portrayal of women. Scientific studies and the most casual viewing yield the same conclusion: Women are shown almost exclusively as housewives or sex objects.

The housewife, pathologically obsessed by cleanliness and 8 lemon-fresh scents, debates cleaning products with herself and worries about her husband's "ring around the collar."

The sex object is a mannequin, a shell. Conventional beauty is 9 her only attribute. She has no lines or wrinkles (which would indicate she had the bad taste and poor judgment to grow older), no scars or blemishes—indeed, she has no pores. She is thin, generally tall and long-legged, and, above all, she is young. All "beautiful" women in advertisements (including minority women), regardless of product or audience, conform to this norm. Women are constantly exhorted to emulate this ideal, to feel ashamed and guilty if they fail, and to feel that their desirability and lovability are contingent upon physical perfection.

Creating Artificiality

The image is artificial and can only be achieved artificially (even the 10 "natural look" requires much preparation and expense). Beauty is something that comes from without; more than one million dollars is spent every hour on cosmetics. Desperate to conform to an ideal and impossible standard, many women go to great lengths to manipulate and change their faces and bodies. A woman is conditioned to view her face as a mask and her body as an object, as *things* separate from and more important than her real self, constantly in need of alteration, improvement, and disguise. She is made to feel dissatisfied with and ashamed of herself, whether she tries to achieve "the look" or not. Objectified constantly by others, she learns to objectify herself. (It is interesting to note that one in five college-age women have an eating disorder.)

"When *Glamour* magazine surveyed its readers in 1984, 75 per-   11
cent felt too heavy and only 15 percent felt just right. Nearly half of those who were actually underweight reported feeling too fat and wanting to diet. Among a sample of college women, 40 percent felt overweight when only 12 percent actually were too heavy," according to Rita Freedman in her book *Beauty Bound*.

There is evidence that this preoccupation with weight begins at   12
ever-earlier ages for women. According to a recent article in *New Age Journal*, "even grade-school girls are succumbing to sticklike standards of beauty enforced by a relentless parade of wasp-waisted fashion models, movie stars, and pop idols." A study by a University of California professor showed that nearly 80 percent of fourth-grade girls in the Bay Area are watching their weight.

A recent *Wall Street Journal* survey of students in four Chicago-   13
area schools found that more than half the fourth-grade girls were dieting and three-quarters felt they were overweight. One student said, "We don't expect boys to be that handsome. We take them as they are." Another added, "But boys expect girls to be perfect and beautiful. And skinny."

Dr. Steven Levenkron, author of *The Best Little Girl in the World*,   14
the story of an anorexic, says his blood pressure soars every time he opens a magazine and finds an ad for women's fashions. "If I had my way," he said, "every one of them would have to carry a line saying, 'Caution: This model may be hazardous to your health.'"

Women are also dismembered in commercials, their bodies sep-   15
arated into parts in need of change or improvement. If a woman has "acceptable" breasts, then she must also be sure that her legs are worth watching, her hips slim, her feet sexy, and that her buttocks look nude under her clothes ("like I'm not wearin' nothin'"). This image is difficult and costly to achieve and impossible to maintain (unless you buy the product)—no one is flawless and everyone ages. Growing older is the great taboo. Women are encouraged to remain little girls ("because innocence is sexier than you think"), to be passive and dependent, never too mature. The contradictory message—"sensual, but not too far from innocence"—places women in a double bind; somehow we are supposed to be both sexy and virginal, experienced and naíve, seductive and chaste. The disparagement of maturity is, of course, insulting and frustrating to adult

women, and the implication that little girls are seductive is dangerous to real children.

Influencing Sexual Attitudes

Young people also learn a great deal about sexual attitudes from the   16
media and from advertising in particular. Advertising's approach to
sex is pornographic; it reduces people to objects and de-emphasizes
human contact and individuality. This reduction of sexuality to a
dirty joke and of people to objects is the real obscenity of the culture.
Although the sexual sell, overt and subliminal, is at a fevered pitch
in most commercials, there is at the same time a notable absence of
sex as an important and profound human activity.

There have been some changes in the images of women. Indeed,   17
a "new woman" has emerged in commercials in recent years. She is
generally presented as superwoman, who manages to do all the
work at home and on the job (with the help of a product, of course,
not of her husband or children or friends), or as the liberated
woman, who owes her independence and self-esteem to the products she uses. These new images do not represent any real progress
but rather create a myth of progress, an illusion that reduces complex sociopolitical problems to mundane personal ones.

Advertising images do not cause these problems, but they con-   18
tribute to them by creating a climate in which the marketing of
women's bodies—the sexual sell and dismemberment, distorted
body image ideal and children as sex objects—is seen as acceptable.

This is the real tragedy, that many women internalize these   19
stereotypes and learn their "limitations," thus establishing a self-
fulfilling prophecy. If one accepts these mythical and degrading images, to some extent one actualizes them. By remaining unaware of
the profound seriousness of the ubiquitous influence, the redundant
message and the subliminal impact of advertisements, we ignore
one of the most powerful "educational" forces in the culture—one
that greatly affects our self-images, our ability to relate to each other,
and effectively destroys any awareness and action that might help to
change that climate.

MEANINGS AND VALUES

1. According to the writer, what does advertising tell women they
    should be, and by what process does it convey this message? Does

the beginning of paragraph 18 accurately summarize the process the writer has been analyzing? If not, what is missing from the summary? Would the essay be stronger if the missing information were included? Why or why not? (See "Guide to Terms": *Evaluation.*)

2. Who or what is the "new woman" (par. 7)? Why does the writer believe that this image does "not represent any real progress"? Why would the absence of any discussion of the "new woman" weaken the expository purpose of the selection? (Guide: *Purpose.*)

3. At several places in the essay, Kilbourne discusses the consequences of advertising on teenagers while in much of the rest of the essay she focuses on women. Does the focus on teenagers undermine the unity of the essay? Why or why not? (Guide: *Unity.*)

EXPOSITORY TECHNIQUES

1. What strategy does Kilbourne use to begin her essay (pars. 1–2)? (Guide: *Introductions.*) Can the opening of this essay be considered ironic? Why or why not? (Guide: *Irony.*) What strategy does she use to conclude the essay? (Guide: *Closings.*)

2. What kinds of evidence does the author provide to support her conclusions about the process of advertising and its consequences? Which kind of evidence do you consider most effective, and which least effective? Why? (Guide: *Evaluation.*)

3. Discuss how Kilbourne varies sentence length (and structure) to achieve emphasis in paragraphs 3, 9, and 15. (Guide: *Emphasis; Syntax.*)

DICTION AND VOCABULARY

1. Where in the essay does the writer use numbers to present information? Be specific. Why can these numbers be considered a form of concrete diction? (Guide: *Concrete/Abstract; Diction.*) What do they contribute to the effects of the various passages in which they appear?

2. If you do not know the meaning of some of the following words, look them up in a dictionary: provocatively, cleavage (par. 1); touting (2); stereotypes; WASP (6); pathologically (8); mannequin, attribute, exhorted, contingent (9); anorexic (14); sensual, disparagement (15); overt, subliminal (16); mundane (17); ubiquitous, redundant (19).

READ TO WRITE

1. **Collaborating:** Working with a group of classmates, spend some time observing advertisements on television or analyzing them in magazines. Take notes on the process by which they achieve their effects as well as the effects themselves. Discuss the notes and arrive at a focus and a thesis for a possible essay.

2. **Considering Audience:** Read (or reread) Brent Staples's essay, "Just Walk on By" (pages 57–63), for another example of an essay that begins with a reversal of readers' expectations. Create an opening for an essay of your own with a reversal of readers' expectations similar to the ones created by Kilbourne and Staples.

3. **Developing an Essay:** Using Kilbourne's essay as a model, discuss the process of advertising as it affects a group or groups other than women in general. Feel free to take a positive view of advertising in contrast to Kilbourne's generally negative perspective.

(NOTE: Suggestions for topics requiring development by means of PROCESS ANALYSIS follow.)

Writing Suggestions for Chapter 7

ANALOGY

From one of the following topics develop a central theme into an informational process analysis, showing:

1. How you selected a college.
2. How you selected your future career or major field of study.
3. How your family selected a home.
4. How an unusual sport is played.
5. How religious faith is achieved.
6. How gasoline is made.
7. How the air (or water) in _____ becomes polluted.
8. How lightning kills.
9. How foreign policy is made.
10. How political campaigns are financed.
11. How _____ Church was rebuilt.
12. How fruit blossoms are pollinated.
13. How a computer chip is designed or made.

COLLABORATIVE EXERCISES

1. As a group write an informative paper on the process of completing a collaborative project. Consider how you plan team meetings, team tasks, team evaluations, etc.

2. For topics 2 a-h, have each member of a group write the directional process for a different audience/reader. Pre-define each person's audience profile using an audience profile sheet.

   a. How to do any of the processes suggested by topics 1a–e. (This treatment will require a different viewpoint, completely objective, and may require a different organization.)

   b. How to overcome shyness.

   c. How to overcome stage fright.

   d. How to make the best use of study time.

   e. How to write a college composition.

   f. How to sell an ugly house.

   g. How to prepare livestock or any other entry for a fair.

   h. How to start a club (or some other kind of recurring activity).

8

Analyzing *Cause-and-Effect* Relationships

Writing built around cause-effect analysis addresses questions like "Why did that happen?" and "What is likely to happen next?" It can grow from simple curiosity about the *why* of events or from a practical desire to avoid unpleasant or unforeseen consequences. Above all, cause-effect analysis focuses on relationships, the links between one phenomenon and another. When you employ the pattern in expository writing, you need to do more than identify possible causes or consequences. You need to establish a reasonable relationship among them by showing how both logic and the available evidence point to the relationship. After all, two things that often occur together, such as storms and tornadoes, are not *necessarily* related. Since many storms occur without the accompaniment of tornadoes, a cause-effect analysis would focus first on identifying those kinds of storms frequently associated with the appearance of tornadoes, then isolate specific causal features that can be demonstrably linked to funnel clouds and destructive winds.

A search for cause and effect can be rigorously scientific ("Researchers debate possible links between caffeine consumption and heart disease") or it can be personal ("Why do I always end up arguing with my parents over things we all know are unimportant?"). It can take the form of causal analysis, trying to identify all the links in a causal chain: remote causes, necessary conditions, and direct causes to immediate effects and on to more distant consequences. Or it can identify the many conditions and forces that work together in no particular pattern to shape a person's life, create a particular situation, or help bring about events.

Most expository uses of the pattern do not require scientific rigor, however. For social or cultural events, like the growth of a political movement or the rise of a new form of art, we can seldom hope to pinpoint exact causes and effects. Instead, we can identify the roots of contemporary phenomena and develop an awareness of the kinds of changes that may be going on today. This is the kind of explanation provided by the following paragraph that looks at the early development of a popular kind of music.

> Rap started in the discos, not the midtown glitter palaces like Studio 54 or New York, New York, but at Mel Quinn's on 42nd Street and Club 371 in the Bronx, where a young Harlemite who called himself D.J. Hollywood spun on the weekends. It wasn't unusual for black club jocks to talk to their audiences in the jive style of the old personality deejays. Two of the top black club spinners of the day, Pete (D.J.) Jones and Maboya, did so. Hollywood, just an adolescent when he started, created a more complicated, faster style, with more rhymes than his older mentors and call-and-response passages to encourage reaction from the dancers. At local bars, discos, and many illegal after-hours spots frequented by street people, Hollywood developed a huge word-of-mouth reputation. Tapes of his parties began appearing around the city on the then new and incredibly loud Japanese portable cassette players flooding into America. In Harlem, Kurtis Blow, Eddie Cheeba, and D.J. Lovebug Star-ski; in the Bronx, Junebug Star-ski, Grandmaster Flash, and Melle Mel; in Brooklyn, two kids from the projects called Whodini; and in Queens, Russell and Joey, the two youngest sons from the middle-class Simmons household—all shared a fascination with Hollywood's use of the rhythmic breaks in his club mixes and his verbal dexterity. These kids would all grow up to play a role in the local clubs and, later, a few would appear on the national scene to spread Hollywood's style. Back in the 1970s, while disco reigned in the media, the Black Main Streets of New York were listening to D.J. Hollywood, and learning.
>
> —Nelson George, *The Death of Rhythm and Blues*

WHY USE CAUSE-EFFECT ANALYSIS?

Some causes and effects are not very complicated; at least their explanation requires only a simple statement. New parking facilities are not built because a college (or town) lacks the money in its budget. But frequently a much more thorough analysis is required. New parking facilities are not built partly because of expense and partly because they simply seem to encourage more traffic and rapidly become jammed. The college (or town) delays the project until it can study *why* parking facilities quickly become overloaded. In writing, cause-effect as an expository pattern helps address these kinds of complicated relationships.

Writers often respond to puzzling or intriguing phenomena with causal explanations. In its simplest form, the strategy consists of a description of a puzzling phenomenon (the persistence of alcoholism in families, for example) followed by an explanation or an examination of possible causes. The simplicity of this pattern gives it considerable power and flexibility. Writers speculating about social patterns and individual behavior often use the strategy or vary it to consider possible consequences. In dealing with effects, the strategy consists of discussion of a new or previously unnoticed phenomenon whose consequences are unfamiliar followed by consideration of its likely effects, or it begins with discussion of desired effects followed by examination of actions or arrangements most likely to produce these consequences.

Causal explanations appear frequently in academic and research writing. Scholars often look for a particularly puzzling element in a subject or a point over which there has been much disagreement and then build an essay in an attempt to explain the phenomena: "Perhaps the most interesting feature of early jazz is . . ."; "Over the last decade researchers have argued about the role of aggressive behavior in corporate organizations . . . ."

CHOOSING A STRATEGY

To explain fully the causes of a phenomenon, writers must seek not only *immediate* causes (the ones encountered first) but also *ultimate* causes (the basic, underlying factors that help to explain the more apparent ones). Business or professional people, as well as students, often have a pressing need for this type of analysis. How else could they fully understand or report on a failing sale campaign, diminishing church membership, a local increase in traffic accidents, or a decline in crime and the use of drugs? The immediate cause of a disastrous warehouse fire could be faulty electrical wiring, but this might be attributed in turn to the company's unwise economy measures, which might be traced even further to undue pressures on the management to show large profits. The written analysis might logically stop at any point of course, with the actual strategy a writer employs depending on the purpose of the writing and the audience for which it is intended.

Similarly, both the immediate and ultimate *effects* of an action or situation may, or may not, need to be fully explored. If a five percent pay raise is granted, what will be the immediate effect on the cost of production, leading to what ultimate effects on prices and, in some cases, on the economy of a business, a town, or perhaps the entire region?

Whatever the extent of the reasoning your writing task demands, you need to make certain strategic choices. Will you focus on causes, effects, or both? Will you focus on a single clear chain of causes and effects or provide a more general discussion, highlighting many contributing factors? How will you use the opening of your writing to convince readers of the importance of understanding the causes or effects of a phenomenon or situation and interest them in reading about the topic?

Because causes and effects often form intricate, potentially confusing relationships, you should develop a straightforward plan for your writing—an organization that will help readers understand the order you have discovered within the complexity. This is particularly important when a phenomenon has multiple causes, as in the following example.

> Introduction: Example of a diverse audience at a horror movie responding with fear and pleasure to the film
> Tentative thesis: People choose to watch horror films for many different reasons, each depending on the individual's taste and psychological makeup
> Cause 1: The "thrill" of being shocked and scared
> > Support: Some people are psychologically disposed to get pleasure from danger, especially when it is imaginary
> > Support: Brain chemistry may mean that (like people who engage in extreme sports) certain people get a feeling of well-being after feeling that they have placed themselves in danger
> Cause 2: The twists and turns of the plot
> > Support: Many people enjoy the kinds of complicated, surprising plots they find in horror movies (similar in some ways to the kinds of plots people enjoy in adventure stories)
> Cause 3: The pleasure of "escape"
> > Support: The dangers faced by characters in the films allow viewers to escape from a short time from their somewhat less serious but more real everyday problems
> Cause 4: Fashion
> > Support: Horror movies are popular. Going to them with friends and talking about them afterwards is a pleasant social experience
> Summary

Your writing will need to do more than identify causes and effects. It will need to provide readers with evidence that you have correctly identified the relationships. As a result, much writing that employs this pattern relies on detailed research. Printed sources, television documentaries, and interviews can provide you with useful information. You should keep such research focused, however, so you don't stray too far into areas that are interesting but not really related to the causes or consequences you will be discussing.

DEVELOPING CAUSE-EFFECT ANALYSIS

Discussions of causes and effects can easily become complex and confusing, so consider using the following strategies for alerting readers to the relationships among causes and effects. A concise statement near the beginning of an essay can point out relationships you plan to examine. Statements in the body of an essay can remind readers of the points you are making and the supporting details and reasoning you are providing. Likewise, terms that identify causes and effects or that indicate their relationships can help guide readers' attention:

result	effect	accomplishment	development
outcome	antecedent	source	first
cause	instrument	as a result	second
means	thus	motive	third
consequence	reason	agent	next

When you analyze causes and effect, your readers must always have confidence in the thoroughness and logic of your reasoning. Here are some ways to avoid the most common faults in causal reasoning:

1. Never mistake the fact that something happens with or after another occurrence as evidence of a causal relationship—for example, that a black cat crossing the road caused the flat tire a few minutes later, or that a course in English composition caused a student's nervous breakdown that same semester.

2. Consider all possible relevant factors before attributing causes. Perhaps studying English did result in a nervous breakdown, but the cause may also have been ill health, trouble at home, the stress of working while attending college, or the anguish of a love affair. (The composition course, by providing an "emotional" outlet, may even have helped postpone the breakdown!)

3. Support the analysis by more than mere assertions: offer evidence. It would not often be enough to *tell* why Shakespeare's wise Othello believed the villainous Iago—the dramatist's lines should be used as evidence, possibly supported by the opinions of at least one literary scholar. If you are explaining that capital punishment deters crime, do not expect the reader to take your word for it—give before-and-after statistics or the testimony of reliable authorities.

4. Be careful not to omit any links in the chain of causes or effects unless you are certain that the readers for whom the writing is intended will automatically make the right connections themselves—and this is frequently a dangerous assumption. To unwisely omit one or more of the links might leave the reader with only a vague, or even erroneous, impression of the causal connection, possibly invalidating all that follows and thus making the entire writing ineffective.

5. Be honest and objective. Writers (or thinkers) who bring their old prejudices to the task of casual analysis, or who fail to see the probability of *multiple* causes or effects, are almost certain to distort their analyses or to make them so superficial, so thin, as to be almost worthless.

Student Essay

As an expository pattern, cause-effect can explore personal matters as well as those of broader public interest. Aware of her difficulties in coming to terms with her mother's death, Sarah Egri used the pattern to explore one possible reason for her feelings.

Gives topic an interesting twist: an absence rather than a presence is the cause.

Thesis statement

How a Public Document
Affected My Life

Public documents are a part of every day life. The presence of these documents can affect a person's life in many different ways. However, the *absence* of such documents may also affect a person's life, such as my own. I believe the absence of my mother's death certificate has affected my life.

When I was around twelve years old, my mother became very ill with cancer. She was diagnosed with Lymphoma, which is can-

Background to help readers understand the cause and the effects

cer within the lymph nodes. She sought several types of medical treatment, but nothing seemed to help her. During this time, the doctor told my family that my mom did not have much longer to live. The doctor also told my mom this, but she did not believe him, nor did she want to. At this point, I did not know what was happening. Since I was so young, I did not understand. I listened to my mom and believed her because I did not want her to die. She and I were quite close. I was able to talk to her about anything and everything. There was still so much I had to learn from her, still so many more memories to be made.

When I was fourteen years old my mother passed away. I will never forget that night, for it seemed like a dream; it seemed as though it were not really happening. I awoke to a phone call at one-thirty in the morning saying that my mom had passed away. No more would I be able to talk with her, or learn from her, or make precious memories. She was gone, yet it felt like it was not real. I could not grasp the concept that she would no longer

One of the effects

be a part of my life. The years passed by and I only got *used to* my mom not being there; I never faced the fact that she had died. The day that my mother died, I never

The cause

saw her death certificate. Perhaps if I had seen it, her death would have seemed more realistic.

Examines and explains the cause

Now as I think back, I *never* saw my mother's death certificate. A death certificate is a document that is signed by a doctor, giving information about the time, place, and cause of a person's death. This

Generalizes about the effects

document finalizes everything. It may be that since I never saw this document, I never came to the realization that she had passed. Since I did not believe she *would* die, I cannot bring myself to believe that she *did* die. If I had seen the death certificate, I would have come to terms with her death.

Explains the force and importance of public documents

How can such a *small* document make such a *big* difference in my life? All a death certificate is, is a small piece of paper with a person's name on it. I think it might have made a difference because it's an *official* notification of my mom's death. It's a *real,* physical thing; it is more real than just *thinking* someone has died.

Explores effects

My mother's death certificate has affected my life, even though I never did see it. The absence of this document affects my life, because if I had seen it, I would have come to the realization that she is really gone. If I had seen that document, her death would have been finalized in my mind and I would not just be *used to* her not being around, I would *know* that she has passed and is no longer with us. The death certificate finalizes a person's death, and if I had seen my mom's it would have finalized her death for me.

Ends with a contrast between absence and presence

Since I did not see this document, I have not brought my mom's death to a close. Perhaps the *absence* of some documents, such as my mother's death certificate, can affect a person's life more than the presence of other documents.

SUSAN PERRY AND JIM DAWSON

Susan Perry is a former staff writer for Time-Life, Inc., and now works full-time as a freelance writer specializing in health, business, and women's issues. Her articles have appeared in such publications as *Ms., The Washington Post,* and the *Minneapolis Star.* She is the author of *Nightmare* (1985) and *Natural Menopause* (1992). James Dawson is a science reporter who writes regularly for the *Minneapolis Star-Tribune.* Perry and Dawson co-authored *The Secrets Our Body Clocks Reveal* (1988).

What's Your Best Time of Day?

This essay, published as a magazine article, is drawn from *The Secrets Our Body Clocks Reveal.* The piece opens with examples of some puzzling behaviors, looks at their causes in the rhythms of our bodies, then examines some further effects of these rhythms. The authors make use of examples, classification, and process to support the cause-effect pattern and provide practical advice for taking advantage of the biological patterns that help govern our lives.

Every fall, Jane, a young mother and part-time librarian, begins to eat more and often feels sleepy. Her mood is also darker, especially when she awakens in the morning; it takes all her energy just to drag herself out of bed. These symptoms persist until April, when warmer weather and longer days seems to lighten her mood and alleviate her cravings for food and sleep. 1

Joseph, a 48-year-old engineer for a Midwestern computer company, feels cranky early in the morning. But as the day progresses, he becomes friendlier and more accommodating. 2

All living organisms, from mollusks to men and women, exhibit biological rhythms. Some are short and can be measured in minutes or hours. Others last days or months. The peaking of body temperature, which occurs in most people every evening, is a daily rhythm. The menstrual cycle is a monthly rhythm. The increase in sexual 3 drive in the autumn—not in the spring, as poets would have us believe—is a seasonal, or yearly, rhythm.

The idea that our bodies are in constant flux is fairly new—and   4
goes against traditional medical training. In the past, many doctors were taught to believe the body has a relatively stable, or homeostatic, internal environment. Any fluctuations were considered random and not meaningful enough to be studied.

As early as the 1940s, however, some scientists questioned the   5
homeostatic view of the body. Franz Halberg, a young European scientist working in the United States, noticed that the number of white blood cells in laboratory mice was dramatically higher and lower at different times of day. Gradually, such research spread to the study of other rhythms in other life forms, and the findings were sometimes startling. For example, the time of day when a person receives X-ray or drug treatment for cancer can affect treatment benefits and ultimately mean the difference between life and death.

This new science is called chronobiology, and the evidence sup-   6
porting it has become increasingly persuasive. Along the way, the scientific and medical communities are beginning to rethink their ideas about how the human body works, and gradually what had been considered a minor science just a few years ago is being studied in major universities and medical centers around the world. There are even chronobiologists working for the National Aeronautics and Space Administration, as well as for the National Institutes of Health and other government laboratories.

With their new findings, they are teaching us things that can   7
literally change our lives—by helping us organize ourselves so we can work *with* our natural rhythms rather than against them. This can enhance our outlook on life as well as our performance at work and play.

Because they are easy to detect and measure, more is known of   8
daily—or circadian (Latin for "about a day")—rhythms than other types. The most obvious daily rhythm is the sleep/wake cycle. But there are other daily cycles as well: temperature, blood pressure, hormone levels. Amid these and the body's other changing rhythms, you are simply a different person at 9 A.M. than you are at 3 P.M. How you feel, how well you work, your level of alertness, your sensitivity to taste and smell, the degree with which you enjoy food or take pleasure in music—all are changing throughout the day.

Most of us seem to reach our peak of alertness around noon.   9
Soon after that, alertness declines, and sleepiness may set in by midafternoon.

Your short-term memory is best during the morning—in fact,   10
about 15 percent more efficient than at any other time of day. So,
students, take heed: when faced with a morning exam, it really does
pay to review your notes right before the test is given.

Long-term memory is different. Afternoon is the best time for   11
learning material that you want to recall days, weeks or months later.
Politicians, business executives or others who must learn speeches
would be smart to do their memorizing during that time of day. If
you are a student, you would be wise to schedule your more difficult
classes in the afternoon, rather than in the morning. You should also
try to do most of your studying in the afternoon, rather than late at
night. Many students believe they memorize better while burning the
midnight oil because their short-term recall is better during the wee
hours of the morning than in the afternoon. But short-term memory
won't help them much several days later, when they face the exam.

By contrast, we tend to do best on cognitive tasks—things that   12
require the juggling of words and figures in one's head—during
the morning hours. This might be a good time, say, to balance a
checkbook.

Your manual dexterity—the speed and coordination with   13
which you perform complicated tasks with your hands—peaks during the afternoon hours. Such work as carpentry, typing or sewing
will be a little easier at this time of day.

What about sports? During afternoon and early evening, your   14
coordination is at its peak, and you're able to react the quickest to an
outside stimulus—like a baseball speeding toward you at home
plate. Studies have also shown that late in the day, when your body
temperature is peaking, you will *perceive* a physical workout to be
easier and less fatiguing—whether it actually is or not. That means
you are more likely to work harder during a late-afternoon or early-
evening workout, and therefore benefit more from it. Studies in-
volving swimmers, runners, shot-putters and rowing crews have
shown consistently that performance is better in the evening than in
the morning.

In fact, all of your senses—taste, sight, hearing, touch and   15
smell—may be at their keenest during late afternoon and early
evening. That could be why dinner usually tastes better to us than
breakfast and why bright lights irritate us at night.

Even our perception of time changes from hour to hour. Not   16
only does time seem to fly when you're having fun, but it also seems
to fly even faster if you are having that fun in the late afternoon or
early evening, when your body temperature is also peaking.

While all of us follow the same general pattern of ups and   17
downs, the exact timing varies from person to person. It all depends
on how your "biological" day is structured—how much of a morning
or night person you are. The earlier your biological day gets going,
the earlier you are likely to enter—and exit—the peak times for performing various tasks. An extreme morning person and an extreme
night person may have circadian cycles that are a few hours apart.

Each of us can increase our knowledge about our individual   18
rhythms. Learn how to listen to the inner beats of your body; let them
set the pace of your day. You will live a healthier—and happier—life.
As no less an authority than the Bible tells us, "To every thing there
is a season, and a time to every purpose under heaven."

MEANINGS AND VALUES

1.   What cause(s) and effect(s) do the writers discuss in this selection?

2.   According to the explanations in this essay, what are the best times to
     undertake the following activities, and why:

     a. play a sport

     b. balance a checkbook

     c. learn a speech

     d. prepare for an exam

EXPOSITORY TECHNIQUES

1.   What functions do the examples that open the essay perform for
     readers? (See "Guide to Terms": *Introductions*.)

2.   Where in the essay do the authors use classification? Why? Where do
     the authors use process analysis? Why?

3.   Would this essay be more effective if discussions of the causes and
     the effects were more clearly separated? Why, or why not? (Guide:
     Evaluation.)

4.   Discuss the arrangement of paragraphs 9–12, paying special atten-
     tion to parallel structures and transitions within and between para-
     graphs. (Guide: *Unity; Parallel Structure*.)

DICTION AND VOCABULARY

1.   In what ways does the diction in paragraphs 1 and 2 emphasize the
     contrasts being illustrated? (Guide: *Diction*.)

2. Discuss how the authors provide explanations of the following scientific or otherwise unfamiliar terms in the text so that readers will not have to pause to look them up: homeostatic (par. 4); circadian (8); cognitive tasks (12); manual dexterity (13).

3. Does the allusion that concludes the essay seem appropriate? Why, or why not? Try looking up the passage in the Bible (Ecclesiastes 3:1) to see if its original meaning is similar to the one it has in the context of this essay.

READ TO WRITE

1. **Collaborating:** Assume for a moment that Perry and Dawson's view of the cause-effect relationship of body cycles and behavior is accurate. In a group, discuss how typical academic or work schedules might need to be altered to take into account the patterns described by the authors. What common practices seem particularly in need of change given the information provided here? As a group, plan an essay with such practical consequences as its topic.

2. **Considering Audience:** In a magazine like *Discover* or *Scientific American,* read an article that offers a physical explanation of human behavior. Or in a magazine like *Psychology Today,* read an article that offers a psychological or social explanation of behavior. Then prepare a brief analysis of the different kinds of audiences to which this article and Perry and Dawson's essay are directed.

3. **Developing an Essay:** Perry and Dawson use numerous examples to explain and confirm the effects of body cycles. Do your experiences agree with what the authors say about the cycles that guide our behavior? In an essay of your own, provide examples that either support or contradict their conclusions, or that do the same for some other well-known explanation of behavior.

(NOTE: Suggestions for topics requiring development by analysis of CAUSE AND EFFECT are on pp. 350–351 at the end of this chapter.)

CULLEN MURPHY

CULLEN MURPHY grew up in Greenwich, Connecticut and attended school in both Greenwich and Dublin, Ireland. He received a B.A. from Amherst College in 1974 and soon after began working in the production department of *Change* magazine. In 1977 he was named editor of *The Wilson Quarterly,* and he has been managing editor of *The Atlantic Monthly* since 1985. In his parallel career, he has written the comic strip Prince Valiant since the middle 1970s (a comic strip which his father draws). Murphy is an essayist and nonfiction writer as well. His essays on many different topics have appeared in *The Atlantic Monthly* and other magazines, including *Harper's.* His first book, *Rubbish!* (with William Rathje), appeared in 1992, and a collection of his essays, *Just Curious,* was published in 1995.

Hello, Darkness

"Hello, Darkness" was first published in *The Atlantic Monthly* in 1996. With touches of humor, Murphy looks at a subject that troubles many people: lack of sleep. His explanations of a phenomenon that most of us view as a matter of personal behavior may at first seem surprising; nonetheless, they point convincingly to technology and social change as the culprits who have stolen sleep.

A mericans today have plenty of reasons to be thankful that they were not Americans a hundred years ago, but they also have more than a few reasons to wish they had been. On the one hand, a hundred years ago there was no Voting Rights Act, no penicillin, and no zipper, and the first daily comic strip was still more than a decade away. On the other hand there was no income tax, no nuclear bomb, and no Maury Povich. Also on the plus side, the average American a hundred years ago was able to sleep 20 percent longer than the average American today.

That last figure, supported by various historical studies over the years, comes from a report released by the Better Sleep Council. Americans in the late 1800s are believed to have slept an average of about nine and a half hours a night. The average today is about seven and a half hours. A survey by the Better Sleep Council reveals that on a typical weeknight almost 60 percent of Americans get *less*

1

2

than seven hours of sleep. Other evidence seems to indicate that the rate of sleep loss is in fact accelerating.

Some may argue that the Better Sleep Council's news should be discounted, on the grounds that the council has an interest in the story—it is supported (comfortably?) by the mattress industry.

I would counter that the data simply confirm what anecdotal evidence already suggests is true. Independent experts at universities and hospitals speak as one on the subject, observing that as a nation we are laboring under a large and increasingly burdensome "sleep deficit," defined as the difference between how much sleep we need and how much we get.

Would that we could pass this particular deficit on to our children! But the only way we can pay it back, the experts say, is by getting more sleep ourselves. Apparently, we're trying. A recent article in *The Wall Street Journal* took note of the growing phenomenon of employees napping at work, but I suspect that this barely covers the interest payments, which go right to Japan. (As you may have noticed, the Japanese are asleep most of the time that we're awake.)

Why, by degrees, are we banishing sleep? In a handful of instances, arguably, the cause has been government over-regulation. I am thinking of the recent case of Sari Zayed, of Davis, California. Ms. Zayed, after being overheard by a neighbor, was awakened at 1:30 A.M. by a municipal "noise-abatement officer" who gave her a $50 citation for snoring too loudly. The amount of money that Ms. Zayed subsequently received in damages from the city of Davis would allow her to pay for nightly snoring citations from now to the end of the year.

America's sleep deficit, though, is surely a systemic phenomenon. Many commentators would blame it on what might be called the AWOL factor—that is, the American Way of Life. We are by nature a busy and ambitious people whom tectonic social forces—declining average wage, high rate of divorce, two-paycheck families, instant telecommunications, jet travel across time zones, growing popularity of soccer for everyone older than four—have turned into a race of laboratory rats on a treadmill going nowhere ever faster. And there is obviously something to this explanation. It is noteworthy that television shows like *Seinfeld* and *Cheers*, on which nobody seems to have any real responsibilities (circumstances that accord more fully with most viewers' fantasies than with their actual lives), have come to constitute a distinct broadcast genre known as "time porn."

It is hard not to credit the importance of the AWOL factor, but I wonder if the driving force behind the sleep deficit is in fact more pervasive, and indeed global in nature: the triumph of light. I am by no means a romantic or a Luddite when it comes to electricity (anyone who is should read Robert Caro's *The Years of Lyndon Johnson* for its haunting description of life in west Texas in the days before rural electrification), and I also don't subscribe to the fashionable opinion that electronic labor-saving devices (personal computers possibly excepted) end up consuming more labor than they save. Yet electricity's ubiquitous and seemingly most innocuous use—to power the common light bulb—could not help exacting a price in sleep. Electricity made it possible for the first time in history for masses of humanity to vanquish darkness.

I had never given much thought to the role of darkness in ordinary human affairs until I read a monograph prepared by John Staudenmaier, a historian of technology and a Jesuit priest, for a recent conference at MIT. (The essay appears in a book called *Progress: Fact or Illusion*, edited by Leo Marx and Bruce Mazlish.) Staudenmaier makes the point—obvious when brought up, though we've mostly lost sight of it—that from the time of the hominid Lucy, in Hadar, Ethiopia, to the time of Thomas Edison, in West Orange, New Jersey, the onset of darkness sharply curtailed most kinds of activity for most of our ancestors. He writes,   9

> Living with electric lights makes it difficult to retrieve the experience of a non-electrified society. For all but the very wealthy, who could afford exorbitant arrays of expensive artificial lights, nightfall brought the works of daytime to a definitive end. Activities that need good light—where sharp tools are wielded or sharply defined boundaries maintained; purposeful activities designed to achieve specific goals; in short, that which we call work—all this subsided in the dim light of evening. Absent the press of work, people typically took themselves safely to home and were left with time in the evening for less urgent and more sensual matters: storytelling, sex, prayer, sleep, dreaming.

Staudenmaier's comments on electric light occupy only a few   10 passages. His larger subject is Western intellectual history, and how metaphors of "enlightenment" came to be associated with orderliness, objectivity, and progress, even as metaphors of darkness came to signify the chaotic, the nonrational, the terrifying. He argues that we have lost, to our detriment, the medieval view that some aspects of life and understanding are not necessarily helped by clarity or harmed by ambiguity. Observing that Enlightenment ideals have "taken a fair beating" in the course of this century, Staudenmaier wonders if it is time to rediscover the metaphysical dark, that place "where visions are born and human purpose renewed."

I'll leave that thought where it is. But the implication of electric- 11
ity in the sleep deficit seems hard to argue with. Whatever it is that
we wish or are made to do—pursue leisure, earn a living—there are
simply far more usable hours now in which to do it. Darkness was
once an ocean into which our capacity to venture was greatly limited; now we are wresting vast areas of permanent lightness from
the darkness, much the way the Dutch have wrested polders of dry
land from the sea. So vast are these areas that in composite satellite
photographs of the world at night the contours of civilization are
clearly illuminated—the boundaries of continents, the metastases of
cities. Even Wrigley Field, once a reliable pool of nocturnal darkness, would now show up seventeen nights during the baseball season. In the United States at midnight more than five million people
are at work at full-time jobs. Supermarkets, gas stations, copy
shops—many of these never close. I know of a dentist in Ohio who
decided to open an all-night clinic, and has had the last laugh on
friends who believed that he would never get patients. The supply-
side theory may not have worked in economics, but it has certainly
worked with regard to light: the more we get, the more we find
ways to put it to use. And, of course, the more we get, the more we
distance ourselves from the basic diurnal rhythm in which our evolution occurred.

Thomas Edison, famous for subsisting on catnaps, would have 12
wanted it this way. In contrast, Calvin Coolidge, a younger man
with an older temperament, slept at least ten and often as much as
eleven hours a day. Two world views collide here, and somewhere
between them is a balance waiting to be struck. Where and how?
The only useful contribution I can make is to recall life in Ireland in
the mid-1960s. One of the elements that made it so congenial was a
shared expertise among engineers at the Electricity Supply Board
which resulted in regular but unpredictably occurring blackouts.
The relentless march of time would suddenly be punctuated by a
limbo of uncertain duration. Lights were extinguished. Clocks
stopped. Television screens went black. Drivers became hesitant and
generous at traffic signals. Society and all its components took a
blessed time out.

There was also something in Ireland called "holy hour," a pe- 13
riod in the afternoon when all the pubs would close. Perhaps what
Americans need is a holy hour in the form of a blackout—a brief
caesura in our way of life that might come every day at perhaps
nine-thirty or ten at night. Not the least of the holy hour's benefits, I
might add, would be an appealing new time slot for Maury Povich.

MEANINGS AND VALUES

1. The writer mentions "anecdotal evidence" of a "'sleep deficit'" (par. 4) but does not present it directly. Why do you think he chose not to offer it in detail? Is the essay weakened—or perhaps strengthened—by this omission? Explain. (See "Guide to Terms": *Evaluation.*)

2. Are we to take the example in paragraph 6 seriously? If not, what is its role in the essay? Is it an indication that we should not take other examples in the essay seriously? Why or why not?

3. Explain why the author might be justified in referring to certain television shows as "time porn." Do you think most readers will agree or disagree with his conclusion? Why?

4. According to this essay, what was lost when electricity made it possible to "vanquish darkness" (8)?

EXPOSITORY TECHNIQUES

1. Where does Murphy first announce the phenomenon he wishes to explain? Should this announcement be considered a thesis? Why or why not? (Guide: *Thesis.*)

2. What is the role of the rhetorical question that opens paragraph 6? (Guide: *Rhetorical Questions.*)

3. Which causes of the sleep deficit does the author consider most important, and how does he signal their importance to readers? Which of the strategies for creating emphasis does he use with frequency in this essay? (Guide: *Emphasis.*)

4. Where in the essay does the author begin discussing the effects of electricity?

5. What is the role of the extended discussion of Staudenmaier's work in paragraphs 10 and 11? To what extent do these paragraphs contradict or complement Murphy's tone and approach in the rest of the essay? (Guide: *Style/Tone.*)

6. What strategy does the writer use to conclude the essay? (Guide: *Closings.*) How effective is the conclusion?

DICTION AND VOCABULARY

1. To what does the title allude? (Guide: *Figures of Speech.*) How is the allusion related to the rest of the essay? Discuss how repetition of the word "darkness," beginning with the title, serves to create unity and coherence in the essay. (Guide: *Unity; Coherence.*) Is the title effective even for readers who do not recognize the allusion? Why or why not?

2. What choices of words and phrases does the writer make in paragraph 8 to indicate the importance of electricity as one of the causes of the sleep deficit and the disappearance of "darkness" in our daily lives? (Guide: *Diction*.) Do you think the diction in this paragraph is appropriate to its purposes, or is it excessive? Explain. (Guide: *Evaluation*.)

3. If you do not know the meaning of some of the following terms, look them up in a dictionary: anecdotal (par. 4); systemic, tectonic (7); Luddite, innocuous, vanquish (8); hominid, curtailed (9); metastases, diurnal (11); subsisting, limbo, duration (12); caesura (13).

READ TO WRITE

1. **Collaborating:** In a group, think of other modern inventions (airplanes, television, internet, credit cards) and the ways they have changed our society and shaped our lives. The inventions can be seemingly insignificant (cup holders in automobiles, telephone calling cards, zippers or velcro) and still be topics worth exploring because of their consequences, both good and bad. Then plan an essay exploring the consequences of one or more of the inventions.

2. **Considering Audience:** This essay is partly humorous, partly serious. Prepare an essay analyzing the role of each element and discussing how readers are likely to respond to the combination.

3. **Developing an Essay:** This essay makes effective use of the concept of a "deficit," that is, the difference between what we have and what we ought to have. Use a similar strategy to begin an essay of your own by introducing some other kind of "deficit" whose causes and consequences are worth exploring.

(NOTE: Suggestions for topics requiring development by analysis of CAUSE AND EFFECT are on pp. 350–351 at the end of this chapter.)

LINDA HASSELSTROM

LINDA HASSELSTROM is an essayist, poet, and environmental writer who is also a rancher in western South Dakota. Her books include *Caught by One Wing* (1984) and *Roadkill* (1987) (poetry); *Windbreak: A Woman Rancher on the Northern Plains* (1987) and *Going over East* (1987) (journals and nonfiction); and *Land Circle: Writings Collected from the Land* (1991) (essays and poetry). Her essays have appeared in many magazines such as *High Country News, Northern Lights, North American Review, Working Parents, Iowa Woman, Whole Earth Review,* and *Utne Reader* as well as newspapers such as the *Los Angeles Times* and *The Christian Science Monitor.*

A Peaceful Woman Explains
Why She Carries a Pistol

This version of the essay "Why One Peaceful Woman Carries a Pistol" first appeared in the *Utne Reader*. In it, Hasselstrom takes a subject (gun ownership) usually dealt with in terms of general principles (the right to bear arms) or social trends and explores it in terms of a particular person in a particular setting. This focus on the individual leads to an analysis of cause and effect relationships that readers are likely to find either invigorating or disquieting, or both.

I am a peace-loving woman. But several events in the past 10 years   1
have convinced me I'm safer when I carry a pistol. This was a personal decision, but because handgun possession is a controversial subject, perhaps my reasoning will interest others.

I live in western South Dakota on a ranch 25 miles from the   2
nearest large town; for several years I spent winters alone here. As a free-lance writer, I travel alone a lot—more than 100,000 miles by car in the last four years. With women freer than ever before to travel alone, the odds of our encountering trouble seem to have risen. And help, in the West, can be hours away. Distances are great, roads are deserted, and the terrain is often too exposed to offer hiding places.

A woman who travels alone is advised, usually by men, to pro-   3
tect herself by avoiding bars and other "dangerous situations," by approaching her car like an Indian scout, by locking doors and windows.

But these precautions aren't always enough. I spent years following them and still found myself in dangerous situations. I began to resent the idea that just because I am female, I have to be extra careful.

A few years ago, with another woman, I camped for several 4 weeks in the West. We discussed self-defense, but neither of us had taken a course in it. She was against firearms, and local police told us Mace was illegal. So we armed ourselves with spray cans of deodorant tucked into our sleeping bags. We never used our improvised Mace because we were lucky enough to camp beside people who came to our aid when men harassed us. But on one occasion we visited a national park where our assigned space was less than 15 feet from other campers. When we returned from a walk, we found our closest neighbors were two young men. As we gathered our cooking gear, they drank beer and loudly discussed what they would do to us after dark. Nearby campers, even families, ignored them; rangers strolled past, unconcerned. When we asked the rangers point-blank if they would protect us, one of them patted my shoulder and said, "Don't worry, girls. They're just kidding." At dusk we drove out of the park and hid our camp in the woods a few miles away. The illegal spot was lovely, but our enjoyment of that park was ruined. I returned from the trip determined to reconsider the options available for protecting myself.

At that time, I lived alone on the ranch and taught night classes 5 in town. Along a city street I often traveled, a woman had a flat tire, called for help on her CB radio, and got a rapist who left her beaten. She was afraid to call for help again and stayed in her car until morning. For that reason, as well as because CBs work best along line-of-sight, which wouldn't help much in the rolling hills where I live, I ruled out a CB.

As I drove home one night, a car followed me. It passed me on a 6 narrow bridge while a passenger flashed a blinding spotlight in my face. I braked sharply. The car stopped, angled across the bridge, and four men jumped out. I realized the locked doors were useless if they broke the windows of my pickup. I started forward, hoping to knock their car aside so I could pass. Just then another car appeared, and the men hastily got back in their car. They continued to follow me, passing and repassing. I dared not go home because no one else was there. I passed no lighted houses. Finally they pulled over to the roadside, and I decided to use their tactic: fear. Speeding, the pickup horn blaring, I swerved as close to them as I dared as I roared past. It worked; they turned off the highway. But I was frightened and angry. Even in my vehicle I was too vulnerable.

Other incidents occurred over the years. One day I glanced out   7
a field below my house and saw a man with a shotgun walking toward a pond full of ducks. I drove down and explained that the land
was posted. I politely asked him to leave. He stared at me, and the
muzzle of the shotgun began to rise. In a moment of utter clarity I realized that I was alone on the ranch, and that he could shoot me and
simply drive away. The moment passed; the man left.

One night, I returned home from teaching a class to find deep   8
tire ruts in the wet ground of my yard, garbage in the driveway, and
a large gas tank empty. A light shone in the house; I couldn't remember leaving it on. I was too embarrassed to drive to a neighboring ranch and wake someone up. An hour of cautious exploration
convinced me the house was safe, but once inside, with the doors
locked, I was still afraid. I kept thinking of how vulnerable I felt,
prowling around my own house in the dark.

My first positive step was to take a kung fu class, which teaches   9
evasive or protective action when someone enters your space without permission. I learned to move confidently, scanning for possible
attackers. I learned how to assess danger and techniques for avoiding it without combat.

I also learned that one must practice several hours every day to   10
be good at kung fu. By that time I had married George; when I practiced with him, I learned how *close* you must be to your attacker to
use martial arts, and decided a 120-pound woman dare not let a six-
foot, 220-pound attacker get that close unless she is very, very good
at self-defense. I have since read articles by several women who
were extremely well trained in the martial arts, but were raped and
beaten anyway.

I thought back over the times in my life when I had been attacked   11
or threatened and tried to be realistic about my own behavior, searching for anything that had allowed me to become a victim. Overall, I
was convinced that I had not been at fault. I don't believe myself to be
either paranoid or a risk-taker, but I wanted more protection.

With some reluctance I decided to try carrying a pistol. George   12
had always carried one, despite his size and his training in martial
arts. I practiced shooting until I was sure I could hit an attacker who
moved close enough to endanger me. Then I bought a license from
the county sheriff, making it legal for me to carry the gun concealed.

But I was not yet ready to defend myself. George taught me that   13
the most important preparation was mental: convincing myself I
could actually *shoot a person*. Few of us wish to hurt or kill another
human being. But there is no point in having a gun—in fact, gun pos-

session might increase your danger—unless you know you can use it. I got in the habit of rehearsing, as I drove or walked, the precise conditions that would be required before I would shoot someone.

People who have not grown up with the idea that they are ca-   14
pable of protecting themselves—in other words, most women— might have to work hard to convince themselves of their ability, and of the necessity. Handgun ownership need not turn us into gun- slingers, but it can be part of believing in, and relying on, *ourselves* for protection.

To be useful, a pistol had to be available. In my car, it's within   15
instant reach. When I enter a deserted rest stop at night, it's in my purse, with my hand on the grip. When I walk from a dark parking lot into a motel, it's in my hand, under a coat. At home, it's on the headboard. In short, I take it with me almost everywhere I go alone.

Just carrying a pistol is not protection; avoidance is still the best   16
approach to trouble. Subconsciously watching for signs of danger, I believe I've become more alert. Handgun use, not unlike driving, becomes instinctive. Each time I've drawn my gun—I have never fired it at another human being—I've simply found it in my hand.

I was driving the half-mile to the highway mailbox one day   17
when I saw a vehicle parked about midway down the road. Several men were standing in the ditch, relieving themselves. I have no ob- jection to emergency urination, but I noticed they'd dumped several dozen beer cans in the road. Besides being ugly, cans can slash a cow's feet or stomach.

The men noticed me before they finished and made quite a per-   18
formance out of zipping their trousers while walking toward me. All four of them gathered around my small foreign car, and one of them demanded what the hell I wanted.

"This is private land. I'd appreciate it if you'd pick up the beer   19
cans."

"What beer cans?" said the belligerent one, putting both hands   20
on the car door and leaning in my window. His face was inches from mine, and the beer fumes were strong. The others laughed. One tried the passenger door, locked; another put his foot on the hood and rocked the car. They circled, lightly thumping the roof, discussing my good fortune in meeting them and the benefits they were likely to bestow upon me. I felt very small and very trapped and they knew it.

"The ones you just threw out," I said politely.   21

"I don't see no beer cans. Why don't you get out here and show   22
them to me, honey?" said the belligerent one, reaching for the han- dle inside my door.

"Right over there," I said, still being polite, "—there, and over   23
there." I pointed with the pistol, which I'd slipped under my thigh.
Within one minute the cans and the men were back in the car and
headed down the road.

I believe this incident illustrates several important principles.   24
The men were trespassing and knew it; their judgment may have
been impaired by alcohol. Their response to the polite request of a
woman alone was to use their size, numbers, and sex to inspire fear.
The pistol was a response in the same language. Politeness didn't
work; I couldn't match them in size or number. Out of the car, I'd
have been more vulnerable. The pistol just changed the balance of
power. It worked again recently when I was driving in a desolate
part of Wyoming. A man played cat-and-mouse with me for 30
miles, ultimately trying to run me off the road. When his car passed
mine with only two inches to spare, I showed him my pistol, and he
disappeared.

When I got my pistol, I told my husband, revising the old Colt   25
slogan, "God made men *and women*, but Sam Colt made them
equal." Recently I have seen a gunmaker's ad with a similar senti-
ment. Perhaps this is an idea whose time has come, though the paci-
fist inside me will be saddened if the only way women can achieve
equality is by carrying weapons.

We must treat a firearm's power with caution. "Power tends to   26
corrupt, and absolute power corrupts absolutely," as a man (Lord
Acton) once said. A pistol is not the only way to avoid being raped
or murdered in today's world, but, intelligently wielded, it can shift
the balance of power and provide a measure of safety.

MEANINGS AND VALUES

1. State in your own words the phenomenon Hasselstrom analyzes in
    this essay. Does she explain causes, effects, or both? Identify specific
    portions of the essay to support your answer.

2. What attitudes towards gun ownership does Hasselstrom probably
    anticipate her readers will bring to the essay? Be specific. Where in
    the essay, if at all, does she acknowledge likely attitudes?

3. What point(s) of view toward gun ownership does the writer encour-
    age readers to adopt? Where does she announce this outlook?

4. How would you characterize the writer's purpose? Explanation?
    Argument? Self-justification? (See "Guide to Terms": *Purpose*.)

EXPOSITORY TECHNIQUES

1. Identify the main examples presented in this essay. Why, if at all, are we justified in considering this essay as primarily concerned with explaining causes and effects when so much of it is devoted to examples?

2. In what ways does the writer use strategies of comparison and contrast in paragraphs 9–11 to consider and dismiss alternatives to gun owning (see Chapter 5)? Explain why her tactics in these paragraphs are successful or unsuccessful. (Guide: *Evaluation.*)

3. What generalities concerning when and how to use a gun correctly does the writer present in paragraphs 12–26? Where in the paragraphs does she announce the generalities? For which does she provide supporting examples? Which of the examples, if any, also illustrate causes or effects of gun ownership?

DICTION AND VOCABULARY

1. Discuss the writer's use of connotation in paragraphs 4, 6–8, and 17–23 to create emotional emphasis that makes her reasons for owning a gun seem plausible and convincing. (Guide: *Connotation/Denotation.*)

2. Tell how the writer's use of qualification and her word choice in the opening paragraph help keep the essay from becoming predominantly argumentative. (Guide: *Qualification; Diction.*)

3. How might this essay have been different had the writer not made such frequent use of "I" in presenting examples and explanations?

READ TO WRITE

1. **Collaborating:** Working in a group, list as many good reasons as you can for owning and carrying a pistol. Then, list reasons for *not* carrying a pistol. Finally, arrange each list in order from most persuasive to least persuasive and provide a brief explanation for ranking of each item.

2. **Considering Audience:** To identify possible topics for writing, think about how people's attitudes about issues like animal rights, gun control, approaches to education, and economic policies are likely to differ according to where they live or according to their economic and social status. Think about how you might identify such differences, their causes, and their effects. You might also wish to identify other facts that affect people's outlooks in substantial ways.

3. **Developing an Essay:** Explore another issue over which there has been considerable public debate. Follow Hasselstrom's lead, and write about it from a personal perspective, exploring causes and effects and providing explanation rather than argument.

(NOTE: Suggestions for topics requiring development by analysis of CAUSE AND EFFECT are on pp. 350–351 at the end of this chapter.)

SUSAN ROACH

Susan Roach is a freelance writer whose work has appeared in a number of magazines. She lives in San Francisco.

My Father the Geezer

In "My Father the Geezer," Susan Roach begins with the assumption that most readers hold negative views about the likely effects of having older parents, then goes on to undermine them by presenting in often humorous detail the consequences in her own life of having a "Geezer" for a parent. This essay first appeared in the *New York Times Magazine*.

My father was 65 when I was born. Even to myself, the statement   1
sits funny, like one of those how-so brain teasers with the hidden loophole—the boy's mother is the doctor. But there is no loophole. He was my biological father, 20 years older than my mother. He had children late because he married late. I came in under the wire.

People invariably want to know what it was like growing up   2
with an old father. Some want to know because they're coming to parenthood relatively late themselves and wonder how it will affect their children. Most are just rubbernecking. There's a "Good God!" in their tone, as though I'd been suckled by wolves. Who fed whom, they're wondering. Did I dress him or did he dress me? To which I reply that he was a young 65, white-haired but red-blooded.

Granted, my upbringing seemed a little odd. I could recite the   3
names of all the members of the Lawrence Welk musical family. I practiced phonemes by reading aloud from Modern Maturity. My first paying job, at age 7, was to sit on my father's lap with a pair of tweezers and cull overgrown ear hairs for 2 cents a pluck.

One thing I didn't do was engage in those "When I'm age X,   4
he'll be X" calculations. Children live in the moment. If he was around next Saturday to drive me to the riding ring, that was good enough. We'd deal with the strangeness when we got to it. How will an 82-year-old cope with a 16-year-old? As best he could, and with frequent naps.

Fortunately for all involved, I wasn't a particularly difficult   5
teen-ager. I remember one summer afternoon, walking out of the A&P with a roll of "Ripe for Tonight" avocado stickers I'd swiped

from a stockboy's cart. My father, who'd been waiting in the car, said, "What's under your sweatshirt?" "Nothing," I lied. He just shook his head and went back to his newspaper. For whatever reason, I never moved on to the big stuff: jewelry, clothing, actual avocados. I like to think my father's indifference took the thrill out of shoplifting. More likely, he was just lucky.

In the end, what most people fixate on is that my father was too old to—as they often put it—play ball with me. This is true. I can't recall ever seeing him run. He didn't swim or ride a bicycle or roller-skate. The extent of my father's physical activity was an evening constitutional to the end of Dogford Road, in his Irish tweed hat, whistling a tune and swinging a Hanover Hardware yardstick as if it were a brass-tipped cane. Perhaps that's why I didn't learn to swim as a child, why I was chosen last for gym teams. Perhaps, and who cares. Show me the support group for children of sedentary parents.

What stands out about my father are not the things he couldn't do but the things he did. That most of them were done from a sitting position hardly seems to matter. My father was an artist, a story-teller, a character. When I was 11, he painted a life-size elephant on the basement floor because elephants were my favorite animal. He taught me to draw, making a squiggle on a sheet of paper and challenging me to finish the picture. He framed my finger paintings and hung them on the living room wall, and when guests commented, he'd make up the name of "a noted abstract artist" and wink at me. My father, in short, was a very cool dad. So he mixed Metamucil in his orange juice. So he turned the TV up loud. So his hands shook on the steering wheel. Of all the undesirable things fathers can be (absent, cruel, cold, immature), old is pretty weak poison.

Parenthood over 60 has its advantages. My father spent a good deal more time with me than the average 30-year-old father can afford to. Retirement is like endless paternity leave. Pop was my day care, my baby sitter, my play date. We didn't break a sweat together, but we had a lot of fun.

To be sure, it could easily have been otherwise. Old fathers are more likely to be invalid fathers, senile fathers, dead fathers. (I like to think I kept mine young at heart.) Sixty-five is not the ideal age to have a baby. You can be too old to be a parent. You can also be too young. Neither has all that much to do with years.

Would my father have been a better parent had he been 30 at the time I was born? Probably not. My father spent his 30's on the road with a theater troupe. He would have resented my arrival, the shelved aspirations, the loss of freedom I represented. As it was, I was a gift (or so I like to think), an unexpected coda on a long, full life.

MEANINGS AND VALUES

1. Why does Roach point out that people "fixated" on the fact that her father was "too old to play ball" (par. 1)? What is the traditional value placed on children playing ball with their fathers? What activities "replaced" this for Roach?

2. Why is the phrase "retirement is endless paternity leave" (par. 8) significant for readers today who often come from homes with two working parents?

3. What is the significance of the last line of the essay? Why is the musical reference appropriate for an essay on Roach's father?

EXPOSITORY TECHNIQUES

1. Roach tells us that her father married late and consequently was an older parent (par. 1). Only at the end of the essay does the reader learn what career Roach's father had and the potential reason that he may have settled into marriage later in life. Is it important for the reader to know why Roach's father had children later in life early on in the essay? Would it have been more effective? Why might Roach have waited to share that information with her readers?

2. What positive and negative effects of having an older father does Roach list in this essay? Do they support her response to people that she shares with her readers at the end of paragraph 2 ("... to which I reply that he was a young 65, white-haired but red-blooded.")?

DICTION AND VOCABULARY

1. What is the tone of Roach's essay? Does she make light of a serious topic, or is her use of humor very deliberate? Explain. (See "Guide to Terms": *Tone*.)

2. At what point does she take on a serious voice? Why might she have chosen this spot?

3. What kinds of readers might enjoy this piece? Explain.

READ TO WRITE

1. **Collaborating:** Roach shares particular memories of episodes and events with her father. Individually, write a list of the times that you remember the most with one of your parents. Compare your list with

a partner and look for any common threads or activities that you might have. Then look at what you did differently. Write an individual comparison and contrast essay of the memories that you and your partner have with your respective parents. Be sure to include a cause-effect analysis explaining the differences.

2. **Considering Audience:** How would readers who have grown up without a father in the household respond to this essay? Would it have the same impact? Rewrite this essay for a reader who might better identify with a mother or some other woman who was a strong role model. Use a woman in your life as the basis for the essay.

3. **Developing an Essay:** Choose a role model in your life who may have been somewhat different from role models in your friend's lives. (i.e. Roach's father was different because of his age.) Write an essay similar in style sharing with your reader the experiences that you remember. Be sure that the experiences reflect the different quality that the person you choose possesses.

(NOTE: Suggestions for topics requiring development by analysis of CAUSE AND EFFECT are on pp. 350–351 at the end of this chapter.)

Issues and Ideas

Work, Success, and Failure

- William Severini Kowinski, *Kids in the Mall: Growing Up Controlled*
- Randall Rothenberg, *What Makes Sammy Walk?*
- Peter Hillary, *Everest Is Mighty, We Are Fragile*

"What do you do (for a living)?" is a question people often ask when they meet someone for the first time. Clearly, we frequently define ourselves and others by our work. But is it appropriate to do this? Does our work shape our personalities and values? If so, how does this happen? Is it a good idea to build our lives around work?

In our society, moreover, work is usually a competitive enterprise: we succeed at work or we fail. Indeed, our entire economic system rests on a belief in the benefits of competition. No wonder, then, that success and failure should have such psychological importance for us, or that we should treat many other activities besides work as challenges at which we succeed and fail.

The links of cause and effect tying together concepts of work, success, failure, and challenge and leading to systems of value and behavior are complex, and certainly beyond the range of a single essay to unravel, if anyone can indeed do so. Nonetheless, the essays that follow address various elements in this complicated relationship. William Severini Kowinski, in "Kids in the Mall: Growing Up Controlled," explores the links between contemporary concepts of work and the self-images and values of teenagers. Randall Rothenberg in, "What Makes Sammy Walk?," asks why people have begun rejecting the importance of work in their lives, and addresses the effects of their following a different system of values. Peter Hillary, in "Everest is Mighty, We are Fragile," looks at the importance for individuals and society as a whole of taking on challenges, even those where failure can lead to disaster and death. Though they raise some serious questions about work, success, and failure, however, in the end, each of the writers affirms the importance of work and challenges in our lives.

WILLIAM SEVERINI KOWINSKI

WILLIAM SEVERINI KOWINSKI grew up in Greensburg, Pennsylvania. In 1964, the year before the first mall was built in Greensburg, he left to attend Knox College in Illinois. While attending Knox he spent a semester studying in the fiction and poetry workshops at the University of Iowa. Kowinski was a writer and editor for the Boston *Phoenix* and the Washington *Newsworks* and has written articles for a number of national newspapers and magazines including *Esquire, New Times,* and *The New York Times Magazine.* His book *The Malling of America: An Inside Look at the Great Consumer Paradise* (1985) is based on his travels to malls throughout the United States and Canada.

Kids in the Mall: Growing Up Controlled

Over the past thirty years, the number, size, and variety of suburban shopping malls have grown at astonishing rates, replacing, in many cases, both plazas and urban shopping districts. They are now important economic and cultural forces in American and Canadian society. In this chapter from *The Malling of America,* Kowinski looks at some of the ways malls have affected the teenagers who spend much of their time shopping, working, or just hanging around at the mall.

Butch heaved himself up and loomed over the group. "Like it was different for me," he piped. "My folks used to drop me off at the shopping mall every morning and leave me all day. It was like a big free baby-sitter, you know? One night they never came back for me. Maybe they moved away. Maybe there's some kind of a Bureau of Missing Parents I could check with."   1

—Richard Peck, *Secrets of the Shopping Mall,* a novel for teenagers

From his sister at Swarthmore, I'd heard about a kid in Florida   2
whose mother picked him up after school every day, drove him straight to the mall, and left him there until it closed—all at his insistence. I'd heard about a boy in Washington who, when his family moved from one suburb to another, pedaled his bicycle five miles every day to get back to his old mall, where he once belonged.

Their stories aren't unusual. The mall is a common experience   3
for the majority of American youth; they have probably been going

there all their lives. Some ran within their first large open space, saw their first fountain, bought their first toy, and read their first book in a mall. They may have smoked their first cigarette or first joint or turned them down, had their first kiss or lost their virginity in the mall parking lot. Teenagers in America now spend more time in the mall than anywhere else but home and school. Mostly it is their choice, but some of that mall time is put in as the result of two-pay-check and single-parent households, and the lack of other viable alternatives. But are these kids being harmed by the mall?

I wondered first of all what difference it makes for adolescents   4
to experience so many important moments in the mall. They are, after all, at play in the fields of its little world and they learn its ways; they adapt to it and make it adapt to them. It's here that these kids get their street sense, only it's mall sense. They are learning the ways of a large-scale artificial environment: its subtleties and flexibilities, its particular pleasures and resonances, and the attitudes it fosters.

The presence of so many teenagers for so much time was not   5
something mall developers planned on. In fact, it came as a big surprise. But kids became a fact of mall life very early, and the International Council of Shopping Centers found it necessary to commission a study, which they published along with a guide to mall managers on how to handle the teenage incursion.

The study found that "teenagers in suburban centers are bored   6
and come to the shopping centers mainly as a place to go. Teenagers in suburban centers spent more time fighting, drinking, littering and walking than did their urban counterparts, but presented fewer overall problems." The report observed that "adolescents congregated in groups of two to four and predominantly at locations selected by them rather than management." This probably had something to do with the decision to install game arcades, which allow management to channel these restless adolescents into naturally contained areas away from major traffic points of adult shoppers.

The guide concluded that mall management should tolerate   7
and even encourage the teenage presence because, in the words of the report, "The vast majority support the same set of values as does shopping center management." *The same set of values* means simply that mall kids are already preprogrammed to be consumers and that the mall can put the finishing touches to them as hard-core, lifelong shoppers just like everybody else. That, after all, is what the mall is about. So it shouldn't be surprising that in spending a lot of time there, adolescents find little that challenges the assumption that the goal of life is to make money and buy products, or that just about everything else in life is to be used to serve those ends.

Growing up in a high-consumption society already adds ines- 8
timable pressure to kids' lives. Clothes consciousness has invaded
the grade schools, and popularity is linked with having the best,
newest clothes in the currently acceptable styles. Even what they
read has been affected. "Miss [Nancy] Drew wasn't obsessed with
her wardrobe," noted *Wall Street Journal.* "But today the mystery in
teen fiction for girls is what outfit the heroine will wear next."
Shopping has become a survival skill and there is certainly no better
place to learn it than the mall, where its importance is powerfully reinforced and certainly never questioned.

The mall as a university of suburban materialism, where Valley 9
Girls and Boys from coast to coast are educated in consumption, has
its other lessons in this era of change in family life and sexual mores
and their economic and social ramifications. The plethora of products in the mall, plus the pressure on teens to buy them, may contribute to the phenomenon that psychologist David Elkind calls
"the hurried child": kids who are exposed to too much of the adult
world too quickly, and must respond with a sophistication that be-
lies their still-tender emotional development. Certainly the adult
products marketed for children—form-fitting designer jeans, sexy
tops for preteen girls—add to the social pressure to look like an
adult, along with the home-grown need to understand adult fi-
nances (why mothers must work) and adult emotions (when parents divorce).

Kids spend so much time at the mall partly because their par- 10
ents allow it and even encourage it. The mall is safe, it doesn't seem
to harbor any unsavory activities, and there is adult supervision; it
is, after all, a controlled environment. So the temptation, especially
for working parents, is to let the mall be their babysitter. At least the
kids aren't watching TV. But the mall's role as a surrogate mother
may be more extensive and more profound.

Karen Lansky, a writer living in Los Angeles, has looked into 11
the subject and she told me some of her conclusions about the effects
on its teenaged denizens of the mall's controlled and controlling environment. "Structure is the dominant idea, since true 'mall rats'
lack just that in their homelives," she said, "and adolescents about to
make the big leap into growing up crave more structure than our
modern society cares to acknowledge." Karen pointed out some of
the elements malls supply that kids used to get from their families,
like warmth (Strawberry Shortcake dolls and similar cute and cuddly merchandise), old-fashioned mothering ("We do it all for you,"
the fast-food slogan), and even home cooking (the "homemade"
treats at the food court).

The problem in all this, as Karen Lansky sees it, is that while   12
families nurture children by encouraging growth through the assumption of responsibility and then by letting them rest in the bosom of the family from the rigors of growing up, the mall as a
structural mother encourages passivity and consumption, as long as
the kid doesn't make trouble. Therefore all they learn about becoming adults is how to act and how to consume.

Kids are in the mall not only in the passive role of shoppers—   13
they also work there, especially as fast-food outlets infiltrate the
mall's enclosure. There they learn how to hold a job and take responsibility, but still within the same value context. When *CBS
Reports* went to Oak Park Mall in suburban Kansas City, Kansas, to
tape part of their hour-long consideration of malls, "After the Dream
Comes True," they interviewed a teenaged girl who worked in a
fast-food outlet there. In a sequence that didn't make the final program, she described the major goal of her present life, which was to
perfect the curl on top of the ice-cream cones that were her store's
specialty. If she could do that, she would be moved from the lowly
soft-drink dispenser to the more prestigious ice-cream division, the
curl on top of the status ladder at her restaurant. These are the
achievements that are important at the mall.

Other benefits of such jobs may also be overrated, according to   14
Laurence D. Steinberg of the University of California at Irvine's social ecology department, who did a study on teenage employment.
Their jobs, he found, are generally simple, mindlessly repetitive and
boring. They don't really learn anything, and the jobs don't lead
anywhere. Teenagers also work primarily with other teenagers;
even their supervisors are often just a little older than they are.
"Kids need to spend time with adults," Steinberg told me.
"Although they get benefits from peer relationships, without parents and other adults it's one-sided socialization. They hang out
with each other, have age-segregated jobs, and watch TV."

Perhaps much of this is not so terrible or even so terribly differ-   15
ent. Now that they have so much more to contend with in their lives,
adolescents probably need more time to spend with other adolescents without adult impositions, just to sort things out. Though it is
more concentrated in the mall (and therefore perhaps a clearer target), the value system there is really the dominant one of the whole
society. Attitudes about curiosity, initiative, self-expression, empathy, and disinterested learning aren't necessarily made in the mall;
they are mirrored there, perhaps a bit more intensely—as through a
glass brightly.

Besides, the mall is not without its educational opportunities. 16
There are bookstores, where there is at least a short shelf of classics at
great prices, and other books from which it is possible to learn more
than how to do sit-ups. There are tools, from hammers to VCRs, and
products, from clothes to records, that can help the young find and
express themselves. There are older people with stories, and places to
be alone or to talk one-on-one with a kindred spirit. And there is always the passing show.

The mall itself may very well be an education about the future. 17
I was struck with the realization, as early as my first forays into
Greengate,[1] that the mall is only one of a number of enclosed and
controlled environments that are part of the lives of today's young.
The mall is just an extension, say, of those large suburban schools—
only there's Karmelkorn instead of chem lab, the ice rink instead of
the gym: It's high school without the impertinence of classes.

Growing up, moving from home to school to the mall—from 18
enclosure to enclosure, transported in cars—is a curiously continu-
ous process, without much in the way of contrast or contract with
unenclosed reality. Places must tend to blur into one another. But
whatever differences and dangers there are in this, the skills these
adolescents are learning may turn out to be useful in their later lives.
For we seem to be moving inexorably into an age of pre-planned
and regulated environments, and this is the world they will inherit.

Still, it might be better if they had more of a choice. One 19
teenaged girl confessed to *CBS Reports* that she sometimes felt she
was missing something by hanging out at the mall so much. "But
I'm here," she said, "and this is what I have."

MEANINGS AND VALUES

1.   Do teenagers who spend their time in malls display any obviously
     unusual behavior? If so, in what ways do they behave? If not, how
     might one describe their behavior?

2.   What question does this essay attempt to answer? Where in the essay
     is the question asked? Other than providing an answer to the ques-
     tion, what purpose or purposes does this selection have? (See "Guide
     to Terms": *Purpose.*)

[1]Greengate Mall in Greesburg, Pennsylvania, where Kowinski began his research on
malls (Editors' note).

3. What does Kowinski see as the major effects of malls on teenagers? What other, less important effects (if any) does he identify? Discuss whether or not the author presents enough evidence to convince most readers that he has correctly identified the effects.

4. Where in the essay does Kowinski consider causes other than the mall environment for the attitudes and behaviors of teenagers? Explain how the alternative explanation either undermines or adds to his view of the malls.

Expository Techniques

1. What strategies does the author employ in the introduction (pars. 1–3) to help convince readers of the importance of reading and thinking about what happens to teenagers as a result of the time they spend at malls? (Guide: *Introductions.*)

2. Discuss how the author uses examples, quotations from authorities, and various strategies of emphasis in paragraphs 8, 9, 11, 13, and 14 to indicate whether or not the effects of malls can be considered harmful. (Guide: *Emphasis.*)

3. Which chapters of the essay are devoted *primarily* to exploring the effects of the mall environment? Which are devoted *primarily* to discussing whether or not the effects are harmful?

4. What use does the author make of qualification in presenting his conclusions in paragraphs 15 and 17–19? (Guide: *Qualification.*) Explain why this strategy adds to or weakens your confidence in his conclusions.

5. Explain how parallelism in paragraphs 17 and 18 helps emphasize similarities in the environments. (Guide: *Parallel Structure.*)

Diction and Vocabulary

1. Who is the Nancy Drew alluded to in paragraph 8? (Guide: *Figures of Speech.*) What is the purpose of this allusion?

2. What transitional devices are used to tie together paragraphs 7–9? (Guide: *Transition.*) Which are used to link paragraphs 10–13?

3. If you do not know the meaning of some of the following words, look them up in the dictionary: loomed, piped (par. 1); viable (3); resonances, fosters (4); incursion (5); inestimable (8); mores, ramifications, plethora (9); surrogate (10); denizens (11); nurture (12); socialization (14); impositions, empathy, disinterested (15); kindred (16); forays, impertinence (17); inexorably (18).

Read to Write

1. **Collaborating:** Working in a group, use these questions to help develop a topic and plan for an essay: Were malls as important to you

as they were to the people Kowinski describes in his essay? Based on your experience and observations, does Kowinski appear to be overstating the effects of malls on teenagers? What other influences on the lives of teenagers are as important or more important than malls (or than shopping in general)? Are malls important in people's lives because of the special experiences they offer, or simply because they bring together large numbers of people and offer work to many individuals?

2.   **Considering Audience:** Kowinski takes a partly negative view of malls and the work they provide. Are readers in general likely to agree or disagree with him? What do you think? Prepare a brief essay analyzing readers' likely reactions to the essay.

3.   **Developing an Essay:** What experiences and activities condition us for success or failure? Which ones give us important goals for work, personal relationships, and civic responsibility? Taking an approach similar to the one Kowinski employs in "Kids in the Mall," criticize the influence of the activities that characterize contemporary teenage life. Or, reverse Kowinski's approach and praise the effects of particular activities and experiences.

(NOTE: Suggestions for topics requiring development by analysis of CAUSE AND EFFECT are on pp. 350–351 at the end of this chapter.)

RANDALL ROTHENBERG

RANDALL ROTHENBERG is a writer whose essays have appeared in a wide variety of magazines. He has also published *The Neoliberals* (1984) and *Where the Suckers Moon* (1994), a chronicle of an advertising campaign.

What Makes Sammy Walk?

Why would people with good jobs stop working? What will happen to them? Why would people who lose their jobs not bother to find new ones? These are some of the questions Rothenberg addresses in this essay, first published in *Esquire* magazine in 1995. By altering the title of a novel from the 1950s, *What Makes Sammy Run,* Rothenberg makes plain his desire to look at the causes of a phenomenon that is a surprising reversal of the characteristic values and behaviors of modern society.

In Northgate, a Seattle neighborhood of sturdy homes and limitless vistas, a support group meets twice a month to help its members through the emotionally wrenching, physically demanding withdrawal from addiction. Among them tonight are an accountant, a college administrator, a computer-company founder, and a state-government employee. They are not dependent on drugs, alcohol, sexual relationships, or the other themes of twelve-step programs. These thirteen men and women are seeking release from their reliance on jobs. 1

"My name is Darrel," says one. He is forty-two, a compact man with neatly trimmed brown hair, dressed comfortably in a sweatshirt and jeans. "My interest is in getting out of the rat race and getting back to simplicity. I think it's a matter of time—not if but when I can do it." To prepare himself, he's deliberately stopped repairing or replacing broken household appliances. "The dryer pooped out, and we can do without the dryer," he says to approving nods. 2

A young woman follows. She is sitting on a couch, under a bookshelf on which newsletters with names like *The Tightwad Gazette* and *Simple Living* are neatly displayed. "My name is Laura," she says, twisting her fingers nervously. "I've decided to quit my job." 3

"Great!" barks the silver-haired man next to her.   4

Emboldened, she continues. "I'm gonna quit my job in June. It's   5
not really that hard." For months already, she and her boyfriend
have been living on one income and banking the second. "So I'm
gonna quit my job," Laura repeats, trying to convince herself. "I'll
get all my time back."

Finally, eyes turn to David Heitmiller. He and his wife Jacque   6
Blix, forty-nine and forty-five, respectively, tall, calm, and articulate,
are stalwarts and stars of this group.

"My name is Dave and I'm married to Jacque, and we've been   7
on a voluntary-simplicity track for close to four years now, and it
worked out," he tells his confidants. "We went through a heavy-
duty yuppie phase in the mid- to late-eighties, like many people
did." But after realizing their folly, they went on a rigid program to
control their spending and expand their savings. "We succeeded in
reaching financial independence one year ago." At about the same
time, U.S. West, where Dave had served in several executive jobs
throughout seventeen years, offered him a buyout. Naturally, he
took it.

"I haven't worked since. In a regular job, I should say. I have,   8
very voluntarily and simplistically, rebuilt my bicycle. I did all the
work myself," he says proudly, "but I got the frame for free."

Do you have a Barnes & Noble superstore near you, one of   9
those giant book emporiums, replete with coffee shop, easy chairs,
and browsable magazine stands? Skulk around one some afternoon and check out how many of its plush settees are occupied—
and by whom. "A lot of people are reexamining," muses Jim Kirk,
a Barnes & Noble vice-president. "A lot who were going a thousand miles an hour in the 1980s are now saying, 'Let's go thirty
miles an hour.'"

Or perhaps you have a nouvelle coffee shop in your   10
neighborhood—not the modern move-'em-in-and-move-'em-out
kind, but one of the Parisian set-a-spell variety popping up of late.
Ever notice who's pausing over that steaming latte and the morning
paper in the hours before noon?

Chances are that, dotted among the expected regulars—the   11
stroller-pushing moms, the aimless students, and the elderly—one
third of the denizens are men, middle-class, middle-aged, and piddling around. Men who, in another life, were managers, financial
planners, sales executives, attorneys, bankers, administrators, and
account executives. White-collar men, "the interchangeable parts of
the big chains of authority that bind the society together," the late

sociologist C. Wright Mills called them. Men like you.[1] Men who should be working. But aren't.

Every week, it seems, I run into an old friend, sometimes two or three—Ivy Leaguers in their late thirties or forties, comfortable but far from rich—who have departed the fast track. Whether they were pushed or not, their reactions have been strikingly similar: After a lot of soul-searching, some agony, and perhaps a tiny bit of self-loathing, they have decided to remain in the slow lane. First it was Peter, Princeton B.A. and Harvard Law Review, who went on hourly wages and then went part-time at his West Coast firm in order to study botany. Then there was Rob, who, fired by his investment bank, decided to work part-time, on contract, so that he might dally with a paintbrush several mornings a week. Al, who'd spent the years after his M.B.A. and law degree planning international real estate ventures, forced his bank to fire him when it started withdrawing from the field. Before making any moves, he's taking at least a year off to spend time with his infant daughter, even as his wife begins her new life as a judicial clerk.

They may seem like cultural quirks—1990s versions of James Dean's causeless heretic, who've substituted loafers for leather in their rebellion against America's Organization Man ethos—but it's not merely the economically and educationally resourceful who are joining the BarcaLounger brigade. Hundreds of thousands, perhaps millions, of otherwise normal men are banding together in a mass mystery that defies easy explanation. They are not turning on. They are not tuning in. But they are dropping out.

Last July, a Gallup poll found that some one third of all Americans said they would take a 20 percent cut in income if they or their spouses could work fewer hours, an unprecedentedly high figure. Mere wishful thinking? When IBM offered employees a departure package in mid–1992, more than thirty-two thousand of the wing-tip warriors—60 percent more than management had anticipated—took the buyout.

All around us are the unmistakable signs of a shift in the American character. Instead of working harder as times get tougher, men, including the salaried shock troops that sustain the corporate world, are working less.

For several years—even as their wives and sisters have continued on the trek toward more hours for higher pay—men have been

---

[1]*Esquire* magazine, where the essay first appeared, is supposedly addressed to a male audience, though a huge proportion of its readers are women. (Editors' note)

drifting away from work. At first, the departures were involuntary, forced almost solely by the continuing disappearance of factory jobs as microchips replaced muscle. In recent years, with corporate downsizing decimating the one fourth of American workers classified as managers and professionals, some experts have begun to notice a surge in deliberate departures.

"This has been going on among a core group of leading-edge boomers, and some older than the boomers, probably since the early seventies. The difference now is that it's going mainstream," says Gerald Celente, director of the Trends Research Institute in Rhinebeck, New York, "What's going on now in a lot of people's minds is, Look, I'm working longer and harder, I'm falling back, I hate my job, I don't know if I'm going to have a job—I don't want to do this anymore!"   17

In the post–Timothy Leary world, this leave-taking lifestyle is no longer referred to as dropping out. Some economists speak of "downshifting," the pursuit and acceptance of slower days and lower pay. Others talk of a "voluntary-simplicity movement." Still others call it a search for "exit strategies." Inferential Focus, a respected New York trend-analysis company, says the desire "to take flight from current employment predicaments has become pandemic."   18

It is evident in many varied phenomena. You can find a hint of it in the Arts and Crafts-style armchairs, lamps, coffee tables, and couches that the Rouse Company, the nation's premier shopping-center developer, placed throughout the public spaces of Atlanta's Perimeter Mall to make it more appealing to people with time on their hands. It's in the baby-changing facilities Barnes & Noble has placed in the men's restrooms of its superstores. And it's in the proliferation of newsletters—like *Living Cheap News* of San Jose, California; *Skinflint News* of Palm Harbor, Florida; and *Simple Living* of Seattlewritten for folks with empty schedules and shallow wallets. (One such journal, *The Tightwad Gazette* of Leeds, Maine, has grown to fifty thousand subscribers from a mere seventeen hundred in less than five years.)   19

Data culled from government, industry, and think tanks point to an astonishing transformation in the nature of work, which we were raised to associate with eight-hour days at offices or factories. The number of men in their traditional prime working years—early twenties to early sixties—who worked full-time for at least eight out of ten years fell nine percentage points from the 1970s to the 1980s. The recession that followed can only have added to their ranks, pulling the current number of "full-time full-timers" below 70 percent   20 of American men. Of those employed, fully one fourth work on a temporary, contract, or part-time basis, according to the Economics Policy Institute in Washington, D.C. Link Resources Corporation, a technology-research company, says the total number of Americans who work at least part of the time at home, for themselves or for their employers, rose to 43.2 million in 1994 from fewer than 25 million just eight years ago.

Like it or not, man by man, modem by modem, we are becoming a freelance nation. We are insecure, sure, but we are also, as the word implies, free.   21

"This whole simple-living phenomenon seems to be marginal, but it's growing. It seems to be exploding," says Harvard economist Juliet B. Schor. The nation's leading critic of drudgery, Schor, in her 1992 book, *The Overworked American*, calculated that between 1969 and 1987, the average employed person put in an extra 163 hours a year on the job. It's a telling sign that her newest study, which began in February, is designed to establish how many Americans are laying back, and why they're doing so.   22

In pursuit of dropouts, Schor distributed a notice at a Massachusetts unemployment center for white-collar workers established along the Route 128 high-tech corridor. The respondents told her similar tales. "Their jobs were too stressful. They were unsatisfied. They were searching for meaning," Schor recalls. "So they found other, lower-paying jobs, or they got themselves fired. They were no longer playing ball."   23

"Most had new jobs or situations that paid much less," she continues, "but they were much happier."   24

In that euphoria lies perhaps the most consequential and troubling aspect of men's move to the sidelines. We were raised to labor— to honor sweat and revere the profit motive. For skilled, educated, and experienced people to find contentment in the absence of effort denotes a historical alteration in the meaning of work and a change in the importance of the work ethic in a nation whose willingness to toil distinguished it from the aristocracies from which our forebears fled. It also indicates an abandonment of the American dream by the people who have benefited from it the most. We are asking ourselves why we should work so hard, if forces beyond our control are determining our fate; we are answering by earning little, consuming less, and opting out.   25

We are becoming, in short, a nation of middle-aged slackers.   26

. . . Its lure is ancient and tempting, the call to abjure work and drop out. Even in "this bustling nineteenth century," Henry David   27

Thoreau found a ready audience for his message that toil was enslaving the American mind. "Men labor under a mistake," he wrote in *Walden Pond.* "The better part of a man is soon plowed into the soil for compost. By a seeming fate, commonly called necessity, they are employed, as it says in an old book, laying up treasures which moth and rust will corrupt and thieves break through and steal. It is a fool's life, as they will find when they get to the end of it."

Thoreau notwithstanding, it would be a mistake to assume that were it not for the drumbeat of commercialism and its appeals to our vanity, we would readily return to a state of nature. Thoreau exasperated his contemporaries: "To a healthy mind," James Russell Lowell wrote of him shortly after his death, "the world is a constant challenge." Such critics understood that, almost from the beginning, the character of Americans was distinguished from that of our European antecedents not by a search for leisure and contemplation but by our willingness to work and seek the rewards. 28

"The workman," wrote Tocqueville of his travels across this new nation, "is filled with new ambition and new desires, he is harassed by new wants. Every instant he views with longing the profits of his employer; and in order to share them, he strives to dispose of his labor at a higher rate and he generally at length succeeds in the attempt." 29

As the decade wore on, Thoreau's message of self-reliance was blended into this obsession with acquisition and fashioned into the American dream, which could be summarized in four words: Work and get rich. 30

The classic expression of this reverie sat prominently on my parents' living-room bookshelf throughout my childhood. It was a thin volume titled *Acres of Diamonds,* a reprint of a motivational lecture that was delivered more than six thousand times in the late nineteenth and early twentieth centuries by Russell H. Conwell, a Baptist minister and the founder of Temple University in Philadelphia. 31

In the speech, Conwell recounted the apocryphal story of Ali Hafed, a Persian farmer who was persuaded by a priest that fields of gemstones lay somewhere beyond the mountains of his domain. For years, Ali Hafed roamed far and wide to find the treasure, eventually selling his farm to finance the expedition, exhausting himself and dying a broke and broken man. Not long after Ali Hafed's death, the farmer who had bought his land was leading a camel across it when a gleam caught his eye. And there he discovered the **acres of diamonds**, right in Ali Hafed's own backyard. 32

Conwell meant his lesson literally. The lecture is filled with in-   33
spiring stories of entrepreneurs who searched their own environs
and found fabulous wealth: the man who made $52,000 inventing a
better hatpin; the fellow who made $90,000 developing rock candy.
"I say you ought to be rich; you have no right to be poor," Conwell
thundered to the multitudes. "You and I know there are some things
more valuable than money. . . . Nevertheless, the man of common
sense also knows that there is not any one of those things that is not
greatly enhanced by the use of money. Money is power." It's no
wonder that with such sentiments, *Acres of Diamonds* to this day remains a favorite motivational reference, cited in life-insurance-sales
guides and at Amway conventions.

Luckily, this work ethic coincided with the needs of industrial   34
capitalism. Competitive success required firms continually to increase their productivity—their ability to get fewer workers to turn
out more goods in less time, which makes products cheaper and,
therefore, more profitable. As large corporations took over the management of the American economy, the workers who made this nation the most productive the world had ever seen were rewarded
with an implied social contract: higher wages and lifetime job security for more and harder work. "What makes the economy function
well," Herbert Stein, the head of President Nixon's Council of
Economic Advisers, once said, "is that a hundred million people get
up every morning and go to work, doing the best for themselves that
they can."

The bargain was a good one for America. In the fifteen years fol-   35
lowing the end of World War II, family income doubled. "Middle
class," a term that applied to only a third of the nation at the start of
the war, referred to two thirds by the mid-1970s.

As material comfort became a given, Americans found fulfill-   36
ment in the social esteem their professions and professional accou-
trements provided. "Satisfaction in work often rests upon status
satisfactions," C. Wright Mills wrote in the 1950s. "Status panic," he
believed, had become an essential motivation for people to work in
the white-collar world. The 1980s provided vigorous support for his
thesis. SUCCESS! shouted this magazine,[2] an avatar of the new work
ethic, on its February 1985 cover, above a photo of a young man, his
red tie flying, his briefcase clutched tightly to his chest. "It is the religion of the eighties. Everyone pursues it. Only the most driven and
talented achieve it. Few know how to live with it. Or without it."

[2]*Esquire.* (Editors' note)

Today, it all seems so dated. Daniel Yankelovich's annual DYG   37
Scan trend-tracking study uncovered striking disaffection from
work, with employees routinely expressing grave doubts about
their futures, their employers' loyalty to them, the value of accrued
professional experience, and even the bedrock tenet of the American
work ethic—that work can set you free from want. In less than ten
years, something has happened, either in our character or our economy, to upend the work ethic.

In large part, this development has arisen because work pro-   38
vides workers with fewer real rewards. Even though the economy,
now in its third solid year of recovery, is booming, the benefits have
been manifested almost entirely in the creation of new jobs, not in
the improvement of existing ones. Real wages have declined in almost every sector of the economy since 1979, according to a
McKinsey analysis of Labor Department data. Benefits, too, are disappearing. Defined-benefit pensions—retirement plans that guarantee fixed payments from departure to death—covered 84 percent of
workers as recently as 1982. Today, slightly more than half of all
workers have their futures thus secured.

"In the aftermath of the recession, we are witnessing a gradual   39
downward revision of expectations about accumulating material
wealth to achieve success," says Yankelovich. "People are lowering
their expectations about what they can get out of their jobs. They are
putting their emotional investment into values and lifestyles that depend less on work and money."

Mark Baron changed his investment portfolio a few months   40
ago, joining the two million men who the U.S. Census Bureau says
are now serving as full-time fathers. I came across his name in a
newsletter called *At-Home Dad,* a publication filled with supportive
assertions ("at-home dads have smarter kids") and practical advice
("pet-sitting for profit").

A thirty-seven-year-old former industrial-tool salesman from   41
Sharon, Massachusetts, Mark started talking two years ago with his
wife, Andrea, about adding to their brood. They already had a three-
year-old son and part-time custody of Mark's twelve-year-old son
from a previous marriage. They calculated the costs, psychic and
physical. He and Andrea, a rising finance-company executive, hated
what Mark called "the nuttiness in the morning—packing lunches,
who's gonna stay home if the kid is sick. You walk in at 6:00 P.M. and
you spend the whole night doing baths, packing kids up, making
lunches for the next day. Nine o'clock at night, you collapse. And
when you finish paying day-care expenses, incremental expenses,

buying clothing for the road, lunches on the road, dry cleaning—was it worth it?" Out of Mark's salary, then in the mid-forties, they were left with $10,000 to $15,000 after taxes.

Instead of sacrificing the job of another baby, they decided to jettison Marks' job. "We asked, 'Is it worth $10,000?' No. Forty, sure, but not for ten." 42

Implicit in the lesson of the work ethic was the idea of control—that we create our own fate, that we are solely responsible for our destiny. If *Acres of Diamonds* retains an appeal, it is in the message that, inevitably, we *will* find our fortune if we search hard enough. But Americans no longer believe in that fervently. Many of those who did believe have had their dreams dashed by the onslaught of statistics, with names and faces attached, that have coursed through American business these past few years. 43

At first, we dismissed it as the curse of the blue-collar class. When the five hundred largest U.S. manufacturing companies slashed payrolls by 4.7 million workers between 1980 and 1993, white-collar America sighed with relief. When the slashers came for the centurions of the "new economy"—when IBM began laying off 171,000 people between 1986 and 1994—the middle class worried a bit but blamed Big Blue's complacency and the recession that had sundered it. But when the recession ended, the assault continued. A week before Christmas, Mattel (a toy maker!) announced the elimination of one thousand jobs, despite record profits; a month later, on the same day it reported a 4 percent increase in fourth-quarter profits, American Home Products Corporation said it would cast off four thousand workers. It was clear the crash had come for everyone. 44

The villain is called downsizing, and it is demolishing the white-collar world. For the first time since the Depression, middle-aged, middle-class, college-educated men are suffering a decline in their standard of living and their prospects for employment. During the last recession, for the first time in history, says Harvard economist James Medoff, the percentage of unemployed white-collar workers grew. What's more, men aged thirty-five to fifty-four who are pitched from their jobs are increasingly unable to find full-time employment: The ranks of those classified as "permanently unemployed" rather than "temporarily unemployed" grew by 25 percent between the 1981 recession and the slump a decade later. Indeed, Medoff labels the 1990s "the era of middle-aged-male permanent-layoff unemployment." 45

The financial—not to mention emotional—impact on the wealthier, and presumably more secure, part of this cohort has been crushing. Massachusetts Institute of Technology economist Frank 46

Levy says that men aged forty-five to fifty-four with four years of college, middle managers who were "earning their age," saw their median earnings drop to $41,898 in 1992 from $48,189 just three years earlier. "This group has taken a pounding," Levy says.

Soon, they will be as dust, if the gurus of the new economy are 47 right. "I think there are a lot of people who will never find a job again," Michael Hammer, coauthor of the best-seller *Re-engineering the Corporation,* said recently. "If you can't design or sell a product, if you can't do real work, I'd get real nervous."

Middle-aged slacking is not a choice. It's a necessity. 48

"Pretty soon, we're all going to have to cut back anyway," says 49 Cecile Andrews [director of a Seattle-area workshop on voluntary simplicity], shrugging. "Are we going to be able to think of creative ways to live?"

At 6:45 on a Friday evening, I go with Cecile to the Phinney 50 Neighborhood Center, a massive brick schoolhouse in northwest Seattle, not far from the Honey Bear Bakery. Thirty-three men and women assemble in the basement auditorium for Cecile's latest voluntary-simplicity workshop, their first stab at exploring life played at 16 rpm. A bit nervously but soon with the unforced camaraderie of a platoon under fire, they introduce themselves to one another.

"Five months ago, I left my company," says a weary, heavyset 51 man in his early forties. "Sixty hours a week there is normal now. Charging forward, giving customers services they don't even want. And I survived four down sizings so far!"

"I'm going through one now," says the woman next to him, of 52 similar age, who's kept on her white anorak to ward off the chill. Her husband nods grimly.

A lithe, angular man introduces himself as a designer and a 53 builder. His eyes are narrow slits and his skin is sallow. "I work all the time," he tells the woman next to him. "I've been trying to cut back, save some money, so I can regain my time."

"I was in secretarial work for twenty-five years," his neighbor 54 responds. She doesn't give details, but somehow that career ended abruptly. "For the last three, I've been driving vans back and forth to the airport. It's heavy pressure. I don't like it. I've paid off my credit cards. Now I want to do what I want to do."

"I just put in a proposal to cut my work back to thirty-two hours 55 a week and take a 20 percent pay cut," says a veterinary clinician. "It's been accepted. I'm so happy."

Corporate downsizing and its requirements—longer hours for 56 less pay, a work environment with no security and little future—

have brought us to a crossroads. The social contract between employees and their bosses has been broken. Without unions to fight for them, and with the political and social environment turned unsympathetically Darwinian, workers—especially managers and professionals with a bit of a nest egg and a sense of emotional and intellectual security—are starting to withhold the one bargaining chip they have left: their time.

Dave Heitmiller and Jacque Blix know this well. They dropped   57
out before the economy dropped them. "Before, in the seventies, you could still maybe get a job in a factory, buy a new car. Property values were appreciating everywhere. You could still count on doing better than your folks did," Dave says. "That's all changed. We're going through a dramatic change in the business world, and that's affecting the worker bees. So some of us are saying, maybe there's a better way."

So enamored is he of that "better way" that Dave has decided to   58
become a proselytizer, writing and perhaps speaking on behalf of the downshifted life. Like new converts to any cause, he wants to surround himself with true believers, whose presence will support his own decision to drop out. And, maybe, reassure himself that he's not a quitter but the advance guard of the weary world order. "I'm thinking that part of my work—and I separate that in my mind from a job— is promoting the concept of simple living," Dave says. "I've come to believe in it as a philosophy and not merely an economic thing."

He remains defiant, though. This is not a career but a move-   59
ment. "I'm not doing it to earn my living," Dave wants me to know, before he and Jacque take their '92 Nissan Sentra (bought used) over to their simplicity-circle meeting. "If I do make some extra money, fine, but that's not the goal."

No, the goal for him and his armchair army is to show the na-   60
tion that living simply is the best revenge.

MEANINGS AND VALUES

1. In what ways do the people quoted in paragraphs 1–8 view work? What reactions are readers likely to have to these views? Be specific.

2. What questions about the new "drop out" phenomenon are readers likely to have after the first eight paragraphs of the essay, and which ones do paragraphs 9–26 attempt to answer? State in your own words the specific answers the writer provides.

3. In paragraphs 27–35, the writer traces changes over the last two hundred years in our view of work's importance. Briefly state the different ways we have regarded work.

EXPOSITORY TECHNIQUES

1. In what ways does the writer present the speakers in paragraphs 1–8 as if they were members of a twelve-step program for addiction? What is his likely purpose for doing so? (Guide: *Purpose.*) Is there any irony in this portrayal? Why or why not? (Guide: *Irony.*)

2. During the course of the essay, the writer reviews many possible causes for the movement away from work. Often he lets others explain the possible causes rather than doing so himself. Where in the essay does he finally summarize his view of the causes? Why do you think he waits so long to do this?

3. Rothenberg begins and concludes this essay with a similar strategy. What is it? In what ways does this structure support, or fail to support, the purposes of the essay? (Guide: *Purpose.*)

4. How would you characterize the tone of this essay? In what ways is the choice of tone related to the expository purposes of the essay? If the essay were more argumentative, strongly endorsing or criticizing the trend, how would the tone be likely to change?

DICTION AND VOCABULARY

1. Discuss the writer's use of diction and concrete detail to present the examples in paragraphs 2–4, 40–42, and 50–59. To what extent are the words and details chosen for expository purposes? What purposes do they serve? To what extent do they reveal the writer's opinions and values? Be specific.

2. Identify the allusions in the last three sentences of paragraph 13 and in paragraph 60. (Guide: *Figures of Speech.*) In what ways does the author reverse the meaning of the original sayings to which they refer? How do the new phrases fit the ideas being explored in the essay?

3. If you do not know the meaning of some of the following words, look them up in a dictionary: articulate, stalwarts (par. 6); settees (9); nouvelle (10); denizens, piddling (11); heretic (13); involuntary (16); avatar (36); tenet (37); manifested (38); incremental (41); implicit, coursed (43); enamored, proselytizer (58).

READ TO WRITE

1. **Collaborating:** Working in a group, make a list of any other traditional values of work, leisure, health, well-being, fashion, art, or polite behavior that are currently being questioned or undermined by a significant number of people. Consider each set of values as a possible

writing topic to which you can address these questions: Why are people questioning this value and in what ways? What are some of the possible consequences of this questioning? Then turn your list and discussions into a plan for an essay.

2. **Considering Audience:** Choose a puzzling, unusual, or new form of behavior (including fashion, expression, or taste) and prepare a short essay describing the different ways people react to it.

3. **Developing an Essay:** Using "What Makes Sammy Walk?" as a model, address some other contemporary trend and explore causes and effects without turning your essay into an argument for or against the trend.

(NOTE: Suggestions for topics requiring development by analysis of CAUSE AND EFFECT are on pp. 350–351 at the end of this chapter.)

PETER HILLARY

> PETER HILLARY is the son of Sir Edmund Hillary, the first man to climb
> Mt. Everest successfully. A well-known mountain climber in his
> own right, Peter Hillary made it to the top of Everest in 1990. He is
> also the author of *A Sunny Day in the Himalayas* (1980).

Everest Is Mighty, We Are Fragile

> If so many people die trying to climb Mt. Everest, why do others con-
> tinue to challenge it? Why is it important for all of us that some peo-
> ple continue to undertake the work of climbing Everest—even if they
> fail? These are some of the questions Peter Hillary addresses in his
> essay, published as an opinion piece in the *New York Times*. Along
> the way, Hillary also manages to explore ways in which failure can
> be a kind of success, and success, in turn, can be a kind of failure
> when it carries with it memories of others who did not succeed.

Over the past few years, I have watched the public perception of   1
Mount Everest drift from awe of the greatest mountain on earth
and respect for anyone who succeeds in scaling it to an assumption
that now things have changed.

Just as computer technology advances almost daily and our   2
back roads become highways and then freeways, people believe that
surely by now the tracks and camps on Everest are permanent fix-
tures that are improved each year. After all, in the Alps you can
climb to huts high above the snow line and sleep in a comfortable
bed and order food and wine from a concierge.

For Everest climbers, there has been progress, too, but it lies   3
only in the technology of our equipment and communications. The
mountain remains the same: huge, steep, cold and impassive toward
our human endeavor.

On the great mountains of the world there is constancy, and the   4
Everest that took the lives of George Leigh Mallory and Andrew
Irvine in the 1920's is the same Everest that was finally climbed by
my father, Sir Edmund Hillary, and Tenzing Norgay in 1953, the
same mountain climbed solo by Reinhold Messner in 1980, the same
summit I climbed on May 10, 1990, with Rob Hall and Gary Ball on a

brilliantly sunny day, and it is the same Everest that took the lives of eight climbers, including Rob, in a terrible storm on May 10, 1996.

Some things never change. While having the right equipment   5
and clothing is essential, it is only 5 percent of the overall mountaineering equation, of what is needed to reach the top. The rest lies with you. Do you have the drive, the psyche, the power?

Perhaps the greatest thing to change on Everest occurred on   6
May 29, 1953, when Dad and Tenzing reached the 29,028-foot summit for the first time.

It was like the breaking of the four-minute mile by Roger   7
Bannister. The way was clear for others to establish records, but now not for humanity but for individuals. This is a new age in which individual participation has usurped national spectatorship. Just about everyone knows somebody who has jumped out of an airplane with a parachute on his back, rappelled down a cliff face, rafted foaming white-water rapids or taken a motorcycle for a 100-mile-per-hour blast around a race track.

And so it is no surprise to me that the 100-year-old profession of   8
guiding clients up mountains has extended to ascents of the world's highest mountain—a mountain that has been climbed by 615 people in 43 years and has taken the lives of about 150. Many clients are expert climbers without time to organize expeditions, while others are more motivated than experienced. Nonetheless, these professional expeditions have succeeded in getting many people to the summit safely.

Surely the time will come when the numbers of climbers on   9
Everest will have to be limited, just as Yosemite National Park has been talking about doing. I would hate to see controls that were anything but first come, first served. The highly distasteful thought of a panel of assessors scrutinizing your qualifications, commenting on your objectives and counting the number of spare underpants in your day pack is objectionable to me. It is anathema to the personal right to challenge oneself.

What happened two weeks ago on Everest demonstrated the   10
unbridled might of the mountain, its furious high-altitude storms and the fact that not even the experience and skill of two outstanding alpine leaders like Rob Hall and Scott Fischer is enough when the Big E stirs.

I have heard people say they don't care about such climbers,   11
who, in their view, take pointless risks. It was suicidal; they knew how dangerous it was. "They have satellite telephones, meteorological reports, Gore-Tex jackets and good jobs. What are they doing?"

So should we discourage the risktakers by despising and shun- 12
ning them? Most of us want the people around us to be the same as
we are and to feel the same as we do—and yet intellectually most of
us will admit that variety is good. We admire people who try a little
harder and who push the envelope a little further. Every success by
an individual is an inspiration for his or her community—just as a
person's failure is a time for the community to take stock.

So while Rob lies stilled on the steep icy flanks of Everest, I take 13
stock both as a mountaineer and as a friend. I wonder about the future of my own mountaineering. The fact that Rob and Gary, with
whom I climbed Everest in 1990, have died on 8,000-meter mountains scares me. This latest alpine horror makes me feel very vulnerable. Despite what some people try to tell themselves, we humans
are very fragile. We die easily.

The death of eight on Everest comes on the heels of my own un- 14
cannily similar experience on K-2, the world's second highest mountain, last year. On Aug. 13, eight climbers from three different
expeditions were ascending the steep ice gully called the Bottleneck,
just below the summit. I was becoming progressively concerned
about the bank of evil-looking clouds encroaching from the north,
from western China, and at midday, in a cloud and falling snow, I
decided to descend alone while the other seven continued on.
(Other climbers went back down earlier that day.) I imagined the
seven descending the following day and boasting of their sunset
photographs from the summit, and asking, "Why didn't you come
on up with us?" None ever came back.

The weather deteriorated steadily, and I spent five hours of 15
lonely anguish, lost in cloud and wind on plunging flanks and
spurs between 26,500 and 24,000 feet. On finding the ledge where a
small tent was pitched, I clipped into the top of our fixed ropes and
began the 5,000-foot rappel down the Black Pyramid to the chim-
neys and couloirs of the lower Abruzzi Spur. As I leaned out over
the great void of the eastern flank of K-2, which was engulfed in a
cloud, the storm struck and I was blown about on the line like a
cork on a string. I knew I had entered a new phase of terrifying uncertainty.

The storm raged into the night and early morning, blasting the 16
mountain with winds over 100 miles per hour. When I reached the
ledge at 22,000 feet where Camp 2 tents were lashed to the rock that
rose above, I joined two others who had turned back for a night of
fear that our tents would be shredded by the screaming storm, leaving us very vulnerable to the raging elements.

In my bones, I knew there was little hope for the seven on the   17
summit. They were no doubt blasted from the mountain by the jet-
stream winds, perhaps falling 12,000 feet to the twisting, turning
Godwin Austen glacier, which flows south through a corridor of
spires and summits.

Surviving is sometimes the most painful role to play in this life.   18
You get the opportunity to re-enact in your mind those closing
scenes again and again and again.

Even though he lived the high-profile life of an eminent adven-   19
turer and mountaineer, Rob Hall was a generous man, a good friend
to many. There are not too many who walk with the mantle of fame
and remain true to themselves.

So for those who wonder "Why do they do it?" I can only say   20
that through the haze of lament and loss that has swept across the
world of mountaineers and those who dream of mountains, I can remember what I would have said before May 10: To climb the great
mountains is to leave the comfort of familiar places and to challenge
the very essence of oneself. Perhaps there is no greater quest.

Meanings and Values

1. According to the writer, the recent, well-publicized deaths of expert
   climbers on Mt. Everest remind us of important lessons the mountain
   and the dangers of mountain climbing have to teach. What are these
   lessons?

2. Hillary seems to be saying that the deaths can be viewed as a good
   thing in some ways, despite the tragedy. In what ways does the essay
   suggest that the deaths have some good consequences? How important is the tone of the essay in getting readers to accept the proposition
   that good can come from tragedy? (See "Guide to Terms": *Style/Tone.*)

3. What answer does the writer offer to the familiar question, "Why
   climb Mt. Everest?" In what ways is his answer satisfactory or unsat-
   isfactory? Be specific in your answer.

Expository Techniques

1. How does Hillary establish himself as an authority on the subject of
   mountain climbing and on issues of success and failure? Where in
   the essay does he do these things? How does he manage to avoid the
   impression that he is gloating over the failures of other climbers?

2. Hillary is a mountaineer, not a professional writer. If he were a professional writer, do you think he would have organized this essay

differently? Why or why not? (Guide: *Evaluation.*) What specific suggestions would you offer him, if any, for reorganizing the essay?

3.   Where in the selection does Hillary provide an extended example? What is his purpose in employing this strategy? (Guide: *Purpose.*) What other expository patterns, if any, are used in the essay?

DICTION AND VOCABULARY

1.   Identify those places in the essay where the writer uses words like "constancy" to describe Everest and words like "fragile" to describe humans. What other words, or groups of words, does he associate with each? How does this pattern of diction reflect important ideas in the essay? In what way is it related to the discussion of causes and effects? (Guide: *Diction.*)

2.   If you do not know the meaning of some of the following terms, look them up in a dictionary: concierge (par. 2); impassive (3); psyche (5); anathema (9); encroaching (14); rappel, couloirs (15); mantle (19).

READ TO WRITE

1.   **Collaborating:** It is easy to identify individual behaviors that are dangerous yet attractive to some people (skydiving, automobile racing, and the like). Societies as a whole can also undertake activities that threaten either individuals or the entire group. Working in a group, make a list of such activities, and develop one of them into a plan for an essay analyzing causes and effects.

2.   **Considering Audience:** Talk to several people about their reactions to dangerous sports like mountain climbing and prepare a brief report of similarities and differences among their responses.

3.   **Developing an Essay:** Many human behaviors seem unwise, wasteful, dangerous, or excessively selfish from one perspective, yet from another point of view they seem necessary, even beneficial. Prepare an essay of your own in which you, like Hillary, look at the causes and consequences of such a behavior and demonstrate its necessity and benefits. (Or take the opposite approach and demonstrate how the causes and consequences of a behavior generally considered good can also be viewed in a negative light.)

(NOTE: Suggestions for topics requiring development by analysis of CAUSE AND EFFECT follow.)

Writing Suggestions for Chapter 8

CAUSE AND EFFECT

Analyze the immediate and ultimate causes and/or effects of one of the following subjects, or another suggested by them. (Be careful that your analysis does not develop into a mere listing of superficial "reasons.")

1. The ethnic makeup of a neighborhood.
2. Some *minor* discovery or invention.
3. The popularity of some modern singer or other celebrity.
4. The popularity of some fad of clothing or hair style.
5. The widespread fascination for antique cars (or guns, furniture, dishes, motorcycles, old bottles, etc.).
6. The widespread enjoyment of fishing or hunting.
7. Student cheating.
8. Too much pressure (on you or an acquaintance) for good school grades.
9. Your being a member of some minority, ethnic, or religious group.
10. Your association, as an outsider, with members of such a group.
11. The decision of some close acquaintance to enter the religious life.
12. Some unreasonable fear or anxiety that afflicts you or someone you know well.
13. The reluctance of many women today to enter what used to be primarily women's professions such as nursing.
14. Your tendency toward individualism.
15. The popularity of computer games.
16. The mainstreaming of handicapped children.
17. The appeal of careers that promise considerable financial rewards.
18. The appeal of a recent movie or current television series.
19. The willingness of some people to sacrifice personal relationships for professional success.
20. The disintegration of a marriage or family.
21. A family's move (or reluctance to move) to a new home.
22. A candidate's success in a local or national election.
23. A recent war or international conflict.

24. A trend in the national economy.

25. The concern with diet and physical fitness.

26. Worry about crime.

27. Attention to gender roles.

28. Personal stress or depression.

29. Desire for success.

30. Willingness to take risks, even extreme ones.

COLLABORATIVE EXERCISES

1. As a group, research the causes of the Gulf War. Decide collectively which causes were most central and together write an essay showing how the combination of such causes led to the war. Look at immediate (direct) causes as well as indirect causes.

2. Split into teams of four. Divide each team into two halves, one which will analyze the causes and one which will analyze the effects of number 20 (p. 350). Create a thesis based on your analyses that would work as a claim for an essay on the topic.

3. Perform the same task for the above question for the topic of "the high percentage of women in the workforce."

9

Using *Definition* To Help Explain

Few barriers to communication are as great as those created by key terms or concepts that have various meanings or shades of meaning. For this reason, expository writing often provides definitions of words and ideas whose precise meaning is important to the writer's purpose. Sometimes definitions merely clarify meanings of concrete or noncontroversial terms. This simple process is similar to that often used in dictionaries:

1) providing a synonym, for example, *cinema:* a motion picture

or

2) placing the word in a class and then showing how it differs from others of the same class, for example

metheglin: an alcoholic liquor made of fermented honey
Term   Class   Details

Often, however, definitions specify the meanings of abstract, unusual, or newly-minted terms. Definitions of this sort are particularly useful when the experiences or knowledge of readers do little to help them with the meaning of a term or idea that is nonetheless a key element of an overall explanation.

Sometimes a term or concept (or perhaps a process, a natural phenomenon, a group of people, or a relationship) is itself the subject of an explanation, leading to an *extended definition,* as in the following example.

This is *orienteering,* a mixture of marathon, hike, and scavenger hunt, a cross-country race in which participants must locate a series of markers set in unfamiliar terrain by means of map and compass. The course, which may range from an acre of city park to twenty square miles of wilderness, is dotted with anywhere from four to fifteen "controls," red-and-white flags whose general locations are marked on the map by small circles. At each control there is a paper punch that produces a distinctive pattern on a card the racer carries. In most events the order in which the card must be punched is fixed; the route taken to reach each control, however, is up to the participant.

—Linton Robinson, "Marathoning with Maps"

Extended definitions may take a paragraph or two or may be the primary pattern for all or most of an essay, depending on the complexity of the subject being defined, the amount of controversy or confusion it has generated, the likely interest of readers in the discussion, and the writer's purpose.

WHY USE DEFINITION?

When your subject requires you to write about terms, ideas, or phenomena likely to be unfamiliar to your audience, or when the concepts and words you are using have conflicting or controversial meanings, then you probably need to prepare an extended definition for your readers. For years, discussions of how much people work each week excluded housework and other time spent on activities important to home and family. The definition of *work* included only labor outside the home for a specific wage. Women were rightly angered by this definition, which excluded the hours many of them labored creating homes and maintaining families. If you were to write today about how much work people do in an average week, you would need to provide an extended definition of work including such activities. Few people would argue your definition, but they would expect you to be aware of the different (and conflicting) meanings of the term and to make your choice among them clear. If some readers are likely to disagree with your choice, however, you will need to present reasons for it. You might even need to stipulate (or dictate) the meaning of the term as you use it in the essay so that your audience will not misread your essay by substituting their preferred meaning for your own.

When your writing focuses on a fashion, artistic trend, social phenomenon, political movement, or set of ideas or behaviors whose impact is widespread enough to interest most readers but new enough to require definition, you might consider creating an essay that presents an *informative definition,* one that explores and explains the various aspects of your subject. In contrast, when your readers already have some ideas about your subject, but you think these ideas (or perspectives) need to be changed, you could create a *redefinition* essay. A redefinition begins with the ideas readers hold and tries to substitute new and different ones. For example, people often try to make pets of wild animals because they consider the creatures cute, cuddly, or amusing. You might attempt to redefine the favorable images people hold of animals like koala bears, monkeys, boa constrictors, ocelots, or raccoons to show that these and similar creatures are likely to make troublesome, unpleasant, or even dangerous pets.

CHOOSING A STRATEGY

Extended definitions, unlike the simple dictionary type, follow no set pattern. Often when extended definitions are part of an essay, readers are not specifically aware of the process of definition. This lack of specific awareness arises because the definitions are frequently part of the overall subject, are written in the same tone as the rest of the exposition, and are closely tied to the writer's thesis and purpose.

When an extended definition is the primary pattern for an essay, however, the essay itself may follow one of several broad strategies. An informative definition often begins by explaining the reason for the subject's current importance and as well as the need to define it. It may then move to a brief, sometimes formal definition; continue with a discussion of the historical background and present instances; and conclude with a review of the subject's features. The following informal plan for an essay includes these strategies in an order appropriate to the subject.

Introduction
>   Tentative thesis: If you look carefully at your calendar for the month of December, you are likely to come across the holiday Kwanzaa, which may be unfamiliar to you, but which is celebrated each year by an increasing number of your friends, coworkers, and neighbors
>   Current importance: Examples
Definition
>   Brief formal definition

Historical background
Features: Seven principles, various activities, clothing, par-
ticipants, meaning of celebration, food, stories, and
materials and resources
Present instances: Current and growing popularity
Conclusion: Summary and sources for further information

A redefinition essay grows from the assumption that readers already have some ideas about the subject but that these ideas should
be modified or discarded altogether. Redefinitions often begin in the
same matter as informative definitions—by creating interest in the
topic. Then they generally proceed to mention the ways the subject
is normally interpreted, following each with an alternate interpretation, or redefinition. Or they review various aspects of the subject
and suggest fresh ways of looking at each.

DEVELOPING DEFINITIONS

A definition helps writers and readers agree on the teaming of a
term, concept, or phenomenon by providing answers to some important questions. As you develop a definition, try keeping in mind
the questions you will need to address in order to help readers understand your subject. These sample questions can provide a start.

For subjects that can be observed, measured, and known	For concepts, values, or terms whose meaning depends on the ways people use them
What are its features?	How do people use it?
What is its history?	What has its meaning been historically, and how has the meaning changed?
What does it do?	
What doesn't it do?	How is this set of values or concepts different from others?
	Similar?

Definitions use many familiar techniques of expository writing,
including examples, comparisons, and classifications. There are,
however, some techniques peculiar to definition. You can give the
background of a word, answering the question "What is the history of

the term or concept?" (that is, its *etymology*) and providing valuable hints to its meanings. For example, *catholic* originally, in ancient times meant pertaining to the universal Christian church. Its present meaning—of or concerning the Roman Catholic Church—retains some of the original force because the Roman Catholic Church views itself as the direct descendant of the ancient, undivided Christian church.

You can also enumerate the *characteristics* of the term or subject, sometimes isolating an essential one for special treatment. In defining a social group, such as triathletes, for example, you might list the physical qualities they share (endurance, strength, versatility, exceptional fitness), their mental qualities (high endurance for pain, desire to exceed normal levels of achievement, pleasure in physical exertion), and social preferences (tolerance for solitary training routines, desire to excel, preference for individual achievement rather than group membership). In so doing, you would be explaining the common elements that define the group and distinguish it from other groups.

You might define by *negation*, sometimes called "exclusion" or "differentiation," by showing what is *not* the meaning of the term, concept, or phenomenon. (This is an important technique for a redefinition essay.) To do this, you answer the question, "What is it *not?*": "*Intelligence* is neither a puzzle-solving activity that enables people to do well on a standardized example like the SAT or ACT, nor the ability to remember columns of facts and figures that may have no real use." If you employ this technique, however, remember that readers will expect you also to provide a positive definition, indicating what the definition *is* as well as what it *is not*.

But perhaps the most dependable techniques for defining are basic expository patterns. You can illustrate the meaning of a term or define a phenomenon by drawing *examples* from your own experience, from newspaper or online reports, from books and magazines, or from interviews and surveys. For instance, you might help explain the range of behaviors included in the term *deviant behavior* by offering examples not only of thieves, drug dealers, and pornographers, but also of people who live alone in the wilderness for spiritual enlightenment or who participate in dangerous sports. You might even include yourself in the category by telling how you climbed the side of a glacier or parachuted from a bridge into a river gorge. Or you might define by *classifying*, sorting kinds of deviant behavior into those that are socially acceptable, even honorable (the search for spiritual enlightenment), those that are harmful only to the individual (dangerous sports), and those that harm other people (thievery and other activities generally considered criminal).

Comparisons are useful, too, both those that identify *synonyms* (*naive* means innocent, unsophisticated, natural, unaffected, and artless) or that distinguish among concepts with similar, though not identical meanings, such as *consensus* (general agreement among a group of people on their attitude toward an issue or problem) and *dissensus* (general agreement among a group of people on the ways their attitudes toward an issue or problem differ). Comparisons respond to the question "What is the subject like or unlike?" So, too, do *similes* and *metaphors,* two techniques that are especially useful in defining concepts and attitudes that are difficult to grasp directly, ("an *epiphany* is a moment of sudden clarity and insight, like the moment your eyes become accustomed to the dark and you can suddenly see your surroundings," "a *transition* in writing is a bridge between ideas").

A narrative or an account of a process can also help you define. An explanation of *courage,* for example, might include the story of a ten-year-old saving a friend from drowning in an icy pond. A discussion of *open-heart surgery* might include a description of the process.

Few extended definitions would use all these methods, but the extent to which you use them should depend on three factors: (1) the term ᴏr concept itself, since some are more elusive and subject to misunderstanding than others; (2) the function the term serves in your writing, since it is foolish to develop several pages defining a term that serves only a casual or unimportant purpose; and (3) your prospective audience, since the extent of your readers' knowledge and their likely responses to your definition of a disputed or controversial concept or phenomenon should lead you to choose the most convincing or persuasive strategies for the particular audience.

Finally, remember that reference works can be valuable sources for definition. The *Oxford English Dictionary,* for example, traces the meanings of a word during various historical periods; the *Dictionary of Slang and Unconventional English* or the *Encyclopedia of Pop, Rock, and Soul* can provide you with surprising and useful information. A reference librarian or an Internet search engine can provide you with many more sources.

Student Essay

In the following essay, Lori L'Heureux uses a variety of definition techniques to define and redefine *stars.*

Stars

Lori L'Heureux

importance of term

How many of us as children longed to be
famous when we grew up? Many of us admired
a certain celebrity and wanted to be just

word/concept to be defined

like him or her when we got older. We
wanted to be a star.

The word "star," used to describe a
celebrity, first came into use around
1830. Before this there was no special
term to label performers who, on their
own, could draw large numbers of specta-
tors to a performance or an athletic con-

background and history

test. The lack of a term for such a
celebrity probably reflected a greater emphasis on the performance or athletic
event than on the individual performer or
athlete. But as the role of talented individuals became more important, a word for
it was needed. Many words, old or newly
fashioned, might have served, but the noun
borrowed from gazing at the night sky somehow captured the emerging role (Braudy 9).

effects and importance

Stars, indeed, have an enormous impact
on our lives. They are recognized throughout society, observed closely onstage and
off, thought about, talked about, emulated, even dreamed about. Stardom is a
vital force in our culture.

Because so many people perceive the work
stars do as a form of upgraded play, they
understand only imperfectly the work life
of celebrity entertainers. According to
Jib Fowles, many stars resent the stereotypes that have been created for them over
the last century. Many people, thinking
that the majority of stars spend the hours
of the day at leisure, imagine them living
a lavish lifestyle characterized by money

define by negation

and glamour. Stars are thought to be greedy and to associate only with people whose social status matches their own. Stars are frequently imagined as leading relaxed lives: this one reclining in a chaise lounge, reading a script; that one stretched out on a massage table, getting worked on by a team's trainer; several others poolside and prone. But in reality, the life of most stars is quite the opposite (Fowles 59).

what readers believe

I conducted a survey of my own to see if most people hold these misconceptions of celebrities' lives. I asked fifteen people to tell me what type of lives they felt celebrities lead. Twelve people said that stars were rich and had easy careers. Only three said celebrities led hard lives in the public eye and had difficult jobs. Two people added that they were never tempted to become stars (L'Heureux).

rhetorical questions provide structure

But what exactly is a star? Is there a downside to being constantly in the public eye? Is being a star really a lot of work? What is the cost of being famous?

It must be understood that being a star is a social role that an individual adopts. Every day of our lives, we, too, take on social roles; we accept the obligations and behaviors of being an employee, a parent, a spouse, and so forth. Celebrity performers are similar; they wake up in the morning and step into the star role.

examples

A star's talent delights audiences of all ages. A star acts or sings or cracks jokes or even just poses, and does these things with such style that we are fascinated and refreshed. We pay attention to stars because their performances are so successful at entertaining us. Because the audience for television shows, films, and recordings has become so large and so appreciative, the acclamation a star receives has become greater and more ferocious in recent decades. Through ticket sales, high ratings, and fan mail, an audience makes known its jubilant or waning response to a star's performance. When the response is good, the flow of good tidings certifies a star in public regard and elevates him or her to a special glory. At some moments for certain stars and their captivated fans, the reaction can be manic, as when the Beatles first toured the U.S. in 1964.

redefining star

Becoming a star is sometimes a difficult task. Trying to become known in the industry, to be liked by directors, and to get parts, hopefuls embark on endless rounds of auditions. Most will spend more time at auditions than they ever will before the camera. Athletes struggling to become star players generally spend many years in the minor leagues (or the equivalent) waiting for a call to "the show."

examples

Meanwhile, between roles, struggling actors have to sustain themselves. Usually this means menial jobs of one sort or another. For example, Marilyn Monroe labored in a wartime defense plant where she packed parachutes. For aspiring athletes, a job in the off season is generally a necessity.

example

Fame may require much in the way of disappointment, strain, and heartache. Since so many people are striving to become stars, and since so few will make it, the

redefining

typical aspirant's work life is a ceaseless round of rejection and exclusion. He
or she may attempt to maintain motivation
with visions of ultimate stardom, but the
daily experience of trudging from audition
to audition can prove devastating.
Celebrity George C. Scott commented about
acting, "I think it is a psychologically
damaging profession, just too much rejection to cope with every day of your life."

example and quote

Aspirants may initially set themselves
on the path to stardom because, in their
rosy view, fame promises freedom beyond
compare. But in fact the job of the
celebrity performer is subject to suffocating impositions and strangling constraints. Asked what it means to become a
star, Cary Grant replied, "Does it mean
happiness? Yeah, for a couple of days. And
then what happens? You find out that your
life is not your own anymore, and that
you're on show every time you step out on
the street."

example and quote

According to Yoti Lane, such a reaction
is altogether typical, for "one of the
most characteristic symptoms of having actually become a celebrity is a certain
disillusionment, which sets in—after the
first thrill of seeing one's name in
headlines—upon discovering the obligations and inconveniences of being known by
everyone everywhere" (130).

Underestimated by the public, a star's
work is one of the most strenuous occupations that a person can have. Fred Astaire
commented, "People will come up to me and
say, 'Boy, it must have been fun making
those old MGM musicals.' Fun? I suppose
you could have considered them that—if you

redefinition continues

like beating your brains and feet out."
Knocking oneself out to deliver first-rate
performances to the public, time after
time, is the fate of those ensconced in
the star role. The occupation calls for
extraordinary effort and ceaseless toil.

process

For most stars the preparation for performing begins with a general readiness.
Professional athletes work out countless
hours to maintain their physical condition. Singers exercise their voices daily,
practicing their delivery and keeping
their vocal cords in shape. Actors take
classes to strengthen their performance or
spend time carefully observing others.

From a base of readiness, the star prepares for the performance. The rock band
practices its songs for a concert; the comedian works on new material; and the actor concentrates on a new character to
become familiar with it. Actors must go
over their lines again and again, working
to get them right. Before going on, the
star has to be costumed and made up, a
process that can be very time-consuming.

The hard work for a star truly begins
when he or she must concentrate on the
task at hand. What a performer must do is
create wonderfully and completely, on cue.
The star has been engaged to deliver,
within the framework of the performance,
the right act at the right moment. The audience expects the comedian to have the
perfect punchline, the centerfielder to
catch the ball in the sun, and the actress
to cry when required.

**effects of
stardom**

Being a star can also be dangerous.
Actor Sylvester Stallone calculates that
in making some of his action films he has

broken his nose three times, his hand twice, and has suffered a concussion and a ruptured stomach. Also a danger to stars is their public. Fan letters pour in by the thousands each day, and the letter writers often want to enter into some sort of transaction with their idols. This can be dangerous when fans strive to encounter a star in person, pushing and shoving for contact, or when outraged fans try to injure a star.

For the privilege of staring at a star, fans will follow an entertainer into parties, restaurants, and even bathrooms. Sometimes stars have to live with the unremitting presence of fans camped at their front doors. The romance and obsession that are in a fan's mind can lead them to stalk an idol. Brooke Shields was the object of the affections of one Mark Bailey who attempted to break into her New Jersey home; the judge put him on five years' probation. While David Letterman was on the West Coast, a mentally ill woman who claimed to be his wife installed herself in his East Coast home (Fowles 310).

The media can also invade the privacy of a star. Interviews may seem endless and prove to be very draining. The press tends to emphasize personal questions that make the subject of an interview understandably uncomfortable. Magazines such as *The National Enquirer* strive to create rumors about different stars, often relying on questionable sources and rumors that later prove to be unfounded. A personal problem that any of us could easily encounter and that most of us would like to face in privacy frequently ends up on the front pages of newspapers, creating stress and embarrassment for the celebrity and threatening his or her career.

Summary   Even if their lives do not fit within stereotypes, stars are not people who lead normal lives. Celebrities are widely admired and often receive considerable money for their work, yet they must face situations that the general public does not fully understand. Stars face danger; give up their privacy; and work long, hard hours. Referring to celebrities as "stars" is quite appropriate because their lives are as far from ours as the stars are distant from the ground we stand on.

Works Cited

Braudy, Leo. *Frenzy of Renown: Fame and Its History.* New York: Oxford UP, 1986.

Fowles, Jib. *Starstruck.* Chicago: Smithsonian, 1992.

Lane, Yoti. *The Psychology of the Actor.* Westport, CT: Greenwood, 1959.

L'Heureux, Lori. Survey. November 7–10, 1995.

ROGER WELSCH

> Roger Welsch was a professor of English and anthropology at the
> University of Nebraska-Lincoln when he decided to move to a small
> tree farm in the central Plains. Since then he has made a living as a
> writer and television and radio columnist and has begun his "rural
> education." His essays on rural life have been collected in *It's Not
> the End of the Earth but You Can See It from Here: Tales of the Great
> Plains* (1990) and he writes a regular column for *Natural History*
> magazine. His other books include *Treasury of Nebraska Pioneer
> Folklore* (1966); *Shingling the Fog and Other Plains Lies* (1980);
> *Mister, You Got Yourself a Horse: Tales of Old-Time Horse Trading*
> (1981); *Omaha Tribal Myths and Trickster Tales* (1981); *Touching
> the Fire* (1992); and *Cather's Kitchens: Foodways in Literature and Life*
> (1987), *Busted Tractors and Rusty Knuckles* (1997) and *Catfish at the
> Pump: Humor and the Frontier* (1987) (both with Linda K. Welsch).

Gypsies

As the title suggests, this essay offers a definition of a group of
people rather than a term or concept. In addition, one of Welsch's
tasks is to redefine a group whose reputation over the centuries
has often been less than positive.

I was once talking with a Lakota wise man, Richard Fool Bull, won-   1
dering at his ability to sense what seemed to me to be mystic occurrences. Magic things seemed to happen to him fairly regularly. A
hundred years ago they would have been called "visions" by the
Indians. A thousand years ago they would have been called "miracles"
even in our culture, but Mr. Fool Bull accepted them as a normal
part of life.

"They *are* a normal part of life," he laughed when I expressed   2
my amazement. "They happen all the time."

"To you maybe, Mr. Fool Bull, but not to me."   3

"Oh yes, to you too," he said, nodding seriously. "That is the   4
sad thing about white culture. You see, Roger, it is not a matter of

me being trained to see such things; *you* have been trained not to
see them."

That's not a new idea. In anthropology classes it is a common 5
teaching trick, for example, to tell students that there are still peoples of this world who do not know the connection between sexual
intercourse and pregnancy. That usually excites astonishment in
the class—how can anyone not understand a cause-and-effect that
obvious?

The professor lets the students throw around their obvious cul- 6
tural superiority for a few minutes and then asks, "What is the result
of eating asparagus?" It is rare that anyone responds with a serious response. "Your urine smells to high heaven for a couple of hours, that's
what. Now, why is it you think these people are so stupid because
they have not realized an association that spans nine months while
you have never figured out a very obvious cause-and-effect relationship that takes place over only a few minutes?" The fact of the matter
is, very obvious things, most not at all mystical, happen around us all
the time and we manage to remain totally oblivious to them.

I enjoy the regular—every few months or so—articles that ap- 7
pear in the Omaha or Rising City newspapers that run pretty much
along these lines:

> The Bleaker County Savings and Loan lost an estimated $900 in an un-
> usual fraud perpetrated against teller Judy Hockworthy last Thursday.
> According to Ms. Hockworthy six or seven swarthy people—probably
> Indians or Iranians—came in to the office at 48th and Caldwell Streets
> looking for change for the parking meter and a fifty-dollar bill with an
> L in the serial number.
>
> Ms. Hockworthy reported that the men spoke broken English and
> the women were dressed in loose, colorful clothing. The men had
> seventeen one-hundred-dollar bills for which they wanted the change
> for the parking meter and the fifty-dollar bills.
>
> After several changes of the bills, the alleged defrauders left the of-
> fice and drove away in late-model pickup trucks, all with campers on
> the beds and all with Illinois license plates.
>
> The police have no suspects.

I love those stories. For one thing, I think it's wonderful that 8
these skilled con men get away with what they do in large part because they have plenty of money in their hands when they enter the
bank. The thesis in our society, evidently, is, "Anyone who has lots
of money is obviously to be trusted" when every indication should
tell us exactly the opposite.

But there is a deeper, philosophical reason for my affection for 9
these enduring, widespread petty bilkers. You see, I like coyotes. I

don't care if coyotes take 15 percent of the lambs and calves on western ranges. To me coyotes represent something very important— that creatures under the pressure of full warfare can survive. Out here coyotes are hunted with high-power rifles, traps, exploding baits, poison, airplanes, calls, chumming, and mobs. And yet survive. They *prosper!* That prospect gives coyotes like me a lot of hope, you see.

Well, newspaper stories like that are about human coyotes, I   10
guess, Gypsies. That's who those "Indians or Iranians" are, Gypsies. Through a thousand years of resistance, through wars and contempt and murder and expulsion, the Gypsies survive. Before Hitler murdered the Jews, he murdered the Gypsies.

And yet here they are, still with us, and so skillfully concealed   11
that most Americans haven't the foggiest notion they are still here.

Before I forget, let me tell you what happened in Germany. The   12
Gypsies were almost totally eradicated in Germany, and do you know what happened after the Second World War? The Gypsies *swarmed* into Germany. Where would they be safer than where they had only a few years before been pariahs? They could still be hated in England or Sweden, but not in Germany. Gypsy caravans parked illegally under Autobahn overpasses and in department-store parking lots because the gypsies knew that here, where they had been most abused, now they would be most tolerated.

I admired especially the ones camped illegally under the over-   13
passes. Can you imagine a better place to set up camp? Families sat at picnic tables and enjoyed supper even when it was raining like crazy or when the sun was blazing, peacefully watching the traffic whiz by. Overpass railings were festooned with wet laundry, a kind of Gypsy flag of resistance.

Gypsies are still visible throughout Europe, where their distinc-   14
tive clothing and wagons and a long tradition make them easily recognized by the citizens of the countries they travel. In America Gypsies are almost invisible. Americans see them not as "Gypsies" but "slightly peculiar, dark people—maybe Iranians or Indians." The average American perceives their pickup trucks with inevitable camper toppers and "For Sale" signs as something strange—but almost never as "Gypsies"!

What I love about American Gypsies is that they are seen only   15
rarely, and then briefly, like comets. I, for one, feel graced when I have the chance to see them, even if only in passing on the highway.

Fremont, Nebraska, used to be a popular place for Gypsies to   16
stop and for all I know may still be. It is on Highway 30, the Lincoln

Highway, and that was the main artery for cross-country travel for many years. For the still nomadic Gypsies, the long, open stretches of the Lincoln Highway must have been like a hometown. And Fremont is about halfway across America, so it was a logical meeting and resting place for the eternal travelers.

As a boy I once read a newspaper report of a time when two rival Gypsy bands wound up at a Gypsy cemetery in Fremont at the same time—both paying respect, as I recall, to the hallowed memory of the same patriarch of the tribe. The result was memorable. My recollection is that something like four hundred shots were fired, and when the police finally sorted things out after the pitched battle, they amassed a huge pile of knives, clubs, guns, brass knuckles, and other weapons of choice. 17

Now, I am not a violent guy and you probably wonder what possible saving grace I could deduce from a violent encounter like that. Well, what I found *glorious* about it was that not a single person was hurt. It was all posturing, maneuvering, threatening, and bluster. Coyotes at play. 18

I've spoken with quite a few people in Fremont about the Gypsies in the old days, and there are a lot of stories. The Gypsies often asked to camp at farms and farmers would usually give them permission in order to avoid later retribution, but they made sure the chickens and children were put to bed early and the mother and father stayed up late to keep an eye on things. 19

Older farm women who remember when Gypsies would camp near their farmsteads tell me that the Gypsy women and children would often come to the house asking for eggs or milk and they were usually given those simple things. Later inspection revealed that the next day tools, cooking utensils, dogs, and even horses or cows showed up missing—or perhaps I should say didn't show up missing. 20

Today, savvy merchants close up the store the minute they hear that the Gypsies are in town. For those too slow or inexperienced to close up shop, the experience is usually that ten or twelve women with voluminous clothing sweep into the store and scatter throughout the aisles. Merchandise disappears within the ample folds of the clothing. The ensuing shouting, arguing, and linguistic confusion makes it impossible for the merchant, security, or even the police to sort out one woman from another, let alone retrieve pilfered goods, and the inventory is shot to hell for the rest of the year. 21

All except the new car and truck dealers. They love to see the Gypsies come to town. The Gypsies frequently buy new vehicles in 22

Fremont, and their mode of operation is always the same. They come onto the lot, point to the vehicle they want, ask how much it is, and without any haggling whatsoever pay the price in cash.

Now, I know what's going to happen when folks read this. 23 Latter-day Gypsies are going to say that I have slandered their people, that Gypsies never steal, that all the stories are fictions, that Gypsies actually travel around the world doing good deeds wherever they can. Well, anyone who tries to sell that sort of nonsense does the Gypsies a gross disservice. By lying about their people, they deny their heritage. I have no sympathy for people like that. Just as surely as Gypsies have leavened the cultural loaf of western civilization with their music, art, and food, they have enriched us all with their irrepressible resistance to change, their thousands of years of resistance to authority and order not their own.

There will be non-Gypsies who say I am real jerk for suggesting 24 that common thievery is anything but common thievery and the Gypsies should learn to behave like Americans if they intend to live in this glorious land of the free, home of the brave. They should learn that nothing is more rewarding than money earned by the sweat of your brow—sort of like Ivan Boesky or Donald Trump or Don King, I guess. No, the Gypsies offer another alternative—survival by wit.

I don't condone cheating and thievery normally, but in the case 25 of the Gypsies it is a cultural inheritance and its cleverness makes me glad to be a member of the same species as the Gypsies.

I used to think that one of the things I wanted to do in my life 26 was to spend an afternoon or evening in a Gypsy camp. My fantasy was that I would spot a bunch of Gypsy pickup trucks in a small park some day, somewhere on the Plains—I know what to look for, after all. I imagined that what I would do on that occasion is walk into the camp with a couple of chickens and maybe a battered banjo I wouldn't mind losing over my shoulder. That way could trade the chickens for something to eat—something *Gypsy*—and play my banjo in exchange for some of their legendary music.

Unfortunately, the closest I have come to realizing that fantasy 27 is one time when some friends and I stopped for a picnic lunch in a public parking place at a large park in South Dakota. We were eating and I was eyeing ten or twelve pickup campers on the other side of the parking lot. I suspected they might be Gypsies.

As we were eating, two five- or six-year-old children ap- 28 proached us from the direction of the trucks. They were beautiful children—dark-skinned with enormous, black eyes. Obviously they were Gypsies. "Would you like a cookie?" I asked them.

They nodded yes.   29

I held out the sack, but to my surprise they backed away a cou-   30
ple steps. No, they explained they would not take the cookies as a
gift. They would accept them only if they could buy them from me.

Hummm. Maybe these weren't Gypsies. Gypsies steal, I   31
thought. They don't *buy*. I was put mentally off balance.

"How much you want for the cookies, Mister?" one of the chil-   32
dren asked.

These were great big chocolate chip cookies, and I had a big bag of 33
about sixty or seventy of them; they had cost me maybe eight dollars
early that morning at the grocery store. "Tell you what, young man," I
said. "How about a penny. Will you pay a penny for a cookie this big?"

He smiled and nodded yes, and I felt like a real prince for being   34
such a nice guy with these kids. And I felt like a real dope for all the
things I had said in the past about Gypsies being—how shall I say
it?—shrewd operators.

The little boy handed me a penny, and I gave him a cookie. His   35
little friend handed me a penny, and I gave him a cookie too. Gosh,
what a pleasant little vignette, I thought.

Then suddenly, out of nowhere, I was surrounded by eighty lit-   36
tle children, all with pennies, all wanting cookies. So we wound up
selling our entire supper, all of it—cookies, sandwiches, candy bars,
chips, everything, for something like eighty-five cents!

These folks were Gypsies, all right—kids and all. I had been   37
had, but good. I had fallen for exactly the routine I had watched
other people fall for decades—my junior deceivers had confused me
with their impressive wealth, they had let me believe that I was being the clever party to the exchange, they had come at me from a direction I would have never thought of looking into, and when it was
all over, I still wasn't sure what had happened to me, how much I
had lost, how it had ever developed, why I had been such a dope.

And I loved it. Every minute of it. I have savored the moment   38
over and over for these twenty years now. Outwitted by the Gypsies,
I was, and not just by Gypsies but by two five-year old Gypsies.

I still keep an old banjo around the house, and a few chickens,   39
just in case.

MEANINGS AND VALUES

1.   In your own words, summarize Welsch's attitudes towards Gypsies.

2. How would you characterize the tone of this essay? (See "Guide to Terms": *Style/Tone.*) How would you characterize its purpose? (Guide: *Purpose.*)

3. Estimate the importance of tone in helping the essay achieve its purpose.

4. Welsch mentions other definitions of Gypsies as part of his attempt to redefine the group and change readers' attitudes. Where does he mention these other definitions, and what are they?

EXPOSITORY TECHNIQUES

1. Tell where the essay makes use of each of the following definition techniques.

   a. background

   b. negation

   c. enumeration

   d. analogy

2. At first, paragraphs 1–7 may appear to be only loosely related to the rest of the essay. Discuss whether they contribute to or undermine the unity of the selection. (Guide: *Unity.*) How, if at all, can these paragraphs be considered part of an effective introduction?

3. What is the central theme or thesis of this essay, and in what ways is it communicated to readers?

4. Which examples in the body of the essay are most successful in creating admiration (or at least respect) for Gypsies? Which are least successful? Why? (Guide: *Evaluation.*)

DICTION AND VOCABULARY

1. Study the word choice in paragraphs 10 and 13 and explain how Welsch uses it to invite sympathy and admiration for his subjects. Pay special attention to repetition and to the connotation of words. (Guide: *Connotation/Denotation.*)

2. What are the synonyms Welsch offers in paragraphs 1–6 for the phenomenon he refers to first as "mystic occurrences"? Offer a definition of the phenomenon yourself using any of the definition strategies discussed in the introduction to Section 9.

3. If you do not know the meaning of any of the following words, look them up in a dictionary: bilkers (par. 9); festooned (13); patriarch, amassed (17); posturing (18); retribution (19); vignette (35).

READ TO WRITE

1. **Collaborating:** Working with classmates, try to think of any other group (or practices) that might be defended in a manner similar to

the way Welsch defends Gypsies. List the kinds of things you might discuss in an essay on the topic and, as a group, create an informal plan for such an essay.

2. **Considering Audience:** Welsch introduces another speaker (parts 1–4) who provides him with important concepts for his definition and acts as an "audience" for him. Employ a strategy like this in an essay of your own. You can introduce the speaker(s) at any point in the essay you consider appropriate.

3. **Developing an Essay:** Do the activity 1, then, working on your own and using "Gypsies" as a model, prepare the essay you have planned.

(NOTE: Suggestions for topics requiring development by use of DEFINITION are on pp. 424–425 at the end of this chapter.)

JOHN BERENDT

JOHN BERENDT was born in Syracuse, New York in 1939. He was a student at Harvard and received his B.A. in 1961. A journalist, essayist,
and writer of nonfiction, he has also worked as an editor and
columnist at *Esquire,* an editor at *Holiday* and *New York* magazines,
and as an associate producer of *The David Frost Show* and the *Dick
Cavett Show.* His essays and articles have appeared in numerous
magazines, including *Forbes, Publisher's Weekly, Esquire, Architectural
Digest,* and the *New Yorker.* His best-selling book, *Midnight in the
Garden of Good and Evil* (1994) is a nonfiction account of unusual
characters and scandalous goings on in Savannah, Georgia.

The Hoax

In this essay, first published in *Esquire,* Berendt takes a relatively
straightforward approach to definition, yet through skillful writing and wit, he manages to offer a fresh and insightful understanding of a familiar term and the behavior it designates.

When the humorist Robert Benchley was an undergraduate at   1
Harvard eighty years ago, he and a couple of friends showed
up one morning at the door of an elegant Beacon Hill mansion,
dressed as furniture repairmen. They told the housekeeper they had
come to pick up the sofa. Five minutes later they carried the sofa out
the door, put it on a truck, and drove it three blocks away to another
house, where, posing as deliverymen, they plunked it down in the
parlor. That evening, as Benchley well knew, the couple living in
house A were due to attend a party in house B. Whatever the outcome—and I'll get to that shortly—it was guaranteed to be a defining example of how proper Bostonians handle social crises. The wit
inherent in Benchley's practical joke elevated it from the level of
prank to the more respectable realm of hoax.

To qualify as a hoax, a prank must have magic in it—the word   2
is derived from *hocus-pocus,* after all. Daring and irony are useful ingredients, too. A good example of a hoax is the ruse perpetrated by
David Hampton, the young black man whose pretense of being
Sidney Poitier's son inspired John Guare's *Six Degrees of Separation.*
Hampton managed to insinuate himself into two of New York's
most sophisticated households—one headed by the president of the
public-television station *WNET,* the other by the dean of the

Columbia School of Journalism. Hampton's hoax touched a number of sensitive themes: snobbery, class, race, and sex, all of which playwright Guare deftly exploited.

Hampton is a member of an elite band of famous impostors that includes a half-mad woman who for fifty years claimed to be Anastasia, the lost daughter of the assassinated czar Nicholas II; and a man named Harry Gerguson, who became a Hollywood restaurateur and darling of society in the 1930s and 1940s as the ersatz Russian prince Mike Romanoff.

Forgeries have been among the better hoaxes. Fake Vermeers painted by an obscure Dutch artist, Hans van Meegeren, were so convincing that they fooled art dealers, collectors, and museums. The hoax came to light when Van Meegeren was arrested as a Nazi collaborator after the war. To prove he was not a Nazi, he admitted he had sold a fake Vermeer to Hermann Göring for $256,000. Then he owned up to having created other "Vermeers," and to prove he could do it, he painted *Jesus in the Temple* in the style of Vermeer while under guard in jail.

In a bizarre twist, a story much like Van Meegeren's became the subject of the book *Fake!*, by Clifford Irving, who in 1972 attempted to pull of a spectacular hoax of his own: a wholly fraudulent "authorized" biography of Howard Hughes. Irving claimed to have conducted secret interviews with the reclusive Hughes, and McGraw-Hill gave him a big advance. Shortly before publication, Hughes surfaced by telephone and denied that he had ever spoken with Irving. Irving had already spent $100,000 of the advance; he was convicted of fraud and sent to jail.

As it happens, we are used to hoaxes where I come from. I grew up just a few miles down the road from Cardiff, New York—a town made famous by the Cardiff Giant. As we learned in school, a farmer named Newell complained, back in 1889, that his well was running dry, and while he and his neighbors were digging a new one, they came upon what appeared to be the fossilized remains of a man twelve feet tall. Before the day was out, Newell had erected a tent and posted a sign charging a dollar for a glimpse of the "giant"— three dollars for a longer look. Throngs descended on Cardiff. It wasn't long before scientists determined that the giant had been carved from a block of gypsum. The hoax came undone fairly quickly after that, but even so—as often happens with hoaxes—the giant became an even bigger attraction *because* it was a hoax. P. T. Barnum offered Newell a fortune for the giant, but Newell refused, and it was then that he got his comeuppance. Barnum simply made a replica and put it on display as the genuine Cardiff Giant. Newell's gig was ruined.

The consequences of hoaxes are what give them spice. Orson 7 Welles's lifelike 1938 radio broadcast of H. G. Well's *War of the Worlds* panicked millions of Americans, who were convinced that martians had landed in New Jersey. The forged diary of Adolf Hitler embarrassed historian Hugh Trevor-Roper, who had vouched for its authenticity, and *Newsweek* and *The Sunday Times* of London, both of which published excerpts in 1983 shortly before forensic tests proved that there were nylon fibers in the paper it was written on, which wouldn't have been possible had it originated before 1950. The five-hundred-thousand-year-old remains of Piltdown man, found in 1912, had anthropologists confused about human evolution until 1953, when fluoride tests exposed the bones as an elaborate modern hoax. And as for Robert Benchley's game on Beacon Hill, no one said a word about the sofa all evening, although there it sat in plain sight. One week later, however, couple A sent an anonymous package to couple B. It contained the sofa's slipcovers.

Meanings and Values

1. State Berendt's definition of a hoax in your own words, and indicate the difference between a hoax and a practical joke or prank. Look up *hoax* in a dictionary, and tell how Berendt's definition differs, if at all, from the one you encounter there.

2. Restate the meaning of this sentence, "The consequences of hoaxes are what give them spice" (par. 7), and discuss whether the examples that follow it provide satisfactory support for the writer's conclusion. (See "Guide to Terms": *Evaluation.*)

3. Other than defining the term *hoax*, what purposes do you think the writer had in mind for this essay? (Guide: *Purpose.*)

Expository Techniques

1. Discuss how the way Berendt presents the examples in paragraphs 2, 3, and 6 makes them seem imaginative (and somewhat harmless) escapades rather than criminal frauds or deceptions.

2. Determine what definition strategies Berendt uses in this essay. Which seem most effective, and why? (Guide: *Evaluation.*)

3. Evaluate the strategy Berendt uses to open and close the essay. What makes it successful or unsuccessful?

DICTION AND VOCABULARY

1. To what extent does Berendt's presentation of the hoaxes described in paragraphs 2, 3, and 6 as escapades rather than crimes depend on the terms he uses to present them? (See Expository Techniques, question 1.) (Guide: *Diction.*)

2. If you do not know the meaning of some of the following terms, look them up in a dictionary: perpetrated (par. 2); ersatz (3); reclusive (5); gypsum, gig (6); vouched, forensic (7).

READ TO WRITE

1. **Collaborating:** Pranks, jokes, humorous events, adventures, and absurd occurrences make enjoyable examples in essays, and they often reveal a good deal about human beings and their relationships. Working in a group, make a list of possible examples of this sort. Then freewrite individually about the examples as a way of discovering a possible topic and thesis for an essay of your own.

2. **Considering Audience:** Make a list of words that most readers are likely to believe imply some sort of trickery and deception. Then prepare an essay in which you *redefine* one of the words and attempt to alter readers' views of its meaning.

3. **Developing an Essay:** Using Berendt's essay as a general pattern, create a definition of your own about a very different subject—such as the greatest loss, the most difficult task, or the biggest disappointment.

(NOTE: Suggestions for topics requiring development by DEFINITION are on pp. 424–425 at the end of this chapter.)

STEPHEN L. CARTER

Stephen L. Carter is Professor of Law at Yale Law School, and the author of several controversial but highly respected and tightly reasoned books that explore controversies in contemporary ethics, politics, and social relationships. After graduating from Yale Law School, he had a variety of professional experiences, including clerking for Supreme Court Justice Thurgood Marshall and working in a prestigious law firm. Carter's books are *Reflections of an Affirmative Action Baby* (1992), *The Culture of Disbelief: How American Law and Politics Trivialize Religious Devotion* (1994), *The Confirmation Mess: Cleaning Up the Federal Appointments Mess,* (1995), *Integrity* (1997), and *Civility* (1999).

The Insufficiency of Honesty

Integrity is not simply a term or idea. It refers to a way of acting and discerning the qualities of our actions. Integrity may be something we all claim to admire and wish to have ourselves, but as Stephen L. Carter points out in this essay first published in the *Atlantic Monthly,* it can be very difficult to achieve.

A couple of years ago I began a university commencement address by telling the audience that I was going to talk about integrity. The crowd broke into applause. Applause! Just because they had heard the word "integrity": that's how starved for it they were. They had no idea how I was using the word, or what I was going to say about integrity, or, indeed, whether I was for it or against it. But they knew they liked the idea of talking about it. 1

Very well, let us consider this word "integrity." Integrity is like the weather: every body talks about it but nobody knows what to do about it. Integrity is that stuff that we always want more of. Some say that we need to return to the good old days when we had a lot more of it. Others say that we as a nation have never really had enough of it. Hardly anybody stops to explain exactly what we mean by it, or how we know it is a good thing, or why everybody needs to have the same amount of it. Indeed, the only trouble with integrity is that everybody who uses the word seems to mean something slightly different. 2

For instance, when I refer to integrity, do I mean simply "honesty"? The answer is no; although honesty is a virtue of importance, it is a different virtue from integrity. Let us, for simplicity, think of honesty as not lying; and let us further accept Sissela Bok's definition of a lie: "any intentionally deceptive message which is *stated.*" 3

Plainly, one cannot have integrity without being honest (although, as we shall see, the matter gets complicated), but one can certainly be honest and yet have little integrity.

When I refer to integrity, I have something very specific in mind. Integrity, as I will use the term, requires three steps: discerning what is right and what is wrong; acting on what you have discerned, even at personal cost; and saying openly that you are acting on your understanding of right and wrong. The first criterion captures the idea that integrity requires a degree of moral reflectiveness. The second brings in the ideal of a person of integrity as steadfast, a quality that includes keeping one's commitments. The third reminds us that a person of integrity can be trusted.   4

The first point to understand about the difference between honesty and integrity is that a person may be entirely honest without ever engaging in the hard work of discernment that integrity requires: she may tell us quite truthfully what she believes without ever taking the time to figure out whether what she believes is good and right and true. The problem may be as simple as someone's foolishly saying something that hurts a friend's feelings; a few moments of thought would have revealed the likelihood of the hurt and the lack of necessity for the comment. Or the problem may be more complex, as when a man who was raised from birth in a society that preaches racism states his belief in one race's inferiority as a fact, without ever really considering that perhaps this deeply held view is wrong. Certainly the racist is being honest—he is telling us what he actually thinks—but his honesty does not add up to integrity.   5

Telling Everything You Know

A wonderful epigram sometimes attributed to the filmmaker Sam Goldwyn goes like this: "The most important thing in acting is honesty; once you learn to fake that, you're in." The point is that honesty can be something one *seems* to have. Without integrity, what passes for honesty often is nothing of the kind; it is fake honesty—or it is honest but irrelevant and perhaps even immoral.   6

Consider an example. A man who has been married for fifty years confesses to his wife on his deathbed that he was unfaithful thirty-five years earlier. The dishonesty was killing his spirit, he says. Now he has cleared his conscience and is able to die in peace.   7

The husband has been honest—sort of. He has certainly unburdened himself. And he has probably made his wife (soon to be his widow) quite miserable in the process, because even if she forgives him, she will not be able to remember him with quite the vivid   8 image of love and loyalty that she had hoped for. Arranging his own emotional affairs to ease his transition to death, he has shifted to his wife the burden of confusion and pain, perhaps for the rest of her life. Moreover, he has attempted his honesty at the one time in his life when it carries no risk; acting in accordance with what you think is right and risking no loss in the process is a rather thin and unadmirable form of honesty.

Besides, even though the husband has been honest in a sense, he 9 has now twice been unfaithful to his wife: once thirty-five years ago, when he had his affair, and again when, nearing death, he decided that his own peace of mind was more important than hers. In trying to be honest he has violated his marriage vow by acting toward his wife not with love but with naked and perhaps even cruel self-interest.

As my mother used to say, you don't have to tell people every- 10 thing you know. Lying and nondisclosure, as the law often recognizes, are not the same thing. Sometimes it is actually illegal to tell what you know, as, for example, in the disclosure of certain financial information by market insiders. Or it may be unethical, as when a lawyer reveals a confidence entrusted to her by a client. It may be simple bad manners, as in the case of a gratuitous comment to a colleague on his or her attire. And it may be subject to religious punishment, as when a Roman Catholic priest breaks the seal of the confessional—an offense that carries automatic excommunication.

In all the cases just mentioned, the problem with telling every- 11 thing you know is that somebody else is harmed. Harm may not be the intention, but it is certainly the effect. Honesty is most laudable when we risk harm to ourselves; it becomes a good deal less so if we instead risk harm to others when there is no gain to anyone other than ourselves. Integrity may counsel keeping our secrets in order to spare the feelings of others. Sometimes, as in the example of the wayward husband, the reason we want to tell what we know is precisely to shift our pain onto somebody else—a course of action dictated less by integrity than by self-interest. Fortunately, integrity and self-interest often coincide, as when a politician of integrity is rewarded with our votes. But often they do not, and it is at those moments that our integrity is truly tested.

Error

Another reason that honesty alone is no substitute for integrity is 12 that if forthrightness is not preceded by discernment, it may result in the expression of an incorrect moral judgment. In other words, I may be honest about what I believe, but if I have never tested my beliefs, I may be wrong. And here I mean "wrong" in a particular sense: the proposition in question is wrong if I would change my mind about it after hard moral reflection.

Consider this example. Having been taught all his life that   13
women are not as smart as men, a manager gives the women on his staff less-challenging assignments than he gives the men. He does this, he believes, for their own benefit: he does not want them to fail, and he believes that they will if he gives them tougher assignments. Moreover, when one of the women on his staff does poor work, he does not berate her as harshly as he would a man, because he expects nothing more. And he claims to be acting with integrity because he is acting according to his own deepest beliefs.

The manager fails the most basic test of integrity. The question   14
is not whether his actions are consistent with what he most deeply believes but whether he has done the hard work of discerning whether what he most deeply believes is right. The manager has not taken this harder step.

Moreover, even within the universe that the manager has constructed for himself, he is not acting with integrity. Although he is   15
obviously wrong to think that the women on his staff are not as good as the men, even were he right, that would not justify applying different standards to their work. By so doing he betrays both his obligation to the institution that employs him and his duty as a manager to evaluate his employees.

The problem that the manager faces is an enormous one in our   16
practical politics, where having the dialogue that makes democracy work can seem impossible because of our tendency to cling to our views even when we have not examined them. As Jean Bethke Elshtain has said, borrowing from John Courtney Murray, our politics are so fractured and contentious that we often cannot even reach *disagreement*. Our refusal to look closely at our own most cherished principles is surely a large part of the reason. Socrates thought the unexamined life not worth living. But the unhappy truth is that few of us actually have the time for constant reflection on our views—on public or private morality. Examine them we must, however, or we will never know whether we might be wrong.

None of this should be taken to mean that integrity as I have described it presupposes a single correct truth. If, for example, your   17
integrity-guided search tells you that affirmative action is wrong, and my integrity-guided search tells me that affirmative action is right, we need not conclude that one of us lacks integrity. As it happens, I

believe—both as a Christian and as a secular citizen who struggles toward moral understanding—that we *can* find true and sound answers to our moral questions. But I do not pretend to have found very many of them, nor is an exposition of them my purpose here.

It is the case not that there aren't any right answers but that, given human fallibility, we need to be careful in assuming that we have found them. However, today's political talk about how it is wrong for the government to impose one person's morality on somebody else is just mindless chatter. *Every* law imposes one person's morality on somebody else, because law has only two functions: to tell people to do what they would rather not or to forbid them to do what they would.   18

And if the surveys can be believed, there is far more moral agreement in America than we sometimes allow ourselves to think. One of the reasons that character education for young people makes so much sense to so many people is precisely that there seems to be a core set of moral understandings—we might call them the American Core— that most of us accept. Some of the virtues in this American Core are, one hopes, relatively noncontroversial. About 500 American communities have signed on to Michael Josephson's program to emphasize the "six pillars" of good character: trustworthiness, respect, responsibility, caring, fairness, and citizenship. These virtues might lead to a similarly noncontroversial set of political values: having an honest regard for ourselves and others, protecting freedom of thought and religious belief, and refusing to steal or murder.   19

Honesty and Competing Responsibilities

A further problem with too great an exaltation of honesty is that it may allow us to escape responsibilities that morality bids us bear. If honesty is substituted for integrity, one might think that if I say I am not planning to fulfill a duty, I need not fulfill it. But it would be a peculiar morality indeed that granted us the right to avoid our moral responsibilities simply by stating our intention to ignore them. Integrity does not permit such an easy escape.   20

Consider an example. Before engaging in sex with a woman, her lover tells her that if she gets pregnant, it is her problem, not his. She says that she understands. In due course she does wind up pregnant. If we believe, as I hope we do, that the man would ordinarily have a moral responsibility toward both the child he will have helped to bring into the world and the child's mother, then his honest statement of what he intends does not spare him that responsibility.   21

This vision of responsibility assumes that not all moral obliga-   22
tions stem from consent or from a stated intention. The linking of
obligations to promises is a rather modern and perhaps uniquely
Western way of looking at life, and perhaps a luxury that only the
well-to-do can afford. As Fred and Shulamit Korn (a philosopher
and an anthropologist) have pointed out, "If one looks at ethno-
graphic accounts of other societies, one finds that, while obligations
everywhere play a crucial role in social life, promising is not preem-
inent among the sources of obligation and is not even mentioned by
most anthropologists." The Korns have made a study of Tonga,
where promises are virtually unknown but the social order is remarkably stable. If life without any promises seems extreme, we
Americans sometimes go too far the other way, parsing not only our
contracts but even our marriage vows in order to discover the absolute minimum obligation that we have to others as a result of our
promises.

That some societies in the world have worked out evidently   23
functional structures of obligation without the need for promise or
consent does not tell us what *we* should do. But it serves as a reminder of the basic proposition that our existence in civil society creates a set of mutual responsibilities that philosophers used to
capture in the fiction of the social contract. Nowadays, here in
America, people seem to spend their time thinking of even cleverer
ways to avoid their obligations, instead of doing what integrity commands and fulfilling them. And all too often honesty is their excuse.

MEANINGS AND VALUES

1. Most readers are likely to consider honesty a good trait. Why, there-
    fore, do you think Carter created a definition that points out its short-
    comings? What do you think was his overall purpose in writing the
    essay? Do you believe the essay has more than one purpose? If so,
    what are they? (See "Guide to Terms": *Purpose.*)

2. List the reasons the author gives for considering honesty insufficient.
    State in your own words why the author believes that the men in
    paragraphs 7–9 and 21 have honesty but lack integrity.

3. Does this essay have a thesis statement? If so, where is it? Does it ade-
    quately sum up the main idea of the entire essay? Why or why not? If
    it does not have a thesis statement, is the essay nonetheless organized
    around a main idea or theme? What is it? (Guide: *Thesis.*) Explain why
    you consider the essay unified or not unified. (Guide: *Unity.*)

Expository Techniques

1. If one of the main purposes of this essay is to define *integrity*, why does the writer spend so much time discussing the meaning of *honesty*? In formulating your answer, take into account various definition strategies and the likely responses of readers to concepts like *honesty.*

2. What is the main definition strategy Carter employs in this essay? How is the organization of the essay related to this strategy? Be specific in answering this question. What other definition patterns does the writer employ, and where in the essay does he use them?

3. Which paragraphs in the essay are devoted wholly, or mostly, to qualification? (Guide: *Qualification.*) What role(s) do they play in helping develop the definitions? Why would the essay be weaker without them?

4. Where in the essay does the writer use transitions at the beginnings of paragraphs to highlight the essay's organization and indicate the definition strategy he is employing? (Guide: *Transition.*)

Diction and Vocabulary

1. Throughout the essay, Carter uses contrasting words and concepts to explain the difference between honesty and integrity. Sometimes the contrasts involve the denotation of words and sometimes the connotations. (Guide: *Connotation/Denotation.*) Discuss the contrasts as they appear in paragraphs 6, 8, and 9, and explain the use Carter makes of them. (Guide: *Diction.*) Explain the extent to which Carter reinforces the contrasts through sentence structure. (Guide: *Syntax.*)

2. In the course of the essay, Carter repeats a small number of words quite frequently, often varying their form. What are the words? How are they related to the essay's thesis (or theme)? How do they contribute to the essay's coherence? (Guide: *Coherence.*)

3. If you do not know the meanings of some of the following terms, look them up in a dictionary: discerning, criterion, steadfast (par. 4); epigram (6); gratuitous, excommunication (10); laudable, counsel (11); forthrightness (12); contentious (16); presupposes (17); fallibility, impose (18); parsing (22).

Read and Write

1. **Collaborating:** Working in a group, create a list of terms naming qualities that most people would agree are virtues (like *honesty* and *integrity*). Choose two and write three brief examples for each word that help define it. Choose examples that indicate what the term means and also some that indicate what it does not or should not mean. Include examples focusing on women as well as men.

2. **Considering Audience:** Rewrite Carter's essay substituting examples from women's experiences, or use the essay as a model for a discussion of moral concepts as they apply to both men and women.

3. **Developing an Audience:** Carter's title, "The Insufficiency of Honesty," suggests both a focus for the essay and an interesting approach, explaining why a particular quality is inadequate. Borrow this approach for an essay. Explain why your subject is inadequate, insufficient, or incomplete.

(NOTE: Suggestions for topics requiring development by use of DEFINITION are on pp. 424–425 at the end of this chapter.)

JAMES COMBS

James Combs has written numerous books on popular culture, pol-
itics, and the functioning of propaganda. They include *Phony
Culture: Confidence and Malaise in Contemporary America* (1994),
The Comedy of Democracy (1996), *The Reagan Range* (1993), and
Nightly Horrors: Crisis Coverage by Television Network News (with
Dan Nimmo) (1985).

Phony Culture

In "Phony Culture," a selection from his book by the same name,
James Combs explains the various meanings of the word *phony*
and tells how they apply to contemporary American culture.
While his primary focus is on explaining the phenomenon of
"phony culture," his secondary purpose, never far from the surface, is to suggest that we need to consider ways to remove the
phoniness from our everyday lives.

There is no other word for it: in the twentieth century, the culture   1
of the United States is becoming *phony*. The vernacular term
"phony" is an American word but of uncertain origin, coming into
common usage about 1900. People would speak of how you could
"phony up," or "phony it up," or say "you can phony anything up,"
i.e., make things up, fake it, talk your way out of it, use a false excuse
or alibi, and so on (interestingly, one proposed origin of the term is
from the appearance of that new invention, the telephone: using talk
"over the phone" to influence people, or actions such as "phoning in
an excuse"; another theory is that it emerged from an itinerant salesman known as a "fawney-man"). Phony quickly came to mean a
wide array of attributes and behaviors: the false, fake, sham, counterfeit, insincere, inauthentic, affected, the not genuine, the
pompous, the punctilious, the snobbish, the histrionic, or anything
whereby outward habits and actions do not reveal one's true character or nature, or whose words and actions are made to impress.
Phoniness soon became associated with other vernacular terms on
the same track, such as bunk, baloney (one great early term was "the
phonus-bolonus"), buncombe, sham, shilling, bamboozle, flim-
flamming, chisel, welsh, snake oil, bluffing, a bum steer, rook, flum-
mox, selling a bill of goods, the put-on, a raw deal, diddling,
swindling, the snow job, the come-on, the gambit, the royal shaft,

the set-up, being fleeced, getting burned, the ream job, and of course, conning. All these terms speak to the sense that in important human relations, both personal and social, all too often "the fix is in," the game is rigged, the cards are stacked, the deal is off the bottom of the deck, and we are the "mark" who is to be "stung."

The vernacular language of the American people indicates an   2 awareness of phony behavior. Now as social psychologists tell us, people anywhere and anytime are quite capable of phony behavior. The social dissembler is someone who puts on false appearances, conceals facts, tells lies, affects a pretense, and so on. The sociologist Erving Goffmann has recounted the many ways in which we can use phony behavior to advantage. The "rational" phony is someone who is likely engaged in a form of activity that conceals from his auditors what his "true intentions" or "real motives" might be, as well as what he or she hopes to gain out of the transaction. Further, the social actor may try to give an impression of infallibility or superiority, to "show" only the finished product of what he is using to impress others, and to omit or deny disturbing or disconfirming elements from a performance. The task of impression management necessitates the use of concealment, deceit, and seduction, what Machiavelli called *froda:* fraud. Goffmann was interested in the operation of "the interaction order," but we here want to expand the investigation of phoniness as a major trend in American society.

It is our contention that *phoniness has emerged as a social principle.*   3 Phoniness in the contemporary United States is much more than an interactive strategy of the con; rather, phony behavior has become a central organizing principle of social activity, an integral part of concerted institutional and organizational enterprises. We have come to expect, and for many to resent, the utilization of phony behavior in virtually every legitimate (and certainly every illegitimate) activity. Dissembling and fraudulence permeate our society simply because *phoniness works.* We now expect social leaders to be phonies because we know that to get to the top of organizations one has to be a phony, to con others into believing in you. We expect the claims of an organization or a product to be fraudulent, because the organization is quite willing to lie, or at least to not tell the truth, in order to get what it wants. When a public relations *"shill"* speaks on behalf of an organization or personage, we assume that this indentured spokesperson is lying, since the truth is not useful in maintaining the advantaged social position at stake. When we see an advertisement for a product or a candidate, we suspect that the claims are exorbitant and the truth is absent. For many Americans, society seems to be a network of falsities, phony messages propagated by interested parties in order to achieve results rather than promote the truth. The more that social organizations say, the less what they say can be trusted.

Nevertheless, the social practice of phony communications has now become for too many Americans part of their world-taken-for-granted, the social "ground" not often reflected upon. But the pervasion of phoniness exacts an awful price, for many of us no longer can discern the genuine or authentic from the fake; many of us now take the fake to be real, the artifice to be natural, the false to be true. The French intellectual Baudrillard writes cryptically of the American as the new pioneer of "the age of simulation" wherein we "substitute signs of the real for the real," because "artifice is at the very heart of reality." The term "simulation" means "to copy, represent, feign," to show off sham objects or replicas, to commit a histrionic act as if it were real (as in "simulated sex"). America, says Baudrillard, is "weightless," a country wherein "the imaginary and the real are fused and indistinguishable. Disneyland is authentic! Television and movies are real! America has created an ideal world from nothing and consecrated it in the cinema." For Americans, ". . . the only context is its own mythic banality."

Baudrillard's views are controversial, but he has focused our attention on the idea that we are becoming creatures of artifice, a society immersed in its own virtual "hyper-reality" increasingly devoid of concrete referentials. We are losing contact with memories of a past dominated by substantial facts—depression, war, industries, stable careers—and live in an eternal present of insubstantial artifices—entertainment, malls, suburbs, theme parks. But what he does not discuss is that this historical development emerged because of the utility of phoniness: in a world where it is becoming increasingly difficult to deliver the real thing, instead social powers could deliver the illusion, or image, or "the real thing," as if it were the real. In the wake of declining social expectations and morale, it became necessary to sustain the extant system with appeals which substituted or complemented real rewards with symbolic ones. Even though the appeal to confidence had always been important, with the threat of the loss of support for established social systems (consumer capitalism, political normalcy, and cultural pluralism), the appeal for acquiescence in if not enthusiasm for the existing system is now crucial to sustain social "development" and "progress" on the lines and terms of powerful institutions and organizations.

As a social principle, then, phoniness has become ascendant at the time we are being transformed into the "post-modern" world of change and confusion. The social phony has an advantage because he or she knows how to affect a stance that is impressive and often persuasive. Since we now live in a world defined by the mastery of artifice, his grasp of the superficials of communication and the syco-phancy of self-presentation make such fraudulence a powerful mode of effective action. The phony acts at role distance, communi-cating influence through the use of the aesthetics of social interac-tion, and utilizing the ethic of expedience. The phony is committed to communicating rather than veracity, since veracity is only useful until the benefits of dissembling outweigh those of truthfulness. The art of the phony is *social pretension,* the ability to exalt make-believe as a credible reality for credulous auditors. The phony's work is to give shared credence to fictive states, raising "extravagant expecta-tions" for a populace desperate to overcome malaise and to believe in something.

The social consequences of the phony principle is that it creates   7
a phony culture permeated by pretense and fraudulence. Everything becomes transformed from a real, thriving, functionality into a pre-tentious and dramatistic symbolicity. The great impulse of the cre-ators of phony culture is to transform everything into a pretentious and preternatural thing to which is attributed playful meaning. A classic example is the transformation of a community into a "tourist trap." Consider, say, a town in the mountains. The town in its origi-nal state had some functional relationship with nature and society, with farms, shops, industries, and so on. But let us suppose the town is "discovered." In a short time, it becomes something different: the town is not longer an original community; rather it has acquired at-tributes through the intrusion of play functions. The instrumentality of the town as a complex of institutions and habits is superseded by a new symbolic significance, the extent to which "developers" can dramatize the place as a playful paradise worthy of visiting and liv-ing. A general store, for example, may have served the rural area for a long time as a place for farmers to buy cheap goods and congre-gate for communal fellowship. But in the phony play world, the gen-eral store becomes a place of dramatized nostalgia for people who have no memory of a real general store to visit and buy imported goods at inflated "tourist" prices. The general store, like the town, has acquired a new function, as a place that is pretentious (claimed to possess attributes that are phony) and preternatural (exceeding what was natural or normal for the original place). The town is now a "resort town" devoid of community and real and thriving social exchange among local neighbors; rather, is has become a dramatic

set with histrionic features (the general store is a stage which we may enter to see how original life was once lived, even though we have no experience of it that exists as an object of play). As the "up-scale" housing developments, fancy restaurants, boutiques, and so forth proliferate, the town loses any semblance of contact with the old world of real functions and people, and acquires the ambience of the artificial, the pretentious, and the superficial. A preternatural world exists outside of nature, and so too does the newly phony town. For older residents or people who lived there and return, it is now unrecognizable: it has taken on fraudulent attributes that are beyond their original understanding of what the town was. The place has become an imposture, the fraudulent representation of a actual town that is lovely and charming; instead it is a contrived stage for paying audiences who wish to visit a symbolic setting created for their playful pleasure.

In the late twentieth century, the culture of the United States is now increasingly defined by what we might call *derivative features.* We have "progressed" beyond the original social forms of instrumentality (e.g., an economy of needs, a politics of material benefit, and a popular culture of mass entertainment) to a state of expanding forms of artifice and dramatistics. Rather than practicing the sensible economics of needs, we have moved toward the symbolics of an economy of wants, with an ever-expanding manipulation of consumer demand through advertising and public relations that, for instance, turns towns into "concepts" for development and tourism. Rather than practicing a politics of real benefits, we now engage in the histrionics of "symbolic politics," the monitoring and manipulating of public opinion, and the personality cult of the political personage as hero-celebrity. Rather than sustaining a popular culture of mass entertainment, we have progressed to the stage of ever-increasing multiplicity and outrageousness, with the celebrity expected to become ever more bizarre and unusual for our enjoyment and revulsion. In all cases, the social consequence is to create a society dominated by derivative functions that diverge ever further from the original functions of the system. When an economy of needs is superseded by an economy of wants, then the consequence is to make us into addicts of change and novelty, for whom new experiences, no matter how phony, become primary. Politics becomes an exercise in creating the illusion of well-being rather than providing well-being. To use a cultural example, the primary function of religion, one might think, would be the primary goal of theological enhancement, relating man to God; but with televangelism, the derivative function of entertainment and fund raising, not to mention enhancing the celebrity status of the televangelist star, becomes more important, in the process debasing the quality and mission of original religion. In a phony culture, it becomes normal and easy for those with organizational goals simply to use the art of the con in order to achieve newly defined purposes. But it has the consequence of further "phonying up" the society, creating the conditions for both credulity and malaise.

The derivative activities of the new American society underwrite the new "service economy," the media politics, and proliferating popular culture. In these kinds of conditions, the results that are sought and gained differ from older forms of social life. In the new American order, the phony culture gives impetus to the values and practices of the confidence man. The republican idealist, we may recall, was traditionally a man of words, and for that "a man of his word," representing the political and moral ideals of democratic community in political honesty and ethical integrity. The charismatic adventurer was a man of action, conquering the not insuperable objects of some frontier, and representing the social ideal that individual action guiding concerted effort could produce desirable results. But the ascendance of the confidence man means something a bit different. Even though he uses words and conducts social action, he operates on a basis of somewhat different principle, one based on symbolic manipulation rather than politic coalition or material production. *The operative principle of a phony culture is hype.* "Hype" is a term (perhaps derived from "hyperbole") related to the tradition of Barnumian showmanship, expanded now to include all those manipulative activities which utilize appearances as if they were reality. The principle of hype operates in a culture for which reality is not an objective condition, but rather an existential creation. The hype artist makes up things which are then marketed and sold by procuring confidence in their phony merits. Like all con men, they do not politic nor do they produce; rather they procure. They procure belief through hyping make-believe. Whereas the republican idealist strives to make community real, and the charismatic adventurer works to make conquest real, the hype artist makes confidence real. Since appearance is reality, then ever-new appearances can be sold as the latest "new and improved" reality. Reality is, as Lily Tomlin joked, a matter of anxiety for those in active contact with it; thus more pleasing appearances—resort towns, planned communities, theme parks, awards shows, political ceremonials, testimonials, the list is endless—can be procured to allay

9

anxiety and supersede quotidian gloominess through play. We do not have to work at understanding hard reality, when we can be diverted and amused through play with soft realities. If the mythic home of the republican idealist is the town, and that of the charismatic adventurer the forest or financial market primeval, the true home of the contemporary hype artist is Hollywood.

We live, then, in an expanding universe of phoniness, constantly created and re-created by confidence men using the artifices of hype. The habits and practices of phoniness are now so familiar to us that we accept them as commonplaces, the way things are done, without reflection on what they mean for our lives. Here we wish to point to the three major characteristics of a phony culture: immediacy, frivolity, and artificiality. The phony culture of contemporary American is characterized by *immediacy.* The constant emphasis is on the now, the new, the fashionable, the thing of the moment, what's happening right now, what's hot, and what's not, where it's at, the immediate experience. What is current and hyped is what is real. Reality is momentary, the symbolic focus of the ephemeral now. In a phony culture, not only do people have no sense of place, they also have no sense of time. Time and the sense of temporality— memory and projection—lose importance. People have little sense of temporal placement, of the continuity of national past and present, of the legacy of history and the promise of posterity, of breadth of perspective. The narrow focus on "now" reinforces the ascendancy of the ephemeral: what is happening now is what is real and important. The unreal and unimportant is associated with what is past, which is easily disposable, yesterday's events or celebrities or music. Everything becomes unmemorable and quite forgettable just because it is old and passing out of the new immediate moment, and thus is boring and spent, "history" in the pejorative sense. The new is always something that can by hyped: the next experience, thing, or personage is given allure and thus desirability. One is hopelessly "out of date" if you don't yearn for the newest, and think that nothing old is worth having. As Christopher Lasch noted, "make it new" is the great message of modern consumerism, expressed through advertising and programming (such as soap operas and tabloid news), making us into "addicts of change" who constantly seek "novelty and fresh stimulation" and exercise "restless mobility." All things old—cars, clothes, presidents, spouses—are potential throwaways. But confidence in the new is something that has to be created, through the good offices of hype artists who "phony up" futures of newfound pleasures and delights. Without either a sense of history or a coherent view of the future, people are easily lured to the phony object of interest at the moment, drawing attention towards the plaything of the now but diverting attention from a larger view of the temporal world which invites self-placement. The news, for example, is hyped to draw our attention to the "hot story" of the moment, but does little to place events in the larger context of historical process; news is sensational in that it plays to immediate interest, and uninformative in that it makes little attempt at more comprehensive understanding. News is hyped "new" information that is sold like any other hot commodity, and there truly is nothing as old as yesterday's news.

A second characteristic of a phony culture is *frivolity.* 11 Democratic culture has long been accused of favoring the lowest common denominator, quantity over quality, and vulgar mass tastes. The quest for, and hype of, the immediate experience intensifies that activity. If people seek the newest thing that is hyped, it is likely to be a frivolity, something of little weight or importance, the amusing trifles of daily play. Consequently, people find it difficult to take things seriously, to consider matters of weight and importance rather than the glittering but banal entertainments of mundane leisure. In a phony culture, people lead lives of endless diversion, which draws them away from serious or earnest considerations. The frivolous is deemed more fun and less demanding than the serious, so we obey the injunction to be happy, and don't worry. And like immediacy, the impact of frivolity on culture and personality becomes cumulative: The superficial, the flighty, the trivial, the sensational, the gossipy, the shallow become the fare of cultural experience; people lack depth, the capacity for reflection, a commitment to values or ethics. A phony culture lacks what the Romans called *gravitas,* the willingness to discern the serious and consider matters of gravity. The grave is fraught with ponderable significance, which major cultural forces array against: we respond to the hype of the light and irrelevant, but not to the appeal to get serious. A phony culture cannot take anything seriously, including its own grave problems and drift towards decline. Since in such circumstances people can no longer distinguish between the important and unimportant, everything is treated as frivolity, even war, love, and death. If life is presented as a big party, then the "party" extends to turning the serious into play. Everything becomes a big joke, making fun of politics, religion, education, indeed all institutions as frivolous and passing trivialities. The stand-up comic who savages everyone and everything becomes a model opinion leader in such a

society. Everything, even the most awful and primal events and relationships (murder, love, charity) translates into the insubstantial
and merely amusing or diverting. Thus a political campaign loses all
its seriousness as both the campaign organization and the media
hype personality, charges and countercharges, the "horse race," rev-
elations about the candidate's past, and so on. What is lost in the glib
and weightless shuffle is any sense that the campaign means anything, since political trivia drives out the importance of the choice.
Indeed, the principle of frivolity affects all news in the era of
"tabloidization": not only does the news have to be immediate, it
also tends to be frivolous, banal, and shallow reporting that focuses
on "playful" rather than serious elements. Indeed, there is a sort of
Gresham's Law of News by which the trivial becomes equal to or superior to the serious and consequential, in a kind of "equality of all
stories." (A melodramatic squabble between two skaters, a trial in-
volving malicious wounding of a spouse, and a peripheral scandal
take precedence in the news at the same time a major disarmament
agreement is reached, the Warsaw pact essentially joins NATO, and
the president reaches an aid agreement with Russia.) All such social
exercises in frivolity give impetus to the ascendancy of the phony. In
a phony culture, frivolity becomes a social principle that supersedes
seriousness. Since frivolity can be hyped, it becomes more important
than matters of importance.

A third characteristic of phony culture is *artificiality*. A phony   12
culture not only lacks a sense of temporal placement and relative
significance, it also devalues rootedness in the past and tradition
and the habit of seriousness and deliberation in favor of the sweet
cheats of artifice. Since our lack of attention span and interest focuses us on the immediate, and since our flippancy and frivolous-
ness will not allow us to sustain seriousness, we then are drawn to
artificialities, social fabrications which hold our immediate attention
and fill our moments with amusing diversions. Thus social experience tends us to artifices, the dramas of simulated life that characterize our politics, economics, and culture. Immediate amusements we
deem to be "lively," when in fact they are synthetic creations which
separate us from our natural condition and unite us with artificial
conditions. A phony culture creates an environment of artifices, so
much so that we come to believe that ephemeral fabrications constitute what is meaningful and real in our existence. In a phony culture, art does not imitate life; it supersedes it, exalting the status of
"created actualities" as the things most real. A walk in the mall is
better than a walk in the woods. A board game at home is mundane;

a game show is hyper-real. A perfume is just a smell until an advertisement for it explains its magical powers to transform you into a creature of irresistible sexual allure. A political convention is of no interest until media managers transform it into a television show. Pseudo-events—events staged for their staginess—are more real than actual events, which tend to be messy, complicated, and inexplicable, lacking in histrionic structure and dramatic force. A televised briefing by a public relations spokesperson comes to be equated with action, since it lives up to our media expectations: the pseudo-event becomes an event, an "actuality" that has ontological status. Similarly, a meadow is not lovely until it has been developed in an expensive housing project, hyped as a "richly appointed" and "naturally appointed" place for the rich to live in prestige. A place is "nowhere" until it becomes a pseudo-place engineered for conspicuous living. The natural meadow is not valuable until it is denatured. When it becomes a pseudo-place, it then has the aura of environmental dramatization and is worthy of substantial investment. Finally, the news has become the purveyor of the pseudo-fact, "factualities" or "factoids" that fit the currently fashionable or ideologically correct story line, or "take" of what's happening. Much news is phony, focusing on "well-founded rumors" or best-of-authority "inside dope" gossip rather than substantive processes (the vaunted national press, recall, celebrated the personality cult of President Reagan, but a Middle Eastern newspaper broke the Iran-contra story, and they missed entirely perhaps the biggest story of the 1980s, the wholesale looting of the savings and loan industry). The ephemeral artificialities of news now have become so irrelevant to people's lives that newspapers and TV news networks are endangered journalistic species.

A phony culture, then, is characterized by immediacy, frivolity, and artificiality. To a large degree, this emerging culture is the creation of the confidence man, who succeeds to the extent he or she can manipulate our penchant for immediate experiences of play in environments of artifice. Phoniness has now become a social fact and a cultural value, transforming the way we live and what we expect. It is our task here to point out the ways in which we have become a phony culture. Later in the book Phony Culture we discuss in turn phony language, phony people, phony places and things, phony events, phony deals, phony politics, and conclude with reflections on the future of phony worlds. We might note at the outset that the popular malaise of which we spoke is a symptom that phony culture is ultimately unsatisfying, that underneath our widespread acquiescence in the pervasiveness of

13

the phony is a desire for something more, what we might call "life in truth." We can only overcome malaise if we face the truth of phony culture, and confront the assertions of confidence which sustain it. Phony artifices sustain our illusions if we willingly suspend disbelief, and in so doing lose contact with whatever grip on the relationship between ourselves and the objectives and dynamic world that exists beyond our hopes, fears, and fantasies.

MEANINGS AND VALUES

1.   In paragraph 4, Combs shares with a French intellectual, Jean Baudrillard, the belief that in America the "imaginary and the real are fused and indistinguishable." Do you agree? What examples does Combs share from Baudrillard? Can you think of other examples where imagination and reality are indistinguishable?

2.   Combs refers to the "phony principle" (par. 7) which leads people to see things that were once real from a symbolic perspective. Explain how the general store to which Combs refers in that same paragraph exemplifies his definition of a phony culture.

3.   At the conclusion of paragraph 9, Combs leads into a statement on Hollywood as the "true home of the contemporary hype artist . . . ." Explain what Combs is trying to emphasize.

EXPOSITORY TECHNIQUES

1.   In paragraph 1, Combs uses etymology (or a lack of available etymology) to begin the extended definition presented in the essay. Why might Combs have pointed out that an etymology doesn't exist? Is this effective as an introduction for an essay on phoniness? Explain.

2.   Combs employs many synonyms in paragraph 1 to give readers a broad perspective of the meaning of the word "phony." Are these synonyms useful for understanding meaning or do they confuse the reader because of the shades of difference in meaning for each of them?

3.   While Combs' essay primarily defines the word "phony" it also provides several sub-definitions. Identify other terms that Combs defines. What are the similarities and differences in the meanings of these words?

DICTION AND VOCABULARY

1.   Throughout the essay, Combs repeats many words frequently. Identify some of these words. How do they contribute to the meaning and coherence of the essay?

2. Is the diction in Combs' essay specific or general? Does Combs use abstractions or concrete evidence? Identify specific and general language in the essay as well as examples of abstract and concrete words. (See "Guide to Terms": *Diction*.)

3. If you do not know the meaning of some of the following terms, look them up in a dictionary: dissembler (par. 2); cryptically (par. 4); banality (par. 4); extant (par. 5); acquiescence (par. 5); sycophancy (par. 6); expedience (par. 6); temporal (par. 10); flippancy (par. 12); ephemeral (par. 12).

READ TO WRITE

1. **Collaborating:** Current television network programming often blurs the lines of reality and imagination by placing nonfiction shows and fiction shows in similar prime time slots. Some television shows seemingly eliminate the line by using nonfiction plot lines with fictional characters. Working in groups list several examples of television shows and programming lineups that you feel help to contribute to our lack of distinction between the phony and the real. Collaboratively, write an essay that discusses the impact of such programming on society's views of reality and imagination.

2. **Considering Audience:** The vocabulary level of Combs' essay clearly indicates that this essay is for an educated reader. Write an analysis of who Combs' target audience might be and why this essay might be appropriate for such an audience.

3. **Developing an Essay:** In the late 1990s, society was inundated with multiple examples of places where reality and imagination cross. Some people might define the Internet as "phony" based on some of Combs' points. Yet, we often use email, (perhaps better referred as "phony" mail following Combs' theory) to maintain contact with people we might otherwise not talk to. Write an essay discussing how computer technology and the notion of "virtual reality" would fit well with Baudrillard's theories that Combs puts forth in paragraph 4.

(NOTE: Suggestions for topics requiring development by DEFINITION are on pp. 424–425 at the end of this chapter.)

Issues and Ideas

Creating New Definitions for our Lives

- Kesaya Noda, *Growing Up Asian in America*
- Michael Dorris, *Father's Day*
- Veronica Chambers, *Mother's Day*
- M.P. Dunleavy, *"Guy" Envy*

Leave It to Beaver represents for many people a time and a culture whose values, relationships, and roles were simple, clear, and unchanging. Things were probably never that simple, though the television program certainly made them appear that way. Nonetheless, identities and relationships are certainly undergoing more changes and redefinition now than they were three decades ago. The changes involve not only the development of new identities but the recognition that all our identities are constructed from multiple—and sometimes seemingly incompatible—elements.

Though we are always the children of our parents, sometimes we end up playing parental roles toward them, offering advice or counsel, just as Veronica Chambers explains in her essay, "Mother's Day." Though we might like to think of ourselves as typically middle class, Middle Western, or business/labor minded in our values and outlooks, few, if any, of us are so easily defined. As Kesaya Noda points out in her essay, "Growing Up Asian in America," to understand her identity she needs to view herself as American, Japanese, and a woman—all simultaneously. Something similar is probably true for all of us, whatever our primary ethnic, social, economic, religious, or gender identification.

Even such seemingly clear roles as "mother" and "father" can be filled by many different people and by more than one person, especially in this age of blended families. Michael Dorris, in "Father's Day," reminds us that even in the age of *Leave It to Beaver*, an allegiance to traditional values, such as fighting (and dying) for one's country, could alter traditional family roles and relationships. The ways we refer to ourselves, as "guys" or "girls" can also communicate and even shape identity, as M. P. Dunleavy points out in "Guy" Envy

Each of these essays reminds us that the need to understand our identities and our roles in relation to other people makes definition an important pattern of thought and analysis. Each essay also demonstrates many other expository patterns.

KESAYA NODA

KESAYA E. NODA was born in California and raised in rural New Hampshire. She did not learn Japanese until she graduated from high school, but she then spent two years living and studying in Japan. After college, she wrote *The Yamato Colony,* based on her research into the history of the California community to which her grandparents came as immigrants and in which her parents were raised. Following this, she worked and traveled in Japan for another year. Noda earned a master's degree from the Harvard Divinity School. She now teaches at Lesley College in Cambridge, Massachusetts.

Growing Up Asian in America

The act of definition in this essay is one of self-definition, both of an individual and, by implication, of a cultural group. This complex task is accomplished in an especially clear manner. In reading, pay attention to the different kinds of expository patterns Noda employs, including comparison and narration. Note, too, how clearly she makes the different pieces of the essay fit together.

Sometimes when I was growing up, my identity seemed to hurtle toward me and paste itself right to my face. I felt that way, encountering the stereotypes of my race perpetuated by non-Japanese people (primarily white) who may or may not have had contact with other Japanese in America. "You don't like cheese, do you?" someone would ask. "I know your people don't like cheese." Sometimes questions came making allusions to history. That was another aspect of the identity. Events that had happened quite apart from the me who stood silent in that moment connected my face with an incomprehensible past. "Your parents were in California? Were they in those camps during the war?" And sometimes there were phrases or nicknames: "Lotus Blossom." I was sometimes addressed or referred to as racially Japanese, sometimes as Japanese American, and sometimes as an Asian woman. Confusions and distortions abounded.

How is one to know and define oneself? From the inside—   2
within a context that is self defined, from a grounding in community
and a connection with culture and history that are comfortably accepted? Or from the outside—in terms of messages received from
the media and people who are often ignorant? Even as an adult I can
still see two sides of my face and past. I can see from the inside out,
in freedom. And I can see from the outside in, driven by the old
voices of childhood and lost in anger and fear.

I Am Racially Japanese

A voice from my childhood says: "You are other. You are less than.   3
You are unalterably alien." This voice has its own history. We have
indeed been seen as other and alien since the early years of our arrival in the United States. The very first immigrants were welcomed
and sought as laborers to replace the dwindling numbers of
Chinese, whose influx had been cut off by the Chinese Exclusion Act
of 1882. The Japanese fell natural heir to the same anti-Asian prejudice that had arisen against the Chinese. As soon as they began striking for better wages, they were no longer welcomed.

I can see myself today as a person historically defined by law   4
and custom as being forever alien. Being neither "free white," nor
"African," our people in California were deemed "aliens, ineligible
for citizenship," no matter how long they intended to stay here.
Aliens ineligible for citizenship were prohibited from owning, buying, or leasing land. They did not and could not belong here. The
voice in me remembers that I am always a *Japanese* American in the
eyes of many. A third-generation German American is an American.
A third-generation Japanese American is a Japanese American.
Being Japanese means being a danger to the country during the war
and knowing how to use chopsticks. I wear this history on my face.

I move to the other side. I see a different light and claim a dif-   5
ferent context. My race is a line that stretches across ocean and time
to link me to the shrine where my grandmother was raised. Two
high, white banners lift in the wind at the top of the stone steps leading to the shrine. It is time for the summer festival. Black characters
are written against the sky as boldly as the clouds, as lightly as kites,
as sharply as the big black crows I used to see above the fields in
New Hampshire. At festival time there is liquor and food, ritual, discipline, and abandonment. There is music and drunkenness and invocation. There is hope. Another season has come. Another season
has gone.

I am racially Japanese. I have a certain claim to this crazy place   6
where the prayers intoned by a neighboring Shinto priest (standing
in for my grandmother's nephew who is sick) are drowned out by
the rehearsals for the pop singing contest in which most of the villagers will compete later that night. The village elders, the priest,
and I stand respectfully upon the immaculate, shining wooden floor
of the outer shrine, bowing our heads before the hidden powers.
During the patchy intervals when I can hear him, I notice the priest
has a stutter. His voice flutters up to my ears only occasionally because two men and a woman are singing gustily into a microphone
in the compound, testing the sound system. A prerecorded tape of
guitars, samisens, and drums accompanies them. Rock music and
Shinto prayers. That night, to loud applause and cheers, a young man
is given the award for the most *netsuretsu*—passionate, burning—
rendition of a song. We roar our approval of the reward. Never
mind that his voice had wandered and slid, now slightly above, now
slightly below the given line of the melody. Netsuretsu. Netsuretsu.

In the morning, my grandmother's sister kneels at the foot of the   7
stone stairs to offer her morning prayers. She is too crippled to climb
the stairs, so each morning she kneels here upon the path. She shuts
her eyes for a few seconds, her motions as matter of fact as when she
washes rice. I linger longer than she does, so reluctant to leave, sa-
voring the connection I feel with my grandmother in America, the
past, and the power that lives and shines in the morning sun.

Our family has served this shrine for generations. The family's   8
need to protect this claim to identity and place outweighs any individual claim to any individual hope. I am Japanese.

I Am a Japanese American

"Weak." I hear the voice from my childhood years. "Passive," I hear.   9
Our parents and grandparents were the ones who were put into
those camps. They went without resistance; they offered cooperation as proof of loyalty to America. "Victim," I hear. And, "Silent."

Our parents are painted as hard workers who were socially un-   10
comfortable and had difficulty expressing even the smallest opinion.
Clean, quiet, motivated, and determined to match the American
way; that is us, and that is the story of our time here.

"Why did you go into those camps," I raged at my parents, fright-   11
ened by my own inner silence and timidity. "Why didn't you do anything to resist? Why didn't you name it the injustice it was?" Couldn't
our parents even think? Couldn't they? Why were we so passive?

I shift my vision and my stance. I am in California. My uncle is   12
in the midst of the sweet potato harvest. He is pressed, trying to get
the harvesting crews onto the field as quickly as possible, worried
about the flow of equipment and people. His big pickup is pulled off
to the side, motor running, door ajar. I see two tractors in the yard in
front of an old shed; the flat bed harvesting platform on which the
workers will stand has already been brought over from the other
field. It's early morning. The workers stand loosely grouped and at
ease, but my uncle looks as harried and tense as a police officer trying to unsnarl a New York City traffic jam. Driving toward the shed,
I pull my car off the road to make way for an approaching tractor.
The front wheels of the car sink luxuriously into the soft, white sand
by the roadside and the car slides to a dreamy halt, tail still on the
road. I try to move forward. I try to move back. The front bites con-
tentedly into the sand, the back lifts itself at a jaunty angle. My uncle
sees me and storms down the road, running. He is shouting before
he is even near me.

"What's the matter with you," he screams. "What the hell are   13
you doing?" In his frenzy, he grabs his hat off his head and slashes it
through the air across his knee. He is beside himself. "Don't you
know how to drive in sand? What's the matter with you? You've
blocked the whole roadway. How am I supposed to get my tractors
out of here? Can't you use your head? You've cut off the whole
roadway, and we've got to get out of here."

I stand on the road before him helplessly thinking, "No, I don't   14
know how to drive in sand. I've never driven in sand."

"I'm sorry, uncle," I say, burying a smile beneath a look of sin-   15
cere apology. I notice my deep amusement and my affection for him
with great curiosity. I am usually devastated by anger. Not this time.

During the several years that follow I learn about the people   16
and the place, and much more about what has happened in this
California village where my parents grew up. The issei, our grandparents, made this settlement in the desert. Their first crops were
eaten by rabbits and ravaged by insects. The land was so barren that
men walking from house to house sometimes got lost. Women came
here too. They bore children in 114 degree heat, then carried the babies with them into the fields to nurse when they reached the end of
each row of grapes or other truck farm crops.

I had had no idea what it meant to buy this kind of land and   17
make it grow green. Or how, when the war came, there was no space
at all for the subtlety of being who we were—Japanese Americans.
Either/or was the way. I hadn't understood that people were liter-

ally afraid for their lives then, that their money had been frozen in banks; that there was a five-mile travel limit; that when the early evening curfew came and they were inside their houses, some of them watched helplessly as people they knew went into their barns to steal their belongings. The police were patrolling the road, interested only in violators of curfew. There was no help for them in the face of thievery. I had not been able to imagine before what it must have felt like to be an American—to know absolutely that one is an American—and yet to have almost everyone else deny it. Not only deny it, but challenge that identity with machine guns and troops of white American soldiers. In those circumstances it was difficult to say, "I'm a Japanese American." "American" had to do.

But now I can say that I am a Japanese American. It means I   18
have a place here in this country, too. I have a place here on the East Coast, where our neighbor is so much a part of our family that my mother never passes her house at night without glancing at the lights to see if she is home and safe; where my parents have hauled hundreds of pounds of rocks from fields and arduously planted Christmas trees and blueberries, lilacs, asparagus, and crab apples; where my father still dreams of angling a stream to a new bed so that he can dig a pond in the field and fill it with water and fish. "The neighbors already came for their Christmas tree?" he asks in December. "Did they like it? Did they like it?"

I have a place on the West Coast where my relatives still farm,   19
where I heard the stories of feuds and backbiting, and where I saw that people survived and flourished because fundamentally they trusted and relied upon one another. A death in the family is not just a death in a family; it is a death in the community. I saw people help each other with money, materials, labor, attention, and time. I saw men gather once a year, without fail, to clean the grounds of a ninety-year-old woman who had helped the community before, during, and after the war. I saw her remembering them with birthday cards sent to each of their children.

I come from a people with a long memory and a distinctive grace.   20
We live our thanks. And we are Americans. Japanese Americans.

I Am a Japanese American Woman

Woman. The last piece of my identity. It has been easier by far for   21
me to know myself in Japan and to see my place in America than it has been to accept my line of connection with my own mother. She was my dark self, a figure in whom I thought I saw all that I feared

most in myself. Growing into womanhood and looking for some model of strength, I turned away from her. Of course, I could not find what I sought. I was looking for a black feminist or a white feminist. My mother is neither white nor black.

My mother is a woman who speaks with her life as much as with her tongue. I think of her with her own mother. Grandmother had Parkinson's disease and it had frozen her gait and set her fingers, tongue, and feet jerking and trembling in a terrible dance. My aunts and uncles wanted her to be able to live in her own home. They fed her, bathed her, dressed her, awoke at midnight to take her for one last trip to the bathroom. My aunts (her daughters-in-law) did most of the care, but my mother went from New Hampshire to California each summer to spend a month living with grandmother, because she wanted to and because she wanted to give my aunts at least a small rest. During those hot summer days, mother lay on the couch watching the television or reading, cooking foods that grandmother liked, and speaking little. Grandmother thrived under her care. 22

The time finally came when it was too dangerous for grandmother to live alone. My relatives kept finding her on the floor beside her bed when they went to wake her in the mornings. My mother flew to California to help clean the house and make arrangements for grandmother to enter a local nursing home. On her last day at home, while grandmother was sitting in her big, overstuffed armchair, hair combed and wearing a green summer dress, my mother went to her and knelt at her feet. "Here, Mamma," she said. "I've polished your shoes." She lifted grandmother's legs and helped her into the shiny black shoes. My grandmother looked down and smiled slightly. She left her house walking, supported by her children, carrying her pocket book, and wearing her polished black shoes. "Look, Mamma," my mom had said, kneeling. "I've polished your shoes." 23

Just the other day, my mother came to Boston to visit. She had recently lost a lot of weight and was pleased with her new shape and her feeling of good health. "Look at me, Kes," she exclaimed, turning toward me, front and back, as naked as the day she was born. I saw her small breasts and the wide, brown scar, belly button to pubic hair, that marked her because my brother and I were both born by Caesarean section. Her hips were small. I was not a large baby, but there was so little room for me in her that when she was carrying me she could not even begin to bend over toward the floor. She hated it, she said. 24

"Don't I look good? Don't you think I look good?" 25

I looked at my mother, smiling and as happy as she, thinking of   26
all the times I have seen her naked. I have seen both my parents
naked throughout my life, as they have seen me. From childhood
through adulthood we've had our naked moments, sharing baths,
idle conversations picked up as we moved between showers and
closets, hurried moments at the beginning of days, quiet moments at
the end of days.

I know this to be Japanese, this ease with the physical, and it   27
makes me think of an old, Japanese folk song. A young nursemaid, a
fifteen-year-old girl, is singing a lullaby to a baby who is strapped to
her back. The nursemaid has been sent as a servant to a place far
from own home. "We're the beggars," she says, "and they are the
nice people. Nice people wear fine sashes. Nice clothes."

> *If I should drop dead,*
> *bury me by the roadside!*
> *I'll give a flower*
> *to everyone who passes.*
>
> *What kind of flower?*
> *The cam-cam-camellia {tsun-tsun-tsubaki}*
> *watered by Heaven:*
> *alms water.*[1]

The nursemaid is the intersection of heaven and earth, the inter-   28
section of the human, the natural world, the body, and the soul. In
this song, with clear eyes, she looks steadily at life, which is sometimes so very terrible and sad. I think of her while looking at my
mother, who is standing on the red and purple carpet before me,
laughing, without any clothes.

I am my mother's daughter. And I am myself.   29
I am a Japanese American woman.   30

Epilogue

I recently heard a man from West Africa share some memories of his   31
childhood. He was raised Muslim, but when he was a young man,
he found himself deeply drawn to Christianity. He struggled against
this inner impulse for years, trying to avoid the church yet feeling
pushed to return to it again and again. "I would have done *anything* to

---

[1]Patia R. Isaku, *Mountain Storm, Pine Breeze: Folk Song in Japan* (Tucson: University of
Arizona Press, 1981), 41.

avoid the change," he said. At last, he became Christian. Afterwards he was afraid to go home, fearing that he would not be accepted. The fear was groundless, he discovered, when at last he returned— he had separated himself, but his family and friends (all Muslim) had not separated themselves from him.

The man, who is now a professor of religion, said that in the   32 Africa he knew as a child and a young man, pluralism was embraced rather than feared. There was "a kind of tolerance that did not deny your particularity," he said. He alluded to zestful, spontaneous debates that would sometimes loudly erupt between Muslims and Christians in the village's public spaces. His memories of an atheist who harangued the villagers when he came to visit them once a week moved me deeply. Perhaps the man was an agricultural advisor or inspector. He harassed the women. He would say:

> "Don't go to the fields! Don't even bother to go to the fields. Let God take care of you. He'll send you the food. If you believe in God, why do you need to work? You don't need to work! Let God put the seeds in the ground. Stay home."

The professor said, "The women laughed, you know? They just   33 laughed. Their attitude was, 'Here is a child of God. When will he come home?'"

The storyteller, the professor of religion, smiled the most fantas-   34 tic, tender smile as he told this story. "In my country, there is a deep affirmation of the oneness of God," he said. "The atheist and the women were having quite different experiences in their encounter, though the atheist did not know this. He saw himself as quite separate from the women. But the women did not see themselves as being separate from him. 'Here is a child of God,' they said. 'When will he come home?'"

MEANINGS AND VALUES

1. Define in your own words each of the identities Noda outlines for herself. How can the last chapter of the essay, "Epilogue" (pars. 31–34), be said to harmonize these identities or at least to suggest a way of building bridges among them?

2. Discuss how the opening chapter of this essay (pars. 1–2) explains the author's need to define herself and suggests indirectly that each of us needs to go through a similar process.

EXPOSITORY TECHNIQUES

1. Apart from definition, what expository technique does Noda use to organize this essay as a whole? What expository pattern does she employ in paragraphs 3–8? In paragraphs 9–20? What pattern or patterns organize paragraphs 21–28? What pattern helps conclude the essay in paragraphs 31–34?

2. This essay makes use of a variety of expository patterns. Explain why it is accurate (or inaccurate) to refer to the overall pattern as one of definition. Be ready to defend your answer with evidence from the text.

3. Tell how paragraph 2 helps predict and justify the organization of the essay. Why is this kind of paragraph a useful part of the essay? For what kinds of essays might a paragraph like this be neither useful nor necessary?

4. Discuss the use of subtitles in organizing the essay. In what ways are they linked to the overall definition pattern? (See "Guide to Terms": *Unity*.)

DICTION AND VOCABULARY

1. Each of the major chapters in the body of the essay uses a different cluster of terms to explore and define a particular part of the author's identity. Tell what the clusters of terms are in each chapter.

2. Tell how the diction in paragraphs 22–28 contributes to their effectiveness. (Consider also the contribution made by the choice of details.) (Guide: *Diction.*)

3. If you do not know the meanings of some of the following terms, look them up in a dictionary: context (par. 2); influx (3); invocation (5); Shinto, samisens (6); issei (16); arduously (18); pluralism, spontaneous, harangued (32).

READ TO WRITE

1. **Collaborating:** The closing example in the essay endorses "pluralism" (par. 32), tolerance for a variety of beliefs. Working in a group, make a list of questions relating to pluralism that might lead to topics for an essay. Here are some to get you started: To what extent is our society already guided by such an attitude? Give some examples. What might be some of the practical consequences (good and bad) of a thoroughgoing pluralism in our society? Is such an attitude really possible for a large society to adopt?

2. **Considering Audience:** For the past several decades, Canada and the U. S. have experienced considerable immigration. Analyze Noda's essay and prepare a written response explaining the extent to which one of her purposes is to explain the effects of immigration to people who might be concerned or worried about its consequences.

3. **Developing an Essay:** Following Noda's example, build an essay of your own around a series of increasingly specific definitions such as her "I am racially Japanese," "I am a Japanese American," and "I am a Japanese American Woman."

(NOTE: Suggestions for topics requiring development by DEFINITION are on pp. 424–425 at the end of this chapter.)

MICHAEL DORRIS

MICHAEL DORRIS (1945–1997) taught in the English Department at Dartmouth College. He was the parent of several adopted children afflicted with Fetal Alcohol Syndrome, an experience and a condition he wrote about movingly in the highly-praised book *The Broken Cord* (1990). Dorris also wrote about contemporary Native American culture (his own heritage) and the historical experience of Native Americans. Essays on these topics (as well as a wide range of other topics) have appeared in numerous magazines, and many are collected in the volume *Paper Trail* (1994). He was also the author of *Native Americans: Five Hundred Years After* and *A Guide to Research on North American Indians* (with Mary Lou Byler and Arlene Hirschfelder). Among his other books are *Working Men* (stories) (1994); *A Yellow Raft in Blue Water* (1989); and *Cloud Chamber* (1997); (novels) *Morning Girl* (young adult book) (1992); and *The Crown of Columbus* (novel, with Louise Erdrich) (1992).

Father's Day

The redefinition of fatherhood that Dorris offers in this essay, based on his own experiences growing up, calls into question conventional images of family roles and relationships. At the same time, however, it affirms many of the values that conventional definitions also embody. This double movement of redefinition and reaffirmation makes the essay particularly interesting.

My father, a career army officer, was twenty-seven when he was killed, and as a result, I can't help but take war personally. Over the years his image has coalesced for me as an amalgam of familiar anecdotes: a dashing mixed-blood man from the Northwest who, improbably, could do the rumba; a soldier who regularly had his uniform altered by a tailor so that it would fit better; a date, according to my mother, who "knew how to order" in a restaurant; the person whom, in certain lights and to some people, I resemble. He is a compromise of his quirkier qualities, indistinct, better remembered for his death—my grandmother still wears a gold star on her best coat—than for his brief life. 1

From the perspective of the present, my father was a bit player on the edges of the movie frame, the one who didn't make it back, 2 whose fatality added anonymous atmosphere and a sense of mayhem to the plot. His grave, in a military cemetery near Tacoma, is located by graph paper like a small town on a map: E-9. He's frozen in age, a kid in a T-shirt, a pair of dog tags stored in a box in my closet. His willingness to die for his country may have contributed in some small part to the fall of the Nazis, but more in the way of a pawn exchanged for its counterpart, a pair of lives eliminated with the result that there were two fewer people to engage in combat. I was a few months old the last time he saw me, and a single photograph of me in his arms is the only hard evidence that we ever met.

The fact of my father's death exempted me, under the classification "sole surviving son" (A-IV), from being drafted during the Vietnam War, but it also obliged me to empathize with the child of every serviceperson killed in an armed engagement. "Glory" is an inadequate substitute, a pale abstraction, compared to the enduring, baffling blankness of a missing parent.   3

There was a children's book in the 1950s—perhaps it still exists—titled *The Happy Family*, and it was a piece of work. Dad toiled at the office, Mom baked in the kitchen, and brother and sister always had neighborhood friends sleeping over. The prototype of "Leave It to Beaver" and "Father Knows Best," this little text reflects a midcentury standard, a brightly illustrated reproach to my own unorthodox household, but luckily that wasn't the way I heard it. As read to me by my Aunt Marion—her acid delivery was laced with sarcasm and punctuated with many a sidelong glance—it turned into hilarious irony.   4

Compassionate and generous, irreverent, simultaneously opinionated and open-minded, iron-willed and ever optimistic, my aunt was the one who pitched a baseball with me in the early summer evenings, who took me horseback riding, who sat by my bed when I was ill. A fierce, lifelong Democrat—a precinct captain even—she helped me find my first jobs and arranged among her friends at work for my escorts to the father-son dinners that closed each sports season. When the time came, she prevailed upon the elderly man next door to teach me how to shave.   5

"Daddy" Tingle, as he was known to his own children and grandchildren, was a man of many talents. He could spit tobacco juice over the low roof of his garage, gum a sharpened mumbly-peg twig from the ground even without his false teeth, and produce, from the Bourbon Stockyards where he worked, the jewel-like cornea of a cow's eye—but he wasn't much of a shaver. After his instruction, neither am I.   6

Aunt Marion, on the other hand, was a font of information and 7
influence. When I was fifteen, on a series of tempestuous Sunday
mornings at a deserted River Road park, she gave me lessons in how
to drive a stick shift. A great believer in the efficacy of the *World Book
Encyclopedia*—the major literary purchase of my childhood—she insisted that I confirm any vague belief by looking it up. To the then-
popular tune of "You, You, You," she counted my laps in the
Crescent Hill pool while I practiced for a life-saving certificate.
Operating on the assumption that anything out of the ordinary was
probably good for me, she once offered to mortgage the house so
that I could afford to go to Mali as a volunteer participant in
Operation Crossroads Africa. She paid for my first Smith-Corona
typewriter in thirty-six $4-a-week installments.

For over sixty years Aunt Marion was never without steady em- 8
ployment: telegraph operator for Western Union, budget officer for
the city of Louisville, "new girl" at a small savings and loan (when, after twenty-five years in a patronage job, the Democrats lost the
mayor's race), executive secretary for a nationally renowned attorney.

Being Aunt Marion, she didn't and doesn't give herself much 9
credit. Unless dragged to center stage, she stands at the periphery in
snapshots, minimizes her contributions. Every June for forty years
I've sent her a Father's Day card.

MEANINGS AND VALUES

1. Dorris presents examples of three different men in the role of father.
   State in your own words the definitions of fatherhood, or of family
   roles, that each of these examples offers. In what sense can each of
   these images be viewed as symbolic? (See "Guide to Terms": *Symbol.*)

2. In what sense are the pictures that represent traditional images of fatherhood and family roles inadequate? Why does the writer view Aunt
   Marion as a better father than the other father figures in the essay?

3. What new definition (or re-definition) of fatherhood is Dorris offering in this essay? Try stating it in your own words. Why do you think
   that Dorris does not offer his own concise definition of fatherhood in
   the essay? Is the essay more—or less—effective without it? (Guide:
   Evaluation.)

EXPOSITORY TECHNIQUES

1. Why do you think the writer offers two negative (or inadequate) examples of fatherhood and family roles before beginning his positive

example in paragraph 5? Why does he interrupt the positive example with another negative one in paragraph 6?

2.   What strategy does Dorris use to move from the negative example in paragraph 4 to the positive one in paragraph 5? (Guide: *Transition.*) What transition strategies does he use to link the other paragraphs in the essay?

3.   Part of the effectiveness of this essay lies in the variety, quantity, and vividness of the details the author provides in the examples. Identify the details in paragraph 2, and indicate whether they are specific or general. (Guide: *Specific/General.*) Look carefully at the sentence structure in paragraphs 2 and 5, and explain how Dorris shaped their syntax to allow for the inclusion of numerous details. (Guide: *Syntax.*)

4.   Why does the writer wait until the last sentence to announce that he regards Aunt Marion as his "father"? Is this strategy effective? Why or why not? Does the last sentence serve to summarize the essay, or should we consider it a thesis statement of sorts? Explain. (Guide: *Thesis.*)

DICTION AND VOCABULARY

1.   Examine the language used to present details in paragraphs 1, 2, and 4, and indicate where most of it seems to fall on a sliding scale from abstract to concrete. (Guide: *Concrete/Abstract.*) Indicate how the relative concreteness or abstractness of the language aids in the effective presentation of the details. (Guide: *Evaluation.*)

2.   If you do not know the meaning of some of the following terms, look them up in a dictionary: coalesced, amalgam, anecdotes, rumba (par. 1); precinct (5); gum, mumbly-peg, cornea (6); tempestuous (7); periphery (9).

READ TO WRITE

1.   **Collaborating:** Think of other situations that rob children of parents, i.e. AIDS, drugs, etc. Working in a group, consider who might step in as role models for these children. Choose one of these topics and plan an essay which redefines that role model as "parent" for victims of biological parental loss. Your group may need to do some outside research to plan your essay.

2.   **Considering Audience:** Think of the parenting roles various people have played in your life, and in the lives of people you know. Think of how people who are not blood relatives have acted like siblings, aunts, uncles, or grandparents. Freewrite about different ways of viewing families and family relationships until you decide on a topic and direction for an essay. Then share your essay ideas with classmates to discover how many of your definitions they (and your potential readers) are likely to share.

3. **Developing an Essay:** Develop a definition essay of your own in which you give new meaning to a term but withhold either the term or the definition until the end of the essay, just as Dorris does.

(NOTE: Suggestions for topics requiring development by use of DEFINITION are on pp. 424–425 at the end of this chapter.)

VERONICA CHAMBERS

VERONICA CHAMBERS is a writer living in New York City. She is a contributing editor for *Glamour* magazine and has recently published a
memoir, *Mama's Girl* (1996).

Mother's Day

In this selection from her book *Mama's Girl,* published as an essay
in *Glamour* magazine, Chambers uses a variety of expository patterns (comparison, example, narrative, cause-and-effect) to help
understand why her Mother's Day gift received such a cool recep-
tion. As she considers the differences between her perspective as
an African-American professional woman, a college-educated
writer, and that of her mother, who struggled to raise her child on
a maid's salary in the days when educational and occupational opportunities for African Americans were strictly limited, Chambers
comes to a deeper appreciation of her mother's achievements.

A couple of years ago, I earned a good salary for the first time and   1
I wanted to do something special for my mother. So I sent her a
gift certificate for a day at Elizabeth Arden. Included were a massage, facial, sauna and makeover—the works, plus tips. My mother
wouldn't have to spend a dime, only the subway token it would
take to get her there. I called here up on Mother's Day, all excited
about the gift. She was excited, too, and described how it had come
gift-wrapped with a big red bow. Then she asked me a question that
broke my heart in two. "Vee?" she whispered. "Do they allow black
people in those places?"

It was 1992 and my mother was asking whether Elizabeth   2
Arden would slam the red door in her black face. "Of course they allow black people!" I said, using an angry voice to conceal how hurt I
felt. "I've paid for everything, including a tip for everyone who
touches your body. So if anybody so much as looks at you funny,
you tell me!"

Months went by and my mother did not use the gift certificate.   3
"You use it," she would tell me. "You work so hard. Burning the

candle at both ends . . . ." Finally, I got furious with her and made some empty threat about refusing to talk to her until she went to Elizabeth Arden. She wouldn't budge.

In my frustration I reimagined the situation as a Daliesque fan-   4
tasy in which I was an avenging angel pushing my mother through the Red Door. When a friend suggested that perhaps my mother did not want to go to Elizabeth Arden alone, I sent her neighbor a gift certificate too, but it didn't help: She turned out to be just as afraid to go as my mother.

Finally, almost a year later, my mother called and said, "Guess   5
where I've just been? Elizabeth Arden."

My heart almost stopped. "How was it?" I asked.   6

"Nice . . . but everyone there was just like you," she said coyly.   7

"Just like *me?*" I repeated disbelievingly, picturing the Fifth   8
Avenue crowd of older white women laid out on massage tables.

"Professionals. Upper-class women. You know," she replied.   9

While I was thrilled that she'd gone, that exchange made me   10
wonder what my mother saw when she looked at me. I wondered if everything about me that she chose to see as being white—my education, my career, my social activities—obscured everything about me that was black—my family, my community, my mother herself. I always knew she saw me as different from her, but not until she went to Elizabeth Arden did I realize how different.

I never stop feeling that I want to make things up to my   11
mother—make up for her difficulties with my father, from whom she was eventually divorced, for my brother's failure to do well in school or in a job, for the ways in which we all left her. So I buy her things. If I'm shopping and I buy myself a suit, I'll get my mother a blouse. I send her vases and candles and antique dolls. One of the first questions I ask when I enter a store is: "Can you ship this somewhere for me?" I'd be a liar if I said my generosity was only about bestowing kindnesses on my mother. It is also about easing my own guilt.

I am more aware now of how my schooling and experiences   12
separate us, but I cannot get used to the distance. She is so much a part of me that I half felt I graduated college for both of us. To me, the newfound abundance of the money I can earn has meaning for both of us. But my mother sees things differently. We are separated by education and economics.

When I was in college, my mother once called me an Oreo—   13
black on the outside, white on the inside. The word, so cruel when it comes from a black person's peers, was like a punch in the face coming from my mother—as if I were a total stranger and not her own

child. Later, when I told her how much it had hurt me, she said, "But I was just joking!"

Now that I am working, she is fond of calling me a Buppie. I   14
hate it, I tell her, and ask her to stop. But if I talk about wanting to
see a certain play or deliberate over whether to buy a painting, she
can't help but let it slip: "You're such a Buppie." There is a texture of
affection and pride in her voice that suggests she's glad I'm not as
poor as she was when she was my age, but it is a pride I have trouble absorbing. Her voice says, "I am proud of you—but you are now
an entirely different being than I am."

Going from poor to middle class was both the longest and the   15
shortest transition I have ever made. Long, because every day that I
went without was just one of an unending stretch of days in which I'd
always done without. Once I'd craved things so deeply that I kept myself away from malls and shops, so as not to preoccupy myself with
what I could not have. In college I collected mail-order catalogs, marking them up with stars and circling the outfits I liked in the colors and
sizes I wanted. Desire became a game and playing the game was satisfying in its own way. At the end of freshman year, a friend asked,
"Why do you always mark up those catalogs when you never order
anything?" I hadn't realized that anyone noticed what had become a
mindless habit, and I didn't know what to say. Was he being cruel?

"I don't know," I said, feigning dumbness and vowing to keep   16
the catalogs out of sight.

But the jump from poverty to solvency seemed short and sud-   17
den because it was one I made alone. It was just me in an apartment,
staring at a paycheck that was bigger than any I'd ever seen. Who
could I call, without it sounding like I was bragging? Who wouldn't
immediately ask for a loan? Who would understand how a thousand dollars could feel so much like a million? I wanted my mother
there on the other end of the phone.

But I also felt guilty, because I felt she was much more deserv-   18
ing of that check than I was. I watched my mother work all her life
with no reward greater than a cost-of-living raise; she was always
just getting by. I knew that hard work was no guarantee of success.
Success was only a dream—the big payoff that never came from my
father's get-rich-quick schemes, or a winning lottery number that
came to you in a vision. My life had been different. And even after
going to college, even after years of hard work, I still felt deep inside
that I was more lucky than successful. As if I had dreamed of a number and that number had come in.

My mother was neither lucky nor successful. She believed in   19
the promise of the civil rights movement, but never really thought

what those rights would mean to her. She taught her children the importance of equality and pride, but never expected to live in equality herself.

I can see now that although she was affected by the benefits of integration—no more sitting in the back of the bus, no more separate water fountains—most of the triumphs of the movement remained for my mother events that happened on TV. In 1970, my mother gave birth to me and worked as a secretary. In the 1990s, my mother is still a secretary. She's worked hard all her life, mostly for white people, and the civil rights movement did not change that. What it changed was me, and I wasn't some bright, young black woman that my mother saw on TV. I was her daughter. My success brought the benefits of integration through her front door, and that scared her. She could call me an Oreo and a Buppie and try to keep what I represented at a safe distance, but the things I bought her, the restaurants I took her to, forced her to consider life differently. Maybe it wouldn't take a winning lottery ticket for her to be able to lead a better life. [20]

I called my mother recently and had a long talk about money. My mother is only 45. She has so much life ahead of her. I was hoping that I could use some of what I've learned about saving and investing to make her life more comfortable, so I began to ask her questions: What do your retirement savings look like? What are your financial goals? She had to stop and think. [21]

"You mean goals besides paying the rent and putting dinner on the table?" She laughed nervously. [22]

"Yes," I said. "What do you want to own? What trips do you want to take?" [23]

There wasn't much she wanted to own. What she really wanted to do was travel. She wanted to go to Jamaica, Ghana, and Brazil. The tentativeness in her voice was so clear, as if just by speaking her wishes aloud, she might cause the genie to dive back into its bottle. My mother had never been able to see further ahead than the next day or next month. I knew then why it had scared her when, as a ten-year-old, I started talking about college. She didn't know what we were going to eat for the next seven days, much less where she would find tuition in seven years. [24]

Now as we discussed *her* money for the first time, I told my mother that if she didn't dream, if she didn't think about what she wanted to have, then she was going to wake up and another 20 years would be gone. "There's nothing to save," she said, I asked if I could see her weekly budget. I told her I knew it was personal, but I needed to know exactly how much she and my stepfather made and where it was going. "What budget?" she said. [25]

I wrote down all my mother's figures—how much she owed,   26
what little she had saved, how much she and my stepfather made. I
did a budget and a savings plan and outlined a retirement plan that
would give her some sort of nest egg.

"It's not a lot," I told her. "You'd probably still need to work.   27
But maybe you could save enough to open a business." I wrote out
the plan and mailed it to her. When she called me back, I could tell
she was impressed. She told me that she and my stepfather had gone
over my plan and they thought they could stick to it.

My mother told me she had tried to save money when we were   28
little, but often she was too embarrassed to take a five dollar bill up
to the teller's window and deposit it, so she would keep it in an envelope. By the next week, it would be gone.

"I feel like I can really be hopeful now," she said. "Like I have   29
something to look forward to besides bills." Then she paused and
added, "I'm still going to play the lottery, and if I hit it, then to hell
with your savings plan." I laughed and said that would be fine.

For the first time in my life, I hear in my mother's voice that she   30
is more than just coping, more than just figuring out how to get by.
When I hear my mother talk, I can hear her dreaming and it's the
sweetest sound in the world to me.

MEANINGS AND VALUES

1.   In what ways does the author's mother define her daughter? In what
ways does the author define her mother? In what ways does the author define herself?

2.   What social movements and changes in values and attitudes make
necessary the redefinition of identity and roles the author undertakes
in this essay? How many of these social movements are mentioned in
the essay, and where are they mentioned?

3.   How are readers likely to react to the question at the end of paragraph 1? What might determine the ways different readers react?
What proportion of readers do you think are likely to react as the
writer does? Why?

EXPOSITORY TECHNIQUES

1.   In what ways does the question at the end of paragraph 1 act as a justification for the redefining of roles that Chambers undertakes in this essay? Does it provide justification for most readers as well as the writer?
If not, how else does the writer justify the need for new definitions?

2.   Can the sentence at the end of paragraph 1 be considered a thesis statement? Why or why not? If not, where else in the essay does the author make plain the purpose or thesis (main theme) of the piece? (See "Guide to Terms": *Thesis; Purpose.*)

3.   Which paragraphs in the essay use comparison as an expository pattern? What do they contribute to the process of definition?

DICTION AND VOCABULARY

1.   Many of the paragraphs in this essay discuss conflicting definitions and misunderstandings. Discuss how the writer uses transitions in paragraphs 12–14 and 17–20 to emphasize such conflicts and contrasting perspectives. (Guide: *Transition; Emphasis.*)

2.   To what does the word "Daliesque" in paragraph 4 allude? (Guide: *Figures of Speech.*) What does this reveal about the speaker's attitudes and perspective? What is a "Buppie"? Why would the writer be offended by the term?

3.   If you do not know the meaning of some of the following words, look them up in a dictionary: sauna (par. 1); disbelievingly (8); bestowing (11); tentativeness (24).

READ TO WRITE

1.   **Collaborating:** Working with a partner, discuss some aspect of your individual upbringings that distinguishes you from each other. Discuss the differences and plan an essay comparing the definition of your childhood lifestyle with that of your partner.

2.   **Considering Audience:** Throughout her essay, Chambers employs definitions of race, education, socio-economic class, and even gender to explain the differences between her thinking and that of her mother. Choose one of these categories or another, similar one to help you better understand some of the differences between you and a member of your immediate family from a previous generation. Write an essay on parent-child relationships that addresses the feelings and values of readers who are in your age group.

3.   **Developing an Essay:** In what ways are college-educated children likely to view the world differently from parents who have not attended college? Are there likely differences in the perspective between children who have attended graduate school and parents who attended college? Do differences in careers and kinds of work also lead to different perspectives? Consider exploring these and other contrasting outlooks (or definitions of values and identities) in an expository essay.

(NOTE: Suggestions for topics requiring development by DEFINITION are on pp. 424–425 at the end of the chapter.)

M.P. DUNLEAVY

M.P. Dunleavy is a staff writer for *Glamour* magazine.

"Guy" Envy

The names we give to ourselves and other people often contain messages about traditional identities. We can also create new names in an attempt to create new identities, and the act of naming is often an attempt to encourage social change. As M.P. Dunleavy points out in this essay (first published in *Glamour*), naming is often a difficult task, especially at a time when attitudes and identities are changing so quickly that we may not be all that sure which name and identity we envision for ourselves.

There are still a few reasons to envy men: that 74-cents-to-the-dollar   1
thing, their choke on Congress, and the word *guy*. On the first two fronts—earning power and political clout—women continue to gain ground. But when it comes to calling ourselves something besides "woman," something that captures our most laid-back, casual sense of ourselves—our *guyness*, if you will—we need a word of our own.

   Not that there's anything wrong with *woman*. Given the   2
umpteen un-wonderful alternatives (*girl, babe, chick, lady, broad, dame, lass*), it's clear why we fought so hard for this non-pejorative term. Woman is admirable. Woman is honorable. Woman speaks of maturity, motherhood and busting through barriers. And that's *exactly* why we need a term to give us a break from all that. A word that would let us kick back and not shave for a couple of days. A word like *guy*.

   Guy is efficient. Think about it: "There's a new guy in marketing—   3
he's got some great ideas." The focus completely skips over *him*—his gender, his maleness—to the important stuff. That he's a man hardly registers. We females, on the other hand, have no shorthand that unhooks us from the biological and political implications of our sex. "We just hired a woman to run the ad-sales division and she's a dynamo." It's hard to hear that without thinking, Oh, she's a *woman*. Is she young, cute, straight, married? Does she market to women? Did they hire her because she's a woman? Will she fit in with the guys?

A few months ago, Natalie Angier, a science reporter for *The   4
New York Times,* gave into her own "guy" envy and confessed her
longing for "a word that conveys snazziness and style, a casual term
for the double-X set . . . a delicious egalitarian word like . . . gal."

Gal? *Gal?* Though Angier insists that "gal has a rich and pris-   5
matic quality to it," *The Oxford English Dictionary* strikes closer to the
vein, revealing that *gal* is nothing more than "a vulgar or dialectal
pronunciation" of *girl.* Oh, that's progress. Besides, as a friend from
Nevada points out, "Gal is from the heartland. Gal has a warm
heart, big hips, and a bad dye job."

What women need is a word that will let us slip into a more   6
easygoing side of ourselves the way men can slip into guyhood.

When men take off their uniforms, jackets, and ties, they're   7
guys. When they put them on again, they're men. In part it's an attitude thing: In the Oval Office, Bill Clinton is a man. Jogging down
Pennsylvania Avenue, he's a guy. Charles Barkley is a guy, unless
he's on the court; then he's a man. Of course, some males favor one
side of the man/guy fence. Hawkeye is a guy. Colonel Potter is a
man. Humphrey Bogart, Robert De Niro, Ronald Reagan—men.
Steve Martin, Jerry Seinfeld, Spike Lee—guys.

But: Mary Tyler Moore, Rita Hayworth, Connie Chung, Hillary   8
Rodham Clinton, Whoopi Goldberg, Julia Louis-Dreyfus, Rosie
Perez—all different, all women. Everyone knows that Whoopi is
much more of a guy than Hillary is, but we don't have the word to
say so. Meanwhile, don't even try plugging female words into classic guy phrases. Whatta *girl!* (Ugh.) She's a great *babe.* (Oh, no.) She's
a *woman's woman?* From time to time we do call ourselves "guys"
(do any of you guys have a spare tampon?), but let's not kid ourselves. We're on borrowed terminology.

This is not just semantics. Until fairly recently, women could   9
not *be* all that guys were and are. It may seem that we've always
lived and worked and dressed as comfortably as one of the fellas,
but until 30 years ago women were constrained by a standard of
femininity that embraced the word *lady* right along with the wearing
of gloves. In the 1950s, women didn't require a word like *guy* because acting like one wasn't written into their parts. Now our roles
have changed, and it's time that language caught up.

The more traditional words that describe women do come in   10
handy; every once in a while you *want* to be a lady, a bitch or a chick,
and having a word for what you're being makes being it easier. But
how do you describe a woman you hang out with who is cool with
herself and others, a woman you can watch the game with and

whose shoulder you can cry on, knowing that she knows where you're coming from? There is no womanly translation of *guy* and yet most women I know aspire to a certain level of guyhood. Just as our mothers longed to be ladies, this confident, centered, sympathetic yet amusing human being is who we'd like to be.

We'll always be women—no one is advocating giving that up.   11
But we need choices, and unless something better comes along we may just have to stake our own claim to *guy*. After all, we successfully co-opted the original guy symbol: blue jeans. There *was* a time when women weren't supposed to touch denim unless they were washing it. Funny how things change. Right, guys?

MEANINGS AND VALUES

1. The opening line of the essay equates the inequality of male and female earnings with male dominance in Congress and the fact that men can define themselves by the word "guy." Why might Dunleavy put the use of a word like "guy" in the same category as such serious gender inequities?

2. Explain what point Dunleavy is trying to make when she says that some aspire "to a certain level of guyhood" (par. 10). How does this differ from the ladies that "our mothers longed to be" (Par. 10)?

3. In paragraph 9 Dunleavy says that "... having a word for what you're being makes it easier." Do you agree with Dunleavy? Explain.

EXPOSITORY TECHNIQUES

1. Dunleavy compares slipping in and out of clothes to "wearing" labels. It this metaphor successful for this essay? Explain.

2. List the different methods of definition that Dunleavy employs in her essay (*background, negation, comparison contrast,* etc.). Discuss the effectiveness of each method.

3. Much of this essay defines a term that doesn't exist. How effective is this ironic use of definition in writing? Does her thorough definition of "guy" make the nonexistent term somehow real?

DICTION AND VOCABULARY

1. Look up the following words in the dictionary and write down the definition: clout (par. 1), non-perjorative (2), egalitarian (4), prismatic (5), dialectal (5), semantics (9).

2. This essay incorporates slang words. Identify slang terms and words in Dunleavy's writing and explain how she uses them to emphasize her point. (See "Guide to Terms": *Slang.*)

READ TO WRITE

1. **Collaborating:** Dunleavy's article was published in a 1990's edition of a woman's magazine. Much of this article helps female readers to identify themselves a members of a gender group. Working in groups, research similar articles from magazines of the past four decades. Plan a collaborative essay comparing the defining qualities of women from each decade.

2. **Considering Audience:** The last line of this essay directly addresses "guys." But the guys to which Dunleavy speaks are women. Would men identify with the examples in this essay as "guys" also? Is the term cross-gendered? Explain in a short response of several paragraphs what parts of this essay might appeal to a male audience and what sections might lead to resistance.

3. **Developing an Essay:** Think of a concept or style that has yet to be coined with a term. Write an essay in a style similar to Dunleavy's in which you look at a concept and try to find a word that might help to clarify it for your readers.

Writing Suggestions for Chapter 9

DEFINITION

Develop a compostion for a specified purpose and audience, using whatever methods and expository patterns will help convey a clear understanding of your meaning of one of the following terms:

1. Country music.	16. Greed.
2. Conscience.	17. Social poise.
3. Religion	18. Intellectual (the person).
4. Bigotry.	19. Pornography.
5. Success.	20. Courage.
6. Empathy.	21. Patriotism.
7. Family.	22. Equility (or equal opportunity).
8. Hypocrisy.	23. Loyalty.
9. Humor.	24. Stylishness (in clothing or behavior).
10. Sophistication.	25. Fame.
11. Naiveté.	26. Obesity.
12. Cowardice.	27. Cheating.
13. Wisdom.	28. Hero.
14. Integrity.	29. Feminine.
15. Morality.	30. Masculine.

COLLABORATIVE EXERCISE

Working in a group, choose a term from the list below. Have each member of your group define the term for a reader/audience of a particular age group. As a group, compare your choices of definition strategies based on each intended audience.

a. success

b. family

c. cowardice

d. loyalty

e. hero

f. integrity

10

Explaining with the Help of
Description

Y ou can make your expository writing more vivid, and hence more
understandable, with the support of description, sometimes even
using the pattern as the basic plan for an exposition. In writing, you
can use sensory details—sight, sound, touch, taste, and smell—to re-
create *places:* a portrait of the steamy closeness of the Brazilian jungle;
the gray stone, narrow streets, tall houses, and church spires of an
eastern European city. You can create portraits of *people, qualities, emotions,* or *moods:* a beloved aunt whose cheerfulness was part of a long
fight against pain and illness; the physical and spatial on-court "intelligence" of a star basketball player; the despair of a child crying for
her puppy just killed by a car; the contrasting moods of a city where
excited theatergoers pass a drunk slumped against a building.

Descriptive writing depends on detail, and your first and most
important job as a writer employing description is to select the details to be included. There are usually many from which to choose,
and it is easy to become so involved in a subject—especially one that
is visually or emotionally intriguing—that you lose sight of the expository purpose of your writing. As you draft and revise, therefore,
you need to keep in mind the kind of picture you want to paint with
words, one that accomplishes *your* purpose for *your* intended audience. Such a word picture need not be entirely visual, for the dimensions of sound, smell, and even touch can create a vivid and
effective image in your readers' minds.

When used as a pattern for much or all of an expository essay,
description does more than set a mood, add a vivid touch to an explanation, or provide an occasional supporting detail. It becomes the
primary strategy for explaining a subject or supporting a thesis, as in
the following example.

425

thesis
supporting
statement

descriptive
details

It's not winter without an icestorm. When Robert Frost gazed at bowed birch trees and tried to think that boys had bent them playing, he knew better: "Icestorms do that." They do that and a lot more, trimming disease and weakness out of the tree—the old tree's friend, as pneumonia used to be the old man's. Some of us provide life-support systems for our precious shrubs, boarding them over against the ice, for the icestorm takes the young or unlucky branch or birch as well as the rotten or feeble. One February morning we look out our windows over yards and fields littered with kindling, small twigs and great branches. We look out at a world turned into one diamond, ten thousand carats in the line of sight, twice as many facets. What a dazzle of spinning refracted light, spider webs of cold brilliance attacking our eyeballs! All winter we wear sunglasses to drive, more than we do in summer, and never so much as after an icestorm, with its painful glaze reflecting from maple and birch, granite boulder and stone wall, turning electric wires into bright silver filaments. The snow itself takes on a crust of ice, like the finish of a clay pot, that carries our weight and sends us swooping and sliding. It's worth your life to go for the mail. Until sand and salt redeem the highway, Route 4 is quiet. We cancel the appointment with the dentist, stay home, and marvel at the altered universe, knowing that midday sun will strip ice from tree and roof and restore our ordinary white winter world.

—Donald Hall, *Seasons at Eagle Pond*

WHY USE DESCRIPTION?

Descriptions help readers create mental images of a subject or scene. To do this, the writing uses concrete, specific detail ("the floodwater turned the carpet into a slippery mess that smelled like dead fish and covered the electronic insides of the TV with a thin coat of black mud") rather than abstract, general impressions ("The flood soaked everything in the living room"). You can put descriptive detail to work for a variety of purposes, however.

You might choose to focus on a particular place or scene, using description to convey and support your thoughts and conclusions about it. Writing of this sort often appears in brief essays focusing on a limited scene: a beach in winter, a small corner of the Sonoran desert, a mall parking lot just before Christmas, for example. On the other hand, a description of a typical family apartment in Cairo might provide important conclusions and support for study of family structure in Egypt or descriptions of the Arctic landscape might contribute to an understanding of the habits of Polar bears. When used for such expository purposes, descriptive writing goes beyond simply recording details to offer conclusions and explanations of the effects of a setting on those who live in it.

You might also use descriptive writing to create a portrait of a person. To do this, you combine descriptive detail with narration (see Chapter 11), usually in the form of brief but representative incidents. Your aim is to highlight the characteristics of your subject: details of appearance, speech, action, and feeling. In such a context, descriptive detail serves to support and convey your understanding of an individual's outlook and motivation, a sense of a personality, and your insight into the individual's influence on others.

Technical descriptions, common in scientific and professional writing, are another use for descriptive writing. In this form of writing, you provide a precise understanding of the elements of a subject and their relationship, and in so doing you convey necessary information or evidence to support your conclusions. Biologists, for example, might describe features of a frog that are marks of evolution or function; art historians might focus on color, line, shape, and brushstroke as a way of supporting a thesis about an artist or a particular painting.

CHOOSING A STRATEGY

Descriptive writing generally follows one of two strategies—*objective* description or *subjective* description—though some overlapping is also common. In objective description you aim at conveying the details of a subject thoroughly and accurately without suggesting your feelings or biases and without trying to evoke an emotional response from readers. Scientific papers, business reports, and academic writing often take this stance. In choosing details, writers of objective descriptions aim at precision and try to avoid emotional overtones. In arranging the details for presentation, writers either pay attention to the need to support a conclusion or to the function of the object or process being presented, as in the following example.

Cathode Ray Tube
    The most familiar example is a television picture tube, and the simplest kind is the black and white. The inside of the tube is coated with a *phosphor*, a substance that glows when struck by electrons. At the

rear of the tube (the neck) is an electron gun that shoots a beam of electrons toward the front. Electromagnetic coils or electrically charged metal plates direct this stream from side to side and top to bottom, forming a glow-picture of the "message" being received by the cathode ray tube. Color tubes are similar except that the face is coated with thousands of groups of dots. Each group, called a *pixel* (picture element), consists of three dots, one for each of the three primary colors—red, green, and blue.

> —Herman Schneider and Leo Schneider, *The Harper Dictionary of Science in Everyday Language*

In subjective description, however, you make your values and feelings clear and often encourage readers to respond emotionally. Often, instead of describing how something *is*, objectively, you describe how it *seems*, subjectively. To do this, you may make occasional use of direct statement, but are likely to find it more effective to rely on choice of vivid, concrete, or emotionally laden detail or the connotations of words. *Connotations* are the feelings or associations that accompany a word, not its dictionary or literal meaning. Subjective descriptions express your conclusions about a subject or your attitudes toward it. Thus, in arranging details for presentation, you should pay attention to the dominant impression or interpretation you wish to convey as well as to the arrangement of details in the setting (right to left, top to bottom, for example).

In creating a subjective description, pay attention to the dominant impression you create, making sure it conveys and supports your overall purpose or interpretation. In the following passage, for example, the dominant impression clearly conveys the writer's insights into the effects of atmosphere—in this case, fog—on human perceptions, even though she does not directly state this conclusion.

> It begins in late afternoon, a wall of gray blocking the entrance to the harbor, moving imperceptibly, closing in. The sun becomes a bright thing in the sky for a moment before a thick grayness takes over. Trails of vapor drift by. Roads taper off into mist. Pine trees, encircled by the fog, take on different shapes. Inside vacation houses, people make tea, read books, play cards with old decks. Outside, the air smells of soaked wharves. Down by the rocks the surf crashes, but it is a muffled sound, heard while asleep. Bay bushes hunch together, woolly and wet. Walking through fields of Queen Anne's lace, lupine, and goldenrod, their colors muted, is like moving through dreamland. A foghorn blows. Other people are out—a figure appears near the raspberry bushes, spectral, with a basket. A dog runs by, and from the leaves drops fall.

> —Susan Minot, *"Lost in the Light of Gray"*

DEVELOPING DESCRIPTION

The first and most important job in descriptive writing is to select the details. The questions you ask about a subject can help you identify significant details and suggest ways of interpreting it.

For scenes or objects:

- What does it look like (colors, shapes, height, depth)?
- What does it sound like (loud, soft, rasping, soothing, musical, like a lawn mower)?
- What does it smell like (smoky, acrid, like gasoline, like soap, like a wood fire)?
- What does it feel like (smooth, sticky, like a cat's fur, like a spider's web, like grease)?
- What does it taste like (bitter, salty, like grass, like feathers)?

For emotions or ideas:

- What effect does it have on behavior (anger: red face, abrupt gestures)?
- What is it like (freedom is like taking a deep breath of air after leaving a smoky room)?

For people:

- What does the person look like (hair neatly combed, rumpled blouse, muddy boots)?
- What are some characteristic behaviors (rubs hands on skirt, picks ear)?
- What has the person done or said (cheated on a chemistry test, said cruel things to friends)?
- How do others respond to the person (turn to her for advice, call him a "slob")?

Successful subjective descriptions generally focus on a single *dominant impression*, which can act in place of a conclusion or thesis. To create a dominant impression, you select those details that will help create a mood or atmosphere or emphasize a feature or quality. But more that the materials themselves are involved in creating a dominant impression. The words you choose, both their literal and suggestive meanings (denotations and connotations) convey an impression. So, too, do the arrangements of words in sentences, as in the use of short, hurried sentences to help convey a sense of urgency or excitement.

The actual arrangement of the material is perhaps less troublesome in description than in most other expository patterns. Nonetheless, you need to follow a sequence that is clear to your reader and helps you achieve your purpose or support your thesis. A clear spatial organization, for example, will help readers understand a visually complex subject. You can move from left to right, top to bottom, or near to far. You can describe a person from head to toe, or vice versa, or begin with the most noticeable feature and work from there. Or you could start with an overall view of a scene and then move to a focal point.

A chronological arrangement enables you to look at a scene from several perspectives: early morning, midday, and night, for example, or in different weather conditions. Such a strategy allows you to make a point by contrasting the scenes, and it provides variety and interest. A thematic organization emphasizes the dominant impression or thesis through focus and repetition. You might emphasize by repeating clusters of key words (grim, grasping, hard, short-tempered) or images (pink ribbons, the scent of violets). You might also arrange segments of the description by increasing order of importance or in a manner that best supports a thesis.

You can also choose a point of view, either first person ("I looked . . .") or third person ("He sighed . . . ," "It moved . . ."). You might also choose a perspective, including the location of the observer and any limitation on the observer's ability to see and understand, perhaps observing a familiar family scene from a child's perspective to provide new understanding of relationships.

Whatever techniques you choose, however, try to avoid excessive description, which creates confusion and boredom, or description without a clear purpose, which offers your readers no goal or reward for their effort.

Student Essay

In preparing the following essay, Carey Braun tried to combine technical descriptions of the effects of light with her subjective responses and perceptions. In linking the two, she makes some interesting observations about the way we humans are linked to the natural world.

Bright Light

Carey Braun

initial setting
time: morning

The sun woke me by sneaking its way through the narrow cracks of the vertical blinds. I squinted at the bright sun, then kept my eyes closed and enjoyed its warmth on my face and shoulders. After a time, I slid across the bed to the window and peeked through the blinds to look out on a day that reminded me of *my* version of Andrew Lloyd Webber's song, "*Light* changes everything"—or at least the sun does.

thesis-stated somewhat indirectly

What better place to see light, feel light, and become one with the sun, I thought, than at the beach. I rushed out of bed, got dressed, had a bite of break-fast, grabbed my bathing suit and suntan lotion, and headed for the beach.

observer moves from place to place— observations show the effect of light at different times of day

As I stepped out of the car in the park-ing lot, I felt a sunwarmed breeze across my face. It blew my hair across my cheek and made me wonder what it would be like to be a bird, about to skim across the waves of wind with the sun on my back. I hurried down the walkway. On each side of the path, dilapidated summer cottages man-aged to look fresh and new in the early morning rays. Crossing the sand, I stepped gingerly on the hot sand, a recognition that even this early in the day we need to shape our actions to the sun's heat and power.

observer is also participant

I sat on the blanket and rubbed the sun-tan lotion over my body. My skin shined, reflecting the sun's rays and making me seem for a moment like a second source of light. But soon I began to feel like a frying pan that would sizzle if a drop of water hit me. In the background I could hear the sound of many boom boxes blending together forming a light-hearted hymn that took away thoughts of everything else but this time and place. People were splashing

detailed, specific observations

midday

the water, sending luminous drops into the air and breaking the surface of the water into a million mirroring pieces. During brief breaks in the music and the sounds of splashing, I could hear the sound of birds singing.

The sun's heat relaxes me so that I fell asleep. When I woke, there was sweat covering my face and my arms and refracting the sun's rays. If I looked just right, I could see rainbow dots on the surface of my skin. I woke up slowly and decided to head for the cool, refreshing water in front of me. I could feel my body temperature dropping as it moved into the water. As I dove into a wave, chills went through my body like shock waves. I was ready to move back to the beach and the sun.

I couldn't taste the sun, but as I walked back to my blanket, I licked the salt off my lips which had dried quickly in the heat. Salt, I decided, must be the taste of light, at least this morning. The salt on my skin made it feel like stretched leather, tight across my cheekbones and shoulders and stiffening at my joints. I walked across the glinting sand, through midday air heated to luminous, shimmering waves to the outdoor shower.

As I let the water wash away the salt, I looked at the sky and realized that the sun was beginning to descend. The subtle change in light made me feel cooler even though the sand was just as hot as I returned to my blanket. As the light turned to afternoon, people began looking at each other, perhaps noticing the growing shadows and the loss of brilliance. Light now turned to haze, luminous and bright, but

Margin notes:

appeals to a variety of senses

more senses

transition to late afternoon

still haze. People began straggling up the sand, looking as if their energy, too, had begun to wane. The music left and the song that remained was the crash of waves, glinting here and there as the growing fog broke to let through a stray ray.

change in mood and efforts of light

I gathered my belongings and shook all the sand off. As I drove away, I took one last look in the mirror to mourn the passing of the sun's power and light; startled by the electrifying colors of reds, yellow, and oranges spreading from the horizon through the sky, I realized once again the power of light to change everything.

restates thesis

SHARON CURTIN

SHARON CURTIN, a native of Douglas, Wyoming, was raised in a family of ranchers and craftspeople. Curtin, a feminist and political leftist, has worked as a nurse in New York and California but now devotes most of her time to writing and to operating a small farm in Virginia.

Aging in the Land of the Young

"Aging in the Land of the Young" is the first part of Curtin's article by that title, as it appeared in the *Atlantic* in July 1972. It is largely a carefully restructured composite of portions of her book *Nobody Ever Died of Old Age,* also published in 1972. It illustrates the subjective form of description, generally known as impressionistic description.

Old men, old women, almost 20 million of them. They constitute 10 percent of the total population, and the percentage is steadily growing. Some of them, like conspirators, walk all bent over, as if hiding some precious secret, filled with self-protection. The body seems to gather itself around those vital parts, folding shoulders, arms, pelvis like a fading rose. Watch and you see how fragile old people come to think they are.

Aging paints every action gray, lies heavy on every movement, imprisons every thought. It governs each decision with a ruthless and single-minded perversity. To age is to learn the feeling of no longer growing, of struggling to do old tasks, to remember familiar actions. The cells of the brain are destroyed with thousands of unfelt tiny strokes, little pockets of clotted blood wiping out memories and abilities without warning. The body seems slowly to give up, randomly stopping, sometimes starting again as if to torture and tease with the memory of lost strength. Hands become clumsy, frail transparencies, held together with knotted blue veins.

Sometimes it seems as if the distance between your feet and the floor were constantly changing, as if you were walking on shifting and not quite solid ground. One foot down, slowly, carefully force the other foot forward. Sometimes you are a shuffler, not daring to lift your feet from the uncertain earth but forced to slide hesitantly forward in little whispering movements. Sometimes you are able to "step out," but this effort—in fact the pure exhilaration of easy movement—soon exhausts you.

The world becomes narrower as friends and family die or move   4
away. To climb stairs, to ride in a car, to walk to the corner, to talk on the telephone; each action seems to take away from the energy needed to stay alive. Everything is limited by the strength you hoard greedily. Your needs decrease, you require less food, less sleep, and finally less human contact; yet this little bit becomes more and more difficult. You fear that one day you will be reduced to the simple acts of breathing and taking nourishment. This is the ultimate stage you dread, the period of helplessness and hopelessness, when independence will be over.

There is nothing to prepare you for the experience of growing old.   5
Living is a process, an irreversible progression toward old age and eventual death. You see men of eighty still vital and straight as oaks; you see men of fifty reduced to gray shadows in the human landscape. The cellular clock differs for each one of us, and is profoundly affected by our own life experiences, our heredity, and perhaps most important, by the concepts of aging encountered in society and in oneself.

The aged live with enforced leisure, on fixed incomes, subject to   6
many chronic illnesses, and most of their money goes to keep a roof over their heads. They also live in a culture that worships youth.

A kind of cultural attitude makes me bigoted against old peo-   7
ple; it makes me think young is best; it makes me treat old people like outcasts.

> *Hate that gray? Wash it away!*   8
> *Wrinkle cream.*   9
> *Monkey glands.*   10
> *Face-lifting.*   11
> *Look like a bride again.*   12
> *Don't trust anyone over thirty.*   13
> *I fear growing old.*   14
> *Feel Young Again!*   15

I am afraid to grow old—we're all afraid. In fact, the fear of   16
growing old is so great that every aged person is an insult and a threat to the society. They remind us of our own death, that our body won't always remain smooth and responsive, but will someday

betray us by aging, wrinkling, faltering, failing. The ideal way to age would be to grow slowly invisible, gradually disappearing, without causing worry or discomfort to the young. In some ways that does happen. Sitting in a small park across from a nursing home one day, I noticed that the young mothers and their children gathered on one side, and the old people from the home on the other. Whenever a youngster would run over to the "wrong" side, chasing a ball or just trying to cover all the available space, the old people would lean forward and smile. But before any communication could be established, the mother would come over, murmuring embarrassed apologies, and take her child back to the "young" side.

Now, it seemed to me that the children didn't feel any particular fear and the old people didn't seem to be threatened by the children. The division of space was drawn by the mothers. And the mothers never looked at the old people who lined the other side of the park like so many pigeons perched on the benches. These well-dressed young matrons had a way of sliding their eyes over, around, through the old people; they never looked at them directly. The old people may as well have been invisible; they had no reality for the youngsters, who were not permitted to speak to them, and they offended the aesthetic eye of the mothers.   17

My early experiences were somewhat different; since I grew up in a small town, my childhood had more of a nineteenth-century flavor. I knew a lot of old people, and considered some of them friends. There was no culturally defined way for me to "relate" to old people, except the rules of courtesy which applied to all adults. My grandparents were an integral and important part of the family and of the community. I sometimes have a dreadful fear that mine will be the last generation to know old people as friends, to have a sense of what growing old means, to respect and understand man's mortality and his courage in the face of death. Mine may be the last generation to have a sense of living history, of stories passed from generation to generation, of identity established by family history.   18

MEANINGS AND VALUES

1. What is the general tone of this writing? (See "Guide to Terms": *Style/Tone.*)

2. If you find it depressing to read about aging, try to analyze why (especially in view of the fact that you are very likely many years from the stage of "a fading rose").

3. Why do you suppose it is more likely to be the mothers than the children who shun old people (pars. 16–17)?

4. Has this author avoided the excesses of sentimentality? Try to discover how. (Guide: *Sentimentality*.) If not, where does she fail?

EXPOSITORY TECHNIQUES

1. Why should this writing be classed as primarily impressionistic, rather than objective? What is the dominant impression?

2. Analyze the role that selection of details plays in creating the dominant impression. Provide examples of the type of details that could have been included but were not. Are such omissions justifiable?

3. Paragraph 5 ends the almost pure description to begin another phase of the writing. What is it? How has the author provided for a smooth transition between the two? (Guide: *Transition*.)

4. Which previously studied patterns of exposition are also used in this writing? Cite paragraphs where each may be found.

DICTION AND VOCABULARY

1. The author sometimes changes person—e.g., "they" to "you" after paragraph 2. Analyze where the changes occur. What justification, if any, can you find for each change?

2. Which two kinds of figures of speech do you find used liberally to achieve this description? (Guide: *Figures of Speech*.) Cite three or more examples of each. As nearly as you can tell, are any of them clichés? (Guide: *Clichés*.)

READ TO WRITE

1. **Collaborating:** Working with a group, to identify and explore topics for writing, think about some of the consequences of current attitudes towards aging (as described by Curtin). Put the group's thoughts in the form of questions you could attempt to answer in an essay. Here are three questions to get you started. If Curtin is correct in her fears expressed in the last two sentences, what could be the consequences for society in general? If many people are still efficient at their jobs at age sixty-five, as is often argued, what practical reasons are there for forcing retirement at that age, and what are the negative consequences? If some very old people are not as affected by aging as the ones Curtin describes, what may account for this difference?

2. **Considering Audience:** Curtin's selection begins with a description of readers' likely attitudes toward old people and the process of aging. Use a similar reader-centered strategy to begin an essay of your own. Start with a description of the people, relationships, or things you plan to explain, and in the course of the description introduce

the main ideas, consequences, or issues you will take up in the rest of the essay.

3.   **Developing an Essay:** A description is not a form of exposition un-
     less it is used for expository purposes, as in "Aging in the Land of the
     Young." Follow Curtin's lead by using detailed description in an es-
     say to explain a relationship, problem, or phenomenon whose impor-
     tance and possible consequences may not be immediately apparent
     to readers, or to encourage readers to view critically actions and atti-
     tudes they take for granted.

(NOTE: Suggestions for topics requiring development by use of DESCRIPTION are on
pp. 477–478 at the end of this chapter.)

GEORGE SIMPSON

> GEORGE SIMPSON, born in Virginia in 1950, received his B.A. in jour-
> nalism from the University of North Carolina. He went to work for
> *Newsweek* in 1972 and in 1978 became public affairs director for
> that magazine. Before joining *Newsweek,* Simpson worked for two
> years as a writer and editor for the *Carolina Financial Times* in
> Chapel Hill, North Carolina, and as a reporter for the *News-Gazette*
> in Lexington, Virginia. He received the Best Feature Writing award
> from Sigma Delta Chi in 1972 for a five-part investigative series on
> the University of North Carolina football program. He has written
> stories for *The New York Times, Sport, Glamour,* the *Winston-Salem
> Journal,* and *New York.*

The War Room at Bellevue

> "The War Room at Bellevue" was first published in *New York* mag-
> azine. The author chose, for good reason, to stay strictly within a
> time sequence as he described the emergency ward. This essay is
> also noteworthy for the cumulative descriptive effect, which was
> accomplished almost entirely with objective details.

Bellevue. The name conjures up images of an indoor war zone: the   1
wounded and bleeding lining the halls, screaming for help while
harried doctors in blood-stained smocks rush from stretcher to
stretcher, fighting a losing battle against exhaustion and the crushing number of injured. "What's worse," says a longtime Bellevue
nurse, "is that we have this image of being a hospital only for . . ."
She pauses, then lowers her voice, "for crazy people."

Though neither battlefield nor Bedlam is a valid image, there is   2
something extraordinary about the monstrous complex that spreads
for five blocks along First Avenue in Manhattan. It is said best by the
head nurse in Adult Emergency Service: "If you have any chance for
survival, you have it here." Survival—that is why they come. Why
do injured cops drive by a half-dozen other hospitals to be treated at
Bellevue? They've seen the Bellevue emergency team in action.

9:00 P.M. It is a Friday night in the Bellevue emergency room. 3
The after-work crush is over (those who've suffered through the
day, only to come for help after the five-o'clock whistle has blown)
and it is nearly silent except for the mutter of voices at the admitting
desk, where administrative personnel discuss who will go for coffee.
Across the spotless white-walled lobby, ten people sit quietly, passively, in pastel plastic chairs, waiting for word of relatives or to see
doctors. In the past 24 hours, 300 people have come to the Bellevue
Adult Emergency Service. Fewer than 10 percent were true emergencies. One man sleeps fitfully in the emergency ward while his
heartbeat, respiration, and blood pressure are monitored by control
consoles mounted over his bed. Each heartbeat trips a tiny bleep in
the monitor, which attending nurses can hear across the ward. A
half hour ago, doctors in the trauma room withdrew a six-inch
stiletto blade from his back. When he is stabilized, the patient will be
moved upstairs to the twelve-bed Surgical Intensive Care Unit.

9:05 P.M. An ambulance backs into the receiving bay, its red and 4
yellow lights flashing in and out of the lobby. A split second later,
the glass doors burst open as a nurse and an attendant roll a mobile
stretcher into the lobby. When the nurse screams, "Emergency!" the
lobby explodes with activity as the way is cleared to the trauma
room. Doctors appear from nowhere and transfer the bloodied body
of a black man to the treatment table. Within seconds his clothes are
stripped away, revealing a tiny stab wound in his left side. Three
doctors and three nurses rush around the victim, each performing a
task necessary to begin treatment. Intravenous needles are inserted
into his arms and groin. A doctor draws blood for the lab, in case
surgery is necessary. A nurse begins inserting a catheter into the victim's penis and continues to feed in tubing until the catheter reaches
the bladder. Urine flows through the tube into a plastic bag. Doctors
are glad not to see blood in the urine. Another nurse records pulse
and blood pressure.

The victim is in good shape. He shivers slightly, although the 5
trauma room is exceedingly warm. His face is bloodied, but shows
no major lacerations. A third nurse, her elbow propped on the treatment table, asks the man a series of questions, trying to quickly outline his medical history. He answers abruptly. He is drunk. His left
side is swabbed with yellow disinfectant and a doctor injects a local
anesthetic. After a few seconds another doctor inserts his finger into
the wound. It sinks in all the way to the knuckle. He begins to rotate
his finger like a child trying to get a marble out of a milk bottle. The
patient screams bloody murder and tries to struggle free.

Meanwhile in the lobby, a security guard is ejecting a derelict 6
who has begun to drink from a bottle hidden in his coat pocket.
"He's a regular, was in here just two days ago," says a nurse. "We
checked him pretty good then, so he's probably okay now. Can you
believe those were clean clothes we gave him?" The old man, blackened by filth, leaves quietly.

9:15 P.M. A young Hispanic man interrupts, saying his pregnant 7
girl friend, sitting outside in his car, is bleeding heavily from her
vagina. She is rushed into an examination room, treated behind
closed doors, and rolled into the observation ward, where, much
later in the night, a gynecologist will treat her in a special room—the
same one used to examine rape victims. Nearby, behind curtains,
the neurologist examines an old white woman to determine if her
headaches are due to head injury. They are not.

9:45 P.M. The trauma room has been cleared and cleaned merci- 8
lessly. The examination rooms are three-quarters full—another
overdose, two asthmatics, a young woman with abdominal pains. In
the hallway, a derelict who has been sleeping it off urinates all over
the stretcher. He sleeps on while attendants change his clothes. An
ambulance—one of four that patrol Manhattan for Bellevue from
42nd Street to Houston, river to river—delivers a middle-aged white
woman and two cops, the three of them soaking wet. The woman
has escaped from the psychiatric floor of a nearby hospital and tried
to drown herself in the East River. The cops fished her out. She lies
on a stretcher shivering beneath white blankets. Her eyes stare at the
ceiling. She speaks clearly when an administrative worker begins
routine questioning. The cops are given hospital gowns and wait to
receive tetanus shots and gamma globulin—a hedge against infection from the befouled river water. They will hang around the E.R.
for another two hours, telling their story to as many as six other policemen who show up to hear it. The woman is rolled into an examination room, where a male nurse speaks gently: "They tell me you
fell into the river." "No," says the woman, "I jumped. I have to commit suicide." "Why?" asks the nurse. "Because I'm insane and I can't
help [it]. I have to die." The nurse gradually discovers the woman
has a history of psychological problems. She is given dry bedclothes
and placed under guard in the hallway. She lies on her side, staring
at the wall.

The pace continues to increase. Several more overdose victims 9
arrive by ambulance. One, a young black woman, had done a
striptease on the street just before passing out. A second black
woman is semiconscious and spends the better part of her time at

Bellevue alternately cursing at and pleading with the doctors. Attendants find a plastic bottle coated with methadone in the pocket of a Hispanic O.D. The treatment is routinely the same, and sooner or later involves vomiting. Just after doctors begin to treat the O.D., he vomits great quantities of wine and methadone in all directions. "Lovely business, huh?" laments one of the doctors. A young nurse confides that if there were other true emergencies, the overdose victims would be given lower priority. "You can't help thinking they did it to themselves," she says, "while the others are accident victims."

10:30 P.M. A policeman who twisted his knee struggling with an   10
"alleged perpetrator" is examined and released. By 10:30, the lobby is jammed with friends and relatives of patients in various stages of treatment and recovery. The attendant who also functions as a translator for Hispanic patients adds chairs to accommodate the overflow. The medical walk-in rate stays steady—between eight and ten patients waiting. A pair of derelicts, each with battered eyes, appear at the admitting desk. One has a dramatically swollen face laced with black stitches.

11:30 P.M. The husband of the attempted suicide arrives. He   11
thanks the police for saving his wife's life, then talks at length with doctors about her condition. She continues to stare into the void and does not react when her husband approaches her stretcher.

Meanwhile, patients arrive in the lobby at a steady pace. A   12
young G.I. on leave has lower-back pains; a Hispanic man complains of pains in his side; occasionally parents hurry through the adult E.R. carrying children to the pediatric E.R. A white woman of about 50 marches into the lobby from the walk-in entrance. Dried blood covers her right eyebrow and upper lip. She begins to perform. "I was assaulted on 28th and Lexington, I was," she says grandly, "and I don't have to take it *anymore.* I was a bride 21 years ago and, God, I was beautiful then." She has captured the attention of all present. "I was there when the boys came home—on Memorial Day—and I don't have to take this kind of treatment."

As midnight approaches, the nurses prepare for the shift   13
change. They must brief the incoming staff and make sure all reports are up-to-date. One young brunet says, "Christ, I'm gonna go home and take a shower—I smell like vomit."

11:50 P.M. The triage nurse is questioning an old black man   14
about chest pains, and a Hispanic woman is having an asthma attack, when an ambulance, its sirens screaming full tilt, roars into the receiving bay. There is a split-second pause as everyone drops what he or she is doing and looks up. Then all hell breaks loose. Doctors

and nurses are suddenly sprinting full-out toward the trauma room. The glass doors burst open and the occupied stretcher is literally run past me. Cops follow. It is as if a comet has whooshed by. In the trauma room it all becomes clear. A half-dozen doctors and nurses surround the lifeless form of a Hispanic man with a shotgun hole in his neck the size of your fist. Blood pours from a second gaping wound in his chest. A respirator is slammed over his face, making his chest rise and fall as if he were breathing. "No pulse," reports one doctor. A nurse jumps on a stool and, leaning over the man, begins to pump his chest with her palms. "No blood pressure," screams another nurse. The ambulance driver appears shaken, "I never thought I'd get here in time," he stutters. More doctors from the trauma team upstairs arrive. Wrappings from syringes and gauze pads fly through the air. The victim's eyes are open yet devoid of life. His body takes on a yellow tinge. A male nurse winces at the gunshot wound. "This guy really pissed off somebody," he says. This is no ordinary shooting. It is an execution. IV's are jammed into the body in the groin and arms. One doctor has been plugging in an electrocardiograph and asks everyone to stop for a second so he can get a reading. "Forget it," shouts the doctor in charge. "No time." "Take it easy, Jimmy," someone yells at the head physician. It is apparent by now that the man is dead, but the doctors keep trying injections and finally they slit open the chest and reach inside almost up to their elbows. They feel the extent of the damage and suddenly it is all over. "I told 'em he was dead," says one nurse, withdrawing. "They didn't listen." The room is very still. The doctors are momentarily disgusted, then go on about their business. The room clears quickly. Finally there is only a male nurse and the still-warm body, now waxy-yellow, with huge ribs exposed on both sides of the chest and giant holes in both sides of the neck. The nurse speculates that this is yet another murder in a Hispanic political struggle that has brought many such victims to Bellevue. He marvels at the extent of the wounds and repeats, "This guy was really blown away."

Midnight. A hysterical woman is hustled through the lobby into an examination room. It is the dead man's wife, and she is nearly delirious. "I know he's dead, I know he's dead," she screams over and over. Within moments the lobby is filled with anxious relatives of the victim, waiting for word on his condition. The police are everywhere asking questions, but most people say they saw nothing. One young woman says she heard six shots, two louder than the other four. At some point, word is passed that the man is, in fact, 15 dead. Another woman breaks down in hysterics; everywhere young Hispanics are crying and comforting each other. Plainclothes detectives make a quick examination of the body, check on the time of pronouncement of death, and begin to ask questions, but the bereaved are too stunned to talk. The rest of the uninvolved people in the lobby stare dumbly, their injuries suddenly paling in light of a death.

12:30 A.M. A black man appears at the admissions desk and says   16
he drank poison by mistake. He is told to have a seat. The ambulance brings in a young white woman, her head wrapped in white gauze. She is wailing terribly. A girl friend stands over her, crying, and a boyfriend clutches the injured woman's hands, saying, "I'm here, don't worry, I'm here." The victim has fallen downstairs at a friend's house. Attendants park her stretcher against the wall to wait for an examination room to clear. There are eight examination rooms and only three doctors. Unless you are truly an emergency, you will wait. One doctor is stitching up the eyebrow of a drunk who's been punched out. The friends of the woman who fell down the stairs glance up at the doctors anxiously, wondering why their friend isn't being treated faster.

1:10 A.M. A car pulls into the bay and a young Hispanic asks if a   17
shooting victim has been brought here. The security guard blurts out, "He's dead." The young man is stunned. He peels his tires leaving the bay.

1:20 A.M. The young woman of the stairs is getting stitches in a   18
small gash over her left eye when the same ambulance driver who brought in the gunshot victim delivers a man who has been stabbed in the back on East 3rd Street. Once again the trauma room goes from 0 to 60 in five seconds. The patient is drunk, which helps him endure the pain of having the catheter inserted through his penis into his bladder. Still he yells, "That hurts like a bastard," then adds sheepishly, "Excuse me, ladies." But he is not prepared for what comes next. An X-ray reveals a collapsed right lung. After just a shot of local anesthetic, the doctor slices open his side and inserts a long plastic tube. Internal bleeding had kept the lung pressed down and prevented it from reinflating. The tube releases the pressure. The ambulance driver says the cops grabbed the guy who ran the eight-inch blade into the victim's back. "That's not the one," says the man. "They got the wrong guy." A nurse reports that there is not much of the victim's type blood available at the hospital. One of the doctors says that's okay, he won't need surgery. Meanwhile blood pours from the man's knife wound and the tube in his side. As the nurses work, they chat about personal matters, yet they respond immedi-

ately to orders from either doctor. "How ya doin'?" the doctor asks
the patient. "Okay," he says. His blood spatters on the floor.

So it goes into the morning hours. A Valium overdose, a woman   19
who fainted, a man who went through the windshield of his car.
More overdoses. More drunks with split eyebrows and chins. The
doctors and nurses work without complaint. "This is nothing, about
normal, I'd say," concludes the head nurse. "No big deal."

MEANINGS AND VALUES

1. What is the author's point of view? (See "Guide to Terms": *Point of
    View*.) How is this reflected by the tone? (Guide: *Style/Tone*.)

2. Does Simpson ever slip into sentimentality—a common failing when
    describing the scenes of death and tragedy? (Guide: *Sentimentality*.) If
    so, where? If not, how does he avoid it?

3. Cite at least six facts learned from reading this piece that are told, not
    in general terms, but by specific, concrete details—e.g., that a high
    degree of cleanliness is maintained at Bellevue, illustrated by "the
    spotless white-walled lobby" (par. 3) and "the trauma room has been
    cleared and cleaned mercilessly" (par. 8). What are the advantages of
    having facts presented in this way?

EXPOSITORY TECHNIQUES

1. Do you consider the writing to be primarily objective or impression-
    istic? What is the dominant impression, if any?

2. What is the value of using a timed sequence in such a description?

3. Does it seem to you that any of this description is excessive—i.e., un-
    necessary to the task at hand? If so, how might the piece be revised?

4. List, in skeletal form, the facts learned about the subject from reading
    the two-paragraph introduction. How well does it perform the three
    basic purposes of an introduction? (Guide: *Introductions*.)

5. What is the significance of the rhetorical question in paragraph 2?
    (Guide: *Rhetorical Questions*.) Why is it rhetorical?

6. Is the short closing effective? (Guide: *Closings*.) Why or why not?

DICTION AND VOCABULARY

1. Cite the clichés in paragraphs 4, 5, 8, and 14. (Guide: *Clichés*.) What
    justification, if any, can you offer for their use?

2. Cite the allusion in paragraph 2, and explain its meaning and source.
    (Guide: *Figure of Speech*.)

3.   Simpson uses some slang and other colloquialisms. (Cite as many of
     these as you can. (Guide: *Colloquial Expressions.*) Is their use justified?
     Why or why not?

READ TO WRITE

1.   **Collaborating:** Working in a group, discuss a job or an activity
     (sport, organization) that to an outsider might seem hectic or haz-
     ardous. Consider describing it in an essay so that readers can come to
     understand it more clearly.

2.   **Considering Audience:** Descriptive writing can create events for read-
     ers who have not experienced it. Much of the power of Simpson's
     writing comes from the sensational nature of the subjects he de-
     scribes and his careful selection of detail. If you have witnessed or
     participated in some other kind of "extreme" experience, help your
     readers understand it by describing and explaining it with the same
     mix of detail and commentary that Simpson offers.

3.   **Developing an Essay:** Consider arranging an expository essay of
     your own by using a time frame as Simpson does. Your purposes for
     using this device need not be the same, however, and you can use
     this strategy for expository patterns other than description.

(NOTE: Suggestions for topics requiring development by use of DESCRIPTION are on
pp. 476–478 at the end of this chapter.)

EDIE CLARK

EDIE CLARK writes regularly for *Yankee* magazine.

Ice Flowers

"Ice Flowers," originally one of the writer's magazine columns, blends objective and subjective description, combining scientific with personal observation. In so doing, it looks at the borders between nature and art. As Clark points out, many of our artistic efforts are derived from beauty created by nature, and we often, in turn, view nature as an artist.

In midwinter, windows become of interest. Back in the 1970s we were bombarded with frightening information such as the statement that 40 percent of a house's heat is lost through its single-pane windows. And so now most of us have windows that are double- or triple-glazed, windows thicker and more impervious to the elements than walls. This is an old house so short of replacing all the windows, we put in storm windows, the newer version with screens that slide down in the summer and extra windows that slide into place in the winter. They do the job, though they're not as sleek as the new double-glazed windows. We are snug behind them in the winter, and we don't need extra sweaters anymore when we sit near a window. They are efficient and we are warmer and our heating bills are lower. But there is one thing that we miss with these window walls: ice flowers. 1

Back before we changed the windows, incredible works of art grew on the inside of our windows, especially at night, when the temperature dropped below zero. We could watch the pattern grow, tiny needles if ice making their way across the glass, like brush strokes creating an incredible silver canvas of cold. 2

On warm days, the ice would melt and water would bead up on the pane. But at night, the painting would return with the cold, and we would read the patterns like clouds, seeing feathers and ferns, lace and doilies, palm fronds, star bursts and pinwheels, birds in flight. Through this windowpane fantasy, ice and cold became masters of creativity. 3

We discovered that if we scratched a message onto the glass with razor blades, the heavy words would appear overnight. Or if we washed the windows with a certain stroke, the next night's pattern 4 would follow that stroke. I used to look forward to the coldest nights because I knew that in the morning, when the sun came up and shone through the bedroom window, there would be a brand-new design. It somehow made the cold more bearable. I would lie there, still snug in bed, and watch the light of the sun bring the night's frost painting alive. I thought of this window as my winter garden, where blooms came faster and more dramatically than any green plant ever could.

Years ago, in Vermont, there was a man who was fascinated by snowflakes, fascinated enough to try to preserve them. Wilson Alwyn Bentley would walk out into a fresh snowstorm in a heavy coat and stand with his arms outstretched, catching the snowflakes on a board covered with black cloth. Using his carefully constructed, blanketed camera rig, he'd photograph the flakes. A frail little man with a bristle-brush mustache who did his work in his farmyard and in his cold shed and inside his farmhouse, he became known as "Snowflake" Bentley, and he changed forever the way we think about snow and about cold. Bentley photographed not just snowflakes, but anything cold: frost, hail, rime, sleet, and dew. He also photographed frost patterns on windowpanes. With no scientific training whatsoever, he carried this hobby on for over 40 years, and when he died in 1931, he left behind him more than 5,000 photographs of snowflakes. It is because of his work that we now maintain, with some certainty, that no two snowflakes are alike. Scientists used his photographs to further their knowledge of snow and cold. Lace makers used his photographs to create new designs for tablecloths and window curtains. Tiffany's used his photographs to create designs for gold pendants and brooches. I use his photographs to remember the gift of our window-born frost gardens and a time when we could wake up in the morning and see the beauty of the cold from beneath our blankets, before we had to emerge into it.

MEANING AND VALUES

1. What might windows symbolize throughout this essay? (See "Guide to Terms": *Symbol.*) Why does the author use this image?

2. What is ironic about the use of the words "ice" and "flowers" together as an expression? (Guide: *Irony.*)

EXPOSITORY TECHNIQUES

1. Is Clark's essay impressionistic or objective? Explain.

2. To what senses does Clark's essay appeal? Point to examples of each appeal.

3. Does Clark's essay successfully use physical description to evoke emotional response? Where in the essay is this most apparent?

DICTION AND VOCABULARY

1. Identify the concrete diction in paragraph 3. How does this contribute to the effectiveness of the essay?

2. Look up the following words in the dictionary and write definitions for any that are unfamiliar to you: impervious (par. 1); hoary (par. 4); rime (par 5)

READ TO WRITE

1. **Collaborating:** Working in a group, list aspects of nature that are highly detailed (i.e. snowflakes, beach sand, etc.). Choose two examples from your group list and collectively write descriptive paragraphs for each. Be sure to use concrete language to "paint" a picture.

2. **Considering Audience:** Would a reader who had never seen ice crystals on a window be able to visualize the phenomenon based on Clark's description? Choose an example that might better suit such an audience and write a descriptive essay in a style similar to Clark's.

3. **Developing an Essay:** Clark's essay uses the changing of windows to create a nostalgic response in a reader. Think of some change that you have made in your own physical surrounding that is an improvement technologically but has reminded you of what is lost with such an advancement. Write an essay similar to Clark's explaining your change.

(NOTE: Suggestions for topics regarding development by use of DESCRIPTION are on pp. 477–478 at the end of this chapter.)

Issues and Ideas

Place and Person

- Barry Lopez, *A Passage of Hands*
- Joyce Maynard, *The Yellow Door House*
- E.B. White, *Once More to the Lake*

Our environments shape us, but we in turn shape them, in large ways and small. This probably seems so obvious to you that you seldom stop to notice the many relationships between place and person. This, however, is exactly what the next three essays ask you to do. Joyce Maynard's "The Yellow Door House," Barry Lopez's "A Passage of the Hands," and E. B. White's "Once More to the Lake" offer three rather different perspectives on the relationship of people and their surroundings.

Though a feeling of nostalgia—a sense of fond memories and loss—might seem most appropriate for journeys back to childhood settings, the tone Barry Lopez creates is far more complex. Joyce Maynard and E. B. White also ask readers to move beyond sentimental responses in their descriptions of places from the past. Indeed, when description is used as an expository strategy, it goes beyond simple re-creation of a setting to analysis and explanation.

An effective analysis of place and its relationship to character needs to focus not only on the details of the setting but also the extent to which they embody and enact social, cultural, and psychological influences. To grow up in a house with abundant artist's supplies (as Joyce Maynard did) is to encounter art not simply as an activity but as a set of values and as a way of living, as "The Yellow Door House" suggests. But while it can be insightful, this use of description is seldom objective, especially when the writer is describing scenes and events from his or her own experience. As a writer, therefore, you should try to remain aware of the extent to which your perspective shapes and reshapes the scenes you are presenting. As a reader, you also need to stay alert to this further dimension of the relationship between person and place.

BARRY LOPEZ

BARRY LOPEZ was born in 1945 in Port Chester, New York. He attended the University of Notre Dame and the University of Oregon and works as a writer and photographer specializing in natural subjects. His writing and photography has been published in *Audubon, National Wildlife, Harper's, National Geographic* and many other magazines. Among his books are *Desert Notes: Reflections in the Eye of the Raven* (1976), *Of Wolves and Men* (1978), *River Notes: The Dance of the Herons* (1979), *Winter Count* (1982), *Arctic Dreams* (1986) (winner of the National Book Award), *The Rediscovery of North America* (1990), and *About This Life* (1998).

A Passage of Hands

In this essay, first published in the collection *About This Life,* Barry Lopez links a number of descriptions as a way of recording and exploring changes in his life as well as the development of his values and a growing sense of self. Though the hands remain physical objects throughout, engaged in all sorts of activities, they simultaneously act as symbols summing up the meaning Lopez discovers in the various activities in which the hands are engaged.

My hands were born breech in the winter of 1945, two hours before 1 sunrise. Sitting with them today, two thousand miles and more from that spot, turning each one slowly in bright sunshine, watching the incisive light raise short, pale lines from old cuts, and seeing the odd cant of the left ring finger, I know they have a history, though I cannot remember where it starts. As they began, they gripped whatever might hold me upright, surely caressed and kneaded my mother's breasts, yanked at the restrictions of pajamas. And then they learned to work buttons, to tie shoelaces and lift the milk glass, to work together.

The pressure and friction of a pencil as I labored down the 2 spelling of words right-handed raised the oldest permanent mark, a callus on the third joint of the middle finger. I remember no trying accident to either hand in these early years, though there must have been glass cuts, thorn punctures, spider bites, nails torn to the cuticle, scrapes from bicycle falls, pin blisters from kitchen grease, splinters, nails blackened from door pinches, pain lingering from having all four fingers forced backward at once, and the first true weariness, coming from work with lumber and stones, with tools made for larger hands.

It is from these first years, five and six and seven, that I am able   3
to remember so well, or perhaps the hands themselves remember, a
great range of texture—the subtle corrugation of cardboard boxes,
the slickness of the oilcloth on the kitchen table, the shuddering
bend of a horse's short-haired belly, the even give in warm wax, the
raised oak grain in my school-desk top, the fuzziness of dead bumblebees, the coarseness of sheaves immediate to the polished silk of
unhusked corn, the burnish of rake handles and bucket bails, the
rigidness of the bony crest rising beneath the skin of a dog's head,
the tackiness of flypaper, the sharpness of saws and ice picks.

It is impossible to determine where in any such specific mem-   4
ory, of course, texture gives way to heft, to shape, to temperature.
The coolness of a camellia petal seems inseparable from that texture,
warmth from the velvet rub of a horse's nose, heft from a brick's dry
burr. And what can be said, as the hand recalls the earliest touch and
exploration, or how texture changes with depth? Not alone the press
of the palm on a dog's head or fingers boring to the roots of wool on
a sheep's flank, but of, say, what happens with an orange: the hands
work in concert to disassemble the fruit, running a thumb over the
beaded surface of the skin, plying the soft white flay of the interior,
the string net of fiber clinging to the translucent skin cases, dividing
the yielding grain of the flesh beneath, with its hard, wrinkled seeds.
And, further, how is one to separate these textures from a memory
of the burst of fragrance as the skin is torn, or from the sound of the
sections being parted—to say nothing of the taste, juice dripping
from the chin, or the urge to devour, then, even the astringent skin,
all initiated by the curiosity of the hands?

Looking back, it's easy to see that the education of the hands   5
(and so the person) begins like a language: a gathering of simple
words, the assembly of simple sentences, all this leading eventually
to the forging of instructive metaphors. Afterward nothing can truly
be separated, to stand alone in the hands' tactile memory. Taking
the lay of the dog's fur, the slow petting of the loved dog is the increasingly complicated heart speaking with the hand.

Still, because of an occasional, surprising flair of the hands, the   6
insistence of their scarred surfaces, it is possible for me to sustain the
illusion that they have a history independent of the mind's perception, the heart's passion; a history of gathering what appeals, of expressing exasperation with their own stupidity, of faith in the
accrual of brute work. If my hands began to explore complex knowledge by seeking and sorting texture—I am compelled to believe
this—then the first names my memory truly embraced came from
the hands' differentiating among fruits and woven fabrics.

Growing on farms and in orchards and truck gardens around   7
our home in rural California was a chaos of fruit: navel and Valencia
oranges, tangerines, red and yellow grapefruit, pomegranates,
lemons, pomelos, greengage and damson plums, freestone and cling
peaches, apricots, figs, tangelos, Concord and muscadine grapes.
Nectarines, Crenshaw, casaba, and honeydew melons, watermel-
ons, and cantaloupes. My boyish hands knew the planting, the
pruning, and picking, and the packing of some of these fruits, the
force and the touch required. I sought them all out for the resilience
of their ripeness and knew the different sensation of each—pips, ra-
dius, cleavage. I ate even tart pomegranates with ardor, from melons I dug gobs of succulent meat with mouth and fingers. Slicing
open a cantaloupe or a melon with a knife, I would hesitate always
at the sight of the cleft fistula of seeds. It unsettled me, as if it were
the fruit's knowing brain.

The fabrics were my mother's. They were stacked in bolts   8
catawampus on open shelves and in a closet in a room in our small
house where she both slept and sewed, where she laid out skirts,
suits, and dresses for her customers. Lawn, organdy, batiste, and
other fine cottons; cambric and gingham; silks—moiré, crepe de
chine, taffeta; handkerchief and other weights of linen; light wools
like gabardine; silk and cotton damasks; silk and rayon satins; cotton and wool twills; velvet; netted cloths like tulle. These fabrics differed not only in their texture and weave, in the fineness of their
threads, but in the way they passed or reflected light, in their drape,
and, most obviously from a distance, in their color and pattern.

I handled these fabrics as though they were animal skins, open-   9
ing out bolts on the couch when Mother was working, holding them
against the window light, raking them with my nails, crumpling
them in my fist, then furling them as neatly as I could. Decades later,
reading "samite of Ethnise" and "uncut rolls of brocade of Tabronit"
in a paperback translation of Wolfram von Eschenbach's *Parzival*, I
watched my free hand rise up to welcome the touch of these cloths.

It embarrassed and confounded me that other boys knew so lit-   10
tle of cloth, and mocked the knowledge; but growing up with orchards and groves and vine fields, we shared a conventional,
peculiar intimacy with fruit. We pelted one another with rotten
plums and the green husks of walnuts. We flipped gourds and
rolled melons into the paths of oncoming, unsuspecting cars. The
prank of the hand—throwing, rolling, flipping—meant nothing
without the close companionship of the eye. The eye measured the distance, the crossing or closing speed of the object, and then the hand—
the wrist snapping, the fingers' tips guiding to the last—decided

upon a single trajectory, measured force, and then a rotten plum hit someone square in the back or sailed wide, or the melon exploded beneath a tire or rolled cleanly to the far side of the road. And we clapped in glee and wiped our hands on our pants.

In these early years—eight and nine and ten—the hands be- 11 came attuned to each other. They began to slide the hafts of pitchforks and pry bars smoothly, to be more aware of each other's placement for leverage and of the light difference in strength. It would be three or four more years before, playing the infield in baseball, I would sense the spatial and temporal depth of awareness my hands had of each other, would feel, short-hopping a sharp grounder blind in front of third base, flicking the ball from gloved-left to bare-right hand, making the cross-body throw, that balletic poise of the still fingers after the release, would sense how mindless the beauty of it was.

I do not remember the ascendancy of the right hand. It was the 12 one I was forced to write with, though by that time the right hand could already have asserted itself, reaching always first for a hammer or a peach. As I began to be judged according to the performance of my right hand alone—how well it imitated the Palmer cursive, how legibly it totaled mathematical figures—perhaps here is where the hands first realized how complicated their relationship would become. I remember a furious nun grabbing my six-year-old hands in prayer and wrenching the right thumb from under the left. Right over left, she insisted. *Right over left.* Right over left in praying to God.

In these early years my hands were frequently folded in prayer. 13 They, too, collected chickens' eggs, contended with the neat assembly of plastic fighter planes, picked knots from bale twine, clapped chalkboard erasers, took trout off baited hooks, and trenched flower beds. They harbored and applauded homing pigeons. When I was eleven, my mother married again and we moved east to New York. The same hands took on new city tasks, struggled more often with coins and with tying the full Windsor knot. Also, now, they pursued a more diligent and precise combing of my hair. And were in anxious anticipation of touching a girl. And that caress having been given, one hand confirmed the memory later with the other in exuberant disbelief. They overhauled and pulled at each other like puppies.

I remember from these years—fourteen and fifteen and sixteen— 14 marveling at the dexterity of my hands. In games of catch, one hand tipped the falling ball to the other, to be seized firmly in the same instant the body crashed to the ground. Or the hands changed effortlessly on the dribble at the start of a fast break in basketball. I remember disassembling, cleaning, and reassembling a two-barrel carburetor, knowing the memory of where all the parts fit was within my hands. I can recall the baton reversal of a pencil as I wrote then erased, wrote then erased, composing sentences on a sheet of paper. And I remember how the hands, so clever with a ball, so deft with a pair of needle-nose pliers, fumbled attaching a cymbidium orchid so close to a girl's body, so near the mysterious breast.

By now, sixteen or so, my hands were as accustomed to books, 15 to magazines, newspapers, and typing paper, as they were to mechanic's tools and baseballs. A blade in my pocketknife was a shape my fingers had experienced years earlier as an oleander leaf. The shape of my fountain pen I knew first as a eucalyptus twig, drawing make-believe roads in wet ground. As my hands had once strained to bring small bluegills to shore, now they reeled striped bass from the Atlantic's surf. As they had once entwined horses' manes, now they twirled girls' ponytails. I had stripped them in those years of manure, paint, axle grease, animal gore, plaster, soap suds, and machine oil; I had cleaned them of sap and tar and putty, of pond scum and potting soil, of fish scales and grass stains. The gashes and cuts had healed smoothly. They were lithe, strenuous. The unimpeded reach of the fingers away from one another in three planes, their extreme effective span, was a subtle source of confidence and wonder. They showed succinctly the physical intelligence of the body. They expressed so unmistakably the vulnerability in sexual desire. They drew so deliberately the curtains of my privacy.

One July afternoon I stood at an ocean breakwater with a friend, 16 firing stones one after another in long, beautiful arcs a hundred feet to the edge of the water. We threw for accuracy, aiming to hit small breaking waves with cutting *thwips.* My friend tired of the game and lay down on his towel. A few moments later I turned and threw in a single motion just as he leaped to his feet. The stone caught him full in the side of the head. He was in the hospital a month with a fractured skull, unable to speak clearly until he was operated on. The following summer we were playing baseball together again, but I could not throw hard or accurately for months after the accident, and I shied away completely from a growing desire to be a pitcher.

My hands lost innocence or gained humanity that day, as they 17 had another day when I was pulled off my first dog, screaming, my hands grasping feebly in the air, after he'd been run over and killed in the road. Lying awake at night I sometimes remember throwing the near deadly stone, or punching a neighbor's horse with my adolescent fist, or heedlessly swinging a 16-gauge shotgun, leading quail—if I hadn't forgotten to switch off the trigger safety, I would have shot an uncle in the head. My hands lay silent at my sides those nights. No memory of their grace or benediction could change their melancholy stillness.

While I was in college I worked two summers at a ranch in 18
Wyoming. My hands got the feel of new tools—foot nips, frog pick, fence pliers, skiving knife. I began to see that the invention, dexterity, and quickness of the hands could take many directions in a man's life; and that a man should be attentive to what his hands loved to do, and so learn not only what he might be good at for a long time but what would make him happy. It pleased me to smooth every wrinkle from a saddle blanket before I settled a saddle squarely on a horse's back. And I liked, too, to turn the thin pages of a Latin edition of the *Aeneid* as I slowly accomplished them that first summer, feeling the impression of the type. It was strengthening to work with my hands, with ropes and bridles and hay bales, with double-bitted axes and bow saws, currying horses, scooping grain, adding my hands' oil to wooden door latches in the barn, calming horses at the foot of a loading ramp, adjusting my hat against the sun, buckling my chaps on a frosty morning. I'd watch the same hand lay a book lovingly on a night table and reach for the lamp's pull cord.

I had never learned to type, but by that second summer, at nine- 19
teen, I was writing out the first few stories longhand in pencil. I liked the sound and the sight of the writing going on, the back pressure through my hand. When I had erased and crossed out and rewritten a story all the way through, I would type it out slowly with two or sometimes four fingers, my right thumb on the space bar, as I do to this day. Certain keys and a spot on the space bar are worn through to metal on my typewriters from the oblique angles at which my fingernails strike them.

Had I been able to grasp it during those summers in Wyoming, 20
I might have seen that I couldn't get far from writing stories and physical work, either activity, and remain happy. It proved true that in these two movements my hands found their chief joy, aside from the touching of other human beings. But I could not see it then. My hands only sought out and gave in to the pleasures.

I began to travel extensively while I was in college. Eventually I 21
visited many places, staying with different sorts of people. Most worked some substantial part of the day with their hands. I gravitated toward the company of cowboys and farmers both, to the work of loggers and orchardists, but mostly toward the company of field biologists, college-educated men and women who worked long

days open to the weather, studying the lives of wild animals. In their presence, sometimes for weeks at a time, occasionally in stupefying cold or under significant physical strain, I helped wherever I could and wrote in my journal what had happened and, sometimes, what I thought of what had happened. In this way my hands came to know the prick and compression of syringes, the wiring and soldering of radio collars, the arming of anesthetizing guns, the setting of traps and snares, the deployment of otter trawls and plankton tows, the operation of calipers and tripod scales, and the manipulation of various kinds of sieves and packages used to sort and store parts of dead animals, parts created with the use of skinning and butchering knives, with bone saws, teasing needles, tweezers, poultry shears, and hemostatic clamps. My hands were in a dozen kinds of blood, including my own.

Everywhere I journeyed I marveled at the hands of other creatures, at how their palms and digits revealed history, at how well they performed tasks, at the elegant and incontrovertible beauty of their design. I cradled the paws of wolves and polar bears, the hooves of caribou, the forefeet of marine iguanas, the foreflippers of ringed seals and sperm whales, the hands of wallabies, of deer mice. Palpating the tendons, muscles, and bones beneath the skin or fur, I gained a rough understanding of the range of ability, of expression. I could feel where a broken bone had healed and see from superficial scars something of what a life must have been like. Deeper down, with mammals during necropsy, I could see how blood vessels and layers of fat in a paw or in a flipper were arranged to either rid the creature or its metabolic heat or hoard it. I could see the evidence of arthritis in its phalanges, how that could come to me. [22]

I have never touched a dead human, nor do I wish to. The living hands of another person, however, draw me, as strongly as the eyes. What is their history? What are their emotions? What longing is there? I can follow a cabinetmaker's hands for hours as they verify and detect, shave, fit, and rub; or a chef's hands adroitly dicing vegetables or shaping pastry. And who has not known faintness at the sight of a lover's hand? What man has not wished to take up the hands of the woman he loves and pore over them with reverence and curiosity? Who has not in reverie wished to love the lover's hands? [23]

Years after my mother died I visited her oldest living friend. We were doing dishes together and she said, "You have your mother's hands." Was that likeness a shade of love? And is now I say out of respect for my hands I would buy only the finest tools, is that, too, not love? [24]

The hands evolve, of course. The creases deepen and the fingers   25
begin to move two or three together at a time. If the hands of a man
are put to hard use, the fingers grow blunt. They lose dexterity and
the skin calluses over like hide. Hardly a pair of man's hands known
to me comes to mind without a broken or dislocated finger, a lost
fingertip, a permanently crushed nail. Most women my age carry
scars from kitchen and housework, drawer pinches, scalds, knife
and glass cuts. We hardly notice them. Sunlight, wind, and weather
obscure many of these scars, but I believe the memory of their occurrence never leaves the hands. When I awaken in the night and
sense my hands cupped together under the pillow, or when I sit
somewhere on a porch, idly watching wind crossing a ripening
field, and look down to see my hands nested in my lap as if asleep
like two old dogs, it is not hard for me to believe they know. They
remember all they have done, all that has happened to them, the
ways in which they have been surprised or worked themselves free
of desperate trouble, or lost their grip and so caused harm. It's not
hard to believe they remember the heads patted, the hands shaken,
the apples peeled, the hair braided, the wood split, the gears shifted,
the flesh gripped and stroked, and that they convey their feelings to
each other.

In recent years my hands have sometimes been very cold for   26
long stretches. It takes little cold now to entirely numb thumbs and
forefingers. They cease to speak what they know. When I was
thirty-one, I accidentally cut the base of my left thumb, severing
nerves, leaving the thumb confused about what was cold, what was
hot, and whether or not it was touching something or only thought
so. When I was thirty-six, I was helping a friend butcher a whale.
We'd been up for many hours under twenty-four-hour arctic daylight and were tired. He glanced away and without thinking drove
the knife into my wrist. It was a clean wound, easy to close, but
with it I lost the nerves to the right thumb. Over the years each
thumb has regained some sensitivity, and I believe the hands are
more sympathetic to each other because of their similar wounds.
The only obvious difference lies with the left hand. A broken
metacarpal forced a rerouting of tendons to the middle and ring fingers as it healed and raised a boss of carpal bone tissue on the back
of the hand.

At the base of the right thumb is a scar from a climbing acci-   27
dent. On the other thumb, a scar the same length from the jagged
edges of a fuel-barrel pump. In strong sunlight, when there is a certain tension in the skin, as I have said, I can stare at my hands for a

while, turning them slowly, and remember with them the days, the weather, the people present when some things happened that left scars behind. It brings forth affection for my hands. I recall how, long ago, they learned to differentiate between cotton and raw silk, between husks of the casaba and the honeydew melon, and how they thrilled to the wire bristle of a hog's back, how they clipped the water's surface in swimming-pool fights, how they painstakingly arranged bouquets, how they swung and lifted children. I have begun to wish they would speak to me, tell me stories I have forgotten.

I sit in a chair and look at the scars, the uneven cut of the nails, and reminisce. With them before me I grin as though we held something secret, remembering bad times that left no trace. I cut firewood for my parents once, winter in Alabama, swamping out dry, leafless vines to do so. Not until the next day did I realize the vines were poison ivy. The blisters grew so close and tight my hands straightened like paddles. I had to have them lanced to continue a cross-country trip, to dress and feed myself. And there have been days when my hands stiffened with cold so that I had to quit the work being done, sit it out and whimper with pain as they came slowly back to life. But these moments are inconsequential. I have looked at the pale, wrinkled hands of a drowned boy, and I have seen handless wrists.   28

If there were a way to speak directly to our hands, to allow them a language of their own, what I would most wish to hear is what they recall of human touch, of the first exploration of the body of another, the caresses, the cradling of breast, of head, of buttock. Does it seem to them as to me that we keep learning, even when the caressed body has been known for years? How do daydreams of an idealized body, one's own or another's affect the hands' first tentative inquiry? Is the hand purely empirical? Does it apply an imagination? Does it retain a man's shyness, a boy's clumsiness? Do the hands anguish if there is no one to touch?   29

Tomorrow I shall pull blackberry vines and load a trailer with rotten timber. I will call on my hands to help me dress, to turn the spigot for coffee, to pull the newspaper from its tube. I will put my hands in the river and lift water where the sunlight is brightest, a playing with fractured light I never tire of. I will turn the pages of a book about the history of fire in Australia. I will sit at the typewriter, working through a story about a trip to Matagorda Island in Texas. I will ask my hands to undress me. Before I turn out the light, I will fold and set my reading glasses aside. Then I will cup my hands, the left in the right, and slide them under the pillow beneath my head, where they will speculate, as will I, about what we shall handle the   30 next day, and dream, a spooling of their time we might later remember together and I, so slightly separated from them, might recognize.

MEANINGS AND VALUES

1. Lopez uses his hands as the thread for an autobiographical essay. Why might he have chosen hands to represent the changes in his life? (See "Guide to Terms": *Symbol*.)

2. Lopez says, "Looking back, it's easy to see that the education of the hands (and so the person) begins like a language: a gathering of simple words, the assembly of simple sentences, all this leading eventually to the forging of instructive metaphors" (par. 5). Why might he have chosen such a simile? What is the connection between hands and language as Lopez explains it?

3. Find all of Lopez's references to writing in the essay. What theme emerges from the repetitive use of the physical act of writing?

EXPOSITORY TECHNIQUES

1. Identify where Lopez uses transition to represent the passage of time. How does he use the subject of hands to link stages in his life? (Guide: *Transitions*.)

2. Does Lopez primarily use concrete or abstract images in this essay? Point to examples of each and analyze their success. (Guide: *Evaluation*.)

3. Compare the references to dogs in paragraph 5 ("Taking the lay of the dog's fur, the slow petting of the loved dog is the increasingly complicated heart speaking with the hand") to that in paragraph 17 ("My hands lost innocence or gained humanity that day, as they had another day when I was pulled off my first dog, screaming, my hands grasping feebly in the air, after he'd been run over and killed in the road"). How do these acts of placing hands on a dog differ? How has the author grown as a result of these experiences?

DICTION AND VOCABULARY

1. Compare the tasks of the hands in paragraphs 1 and 30. What words and actions are repeated? Explain the significance of Lopez's linked introduction and conclusion in this essay. (Guide: *Introductions, Conclusions*.)

2. Why does Lopez emphasize his right hand throughout the essay? What connotation does the left hand evoke in many readers? (Guide: *Denotation/Connotation*.)

3. Look up any of the following words with which you are unfamiliar: heft (par. 4); casaba (par. 7); cambric (par. 8); hafts (par. 11); necropsy (par. 22).

READ TO WRITE

1. **Collaborating:** Lopez "grows up" in this essay. Consider the various stages in your own lives. List those stages in an outline. Working in a group identify the specific passages which indicate a new phase of Lopez's life and outline them. Compare Lopez's stages with your own and with those of other group members. Write a paragraph analyzing the similarities and differences among your choices.

2. **Considering Audience:** Lopez shares many experiences with his audience. With how many of these experiences might a majority of his readers be familiar? Can you think of any personal experiences with your hands that could be added and that readers would readily understand? Choose one and write a paragraph that could fit into Lopez's essay.

3. **Developing an Essay:** "A Passage of the Hands" relies on clear description of touch. Choose one of your other five senses and write an autobiographical essay similar to Lopez's.

(NOTE: Suggestions for topics regarding development by use of DESCRIPTION are on pp. 477–478 at the end of this chapter.)

JOYCE MAYNARD

> JOYCE MAYNARD was born in 1953 and spent her childhood in Durham, New Hampshire, where her father taught at the nearby University of New Hampshire. At 19, while she was still a sophomore at Yale University, her first book appeared: *Looking Backward: A Chronicle of Growing Up Old in the Sixties* (1973). Maynard was a reporter for *The New York Times* and currently writes a syndicated newspaper column. She has also written monthly for *Parenting* magazine and has published three novels, *Baby Love* (1981), *To Die For* (1992), and *Where Love Goes* (1995). Many of her columns were reprinted in the collection *Domestic Affairs* (1987).

The Yellow Door House

> Permanence, continuity, and change in place and personality are some of the ideas explored through description in this essay, originally published as one of the author's columns. Comparison plays an important part in the exposition as well, particularly in juxtaposing Maynard's memories of the house with its present reality.

I've known only two homes in my life: the one I live in now, with my husband and children, and another one, just sixty miles from here, where I grew up. My father's dead now, and even before that, my parents were divorced and my mother moved away from our old house. But though she rents the house out nine months of the year and hasn't spent a winter there for thirteen years, she hasn't sold our old house yet. It's still filled with our old belongings from our old life. And though my mother has another house now, and a good life, with another man, in a new place, she still comes back to the old house for a couple of months every summer. Every year I ask her, "Have you considered putting the house on the market?" And every summer the answer is "not yet."

My children call the place where I grew up the yellow door house. They love the place, with its big, overgrown yard, the old goldfish pond, the brick walkway, the white picket fence. On the front door there's a heavy brass knocker my sons like to bang on to

1

2

announce their arrival for visits with their grandmother, and French windows on either side that I was always cautioned against breaking as a child. (As now I caution my children.) There's a brass mail slot I used to pass messages through to a friend waiting on the other side. Now my daughter Audrey does the same.

It's a big house, a hip-roofed colonial, with ceilings higher than anybody needs, and a sweeping staircase rising up from the front hall, with a banister that children more adventurous than my sister and I (mine, for instance) are always tempted to slide on. There are plants everywhere, paintings my father made, Mexican pottery, and a band of tin Mexican soldiers—one on horseback, one playing the flute, one the tuba. We bought those soldiers on the first trip I ever made to New York City. They cost way too much, but my mother said we could get them if we took the bus home instead of flying. So we did.

One room of the yellow door house is wood paneled and lined with books. There used to be a big overstuffed armchair in it that I'd settle into with my cookies and milk, when I came home from school, to do my homework or watch "Leave It to Beaver." (That chair is in my house now.) There's a porch with a swing out back, and a sunny corner in the kitchen where I always ate my toast—grilled in the oven, sometimes with cinnamon sugar and sometimes jam, but always the way my mother made it, buttered on both sides. My mother is a wonderful, natural cook, who would announce, on a typical night, three different dessert possibilities, all homemade. Now I wouldn't think of eating a third piece of blueberry pie. But the old habits return when I walk into my mother's kitchen. The first thing I do is go see what's in the refrigerator.

It's been fourteen years since I lived in the yellow door house, but I could still make my way around it blindfolded. There are places where the house could use some work now, and my mother never was the best housekeeper. I open a drawer in the big Welsh dresser in the dining room, looking for a safety pin, and so much spills out (though not safety pins) that I can't close it again. A person can choose from five different kinds of cookies in this house. There's a whole closetful of fabric scraps and antique lace. Eight teapots. But no yardstick, no light bulbs, no scissors.

My children's favorite place in the house is the attic. The front half used to be the studio where my father painted, at night, when he came home from his job as an English teacher. The paintings and paints are long gone now; but my father was a lover of art supplies and hopelessly extravagant when it came to acquiring them, so every once in a while, even now, thirteen years since he's been here, I'll come upon a box of unopened pastels, or watercolor pencils, or the kind of art gum eraser he always used. I'll pick up a stub of an oil pastel and hold it up to my nose, and a wave of feeling will wash over me that almost makes my knees weak. Cadmium yellow light. Cerulean blue. Suddenly I'm ten years old again, sitting on the grass in a field a couple of miles down the road from here, with a sketch pad on my lap and my father beside me, drawing a picture of Ski Jump Hill.

Beyond the room that was my father's studio is the part of our attic where my mother—a hoarder, like me—has stored away just about every toy we ever owned, and most of our old dresses. A ripped Chinese umbrella, a broken wicker rocker, a hooked rug she started and never finished, an exercise roller, purchased around 1947, meant to undo the damage of all those blueberry pies. Songs I wrote when I was nine. My sister's poems. My mother's notes from college English class. My father's powerfully moving proclamations of love to her, written when she was eighteen and he was thirty-eight, when she was telling him she couldn't marry him and he was telling her she must.

Every time we come to the yellow door house to visit, Audrey and Charlie head for the attic—and though we have mostly cleaned out my old Barbies now (and a Midge doll, whose turned-up nose had been partly nibbled off by mice), we never seem to reach the end of the treasures: My homemade dollhouse furniture (I packed it away, room by room, with notes enclosed, to the daughter I knew I would someday have, describing how I'd laid out the rooms.) An old wooden recorder. A brass doll bed. Wonderfully detailed doll clothes my mother made for us every Christmas (at the time, I longed for store-bought). One year she knit a sweater, for a two-inch-tall bear, using toothpicks for knitting needles. Another year she sewed us matching skirts from an old patchwork quilt.

The little town where I grew up (and where I used to know just about everyone) has been growing so fast that my mother hardly knows anyone on our street anymore. A house like hers has become so desirable that within days of her arrival this summer, my mother got a call from a realtor asking if she'd be interested in selling. He named as a likely asking price a figure neither one of us could believe. My parents bought the house, thirty years ago, for a fifth of that amount, and still, they sometimes had to take out loans to meet the mortgage payments.

For years now, I have been telling my mother that it makes little sense to hold on to the yellow door house (and to worry about tenants, make repairs, put away the Mexican tin soldiers every Labor

Day and take them out again every Fourth of July). But I suddenly realized, hearing about this realtor's call, that when the day comes that my mother sells the house, I will be deeply shaken. I doubt if I will even want to drive down our old street after that, or even come back to the town, where I scarcely know anybody anymore. I don't much want to see some other family inventing new games, new rituals, in our house. Don't want to know where they put their Christmas tree, or what sort of paintings they hang on their walls. It would be crazy—impossible—to pack up and haul away all those dress-up clothes and bits of costume jewelry and boxes of old book reports and crumbs of pastels. But neither do I relish the thought of someday having to throw them out.

My mother's yellow door house is a perfect place to play hide-and-seek, and last weekend, when I was there visiting with my three children, that's what my two sons and I did. I found a hiding place in the wood-paneled room, behind the couch. I scrunched myself up so small that several minutes passed without my sons' finding me, even though they passed through the room more than once. 11

Many families have rented the house since my mother ceased to make it her full-time home, but the smell—I realized—hasn't changed. Listening to my children's voices calling out to me through the rooms, I studied a particular knothole in the paneling, and it came back to me that this knothole had always reminded me of an owl. I ran my finger over the wood floors and the upholstery on the side of the couch, and noted the dust my mother has always tended to leave in corners. I heard the sewing machine whirring upstairs: my mother, sewing doll clothes with Audrey. I smelled my mother's soup on the stove. And for a moment, I wanted time to freeze. 12

But then I let myself make a small noise. "We found you, we found you," my boys sang out, falling into my arms. And then we all had lunch, with my mother's chocolate chip cookies for dessert—and headed back to the house I live in now. Whose door is green. 13

MEANINGS AND VALUES

1. What connections between place and personality (her parents' or her own) does Maynard discuss directly or by implication in paragraphs 6, 7, 8, and 10?

2. Where in the opening paragraph does Maynard introduce the themes of change and continuity?

3.   What does the author believe will be lost if her mother sells the house?

4.   What is meant by the phrase "I wanted time to freeze" in paragraph 12? What actions does the author take in the next paragraph that undermine this wish and the values implied by it?

Expository Techniques

1.   Identify the subjects Maynard describes in each of the paragraphs following the opening. Do these paragraphs generally focus on a single scene (or subject) or on several? Be ready to support your answer with examples from the text.

2.   Can the descriptions in paragraphs 4 and 10 be considered unified? Why or why not? (See "Guide to Terms": *Unity.*)

3.   What use does Maynard make of comparison in paragraphs 2, 12, and 13 to suggest ways that values and patterns of behavior are passed from generation to generation?

Diction and Vocabulary

1.   Identify the concrete diction in paragraph 6 and discuss how it contributes to the effectiveness of the passage. (Guide: *Evaluation.*) What are the technical terms used in the passage, and how do they contribute to its effect? (Guide: *Diction.*)

2.   Why does the author mention the television program "Leave It to Beaver" (par. 4)? In what ways did her home and family life resemble those depicted in the series? In what way did they differ?

Read to Write

1.   **Collaborating:** Working in a group, use the following questions and make up others like them in order to examine the relationship between place, personality, and values, and develop a list of possible topics for writing. Do many people today have a chance to return to the homes, apartments, or neighborhoods in which they grew up and which helped shape their values and personalities? Is it likely that many spent their entire childhoods living in a single house or apartment? How are the childhood memories of people whose families often moved likely to differ from those of Maynard? Are their values likely to differ also?

2.   **Considering Audience:** Consider how readers who grew up in setting very different from the one Maynard describes are likely to respond to her essay. Write an essay describing the likely reactions of such readers, focusing especially on passages they might not fully appreciate or to which they might respond negatively.

3.   **Developing an Audience:** Prepare an essay describing one or more places where you lived as a child. In the course of the description, fol-

low Maynard's lead and deal with questions of place, personality, change, loss, growth, continuity, and related matters, offering your insights, of course, and not Maynard's.

(NOTE: Suggestions for topics requiring development by use of DESCRIPTION are on pp. 477–478 at the end of this chapter.)

E. B. WHITE

E. B. WHITE, distinguished essayist, was born in Mount Vernon, New York, in 1899 and died in 1985 in North Brooklin, Maine. A graduate of Cornell University, White worked as a reporter and advertising copywriter, and in 1926 he joined the staff of the *New Yorker* magazine. After 1937 he did most of his writing at his farm in Maine, for many years contributing a regular column, "One Man's Meat," to *Harper's* magazine and freelance editorials for the "Notes and Comments" column of the *New Yorker.* White also wrote children's books, two volumes of verse, and, with James Thurber, *Is Sex Necessary?* (1929). With his wife, Katherine White, he compiled *A Subtreasury of American Humor* (1941). Collections of his own essays include *One Man's Meat* (1942), *The Second Tree from the Corner* (1953), *The Points of My Compass* (1962), and *Essays of E. B. White* (1977). In 1959 he revised and enlarged William Strunk's *The Elements of Style,* a textbook still widely used in college classrooms. White received many honors and writing awards for his crisp, highly individual style and his sturdy independence of thought.

Once More to the Lake

In this essay White relies primarily on description to convey his sense of the passage of time and the power of memory. The vivid scenes and the clear yet expressive prose in this essay are characteristic of his writing.

August 1941

One summer, along about 1904, my father rented a camp on a   1
lake in Maine and took us all there for the month of August. We all got ringworm from some kittens and had to rub Pond's Extract on our arms and legs night and morning, and my father rolled over in a canoe with all his clothes on; but outside of that the vacation was a success and from then on none of us ever thought there was any place in the world like that lake in Maine. We returned summer after summer—always on August 1 for one month. I have since be-

come a salt-water man, but sometimes in summer there are days when the restlessness of the tides and the fearful cold of the sea water and the incessant wind that blows across the afternoon and into the evening make me wish for the placidity of a lake in the woods. A few weeks ago this feeling got so strong I bought myself a couple of bass hooks and a spinner and returned to the lake where we used to go, for a week's fishing and to revisit old haunts.

I took along my son, who had never had any fresh water up his nose and who had seen lily pads only from train windows. On the journey over to the lake I began to wonder what it would be like. I wondered how time would have marred this unique, this holy spot—the coves and streams, the hills that the sun set behind, the camps and the paths behind the camps. I was sure that the tarred road would have found it out, and I wondered in what other ways it would be desolated. It is strange how much you can remember about places like that once you allow your mind to return into the grooves that lead back. You remember one thing, and that suddenly reminds you of another thing. I guess I remembered clearest of all the early mornings, when the lake was cool and motionless, remembered how the bedroom smelled of the lumber it was made of and of the wet woods whose scent entered through the screen. The partitions in the camp were thin and did not extend clear to the top of the rooms, and as I was always the first up I would dress softly so as not to wake the others, and sneak out into the sweet outdoors and start out in the canoe, keeping close along the shore in the long shadows of the pines. I remembered being very careful never to rub my paddle against the gunwale for fear of disturbing the stillness of the cathedral.

The lake had never been what you would call a wild lake. There were cottages sprinkled around the shores, and it was in farming country although the shores of the lake were quite heavily wooded. Some of the cottages were owned by nearby farmers, and you would live at the shore and eat your meals at the farmhouse. That's what our family did. But although it wasn't wild, it was a fairly large and undisturbed lake and there were places in it that, to a child at least, seemed infinitely remote and primeval.

I was right about the tar: it led to within half a mile of the shore. But when I got back there, with my boy, and we settled into a camp near a farmhouse and into the kind of summertime I had known, I could tell that it was going to be pretty much the same as it had been before—I knew it, lying in bed the first morning, smelling the bedroom and hearing the boy sneak quietly out and go off along the shore in a boat. I began to sustain the illusion that he was I, and therefore, by simple transposition, that I was my father. This sensation persisted, kept cropping up all the time we were there. It was not an entirely new feeling, but in this setting it grew much stronger. I seemed to be living a dual existence. I would be in the middle of some simple act, I would be picking up a bait box or laying down a table fork, or I would be saying something, and suddenly it would be not I but my father who was saying the words or making the gesture. It gave me a creepy sensation.

We went fishing the first morning. I felt the same damp moss   5 covering the worms in the bait can, and saw the dragonfly alight on the tip of my rod as it hovered a few inches from the surface of the water. It was the arrival of this fly that convinced me beyond any doubt that everything was as it always had been, that the years were a mirage and that there had been no years. The small waves were the same, chucking the rowboat under the chin as we fished at anchor, and the boat was the same boat, the same color green and the ribs broken in the same places, and under the floorboards the same fresh-water leavings and débris—the dead helgramite, the wisps of moss, the rusty discarded fishhook, the dried blood from yesterday's catch. We stared silently at the tips of our rods, at the dragonflies that came and went. I lowered the tip of mine into the water, tentatively, pensively dislodging the fly, which darted two feet away, poised, darted two feet back, and came to rest again a little farther up the rod. There had been no years between the ducking of this dragonfly and the other one—the one that was part of memory. I looked at the boy, who was silently watching his fly, and it was my hands that held his rod, my eyes watching. I felt dizzy and didn't know which rod I was at the end of.

We caught two bass, hauling them in briskly as though they   6 were mackerel, pulling them over the side of the boat in a businesslike manner without any landing net, and stunning them with a blow on the back of the head. When we got back for a swim before lunch, the lake was exactly where we had left it, the same number of inches from the dock, and there was only the merest suggestion of a breeze. This seemed an utterly enchanted sea, this lake you could leave to its own devices for a few hours and come-back to, and find that it had not stirred, this constant and trustworthy body of water. In the shallows, the dark, water-soaked sticks and twigs, smooth and old, were undulating in clusters on the bottom against the clean ribbed sand, and the track of the mussel was plain. A school of minnows swam by, each minnow with its small individual shadow, doubling the attendance, so clear and sharp in the sunlight. Some of the other campers were in swimming, along the shore, one of them with a cake of soap, and the water felt thin and clear and unsubstantial. Over the years there had been this person with the cake of soap, this cultist, and here he was. There had been no years.

Up to the farmhouse to dinner through the teeming, dusty field, the road under our sneakers was only a two-track road. The middle track was missing, the one with the marks of the hooves and the splotches of dried, flaky manure. There had always been three tracks to choose from in choosing which track to walk in; now the choice was narrowed down to two. For a moment I missed terribly the middle alternative. But the way led past the tennis court, and something about the way it lay there in the sun reassured me; the tape had loosened along the backline, the alleys were green with plantains and other weeds, and the net (installed in June and removed in September) sagged in the dry noon, and the whole place steamed with midday heat and hunger and emptiness. There was a choice of pie for dessert, and one was blueberry and one was apple, and the waitresses were the same country girls, there having been no passage of time, only the illusion of it as in a dropped curtain—the waitresses were still fifteen; their hair had been washed, that was the only difference—they had been to the movies and seen the pretty girls with the clean hair.

Summertime, oh, summertime, pattern of life indelible, the fade-proof lake, the woods unshatterable, the pasture with the sweetfern and the juniper forever and ever, summer without end; this was the background, and the life along the shore was the design, their tiny docks with the flagpole and the American flag floating against the white clouds in the blue sky, the little paths over the roots of the trees leading from camp to camp and the paths leading back to the outhouses and the can of lime for sprinkling, and at the souvenir counters at the store the miniature birch-bark canoes and the postcards that showed things looking a little better than they looked. This was the American family at play, escaping the city heat, wondering whether the newcomers in the camp at the head of the cove were "common" or "nice," wondering whether it was true that the people who drove up for Sunday dinner at the farmhouse were turned away because there wasn't enough chicken.

It seemed to me, as I kept remembering all this, that those times and those summers had been infinitely precious and worth saving. There had been jollity and peace and goodness. The arriving (at the beginning of August) had been so big a business in itself, at the railway station the farm wagon drawn up, the first smell of the pine-laden air, the first glimpse of the smiling farmer, and the great importance of the trunks and your father's enormous authority in such matters, and the feel of the wagon under you for the long ten-mile haul, and at the top of the last long hill catching the first view of the lake after eleven months of not seeing this cherished body of water. The shouts and cries of the other campers when they saw you, and the trunks to be unpacked, to give up their rich burden. (Arriving was less exciting nowadays, when you sneaked up in your car and parked it under a tree near the camp and took out the bags and in five minutes it was all over, no fuss, no loud wonderful fuss about trunks.)

Peace and goodness and jollity. The only thing that was wrong   10
now, really, was the sound of the place, an unfamiliar nervous sound of the outboard motors. This was the note that jarred, the one thing that would sometimes break the illusion and set the years moving. In those other summertimes all motors were inboard; and when they were at a little distance, the noise they made was a sedative, an ingredient of summer sleep. They were one-cylinder and two-cylinder engines, and some were make-and-break and some were jump-spark, but they all made a sleepy sound across the lake. The one-lungers throbbed and fluttered, and the twin-cylinder ones purred and purred, and that was a quiet sound, too. But now the campers all had outboards. In the daytime, in the hot mornings, these motors made a petulant, irritable sound; at night, in the still evening when the afterglow lit the water, they whined about one's ears like mosquitoes. My boy loved our rented outboard, and his great desire was to achieve single-handed mastery over it, and authority, and he soon learned the trick of choking it a little (but not too much), and the adjustment of the needle valve. Watching him I would remember the things you could do with the old one-cylinder engine with the heavy flywheel, how you could have it eating out of your hand if you got really close to it spiritually. Motorboats in those days didn't have clutches, and you would make a landing by shutting off the motor at the proper time and coasting in with a dead rudder. But there was a way of reversing them, if you learned the trick, by cutting the switch and putting it on again exactly on the final dying revolution of the flywheel, so that it would kick back against compression and begin reversing. Approaching a dock in a strong following breeze, it was difficult to slow up sufficiently by the ordinary coasting method, and if a boy felt he had complete mastery over his motor, he was tempted to keep it running beyond its time and then reverse it a few feet from the dock. It took a cool

nerve, because if you threw the switch a twentieth of a second too soon you would catch the flywheel when it still had speed enough to go up past center, and the boat would leap ahead, charging bull-fashion at the dock.

We had a good week at the camp. The bass were biting well and   11
the sun shone endlessly, day after day. We would be tired at night and lie down in the accumulated heat of the little bedrooms after the long hot day and the breeze would stir almost imperceptibly outside and the smell of the swamp drift in through the rusty screens. Sleep would come easily and in the morning the red squirrel would be on the roof, tapping out his gay routine. I kept remembering everything, lying in bed in the mornings—the small steamboat that had a long rounded stern like the lip of a Ubangi, and how quietly she ran on the moonlight sails, when the older boys played their mandolins and the girls sang and we ate doughnuts dipped in sugar, and how sweet the music was on the water in the shining night, and what it had felt like to think about girls then. After breakfast we would go up to the store and the things were in the same place—the minnows in a bottle, the plugs and spinners disarranged and pawed over by the youngsters from the boys' camp, the Fig Newtons and the Beeman's gum. Outside, the road was tarred and cars stood in front of the store. Inside, all was just as it had always been, except there was more Coca-Cola and not so much Moxie and root beer and birch beer and sarsaparilla. We would walk out with the bottle of pop apiece and sometimes the pop would backfire up our noses and hurt. We explored the streams, quietly, where the turtles slid off the sunny logs and dug their way into the soft bottom; and we lay on the town wharf and fed worms to the tame bass. Everywhere we went I had trouble making out which was I, the one walking at my side, the one walking in my pants.

One afternoon while we were there at that lake a thunderstorm   12
came up. It was like the revival of an old melodrama that I had seen long ago with childish awe. The second-act climax of the drama of the electrical disturbance over a lake in America had not changed in any important respect. This was the big scene, still the big scene. The whole thing was so familiar, the first feeling of oppression and heat and a general air around camp of not wanting to go very far away. In mid-afternoon (it was all the same) a curious darkening of the sky, and a lull in everything that had made life tick; and then the way the boats suddenly swung the other way at their moorings with the coming of a breeze out of the new quarter, and the premonitory rumble. Then the kettle drum, then the snare, then the bass drum

and cymbals, then crackling light against the dark, and the gods grinning and licking their chops in the hills. Afterward the calm, the rain steadily rustling in the calm lake, the return of light and hope and spirits, and the campers running out in joy and relief to go swimming in the rain, their bright cries perpetuating the deathless joke about how they were getting simply drenched, and the children screaming with delight at the new sensation of bathing in the rain, and the joke about getting drenched linking the generations in a strong indestructible chain. And the comedian who waded in carrying an umbrella.

When the others went swimming, my son said he was going in, too. He pulled his dripping trunks from the line where they had hung all through the shower and wrung them out. Languidly, and with no thought of going in, I watched him, his hard little body, skinny and bare, saw him wince slightly as he pulled up around his vitals the small, soggy, icy garment. As he buckled the swollen belt, suddenly my groin felt the chill of death.   13

Meanings and Values

1. In what ways have the lake and its surroundings remained the same since White's boyhood? Be specific. In what ways have they changed?

2. Can the lake be considered a personal symbol for White? (See "Guide to Terms": *Symbol.*) If so, what does it symbolize?

3. At one point in the essay White says, "I seemed to be living a dual existence" (par. 4). What is the meaning of this statement? How does this "dual existence" affect his point of view in the essay? (Guide: *Point of View.*) Is the "dual existence" emphasized more in the first half of the essay or the second half? Why?

4. Where in the essay does White link differences between the lake now and in his youth with a difference between his son's outlooks and his own? Is this distance between father and son caused by changes in the world around them or merely the passage of time? Explain.

5. After spending a day on the lake, White remarks, "There had been no years" (par. 6). What other direct or indirect comments does he make about time and change? Be specific.

6. What is the tone of the essay? (Guide: *Style/Tone.*) Does the tone change or remain the same throughout the essay?

7. What is meant by the closing phrase of the essay, "suddenly my groin felt the chill of death" (par. 13)? Is this an appropriate way to end the essay? Why or why not?

EXPOSITORY TECHNIQUES

1. In the first part of the essay White focuses on the unchanged aspects of the lake; in the second part he begins acknowledging the passage of time. Where does this shift in attitude take place? What strategies, including transitional devices, does White use to signal to the reader the shift in attitude? Be specific.

2. How does White use the discussion of outboard motors and inboard motors (par. 10) to summarize the differences between life at the lake in his youth and at the time of his return with his son?

3. Many of the descriptive passages in this essay convey a dominant impression, usually an emotion or mood. Discuss how the author's choice of details and author's comments suggest that the impressions are more a reflection of the observer's perspective than an objective description of the lake. (Guide: *Syntax; Diction.*)

4. In many places the author combines description and comparison. Select a passage from the essay and discuss in detail how he combines the patterns. In what ways is the combination of description and comparison appropriate to the theme and the point of view of the essay?

DICTION AND VOCABULARY

1. How much do the connotations of the words used in paragraph 8 contribute to the dominant impression the author is trying to create? (Guide: *Connotation/Denotation.*) In paragraph 10? What do these connotations suggest about the relation of person to place? Of observer to subject of observation?

2. Is the diction in this passage sentimental: "Summertime, oh, summertime, pattern of life indelible, the fade-proof lake, the woods unshatterable, the pasture with the sweetfern and the juniper forever and ever, summer without end . . ." (par. 8)? (Guide: *Sentimentality.*) If so, why would the author choose to use this style in the passage? Does the passage contain an allusion? If so, what is alluded to and why? (Guide: *Figures of Speech.*)

3. In what sense can a tennis court steam "with midday heat and hunger and emptiness" (par. 7)?

4. What kind of paradox is presented in this passage: ". . . the waitresses were the same country girls, there having been no passage of time, only the illusion of it as in a dropped curtain—the waitresses were still fifteen; their hair had been washed, that was the only difference—they had been to the movies and seen the pretty girls with the clean hair" (par. 7)? (Guide: *Paradox.*)

5. Study the author's uses of the following words, consulting the dictionary as needed: incessant, placidity (par. 1); gunwale (2); primeval (3); transposition (4); helgramite, pensively (5); petulant (10); premonitory (12); languidly (13).

READ TO WRITE

1. **Collaborating:** Working with a group, make a list of your memorable vacations and holidays, then choose three and develop for each a tentative thesis statement that sums up the meaning of the event.

2. **Considering Audience:** In his descriptions, White creates symbols to convey his ideas about the passing of time. How else might readers respond to the incidents White describes? To what extent might responses be shaped by differing religious, social, economic, or cultural backgrounds? Prepare a short essay considering the possible range of reactions.

3. **Developing an Essay:** Drawing on the strategies White employs in "Once More to the Lake," choose some place you remember from your childhood and have seen recently, and write a description of it comparing its present appearance with your memories of it. As you write, take into account the relationships of place and person, permanence and change, and the effect of experience on perception.

(NOTE: Suggestions for topics requiring development by use of DESCRIPTION follow.)

Writing Suggestions for Chapter 10

DESCRIPTION

1. Primarily by way of impressionistic description that focuses on a single dominant impression, show and explain the mood, or atmosphere, of one of the following:

   a. A country fair.

   b. A ball game.

   c. A rodeo.

   d. A wedding.

   e. A funeral.

   f. A busy store.

   g. A ghost town.

   h. A cave.

   i. A beach in summer (or winter).

   j. An antique shop.

   k. A party.

   l. A family dinner.

   m. A traffic jam.

   n. Reveille.

   o. An airport (or a bus depot).

   p. An automobile race (or a horse race).

   q. A home during one of its rush hours.

   r. The last night of holiday shopping.

   s. A natural scene at a certain time of day.

   t. The campus at examination time.

   u. A certain person at a time of great emotion—e.g., joy, anger, grief.

2. Using objective description as your basic pattern, explain the functional qualities or the significance of one of the following:

   a. A house for sale.

   b. A public building.

   c. A dairy barn.

   d. An ideal workshop (or hobby room).

   e. An ideal garage.

    f. A fast-food restaurant.

    g. The layout of a town (or airport).

    h. The layout of a farm.

    i. A certain type of boat.

    j. A sports complex.

COLLABORATIVE EXERCISES

1. Have each member of your team brainstorm a list of words that describe the mood or atmosphere when attending any one of the events listed in 1 a–c. From your individual lists look for similar experiences and moods. Collaboratively write an essay based on one of those events and the team similarities.

2. Have each member of the group describe a designated building on campus. Compare and contrast your descriptions.

3. Consider an ideal gymnasium or dormitory. Have each student in the group research this building by talking to other students on campus. Share your results and write a collaborative essay incorporating each member's research.

11

Using *Narration* as an Expository Technique

When is narration a pattern of exposition rather than a story told for its own purposes? When it serves to explain a subject, present conclusions, or support an interpretation or a thesis. For example, a writer who wishes to explain the role of risk-taking individuals (rather than corporations) in developing new ideas and products might tell the story of an entrepreneur who perfected the frozen French fry in the early 1950s only to discover that there was little demand for his product. The story would emphasize his perseverance in struggling to develop a market for the product—a perseverance that paid off for all concerned a decade later when the rapidly growing fast food industry discovered the usefulness of frozen fries for ready-in-a-minute menus.

Whether you use narration as the pattern for an entire essay or for support and explanation within an essay, your readers will expect you to do certain things. They will expect your narrative to help them understand *what happened,* including the *who, where, what,* and *to whom* of events. They will expect the narrative to *re-create* events, showing (through concrete detail or the actual words of participants) rather than merely telling what happened (through summary). Finally, your readers will expect your narrative to help them understand the *significance* of the events. They will look for the point you are making, for what you have to say about the events, or for the way the events support your thesis.

In a book explaining the extraordinary character and physical courage of early Antarctic explorers, the writer Edwin Mickleburgh offers the following narrative to support his thesis about the explorer Shackleton's abilities as a leader and the courage of his crew.

Introduces narrative and its relation to writer's main point

narrative

For anyone who has looked up from the sullen South Georgia shore [island near Antarctica] towards the soaring, razor-edged peaks and the terrible chaos of glaciers topped by swirling clouds and scoured by mighty winds, the knowledge of the crossing made by these three men adds a wider dimension to an already awe inspiring sight. How they did it, God only knows, but they crossed the island in thirty-six hours. They were fortunate that the weather held, although many times great banks of fog rolled in from the open sea, creeping toward them over the snow and threatening to obscure their way. Confronted by precipices of ice and walls of rock they had often to retrace their steps adding many miles to the journey. They walked almost without rest. At one point they sat down in an icy gully, the wind blowing the drift around them, and so tired were they that Worseley and Crean fell asleep immediately. Shackleton, barely able to keep himself awake, realized that to fall asleep under such conditions would prove fatal. After five minutes he woke the other two, saying that they had slept for half an hour.

—Edwin Mickleburgh, *Beyond the Frozen Sea: Visions of Antarctica*

WHY USE NARRATION?

Perhaps the most familiar form of expository narrative is the personal narrative, based on personal experience or observation, that offers insights into events or conclusions about relationships and the importance of certain kinds of experience. These include memoirs focusing on the author's personal and intellectual development or on an unusual and significant childhood event or other experiences. They include autobiographies of media stars, politicians, and other well-known people, especially those that shed light on the fields in which they have worked or the important events they have witnessed. And they include personal narratives embedded in other kinds of works in order to give them a sense of authenticity.

Another use of narrative is to present a profile on an unfamiliar or unusual activity or the people involved. Typically, such a narrative begins by presenting an interesting person in action (a day in the life of a computer game creator, for example) or focuses on an activity (workers changing light bulbs on the spire of the Empire State Building; divers searching in deep water for wreckage from an airplane crash).

As a way of creating drama and interest, such narratives frequently reveal surprising tensions or contradictions, such as the quiet home life and personal kindness of an offshore boat racer also known for his fearlessness, abrasiveness, spectacular crashes, and narrow escapes from death.

A narrative can also provide a framework for commentary and analysis, with passages of narrative interspersed with discussions of the significance and implications of the events. Or narratives can add convincing detail or emotional force to explanations built around some other expository pattern, such as comparison (Chapter 5), cause-effect (Chapter 8), or definition (Chapter 9).

CHOOSING A STRATEGY

A narrative is a chronological account of events. You do not always have to present the events in chronological order nor give them all equal emphasis. When you are creating an event for expository purposes, begin your planning process with questions like these:

- What events are most important to my purpose for writing?
- What ideas and emotions surrounding the events are worth sharing with my readers?
- What point do I want to make with this narrative?

Your answers to questions like these should help you limit the time frame of your narrative and focus on the most important events of the story. Many writers are gripped by a compulsion to get all the details of a story down—important and unimportant. Radical surgery often helps. Instead of covering a whole week or day, consider focusing on the single most important incident—the four or five minutes when all the forces came together—and summarize the rest.

Remember that you can arrange the events to suit your purpose(s). In basic form, a narrative sets the scene, introduces characters, then presents, in chronological order, episodes that introduce a conflict or prepare for the central event. Finally, it explores in detail the most important incident in which the conflict is resolved or the writer's outlook is made clear. Yet the chronological approach can make it hard to emphasize the most important element. You may instead want to start in the middle of things, perhaps at the climactic episode, and fill in prior events through flashbacks. Or you might stop in the middle of events to provide important background information or comment on the characters and their actions.

And you need to choose whether to provide an explicit thesis statement to organize your narrative and direct commentary on the events, or to let the events speak for themselves, assuming that their relationship to your main point will be sufficiently clear to readers.

DEVELOPING A NARRATIVE

As you draft and revise a narrative, pay attention to the following concerns which can contribute to the success (or failure) of your efforts.

- **Selection of Details.** You will probably have many more details you might include in a narrative than you need. Keep in mind that too many details can overwhelm readers, making them lose sight about the point the narrative is making or the explanation it is offering. Focused, unified writing makes use only of those details that are most relevant to the writer's purpose and desired effect. Whenever possible, try to include concrete, specific details that make the narrative vivid and believable and that will be likely to hold your readers' interest.
- **Time order.** You can employ straight chronology, relating events as they happened, or the flashback method, leaving the sequence temporarily in order to go back and relate some now-significant happening of a time prior to the main action. If you use flashback, do so deliberately, not merely because you neglected to mention the episode earlier.
- **Transitions.** Watch out for overly simple and repetitive transitions between events in the narrative: ". . . And then we . . . And then she . . . And then we . . . ." As you revise, make a conscious effort to creative variety in transitions: "next," "following," "subsequently," "as a consequence," "reacting to," "later," "meanwhile," "at the same time," "concurrently," and the like.
- **Point of View.** Decide whether you want to tell the story from the point of view of a participant, yourself or a character, or from the overall perspective of a spectator. The vividness and immediacy possible from a participant's point of view can make the narrative more dramatic, but the spectator's point of view can allow for an easier transition from narrative to commentary and may be especially useful in expository writing. Whichever point of view you choose, keep it consistent throughout the narrative.
- **Dialogue.** Remember that quoting the words of participants can help make a narrative more convincing, and dialogue, which can reveal conflicting perspectives among the participants, can also be a springboard to your commentary on the meaning of the events.

Student Essay

One important use of narrative in expository writing is to explore values and the ways they change. In the following essay, Hrishikesh Unni uses flashback and a dream sequence to explain a set of personal values—love of ivory and of ivory carvings—that may be unfamiliar to many of his readers. He then returns to the main narrative of his encounter with a herd of elephants in Zambia and uses it to explain his change in attitude toward ivory collecting.

Elephants, Ivory, and
an Indelible Experience
Hrishikesh Unni

opening incident— starts in the middle of events

The roar of the engine increased to a crescendo as the driver revved the engine of the open van. This sound broke the monotonous atmosphere of the dry and deserted African grassland of the Luangwa Valley in Zambia and made me shift in my rear seat. I had been sitting there for at least three hours since noon and had not seen any game, apart from the impala and zebra that intermittently spotted the grasslands. These creatures are a common sight in all national parks in Zambia, including the Luangwa. The drought had taken its toll. What was once a land filled with green vegetation was turned into a brown and heavily scorched area by the menacing October sun that was callously beating down on my back. I clutched my Canon camera even more firmly and could feel the heat radiating from the surface of its black case.

unusual, exotic—gets readers' attention

appeals to senses

uses quotation

"You sure are unlucky, aren't you, Hrishi. No elephants yet!" said Musa, the guide, who was the only other person in the spacious van, besides Banda.

fills in background of events

Banda was a local driver who could only speak the local language, Nyanga. I merely nodded to this statement, admitting my

disappointment. I had come all the way
from Ndola (another town in Zambia) to see
the well-known elephants of the Luangwa
National Park. I had given up hope because
it was the third and final day of my
visit, and I had not seen any so far. What
irritated me was the fact that I had lost
a long-awaited opportunity to see these
beasts. To overcome my disappointment, I
looked at the metallic body of the van
that was painted white. It blazed in the
sun and blinded my eyes. It reminded me of
something I had once loved and treasured:
Ivory.

uses key word to set off flashbacks

introduces his values

I had an affinity for ivory. I loved its
color, texture, and appearance. My positive feelings for this substance had begun

flashbacks— source of values

after I received my first ivory carving
for my ninth birthday from a Zambian
friend. It was a superb carving of a baby
elephant, and I instantly liked it. I
would gaze at it, admiring its dominant
white color and its smooth texture. Also
its different shades of light brown never
seemed to bore me. Since receiving that
gift, I had bought every ivory item I
could get my hands on and had a magnifi-
cent collection that I kept in my room.

back to main narrative

My eyes could no longer take the glare
and in an attempt to reduce the strain, I
allowed my eyelids to drop over them. I
realized how tired I was when I closed by
eyes. Every muscle in my body seemed to be
screaming in desperation, ordering my
brain to sleep. I felt sleep gradually

dream event

overtake me like an ivy conquering an old
dilapidated castle. Soon I was fast asleep
and dreaming of the time . . . .

I entered my room and switched on my titanium-white tube light. I stared in awe as the light fell on my ivory collection, enhancing its already immaculate white coating. The furniture in my room consisted of a bed, table, chair, and a couple of shelves that were attached to the wall. It was decorated with my extravagant ivory collection. I stood at the doorway and began surveying the room, casting my eyes on each and every piece of ivory. I admired and absorbed every detail of the carvings and was aware of the hours of work involved in creating a single delicate carving from a long curved elephant tusk. The dexterity and skill the African craftsmen possessed amazed me, and I never got tired of looking at my collection. I saw a variety of things: old traditional men, dogs, a range of birds, daggers, kudu, impala, elephants, rhino, leopards, cheetahs—all in ivory. My eyes finally came to rest on the carving I admired the most—an elephant bull, which I had named Tusker Bull. It was the largest piece I had. Its place on the highest shelf and its majestic posture gave it an authority over the other animals in my collection. Its ominous, evil eyes and its cocked ears portrayed tyranny. I had a sudden urge to look into its lifeless eye. I daringly did this and saw a look I had never seen before. It was one of anger and rage. This look sent a chill down my spine as I wondered if my imagination was mocking me. The look in its eye seemed to be saying . . .

explains values; love of ivory helps readers understand appeal of art that may be unfamiliar to them

brief
transition
paragraph

back to main
narrative

"Wake up, Hrishi, elephants!" shouted the guide.

I awoke with a jump, expecting to see my room, but the heat waves of the national park that enveloped me made me aware that I was a long way away from there. The painful process of adjusting to the amber sunlight took quite a while. The sky was an orange-yellow, and the ground seemed to have darkened to a beige color. It was nearly dusk, and I realized I had been sleeping for at least two hours. Musa repeated the word "elephant," the word I longed to hear. I knew he had spotted a couple of them.

"Where?" I asked anxiously.

He pointed in between two brown colored thickets and said, "By that dry waterhole."

He was right, and I could see the posterior of two African elephants. I could not see the entire waterhole because the dry trees and scrub that had adapted to drought conditions partially obliterated our view. I was filled with excitement as images of elephants and my ivory collection flashed in my mind. I quickly set my camera to "operate" as the driver steered the van towards the elephants. We took an unorthodox and meandering path towards the elephants. As the van cut through the dry scrub, I could hear the twigs being crushed by its enormous tires and the dry grass, grazing and caressing the sides of the van. We finally reached the brown-colored thicket, and the driver deftly steered around it enabling us to see the entire expanse of the waterhole that merely had shallow puddles of water.

What we saw shocked us. There were not two elephants; there were two thousand of them! From where we were before, we could only get a glimpse of this enormous herd.

"What a sight! Ten years in this business, and I have not seen this many at once!" exclaimed Musa.

"Hitut, hitut!" said Banda, in awe.

Everywhere I looked, I only saw elephants. They completely superimposed the entire landscape, which now looked like a dark gray Persian carpet. The faint sunlight that reflected off the elephants transformed the color of their bodies to a stone-gray. It was an absolutely fantastic and awesome sight! I began surveying them, in the manner I surveyed my ivory collection in my dream; slowly and meticulously, but this time I wasn't looking at elephant ivory carvings but at real elephants. My eyes swept across the herd, and I was amazed at the unique behavior of each individual elephant I saw. There were numerous bulls with gigantic tusks. Their white tusks contrasted with their black bodies and made me think of ivory. From our position the tusks looked like curved toothpicks. The females were nurturing and tending to their playful calves. The elephants were of different sizes, but all the bulls were above eleven feet. Their postures conveyed a strong sense of magnanimity as they marched slowly in unison, every step serving a purpose. I admired the ease with which they moved, taking all the time in the world. They deliberately swung their trunks from side to side, like pendulums, and their tails moved naturally to their rhythmic walk. The mild deep

experience of seeing elephants more dramatic and moving than their representations in ivory

concrete details appeal to senses throughout narrative

grunts of the bulls were amplified by the wind that blew towards us. This natural sound enabled them to coax the members of the herd that were extremely slow. The pitch of this sound was lower than the sound the baby elephants made, which was like notes played on a trumpet that was not in tune. The calves pranced around playfully and used their trunks to mock and tease each other, not aware of their vulnerability to predators. A huge bull raised its head and arched its trunk in a form of imperious salute. He was definitely the largest and seemed to be leading the herd, ready to admonish the herd

dialogue

of any potential danger. I wanted a photo of this elephant.

"Let's get closer, I want a photo of that bull," I said, pointing to the conspicuous animal.

"I think we'll be asking for trouble if we get any closer. This herd if definitely over-protective because there are so many young," replied Musa.

"Oh, come on, this is the only opportunity we've had of seeing so many elephants. I mean, this is a rare sight, and we haven't seen any all day. I want that bull. We must get closer," I persisted.

Musa and Banda conversed in the local language about my idea. I could tell Banda was not pleased, but finally he reluctantly nodded his head in apparent consent.

"Okay, but Banda says only a couple of meters," he said firmly.

I gave them both a "thumbs up" sign showing my appreciation. Banda furtively drove the van towards the herd that had

not noticed us yet and stopped near it. As
a precaution he left the engine on and did
not remove his foot from the accelerator,
establishing a ready position to take off
if something went terribly wrong. From the
expression on Banda's and Musa's faces, I
could tell that they were not pleased. I
was told that the elephants were used to
the sound of the van, and if you maintained a safe distance, you would be fine
even if they were aware of you. I knew the
elephants had seen us because some turned
their heads in our direction.

Now we were a dangerous fifteen meters
from the herd, and I was now in a position
to take a photo of the largest elephant
that was closer to us than the rest of the
herd. I set the flash on my camera and
peered at the bull through the eyepiece.
It was out of focus, and I had the lateral
view of the elephant. I quickly brought it
into focus and waited, hoping it would
turn towards me. I had to wait for approx-

**link to dream
sequence—
effect on his
values**

imately forty seconds until the moment I
longed for arrived, but it was a moment I
have never forgotten to this day. The bull
turned its head towards me, and I stared
into its eye the way I stared into the
eye of the elephant carving in my dream.
I saw the same look of rage and anger in
its eye. The menacing look seemed to be
accusing me of an unforgivable crime I
seemed to have committed. I avoided its
eyes and pressed the button on my camera.
This was a big mistake because the flash
disturbed the elephant, and it let out an
ear-shattering sound that I had never
heard before. This sound seemed to be the
warning alarm because it caused the whole

herd to simultaneously bellow in this fashion. It sounded like a loud never-ending echo, which punished our ears. The ground reverberated beneath us as they moved impetuously and tried to form a cordon around their young. There were so many of them, causing them to nearly trample on each other. Some began running away from us, while others advanced towards us, their ears flapping rapidly and fervently in a form of defense. What had once been a calm and benign atmosphere turned into a calamitous one at the push of a camera button.

I was speechless and could hear Musa shouting, "Tieni, tieni fast!" to the driver. Instinctively, Banda slammed the foot on the accelerator causing the engine to roar strongly, but this sound was barely audible due to the louder angry grunts of the elephants. He then turned the van away from the herd in an attempt to reach safety.

dramatic climax of narrative

"Abuil abuil ei tiuti hamba isa tieni tieni fast!" shouted Musa frantically to Banda as he ducked below a seat. I did not know what this had meant, but I soon found out. The massive bull, which I had tried to photograph, began charging at us from the rear, flapping its ears vigorously and grunting vehemently. Its tusks were raised, like a tank with two white-colored barrels, ready for battle. I had a clear view of its tusks and they made me think of ivory—yet not as a smooth and attractive substance, as I once did, but as something dangerous to be in possession of. Now the thought of ivory did not amaze me but frightened me. I have never seen

reference to dream sequence and to underlying discussion of values

ivory the same way since that day. At that moment, the image of Tusker Bull, my biggest piece in the ivory collection, flashed into my mind. It seemed as if it had come alive and was after me. I was surprised at the pace the bull was running because I didn't expect such a large animal to run at such a fast speed. I honestly thought I was going to die and was terrified because it was merely ten feet away from the van and was gaining on us. I held on to the side of the van and shut my eyes, not looking behind me. Yet, I could see the elephant in my mind, charging angrily at us. Banda was doing his best to escape from this animal, but his efforts seemed to be futile.

It seemed hours had passed when suddenly Musa yelled in relief, "It's stopped! It's stopped!" pointing at the elephant that had become stationary.

warning symbolic of writer's changed perspectives

It gave an indignant salute that meant to say, "Don't ever come near my herd again. We are much more powerful than you."

"Hiny in hyi it fl,ungo," replied Banda in a tone of relief.

"Are you all right?" Musa asked me.

Since I was in a state of shock, I did not say a word and merely nodded.

"We'll be at the lodge soon so don't worry. It's over, and everything will be all right," said Musa.

I responded to him with a slight smile and then closed my eyes, while thinking of my close brush with death. The roar of the engine increased to a crescendo as the driver revved the engine of the open van and followed the dusty route to Mfuwe

Lodge of the Luangwa National Park of Zambia.

discussion of changed values— summarizes main ideas of essay

The ten-minute encounter with the elephants and the charging bull changed my perspective of elephants and gave me second thoughts about collecting ivory. This frightening experience made me aware of how protective an elephant community is and of the similarities in its character to that of a human society. It was during this time that I realized the natural power these animals possess and that a human is only able to overpower them with the use of guns and other weapons. My respect for these animals and nature in general has increased. I felt that the elephants were trying to make me aware of the cruelty of people and how they have killed elephants to get ivory. Just the fact that I collected ivory betrayed my insensitivity toward these creatures. I burned my collection when I got home, and now I am no longer interested in collecting ivory. Now I don't value my collection in terms of money but in terms of the amount of life that is wasted in obtaining every piece that was present in my collection. I was taught a lesson by the victims and that I feel is the best way to be punished. I will never collect ivory again, and I am planning to become part of the organization that plans to ban ivory and abolish poaching. Yes, the actual substance of ivory I will continue to admire; but differently, because I now think that ivory looks best on an elephant and not as carvings placed on a shelf in my room.

MARTIN GANSBERG

MARTIN GANSBERG, born in Brooklyn, New York, in 1920, received a Bachelor of Social Sciences degree from St. John's University. He has been an editor and reporter for *The New York Times* since 1942, including a three-year period as editor of its international edition in Paris. He also served on the faculty of Fairleigh Dickinson University. Gansberg has written for many magazines, including *Diplomat, Catholic Digest, Facts,* and *U.S. Lady.*

38 Who Saw Murder Didn't Call the Police

"38 Who Saw Murder . . ." was written for the *New York Times* in 1964, and for obvious reasons it has been anthologized frequently since then. Cast in a deceptively simple news style, it still provides material for serious thought, as well as a means of studying the use and technique of narration.

For more than half an hour 38 respectable, law-abiding citizens in Queens watched a killer stalk and stab a woman in three separate attacks in Kew Gardens. 1

Twice their chatter and the sudden glow of their bedroom lights interrupted him and frightened him off. Each time he returned, sought her out, and stabbed her again. Not one person telephoned the police during the assault; one witness called after the woman was dead. 2

That was two weeks ago today. 3

Still shocked is Assistant Chief Inspector Frederick M. Lussen, in charge of the borough's detectives and a veteran of 25 years of homicide investigations. He can give a matter-of-fact recitation on many murders. But the Kew Gardens slaying baffles him—not because it is a murder, but because the "good people" failed to call the police. 4

"As we have reconstructed the crime," he said, "the assailant had three chances to kill this woman during a 35-minute period. He returned twice to complete the job. If we had been called when he first attacked, the woman might not be dead now." 5

This is what the police say happened beginning at 3:20 A.M. in 6
the staid, middle-class, tree-lined Austin Street area:

Twenty-eight-year-old Catherine Genovese, who was called 7
Kitty by almost everyone in the neighborhood, was returning home
from her job as manager of a bar in Hollis. She parked her red Fiat in
a lot adjacent to the Kew Gardens Long Island Rail Road Station,
facing Mowbray Place. Like many residents of the neighborhood,
she had parked there day after day since her arrival from
Connecticut a year ago, although the railroad frowns on the practice.

She turned off the lights of her car, locked the door, and started 8
to walk the 100 feet to the entrance of her apartment at 82–70 Austin
Street, which is in a Tudor building, with stores in the first floor and
apartments on the second.

The entrance to the apartment is in the rear of the building be- 9
cause the front is rented to retail stores. At night the quiet neighborhood is shrouded in the slumbering darkness that marks most
residential areas.

Miss Genovese noticed a man at the far end of the lot, near a 10
seven-story apartment house at 82–40 Austin Street. She halted.
Then, nervously, she headed up Austin Street toward Lefferts
Boulevard, where there is a call box to the 102nd Police Precinct in
nearby Richmond Hill.

She got as far as a street light in front of a bookstore before the 11
man grabbed her. She screamed. Lights went on in the 10-story
apartment house at 82–67 Austin Street, which faces the bookstore.
Windows slid open and voices punctuated the early-morning stillness.

Miss Genovese screamed: "Oh, my God, he stabbed me! Please 12
help me! Please help me!"

From one of the upper windows in the apartment house, a man 13
called down: "Let that girl alone!"

The assailant looked up at him, shrugged and walked down 14
Austin Street toward a white sedan parked a short distance away.
Miss Genovese struggled to her feet.

Lights went out. The killer returned to Miss Genovese, now try- 15
ing to make her way around the side of the building by the parking
lot to get to her apartment. The assailant stabbed her again.

"I'm dying!" she shrieked, "I'm dying!" 16

Windows were opened again, and lights went on in many apart- 17
ments. The assailant got into his car and drove away. Miss Genovese
staggered to her feet. A city bus, Q–10, the Lefferts Boulevard line to
Kennedy International Airport, passed. It was 3:35 A.M.

The assailant returned. By then, Miss Genovese had crawled to   18
the back of the building, where the freshly painted brown doors to
the apartment house held out hope for safety. The killer tried the
first door; she wasn't there. At the second door, 82–62 Austin Street,
he saw her slumped on the floor at the foot of the stairs. He stabbed
her a third time—fatally.

It was 3:50 by the time the police received their first call, from a   19
man who was a neighbor of Miss Genovese. In two minutes they were
at the scene. The neighbor, a 70-year-old woman, and another woman
were the only persons on the street. Nobody else came forward.

The man explained that he had called the police after much de-   20
liberation. He had phoned a friend in Nassau County for advice and
then he had crossed the roof of the building to the apartment of the
elderly woman to get her to make the call.

"I didn't want to get involved," he sheepishly told the police.   21

Six days later, the police arrested Winston Moseley, a 29-year-   22
old business-machine operator, and charged him with homicide.
Moseley had no previous record. He is married, has two children
and owns a home at 133–19 Sutter Avenue, South Ozone Park,
Queens. On Wednesday, a court committed him to Kings County
Hospital for psychiatric observation.

When questioned by the police, Moseley also said that he had   23
slain Mrs. Annie May Johnson, 24, of 146–12 133rd Avenue, Jamaica,
on Feb. 29 and Barbara Kralik, 15, of 174–17 140th Avenue,
Springfield Gardens, last July. In the Kralik case, the police are holding Alvin L. Mitchell, who is said to have confessed to that slaying.

The police stressed how simple it would have been to have got-   24
ten in touch with them. "A phone call," said one of the detectives,
"would have done it." The police may be reached by dialing "O" for
operator or SPring 7–3100.

Today witnesses from the neighborhood, which is made up of   25
one-family homes in the $35,000 to $60,000 range with the exception
of the two apartment houses near the railroad station, find it difficult to explain why they didn't call the police.

A housewife, knowingly if quite casually, said, "We thought it   26
was a lover's quarrel." A husband and wife both said, "Frankly, we
were afraid." They seemed aware of the fact that events might have
been different. A distraught woman, wiping her hands on her
apron, said, "I didn't want my husband to get involved."

One couple, now willing to talk about that night, said they   27
heard the first screams. The husband looked thoughtfully at the
bookstore where the killer first grabbed Miss Genovese.

"We went to the window to see what was happening," he said, 28 "but the light from our bedroom made it difficult to see the street." The wife, still apprehensive, added: "I put out the light and we were able to see better."

Asked why they hadn't called the police, she shrugged and 29 replied: "I don't know."

A man peeked out from the slight opening in the doorway to 30 his apartment and rattled off an account of the killer's second attack. Why hadn't he called the police at the time? "I was tired," he said without emotion. "I went back to bed."

It was 4:25 A.M. when the ambulance arrived to take the body of 31 Miss Genovese. It drove off. "Then," a solemn police detective said, "the people came out."

MEANINGS AND VALUES

1. What is Gansberg's central (expository) theme? How might he have developed this theme without using narration at all? Specify what patterns of exposition he could have used instead. Would any of them have been as effective as narration *for the purpose*? Why or why not?

2. Why has this narrative account of old news (the murder made its only headlines in 1964) retained its significance to this day? Are you able to see in this event a paradigm of any larger condition or situation? If so, explain, using examples as needed to illustrate your ideas.

EXPOSITORY TECHNIQUES

1. What standard introductory technique is exemplified in the first paragraph? (Guide: *Introductions.*) How effective do you consider it? If you see anything ironic in the fact stated there, explain the irony. (Guide: *Irony.*)

2. Where does the main narration begin? What, then, is the function of the preceding paragraphs?

3. Study several of the paragraph transitions within the narration itself to determine Gansberg's method of advancing the time sequence (to avoid overuse of "and then"). What is the technique? Is another needed? Why or why not?

4. What possible reasons do you see for the predominant use of short paragraphs in this piece? Does this selection lose any effectiveness because of the short paragraphs?

5. Undoubtedly, the author selected with care the few quotations from witnesses that he uses. What principle or principles do you think applied to his selection?

6. Explain why you think the quotation from the "solemn police detective" was, or was not, deliberately and carefully chosen to conclude the piece. (Guide: *Closings.*)

7. Briefly identify the point of view of the writing. (Guide: *Point of view.*) Is it consistent throughout? Show the relation, as you see it, between this point of view and the author's apparent attitude toward his subject matter.

DICTION AND VOCABULARY

1. Why do you think the author used no difficult words in this narration? Do you find the writing at all belittling to college people because of this fact? Why or why not?

READ TO WRITE

1. **Collaborating:** Gansberg's narration is written as a news account except that it clearly editorializes about the apathetic attitude of citizens. Working in a group, identify the places in the essay that Gansberg injects his bias. With your group, rewrite those sections where Gansberg expresses his perspective, taking the opposite point of view—supporting people who do not get involved in a situation like the one presented in the essay.

2. **Considering Audience:** The general plot of this story is as believable for audiences of the 1990s as it was for audiences of the 1960s—perhaps even more so because levels of violence in society have increased in the intervening decades. However, how might the behaviors of the people involved have been different if the incident had occurred in the late 1990s? Write out your answer and a brief explanation of it.

3. **Developing an Essay:** Though he certainly has his own view of the events he reports, Gansberg allows readers to question the motivations of the observers and to make their own judgments about the lack of involvement. Prepare an account of some incident you witnessed and use a similar approach. Call attention to the various motivations expressed by the participants, to any inconsistencies in their behavior, and to any other elements you wish readers to analyze and question. The event itself need not be of more than local significance (an account of a meeting or a sports event can offer interesting insights, for example), but your exposition should offer readers insights worth considering.

(NOTE: Suggestions for topics requiring development by NARRATION are on pp. 535–536 at the end of this chapter.)

LYDIA MINATOYA

> Lʏᴅɪᴀ Mɪɴᴀᴛᴏʏᴀ was born in Albany, New York in 1950. She received her PhD in psychology from the University of Maryland in 1981 and is currently a college professor. She has written about her experiences growing up as an Asian American and her travels of self-discovery in Asia in *Talking to Monks in High Snow: An Asian-American Odyssey* (1993). She has also published a novel, *The Strangeness of Beauty* (1999), about several generations of Japanese Americans who return to Japan just before World War II and view the conflict from the perspective of insiders who are also outsiders.

Transformation

In "Transformation," a selection from *Talking to Monks in High Snow,* Minatoya uses narrative to give a specific meaning to her claim that "many Japanese Americans never quite understood that the promise of America was not truly meant for them."

Call it denial, but many Japanese Americans never quite under- 1
stood that the promise of America was not truly meant for
them. They lived in horse stalls at the Santa Anita racetrack and said
the Pledge of Allegiance daily. They rode to Relocation Camps under armed guard, labeled with numbered tags, and sang "The Star-
Spangled Banner." They lived in deserts or swamps, ludicrously
imprisoned—where would they run if they ever escaped—and
formed garden clubs, and yearbook staffs, and citizen town meetings. They even elected beauty queens.

My mother practiced her okoto and was featured in a recital. She 2
taught classes in fashion design and her students mounted a show.
Into exile she had carried an okoto and a sewing machine. They were
her past and her future. She believed in Art and Technology.

My mother's camp was the third most populous city in the en- 3
tire state of Wyoming. Across the barren lands, behind barbed wire,
bloomed these little oases of democracy. The older generation bore
the humiliation with pride. "*Kodomo no tame ni,*" they said. For the
sake of the children. They thought that if their dignity was great,
then their children would be spared. Call it valor. Call it bathos.
Perhaps it was closer to slapstick: a sweet and bitter lunacy.

Call it adaptive behavior. Coming from a land swept by savage 4
typhoons, ravaged by earthquakes and volcanoes, the Japanese have

evolved a view of the world: a cooperative, stoic, almost magical way of thinking. Get along, work hard, and never quite see the things that can bring you pain. Against the tyranny of nature, of feudal lords, of wartime hysteria, the charm works equally well.

And so my parents gave me an American name and hoped that I could pass. They nourished me with the American dream: Opportunity, Will, Transformation.   5

When I was four and my sister was eight, Misa regularly used me as a comic foil. She would bring her playmates home from school and query me as I sat amidst the milk bottles on the front steps.   6

"What do you want to be when you grow up?" she would say. She would nudge her audience into attentiveness.   7

"A mother kitty cat!" I would enthuse. Our cat had just delivered her first litter of kittens and I was enchanted by the rasping tongue and soft mewings of motherhood.   8

"And what makes you think you can become a cat?" Misa would prompt, gesturing to her howling friends—wait for this; it gets better yet.   9

"This is America," I stoutly would declare. "I can grow up to be anything that I want!"   10

My faith was unshakable. I believed. Opportunity. Will. Transformation.   11

When we lived in Albany, I always was the teachers' pet. "So tiny, so precocious, so prettily dressed!" They thought I was a living doll and this was fine with me.   12

My father knew that the effusive praise would die. He had been through this with my sister. After five years of being a perfect darling, Misa had reached the age where students were tracked by ability. Then, the anger started. Misa had tested into the advanced track. It was impossible, the community declared. Misa was forbidden entry into advanced classes as long as there were white children being placed below her. In her defense, before an angry rabble, my father made a presentation to the Board of Education.   13

But I was too young to know of this. I knew only that my teachers praised and petted me. They took me to other classes as an example. "Watch now, as Lydia demonstrates attentive behavior," they would croon as I was led to an empty desk at the head of the class. I had a routine. I would sit carefully, spreading my petticoated skirt neatly beneath me. I would pull my chair close to the desk, crossing my swinging legs at my snowy white anklets. I would fold my hands carefully on the desk before me and stare pensively at the blackboard.   14

This routine won me few friends. The sixth-grade boys threw   15
rocks at me. They danced around me in a tight circle, pulling at the
corners of their eyes. "Ching Chong Chinaman," they chanted. But
teachers loved me. When I was in first grade, a third-grade teacher
went weeping to the principal. She begged to have me skipped. She
was leaving to get married and wanted her turn with the dolly.

When we moved, the greatest shock was the knowledge that I   16
had lost my charm. From the first, my teacher failed to notice me.
But to me, it did not matter. I was in love. I watched her moods, her
needs, her small vanities. I was determined to ingratiate.

Miss Hempstead was a shimmering vision with a small up-   17
turned nose and eyes that were kewpie-doll blue. Slender as a sylph,
she tripped around the classroom, all saucy in her high-heeled
shoes. Whenever I looked at Miss Hempstead, I pitied the Albany
teachers whom, formerly, I had adored. Poor old Miss Rosenberg.
With a shiver of distaste, I recalled her loose fleshy arms, her mottled hands, the scent of lavender as she crushed me with her heavy
breasts.

Miss Hempstead had a pet of her own. Her name was Linda   18
Sherlock. I watched Linda closely and plotted Miss Hempstead's
courtship. The key was the piano. Miss Hempstead played the piano. She fancied herself a musical star. She sang songs from
Broadway revues and shaped her students' reactions. "Getting to
know you," she would sing. We would smile at her in a staged manner and position ourselves obediently at her feet.

Miss Hempstead was famous for her ability to soothe. Each day   19
at rest time, she played the piano and sang soporific songs. Linda
Sherlock was the only child who succumbed. Routinely, Linda's
head would bend and nod until she crumpled gracefully onto her
folded arms. A tousled strand of blonde hair would fall across her
forehead. Miss Hempstead would end her song, would gently lower
the keyboard cover. She would turn toward the restive eyes of the
class. "Isn't she sweetness itself!" Miss Hempstead would declare. It
made me want to vomit.

I was growing weary. My studiousness, my attentiveness, my   20
fastidious grooming and pert poise: all were failing me. I changed
my tactics. I became a problem. Miss Hempstead sent me home with
nasty notes in sealed envelopes: Lydia is a slow child, a noisy child,
her presence is disruptive. My mother looked at me with surprise,
"Nani desu ka? Are you having problems with your teacher?" But I
was tenacious. I pushed harder and harder, firmly caught in the ob-
sessive need of the scorned.

One day I snapped. As Miss Hempstead began to sing her   21
wretched lullabies, my head dropped to the desk with a powerful
CRACK! It lolled there, briefly, then rolled toward the edge with a
momentum that sent my entire body catapulting to the floor. Miss
Hempstead's spine stretched slightly, like a cat that senses danger. Otherwise, she paid no heed. The linoleum floor was smooth
and cool. It emitted a faint pleasant odor: a mixture of chalk dust
and wax.

I began to snore heavily. The class sat electrified. There would   22
be no drowsing today. The music went on and on. Finally, one boy
could not stand it. "Miss Hempstead," he probed plaintively, "Lydia
has fallen asleep on the floor!" Miss Hempstead did not turn. Her
playing grew slightly strident but she did not falter.

I lay on the floor through rest time. I lay on the floor through   23
math drill. I lay on the floor while my classmates scraped around
me, pushing their sturdy little wooden desks into the configuration
for reading circle. It was not until penmanship practice that I finally
stretched and stirred. I rose like Sleeping Beauty and slipped back
into my seat. I smiled enigmatically. A spell had been broken. I
never again had a crush on a teacher.

MEANINGS AND VALUES

1. Explain Minatoya's reference to "Art" and "Technology" (par. 2).
   Why does she capitalize these words?

2. What is the significance of the references to an American name and
   the American Dream (par. 5)? Why might Minatoya have chosen
   "Opportunity," "Will," and "Transformation" as defining terms for
   the American Dream?

3. Explain the meaning of the essay's conclusion (par. 23). What has
   Miss Hempstead taught the young Minatoya? How does this connect
   with the images presented earlier in the essay?

EXPOSITORY TECHNIQUES

1. Throughout the narration, Minatoya carries the theme of America
   and its culture. How effective is this theme in unifying the essay?
   (See "Guide to Terms": *Unity.*)

2. What organizational pattern does Minatoya use in her narration?
   How successful is she at creating transitions between the stages of
   her life presented in the essay? (Guide: *Transitions.*) Be ready to explain your answer.

3. Identify the places in the essay where Minatoya uses dialogue. In what ways and for what purpose does she incorporate it? Does the dialogue serve to keep the narrative moving forward?

4. What is Minatoya's tone in this essay? (Guide: *Tone.*) Point to specific passages to support your response.

DICTION AND VOCABULARY

1. How "difficult" are the diction and the level of vocabulary Minatoya employs in the quotations she presents in the selection? (Guide: *Diction.*) Why do you think she chose this particular level of vocabulary?

2. Look up in a dictionary any of the following words with which you are unfamiliar: ludicrously (par. 1); bathos (par. 3); rabble (par. 13); croon (par. 14); ingratiate (par. 16); soporific (par. 19); and tenacious (par. 20).

READ TO WRITE

1. **Collaborating:** Working in a group, list and describe briefly the earliest recollections that each group member has of either meeting someone who was part of a minority group or of realizing that you were part of a minority group. From the list, choose several that your group finds particularly intriguing and plan a narrative essay around each one.

2. **Considering Audience:** How might American readers of 1950 have reacted to Minatoya's essay? Talk to people who might remember the era in which Minatoya was a little girl (just after World War II). Write an analysis of how Asian Americans (as individuals or as a group) were treated at that time compared to their relationships to the rest of society now.

3. **Developing an Essay:** Think of some identifying characteristic that you have. Write an autobiographical narrative similar to Minatoya's, emphasizing that distinguishing part of you. Remember to include your point of view and the reactions of others to you.

SEBASTIAN JUNGER

SEBASTIAN JUNGER writes on the natural world and the people who meet its challenges and dangers. His articles have appeared in a variety of magazines. His book *The Perfect Storm: A True Story of Men Against the Sea* appeared in 1997.

The Storm

"The Storm," first published in 1994 in *Outside* magazine later became the basis for Junger's book *The Perfect Storm*. In the essay, Junger blends narrative with commentary and explanation to give readers an understanding of the workings, challenges, and dangers of commercial fishing in the North Atlantic while at the same time telling a dramatic tale of how an experienced crew was lost at sea.

"They that go down to the sea in ships . . . see the deeds of the Lord. They reel and stagger like drunken men, they are at their wits' end."

—Psalm 107

Gloucester, Massachusetts, a town of 28,000 people, is squeezed   1
between a rocky coast and a huge tract of scrub pine and boulders called Dogtown Common. Local widows used to live in Dogtown, along with the forgotten and the homeless, while the rest of the community spread out along the shore. Today a third of all jobs in Gloucester are fishing related, and the waterfront bars—the Crow's Nest, the Mariners Pub, the Old Timer's Tavern—are dark little places that are unmistakably not for tourists.

One street up from the coastline is Main Street, where the bars   2
tend to have windows and even waitresses, and then there is a rise called Portugee Hill. Halfway up Portugee Hill is Our Lady of Good Voyage Church, a large stucco construction with two bell towers and a statue of the Virgin Mary, who looks down with love and concern at the bundle in her arms. The bundle is a Gloucester fishing schooner.

September 18, 1991, was a hot day in Gloucester, tourists shuf-   3
fling down Main Street and sunbathers still crowding the wide expanses of Good Harbor Beach. Day boats bobbed offshore in the heat shimmer, and swells sneaked languorously up against Bass Rocks.

At Gloucester Marine Railways, a haul-out place at the end of   4
the short peninsula. Adam Randall stood contemplating a boat named the *Andrea Gail*. He had come all the way from Florida to go

swordfishing on the boat, and now he stood considering her un-
easily. The *Andrea Gail* was a seventy-foot long-liner that was leaving for Canada's Grand Banks within days. He had a place on board
if he wanted it. "I just had bad vibes." He would say later. Without
quite knowing why, he turned and walked away.

Long-liners are steel-hulled fishing boats that can gross as much   5
as $1 million in a year. Up to half of that can be profit. Swordfish
range up and down the coast from Puerto Rico to Newfoundland,
and the long-liners trail after them all year like seagulls behind a day
trawler. The fish are caught with monofilament lines forty miles long
and set with a thousand hooks. For the crew, it's less a job than a
four-week jag. They're up at four, work all day, and don't get to bed
until midnight. The trip home takes a week, which is the part of the
month when swordfishermen sleep. When they get to port the owner
hands each of them several thousand dollars. A certain amount of
drinking goes on, and then a week later they return to the boat, load
up, and head back out.

"Swordfishing is a young man's game, a single man's game,"   6
says the mother of one who died at it. "There aren't a lot of Boy
Scouts in the business," another woman says.

Sword boats come from all over the East Coast—Florida, the   7
Carolinas, New Jersey. Gloucester, which is located near the tip of
Cape Ann, a forty-five-minute drive northeast from Boston, is a
particularly busy port because it juts so far out toward the summer
fishing grounds. Boats load up with fuel, bait, ice, and food and
head out to the Grand Banks, about ninety miles southeast from
Newfoundland, where warm Gulf Stream water mixes with the
cold Labrador current in an area shallow enough—or "shoal"
enough, as fishermen say—to be a perfect feeding ground for fish.
The North Atlantic weather is so violent, though, that, in the early
days, entire fleets would go down at one time, a hundred men lost
overnight. Even today, with loran navigation, seven-day forecasts,
and satellite tracking, fishermen on the Grand Banks are just
rolling the dice come the fall storm season. But swordfish sell for
around six dollars a pound, and depending on the size of the boat a
good run might take in thirty thousand to forty thousand pounds.
Deckhands are paid shares based on the catch and can earn ten
thousand dollars in a month. So the tendency among fishermen in
early fall is to keep the dice rolling.

The *Andrea Gail* was one of maybe a dozen big commercial boats   8
gearing up in Gloucester in mid-September 1991. She was owned by
Bob Brown, a long-time fisherman who was known locally as Suicide

Brown because of the risks he'd taken as a young man. He owned a second long-liner, the *Hannah Boden,* and a couple of lobster boats. The *Andrea Gail* and the *Hannah Boden* were Brown's biggest investments, collectively worth well over a million dollars.

The *Andrea Gail,* in the language, was a raked-stem, hard- 9 chined, western-rig boat. That meant that her bow had a lot of angle to it, she had a nearly square cross-section, and her pilothouse was up front rather than in the stern. She was built of welded steel plate, rust-red below the waterline, green above, and she had a white wheelhouse with half-inch-thick safety-glass windows. Fully rigged for a long trip, she carried hundreds of miles of monofilament line, thousands of hooks, and ten thousand pounds of bait fish. There were seven life preservers on board, six survival suits, an emergency position-indicating radio beacon, and one life raft.

The *Andrea Gail* was captained by a local named Frank "Billy" 10 Tyne, a former carpenter and drug counselor who had switched to fishing at age twenty-seven. Tyne had a reputation as a fearless captain, and in his ten years of professional fishing he had made it through several treacherous storms. He had returned from a recent trip with almost forty thousand pounds of swordfish in his hold, close to a quarter of a million dollars' worth. Jobs aboard Tyne's boats were sought after. So it seemed odd, on September 18, when Adam Randall walked back to the dock at Gloucester Marine Railways and returned to town.

Randall's replacement was twenty-eight-year-old David Sullivan, 11 who was mildly famous in town for having saved the lives of his entire crew one bitter January night two years before. When his boat, the *Harmony,* had unexpectedly begun taking on water, Sullivan had pulled himself across a rope to a sister ship and got help just in time to rescue his sinking crew. Along with Sullivan were a young West Indian named Alfred Pierre; thirty-year-old Bobby Shatford, whose mother, Ethel, tended bar at the Crow's Nest on Main Street; and two men from Brandenton Beach, Florida—Dale Murphy, thirty, and Michael "Bugsy" Moran, thirty-six.

On September 20, Billy Tyne and his crew passed Ten Pound 12 Island, rounded Dogbar Breakwater, and headed northeast on a dead-calm sea.

For several generations after the first British settlers arrived in 13 Gloucester, the main industries on Cape Ann were farming and logging. Then around 1700 the cod market took off, and Gloucester schooners began making runs up to the Grand Banks two or three times a year. French and Basque fishermen had already been working the area since 1510, perhaps earlier. They could fill their holds faster by crossing the Atlantic and fishing the rich waters of the Banks than by plying their own shores.

The Gloucester codfisherman worked from dories and returned   14
to the schooners each night. Payment was reckoned by cutting the tongues out of the cod and adding them up at the end of the trip. When fog rolled in, the dories would drift out of earshot and were often never heard from again. Occasionally, weeks later, a two-man dory crew might be picked up by a schooner bound for, say, Pernambuco or Liverpool. The fishermen would make it back to Gloucester several months later, walking up Main Street as if returning from the dead.

The other danger, of course, was storms. Like a war, a big storm   15
might take out all the young men of a single town. In 1862, for example, a winter gale struck seventy schooners fishing the dangerous waters of Georges Bank, east of Cape Cod. The ships tried to ride out fifty-foot seas at anchor. By morning fifteen Gloucester boats had gone down with 125 men.

At least four thousand Gloucestermen have been lost at sea, but   16
some estimates run closer to ten thousand. A bronze sculpture on the waterfront commemorates them: THEY THAT GO DOWN TO THE SEA IN SHIPS 1623–1923. It shows a schooner captain fighting heavy weather, his faced framed by a sou'wester hat.

In the early days, a lot of superstition went into seafaring.   17
Occasionally men stepped off ill-fated boats on a hunch. Captains refused to set sail on Fridays, since that was the day their Lord had been crucified. Boats often had lucky silver coins affixed to the base of their masts, and crew members took care never to tear up a printed page because they never knew—most of them being illiterate—whether it was from the Bible.

The *Andrea Gail* took nearly a week to reach the fishing grounds.   18
The six crewmen watched television, cooked and ate, slept, prepared the fishing gear, talked women, talked money, talked horse racing, talked fish, stared at the sea. Swordfishermen seldom eat swordfish when they're out. Like many ocean fish, it's often full of sea worms, four feet long and thick as pencils, and though the worms are removed prior to market, many of the men who catch swordfish consider it fit only for the landlubbing public. At sea a fisherman will eat steak, spaghetti, chicken, ice cream, anything he wants. On ice in the *Andrea Gail*'s hold was three thousand dollars' worth of groceries.

The boat arrived at the Grand Banks around September 26 and   19
started fishing immediately. On the main deck was a huge pool of

six-hundred-pound-test monofilament, the mainline, which passed across a bait table and paid out off the stern. Baiters alternate at the mainline like old-time axmen on a Douglas fir. They are expected to bait a hook with squid or mackerel every fifteen seconds; at this rate it takes two men four hours to set forty miles of line. After they are done they shower and retire to their bunks. Around four in the morning, the crew gets up and starts hauling the line. A hydraulic drum on the wheelhouse deck slowly pulls it in, and the crew un-clips the leaders as they come. When there's a fish at the end of a leader, deckhands catch it with steel gaffs and drag it, struggling, aboard. They saw the sword off, gut and behead the fish with a knife, and drop it into the hold.

The crew has dinner in midafternoon, baits the line again, and sets it back out. They might then have a couple of beers and go to bed.   20

The *Andrea Gail* had been out thirty-eight days when the National Weather Service suddenly started issuing fax bulletins about a low-pressure system that was building over southern Quebec and heading out to sea: "DEVELOPING STORM 45N 73W MOVING E 24 KTS. WINDS INCREASING TO 35 KTS AND SEAS BUILDING TO 16 FT." Meanwhile, the Weather Service was keeping a close eye on the mid-Atlantic, where Hurricane Grace, which had developed in the vicinity of Bermuda two days before, was now tracking steadily northwest toward the Carolina coast.   21

It was Sunday, October 27, very late to be pushing one's luck on the Grand Banks. Most of the fleet was well to the east of Tyne, out on the high seas, but a 150-foot Japanese swordboat named the *Eishan Maru* and the 77-foot *Mary T* were fishing nearby. Tyne told Albert Johnston, the *Mary T*'s captain, that he had forty thousand pounds of fish in his hold—an impressive catch—and now he was heading home.   22

The question was, could he make it through the Canadian storm that was rapidly coming his way? He would have to cross some very dangerous water while passing Sable Island, a remote spit 120 miles southeast of Nova Scotia, whose shoals are known to fishermen as the Graveyard of the Atlantic. That night Linda Greenlaw, the captain of Bob Brown's other long-liner, the *Hannah Boden*, radioed in and asked Tyne if he'd received the weather chart. "Oh, yeah, I got it," Tyne replied. "Looks like it's gonna be wicked." They set some channels to relay information to Bob Brown and de-cided to talk the following night.   23

Though Billy Tyne had no way of knowing it, the heavy weather that was now brewing in the North Atlantic was an anomaly   24 of historic proportions. Three years later, professional meteorologists still talk animatedly about the storm of '91, debating how it formed and exactly what role Hurricane Grace played in it all. Generally, hurricanes this late in the season are anemic events that quickly dissipate over land. Hurricane Grace, though, never made it to shore; a massive cold front, called an anticyclone, was blocking the entire eastern seaboard. Well off the Carolinas, Grace ran up against the cold front and literally bounced off. She veered back out to sea and, though weakened, churned northeast along the warm Gulf Stream waters.

At the same time, the low-pressure system that had developed   25
over Quebec and moved eastward off the Canadian Maritimes was beginning to behave strangely. Normally, low-pressure systems in the region follow the jet stream offshore and peter out in the North Atlantic, the usual pattern of the well-known nor'easter storms. But this system did the opposite: On Monday, October 28, it unexpectedly stalled off the coast of Nova Scotia and began to grow rapidly, producing record high seas and gale-force winds. Then it spun around and headed back west, directly at New England, a reversal known as a retrograde.

Meteorologists still disagree about what caused the storm to   26
grow so suddenly and then to retrograde. But the best theory offered by the National Weather Service and its Canadian equivalent, Environment Canada, is that it was caught between the counterclockwise spin of the dying hurricane and the clockwise swirl of the anticyclone, creating a funnel effect that forced it toward the coast at speeds of up to ten knots. The farther west it tracked, the more it absorbed moisture and energy from the remnants of Hurricane Grace—and the more ferocious it became.

The technical name for the new storm was *midlatitude cyclone.*   27
The people in its path, however, would later call it the No Name Hurricane, since it had all the force of a hurricane but it was never officially designated as one. And because the brunt of the storm would strike the eastern seaboard around October 31, it would also acquire another name: the Halloween Gale.

Around 6:00 P.M. on Monday, October 28, Tyne told the skipper   28
of a Gloucester boat named the *Allison* that he was 130 miles north-northeast of Sable Island and experiencing eighty-knot winds. "She's comin' on, boys, and she's comin' on strong," he said. According to Tyne, the conditions had gone from flat calm to fifty knots almost without warning. The rest of the fleet was farther east and in relative safety, but the *Andrea Gail* was all alone in the path of the

fast-developing storm. She was probably running with the waves and slightly angled toward them—"quartering down-sea," as it's called—which is a stable position for a boat; she'll neither plow her nose into the sea nor roll over broadside. A wave must be bigger than a boat to flip her end over end, and the *Andrea Gail* was seventy feet long. But by this point, data buoys off Nova Scotia were measuring waves as high as one hundred feet—among the highest readings ever recorded. Near Sable Island the troughs of such monsters would have reached the ocean floor.

Tyne would have radioed for help if trouble had come on slowly—a leak or a gradual foundering, for example. "Whatever happened, happened quick," a former crew member from the *Hannah Boden* later said. Tyne didn't even have time to grab the radio and shout.   29

Waves of unimaginable proportions have been recorded over the years. When Sir Ernest Shackleton skippered an open sailboat off the South Georgian Islands on May 1916, he saw a wave so big that he mistook the foaming crest for a break in the clouds. "It's clearing boys!" he yelled to his crew, and then, moments later: "For God's sake, hold on, it's got us!" By some miracle they managed to survive. In 1933 in the South Pacific an officer on the USS *Ramapo* looked to stern and saw a wave that was later calculated to be 112 feet high. In 1984 a three-masted schooner named the *Marques* was struck by a single wave that sent her down in less than a minute, taking nineteen people with her. Nine survived, including a strapping young Virginian who managed to force his way up through a rising column of water and out an open hatch.   30

Oceanographers call these "extreme waves" or "rogues." Old-time Maine fishermen call them "queer ones." They have roared down the stacks of navy destroyers, torn the bows off container-ships, and broken cargo vessels in two.   31

When the rogue hit the *Andrea Gail*, sometime between midnight and dawn on October 29, Tyne would probably have been alone in the wheelhouse and already exhausted after twenty-four hours at the helm. Captains, unwilling to relinquish the wheel to inexperienced crew, have been known to drive for two or even three days straight. The crew would have been below deck, either in the kitchen or in their staterooms. Once in a while one of the men would have come up to keep Tyne company. In the privacy of the wheelhouse he might have admitted his fears: This is bad, this is the worst I've ever seen. There's no way we could inflate a life raft in these conditions. If a hatch breaks open, if anything lets go . . .   32

Tyne must have looked back and seen an exceptionally big   33
wave rising up behind him. It would have been at least seventy feet
high, maybe a hundred. The stern of the boat would have risen up
sickeningly and hurled the men from their bunks. The *Andrea Gail*
would have flipped end over end and landed hull up, exploding the
wheelhouse windows. Tyne, upside down in his steel cage, would
have drowned without a word. The five men below deck would have
landed on the ceiling. The ones who remained conscious would have
known that it was impossible to escape through an open hatch and
swim out from under the boat. And even if they could, what then?
How would they have found their survival suits, the life raft?

The *Andrea Gail* would have rolled drunkenly and started to fill.   34
Water would have sprayed through bursting gaskets and risen in a
column from the wheelhouse stairway. It would have reached the
men in their staterooms, and it would have been cold enough to take
their breath away. At least the end would have come fast.

It wasn't until Tuesday afternoon that the boats on the Grand   35
Banks were able to check in with one another. The *Eishan Maru*,
which was closest to Billy Tyne's last known location, reported that
she was completely rolled by one huge wave; her wheelhouse windows were blown out, and she was left without rudder or electronics. The *Lori Dawn Eight* had taken so much water down her vents
that she lost an engine and headed in. The *Mary T* had fared well but
had already taken $165,000 worth of fish in nine days, so she headed
in, too. The *Hannah Boden,* the *Allison,* the *Mr. Simon,* and the *Miss
Millie* were way to the east and "had beautiful weather," in Albert
Johnston's words. That left the *Andrea Gail.*

By Wednesday, October 30, the storm had retrograded so far to   36
the west that conditions at sea were almost tolerable. At that point
the worst of it was just hitting Gloucester. The Eastern Point neighborhood, where the town's well-to-do live, had been cut in half.
Waves were rolling right through the woods and into some of the
nicest living rooms in the state. On the Back Shore, thirty-foot waves
were tearing the façades off houses and claiming whole sections of
Ocean Drive. The wind, whipping through the power lines, was hitting pitches that no one had ever heard before. Just up the coast in
Kennebunkport, some Democrats cheered to see boulders in the
family room of President Bush's summer mansion.

"The only light I can shed on the severity of the storm is that un-   37
til then, we had never—ever—had a lobster trap move offshore,"
said Bob Brown. "Some were moved thirteen miles to the west. It
was the worst storm I have ever heard of, or experienced."

By now the storm had engulfed nearly the entire eastern   38
seaboard. Even in protected Boston Harbor, a data buoy measured
wave heights of thirty feet. A Delta Airlines pilot at Boston's Logan
Airport was surprised to see spray topping two-hundred-foot construction cranes on Deer Island. Sitting on the runway waiting for
clearance, his air-speed indicator read eighty miles per hour. Off Cape
Cod, a sloop named the *Satori* lost its life raft, radios, and engine. The
three people in its crew had resigned themselves to writing goodbye
notes when they were finally rescued two hundred miles south of
Nantucket by a Coast Guard swimmer who jumped, untethered,
from a helicopter into the roiling waves. An Air National Guard helicopter ran out of fuel off Long Island, and its crew had to jump one at
a time through the darkness into the sea. One man was killed; the
other four were rescued after drifting throughout the night. All along
the coast, waves and storm surge combined to act as "dams" that prevented rivers from flowing into the sea. The Hudson backed up one
hundred miles to Albany and caused flooding; so did the Potomac.

Brown tried in vain all day Wednesday to radio Tyne. That   39
evening he finally got through to Linda Greenlaw, who said she'd
last heard Billy Tyne talking to other boats on the radio Monday
night. "Those men sounded really scared, and we were scared for
them," she said later. Later that night Brown finally alerted the U.S.
Coast Guard.

"When were they due in?" the dispatcher asked.   40

"Next Saturday," Brown replied.   41

The dispatcher refused to initiate a search because the boat   42
wasn't overdue yet. Brown then got the Canadian Coast Guard on
the line. "I'm afraid my boat's in trouble, and I fear the worst," he told
the dispatcher in Halifax. At dawn Canadian reconnaissance planes,
which were already in the area, began sweeping for the *Andrea Gail.*

Two days later, a U.S. Coast Guard cutter and five aircraft were   43
also on the case. But there was no clue about the missing boat until
November 5, when the Coast Guard positively identified the *Andrea
Gail*'s radio beacon and propane tank, which had washed up on
Sable Island. "The recovered debris is loose gear and could have
washed overboard during heavy weather," said Petty Officer
Elizabeth Brannan. "No debris has been located that indicates the
Andrea Gail has been sunk."

The search had covered more than sixty-five thousand square   44
miles at that point. In heavy seas it's hard for a pilot to be sure he
is seeing everything—one Coast Guard pilot reported spotting a
five-hundred-foot ship that he had completely missed on a previous

flight—so no one was leaping to any conclusions. Two days and thirty-five thousand square miles later, though, it was hard not to assume the worst: Now the *Andrea Gail*'s emergency position-indicating radio beacon (EPIRB) had been found. It, too, had washed up on the beaches of Sable Island.

An EPIRB is a device about the size of a bowling pin that auto-   45
matically emits a radio signal if it floats free of its shipboard holster. The signal travels via satellite to onshore listening posts, where Coast Guard operators decode the name of the boat and her location to within two miles. EPIRBs have been required equipment for fishing vessels on the high seas since 1990. The only catch is that the device must be turned on, something captains do automatically when they leave port. ("It's not the sort of thing you forget," says one captain.) Though Bob Brown insists that the *Andrea Gail*'s EPIRB had been turned on when it left port, it was found on Sable Island disarmed.

The Coast Guard called off the search on November 8, eleven   46
days after the *Andrea Gail* had presumably gone down. Search planes had covered 116,000 square miles of ocean. "After taking into account the water temperature and other factors, we felt the probability of survival was minimal," Coast Guard lieutenant Brian Krenzien told reporters at the time. The water temperature was forty-six degrees. When a man falls overboard on the Grand Banks that late in the year, there usually isn't even time to turn the boat around.

"I finally gave up hope after the Coast Guard called the search   47
off," says Ethel Shatford, Bobby Shatford's mother, at the Crow's Nest. "It was very hard, though. You always read stories about people being found floating around in boats. The memorial was on November 16. There were more than a thousand people. This bar and the bar next door were closed, and we had enough food for everyone for three days. Recently we had a service for a New Bedford boat that went down last winter. None of the crew was from here, but they were fishermen."

The Crow's Nest is a low, dark room with wood-veneer panel-   48
ing and a horseshoe bar where regulars pour their own drinks. On the wall below the television is a photo of Bobby Shatford and another of the *Andrea Gail*, as well as a plaque for the six men who died. Upstairs there are cheap guest rooms where deckhands often stay.

Ethel Shatford is a strong, gray-faced Gloucester native in her   49
late fifties. Three of her own sons have fished, and over the years she has served as den mother to scores of young fishermen on the Gloucester waterfront. Four of the six men who died on the *Andrea Gail* spent their last night onshore in the rooms of the Crow's Nest.

"My youngest graduated high school last June and went fishing   50
right off the b-a-t," she says. "That was what he always wanted to
do, fish with his brothers. Bobby's older brother, Rick, used to fish
the *Andrea Gail* years ago."

She draws a draft beer for a customer and continues. "The *Andrea*   51
Gail crew left from this bar. They were all standing over there by the
pool table saying good-bye. About the only thing different that time
was that Billy Tyne let them take our color TV on the boat. He said,
'Ethel, they can take the TV, but if they watch it instead of doing their
work, the TV's going overboard.' I said, 'That's fine, Billy, that's fine.'"

That was the last time Shatford ever saw her son. Recently, a   52
young guy drifted into town who looked so much like Bobby that people were stopping and staring on the street. He walked into the Crow's
Nest, and another bartender felt it necessary to explain to him why
everyone was looking at him. "He went over to the picture of Bobby
and says, 'If I sent that picture to my mother, she'd think it was me.'"

Linda Greenlaw still comes into the bar from time to time, be-   53
tween trips, swearing that someday she's going to "meet the right
guy and retire to a small island in Maine," Bob Brown settled out of
court with several of the dead crewmembers' families after two
years of legal wrangles. Adam Randall, the man who had stepped
off the *Andrea Gail* at the last minute, went on to crew with Albert
Johnston on the *Mary T.* When he found out that the *Andrea Gail* had
sunk in the storm, all he could say was, "I was supposed to have
been on that boat. That was supposed to have been me."

During the spring of 1993 the *Mary T* was hauled out for re-   54
pairs, and Randall picked up work on a tuna long-liner, the *Terri Lei,*
out of Georgetown, South Carolina. On the Evening of April 6, 1993,
the crew of the *Terri Lei* set lines. In the early morning, there were reports of gusty winds and extremely choppy seas in the area. At 8:45
A.M. the Coast Guard in Charleston, South Carolina, picked up an
EPIRB signal and sent out two aircraft and a cutter to investigate. By
then the weather was fair and the seas were moderate. One hundred
and thirty-five miles off the coast, they found the EPIRB, some fishing gear, and a self-inflating life raft. The raft had the name *Terri Lei*
stenciled on it. There was no one on board.

MEANINGS AND VALUES

1. Why does Junger discuss the selling price of swordfish (par. 7) di-
    rectly following a discussion of the violent weather in the Atlantic?

2.   In paragraph 11, Junger describes Adam Randall's replacement as
     "... mildly famous in town for having saved the lives of his entire
     crew one bitter January night two years before." Why is this man
     only "mildly" famous in a small town like Gloucester? Is the state-
     ment ironic in any way? (See "Guide to Terms": *Irony*.)

3.   Junger shares with us the brief account of Adam Randall's decision
     to bow out of the trip on the *Andrea Gail* (par. 4) because of "bad
     vibes." He concludes the essay with an account of Adam Randall's
     death (par. 52). Why is Randall's death significant in this essay?

EXPOSITORY TECHNIQUES

1.   Junger uses several examples of foreshadowing later events in the
     early sections of the essay. Identify as many examples of it as you
     can. How successful is foreshadowing at setting a tone for the subse-
     quent events? (Guide: *Tone*.)

2.   In paragraph 14, Junger uses a simile to compare war and storms.
     Compare the risks of storms and war as Junger presents them.
     (Guide: *Figures of Speech: Simile*.) Is this an effective use of simile?
     Please explain.

3.   What is ironic about Junger's emphasis on the men's diets at sea (par.
     18)? What symbolic meaning might this have in the essay? (Guide:
     Symbol.)

DICTION AND VOCABULARY

1.   Though Junger does not use excessive dialogue, he does incorporate
     it at some key points. Identify the places where the characters speak.
     Why might Junger have chosen these particular parts of the essay to
     incorporate dialogue? How advanced or involved is the speech of the
     characters?

2.   Throughout paragraphs 29–32, Junger uses the verb form *would have*
     repeatedly. Why might he have chosen this style? Is it effective for
     his narration? Why, or why not?

READ TO WRITE

1.   **Collaborating:** Junger's essay is broken into several sections: pars. 1–2;
     pars. 3–27; pars. 28–32; pars. 33–44; and pars. 45–52. Working in a
     group compare and contrast the narrative techniques in each of these
     sections. Do they have different organization patterns? Different
     points of view? A variety of tones? Then write your own essay, incor-
     porating the group's collective analysis as well as your own insights.

2.   **Considering Audience:** People who have never experienced a
     coastal storm may not respond to Junger's essay as those readers
     who have grown up with such experiences. What might be a more

appropriate natural disaster around which to build a story for a reader from some part of North America that is not close to the ocean? Write an outline for such an essay, and write the introductory paragraphs for it.

3. **Developing an Essay:** List several natural phenomenon that you have experienced in your life (storms, earthquakes, forest fires, etc.). Using descriptions of your local town (where the event occurred), write an essay similar in style and approach to Junger's in which you focus on a particular character or group of characters.

(NOTE: Suggestions for topics requiring development by NARRATION are on pp. 535–536 at the end of this chapter.)

Issues and Ideas

Stories and Values

- George Orwell, *A Hanging*
- Wayne Worcester, *Arms and the Man*
- Chang-Rae-Lee, *Uncle Chul Gets Rich*

Sometimes speaking directly about our values or perspectives does not clarify them or convey them effectively. The situation which gives rise to a particular moral judgment or leads to an ethical perspective can give someone else a better understanding than a detailed definition or even a careful comparison of differing perspectives. The more complex the idea or outlook, the more we may need to know about the events surrounding it. A detailed narrative can perhaps give readers a better understanding of causes and effects than an explanation that attempts to isolate them from the surrounding details.

The three essays that follow demonstrate the effectiveness of narration as an expository pattern for dealing with questions of value. Capital punishment has been the subject of many argumentative and expository essays, but few have offered the kind of insight into the minds of the prisoner and of those responsible for carrying out the sentence that George Orwell provides in "A Hanging." And few essays explore the moral ambiguities surrounding the practice as well as Orwell does.

Wayne Worcester's "Arms and the Man" provides an insider's view of some of the values associated with gun ownership and use. While his perspective is in one way linked to his (and his friend's) experience, it nonetheless gains power and depth for others from the same experience. Finally Chang-Rae Lee, in "Uncle Chul Gets Rich" uses narrative to explore interesting sets of values: personal, family, and cultural. He also uses the immigrant experience to explore American values from the perspective of outsiders struggling to become insiders.

GEORGE ORWELL

Gᴇᴏʀɢᴇ Oʀᴡᴇʟʟ (1903–1950), whose real name was Eric Blair, was a British novelist and essayist, well known for his satire. He was born in India and educated at Eton in England; he was wounded while fighting in the Spanish Civil War. Later he wrote the books *Animal Farm* (1945), a satire on Soviet history, and *1984* (1949), a vivid picture of life in a projected totalitarian society. He was, however, also sharply aware of injustices in democratic societies and was consistently socialistic in his views. Many of Orwell's essays are collected in *Critical Essays* (1946), *Shooting an Elephant and Other Essays* (1950), and *Such, Such Were the Joys* (1953).

A Hanging

"A Hanging" is typical of Orwell's essays in its setting—Burma—and in its subtle but biting commentary on colonialism, on capital punishment, even on one aspect of human nature itself. Although he is ostensibly giving a straightforward account of an execution, the author masterfully uses descriptive details and dialogue to create atmosphere and sharply drawn characterizations. The essay gives concrete form to a social message that is often delivered much less effectively in abstract generalities.

It was in Burma, a sodden morning of the rains. A sickly light, like yellow tinfoil, was slanting over the high walls into the jail yard. We were waiting outside the condemned cells, a row of sheds fronted with double bars, like small animal cages. Each cell measured about ten feet by ten and was quite bare within except for a plank bed and a pot for drinking water. In some of them brown, silent men were squatting at the inner bars, with their blankets draped round them. These were the condemned men, due to be hanged within the next week or two.

One prisoner had been brought out of his cell. He was a Hindu, a puny wisp of a man, with a shaven head and vague liquid eyes. He had a thick, sprouting mustache, absurdly too big for his body, rather like the mustache of a comic man on the films. Six tall Indian warders were guarding him and getting him ready for the gallows. Two of them stood by with rifles and fixed bayonets, while the others hand-cuffed him, passed a chain through his handcuffs and fixed it to their belts, and lashed his arms tight to his sides. They crowded very close about him, with their hands always on him in a careful, caressing grip, as though all the while feeling him to make sure he was there. It was like men handling a fish which is still alive and may jump back into the water. But he stood quite unresisting, yielding his arms limply to the ropes, as though he hardly noticed what was happening.

Eight o'clock struck and a bugle call, desolately thin in the wet 3 air, floated from the distant barracks. The superintendent of the jail, who was standing apart from the rest of us, moodily prodding the gravel with his stick, raised his head at the sound. He was an army doctor, with a grey toothbrush mustache and a gruff voice. "For God's sake, hurry up, Francis," he said irritably. "The man ought to have been dead by this time. Aren't you ready yet?"

Francis, the head jailer, a fat Dravidian in a white drill suit and 4 gold spectacles, waved his black hand. "Yes sir, yes sir," he bubbled. "All iss satisfactorily prepared. The hangman iss waiting. We shall proceed."

"Well, quick march, then. The prisoners can't get their breakfast 5 till this job's over."

We set out for the gallows. Two warders marched on either side 6 of the prisoner, with their rifles at the slope; two others marched close against him, gripping him by arm and shoulder, as though at once pushing and supporting him. The rest of us, magistrates and the like, followed behind. Suddenly, when we had gone ten yards, the procession stopped short without any order or warning. A dreadful thing had happened—a dog, come goodness knows whence, had appeared in the yard. It came bounding among us with a loud volley of barks and leapt round us wagging its whole body, wild with glee at finding so many human beings together. It was a large woolly dog, half Airedale, half pariah. For moment it pranced around us, and then, before anyone could stop it, it had made a dash for the prisoner, and jumping up tried to lick his face. Everybody stood aghast, too taken aback even to grab the dog.

"Who let that bloody brute in here?" said the superintendent 7 angrily. "Catch it, someone!"

A warder detached from the escort, charged clumsily after the 8 dog, but it danced and gambolled just out of his reach, taking every-thing as part of the game. A young Eurasian jailer picked up a handful of gravel and tried to stone the dog away, but it dodged the stones and came after us again. Its yaps echoed from the jail walls. The prisoner, in the grasp of the two warders, looked on incuriously, as though this was another formality of the hanging. It was several minutes before someone managed to catch the dog. Then we put my handkerchief through its collar and moved off once more, with the dog still straining and whimpering.

It was about forty yards to the gallows. I watched the bare   9
brown back of the prisoner marching in front of me. He walked clumsily with his bound arms, but quite steadily, with that bobbing gait of the Indian who never straightens his knees. At each step his muscles slid neatly into place, the lock of hair on his scalp danced up and down, his feet printed themselves on the wet gravel. And once, in spite of the men who gripped him by each shoulder, he stepped lightly aside to avoid a puddle on the path.

It is curious; but till that moment I had never realized what it   10
means to destroy a healthy, conscious man. When I saw the prisoner step aside to avoid the puddle, I saw the mystery, the unspeakable wrongness, of cutting a life short when it is in full tide. This man was not dying, he was alive just as we are alive. All the organs of his body were working—bowels digesting food, skin renewing itself, nails growing, tissues forming—all toiling away in solemn foolery. His nails would still be growing when he stood on the drop, when he was falling through the air with a tenth-of-a-second to live. His eyes saw the yellow gravel and the grey walls, and his brain still remembered, foresaw, reasoned—even about puddles. He and we were a party of men walking together, seeing, hearing, feeling, understanding the same world; and in two minutes, with a sudden snap, one of us would be gone—one mind less, one world less.

The gallows stood in a small yard, separate from the main   11
grounds of the prison, and overgrown with tall prickly weeds. It was a brick erection like three sides of a shed, with planking on top, and above that two beams and a crossbar with the rope dangling. The hangman, a greyhaired convict in the white uniform of the prison, was waiting beside his machine. He greeted us with a servile crouch as we entered. At a word from Francis the two warders, gripping the prisoner more closely than ever, half led, half pushed him to the gallows and helped him clumsily up the ladder. Then the hangman climbed up and fixed the rope round the prisoner's neck.

We stood waiting, five yards away. The warders had formed in a   12
rough circle round the gallows. And then, when the noose was fixed, the prisoner began crying out to his god. It was a high, reiterated cry

of "Ram! Ram! Ram! Ram!" not urgent and fearful like a prayer or cry for help, but steady, rhythmical, almost like the tolling of a bell. The dog answered the sound with a whine. The hangman, still standing on the gallows, produced a small cotton bag like a flour bag and drew it down over the prisoner's face. But the sound, muffled by the cloth, still persisted, over and over again: "Ram! Ram! Ram! Ram! Ram!"

The hangman climbed down and stood ready, holding the   13
lever. Minutes seemed to pass. The steady, muffled crying from the prisoner went on and on, "Ram! Ram! Ram!" never faltering for an instant. The superintendent, his head on his chest, was slowly poking the ground with his stick; perhaps he was counting the cries, allowing the prisoner a fixed number—fifty, perhaps, or a hundred. Everyone had changed colour. The Indians had gone grey like bad coffee, and one or two of the bayonets were wavering. We looked at the lashed, hooded man on the drop, and listened to his cries—each cry another second of life; the same thought was in all our minds; oh, kill him quickly, get it over, stop that abominable noise!

Suddenly the superintendent made up his mind. Throwing up   14
his head he made a swift motion with his stick. "Chalo!" he shouted almost fiercely.

There was a clanking noise, and then dead silence. The prisoner   15
had vanished, and the rope was twisting on itself. I let go of the dog, and it galloped immediately to the back of the gallows; but when it got there it stopped short, barked, and then retreated into a corner of the yard, where it stood among the weeds, looking timorously out at us. We went round the gallows to inspect the prisoners's body. He was dangling with his toes pointed straight downwards, very slowly revolving, as dead as a stone.

The superintendent reached out with his stick and poked the   16
bare brown body; it oscillated slightly. "*He's* all right," said the superintendent. He backed out from under the gallows, and blew out a deep breath. The moody look had gone out of his face quite suddenly. He glanced at his wrist-watch. "Eight minutes past eight. Well, that's all for this morning, thank God."

The warders unfixed bayonets and marched away. The dog,   17
sobered and conscious of having misbehaved itself, slipped after them. We walked out of the gallows yard, past the condemned cells with their waiting prisoners, into the big central yard of the prison. The convicts, under the command of warders armed with lathis, were already receiving their breakfast. They squatted in long rows, each man holding a tin pannikin, while two warders with buckets

marched around ladling out rice; it seemed quite a homely, jolly scene, after the hanging. An enormous relief had come upon us now that the job was done. One felt an impulse to sing, to break into a run, to snigger. All at once everyone began chattering gaily.

The Eurasian boy walking beside me nodded towards the way we had come, with a knowing smile. "Do you know, sir, our friend (he meant the dead man) when he heard his appeal had been dismissed, he pissed on the floor of his cell. From fright. Kindly take one of my cigarettes, sir. Do you not admire my new silver case, sir? From the boxwallah, two rupees eight annas. Classy European style." 18

Several people laughed—at what, nobody seemed certain. 19

Francis was walking by the superintendent, talking garrulously: "Well, sir, all has passed off with the utmost satisfactoriness. It was all finished—flick! Like that. It iss not always so—oah, no! I have known cases where the doctor was obliged to go beneath the gallows and pull the prissoner's legs to ensure decease. Most disagreeable!" 20

"Wriggling about, eh? That's bad," said the superintendent. 21

"Ach, sir, it iss worse when they become refractory! One man, I recall, clung to the bars of hiss cage when we went to take him out. You will scarcely credit, sir, that it took six warders to dislodge him, three pulling at each leg. We reasoned with him, 'My dear fellow,' we said, 'think of all the pain and trouble you are causing to us!' But no, he would not listen! Ach, he wass very troublesome!" 22

I found that I was laughing quite loudly. Everyone was laughing. Even the superintendent grinned in a tolerant way. "You'd better all come out and have a drink," he said quite genially. "I've got a bottle of whisky in the car. We could do with it." 23

We went through the big double gates of the prison into the road. "Pulling at his legs!" exclaimed a Burmese magistrate suddenly, and burst into a loud chuckling. We all began laughing again. At that moment Francis' anecdote seemed extraordinarily funny. We all had a drink together, native and European alike, quite amicably. The dead man was a hundred yards away. 24

MEANINGS AND VALUES

1. What was the real reason for the superintendent's impatience?

2. On first impression it may have seemed that the author gave undue attention to the dog's role in this narrative. Why was the episode

such a "dreadful thing" (par. 6)? Why did the author think it worth noting that the dog was excited at "finding so many human beings together"? Of what significance was the dog's trying to lick the prisoner's face?

3. Explain how the prisoner's stepping around a puddle could have given the author a new insight into what was about to happen (par. 10).

4. Why was there so much talking and laughing after the hanging was finished?

5. What is the broadest meaning of Orwell's last sentence?

EXPOSITORY TECHNIQUES

1. Cite examples of both objective and impressionistic description in the first paragraph.

2. What is the primary time order used in this narrative? If there are any exceptions, state where.

3. Considering the relatively few words devoted to them, several of the characterizations in this essay are remarkably vivid—a result, obviously, of highly discriminating selection of details from the multitude of those that must have been available to the author. For each of the following people, list the character traits that we can observe, and state whether these impressions come to us through details of description, action, and/or dialogue.

    a. The prisoner.

    b. The superintendent.

    c. Francis.

    d. The Eurasian boy.

4. Why do you think the author included so many details of the preparation of the prisoner (par. 2)? Why did he include so many details about the dog and his actions? What is gained by the assortment of details in paragraph 10?

5. How would your characterize the tone of this selection? (Guide: *Style/Tone*)?

DICTION AND VOCABULARY

1. A noteworthy element of Orwell's style is his occasional use of figurative language. Cite six metaphors and similes, and comment on their choice and effectiveness. (Guide: *Figures of Speech.*)

2. Orwell was always concerned with the precise effects that words could give to meaning and style. Cite at least six nonfigurative words that seem to you particularly well chosen for their purpose. Show what their careful selection contributes to the description of atmosphere or to the subtle meanings of the author. (Guide: *Style/Tone.*)

READ TO WRITE

1. **Collaborating:** Discuss in a group people who have jobs which places their "duty" in conflict with their "conscience." Choose one such person or profession and write a collaborative essay similar in style to Orwell's. You may choose to have group members responsible for one or two concrete examples each, to be combined into a unified paper.

2. **Considering Audience:** Orwell's approach in his essay makes his discussion of capital punishment approachable even to readers who may be in disagreement with his views. Identify places in the essay where Orwell deals with opposing views, and prepare an analysis of his success in dealing with them.

3. **Developing an Essay:** Draw on Orwell's expository technique in an essay of your own by recounting a minor incident (like the actions of the dog in "A Hanging") that led to much deeper insight. Or use a minor incident to reveal and emphasize insights that readers probably have not considered before.

(NOTE: Suggestions for topics requiring development by NARRATION are on pp. 535–536 at the end of this chapter.)

WAYNE WORCESTER

WAYNE WORCESTER is a former newspaper reporter and editor. He now teaches journalism at the University of Connecticut.

Arms and the Man

In "Arms and the Man," first published as a newspaper essay, Wayne Worcester narrates a brief incident, largely through dialogue, that explores a variety of values and issues associated with guns and their personal use.

In an especially rural part of southern New Hampshire, where the 1
hills in early spring roll to mottled green and the roads turn to
deep mud-brown, I have two old friends who live as they please.

He drives a truck. She works in a dentist's office. They have 2
three children, and on most days the kids' toys sprawl in abandon
across the living-room floor, directly in front of the gun cabinet,
which has no lock.

"Doesn't it bother you?" I asked on a recent visit. "The kids' 3
playing around the gun cabinet?"

"Nope. We brought 'em up to not touch it." 4

He handed me his newest gun. It was flat and small, only 5
slightly larger than my hand, and the room's bright light died on its
coal-black barrel. No reflection. Not a hint.

"Isn't that a sweetheart?" 6

"Very small." 7

"It's hers, but it's got real stoppin' power. Great protection." 8

I popped the magazine out, and saw the stack of bullets. 9

"You always keep it loaded?" I asked. 10

"Course." 11

"She carry it?" 12

"No point havin' it, she gonna leave it to home." 13

"She works for a dentist, for Chrissake! He use this instead of 14
Novocain? What's she need a gun for?"

His lips went tight, as though I'd insulted him, which I had. 15

"You never know." 16

"How did she get a permit?" 17

"A what? C'mon." 18

"Well, why's she carrying?" 19

"I told you. Protection."   20

"Right. What else have you got in there?"   21

"Couple rifles. Shotgun. My AR 15. God, that's fun. Last year,   22
me and a couple guys from work, we just went out and set up a target on a red oak out back, and we hit it with the AR so many times
the damned tree just broke in half like we'd sawed it off. Thing just
toppled right over."

"Your neighbor must love you."   23

"Yeah, he called the cops up, but they didn't do nothing—just   24
checked to see we was on our own property."

"'Live free or die,' right? What'd the neighbor do?"   25

"Bout three days later, he comes over. His wife's bein' a pain in   26
the ass. He says, 'We're moving in two months, but if you keep the
shootin' down till then, you can have this.'"

From the top shelf of the cabinet, my friend took down a long-   27
barreled, chrome-plated .357-magnum, the kind of handgun that'll
stop a speeding car, or most anything else.

"But this one here's my pride 'n' joy," he said. It was a .22-caliber   28
handgun, jet black with a long, heavy barrel.

"Real accurate. Wanna try her out?"   29

We walked to the edge of the woods, and he set a bright-blue   30
Maxwell House can swinging from a tree limb.

For a small-caliber weapon, the gun was bone-heavy, and in the   31
palm of my hand it felt oddly substantial, as though it were even
more than its true weight. I walked slowly back toward the house,
flipped off the safety, turned—quickly, for some reason—and
squeezed the trigger the instant the barrel fell in line with the target.
The shot was loud. It was sharp and clear and flat, as though it had
hard, cutting edges, and before the sound had died the can had
jumped and the chamber slide had recoiled and kicked out a casing
with that matchlessly pleasing sound that metal on metal can make
only when the parts have been properly and ever-so-precisely ma-
chined. I was pleased, and I fired again, and then, quickly in the
echo, twice again, and I could smell the shots and feel the recoil of the
bone-weight as though it were an extension of me, and I squeezed
the trigger again, and then again in affirmation, counting silently in
the loud and hard flat noise and clink-sliding of the chamber—seven
shots now—and the can danced some more and in a far shadow I
thought I could see old man Bergevin, whom I'd worked for as a
teenager and hated and do to this day, though he is long dead and
not thought of in years. I considered him in his grave, all scraps and
maggoty bone, and was glad. Eight shots, and the can finally fell to

the ground, and I lowered the gun toward the fallen target and squeezed the trigger for the ninth time and sent the can skittering.

We were quiet on the way back. I was still listening to the gun,   32
feeling its weight, thinking about a quip I'd overheard: "You know what N.R.A. stands for? Not a Rational Adult." I chuckled aloud.

"What?" my friend asked.   33

"Just thinking. You ever wonder who you really need protect-   34
ing from?"

He just smiled.   35

MEANINGS AND VALUES

1. Why, in paragraph 2, does Worcester discuss the parents' careers, present a description of the toys, and mention the gun cabinet? What is the significance of these three topics mentioned in conjunction with each other?

2. Worcester says, "His lips went tight as though I'd insulted him, which I had" (par. 14). What did he say that was potentially offensive? Was his friend justified in being insulted? Why, or why not?

3. What is the overall meaning of the last four paragraphs of the essay (31–34)? Who needs protecting and from whom?

EXPOSITORY TECHNIQUES

1. Worcester uses dialogue to present much of his narrative. How does this dialogue provide a context for the only substantially non-conversational section (par. 30)? Is this heavy use of dialogue an effective technique? Please explain.

2. Identify the descriptive details in paragraph 30. What ideas or qualities do they emphasize? (See "Guide to Terms: *Emphasis*.) How does this paragraph serve to unify the essay? (Guide: *Unity*.)

DICTION AND VOCABULARY

1. Why does Worcester use few difficult words in this essay? Who is his target audience? Is it fair to say that he is belittling the characters in this essay by using such relatively simple language? Why, or why not?

READ TO WRITE

1. **Collaborating:** "Arms and the Man" could serve as an introduction to a larger research essay on gun control. Working in a group, choose

another controversial issue and write an anecdote similar in style to Worcester's (either fiction or nonfiction) that could be an introduction to an essay on that issue.

2. **Considering Audience:** What does Worcester assume about the attitude most of his readers will have toward gun use? Identify those places in the essay where he makes his assumptions about his audience clear. Then prepare an essay analyzing the way Worcester addresses, identifies, and interacts with his audience's attitudes.

3. **Developing an Essay:** Think of a time you disagreed with the course of behavior or values of a friend because of the implications of the action or behavior. Write an essay about that relationship, similar to Worcester's essay, and incorporate dialogue and detailed description in your narration.

(NOTE: Suggestions for topics requiring development by NARRATION are on pp. 535–536 at the end of this chapter.)

CHANG-RAE LEE

Chang-rae Lee was born in South Korea in 1967. When he was three years old, he and his family emigrated to the United States. He is a graduate of Phillips Exeter Academy and Yale University. He earned his M.F.A. degree from the University of Oregon where he taught creative writing. Lee's novel, *Native Speaker* (1996), was awarded the Ernest Hemingway Foundation/PEN Award for First Fiction. His second novel is entitled *A Gesture of Life* (1999).

Uncle Chul Gets Rich

In "Uncle Chul Gets Rich," first published in 1996, Lee offers a familiar narrative form—a story of success in business—set amid contrasting values and cultures typical of immigrant experiences. The issues Lee explores, however, will be familiar and important for most readers.

M y father's youngest brother, Uncle Chul, shared the Lees' famously bad reaction to liquor, which was to turn beet-red in the face, grow dizzy and finally get sick. In spite of this, he was always happy to stay up late at family gatherings. After a few Scotches he would really loosen up, and, with the notable exception of my mother, we all appreciated his rough language and racy stories. Only when Mother came in from the kitchen would his talk soften, for he knew he had always fallen short in her eyes. If they were ever alone together, say in the kitchen, after dinner, he would use the most decorous voice in asking for a glass or a fresh bucket of ice, and even offer to help load the dishwasher or run an errand to the store.

On one of those nights we sped off, both happy for a break in the long evening. He asked me about school, what sports I was playing, but the conversation inevitably turned toward my parents, and particularly my mother—how much she had invested in me, that I was her great hope. I thought it was odd that he was speaking this way, like my other relatives, and I answered with some criticism of her—that she was too anxious and overbearing. He stared at me and, with a hard solemnity I had not heard from him before, said that my

1

2

mother was one of the finest people one could ever know. He kept a grip on the wheel and in the ensuing quiet of the drive I could sense how he must have both admired and despised her. In many respects, my mother was an unrelenting woman. She tended to measure people by the mark of a few principles of conduct: ask no help from anyone, always plan for the long run and practice (her own variation of) the golden rule, which was to treat others much better than oneself.

In her mind, Uncle Chul sorely lacked on all these accounts. In the weeks following our drive, my father would be deciding whether to lend him $10,000 to start a business. As always after dinner, my parents sat in the kitchen (the scent of sesame oil and pickled vegetables still in the air) and spoke in Korean, under the light of a fluorescent ring. My mother, in many ways the director of the family, questioned my uncle's character and will. Hadn't he performed poorly in school, failed to finish college? Hadn't he spent most of his youth perfecting his skills as a black belt in taekwondo and his billiards game? Wasn't he a gambler in spirit?

My father could defend him only weakly. Uncle Chul had a history of working hard only when reward was well within sight, like cash piled high on the end of a pool table. His older brothers were all respected professionals and academics. My father was a doctor, a psychiatrist who had taught himself English in order to practice in America. Uncle Chul had left Korea after a series of failed ventures and odd jobs, and found himself broke with a wife and new baby. How valuable were his taekwondo trophies now? What could he possibly do in this country?

My parents argued fiercely and my father left the kitchen. But as was my mother's way, she kept on pushing her side of the issue, thinking aloud. My father was throwing away his hard-earned money on the naïve wish that his little brother had magically changed. Uncle Chul was a poor risk and even now was complaining about his present job, hauling and cleaning produce for a greengrocer in Flushing. He would get to the store at 4 A.M. to prepare vegetables for the day's selling. While he shared a sofa bed with his nephew in his older brother's tiny apartment, his wife and infant daughter were still in Seoul, waiting for him to make enough money to send for them.

But his wages were only $250 a week for 70 hours of work and he loathed the job, the brutal effort that went into clearing a few cents a carrot, a quarter a soda, the niggling, daily accrual. The owners themselves would toil like slaves to see a till full of tattered ones and fives at day's end.

I knew Uncle Chul craved the big score, the quick hit, a rain of   7
cash. For the very reasons my mother had so little faith in him—his
brashness, his flagrant ambitions—I admired him. Over Scotch and
rice crackers, he would tell my father about the millions he was going to make by moving merchandise wholesale, in bigger-ticket
items with decent margins. He would never touch another orange
again. I remember my father absently nodding his head at each
vague and grandiose idea, probably hearing my mothers' harangues.

The other men in my father's family were thick-lensed scrib-   8
blers who worked through their days from A to Z, assiduously removing uncertainty by paying close attention to the thousand
details of each passing hour. My father worked long days at the hospital, and spent weekends pouring over volumes of Freud and Rank
and Erickson in his second language, to "catch up" with the
American doctors. When my father decided to lend Uncle Chul the
$10,000, making it clear that no further discussion was needed, my
mother transferred her worrying energy squarely onto me. It
seemed no accident that her latest criticism was that I was "always
looking for the easy way." I had, in fact, been feeling moody and re-
bellious, weary of being a good student and good boy. I was in the
eighth grade, and my friends were beginning to drink beer and
smoke pot. I secretly resolved to join them.

I was also taking solo train trips from Pleasantville, N.Y., down   9
to the city to visit my older cousins on the weekends, prompting
questions from my mother about what kind of fun we were having.
I didn't tell her that what thrilled me most was riding the elevated
trains between Flushing and Grand Central, shuttling back and
forth with the multitude. My new comer's heart was fearful and en-
thralled, and I naïvely thought Uncle Chul felt the same way. He
had quit working for the greengrocer after getting the money, and
brought over his wife and child. He was busy scouting out stores for
his first business in America.

But Uncle Chul found that the leases for even the smallest stores   10
were $4,000 a month, and he seemed tense and even a little scared. I
felt a strange pang of guilt because of the extra pressure on him—the
$10,000 and the tenuous faith behind it. The only thing worse than
losing the money was what my mother would never have to mention again: that he started working a little too late.

But he did find a store, in the Bronx, and we drove down one   11
Sunday to see it in all its new glory. It seemed as if half the tenement
buildings on the block were burned out or deserted, and the sidewalks were littered with garbage, broken glass and the rubble of

bricks and mortar. My father pulled up behind Uncle Chul's car and we peered out to see if we had the right address. The shop couldn't have been more than eight feet wide. A single foot-wide corridor running its length was lined with accessories, odd-lot handbags and tie clips and lighters; the stuff hung on plastic grids on the walls and overhead. In the back, there was a hot plate on the floor, two stools and a carton of instant ramen noodles.

Uncle Chul proudly showed us the merchandise and, from a glass   12
display box, gave me a watch; my sister got a faux-pearl necklace. A customer peered in but waved her hand and scurried away. My mother said that we were disturbing the business, and after a rush of bows and goodbyes we were in the car, heading back to Westchester.

Uncle Chul had no choice but to be in that neighborhood, in that   13
quarter-size store, with the risk of crime and no insurance. The trade-off was the low rent, and it soon became clear that he had made an excellent choice. With little competition on the block, the money started coming in, and soon he moved to a larger store nearby, and then moved again. His volume and cash flow surged, and after sell-ing each successive business, he staked his profit on the next store.

We didn't see him much during this time, but when we did he   14
made sure to show off his success to my parents. My aunt wore de-signer clothes, and Uncle Chul sported a fat gold Rolex. If we were out somewhere, he would casually pull out a rolled wad of $100's when a check arrived, proclaiming affably to his brothers that it was his turn to pay.

But I noticed, too, that he and my aunt looked haggard and   15
pressed. They spoke hurriedly and ate as quickly as they could. My mother would say something like, 'You've developed such expen-sive tastes,' and tell him that he was still frittering away his money on useless luxuries.

When Uncle Chul amassed the war chest he needed to open the   16
wholesale business he had hoped for, he moved away from New York. He had heard of opportunities in Texas, where goods could be imported across the border and sold at big profits. Within a few years he had more than 50 people working for him, selling, by containers and truckloads, the same purses and belts he started with years before.

He bought a sprawling ranch house, brand-new and fitted with   17
jet-action bathtubs and wide-screen televisions. He hired a team of Mexican maids to keep the place running. He traded in his Cadillacs for BMW's and sent his daughters to private school. One summer he paid my sister outrageous wages to sit in his air-conditioned office and practice her Spanish with the retailers. The business was on

automatic pilot—effortless. Uncle Chul was now a millionaire several times over, richer than all his brothers combined.

I spent time with him again years later, when my mother became terminally ill. He visited regularly, always bearing gifts for the family. To me, he simply gave money. He knew I had quit my first job to become a writer, which meant little to him, except that I would be poor forever. Maybe, someday, my name would be famous, and he invested in that possibility, slipping me a couple of $100's when my mother wasn't looking. He did this naturally, with an ease and power in his grip full of cash. His money was like a weight outside his body, which he could press upon others, like me. But in my mother's presence, his swagger vanished, and he was just Uncle Chul again, prodigal and bereft.   18

He was especially solemn on the day of her funeral. Of the many people who made their way to the cemetery and later to the house, I suspect Uncle Chul knew he was among those she would be most closely watching. My mother's friends had brought food and electric rice cookers and the men were in the living room, drinking companionably, speaking in low voices. My mother had been dying for nearly two years, and now that it was over waves of exhaustion and relief were washing over everyone in the house.   19

I remember Uncle Chul padding softly about the house, wary of disturbing even the layer of dust on her furniture. He was speaking in a soft register, his voice faltering, like a nervous young minister on his first encounter with the bereaved. He was nodding and bowing, even helping the ladies gather cups and plates, exercising until the last visitor left a younger brother's respect and obedience to the family and the dead.   20

In the Korean tradition, mourners brought offerings of money, all token amounts, except for Uncle Chul's fat envelope, which held thousands of dollars. He would have given more, he said, but his wholesale business wasn't doing so well anymore. I knew that wasn't the real reason. He must have known what my mother would have said, perhaps was telling him now—that he couldn't help but be the flashy one again.   21

MEANINGS AND VALUES

1. How would you define an "All-American Success Story"? In what ways is Uncle Chul's story like an all-American success story? Be specific.

2. How do the values embodied by Uncle Chul and the narrative of his success differ from those embodied and expressed by the writer's mother?

3. Does the writer endorse either his mother's values or Uncle Chul's? If so, why and how? If not, why do you think he refrains from making his own opinion known?

EXPOSITORY TECHNIQUES

1. What strategy does the writer use to begin this selection? To conclude it? (See "Guide to Terms": *Introductions; Closings.*) Are both strategies effective? Why or Why not? (Guide: *Evaluation.*)

2. What ideas does the writer highlight or emphasize by his choice of opening and closing strategies? Where else in the essay do these ideas receive emphasis, and through what means? (Guide: *Emphasis.*)

3. Where and for what purposes does this essay employ comparison/ contrast as an expository pattern? (See Chapter 5.) Why should we consider narration, not comparison/contrast, as the dominant expository pattern in the selection?

DICTION AND VOCABULARY

1. Choose a paragraph describing one of the characters and explain how the terms the writer has chosen reflect the values of the character. (Guide: *Diction.*)

2. If you do not know the meaning of some of the following terms, look them up in a dictionary: decorous (par. 1); taekwondo (3); niggling, accrual (6), tenuous (10).

READ TO WRITE

1. **Collaborating:** Uncle Chul seems to believe he can get wealthy quickly. Working in a group, discuss what you consider to be the American Dream. Did Uncle Chul leave Korea for an American Dream? Did the dream exist in the form that he perceived it? Draw on your notes of the group's discussion to write an essay about a person you know or a particular experience that helps define that American Dream.

2. **Considering Audience:** Many of the situations in Lee's essay cross cultural boundaries. "Get rich quick" schemes and disagreements over family members are widespread. Identify situations that Lee presents which are relevant for most readers. Choose one that resonates as part of your life and narrate it in a short essay.

3. **Developing an Essay:** Create a narrative essay using selected scenes from over a considerable period of time. Choose the scenes so that

they reflect differing outlooks or perspectives, and arrange them as Lee does, for an expository purpose.

(NOTE: Suggestions for topics requiring development by NARRATION follow.)

Writing Suggestions for Chapter 11

NARRATION

Use narration as a primary partial pattern (e.g., in developed examples or in comparison) for one of the following expository themes or another suggested by them. Avoid the isolated personal account that has little broader significance. Remember, too, that development of the essay should itself make your point, without excessive moralizing.

1. People can still succeed without a college education.
2. The frontiers are not all gone.
3. When people succeed in communicating, they can learn to get along with each other.
4. Even with "careful" use of capital punishment, innocent people can be executed.
5. Sports don't always build character.
6. Physical danger can make us more aware of ourselves and our values.
7. Conditioning to the realities of the job is as important to the police officers as professional training.
8. It is possible for employees themselves to determine when they have reached their highest level of competence.
9. Wartime massacres are not a new development.
10. "Date rape" and sexual harassment on the job are devastating and generally unexpected.
11. Both heredity and environment shape personality.
12. Physical and mental handicaps can be overcome in some ways, but they are still a burden.
13. Toxic wastes pose a problem for many communities.
14. Hunting is a worthwhile and challenging sport.
15. Lack of money places considerable stress on a family or a marriage.
16. Exercise can become an obsession.
17. People who grow up in affluent surroundings don't understand what it is like to worry about money, to be hungry, or to live in a dangerous neighborhood.
18. Some jobs are simply degrading, either because of the work or because of the fellow workers.

Collaborative Exersises

1. Consider item 6 from the list of writing suggestions. Have each member of a group relate a story of physical danger and self-awareness that affected a friend or the group member himself or herself. Each group member can then combine the examples into a unified paper narrating the effects that physical dangers may have upon people. When the papers are completed, group members can compare them and discuss the different choices the writers made.

2. Item 9 from the writing suggestions mentions as a topic analyzing wartime massacres. Have each member of your group choose some wartime atrocity (e.g. from the Gulf War, the Holocaust, or the like). Group members can then choose from these examples to create unified narratives.

12

Reasoning by Use of *Induction* and *Deduction*

Sometimes you can best explain a subject by asking readers to follow the line of reasoning you use to *understand it:* either *inductive reasoning* or *deductive reasoning. Induction* is the process by which we accumulate evidence until, at some point, we can make the "inductive leap" and thus reach a useful *generalization.* The science laboratory employs this technique; hundreds of tests and experiments and analyses may be required before the scientist will generalize, for instance, that a disease is caused by a certain virus. It is also one of the primary techniques of the prosecuting attorney who presents pieces of inductive evidence, asking the jury to make the inductive leap and conclude that the accused did indeed kill the victim.

Whereas induction is the method of reaching a potentially useful generalization, (for example, people attending meetings after lunch are invariably less attentive than those at morning meetings), *deduction* is the method of *using* such a generality, now accepted as a fact (for example, because we need an attentive audience, we had better schedule this meeting at 10:30 AM rather than 1:00 PM). Working from a generalization already formulated—by ourselves, by someone else, or by tradition—we may deduce that a specific thing or circumstance that fits into the generality will act the same. Hence, if convinced that orange-colored food tastes bad, we will be reluctant to try pumpkin pie.

A personnel manager may have discovered over the years that electrical engineering majors from Central College are invariably well trained in their field. His induction may have been based on the evidence of observations, records, and opinions of people at his company; and, perhaps without realizing it, he has made the usable generalization about the training of Central College electrical engineering majors. Later, when he has an application from Nancy Ortega, a graduate of Central College, his deductive process will probably work as follows: Central College turns out well-trained electrical engineering majors; Ortega was trained at Central; therefore, Ortega must be well trained. Here he has used a generalization for a specific case.

In written form, you can use inductive reasoning to help readers explore the details of a subject and arrive at the same conclusion or interpretation you do, as in the following paragraph.

preliminary observation states topic	Roaming the site, I can't help noticing that when men start cooking, the hardware gets complicated. Custom-built cookers—massive contraptions of cast iron and stainless steel—may cost $15,000 or more; they incorporate the team's barbecue philosophy. "We burn straight hickory under a baffle," Jim Garts,
inductive evidence/ details	coleader of the Hogaholics, points out as he gingerly opens a scorching firebox that vents smoke across a water tray beneath a 4-by-8-foot grill. It's built on a trailer the size of a mobile home. Other cookers have been fashioned from a marine diesel engine; from a '76 [Nissan], with grilling racks instead of front seats, a chimney above the dash, and coals under the hood; and as a 15-foot version of Elvis Presley's guitar (by
inductive generalization	the Graceland Love Me Tenderloins). It's awesome ironmongery.

—Daniel Cohen, "Cooking-Off for Fame and Fortune"

You can use deductive reasoning to help readers use a generalization as a way of understanding a complex situation or complicated evidence and details, as in this paragraph.

background for generalization	It is an everyday fact of life that competitors producing similar products claim that their own goods or services are better than those of their rivals. Every product advertised—from pain relievers to fried chicken—is claimed to be better than its competitor's. If all these
deductive generaliza- tions	companies sued for libel, the courts would be so overloaded with cases that they would grind to a halt. For years courts dismissed criticisms of businesses, products, and performances as expressions of opinion.
specific instance to be explained using the generaliza- tions	When a restaurant owner sued a guidebook to New York restaurants for giving his establishment a bad review, he won a $20,000 verdict in compensatory damages and $5 in punitive damages. But this was overturned by the court of appeals. The court held that, with the exception of one item, the allegedly libelous statements were expressions of opinion, not

fact. Among these statements were that the "dumplings, on our visit, resembled bad ravioli . . . chicken with chili was rubbery and the rice . . . totally insipid . . . ." Obviously, it would be impossible to prove the nature of the food served at that particular meal. What is tender to one palate may be rubbery to another. The one misstatement of fact, that the Peking duck was served in one dish instead of three, was in my opinion, a minor and insignificant part of the entire review. Had the review of the restaurant been considered as a whole . . . , this small misstatement of fact would have been treated as *de minimis*. That is a well established doctrine requiring that minor matters not be considered by the courts. In this case, the court held that the restaurant was a public figure and had failed to prove actual malice.

—Lois G. Forer, *A Chilling Effect: The Mounting Threat of Libel and Invasion of Privacy Actions to the First Amendment*

WHY USE INDUCTION AND DEDUCTION?

One useful way to think of induction and deduction is as a way of arriving at a generalization (induction) and of applying a generalization as an explanatory strategy. Once you start thinking of the patterns this way, you can develop questions to help you decide when to employ them in your writing. You might ask, for example, "Why should I lead readers through the process of arriving at a generalization when I could simply announce it at the beginning of an essay and then provide examples, comparisons, and other kinds of evidence to explain the generalization and show how reasonable it is?" One answer is that you employ deduction whenever the process of arriving at a generalization is as important as the conclusion itself. For example, in explaining a particular kind of childhood behavior, you may also wish to model for readers a way of drawing conclusions about such behavior.

Another occasion when induction is an appropriate pattern of explanation is when the evidence leading to your conclusion is quite complicated or your conclusion is unusual or surprising. In such cases, readers may be more likely to understand and agree with your conclusion if you lead them through the process of reasoning. Inductive reasoning is also appropriate when you want to create tension or drama by building toward your conclusion or when you want to arrive at it by considering and rejecting other explanations until you arrive at a satisfactory one.

Before employing deduction as an explanatory strategy, you might ask, "How will my readers benefit if I use deductive reasoning to guide my explanation?" The importance of deductive reasoning as an explanatory pattern lies in the careful logic (and hence reliability) it can lend to conclusions. Put in simplified form (which, in writing, it seldom is), the deductive process is also called a "syllogism"—with the beginning generality known as the "major premise" and the specific that fits into the generality known as the "minor premise." For example:

> *Major premise*—orange-colored food is not fit to eat.
> *Minor premise*—Pumpkin pie is orange-colored.
> *Conclusion*—Pumpkin pie is not fit to eat.

As this example makes clear, however, deductive reasoning can be only as reliable as the original generalizations that were used as deductive premises. If the generalizations themselves were based on flimsy or insufficient evidence, any future deduction using them is likely to be erroneous.

Working together, induction and deduction can be good strategies for exploring an unfamiliar or complicated topic. Inductive reasoning can suggest a generalization about the topic; deductive reasoning can use the generalization to explore and explain whatever details, applications, and consequences call for understanding.

CHOOSING A STRATEGY

The organization of writing employing induction, deduction, or both generally parallels the process of reasoning. The following example may perhaps make this clear. Suppose that after a careful process of reasoning, you concluded that you family's dog treats you and other family members as if they were part of her own dog pack. This would be a somewhat startling conclusion for many readers, so to help make your explanation convincing, you might wish to follow an inductive-deductive pattern.

> *Tentative thesis* (to be presented in full at the end of the essay): My family's dog treats my parents and my siblings as if we were all members of the same pack of dogs.
> *Inductive Explanation*: Dogs behave in ways that surprise humans.
> 　　1. They often try to sleep with their owners or members of the family. Dogs in packs like to sleep together.

2. Dogs often like to carry around bits of smelly clothing (ugh!) from their owners or family members. Dogs in packs recognize and relate to each other through scent.
3. Dogs often choose one family member as most important and others as less so. Dog packs are strictly hierarchical; a dog is content when he or she can recognize the "Alpha" dog and his or her own place in the pack.
    4, 5, 6 . . .

Inductive Generalization: Dogs relate to humans in ways similar to the ways they relate to other dogs in a pack.

Deductive Explanation: Much of my dog's behavior can be explained by considering my family as her pack.

1. Every time one of the family sits down, our female beagle comes over and falls asleep on one of our feet. She's "cuddling" with us and feeling comfortable when she is literally "in touch" with her pack.
2. I have lots of single socks; the dog has the other ones which she chews, then "lovingly" drapes over her head or muzzle when she falls asleep in her bed. My dog isn't trying to be a pest or to cause me trouble. She's "complimenting" me by letting me know that my scent is an important element in her life.
3. My mother says that even though she feeds and walks the dog, our beagle still thinks my father and my brothers are the most important people in the house. Beagles aren't politically correct; the lead dog is still generally a male, even if the "dog" walks on two legs.
    4, 5, 6 . . .

One particularly effective and familiar pattern of induction in writing is the "process of elimination." If it can be shown, for instance, that "A" does not have the strength to swing the murder weapon, that "B" was in a drunken sleep at the time of the crime, and that "C" had recently become blind and could not have found her way to the boathouse, then we may be ready for the inductive leap—that the foul deed must have been committed by "X," the only other person on the island. This organization can help you explain to readers why a particular explanation or interpretation of a subject is the only reasonable one.

Details of the subject to be explained.
Explanation 1
    Strengths and weaknesses

Explanation 2
>   Strengths and weaknesses

Explanation 3
>   Strengths and weaknesses

4, 5 . . .

Deductive Generalization
>   This explanation is the only one with significant strengths and few significant weaknesses. It is probably the most accurate one.

DEVELOPING INDUCTION AND DEDUCTION

To develop an explanation using induction and deduction, you need to pay attention to the logic of your reasoning. These two faults are common in induction: (1) the use of *flimsy* evidence— mere opinion, hearsay, or analogy, none of which can support a valid generalization—instead of verified facts or opinions of reliable authorities; and (2) the use of *too little* evidence, leading to a premature inductive leap. The amount of evidence needed in any situation depends, of course, on purpose and audience. The success of two Central College graduates might be enough to convince some careless personnel director that all Central College electronics graduates would be good employees, but two laboratory tests would not convince medical researchers that they had learned anything worthwhile about a disease-causing virus.

Deductive reasoning can fall victim to questionable premises or any of a number of flaws in logic (see Chapter 13, p. 584). Induction and deduction are highly logical processes, and any trace of weakness can seriously undermine an exposition that depends on their reasonableness. Although no induction or deduction ever reaches absolute, 100 percent certainty, we should try to get from these methods as high a degree of *probability* as possible.

Student Essay

In the following essay, Sheilagh Brady shows how an essay can use induction and deduction to organize a complicated explanation in a way readers will consider clear and easy to understand. She takes readers through the history of MADD, leading up to some of its key positions, then explores the positions in detail.

Mad about MADD
Sheilagh Brady

background   On May 3, 1980, Cari Lightner was walking through a suburban neighborhood on her
way to a church carnival in Fair Oaks,
California, when she was killed by a hit-
and-run drunk driver. The driver was
Clarence Busch, forty-six years old with
four prior arrests for drunk driving.
Busch had just been released on bail for a
hit-and-run drunk-driving charge a week
before.

Cari's mother, Candy Lightner, was
thirty-three at the time, a divorced
mother of two other children working as a
real estate agent. She was told by two police officers investigating the accident
that Busch would probably receive little
jail time, if any, because "'That's the
way the system works'" (Lightner and
Hathaway 224).

Faced with these circumstances, many of
us might have concluded that the only possible responses were despair and frus-
trated rage. Candy Lightner reached
another conclusion. Mulling over the police officers' words during dinner the
same night, Lightner conceived of the or-
events in the   ganization that eventually became MADD,
history of   Mothers Against Drunk Driving. She felt
MADD and its   the need to do something to take away her
efforts lead   pain. MADD became a way for her to use her
up to the   anger and to come to terms with the death
inductive   of her daughter. For the next five years,
conclusion   Lightner devoted her time and effort to
the creation of MADD.

Lightner moved to Dallas, Texas, the
eventual headquarters of MADD, to begin
working on organizing the new group. In

March, 1983, NBC aired a documentary,
"Mothers Against Drunk Driving: The Candy
Lightner Story." According to James B.
Jacobs, MADD chapters doubled across the
United States by 1985, and in the same
year *Time* magazine reported that there
were 320 chapters nationwide, and 600,000
volunteers and donors (Otto 41).

MADD's response to drunk driving has
been to emphasize jail sentences and legislation. MADD members get angry when people feel "that a killer drunk driver
deserves a lesser penalty than other homi-
cidal offenders" (Jacobs). MADD has been
successful in focusing public attention on
the problems associated with drinking and
driving and mobilizing legal changes to
create stiffer penalties for drunk driving. MADD aims to have these stiffer
penalties made mandatory and plea bargaining abolished (Voas and Lacey 126-127).

Not only has MADD focused public attention but it has also had considerable effect on local, state, and federal
governments. In 1988, S. Ungerleider and
S.A. Bloch did an evaluation of MADD which
has been summarized as concluding that
MADD was "more successful in state legislatures where a large number of laws were
enacted in an effort to produce more severe sanctions for the drunk driving offense" (Voas and Lacey 137).

Yet according to Dave Russel, a member
of the Rhode Island Chapter of MADD, the
past few years have been difficult. During
the 1980s legislation was passed quickly
because of the sudden public support
through pressure groups concerned about
drinking and driving. Since then, the

progress of drunk-driving legislation has
slowed considerably. Russel says that the
number of deaths per year has steadily decreased since 1980 but that alcohol related accidents still take close to 19,000
lives each year. As a response to this
situation, MADD chapters nationally have
concluded that there is still a need for
more drunk-driving legislation, even if
legislators do not see it.

**inductive
generalization**

Having reached this conclusion, MADD
chapters nationwide have decided to submit
three different bills annually to their
state legislatures. Some states have
turned these bills into laws, but many
have not. Just what are these MADD chapters proposing? Are the laws they want enacted reasonable or unreasonable?

**first
deductive
explanation**

One bill aims to reduce the BAC (Blood
Alcohol Content) level from .10 to .08 as
the legal limit of intoxication. In 1988
in a report focusing on BAC levels, researchers Moskowitz and Robinson found
that although theoretically impairment begins with the first drink, significant impairment occurs in most people at .05 BAC
or lower. At the Surgeon General's
Workshop, December 14–16, 1988, C. Everett
Koop called for lowering the BAC limit in
all states to .08, as did the National
Highway Transportation Safety
Administration in reports sent to the
United States Congress. According to MADD
national office, lowering the BAC level to
.09 will reduce drunk driving by making it
more likely that drunk drivers will be
caught, and also acting to discourage driving under the influence. If research evidence and reliable authorities suggest

reducing the BAC level from .10 to .08
will save lives, then most of us are
likely to conclude that the legislative
proposal seems reasonable.

**second
deductive
explanation**

Another bill is the ALR Bill or the
Administrative License Revocation. This
law would eliminate the period between the
arrest of a drunk driver and the hearing
suspending the license. Right now, in many
states, that period is supposed to be
around thirty days, but inevitably becomes
much longer, a delay which allows the
drunk driver to continue driving for that
much longer legally under a valid license.
The ALR would be a process that would allow the police officer to take the drunk
driver's license if there is a refusal to
take the breathalyzer test. In return, the
driver would be given a temporary permit,
good for ten to fifteen days, following an
appearance at a hearing. If the driver
does not appear for the hearing or cannot
provide reasonable evidence for refusing
the test, the license is suspended. In the
case of a "no show," the driver must appear
later to answer to the charge against him
or her, but what is important is that the
license will have already been suspended.

The Administrative License Revocation
was recommended by the Presidential
Commission on Drunk Driving which developed the National Commission Against Drunk
Driving. According to several researchers,
"administrative revocation has widespread
support among researchers, highway safety
experts, and the public in general because
it has been shown to be an effective administrative action that protects innocent
drivers" in an experiment conducted in

California, Washington, and Minnesota
(Peck, Sadler, and Perrine). Most of us
would probably conclude that ALR is a reasonable procedure, yet seventeen states
have not yet turned the ALR bill into a
law.

**third
deductive
explanation**

   Last, MADD chapters propose annually an
Open Container Law requiring that open
containers of alcohol not be allowed in
the passenger compartments of vehicles.
According to MADD's national chapter, it
is fundamental to separate drinking and
driving because this separation is essential to the public interest and to the
public's understanding of the crisis created by drunk driving. MADD argues that
banning open containers of alcoholic bev-
erages in a vehicle is one way to make
sure drivers do not start drinking while
driving or to become even more intoxicated
while driving. Moskowitz and Robinson, in
*Effects of Low Doses of Alcohol on Driving
Skills,* report that drinking while driving
is dangerous because ingesting even a
small amount of alcohol begins the impairment process. For most of us, the Open
Container Law probably also seems quite
reasonable.

   Even though the bills proposed by MADD
chapters are likely to seem reasonable to
most people, many states have not turned
them into laws. At the same time, the combination of alcohol and driving remains a
problem. 19,000 deaths per year may be
lower than in previous years, but this is
still too many avoidable tragedies. One
appropriate response is for each of us to
become involved in working for a solution.
If MADD's three proposals seem reasonable

to you, if they are not yet law in your
state, and if you want these policies in
place to protect you, your family, and
your friends, call your local MADD chapter
and ask what you can do to help.

Works Cited

Lightner, Candy and Nancy Hathaway. "The
Other Side of Sorrow." *Ladies Home
Journal* Sept. 1990: 158.

Jacobs, James B. *Drunk Driving: An
American Dilemma.* Chicago: U of Chicago
P, 1989.

Moskowitz, H. and Robinson, C.D. *Effects
of Low Doses of Alcohol on Driving
Skills.* Washington: National Highway
Traffic Safety Administration, 1988.

Otto, Freidrich. "Seven Who Succeeded."
Time 7 Jan. 1985: 40.

Peck, Raymond C., Sadler, D.D., and
Perrine, M.W. "The Comparative
Effectiveness of Alcohol Rehabilitation
and Licensing Control Actions for Drunk
Driving Offenders: A Review of the
Literature." *Alcohol, Drugs and Driving:
Abstracts and Reviews* 1 (1985): 15–39.

Russel, Dave. Personal Interview. 19 Nov.
1993.

Voas, Robert B. and John H. Lacey. "Drunk
Driving Enforcement Adjudication, and
Sanctions in the United States;"
*Drinking and Driving: Advances in
Research and Prevention.* Ed. Robert E.
Mann and R. Jean Wilson. New York:
Guilford, 1990. pp. 130–145.

WENDY KAMINER

WENDY KAMINER is a public-policy fellow at Radcliffe College, and she is president of the National Coalition Against Censorship. She is also a contributing editor of the *Atlantic* magazine. Her books include *I'm Dysfunctional, You're Dysfunctional: The Recovery Movement and Other Self-Help Fashions* (1992); *It's All the Rage: Crime and Culture* (1995); and *True Love Waits* (1992), a collection of essays.

A Civic Duty to Annoy

In this essay, first published in the *Atlantic*, Kaminer presents a number of experiences from which she draws an inductive generalization (presented in the form of questions) and then goes on to explain this generalization and how it might be applied to our daily lives.

What is there about being in a room filled with people who   1
agree with me that makes me want to change my mind? Maybe it's the self-congratulatory air of consensus among people who consider themselves and one another right-thinking. Maybe it's the consistency of belief that devolves into mere conformity. Maybe it's just that I can no longer bear to hear the word "empower."

At self-consciously feminist gatherings I feel at home in the worst   2
way. I feel the way I do at family dinners, when I want to put my feet up on the table and say something to provoke old Uncle George. To get George going, I defend affirmative action or the capital-gains tax. To irritate my more orthodox feminist colleagues, I disavow any personal guilt about being born white and middle-class. I scoff every time I hear a Harvard student complain that she's oppressed.

I'm not alone in my irreverence, but feminist pieties combined   3
with feminine courtesy keep most of us in line. Radcliffe College, where I am based, is devoted to nurturing female undergraduates. We're supposed to nod sympathetically, in solidarity, when a student speaks of feeling silenced or invisible because she is female, of color, or both. We're not supposed to point out that Harvard students are among the most privileged people in the universe, regardless of race or sex.

I don't mean to scoff at the discrimination that a young woman   4
of any color may have experienced or is likely to experience someday.

I do want to remind her that as a student at Harvard/Radcliffe or any other elite university she enjoys many more advantages than a working-class white male attending a community college. And the kind of discrimination that students are apt to encounter at Harvard—relatively subtle and occasional—is not "oppression." It does not systematically deprive people of basic civil rights and liberties and is not generally sanctioned by the administration.

Besides, everyone is bound to feel silenced, invisible, or unappreciated at least once in a while. Imagine how a white male middle manager feels when he's about to be downsized. Like laments about dysfunctional families, complaints about oppression lose their power when proffered so promiscuously. Melodramatic complaints about oppression at Harvard are in part developmental: students in their late teens and early twenties are apt to place themselves at the center of the universe. But their extreme sensitivity reflects frequently criticized cultural trends as well. An obsession with identity and self-esteem has encouraged students to assume that every insult or slight is motivated by racist, sexist, or heterosexist bias and gravely threatens their well-being. What's lost is a sense of perspective. If attending Harvard is oppression, what was slavery? 5

Sometimes nurturing students means challenging their complaints instead of satisfying their demands for sympathy. I've heard female students declare that any male classmate who makes derogatory remarks about women online or over the telephone is guilty of sexual harassment and should be punished. What are we teaching them if we agree? That they aren't strong enough to withstand a few puerile sexist jokes that may not even be directed at them? That their male classmates don't have the right to make statements that some women deem offensive? There would be no feminist movement if women never dared to give offense. 6

When nurturing devolves into pandering, feminism gives way to femininity. Recently a small group of female students called for disciplinary proceedings against males wearing "pornographic" T-shirts in a dining hall. They found it difficult to eat lunch in the presence of such unwholesome, sexist images. Should we encourage these young women to believe that they're fragile creatures, with particularly delicate digestive systems? Should we offer them official protection from T-shirts? Or should we point out that a group of pro-choice students might someday wear shirts emblazoned with words or images that pro-life students find deeply disturbing? Should we teach them that the art of giving and taking offense is an art of citizenship in a free society? 7

That is not a feminine art. Radcliffe, for example, is an unfail- 8
ingly polite institution. Criticism and dissatisfaction are apt to be expressed in a feminine mode, covertly or indirectly. It's particularly
hard for many of us not to react with great solicitude to a student
who declares herself marginalized, demeaned, or oppressed, even if
we harbor doubts about her claim. If she seeks virtue in oppression,
as so many do, we seek it in maternalism.

We tend to forget that criticism sometimes expresses greater re- 9
spect than praise. It is surely more of an honor than flattery. You
challenge a student because you consider her capable of learning.
You question her premises because you think she's game enough to re-
examine them. You do need to take the measure of her self-confidence,
and your own. Teaching—or nurturing—requires that you gain students' trust and then risk having them not like you.

Sometimes withholding sympathy feels mean, insensitive, and 10
uncaring; you acquire all the adjectives that aren't supposed to attach to women. You take on the stereotypically masculine vices at a
time when the feminine virtue of niceness is being revived: Rosie
O'Donnell is the model talk-show host, civility the reigning civic
virtue, and communitarianism the paradigmatic political theory.
Communities are exalted, as if the typical community were composed solely of people who shared and cared about one another and
never engaged in conflict.

In fact communities are built on compromise, and compromise 11
presupposes disagreement. Tolerance presupposes the existence of
people and ideas you don't like. It prevails upon you to forswear
censoring others but not yourself. One test of tolerance is provocation. When you sit down to dinner with your disagreeable relations,
or comrades who bask in their rectitude and compassion, you have a
civic duty to annoy them.

Meanings and Values

1. Explain the point that Kaminer is trying to make when she asks in the
   opening of the essay, "What is there about being in a room filled with
   people who agree with me that makes me want to change my mind?"
   Does her essay answer this question? Why, or why not?

2. Why does Kaminer "scoff" (par. 2) when she ". . . hear[s] a Harvard
   student complain that she's oppressed . . ." (par. 2)?

3. What display of feminism does Kaminer question in her essay? How
   does she react to women who are easily offended by derogatory

remarks (par. 6) or "pornographic T-shirts" (par. 7)? Please explain your answer.

EXPOSITORY TECHNIQUES

1.   Kaminer's essay addressed two topics: one mentioned in the introduction and conclusion and one focused on in the body of the essay. Identify the two topics. How are they connected? Is there an inductive or deductive mechanism that is used to link the ideas? If so, how does it work?

2.   Identify the concrete examples in Kaminer's essay. (See "Guide to Terms": *Concrete/Abstract*.) How successful are they at illustrating her point? (Guide: *Evaluation*.)

3.   What is Kaminer's tone in this essay? (Guide: *Tone*.) Could she have used the same tone if she were a male author? Be ready to explain your response.

DICTION AND VOCABULARY

1.   Kaminer uses many interrogative sentences in her essay. What is the desired effect of these questions? Can they be considered rhetorical questions? (Guide: *Rhetorical Questions*.) Why, or why not? Would the essay have been better if she had answered all of the questions? If she had phrased them as declaratives instead?

2.   Look up any of the following words with which you are unfamiliar: disavow (par. 2), irreverence (par. 3); pieties (3); puerile (6); and solicitude (8).

READ TO WRITE

1.   **Collaborating:** A "room filled with people who agree with me" is a common and comfortable place for many of us to be. Working in a group, list social events that you have attended where people all tend to be in agreement. Compare your lists. Are your social events and the subjects upon which people agree similar to those of your teammates? Individually write a short analysis essay of your findings.

2.   **Considering Audience:** Kaminer may potentially offend some of her feminist colleagues with the examples that she uses in this essay. Does this serve to illustrate the point that she had made in the introduction and conclusion sections of the essay? How might male readers react to Kaminer's work? Think of two examples that could be added to her essay to make her male audience potentially as uncomfortable as some of her female readers. Incorporate your examples into Kaminer's essay using appropriate transitions.

3.   **Developing an Essay:** List several groups of people whom you know whose members tend to agree with each other. (You might consider

people in your major, your family, teammates in a sport, or the like.) Write an essay similar to Kaminer's which identifies the areas on which these people agree and present in the form of examples what you would do to fulfill your "civic duty" as Kaminer defines it.

(NOTE: Essays requiring development by means of INDUCTION and DEDUCTION are on p. 576 at the end of this chapter.)

NANCY FRIDAY

NANCY FRIDAY is the author of numerous books, including *My Mother, My Self: The Daughter's Search for Identity* (1977); *My Secret Garden: Women's Sexual Fantasies* (1988); *Jealousy* (1997); and *Our Looks, Our Lives: Sex, Beauty, Power, and the Need to Be Seen* (1999).

The Age of Beauty

In "The Age of Beauty," first published in the *New York Times Magazine*, Friday uses induction and deduction to explain a parallel process of personal discovery and change. Her effective use of the pattern illustrates its versatility.

I had stood, all eagerness and impatience, while my sister's old   1
evening dress was pinned on me before that fateful dance at the yacht club. I didn't even know enough to look critically at the mirror and see that the strapless gown didn't suit me, especially after the dark brown velvet straps had been added to keep the dress up on my flat chest. I placed no value on looks. Having not had this rite of passage explained to me, I hadn't a clue that beauty was *the* prerequisite to adolescent stardom. Certainly, this new longing for boys had made me awkward in their presence; but I had noticed that they were awkward, too. Accustomed to being chosen first for any team of girls, I didn't question success that night, couldn't remember failure, so carefully had I buried nursery angers under trophies of recent accomplishments. I'm sure I was prepared to solve any hesitancy the boys might have in approaching us girls by taking the initiative myself. Assuming responsibility was who I was. In recent years my life had been a great adventure, in which there had been no comparisons made to my mother and sister. In my mind, they were boring in their tedious arguing over my sister's looks and her evenings with boys.

That night at the yacht club marked the end of childhood, the   2
finish of that adventure story with me as heroine. In one momentous night I took it all in and made my concession speech to myself. I watched my friends, whose leader I had been for years, watched them happy in the arms of desirable boys, and I recognized what they had that I lacked; saw it so clearly that I can recreate the film today, frame by frame: they had a look I lacked that went beyond

beauty. It wasn't curls, breasts, prettiness, but a quality of acquiescence: the agreeable offer to be led instead of to lead. My own face was too eager, too open, too sure of itself. I needed a mask. I needed a new face that belied the intelligent leader inside and portrayed the little girl, no, the tiny, helpless baby who hadn't been held enough in the first years of life and had been waiting all these years for boys now to care for her.

I stood in my horrible dress, shoulder blades pressing into the 3 wall, watching my dear friends dance by in the arms of handsome boys, with a frozen, ghastly smile on my face, denying I needed to be rescued. Why, even the girl who couldn't hit a ball danced by. Though they all whispered for me to hide in the ladies' room, I stood my ground.

Miserable as I was, I recognized the work ahead: the girl I had 4 invented, so full of words waiting to be spoken and skills to be mastered, she had to be pushed down like an ugly jack-in-the-box. No boy was going to take a package like me.

A part of me was filled with rage at having to abandon what I 5 thought to be a fine person. But I had no voice for rage. I belonged to a family of women who wept, and by not weeping I had made myself different from my mother and sister. But that night I became a woman; I wept and wept after someone's father drove me home while the rest of my group went off to a late party with boys. I showed my grief but not my rage. I did what most women still do: I swallowed anger, choked on it. I bowed my head, in part to be shorter, but also, like a cornered cow, to signal I had given up.

By morning I had buried and mourned my 11-year-old self, the 6 leader, the actress, the tree climber, and had become an ardent beauty student. From now on I would ape my beautiful friends, smile the group smile, walk the group walk and, what with hanging my head and bending my knees, approximate as best I could the group look.

I have a photograph of myself taken in our yard on what looks 7 like The First Day of Adolescence. I am sitting in a white wicker chair, hunched forward, staring at the ground, hands tightly clasped in my lap, swathed in the loser's agony of defeat. I remember the box camera aimed at me and that awful skirt and sweater, which had been my sister's—as had the awful dress at the yacht club, fine for a beauty but oh, so wrong for the tomboy I had been.

Twenty years later, I would go through countless hours of 8 physical therapy to realign my spine, which has never recovered from the bent-leg posture I mastered in learning the art of being less.

Neither professional success, great friendships nor the love of men could recapture the self-confidence, the inner vision and, yes, the kindness of generosity I owned before I lost myself in the external mirrors of adolescence.

MEANINGS AND VALUES

1. In paragraph 2, Friday says, "That night at the yacht club marked the end of childhood, the finish of that adventure story with me as the heroine." Explain the significance of that one evening. What did it symbolize for Friday? (See "Guide to Terms": *Symbol*.)

2. What does Friday mean when she says "It wasn't curls, breast, prettiness, but a quality of acquiescence: the agreeable offer to be led instead of to lead" (par. 2)? How is Friday defining the "role" of a successful woman from her adolescent perspective?

3. Why did Friday have to undergo physical therapy for her spine (par. 8)? What is the significance of this reference as the conclusion of her essay?

EXPOSITORY TECHNIQUES

1. What inductive generalizations does the adolescent Friday make? Does the author still regard that generalization as valid? Why, or why not?

2. Throughout the essay, the author uses masculine imagery to describe her youthful self i.e. "adventure story" (par. 2), ". . . the girl who couldn't hit a ball" (par. 3), "the loser's agony of defeat" (par. 7). Why might she have used such masculine and athletic references?

3. What is the tone of Friday's essay? (Guide: *Tone*.) Is it successful in supporting the inductive pattern that she presents?

DICTION AND VOCABULARY

1. Look up any of the following words with which you may be unfamiliar: tedious (par. 1); acquiescence (2); ardent (6); and swathed (7).

READ TO WRITE

1. **Collaborating:** In a group, share stories from your adolescence that had a particular impact on the way that you defined yourself. Do group members share any similar experiences? Write a collaborative essay using one of those similar experiences as a basis for an inductive essay.

2. **Considering Audience:** Most women who read this essay would have some understanding of Friday's experiences. The image of the dress, the moving from "tomboy" to adolescent "girl," and the effort to "fit" are somewhat universal examples for young women. What images might be universal for men? Think of experiences that young boys have that mark their adolescence. Write an essay similar to Friday's looking at some adult male behaviors that may be outcomes of adolescent experiences. You may have to do some research in the form of interviews.

3. **Developing an Essay:** Think of something physical or emotional that is part of your adult character and that developed as a result of adolescent experiences. Write an essay incorporating an inductive generalization like Friday's to help your reader understand the impact of adolescence on your life.

(NOTE: Essays requiring development by means of INDUCTION and DEDUCTION are on p. 576 at the end of this chapter.)

Issues and Ideas

Digital Realities

- Maia Szalavitz, *A Virtual Life*
- J. C. Herz, *Superhero Sushi*
- Nicholas Negroponte, *A Place Without Space*

To some people, computers may be simply one more appliance whose effects on daily life seem to be minimal. However, the number of people who can avoid working on computers seems to be shrinking, just as computer influence seems to be growing. Computers, the software they run, and their many networked connections, change the way we run our lives. They alter the time we need to spend at a task, the kind of tasks we can undertake, and our creative abilities. They alter our schedules, our places of work and play, and maybe even our friendships and personal relationships.

In very specific ways computers alter our concepts of time and space, of work and leisure, and of ourselves and others. We can say that computers create new realities for us, digital realities. The essays that follow use inductive and deductive reasoning to explore these digital realities. Maia Szalavitz in "A Virtual Life," considers her experiences as a computer user, sums them up, and then reviews her experiences to see if her perceptions and values have indeed changed as much as she suspects. J. C. Herz, in "Superhero Sushi," shows how cultures blend in remarkable ways once they are drawn into cyberspace. Nicholas Negroponte, in "Place without Space," discusses some of the changes in thinking and relationships that computers make possible and considers some of their possible consequences. Both authors are a bit tentative in their conclusions because new digital realities may emerge in just a few years.

MAIA SZALAVITZ

Maia Szalavitz, formerly a television producer, now spends her time as a writer. She lives in New York City and is working on a book about drug policy.

A Virtual Life

In this essay from *The New York Times Magazine,* Szalavitz uses induction and deduction to explore digital reality and its consequences. Along the way, she compares the digital world to the "real" world, acknowledging the attractions of the electronic dimension.

After too long on the Net, even a phone call can be a shock. My 1 boyfriend's Liverpudlian accent suddenly becomes indecipherable after the clarity of his words on screen; a secretary's clipped tonality seems more rejecting than I'd imagined it would be. Time itself becomes fluid—hours become minutes, and alternately seconds stretch into days. Weekends, once a highlight of my week, are now just two ordinary days.

For the last three years, since I stopped working as a producer 2 for Charlie Rose, I have done much of my work as a telecommuter. I submit articles and edit them via E-mail and communicate with colleagues on Internet mailing lists. My boyfriend lives in England, so much of our relationship is also computer-mediated.

If I desired, I could stay inside for weeks without wanting any- 3 thing. I can order food, and manage my money, love and work. In fact, at times I have spent as long as three weeks alone at home, going out only to get mail and buy newspapers and groceries. I watched most of the blizzard of '96 on TV.

But after a while, life itself begins to feel unreal. I start to feel as 4 though I've merged with my machines, taking data in, spitting them back out, just another node on the Net. Others on line report the same symptoms. We start to feel an aversion to outside forms of socializing. It's like attending an A.A. meeting in a bar with everyone holding a half-sipped drink. We have become the Net naysayers' worst nightmare.

What first seemed like a luxury, crawling from bed to com-   5
puter, not worrying about hair, and clothes and face, has become an
evasion, a lack of discipline. And once you start replacing real human contact with cyber-interaction, coming back out of the cave can
be quite difficult.

I find myself shyer, more circumspect, more anxious. Or, con-   6
versely, when suddenly confronted with real live humans, I get
manic, speak too much, interrupt. I constantly worry if I'm dressed
appropriately, that perhaps I've actually forgotten to put on leggings
and walked outside in the T-shirt and underwear I sleep and live in.

At times, I turn on the television and just leave it to chatter in the   7
background, something that I'd never done previously. The voices of
the programs soothe me, but then I'm jarred by the commercials. I
find myself sucked in by soap operas, or compulsively needing
to keep up with the latest news and the weather. "Dateline,"
"Frontline," "Nightline," CNN, New York 1, every possible angle of
every story over and over and over, even when they are of no possible use to me. Work moves from foreground to background. I decide
to check my E-mail.

On line, I find myself attacking everyone in sight. I am irritable,   8
and easily angered. I find everyone on my mailing list insensitive,
believing that they've forgotten that there are people actually reading their invective. I don't realize that I'm projecting until after I've
been embarrassed by someone who politely points out that I've
flamed her for agreeing with me.

When I'm in this state, I fight with my boyfriend as well, misin-   9
terpreting his intentions because of the lack of emotional cues given
by our typed dialogue. The fight takes hours, because the system
keeps crashing. I say a line, then he does, then crash! And yet we
keep on, doggedly.

I'd never realized how important daily routine is: dressing for   10
work, sleeping normal hours. I'd never thought I relied so much on
co-workers for company. I began to understand why long-term unemployment can be so insidious, why life without an externally supported daily plan can lead to higher rates of substance abuse, crime,
suicide.

To counteract my life, I forced myself back into the real world. I   11
call people, set up social engagements with the few remaining friends
who haven't fled New York City. I try to at least get to the gym, so as
to differentiate the weekend from the rest of my week. I arrange interviews for stories, doctor's appointments—anything to get me out of
the house and connected with others.

But sometimes, just one engagement is too much. I meet a 12
friend and her ripple of laughter is intolerable—the hum of conversation in the restaurant, overwhelming. I make my excuses and flee.
I re-enter my apartment and run to the computer as though it were a
sanctuary.

I click on the modem, the once-grating sound of the connection 13
now as pleasant as my favorite tune. I enter my password. The real
world disappears.

MEANINGS AND VALUES

1. What is the inductive generalization the author arrives at after
   spending "too long on the Net" (par. 1)? Where does she state it?

2. In which paragraphs does she apply this generalization in a deductive manner?

3. Explain the meaning of the following phrases: "I've flamed her for
   agreeing with me" (par. 8); "just another node on the Net" (4); and
   "The fight takes hours, because the system keeps crashing"(9).

EXPOSITORY TECHNIQUES

1. How does the essay's conclusion re-enforce the inductive generalization arrived at earlier in the essay? What strategy does the writer employ to conclude the essay? (See "Guide to Terms": *Closings.*)

2. What do the beginning sentences of paragraphs 6–13 have in common in terms of wording or structure? (Guide: *Syntax.*) In what ways
   are these similarities related to the inductive generalization? Discuss
   how they help create coherence in the essay. (Guide: *Coherence.*)

3. Discuss the use of parallelism to provide emphasis in the sentences in
   paragraphs 3 and 11. (Guide: *Parallel Structure.*)

DICTION AND VOCABULARY

1. Discuss the essay's use of computer terminology and slang used by
   people familiar with computers. Does this add to or detract from most
   readers' understanding of the essay? How would the essay be different if the terminology and slang were not used? (Guide: *Colloquial
   Expressions.*)

2. If you do not know the meaning of some of the following words, look
   them up in a dictionary: mediated (par. 2); aversion (4); evasion, cy-
   ber (5); circumspect, manic (6); invective (8); doggedly (9); insidious
   (10); counteract (11).

READ TO WRITE

1. **Collaborating:** Freewrite about your computer experiences or about typical behaviors of computer users that you have observed. Compare your freewrite with other members of a group. As a team, focus on one or two particularly interesting areas, examples, or topics that you have in common. Develop these areas into passages that might be collected for a collaborative essay.

2. **Considering Audience:** By 1996, most readers would have experienced the on-line environment to which Szalavitz refers in her essay. Most readers, therefore, would understand her references to the "virtual life." List other mechanical/technical devices that have removed people from human contact in past generations. Choose one with which you are familiar and write an essay similar to Szalavitz's, making an inductive generalization about the consequences of this other device.

3. **Developing an Essay:** Draw on Szalavitz's comparisons of the digital and the physical world in order to develop further comparisons in an essay of your own.

(NOTE: Suggestions for essays requiring development by INDUCTION and DEDUCTION are on p. 576 at the end of this chapter.)

J. C. HERZ

J. C. HERZ was a graduate student at Harvard University when she set out to explore the world of video games. Her reports on this virtual world have appeared in numerous magazines and in two books, *Surfing on the Internet* (1995) and *Joystick Nation: How Videogames Ate Our Quarters, Won Our Hearts, and Rewired Our Minds* (1997).

Superhero Sushi

For J. C. Herz, induction and deduction serve to explain the complicated mixture of American and Japanese characteristics and cultures that appear in the figures of video game heroes. The essay is a detailed and sometimes disturbing (though entertaining) exploration of the worlds of virtual reality and their complex relationships to everyday life. This essay first appeared in *Joystick Nation*.

A fter walloping her opponent, *Tekken 2*'s heroine, Michelle   1
Chang, swivels within the videogame arena and turns to face the camera, the viewer, the players. And it's a disconcerting moment, because she looks at you intelligently, and there are so many polygons in her face that she almost seems real, and because she is such a confusing mix of signals. She's a slender girl who beats up rippling hypermasculine bruisers. She's computer generated, yet more true-to-life than most of the silicon-enhanced, digitally retouched dreamgirls staring vacantly out from real world magazine racks. She's got an Asian name but ambiguous features—a Western nose, almond-shaped eyes. If you saw her on the street, you'd peg her as Amerasian.

In a way, she is a perfect metaphor for videogames themselves.   2
She's a hybrid, of mixed Asian and American heritage, a creature made possible by the technological innovation of two hemispheres. Videogame characters are a bicontinental crossbreed of American and Japanese pop culture, with elements of Japanese comic books (manga) and animation as well as Western comics and science fiction.

On the Pacific side, videogames' family resemblance to manga   3
and Japanimation are undeniable. In some cases, the games themselves are playable translations of popular Japanese comic books and animated films. In the last decade, hundreds of manga titles have been made into videogames in Japan, crossing over into the

United States as manga shifts from cult status to mass acceptance, mostly via MTV. *Dragonball* alone has spawned six arcade games, a dozen titles for the Super Famicon (the Japanese equivalent of the Super NES), and a *Dragonball* Game Boy cartridge.

The salient feature of manga heroes—and the game characters based on them—is a preternatural cuteness and almost freakish babylike quality, which takes the form of oversized heads, tiny noses, and saucerlike, impossibly liquid eyes. This way of drawing characters translated easily into early videogames, which didn't have the graphic resolution to represent characters with adult proportions. Small, cute characters had fewer pixels per inch and were easier to use, and so videogames borrowed, for reasons of expediency, what manga had developed as a matter of convention. Even a character like Mario the Plumber, who's supposed to be an adult, with facial hair no less, is rendered with the roly-poly proportions of a child, like a manga character. You would expect characters to take on mature dimensions as technology enables videogame manufacturers to animate large, complex, realistic forms. But instead, companies like Sega hew even closer to the babyland aesthetic. To paraphrase Gordon Gekko in *Wall Street,* cuteness is good. Cuteness works. 4

The reason cuteness works, as Scott McCloud notes in *Understanding Comics,*[1] is that abstraction fosters identification. It is only because an animated character is abstract and cartoony that we can project our own expressions onto him. We can't really map ourselves onto truly realistic characters—we see them as objects, separated from us by their details. To use an annoying but useful postmodern term, they read as the Other. The most realistically rendered characters in videogames are usually enemies. The good guys are rounded, simplified, and childlike, a puttylike visual glove into which our own hands and faces fit. If anything, early videogames were especially powerful in this sense. The more photorealistic characters become, the less we relate to them. Seeing a cast of TV actors in a full-motion video makes you into more of a spectator or an editor than a part of the story, whereas the polygon people in *Tekken 2* are easy to slide into, and a character like Mario or Sonic is even easier to identify with. A primitive, completely minimal figure like Pac-Man takes this link between pixel and personality to the nth degree. Characters in *Mortal Kombat* have fingers and stubble. You watch them. Pac-Man has one black dot for an eye, and you *become* him. 5

[1]Scott McCloud, *Understanding Comics: The Invisible Art* (New York: HarperCollins, 1993).

Videogame companies are well aware of this, which is why   6
their figureheads are all round and minimal and cute, just like, well,
jeepers, just like Mickey Mouse. Sega is even working on a version
of *Virtua Fighter 2* called *Virtua Fighter Kizu* ("kizu" is Japlish for
"kids") where all the adult martial arts characters are rendered with
gigantic toddler heads. From a distance, it looks like ferocious duel-
ing lollipops. If you count the height of their hair, the giant toddlers'
heads are as tall as the rest of their bodies. The eyes are bigger than
their flying fists.

Americans usually read these saucer eyes as Western, as a sign   7
of whiteness. After all, the reasoning goes, Western eyes are bigger
and rounder than Asian eyes. This must be the way that they see us.
And for some strange reason, they're drawing us all over their comic
books. But actually, that's not the case, says Matt Thorn, a doctoral
candidate at Columbia University who is writing his dissertation on
teen-girl comic books in Japan. "Japanese readers don't think of the
characters as white," he says. "Of course, they have these huge eyes.
And so to us, the characters do look white, because Westerners expect that the Japanese will represent themselves the way that
Westerners represent them. That is, we have these certain standardized ways of indicating to a viewer this character is Asian or this
character is black or this character is anything but white, including
the slanty eyes and the black hair. And of course, the Japanese don't
draw themselves that way. Those characters aren't white, and the
readers don't think of them as being white, despite those features.
There's a concept in linguistics called the unmarked category. And
in the West, which is white-dominated, white is the unmarked category. Everything else is marked and has to be indicated, but white is
taken for granted. But in Japan, Japanese is the unmarked category,
the one that's taken for granted. They've developed that style with
the huge eyes—that's the way that they've developed for drawing
people, which means Japanese people. And when they want to indicate that a character is not Japanese, they have different ways of doing it. Like, for white people and black people they use exaggerated
features. Like for white people, they'll have big noses or really big
bodies or really sharply defined eyelashes."

So within a typical martial arts videogame, the racial contin-   8
uum is deceptive. It's not a simple matter of ethnic blur. It's a matter
of reading the signs in completely different ways. All the indetermi-
nate characters that to Western eyes would read as white look
Japanese to kids playing the games in Tokyo. Figuratively speaking,
we read these faces left to right. The Japanese read them up and

down. This isn't their way of drawing us. It's their way of drawing themselves. Meanwhile, both sets of videogame players look at the screen and think the characters look native. It's counterintuitive. But when you think about it, really, *no one* has eyes that big.

There are characters in videogames that are visibly Asian, the   9
way Westerners would draw Asians. But these characters are never supposed to be from Japan. They are supposed to be from China or Korea or Mongolia or some other part of Asia. "The irony," says Thorn, "is that the techniques that Westerners use to draw Asians are the same techniques the Japanese use when they're drawing Asians other than themselves. So you'll have a manga in which there are Japanese characters, which to us read as white. And then you'll have a Chinese character, and the Chinese character is drawn in such a way as to indicate to players that this character is not Japanese but Chinese. And they'll use the same kinds of techniques that we use: the straight black hair, the slanty eyes, etc."

And Americans? Usually, when a videogame character hails   10
from the United States, he's blond. He's broad. He's buff. And he's larger than life, or at least larger than the other videogame characters. He looks more like an American comic book character than a manga hero. And he's not nearly as unassuming and cute. In fact, the more videogames borrow from American comic books, the less cute they get. Whereas Japanese manga characters are generally childlike and unassuming, American cartoon heroes in the Marvel/DC vein are, if anything, hyperadult. "In America," writes comic book historian Fred Schodt, "almost every comic book hero is a 'superhero' with bulging biceps (or breasts, as the case may be), a face and physique that rigidly adhere to the classical traditions, invincibly accompanied by superpowers, and a cloying, moralistic personality."[2] Like the drawings in a Western superhero comic, American characters in Japanese fighting games have wildly distorted, hyperrealistic, hypersexual bodies. And in American software houses, where Superman takes native precedence over Speed Racer and Astro Boy, the videogames themselves are absolutely devoid of blinking sweetness, offering instead the beloved stateside menagerie of larger-than-life comic book mutants. Capcom's *Marvel Superheroes* arcade cabinet, which is seven feet tall and physically towers over its Japanese counterparts, pumps out sound effects at blockbuster volume and stars veiny, spandex-clad standbys like the Incredible Hulk, Spiderman,

[2]Frederik Schodt, *Manga Manga: The World of Japanese Comics* (Tokyo: Kodansha, 1983) 77, 78.

and Captain America. The arcade game is, essentially, a moving comic book that replaces Pow! Boom! Zap! bubbles with gut-rattling audio effects. In this way, a Marvel Comics videogame is a more intense comic book experience than the paper it's based on. Comic book characters have always been drawn swooping and swinging and flying through the air. Now they can do it in real time. Comic book videogames are comic books squared. And with this added dimension the blurry line between comic books and videogames finally dissolves.

This blur between media is epitomized by *Comix Zone,* a   11
videogame for the Sega Saturn. The premise, whose only precedent is Swedish pop group A-Ha's *Take On Me* video, is that your character, Sketch, is trapped in a Marvelesque comic book universe and forced to battle through it, panel by panel, combating enemies drawn by Mortus, an evil comic book artist. Along the way, helper characters yell out from the corner of the screen ("Watch out, Sketch!") in comic book dialogue boxes. The object, ultimately, is to defeat the evil illustrator and rip yourself out of his two-dimensional paper universe. It's like an Escher drawing, where you break out of one trompe l'oeil tableau only to find yourself in another impossible illusion. Beyond the simulated comic book page is a simulated TV cartoon, when, really, there aren't any pages, or any television, for that matter. There are only the conventions of paper and television, twined around each other, to float the action of a videogame.

Of course, to kids playing *Comix Zone* or *Marvel Superheroes* or   12
Tekken 2, the distinction between comic book and videogame or Asian and Western is completely irrelevant. The only categories they recognize are "fun" and "not fun." If you walk into an arcade, you don't see white kids choosing white characters and black kids choosing black characters. Kids routinely choose any and all of these options and don't think twice about it, because the only factor in their decision is a given character's repertoire of kick-ass fighting moves. Ironically, all considerations of race, sex, and nationality are shunted aside in the videogame arena, where the only goal is to clobber everyone indiscriminately.

But on a deeper level, the kids playing these games intuitively   13
understand that they're operating in a disembodied environment where your virtual skin doesn't have to match your physical one, and that you can be an Okinawan karate expert, a female Thai kickboxer, a black street fighter from the Bronx, or a six-armed alien from outer space, all within the span of a single game. Members of

the previous generation might have a problem with the idea of playing a Japanese schoolgirl in a combat game. At the very least, they would be aware of their decision to choose this character, and maybe even a little smug about being enlightened enough to do so. For kids of the eighties and nineties, shuffling videogame bodies and faces is like playing with a remote control. The game starts, cycles through a bunch of avatars, and you punch the fire button when you see one you like. It's channel surfing.

In this milieu, the classic distinctions between heroes and villains break down. In older videogames, and in all previous media, the good guys look one way and the bad guys look another. It may be as simple as black hats and white hats or as fraught as cowboys and Indians. In movies and TV shows, we know what the hero and the villain are supposed to look like, and those images are very loaded. Heroes talk like midwestern news anchors and own dogs. Bad guys speak with foreign accents and stroke cats. Heroines are slender and blond and adorably helpless. Bad girls have dark hair and red nails and hips and guns they're ready to use. And because of the way these people look, and the way they're lit, it's clear for whom you're supposed to root.   14

But in an arcade fighting game like *Virtua Fighter 2*, you can't do that, because those categories don't exist at all. You can play any character, and it's every gladiator for himself. This type of videogame doesn't label opposing forces as evil or good, because that would imply a scripted outcome, that the designated "hero" is supposed to win, when really no one is supposed to win. Everyone is supposed to play. It's the skill of the competitors that determines who wins and who loses. In a videogame, unlike in novels or movies or other fictions like history, no one—not even the game designer—knows the outcome of a given contest. And so it's impossible to cast a moral hair light on one character versus another.[3] There are no heroes and villains in a round-robin martial arts game. There are only combatants, each with his or her own special weapons, attributes, and fighting style. In the post-Cold War world, this seems an evenhanded approach. Everyone's a hero. Everyone is also a monster.   15

Or, to paraphrase the Red Dog beer motto, you are your own monster. Now that the videogame hero is freed from the cosmetic   16

---

[3]This becomes patently obvious when you play a game like *Tekken 2*, where even the more wholesome characters are monstrously broad-shouldered, earnest, square-jawed, and monumental in the style of socialist realism. This is when you realize that monstrosity is in the eye of the beholder. This is also when you realize that most of the superheroes we hold up for children to admire are freaks.

constraints of gallant poster boyhood, you can play a whole menagerie of creatures, from werewolves to ice creatures to dinosaurs. Superhuman strength and/or demonic powers seem to be the only prerequisites for inclusion in the videogame bestiary, which draws from martial arts movies, Arthurian legend, the Greek pantheon, science fiction, Norse mythology, and Jurassic Park. And that's just *Primal Rage*, one of the hotter fighting games of 1996.

Primal Rage is mythic stuff. It's a fight-to-the-death among angry, violent demigods who are also dinosaurs. According to the epic back story, "Before there were humans, gods walked the earth. They embodied the essence of Hunger, Survival, Life, Death, Insanity, Decay, Good, and Evil. They fought countless battles up through the Mesozoic Wars." When these conflicts threatened to destroy the planet, a wiser, more mature deity in another dimension decided to launch a kind of mythological NATO peacekeeping mission to shut them up. "He was not powerful enough to kill the gods," the story goes, "so instead he banished one to a rocky tomb within the moon. This disrupted the fragile balance between the gods; pandemonium ensued, and a great explosion threw clouds of volcanic dust into the atmosphere. The dinosaurs died out, and the surviving gods went into suspended animation. Now, the impact of a huge meteor strikes the Earth. Its destructive force wipes out civilization, rearranges the continents, and frees the imprisoned gods. Get ready to rumble . . ."   17

The game ensues, throwing you into a kind of fossil fantasy Ragnarok scenario where you choose one of these reptilian gods to fight against all the others. Each of them has its own repertoire of decay-related weapons, most of which involve bodily functions. The God of Survival is a crafty velociraptor lacking in brute strength but incredibly agile and slippery.   18

In addition to its personal eccentricities, each character also has a coordinated epic backdrop. The fire-breathing Tyrannosaurus rex dukes it out in the Inferno, an active volcanic island oozing lava. The serpentine Goddess of Insanity fights on a Stonehengian knoll under a full moon with petrified enemies planted like lawn sculptures in the background. And, if you make it through all these themed battlegrounds, the final scene of *Primal Rage* is set in a dinosaur graveyard littered with the bones of fallen reptiles. Red cracks split the ground, and a huge vortex swirls in the sky as you leap, bite, and strike as best you can against a very scary-looking, dragonish God of Death. It's a perfect frappé of paleontology and the supernatural, prehistory and the apocalypse. Like the science fiction universe, videogames are where technology melts into the occult. This is a place where missile   19 launchers and mojo are both legitimate weapons. All the old monsters, harpies, dragons, and divinities are excavated from their mythological sediment, sampled, looped, remixed, cross-faded, and digitally recycled. Videogames do to dusty legends what deejays do to vintage vinyl. They weave the old grooves into something accessible to teenagers.

And increasingly, it doesn't matter where those teenagers are.   20
The same way a transcendent house mix leaps from a mixing board in London to sound systems in Tokyo, Los Angeles, and Helsinki, good videogames have a way of becoming popular everywhere. It's all digital. And a certain echelon of global youth all have access to the technology. So if it's fun, it quickly goes transnational. And in the process, it ceases to connote nationality. A successful dance track or videogame doesn't read Japanese or American, German, or British. It's all just pop. And it's yours for fifty cents.

The finest digital architects on the planet have built these play-   21
grounds out of comic books, Hong Kong cinema, scroll paintings and music videos, ancient monsters and digital technology. They pour in their myths and suck out quarters.

And this is what it's about, finally, as the cultural streams of   22
East and West swirl into the Tastee-Freez of global entertainment. Mythic figures resonate, all the more if they're engaged in some kind of combat or action adventure, real or simulated, the most popular forms being basketball and video games. They resonate for the same reasons mythic figures have always resonated. Only now, the audience numbers in the millions, and the object is not to celebrate ancestors or teach lessons or curry favor with the spirits. It's commerce. And the people transmitting their stories to the next generation aren't priests or poets or medicine women. They're multinational corporations. And they are not trying to appease the gods. They are trying to appease the shareholders. It's not just videogames. It's everything, with the possible exception of the Internet. All the mythic pop stars in Hollywood, the NBA, and MTV are purchasable commodities. Videogames are just the logical extreme, because all the superheroes in them are computer generated for maximum resonance and marketing kick. Unlike sports stars or actors, they don't get addicted, arrested, or petulant. They perform. They may look and act superhuman. They may throw lightning or breathe fire. And when you're in the game, they may really inspire or scare you. But unlike the mythic monsters that preceded them, videogame demons are caged in their arcade cabinets, firmly under the control of their corporate wardens. Demigods used to make people docile. Now it's the

other way around. It is Sega and Namco and Capcom and Williams Entertainment, finally, that have tamed the dragons.

MEANINGS AND VALUES

1. Explain the significance of the title of the essay. How does it connect to Herz's message?

2. Why does Herz open with a description of a female, Japanese video character? What is significant about this character as opposed to other characters that Herz might have chosen to use in an introduction?

3. What is the significance of paragraph 4? Does technology control other images that we see? Can it define or create stereotypes? Please explain.

4. In the first section of this essay (par. 1–11), Herz explains the different images of heroes from different nations. But in paragraph 12, she makes a clear shift into limiting the importance of gender, race, and nationality. What is the significance of this shift?

EXPOSITORY TECHNIQUES

1. Herz repeatedly uses comparison and contrast in this essay. Identify the different things that she compares. How successful is this technique for a reader who may have limited knowledge of video games?

2. What is the thesis of this essay? (See "Guide to Terms": *Thesis*.) What type of reasoning (inductive, deductive, or a combination of both) does Herz employ to clarify and support the thesis?

3. Herz uses the second person (you) at various points in the essay. How effective is this? Why might she have chosen that technique in that places that she did?

DICTION AND VOCABULARY

1. Identify slang and jargon in "Superhero Sushi." (Guide: *Slang.*) Is the use of such language excessive? Could a person unfamiliar with video games and the language associated with them understand the essay? Please explain.

2. To what age group(s) is this essay targeted? Explain how Herz's language helps to define the age of her intended audience.

READ TO WRITE

1. **Collaborating:** List as many video game characters as you can think of and identify their race, gender, nationality, or species (if appropriate).

Working with a group, compare your lists. Write a plan for an essay analyzing the various trends in video game characters.

2. **Considering Audience:** This essay clearly will be more easily understood by readers who have played video games or at least observed others play them. Using Herz's thesis as the basis for an essay, write a similar piece for an audience that might be less familiar with such technology.

3. **Developing an Essay:** Choose two or three virtual characters with which you are familiar then go to a local arcade and study the newest games. Write an essay similar to Herz's which uses these characters collectively as a basis for an inductive generalization about the latest trends in video game characters.

(NOTE: Essays requiring development by use of INDUCTION and DEDUCTION are on p. 576 at the end of this chapter.)

NICHOLAS NEGROPONTE

NICHOLAS NEGROPONTE teaches at the Massachusetts Institute of Technology where he is Professor of Media Technology and Founding Director of the Media Lab. He is the author of *Being Digital* (1995).

Place Without Space

In this selection from *Being Digital*, Negroponte uses deductive reasoning to speculate about the effects of electronic technology on our lives. While we cannot predict the future with any certainty, by applying a deductive generalization to real and possible circumstances, we can arrive at some idea of what *might be*, just as Negroponte does in this selection.

In the same ways that hypertext removes the limitations of the printed page, the post-information age will remove the limitations of geography. Digital living will include less and less dependence upon being in a specific place at a specific time, and the transmission of place itself will start to become possible.

If I really could look out the electronic window of my living room in Boston and see the Alps, hear the cowbells, and smell the (digital) manure in summer, in a way I am very much in Switzerland. If instead of going to work by driving my atoms into town, I log into my office and do my work electronically, exactly where is my workplace?

In the future, we will have the telecommunications and virtual reality technologies for a doctor in Houston to perform a delicate operation on a patient in Alaska. In the nearer term, however, a brain surgeon will need to be in the same operating theater at the same time as the brain; many activities, like those of so-called knowledge workers, are not as dependent on time and place and will be decoupled from geography much sooner.

Today, writers and money managers find it practicable and far more appealing to be in the Caribbean or South Pacific while preparing their manuscripts or managing their funds. However, in some countries, like Japan, it will take longer to move away from space and time dependence, because the native culture fights the trend. (For example: one of the main reasons that Japan does not move to daylight savings time in the summer is because going home "after dark" is considered necessary, and workers try not to arrive after or go home before their bosses.)

In the post-information age, since you may live and work at one or many locations, the concept of an "address" now takes on new meaning. 5

When you have an account with America Online, CompuServe, or Prodigy, you know your e-mail address, but you do not know where it physically exists. In the case of America Online, your Internet address is your ID followed by @aol.com—usable anywhere in the world. Not only do you not know where @aol.com is, whosoever sends a message to that address has no idea of where either it or you might be. The address becomes much more like a Social Security number than a street coordinate. It is a virtual address. 6

In my case, I happen to know where my address, @hq.media.mit.edu, is physically located. It is a ten-year-old HP Unix machine in a closet near my office. But when people send me messages they are sending them to me, not to that closet. They might infer I am in Boston (which is usually not the case). In fact, I am usually in a different time zone, so not only space but time is shifted as well. 7

MEANINGS AND VALUES

1. Where does Negroponte announce his deductive generalization, and what is it?

2. To what situations, real or imagined, does Negroponte apply the generalization? Be specific. What conclusions does he draw from the application of the generalization? Which of his predictions seem most probable to you, and why? Which seem less likely? Why?

3. Are there ways we can judge the quality of reasoning in an essay that looks toward the future? If so, what are they? (Use examples from this selection in answering this question.) If not, how can we evaluate an essay like this? (See "Guide to Terms": *Evaluation*.)

EXPOSITORY TECHNIQUES

1. What patterns other than deduction does Negroponte use in this selection? Where does he employ them and for what purposes?

2. Is paragraph 5 simply a transition between other paragraphs, or does it constitute another deductive generalization? Why? (Guide: *Transition*.) If it is another generalization, does it disrupt the unity of the writing? (Guide: *Unity*.)

DICTION AND VOCABULARY

1. Discuss how Negroponte uses pairs of terms like physical and virtual to designate different kinds of reality. Identify any other pairs of terms he uses in the essay and discuss their use.

2. If you do not know the meaning of some of the following terms, look them up in a dictionary: hypertext, digital (par. 1); narrowcasting (2); extrapolation, demographic (3); correlation (4); infinitesimal (5); idiosyncrasies (6); Chardonnay (7). (Note: you may have to consult a dictionary of computer terms for some of these words.)

READ TO WRITE

1. **Collaborating:** Think of the different "places" you can go with a computer. Working in a group, freewrite about the different kinds of reality you can encounter and share your freewriting with the rest of the group. From your group discussion, develop a focus for an essay and prepare a plan for it.

2. **Considering Audience:** The year is 2010. Using Negroponte's discussion as a model, try to predict some other future possibilities in the "post-information" or "digital" world. Write an essay similar to Negroponte's for the 2010 audience.

3. **Developing an Essay:** Use the uncoupling of places and times that Negroponte observes as a key idea for an essay of your own about future possiblities.

(NOTE: Suggestions for essays requiring development by INDUCTION and DEDUCTION follow.)

Writing Suggestions for Chapter 12

INDUCTION AND DEDUCTION

Choose one of the following unformed topics and shape your central theme from it. This could express the view you prefer or an opposing view. Develop your composition primarily by use of induction, alone or in combination with deduction. Unless otherwise directed by your instructor, be completely objective and limit yourself to exposition, rather than engaging in argumentation.

1. Little League baseball (or the activities of 4-H clubs, Boy Scouts, Girl Scouts, etc.) as a molder of character.
2. Conformity as an expression of insecurity.
3. Pop music as a mirror of contemporary values.
4. The status symbol as a motivator to success.
5. The liberal arts curriculum and its relevance to success in a career.
6. Student opinion as the guide to better educational institutions.
7. The role of public figures (including politicians, movie stars, and business people) in shaping attitudes and fashions.
8. The values of education, beyond dollars and cents.
9. Knowledge and its relation to wisdom.
10. The right of individuals to select the laws they obey.
11. Television commercials as a molder of morals.
12. The "other" side of one ecological problem.
13. The value of complete freedom from worry.
14. Homosexuality as in-born or as voluntary behavior.
15. Raising mentally challenged children at home.
16. Fashionable clothing as an expression of power (or a means of attaining status).

COLLABORATIVE EXERCISE

Using #3, 5, or 10 from the Writing Suggestions list above, have each member of your group team write an inductive generalization for the topic. Then as a group, create a plan for a unified essay which presents one of the inductive generalizations.

13

Using Patterns for *Argument*

Argument and exposition have many things in common. They both use the basic patterns of exposition; they share a concern for the audience; and they often deal with similar subjects, including social trends (changing social relationships, the growth of the animal rights movement), recent developments (the creation of new strains of plants through genetic manipulation, developments in health care), and issues of widespread concern (the quality of education, the effects of pollution). As a result, the study of argument is a logical companion to the study of exposition. Yet the two kinds of writing have very different purposes.

Expository writing shares information and ideas; it explores issues and explains problems. Argumentative writing has a different motivation. It asks readers to choose one side of an issue or take a particular action, whether it is to choose a career, vote for a candidate, or build a new highway. In exposition we select facts and ideas to give a clear, interesting, and thorough picture of a subject. In argument we select facts and ideas that provide strong support for our point of view and arrange this evidence in the most logical and persuasive order, taking care to provide appropriate background information and to acknowledge and refute opposing points of view.

The evidence we choose for an argument is determined to a great extent by the attitudes and needs of the people we are trying to persuade. For example, suppose you want to argue successfully for a new approach to secondary education in your community—an approach that enrolls students in "mini-schools" according to their interests. Your essay would need to provide enough examples, facts, and reasons to convince parents and community leaders that the approach would be best for *their* children, not just for children in general. You would need to show that the community could afford the approach and that the benefits would justify the added expense. To be effective, moreover, your essay would also need to answer possible objections to the proposal and demonstrate that it is preferable to other approaches a reasonable school board and community might consider.

Your argumentative writing needs to focus on your thesis: the opinion you wish readers to share, the action you want them to undertake, or the assertion you wish them to endorse. The twin poles of argumentative writing—your thesis and the needs and values of your readers—need to be linked by evidence and reasoning. Evidence and reasoning extend your thesis to readers, and they bring readers closer to it.

WHY USE ARGUMENT?

Argumentative writing responds to situations in which there are two or more conflicting points of view. An argument attempts to resolve or at least modify disagreements by encouraging people to agree upon an action or a point of view. You can recognize an argumentative thesis and an argumentative essay by the writer's evident awareness of opposing perspectives. When readers are likely to require good reasons before they will agree with your thesis or when they are likely to resist your point of view, your situation is one that calls for argumentative writing.

In addition, a simple argumentative essay can serve one of three purposes. Some essays ask readers to agree with a *value judgment* ("The present day care system is inadequate and inefficient"). Others propose a *specific action* ("Money from the student activity fee at this college should be used to establish and staff a fitness program available to all students"). And still others advance an *opinion* quite different from that held by most people ("The supposed "revolution" of Internet shopping is no more than the logical next step in catalog retailing").

In situations calling for more complex arguments, however, you should feel free to combine these purposes as long as the relationship among them is made clear to the reader. In a complex argument, for instance, you might *first* show that the city government is inefficient and corrupt and *then* argue that it is better to change the city charter to eliminate the opportunities for the abuse of power than it is to try to vote a new party into office or to support a reform faction within the existing political machine.

Some people draw a distinction between situations calling for *logical argument* (usually called, simply, *argument*) and *persuasive ar-*

gument (usually termed *persuasion*). Whereas logical argument appeals to reason, persuasive argument appeals to the emotions. The aim of both, however, is to convince, and they are nearly always blended into whatever mixture seems most likely to do the convincing. After all, reason and emotion are both important human elements. The two often work together, with reason helping to change minds and emotion helping to prompt action.

CHOOSING A STRATEGY

Argument begins with an issue, moves to a thesis (or assertion) addressing the issue, and concludes with evidence and reasoning to convince readers and deal with opposing perspectives. This is an admittedly oversimplified view of the components of an argument (and the process of composing), yet it serves to point out that choosing strategies for an argumentative essay calls for a number of different activities.

First, you need to *identify an issue* that you can effectively address through argument. Without an issue—a difference in point of view— you have nothing to argue about. Some issues will take a clear shape before you begin writing: matters of social justice, environmental regulation, civil and criminal law, education, community relationships, and the like are filled with familiar and significant matters of disagreement and difference. In preparing to address such an issue, you need to make sure that you understand them well enough to present them in clearly defined form to readers and to provide appropriate background. You should be ready to stress the significance of an issue, and the need to make a judgment or take an action.

Some familiar issues have been argued so often that readers are not likely to be receptive to further argument; others are matters of taste that are beyond argument. For instance, no amount of reasoning is likely to convince people who dislike action movies to begin enjoying them. And some issues involve matters of deeply held religious or ethical beliefs that are difficult, if not impossible to address through logical argument.

Many issues will take a clear shape only when you think and write about them, however. Perhaps you have been irritated for some time by the concert arrangements at a local civic center, and you believe other people share your irritation. Your irritation is not itself an issue, but it can point to one. If you propose changing the arrangements, and you realize that your proposals are not the only ones that ought to be considered, then you have begun to shape an issue. As you write, you need to be ready to explain the issue to your readers, perhaps drawing on their own irritation with the arrangements to stress the importance of considering changes. Of course, when an issue takes shape in your writing, the opposing points of view are probably not well developed, if at all. For instance, you may not be aware of any alternate concert arrangements that other people have proposed, but you can probably think of some plausible alternatives to your own. In exploring them for readers, however, you identify the opposing points of view that create the issue.

Next, you need to *articulate your stance*. At the heart of an argumentative essay is the opinion you want readers to share or the action you are proposing they undertake. Being able to state this *thesis* (or *proposition*) concisely and clearly to yourself is essential to developing your strategy for an argumentative essay. Conveying your thesis in convincing form is, after all, the main purpose of the essay. Expressing your stance concisely and clearly in a *thesis statement* is perhaps the best way to alert readers to the point of your argument.

Some writers like to arrive at a sharply focused thesis statement early in the process of composing and use it to guide the selection and arrangement of evidence, for example,

> The inconvenience and discontent that accompanies concerts at the Civic Center can be greatly reduced by moving the box office further away from the main entrance doors, doubling the number of restrooms, improving the lighting, and removing the temporary seating that partially obstructs the central aisles.

Other writers settle on a tentative ("working") thesis which they revise as an essay takes shape. In either case, checking frequently to see that factual evidence and supporting ideas or arguments are clearly linked to the thesis is a good way for writers to make sure their finished essays are coherent, unified arguments.

Finally, you need to develop evidence and reasoning that supports your thesis and arrange it in ways that readers will consider clear and convincing. Variety in evidence gives writers a chance to present an argument fully and persuasively. Examples, facts and figures, statements from authorities, personal experience, or the experience of other people—all these can be valuable sources of support. The basic patterns of exposition, too, can be supporting strategies. For example, to persuade people to take driving lessons at an automobile racing school, you might tell the story of someone whose life was saved through the evasive maneuver she learned in her first day at such a school. Or you might follow this narrative example with a classification of the most common kinds of accidents, comparing them, in turn, with the parallel kinds of safety lessons the schools provide.

The expository patterns can also be easily adapted to argumentative purposes. Writers frequently turn to example, comparison and contrast, cause and effect, definition, and induction or deduction to organize arguments. A series of *examples* can be an effective way of showing that a government social policy does not work and in fact hurts the people it is supposed to serve. *Cause and effect* can organize an argument over who is to blame for a problem or over the possible consequences of a new program. *Comparison and contrast* can guide choices among competing products, among ways of disposing toxic waste, or among ways of revising student loan policies. *Definition* is helpful when a controversy hinges on the interpretation of a key term or when the meaning of an important word is itself the subject of disagreement. *Induction* and *deduction* are useful in argument because they provide the kind of careful, logical reasoning necessary to convince many readers, especially those who may at first have little sympathy for the writer's opinion.

An argument need not be restricted to a single pattern. The choice of a pattern or a combination of patterns depends on the subject, the specific purpose, and the kinds of evidence needed to convince the audience to which the essay is directed. Some arguments about complicated, significant issues use so many patterns that they can be called *complex arguments.*

In arranging your evidence and reasoning, you should also consider the potential impact on readers. Three common and effective arrangements from which you can choose are ascending order, refutation-proof, and pro-con. In *ascending order,* the strongest, most complex, or most emotionally moving evidence comes last, where it can build on the rest of the evidence in the essay and is likely to have the greatest impact on readers, as in the following example.

> Introduction: The issue—some people are trying to have genetically altered farm products banned while others are arguing for an increase in the number of such products.
>
> Tentative thesis: Despite a few drawbacks, genetically altered farm products are a great benefit to us all.
>
> Support 1: The regulations governing genetic alteration and extensive testing means the products are generally quite safe; problems have been minor and worries have not been warranted by experience.

Support 2: Genetic alteration can create crops that are less resistant to disease and that are easier to cook and digest.

Support 3: Genetic alteration can make farms more productive and in so doing lower food costs, make more food available, and help fight undernourishment throughout the world [strongest, most moving support; even if there are some problems, these benefits may outweigh them].

Conclusion: Sums up, restates, and reinforces the thesis and the evidence.

In *refutation-proof*, the writer acknowledges opposing points of view early in the essay and then goes on to show why the author's outlook is superior.

Tentative thesis: Genetically altered farm products benefit farmers and consumers.

Opposing Points of View: genetically engineered products are often less tasty and less nutritious; they can have unintended health consequences for farmers and consumers.

Refutation: the products can be engineered to be both tasty and nutritious—the choice is up to the producers and consumers; all natural products can have unintended consequences, and we forget this when dealing with "scientific products"; more extensive testing can help us deal with any unfortunate consequences.

Support 1: Genetically altered products can be more disease and pest-resistant, reducing the dangers of exposure to pesticides and other chemicals.

Support 2: Genetically altered products provide greater variety for consumers and choices for farmers looking for products appropriate for their soil and climate.

Support 3, 4, 5 . . .

Conclusion

A *pro-con* arrangement allows the writer to present an opposing point of view and then refute it, continuing until all opposition has been dealt with and all positive arguments voiced. This strategy is particularly useful when there is a strong opposition to the writer's thesis.

Tentative thesis: The benefits of genetically altered farm products far outweigh the liabilities.

Con 1: The engineered products may end up replacing "natural" ones.

Pro 1: Some "natural" products may be less common, but the success of organic and other specialty products indicates that there will be a demand for both "new" and "natural" foods.

Con 2: Genetically altered products are often designed for the needs of large corporate farms and will contribute to the demise of smaller, family farms.

Pro 2: The shift to larger farms and agribusinesses has been occurring for many reasons other than genetic engineering of crops; the new crops will have only a small effect, if any.

Con 3, 4, 5 . . .

Pro 3, 4, 5 . . .

Conclusion

DEVELOPING ARGUMENTS

In developing an argument, you need to pay attention to your choice of evidence and to make sure your reasoning is clear and logical. It is never possible to arrive at absolute proof—argument, after all, assumes that there are at least two sides to the matter under discussion— yet a carefully constructed case will convince many readers.

One way to construct arguments is to follow the pattern of *data-warrant-claim reasoning* as outlined by the philosopher Stephen Toulmin. *Data* corresponds to your evidence and *claim* to your thesis or assertion. *Warrant* refers to the mental process by which a reader connects the data to the claim. To argue effectively, you need to show your readers how the warrant connects the data to your claim, as in the following sequence.

Data: Children's books are relatively expensive, generally costing between ten and thirty dollars.

Warrant: Buying children a variety of books can be very expensive.

Warrant: Children learn to love books and by reading; playing with books on a regular basis is something that also helps them become good readers.

Warrant: Children get easily bored with a book, so they need a variety of books to keep them occupied—though the book that bores them today will interest them tomorrow and the day after.

Claim: The high cost of children's books keeps many children from learning to love books and becoming better readers

At the same time, a flaw in logic can undermine an otherwise reasonable argument and destroy a reader's confidence in its conclusions. The introduction to Chapter 12, "Reasoning by Use of *Induction* and *Deduction*," discusses some important errors to avoid in reasoning or in choosing evidence. Here are some others:

Post hoc ergo propter hoc ("After this therefore because of this")—Just because one thing happened *after* does not mean that the first event caused the second. In arguing without detailed supporting evidence that a recent drop in the crime rate is the result of a newly instituted anticrime policy, a writer might be committing this error, because there are other equally plausible explanations: a drop in the unemployment rate, for example, or a reduction in the number of people in the fifteen to twenty-five age bracket, the segment of the population that is responsible for a high proportion of all crimes.

Begging the question—A writer "begs the question" when he or she assumes the truth of something that is still to be proven. An argument that begins this way, "The recent, unjustified rise in utility rates should be reversed by the state legislature," assumes that the rise is "unjustified," though this important point needs to be proven.

Ignoring the question—A writer may "ignore the question" by shifting attention away from the issue at hand to some loosely related or even irrelevant matter: for example, "Senator Jones's plan for encouraging new industries cannot be any good because in the past he has opposed tax cuts for corporations" (this approach shifts attention away from the merits of Senator Jones's proposal). A related problem is the *ad hominem* (toward the person) argument, which substitutes personal attack for a discussion of the issue in question.

Student Essay

In recent years, many new foods have been developed, including some that are substitutes for "natural foods." The development of these products has gone hand-in-hand with growing controversies over their safety, with most people willing to at least listen to the criticisms on the grounds that food safety is one of the most important public health issues all of us face. In the face of such controversy, Julie Richardson sets out to defend an "artificial" food, olestra, in her essay, "The Fight on Fat Controversy."

background

importance of topic for readers

information about specific issue/ disagreement

"confusion" suggests potential disagreements

The Fight on Fat Controversy

Today, Americans are realizing the importance of a healthy lifestyle, which includes exercising and following a balanced diet. Reducing fat in the diet decreases the risk of health problems such as heart disease and obesity and is a vital step in achieving an improved lifestyle. Food manufacturers are responding to the consumer's needs by adding more reduced-fat foods to product lines. A trip down the grocery aisle is evidence of the increased "better-for-you" products, tempting the consumer with less salt, less sugar, sugarless, lower fat, and non-fat items.

After nine years of research, the U.S. Food & Drug Administration approved a fat-free cooking oil known as olestra to be used in frying savory snacks. Olestra has been hailed as a breakthrough solution for millions of Americans who are looking to reduce fat and calories from the foods they want to eat without sacrificing the quality of taste. Excitement, curiosity, and confusion have followed the new lineup of products made with olestra. This new discovery is slowly, yet dramatically changing food processing; and consumers need to educate themselves on the facts surrounding this innovative alternative to fat.

Olestra, marketed by Procter & Gamble as Olean®, is made from vegetable oil and

sugar, then used in place of regular cooking oils or fats. This revolutionary fat
substitute does not break down like other
fats; instead, it passes through the stomach and intestines without being digested
or absorbed by the body. As a result,
olestra provides all the taste of vegetable
oil; but none of the calories or harmful
saturated fats of regular vegetable oils.
The results are snacks that taste great
with no fat and half of the calories.

**concise
statement of
issue**

Heralded as a waistline-whittling savior
by millions of consumers; olestra has been
condemned by others as nutritional sabo-
teur with distressing gastrointestinal
side effects. The Center for Science in
the Public Interest, (CSPI) believes there
are serious health risks when products
made with olestra are consumed. This nonprofit health group believes the FDA
should ban olestra or, at the very least,
require a prominent warning label on the
front of packages stating that olestra can
cause severe side effects. Currently there
is only a small warning on the back of
packaging, warning consumers that they
could experience soft stools when consuming olestra.

**arguments
against the
product**

**more
arguments
against**

Challengers of olestra also advocate
that the body is robbed of vitamins or
carotenoids (found in fresh fruits and
vegetables) that have already been digested. Michael Jacobson, Executive
Director of CSPI reveals that carotenoids
protect against chronic diseases. Jacobson
also states that long-term use of olestra
in snack foods is likely to cause thousands of cases of cancer and heart disease
each year. Opponents of olestra believe

additional research should be completed to ensure the protection of consumers' health.

arguments and evidence for the product— refuting opponents of olestra

Proponents of olestra, including Procter & Gamble and the FDA, are quick to point out the fallacy of olestra "robbing" the body of vitamins and carotenoids that have already been digested, as Jacobson implies. Olestra can only interact with vitamins or carotenoids that are in the digestive system at the exact same time as the olestra; and even then, the level of interaction has not been outside the acceptable range. Results from the FDA Advisory Committee Review in June, 1998 determined there is no direct evidence that carotenoids are responsible for lower risk of disease, which disproves Jacobson's theory that carotenoids protect against chronic diseases. These results also show the absurdity of Jacobson's claim that long term use of olestra causes cancer.

Frito-Lay has been allowed to fortify their WOW! Chips with extra vitamins to insure there is no net loss or reduction in vitamin levels due to normal absorption. However, the FDA is preventing Frito-Lay from adding extra carotenoids to their WOW! Chips because the jury in the scientific community is still out as to whether or not carotenoids are actually good or bad. In a study conducted in Sweden, a compelling argument raises the possibility of carotenoids actually causing cancer.

admits to some validity in worries about the product

Michael Jacobson's research is anecdotal and unscientific. Most of his research is obtained through questionnaires completed on the CSPI website, not in a laboratory

direct refutation of major objections supported by statistics and authoritative testimony

by scientists. In contrast, P&G has spent 25 years and $200 million researching olestra, in one of the most comprehensive reviews of any food additive in history. The FDA received 150,000 pages of data from studies of 8,000 adults and children. Results from a follow-up study were reviewed in June, 1998 by a FDA panel of leading health, medical and nutrition experts who overwhelmingly reaffirmed the safety of Olean®. The committee also discussed the possibility of removing or rewording the warning label on Frito-Lay's WOW! Chips.

agrees with objections to packaging of product

Another issue of concern with olestra rivals is the labeling of 'fat-free' on snacks made with olestra. Opponents feel the packaging is misleading to consumers since olestra is an indigestible fat. I do understand the dispute over labeling, even though olestra technically is a fat substitute and does not have the same effect as regular fat in the body.

another objection

followed by two paragraphs of refutation

Side effects from olestra in some people have given way for public scrutiny. Olestra's larger and tighter molecules pass through the body undigested. Since the olestra is mixed in with other food products in the digestive system, it may physically soften the stool, similar to adding oil or water to bread dough. The symptoms experienced may depend on consumption, other eaten foods, and the individual body reaction.

Prior to olestra's approval, it was determined that digestive symptoms were common among the general population. As recorded in the FDA's report on olestra in 1996, 40% of adults noted that they experienced some digestive effect within the past month. Also, a study published in the Journal of American Medical Association (January 1998) said that potato chips made with Olean® are no more likely to cause digestive changes than potato chips made with regular vegetable oil.

Common digestive symptoms are caused by a range of other foods, such as beans, some milk products, and fruit, especially in those who eat too much. Usually when people determine that certain foods do not agree with them, they avoid them. To ban olestra since it may cause diarrhea in some instances is like banning milk because it causes illness for those that are lactose intolerant.

questions motivation of opponents

Opponents of olestra, namely the CSPI group, have fought loud and hard at attacking the new fat substitute by relying on the media to circulate their allegations. They have become the nation's most familiar nutrition watchdog group; however, some people may view CSPI's intentions as being more interested in publicity rather than protecting the public's interest. Let's face it, the media loves drama brought on by interest groups representing "victims" and CSPI is good at digging out victims from their website. According to a Reader's Digest Article titled, "Attack of the Food Police," Jacobson has not only thrashed olestra, but has attempted bans on movie theater popcorn and Chinese food.

CSPI has also petitioned the Federal Trade Commission to stop deceptive multimillion dollar advertising campaigns for Olean® and products made with it. As a result, Michael Jacobson persuaded The New England Journal of Medicine to pull Olean® advertisements on the basis that NEJM was biased and had received funds from manufacturer, Procter & Gamble, for its support.

refutes the reasoning of criticisms of the product

The truth of the matter is, NEJM elected to discontinue the Olean® ad because it did not want to compromise its position while receiving advertising money from P&G. It is common for prestigious magazines to make decisions such as this to protect their interests; however, it was even more critical with Olean®. The backlash and rhetoric the magazine would receive from Jacobson if it were to publish a positive report on olestra while still accepting ad funds from P&G would be damaging to its credibility. This is a good example of the effectiveness of Jacobson's scare tactics and persuasiveness.

pro-evidence of safety (facts)

Since Olean's approval, tens of millions of people have eaten over half-a-billion servings of new snacks made with this ingredient. These consumers have avoided more than 10 million pounds of fat and 40 billion calories, fat and calories they would have eaten in full-fat snacks. That's particularly noteworthy, considering the country's struggle with obesity and concern for cardiovascular diseases.

evidence of trustworthiness of the manufacturer

Proctor & Gamble is continuing to study olestra, including possible nutrient depletion, and will report findings to the FDA. The company has signed agreements with 12 other firms interested in making olestra snacks. P&G has tested olestra in several other foods, such as ice cream and mayonnaise, and states it will submit another application to the FDA for olestra's use within a year.

argumentative proposition implied throughout— now stated directly

I believe the protests made by opponents of olestra to be over exaggerated, unfounded, and sensationalized. The Center for Science in the Public Interest is leading the crusade against olestra in its typical melodramatic fashion by twisting and eliminating the true facts. Consumers owe it to themselves to be aware of the organizations supporting olestra, such as The Food & Drug Administration, The American Medical Association, The American Dietetics Association, The American Academy of Pediatrics, and The National Consumer League.

summarizes evidence for and ends with a quotation summing up the writer's opinion of critics.

The evidence from years of research has proven that olestra can be worked into a healthy diet, just like any other food. Olestra has confirmed its safety and effectiveness to the medical and scientific community as well as gained momentum in the consumer's "fight on fat" battle. Olestra alone is not the answer to trim the fat off America's belly; however, it is a safe and effective way to enjoy favorite foods without sacrificing the taste. Olestra has opened the doors, now it's up to the American people to open their eyes to the truth. As Abraham Lincoln said "truth is generally the best vindication against slander", and the truth of olestra's safety will prevail over Michael Jacobson and the CSPI group.

Issues and Ideas

Current Controversies

- Christopher B. Daly, *How the Lawyers Stole Winter*
- Richard Lynn, *Why Johnny Can't Read, but Yoshio Can*
- Castle Freeman, Jr., *Surviving Deer Season*
- Jane Smiley, *The Call of the Hunt*
- Barbara Lawrence, *Four-Letter Words Can Hurt You*
- Sarah Min, *Language Lessons*

An issue is a subject on which there is more than one point of view. Since arguments address differences and disagreements, they necessarily begin with an issue. When an issue disappears, however, so does the usefulness and relevance of an argument, unless, of course, the argument is expressed in language so moving and effective or with reasoning so precise and convincing that it remains admirable though the immediate concerns of the author and the audience may pass away.

The essays in this chapter address contemporary questions, though the issues themselves have been around in some form for quite a while and are likely to remain with us in coming years. Christopher B. Daly's "How the Lawyers Stole Winter" focuses not only on concerns about children's safety and legal liability, but also on the much larger issue of personal responsibility. Richard Lynn's "Why Johnny Can't Read, but Yoshio Can," reflects continuing concerns about the failures of our educational system and worries that other countries are doing a better job. Castle Freeman, Jr.'s "Surviving Deer Season" and Jane Smiley's "The Call of the Hunt" focus on issues surrounding hunting, each from a different perspective. Barbara Lawrence's Essay, "Four-letter Words Can Hurt You," was first published a little more than twenty years ago. Nonetheless, while the particular words we use may have changed somewhat, the issues are still alive. Sarah Min takes a personal and refreshing approach to the issue of bilingualism. Finally, Barbara Ehrenreich offers an inductive argument designed to resolve many long-standing controversies over gender differences.

ARGUMENT THROUGH COMPARISON AND CONTRAST

CHRISTOPHER B. DALY

> CHRISTOPHER DALY grew up in Medford, Massachusetts. He now lives
> with his family in Newton, Massachusetts and is a free lance writer
> and contributor to magazines.

How the Lawyers Stole Winter

> In this essay, which appeared first in *Atlantic Monthly*, Daly uses
> comparison to make the case that in our attempts to prevent dan-
> gerous accidents, we (and in particular, the lawyers among us)
> have not only stolen some enjoyment from our lives but also less-
> ened responsibility for our own actions. He suggests that the result
> may be more danger, not less.

When I was a boy, my friends and I would come home from   1
school each day, change our clothes (because we were not allowed to wear "play clothes" to school), and go outside until din-
nertime. In the early 1960s in Medford, a city on the outskirts of
Boston, that was pretty much what everybody did. Sometimes there
might be flute lessons, or an organized Little League game, but usually not. Usually we kids went out and played.

In winter, on our way home from the Gleason School, we would   2
go past Brooks Pond to check the ice. By throwing heavy stones onto
it, hammering it with downed branches, and, finally, jumping on it,
we could figure out if the ice was ready for skating. If it was, we would
hurry home to grab our skates, our sticks, and whatever other gear we
had, and then return to play hockey for the rest of the day. When the
streetlights came on, we knew it was time to jam our cold, stiff feet
back into our green rubber snow boots and get home for dinner.

I had these memories in mind recently when I moved, with my   3
wife and two young boys, into a house near a lake even closer to
Boston, in the city of Newton. As soon as Crystal Lake froze over, I
grabbed my skates and headed out. I was not the first one there,
though: the lawyers had beaten me to the lake. They had warned the

town recreation department to put it off limits. So I found a sign that said DANGER. THIN ICE. NO SKATING.

Knowing a thing or two about words myself, I put my own   4
gloss on the sign. I took it to mean *When the ice is thin, there is danger and there should be no skating.* Fair enough, I thought, but I knew that the obverse was also true: *When the ice is thick, it is safe and there should be skating.* Finding the ice plenty thick, I laced up my skates and glided out onto the miraculous glassy surface of the frozen lake. My wife, a native of Manhattan, would not let me take our two boys with me. But for as long as I could, I enjoyed the free, open-air delight of skating as it should be. After a few days others joined me, and we became an outlaw band of skaters.

What we were doing was once the heart of winter in New   5
England—and a lot of other places, too. It was clean, free exercise that needed no StairMasters, no health clubs, no appointments, and hardly any gear. Sadly, it is in danger of passing away. Nowadays it seems that every city and town and almost all property holders are so worried about liability and lawsuits that they simply throw up a sign or a fence and declare that henceforth there shall be no skating, and that's the end of it.

As a result, kids today live in a world of leagues, rinks, rules,   6
uniforms, adults, and rides—rides here, rides there, rides everywhere. It is not clear that they are better off; in some ways they are clearly *not* better off.

When I was a boy skating on Brooks Pond, there were no   7
grown-ups around. Once or twice a year, on a weekend day or a holiday, some parents might come by with a thermos of hot cocoa. Maybe they would build a fire (which we were forbidden to do), and we would gather round.

But for the most part the pond was the domain of children. In   8
the absence of adults, we made and enforced our own rules. We had hardly any gear—just some borrowed hockey gloves, some hand-me-down skates, maybe an elbow pad or two—so we played a clean form of hockey, with no high-sticking, no punching, and almost no checking. A single fight could ruin the whole afternoon. Indeed, as I remember it, thirty years later, it was the purest form of hockey I ever saw—until I got to see the Russian national team play the game.

But before we could play, we had to check the ice. We became   9
serious junior meteorologists, true connoisseurs of cold. We learned that the best weather for pond skating is plain, clear cold, with starry nights and no snow. (Snow not only mucks up the skating surface but also insulates the ice from the colder air above.) And we learned

that moving water, even the gently flowing Mystic River, is a lot less likely to freeze than standing water. So we skated only on the pond. We learned all the weird whooping and cracking sounds that ice makes as it expands and contracts, and thus when to leave the ice.

Do kids learn these things today? I don't know. How would   10
they? We don't let them. Instead we post signs. Ruled by lawyers, cities and towns everywhere try to eliminate their legal liability. But try as they might, they cannot eliminate the underlying risk. Liability is a social construct; risk is a natural fact. When it is cold enough, ponds freeze. No sign or fence or ordinance can change that.

In fact, by focusing on liability and not teaching our kids how to   11
take risks, we are making their world more dangerous. When we were children, we had to learn to evaluate risks and handle them on our own. We had to learn, quite literally, to test the waters. As a result, we grew up to be savvier about ice and ponds than any kid could be who has skated only under adult supervision on a rink.

When I was a boy, despite the risks we took on the ice no one I   12
knew ever drowned. The only people I heard about who drowned were graduate students at Harvard or MIT who came from the tropics and were living through their first winters. Not knowing (after all, how could they?) about ice on moving water, they would innocently venture out onto the half-frozen Charles River, fall through, and die. They were literally out of their element.

Are we raising a generation of children who will be out of their   13
element? And if so, what can we do about it? We cannot just roll back the calendar. I cannot tell my six-year-old to head down to the lake by himself to play all afternoon—if for no other reason than that he would not find twenty or thirty other kids there, full of the collective wisdom about cold and ice that they had inherited, along with hockey equipment, from their older brothers and sisters. Somewhere along the line that link got broken.

The whole setting of childhood has changed. We cannot change   14
it again overnight. I cannot send my children out by themselves yet, but at least some of the time I can go out there with them. Maybe that is a start.

As for us, last winter was a very unusual one. We had ferocious   15
cold (near-zero temperatures on many nights) and tremendous snows (about a hundred inches in all). Eventually a strange thing happened. The town gave in—sort of. Sometime in January the recreation department "opened" a section of the lake, and even dispatched a snowplow truck to clear a good-sized patch of ice. The boys and I skated during the rest of winter. Ever vigilant, the town

officials kept the THIN ICE signs up, even though their own truck could safely drive on the frozen surface. And they brought in "lifeguards" and all sorts of rules about the hours during which we could skate and where we had to stay.

But at least we were able to skate in the open air, on real ice.   16
And it was still free.   17

Meanings and Values

1. Summarize in your own words the issue the author is addressing in this essay. In what ways is this issue representative of similar issues in other settings and climates? Explain. Does this "representativeness" make the argument significant and interesting for people who are not worried about thin ice and have no interest in skating? Why or why not? (See "Guide to Terms": *Evaluation.*)

2. Daly presents his examples of growing up in the early 1960s as illustrations of a good way to teach children responsibility and to allow them to have healthy fun. Does he succeed in doing so? If so, what details in the examples or statements of interpretation are most convincing? If not, what keeps the examples from being successful?

3. What opposing points of view, if any, does Daly acknowledge? Would the essay be more (or less) effective if he spent more time dealing with possible objections to his argument? Make a list of possible objections to his argument and evidence that could be used to support them.

4. Does the writer offer possible answers to the problem he identifies? If so, what are they? Does the essay make a clear case that lawyers are to blame for the problem? If not, does this weaken the essay? Why or why not?

Argumentative Techniques

1. Why does the writer wait until paragraph 6 to offer an argumentative proposition (thesis)? What role(s) do the opening paragraphs play? Do they explain an issue or problem? Do they provide evidence that can be used to support the thesis? Be specific in your answer, and point to specific evidence to support your conclusions. (Guide: *Introductions.*)

2. Which sentence or sentences state the argumentative proposition (thesis)? (Guide: *Thesis.*) Restate it in your own words. Are all parts of the essay clearly related to this thesis? If not, what are the functions of any parts not clearly related to the thesis? (Guide: *Unity.*) How is the comparison-contrast pattern related to the thesis? Explain. Would another arrangement of ideas and evidence be likely to pro-

vide more convincing development and support for the thesis? What arrangement, and why?

3. In what ways does the concluding sentence "echo" the beginning of the essay? Which paragraphs should be considered the conclusion of the essay? What functions do they perform? (Guide: *Closings.*)

DICTION AND VOCABULARY

1. The effectiveness of this essay depends to a considerable extent on the writer's ability to make the account of his childhood experiences seem like a realistic ideal and not merely a sentimental, nostalgic excursion. How does the diction in paragraphs 1–2 and 7–9 aid him in staying away from too much sentimentality while at the same time making the experience seem attractive and worth reclaiming? If you think the examples are overly sentimental, explain why. (Guide: *Sentimentality.*)

2. What words with positive connotations does Daly associate with skating and playing hockey (see pars. 4 and 8)? (Guide: *Connotation/ Denotation*). How do the connotations of these words help support his thesis?

3. If you do not know the meaning of some of the following words, look them up in a dictionary: gloss, obverse (par. 4); high-sticking, checking (8); meteorologists, connoisseurs (9); liability, construct (10); vigilant (15).

READ TO WRITE

1. **Collaborating:** Working in a group, make a list of other valuable childhood activities that have been curtailed, limited, or threatened by legal concerns. Should we ignore these concerns, find a way to accommodate them, or come up with different and less dangerous activities? Consider making an issue from this general subject area the focus of an argumentative essay.

2. **Considering Audience:** Using Daly's essay as a model, argue that in an attempt to deal with a problem, threat, or danger, we have taken steps that create more problems and dangers by taking away the need to be responsible for our actions. In developing the essay, acknowledge that many readers have legitimate fears, and avoid being too critical of such readers.

3. **Developing an Essay:** Begin an argumentative essay of your own with examples of how things should be, then develop your argument by contrasting how they are with how they ought to be.

(NOTE: Suggestions for topics requiring development by ARGUMENT are on pp. 635–636 at the end of this chapter.)

ARGUMENT THROUGH COMPARISON AND CONTRAST

RICHARD LYNN

Richard Lynn was born in London, England, in 1930. He received a B.A. from King's College, Cambridge, in 1953 and was awarded a Ph.D. in 1956. He has taught at Exeter University and the Economic and Social Research Institute, Dublin, and is currently a professor of psychology at the University of Ulster. Among his books are *Personality and National Character* (1971), *An Introduction to the Study of Personality* (1971), *The Entrepreneur* (1974), and *Educational Achievement in Japan* (1988).

Why Johnny Can't Read, but Yoshio Can

This essay was first published in the *National Review,* a magazine noted for its advocacy of conservative social, economic, and political policies. In the selection, Lynn compares the Japanese educational system to those of the United States and England in order to argue for changes in the latter two systems. Of particular interest in this essay is the way the comparison pattern lends itself to arguments urging the adoption of policies that have worked in another setting.

There can be no doubt that American schools compare poorly   1
with Japanese schools. In the latter, there are no serious problems with poor discipline, violence, or truancy; Japanese children take school seriously and work hard. Japanese educational standards are high, and illiteracy is virtually unknown.

The evidence of Japan's high educational standards began to appear as long ago as the 1960s. In 1967 there was published the first of a   2
series of studies of educational standards in a dozen or so economically developed nations, based on tests of carefully drawn representative samples of children. The first study was concerned with achievement in math on the part of 13- and 18-year-olds. In both age groups the Japanese children came out well ahead of their coevals in other countries. The American 13-year-olds came out second to last for

their age group; the American 18-year-olds, last. In both age groups, European children scored about halfway between the Japanese and the Americans.

Since then, further studies have appeared, covering science as   3
well as math. The pattern of results has always been the same: the Japanese have generally scored first, the Americans last or nearly last, and the Europeans have fallen somewhere in between. In early adolescence, when the first tests are taken, Japanese children are two or three years ahead of American children; by age 18, approximately 98 percent of Japanese children surpass their American counterparts.

Meanwhile, under the Reagan Administration, the United States   4
at least started to take notice of the problem. In 1983 the President's report, *A Nation at Risk,* described the state of American schools as a national disaster. A follow-up report issued by the then-secretary of education, Mr. William Bennett, earlier this year[1] claims that although some improvements have been made, these have been "disappointingly slow."

An examination of Japan's school system suggests that there are   5
three factors responsible for its success, which might be emulated by other countries: a strong national curriculum, stipulated by the government; strong incentives for students; and the stimulating effects of competition between schools.

The national curriculum in Japan is drawn up by the Department   6
of Education. It covers Japanese language and literature, math, science, social science, music, moral education, and physical education. From time to time, the Department of Education requests advice on the content of the curriculum from representatives of the teaching profession, industry, and the trade unions. Syllabi are then drawn up, setting out in detail the subject matter that has to be taught at each grade. These syllabi are issued to school principals, who are responsible for ensuring that the stipulated curriculum is taught in their schools. Inspectors periodically check that this is being done.

The Japanese national curriculum ensures such uniformly high standards of teaching that almost all parents are happy to send their   7
children to the local public school. There is no flight into private schools of the kind that has been taking place in America in recent years. Private schools do exist in Japan, but they are attended by less than 1 per cent of children in the age range of compulsory schooling (six to 15 years).

---

[1]1988, the year this essay was first published (Editors' note).

This tightly stipulated national curriculum provides a striking   8
contrast with the decentralized curriculum of schools in America.
Officially, the curriculum in America is the responsibility of school
principals with guidelines from state education officials. In practice,
even school principals often have little idea of what is actually being
taught in the classroom.

America and Britain have been unusual in leaving the curricu-   9
lum so largely in the hands of teachers. Some form of national curriculum is used throughout Continental Europe, although the
syllabus is typically not specified in as much detail as in Japan. And
now Britain is changing course: legislation currently going through
Parliament will introduce a national curriculum for England and
Wales, with the principal subjects being English, math, science,
technology, a foreign language, history and geography, and art, music, and design. It is envisioned that the new curriculum will take up
approximately 70 per cent of teaching time, leaving the remainder
free for optional subjects such as a second foreign language, or extra
science.

Under the terms of the new legislation, school children are go-   10
ing to be given national tests at the ages of seven, 11, 14, and 16 to
ensure that the curriculum has been taught and that children have
learned it to a satisfactory standard. When the British national curriculum comes into effect, America will be left as the only major economically developed country without one.

To achieve high educational standards in schools it is necessary   11
to have motivated students as well as good teachers. A national curriculum acts as a discipline on teachers, causing them to teach efficiently, but it does nothing to provide incentives for students, an
area in which American education is particularly weak.

One of the key factors in the Japanese education system is that   12
secondary schooling is split into two stages. At the age of 11 or 12,
Japanese children enter junior high school. After three years there,
they take competitive entrance examinations for senior high schools.
In each locality there is a hierarchy of public esteem for these senior
high schools, from the two or three that are regarded as the best in
the area, through those considered to be good or average, down to
those that (at least by Japanese standards) are considered to be poor.

The top schools enjoy national reputations, somewhat akin to   13
the famous English schools such as Eton and Harrow. But in
England the high fees exacted by these schools mean that very few
parents can afford them. Consequently there are few candidates for
entry, and the entrance examinations offer little incentive to work

for the great mass of children. By contrast, in Japan the elite senior high schools are open to everyone. While a good number of these schools are private (approximately 30 per cent nationwide, though in some major cities the figure is as high as 50 per cent), even these schools are enabled, by government subsidies, to keep their fees within the means of a large proportion of parents. The public schools also charge fees, but these are nominal, amounting to only a few hundred dollars a year, and loans are available to cover both fees and living expenses.

Thus children have every expectation of being able to attend   14
the best school they can qualify for; and, hence, the hierarchical rankings of senior high schools act as a powerful incentive for children preparing for the entrance examinations. There is no doubt that Japanese children work hard in response to these incentives. Starting as early as age ten, approximately half of them take extra tuition on weekends, in the evenings, and in the school holidays at supplementary coaching establishments known as *juku,* and even at that early age they do far more homework than American children. At about the age of 12, Japanese children enter the period of their lives known as *examination hell:* during this time, which lasts fully two years, it is said that those who sleep more than five hours a night have no hope of success, either in school or in life. For, in addition to conferring great social and intellectual status on their students, the elite senior high schools provide a first-rate academic education, which, in turn, normally enables the students to get into one of the elite universities and, eventually, to move into a good job in industry or government.

Although Japanese children are permitted to leave school at the   15
age of 15, 94 per cent of them proceed voluntarily to the senior high schools. Thus virtually all Japanese are exposed in early adolescence to the powerful incentive for academic work represented by the senior-high-school entrance examinations. There is nothing in the school systems of any of the Western countries resembling this powerful incentive.

The prestige of the elite senior high schools is sustained by the   16
extensive publicity they receive from the media. Each year the top hundred or so schools in Japan are ranked on the basis of the percentage of their pupils who obtain entry to the University of Tokyo, Japan's most prestigious university. These rankings are widely reported in the print media, and the positions of the top twenty schools are announced on TV news programs, rather like the scores made by leading sports teams in the United States and Europe. At a

local level, more detailed media coverage is devoted to the academic achievements of all the schools in the various localities, this time analyzed in terms of their pupils' success in obtaining entry to the lesser, but still highly regarded, local universities.

Thus, once Japanese 15-year-olds have been admitted to their senior high schools, they are confronted with a fresh set of incentives in the form of entrance examinations to universities and colleges, which are likewise hierarchically ordered in public esteem. After the University of Tokyo, which stands at the apex of the status hierarchy, come the University of Kyoto and ten or so other highly prestigious universities, including the former Imperial Universities in the major provincial cities and the technological university of Hitosubashi, whose standing and reputation in Japan resembles that of the Massachusetts Institute of Technology in the United States.   17

Below these top dozen institutions stand some forty or so less prestigious but still well-regarded universities. And after these come numerous smaller universities and colleges of varying degrees of standing and reputation.   18

To some extent the situation in Japan has parallels in the United States and Europe, but there are two factors that make the importance of securing admission to an elite university substantially greater in Japan than in the West. In the first place, the entire Japanese system is geared toward providing lifelong employment, both in the private sector and in the civil service. It is practically unheard of for executives to switch from one corporation to another, or into public service and then back into the private sector, as in the United States and Europe. Employees are recruited directly out of college, and, needless to say, the major corporations and the civil service recruit virtually entirely from the top dozen universities. The smaller Japanese corporations operate along the same lines, although they widen their recruitment net to cover the next forty or so universities in the prestige hierarchy. Thus, obtaining entry to a prestigious university is a far more vital step for a successful career in Japan than it is in the United States or Europe.   19

Secondly, like the elite senior high schools, the elite universities are meritocratic. The great majority of universities are public institutions, receiving substantial government subsidies. Again, as with the senior high schools, fees are quite low, and loans are available to defray expenses. In principle and to a considerable extent in practice, any young Japanese can get into the University of Tokyo, or one of the other elite universities, provided only that he or she is talented enough and is prepared to do the work necessary to pass the   20 entrance examinations. Knowing this, the public believes that *all* the most talented young Japanese go to one of these universities—and, conversely, that anyone who fails to get into one of these schools is necessarily less bright. Avoiding this stigma is, of course, a further incentive for the student to work hard to get in.

The third significant factor responsible for the high educational standards in Japan is competition among schools. This operates principally among the senior high schools, and what they are competing for is academic reputation. The most prestigious senior high school in Japan is Kansei in Tokyo, and being a teacher at Kansei is something like being a professor at Harvard. The teachers' self-esteem is bound up with the academic reputation of their schools—a powerful motivator for teachers to teach well. 21

In addition to this important factor of self-esteem, there is practical necessity. Since students are free to attend any school they can get into, if a school failed to provide good-quality teaching, it would no longer attract students. In business terms, its customers would fade away, and it would be forced to close. Thus the essential feature of the competition among the Japanese senior high schools is that it exposes the teachers to the discipline of the free-enterprise system. In the case of the public senior high schools, the system can be regarded as a form of market socialism in which the competing institutions are state-owned but nevertheless compete against each other for their customers. Here the Japanese have been successfully operating the kind of system that Mikhail Gorbachev may be feeling his way toward introducing in the Soviet Union. The Japanese private senior high schools add a further capitalist element to the system insofar as they offer their educational services more or less like firms operating in a conventional market. 22

The problem of how market disciplines can be brought to bear on schools has been widely discussed in America and also in Britain ever since Milton Friedman raised it a quarter of a century or so ago, but solutions such as Friedman's voucher proposal seem as distant today as they did then. Although the proposal has been looked at sympathetically by Republicans in the United States and by Conservatives in Britain, politicians in both countries have fought shy of introducing it. Probably they have concluded that the problems of getting vouchers into the hands of all parents, and dealing with losses, fraud, counterfeits, and so forth, are likely to be too great for the scheme to be feasible. 23

The Japanese have evolved a different method of exposing schools to market forces. Subsidies are paid directly to the schools 24 on a per-capita basis in accordance with the number of students they have. If a school's rolls decline, so do its incomes, both from subsidies and from fees. This applies to both the public and private senior high schools, although the public schools obviously receive a much greater proportion of their income as subsidies and a smaller proportion from fees.

A similar scheme is being introduced in Britain. The Thatcher   25
government is currently bringing in legislation that will permit public schools to opt out of local-authority control. Those that opt out will receive subsidies from the central government on the basis of the number of students they have. They will then be on their own, to sink or swim.

There is little doubt that this is the route that should be fol-   26
lowed in America. The exposure of American schools to the invigorating stimulus of competition, combined with the introduction of a national curriculum and the provision of stronger incentives for students, would work wonders. Rather than complaining about Japanese aggressiveness and instituting counterproductive protectionist measures, Americans ought to be looking to the source of Japan's power.

Meanings and Values

1. What is the issue or problem Lynn identifies in paragraphs 1–4?

2. Summarize briefly the main reasons Lynn offers for the success of the Japanese school system.

3. How does the curriculum in Japanese schools contrast with those in American and British schools, especially in motivating students to excel?

4. One possible weakness in this argument is that the author pays little attention to opposing points of view. Think of some reasonable objections a North American reader might have to the Japanese educational system. Try to identify some practical difficulties that stand in the way of the reforms the author proposes based on the Japanese model. Explain how you think the author might respond to these objections and possible problems.

Argumentative Techniques

1. What kinds of evidence does the author offer to demonstrate the seriousness of the problem he describes in the opening of the essay? (See "Guide to Terms": *Argument*.)

2. Why might the author have chosen to summarize his main supporting arguments in paragraph 5, early in the essay?

3. Discuss the strategies Lynn employs in paragraphs 11 and 21, which act as transitions between major segments of the essay. (Guide: *Transition.*) Tell how these two paragraphs, along with paragraphs 5 and 6, contribute to the overall coherence of the essay. (Guide: *Coherence.*)

4. How would you describe the tone of the essay? In what ways does the tone add to the persuasiveness of the argument? (Guide: *Style/Tone.*)

DICTION AND VOCABULARY

1. Examine the diction in paragraphs 7, 14, and 22 to decide whether it is designed to appeal primarily to readers' emotions, reason, or both. (See the introduction to Chapter 13, p. 577, and Guide: *Diction.*) On the whole, would you characterize the writing in this selection as objective or subjective? Why? (Guide: *Objective/Subjective.*)

2. Identify the uses Lynn makes of parallel structures and contrasts in diction to emphasize the seriousness of the problem described in paragraphs 2 and 3. (Guide: *Parallel Structure.*)

3. Point out the transitional devices used in paragraphs to emphasize contrasts between the Japanese educational system and those of Britain and America. (Guide: *Transition.*)

READ TO WRITE

1. **Collaborating:** Working in a group, prepare a thesis for an essay in which you consider the recommendations in this essay and propose some educational reforms of your own that you believe would be just as effective—perhaps even more so.

2. **Considering Audience:** Prepare an essay for a group of readers in your community. Using comparison as a strategy, argue for some solutions to a local problem such as disposal of solid waste, improvement of the transportation system, better administration of school athletics, or control of drug and alcohol abuse.

3. **Developing an Essay:** In what other ways do you think North Americans can learn from the economic or social systems of other countries? Following Lynn's essay as a model, discuss this question as it applies to some specific issues. Pay particular attention to countries such as Japan that have been especially successful in recent decades.

(NOTE: Suggestions for topics requiring development by ARGUMENT are on pp. 635–636 at the end of this chapter.)

ARGUMENT THROUGH EXAMPLE

CASTLE FREEMAN, JR.

CASTLE FREEMAN, JR. is an essay and short story writer as well as a novelist. His books include *The Bride of Ambrose and Other Stories* (1987), *Spring Snow: The Seasons of New England from "The Old Farmer's Almanac"* (1995), and *Judgment Hill: A Novel* (1997). He has also written for a number of magazines.

Surviving Deer Season

This writer claims to be able to tolerate deer hunting, yet to read his essay is to discover that he tolerates it with great difficulty and sadness. And he clearly wishes his readers would choose not to go hunting. To make this argument indirectly though effectively, Freeman relies on the power of examples. His carefully chosen examples convey his perspective without alienating people who support deer hunting; they have the further effect of encouraging deer hunters to reconsider their pastime, which is, after all, an important part of Freeman's purpose in this essay. "Surviving Deer Season" was first published in the *Atlantic* magazine.

The foothills of southeastern Vermont were once dairy country, 1 although by the time I arrived, twenty years ago, dairying was mostly finished. One farm in the neighborhood still kept a few milkers, though, and it was there that I became acquainted with a particular local custom that is, I find, rarely celebrated in articles on endearing rural ways through the seasons. Their authors will tell you how to tap a maple in March, mow hay in June, and make cider in October, but by failing to touch on the subject I refer to, they neglect a passage in the turning year that is as venerable as these but darker and more pointed.

One morning in November, looking into my neighbor's pas- 2 ture, I observed an uncanny thing: on the nearest of his animals the word COW had been painted with whitewash in letters two feet high. A further look revealed that the entire herd had been painted the same way. What was this? Was the herd's owner perhaps expecting a visit from city people in need of rural education? Was his tractor painted TRACTOR, his barn BARN? I asked him.

"Well, you know what tomorrow is," my neighbor said.   3

"Saturday?" I said.   4

"You're new around here," he said. "You'll see."   5

I saw, all right. More precisely, I heard. The next morning   6
Vermont's two-week deer-hunting season began. Just before dawn
the slumbering woods erupted with the fell echo of small arms. Single
gunshots, doubles, volleys of three or four, came from all points of the
compass, some far off, others seemingly in the living room. By eleven
the fire had mounted to a fusillade worthy of Antietam. Across the
road, however, my neighbor's cows survived. They hugged the earth
fearfully, like Tommies at the Somme, but they were alive. After all,
no deer hunter who could read would shoot a cow.

Since then I have become a close student of the lengths to which   7
people go each year on the eve of deer season to provide a margin of
safety for themselves, their loved ones, their livestock, their pets.
This is the season when dogs wear brightly colored bandannas
around their necks, like John Wayne and Montgomery Clift in *Red
River.* Cats and smaller dogs, as far as I can tell, have to take their
chances along with the deer, although I don't know why the kind of
elegant dog vest to be seen on the Pekingeses of Park Avenue
shouldn't be produced in hunter orange for the greater safety of
their country cousins.

That same hunter orange, a hideous toxic color, suddenly ap-   8
pears everywhere in mid-November, like the untimely bloom of an
evil flower. Hunters themselves, of course, wear hunter orange to
make it less likely that they'll be shot by their peers. But civilians, too,
turn up in hunter-orange caps, vests, sweaters, and jackets, as they go
about their business outdoors during this uneasy fortnight in the year.

Uneasy indeed. Are you a hiker, a birder, an idle tramper   9
through the woods? In deer season you think twice before setting
out—think twice and then stay home. If you're a non-hunter, it's
painful to avoid the woods and fields as though they were a deserted street in the South Bronx. There is also the trouble of preparing for deer season. It's not as though you don't have enough to do
to get the place ready for winter without having to find time to paint
the cow, flag the dog, pray for the cat, and plan two weeks' worth of
useful projects to do in the cellar.

The heaviest demands that deer season makes on the non-   10
hunter, however, it makes not on his time but on his mind. You have
to reflect. You have to collect your thoughts. You don't want to
move into deer season without having examined your responses,
your beliefs.

I don't object to deer hunting: let everyone have his sport, I say.   11
I don't for a moment doubt the value, importance, and dignity of

hunting for those who do it. Deer hunting teaches skill, discipline, and patience. More than that, it teaches the moral lesson of seriousness—that certain things must be entered into advisedly, done with care, and done right. That hunting provides an education I am very willing to believe. And yet deer season is for me a sad couple of weeks. Because with all its profound advantages for the hunter, the fact remains that deer season is a little tough on the deer.

Suddenly deer turn up in strange places: thrown down in the backs of pickup trucks; roped on top of cars; hanging in front of barns; flopped in blood across platform scales in front of country stores and gas stations. It's hard to recognize in those abject, inert cadavers the agile creatures you surprise along the roads at night or see sometimes in the woods picking their way on slender legs and then bounding off, the most graceful animals in North America. It's hard to see them so defeated, so dead.   12

It's particularly hard for children, those instinctive animal lovers, to see deer season's bloody harvest hauled out of the woods. It's especially hard to explain to them why it isn't wrong to kill deer—or, if it is wrong, why nobody can stop it, and how it is that the hunters themselves, who are also your friends and neighbors, are otherwise such familiar, decent, innocent people. It's a lesson in ambiguity, I guess—a lesson in tolerance.   13

I had a number of conversations along these lines with my children when they were young, inconclusive conversations with on their side conviction and passion, and on my own . . . nothing satisfactory. What do you tolerate, why, and how? How do you separate the act from the friend, and condemn the one but not the other? Not an easy matter at any age, in any season.   14

We don't have those talks anymore. The children are older now. They know that with some things all you can do is figure out how you will conduct your own life and let others do the same. Perhaps they have learned this in part from deer season. If so, I'm content. Let the gunners fire at will—and as for the nonhunters, good luck to them, too. It's not only hunters who can learn from hunting.   15

Meanings and Values

1. Why has Freeman's neighbor painted the word "COW" on his cows? Why do you think Freeman chose cows as the first example in his essay?

2. Freeman says, "I don't know why the kind of elegant dog vest to be seen on the Pekingeses of Park Avenue shouldn't be produced in hunter orange for the greater safety of their country cousins" (par. 7). Explain why Freeman makes this comparison between city and country dogs. Where else in this essay does he compare city and country dwellers?

3. What does Freeman mean when he says that learning about deer season is "a lesson in ambiguity" (par. 13)? Do you agree? Why, or why not?

ARGUMENTATIVE TECHNIQUES

1. What is Freeman's thesis? Is it clearly stated at an appropriate point in the essay, or is it implied? Be ready to explain your answer. How else might he have chosen to present his thesis?

2. Identify the different patterns of development that Freeman incorporates. Which are the most effective and why? (See "Guide to Terms": *Evaluation.*)

3. Does Freeman acknowledge opposing points of view? Where? Is he fair to those who view deer hunting from a perspective other than his own? Please explain.

DICTION AND VOCABULARY

1. Compare the tone of paragraph 1 and of paragraph 6. (Guide: *Tone.*) Why might he have chosen such opposite images for these two paragraphs? Is his language concrete or abstract? (Guide: *Abstract/ Concrete.*) Please explain your response.

2. Paragraphs 3, 4, and 5 are one-line quotations. Explain the significance of these three lines. How do they help Freeman organize his essay and prepare readers for what he has to say?

3. Look up any of the following words with which you are unfamiliar: Antietam (par. 6); fortnight (8); and abject (11).

READ TO WRITE

1. **Collaborating:** Working in a group, list childhood experiences that gave you an ambiguous perspective. Decide with your group which patterns of development might be used for an essay explaining the importance of one of the recollections.

2. **Considering Audience:** Envision yourself as a deer hunter reading Freeman's essay. Write a letter to the editor of the magazine in which it appeared (*Atlantic*), responding to the issue from your perspective as a hunter.

3. **Developing an Essay:** Freeman clearly lets his reader know how he feels about deer hunting without excessive moralizing. Choose a

controversial issue concerning animals and write an essay similar to Freeman's in which you share your belief without judging harshly or openly criticizing those in opposition.

(NOTE: Suggestions for essays requiring development by ARGUMENT are on pp. 635–636 at the end of this chapter).

ARGUMENT THROUGH EXAMPLE

JANE SMILEY

JANE SMILEY is a Pulitzer Prize-winning novelist who teaches at Iowa State University. Her books include *The Age of Grief* (1991), *The All-True Travels and Adventures of Lidie Newton* (1998), *Moo* (1995), and *A Thousand Acres* (1991) (which won the 1992 Pulitzer Prize). She has also published essays in magazines like *Harper's* and *Outside*.

The Call of the Hunt

In this essay, published in 1994 in *Outside* magazine, Smiley draws examples from her own experience to argue that there is something primal and natural about hunting, even though she finds plenty to criticize in the sport and in the people who practice it.

Back when I was on the very lowest reaches of the educational slopes, before any of my present opinions were formed, I used to ponder Oscar Wilde's characterization of foxhunting as "the unspeakable in pursuit of the uneatable." Like almost every other expression that had to do with foxhunting, Wilde's mot seemed to me like a magic charm, or what I would later know as a mantra—an almost unintelligible set of words that others seemed to understand and use with ease but that I found mysterious and fascinating. Just because I was an Anglophile (I had read all of Mary Poppins, Sherlock Holmes, and Prince Valiant by that time) didn't mean I knew what "view halloo" or "gone to earth" or "whipper in" meant. "Hounds" were not dogs. They had "sterns," not tails, and they were counted in "couples," not one by one. Red woolen hunting coats, worn only by men, were actually "pink." Before the hunt everyone partook of the "stirrup cup," which came in a chased silver vessel with a pointed bottom that couldn't be set down but had to be brought around and taken away by servants. Foxes had no tails, faces, or feet, but "brushes," "masks," and "pads," and these were ritually cut from the corpse after the "death" and awarded to especially avid members of the "field" who had been "in at the death." 1

I came to foxhunting through horseback riding, which was my overwhelming obsession. The hunt in my town, St. Louis, was called the Bridlespur Hunt, and most of the horsey types there, from the Busches on down, were members, whether they actually "rode to 2 hounds" or not. If you were a member of the hunt and had "earned your colors," you could wear robin's-egg blue on the collar of your melton jacket. The western environs of St. Louis and St. Charles counties, just north of the Missouri River as it approaches the Mississippi, were and may still be good hunt country, with broad, rolling fields and open woodland, plenty of foxes, and good scenting conditions for the hounds, which I understood then to be light winds and sufficient humidity. Nonetheless, Bridlespur country was not England, and the master, the huntsman, and the members of the field spoke regular American when they weren't hunting, and sometimes when they were. They were probably less afraid of breaking the linguistic rules than I was.

Anything about hunting that other sorts of hunters might cite to justify their sport is not citable about foxhunting. The fox is truly uneatable, even for the hounds, who mill about excitably after the death until the whippers-in whip them back into a pack and the huntsmen and the master decide whether and where to find another. Besides, probably no one in the field has ever gone without a meal anyway. Foxhunters do not commune with nature. The huntsman controls the hounds, the whippers-in look for the fox, and the members of the field spend their nongalloping time gossiping among themselves or attending to their horses. The history of foxhunting (or stag hunting) over the centuries is, in every particular, the history of a privileged class riding roughshod (the horses' iron shoes caulked to provide more secure footing in the mud) over everything in its path. When I saw the movie *Tom Jones*, right in the midst of my foxhunting career, I could at least understand the moment when the farmer emerges from his hovel after the passing of the field and lifts up his prize goose, trampled and broken by the galloping horses. These days, much better read, I understand the "unspeakable" part of Wilde's remark, and I surely wouldn't go foxhunting again, but all the same, like most of the educated, I do harbor a fondness for the sins of my ignorant past.

As a parent, I cannot imagine the abdication of good sense that allowed my parents to allow me to "ride to hounds," but they did. Probably I wore them down drop by drop, as I did about every equestrian venture, overcoming their perfectly reasonable objections on the grounds of safety and expense with the sheer tenacity of my desire. I had gotten them to pay for the riding lessons, then to allow me to jump, then to let me go to the Pony Club rally, which entailed a lot of jumping. I had shown devotion to the horse. After breaking my arm high-jumping (I never suffered a single equestrian injury, but track and field was my undoing), I'd gone to the horse every chance I could anyway and cleaned her stall one-handed. That persuaded them to buy me the horse. She was a dark bay Thoroughbred mare with a kindly nature and a beautiful head. Under saddle, she was a little hot for me, but I had her in control most of the time. It didn't really matter, though, how good or bad she was objectively—she was my destined mate, and I was ready to take the good with the bad.

I rode her and jumped her all summer and into the fall. After   5
the fields were harvested, everyone else in the barn loaded their horses into trailers on Sundays and sometimes on Wednesdays (remember, this was the leisure class) and went out to the various areas where the master had secured permission to hunt, and they galloped and jumped for hours on end. The other girls went. Surely that must have been an element of my argument, and there was probably some phoning among parents. Thanksgiving loomed, and I set my sights upon that Thursday hunt. What better way to celebrate the coming of the English to Virginia—the true origin of our country, forget those nonfoxhunting Puritans—than rising at 5:00 A.M., riding all day, and coming home too exhausted toward the late afternoon to partake of the family feast?

It seems to be the case that experienced horses do like foxhunt-   6
ing. Horses will respond to the sound of the horn and hounds and the sight of the field galloping away by whinnying and fighting to join the hunt. Some horses, if they lose their riders, will keep galloping and jumping with the group until caught and led away.

Writers and artists of foxhunting also maintain that the fox en-   7
joys the hunt. There are many paintings of a fox standing alertly on a stone wall in the foreground, watching the hounds and the horses gallop into the empty distance. Certainly the fox has plenty of warning that it is being hunted—foxhunting makes a virtue of noise—the liquid call of the horn, the seismic boom of forty horses galloping over the earth, and the cry of the hounds, whether is neither barking nor howling, but a high, desperate, glad yodeling called "giving voice." When the hounds are fast on the trail of the fox, they are said to be "in full cry," which means that the noise and speed and adrenaline are peaking in horse and hound and human, and possibly, too, in the fox.

There are other, more efficient mechanisms for disposing of a   8
chicken-killing fox than foxhunting, though characterizing the fox as a verminous nuisance has always been the foxhunter's single limp rationalization for the whole colorful enterprise.

And the hounds undoubtedly like it, because, like all hunting   9
dogs, this is what they are bred to do, and because for the rest of
their time they live in the kennel, and because, unlike Labs and
pointers and German shorthairs, they work in a group.

And so I set the clock for 5:00 A.M., and I rose and dressed care-   10
fully in my high black boots, my thick wool "canary" (yellow)
breeches (in those days before stretch fabrics, wide-pegged at the
thigh for ease in mounting), my black melton jacket, my white cotton "stock" (a four-inch wide tie wrapped two or three times around
the neck, intended for use as a bandage or tourniquet in case of
emergency), my hair net, and my velvet hard hat, in which my
mother vested a great deal of faith concerning head injuries. I was
chauffered by my mother in her robe to the stable, where I accompanied my horse and the other members of the elect to the wildlife area
in St. Charles County where the hunt was to commence. We were
mounted by eight.

Maybe the best thing about a foxhunt is the sight of all the   11
horses and riders gathered together early in the morning, waiting to
set off. The horses are impeccably clean and fitted out—in any
equestrian endeavor there is a high premium placed on making a
pristine appearance that I see now is a sort of conspicuous consumption rooted in the days of grooms and servants—and they are
fresh and eager, too, striding about in an informal ballet, long-
necked and long-limbed and long-tailed, giving off their horsey
scent to the accompaniment of the happy chatter of many riders
who know one another and are secure in sharing social rituals of
long standing.

When the huntsman and the whips bring in the hounds, the   12
hounds introduce an entirely different energy, noisy and single-
minded, that focuses the field upon the task at hand and reminds
them that this isn't just a ride in the park. They are giving themselves
up to the fox, which, once found, will lead them across all sorts of
country, and they and their horses will have to be ready for anything—
any sort of ground, any sort of fence, any sort of incline, any sort of
woodlot. This is the "chase," not the "stalk." Not much care will be
taken once the apotheosis is achieved: the hounds in full cry.

I was nervous about the jumping. I had heard, though I hadn't   13
told my mother, that the fences could be as high as four feet, and I
wasn't used to jumping much higher than three feet. I fixed my hard
hat more firmly on my head. Four feet and solid. Unlike jumps in a
ring, these were not made of poles on standards that would fall if
hit. They were telephone poles and chicken coops and railroad ties. I

kept my fears to myself, but I did hear someone else say, "Usually there's a lower part to one side that you can go for." I decided to stay close to that woman and discreetly fell in not far from her.

I was proud of my mare. She looked sleek and fit, rangy and ea- 14
ger, which is often the special charm of a Thoroughbred. She was somewhat calmer than usual, probably taking pleasure and reassurance from the presence of the other horses. She had never hunted before, but she had raced. Perhaps the situation she found herself in suggested to her that there would be the opportunity to GO. Most Thoroughbreds, even failed racehorses, like very much to GO.

The huntsman set off with the hounds and the whips. When they 15
were just out of sight, the hounds began to give voice. That was the master's signal to follow, and we followed him—more experienced members of the field in front, less experienced or less eager ones behind. It was a dank late autumn day. The sky promised to be a clear, platinum blue, but mist rose from the muddy brown fields and leafless dark woodland, softening the chilly air. The riders and the horses gave off a mist, too, of breath and evaporating perspiration. Like duck and deer hunting, foxhunting is a sport that gives late autumn and early winter a point, that lures the hunter out of the warm house into the strange, coldly lit charms of the dying year. Soon we were cantering after the hounds, which we could hear but not see. I wasn't looking for anything except the tails of the horses in front of me. I thought I would manage my horse for now, and learn about the niceties of actually chasing and killing a fox at some later date.

I should mention here that in England foxhunting is often car- 16
ried out without the fox, revealing that galloping and jumping and listening to the hounds is the real point of the sport. "Draghunts" are common in England—hours before the hunt, someone drags a sack impregnated with fox scent over the countryside, more or less diabolically mimicking foxy strategies, taking care to challenge the field. Draghunting isn't the only death-free alternative. In her memoirs, Jessica Mitford, another left-winger who once adored foxhunting, recalls that her father, Lord Redesdale, was especially fond of hunting his children, a memory corroborated by Nancy Mitford in her novels.

Here is where education interferes with narrative. I know what 17
we would have done next, but the nugget of memory has accreted too many images from later riding experiences, later experiences of horse manuals, English literature, social class, England itself, and even conversations with others. Images that arose as a response of the imagination offer themselves as memories. All I know about

what happened next is that we followed the hounds for an hour or more, and that I grew more self-confident and relaxed.

The next thing I remember is the sight of a large fence, and my-   18
self pausing to wait for other riders to clear it. We gathered at the edge of the field, under the overhang of the woodland, trying to avoid the mud. My turn came up. I followed four or five strides be-hind the woman in front of me, knowing her horse's willingness would influence my horse. But I didn't have anything to worry about. My mare was happy to jump. The fence loomed, brown and upright, in front of us, got larger, and was gone. I felt her forelegs land and saw that we were in a wide, muddy lane that veered to the right toward a dirt road. I saw the other horses galloping away.

Of course, accompanying these visual memories are sensory   19
ones, particularly the feeling of the presence of the horse as I gripped her sides with my legs, moved my own body with the rhythm of her gait, leaned close to her neck, felt the tug of her mouth through the reins in my hands. Two strides after the fence, our momentum was still carrying us forward. I twitched the right rein to remind her to follow the others, and I felt her right hind leg slip in the mud and go out from underneath us.

The fall was a slow one—not a toppling or a pitching forward   20
off the horse, but a sideways fall with the horse. The mud was soft, and I was on my feet almost before I hit the ground, reassuring those who followed that I was all right. Perhaps I remember the sensation of pulling my leg from under my mare, but perhaps I don't. She was on her feet nearly as fast as I was. I do remember the strangeness of the feeling that now we were no longer going, now we were stopped, and I was standing on my feet rather than mounted on my horse. One step forward revealed that my mare was limping badly, so it was clear that going was over for the day.

The next thing I remember is the diagnosis, a break at the stifle   21
joint of the left hind leg. The stifle joint is the joint at the top of the leg, close to the body, comparable to a human knee. I knew from all the horse stories I had read by then that a broken leg was fatal to a horse. I knew that all discussion of healing her and maybe breeding her was done for my benefit, to put off the final blow. But a broken stifle joint was too much of a challenge to veterinary medicine of the period. After pretending to consider other alternatives, my stepfather and the vet told me that the mare would be trailered out to the kennel where the Bridlespur hounds were kept, and put down. An electrical device of some sort would be put to her head, the current would run to her iron shoes, and she would die, be butchered, and be fed to the hounds, a common and entirely appropriate use for old hunters.

Early in the fall, when it was still almost summer, I had been   22
riding my mare alone one Sunday afternoon when I saw my summer riding friend, Dorothy, being driven past in her mother's car.
Dorothy's family raised Connemara ponies, and Dorothy rode a
gray mare named Larkspur. She had been riding for years and had
shown me all the trails and fields around the club where I kept my
mare. Dorothy, teary and disheveled, didn't respond when I called
out to her, but her mother stopped the car and leaned across her
daughter toward the open passenger window. She said, "Dorothy's
pony's just been killed hunting. She fell at a fence and broke her
neck." They drove off. I'm sure I looked stricken and sympathetic,
although I don't know whether, at fourteen, I knew the right thing
to say. Later I heard that Dorothy had given up riding entirely, even
though her family had ten or fifteen other possible mounts for her. I
certainly considered forsaking all equestrian activity, a reasonable
reaction to the death of one's destined equine mate, rather like taking the veil upon the death of one's spouse.

But I found myself cool and remote from my own mare. She   23
stood still in her stall, her eyes half shut, her head down, her coat
staring. She had lost her very horseness, a larger-than-human vitality that makes equine alertness and beauty compelling to people like
me. I saw with her and groomed her and gave her carrots, but I
wasn't drawn to her. A day and a half after her accident, she was
gone from her stall, and I was back to square one, horsewise. I did
not think it likely that my parents would replace her.

None of this meant that I had learned anything about the dan-   24
gers and difficulties of my chosen sport. My obsession flourished as
green as ever; unlike Dorothy, I was uneducable. Experience did
nothing to me.

Now for the peripeteia. The damp, muddy fall progressed into   25
a crisp, frosty winter. The once distant gray-blue sky became a brilliant glare that surrounded us with light. I was again in the field, this
time on a rented horse, also a bay mare. We all, riders and horses,
seemed to shine in the sunlight, from our glossy black velvet caps
down to the caulked shoes of our mounts, which glinted and
winked with each stride and rang on the frozen gravel roads. This
was the New Year's hunt, its venue a part of the wildlife area that
had no fences. For some reason. I resolved to stay near the master
and watch the actual chase after the fox. I don't remember what the
chase looked like. I know there was a fox out there, but I don't remember what it looked like. I know the sterns of the bunched, cours-
ing, vocalizing hounds pointed up like miniature pikes as the pack
ran and scrabbled over the countryside in glorious full cry. I do

remember the sight of the master's horse in front of me, as well as the sunlight on the white stock and gold stock pin of the rider beside me. I remember the long, tireless gallop and the relief I felt at there being no jumping. Then I remember the way we came upon the hounds and the huntsman and the whips just where a clearing gave way to light oak woodlands. The liver-and-white hounds were yodeling and whining, and the huntsman vaulted off his mount and waded into the pack while the whippers-in unfurled the long lashes of their whips and began driving the hounds away from the focus of their attention. The huntsman was leaning down, and then he held the quarry aloft, a dead gray fox.

Yes, I felt exhilarated at the sight, pumped up by the vigor of   26
the galloping and the sensation of having ridden in front of the field, of having been in at the death. I wasn't at all repelled or moved by the sight of the dead fox, and my reaction was entirely visceral, not at all intellectual. We had wanted to kill him and now he was dead, a stillness at the center of human, canine, and equine tumult. Good for us, good for me, good for my rented mount, who had been both willing and controllable. The huntsman drew his knife.

Maybe this is the ugliest face of foxhunting, the group blood-   27
lust. How is the field different from any other mob, except that its members are mounted? A significant portion of my subsequent education would invite and even force me to conclude that the pink coats and the high boots, the elaborate costume and ritual and language of foxhunting, the very expense of it, is really the merest film of respectability designed to camouflage the mob and allow it to reassure itself that it is far more civilized than other mobs, when it is actually far worse—caught up in irresponsible and destructive blood-lust, the object of which is not social justice or even retribution for felt wrongs, but the trivial pursuit of unworthy prey. I could talk myself into class hatred here.

On the other hand, foxhunting is a form of aggression, and it   28
seems clear by now that human aggression is so inherent that it must and will take a form. Inclination, cultural history, and education, too, predispose me to prefer elaborate forms that break down inherent drives into parts, ritualizing them and presenting them for both appreciation and interpretation. Beauty, always morally neutral, resides in rituals of aggression as much as it does in rituals of religious faith or love or art. Foxhunting need not be unmediated or mindless aggression, partly because the hunt must receive permission to ride over land owned by others. The responsibility of the master, the huntsman, the whips, and the field is to understand the

potential for destruction that foxhunting presents and to mitigate the destruction—riding fit and experienced horses, taking responsibility for younger members of the field, never galloping across agricultural ground but always keeping to its margins, hunting in winter when much of the agricultural and natural world is dormant, never blocking the fox's escape strategies, promoting courtesy among the members of the field through severe social strictures. In traditional foxhunting, as in the Catholic Church, there is a name for every occasion of sin as well as every occasion of transcendence. The aggressive impulse is developed and restrained by form that may look like obscure and arbitrary formality.

My teenaged self wasn't engaging in any of these arguments. She 29 was panting and excited, warmed in the chilly sunlight by the exertion of the chase. When the huntsman came around to "blood" me, that is, to dab my cheek with the fox's blood to signify that I had witnessed my first death, the warmth and thickness of it on my cheek and neck was an unalloyed thrill. Of course, now I read many meanings into that gory signifier—the end of virginity, blood on my conscience, feeling death as well as seeing it, making the fox's self part of my own.

I also clearly remember seeing the master look around and 30 smile as the huntsman was taking the trophies from the fox—he smiled at me and told the huntsman to give me one of the pads, rewarding my eagerness and interest in the progress of the chase. Perhaps in addition to keeping close to the master, I had peppered him with respectful questions. I was known for asking a tiresome number of questions in those days. If I did, I don't remember it now.

I took the pad in my hand. It was the small, dark foreleg of the 31 fox, maybe three inches long, with toes and nails like those of a little dog. It hadn't stiffened yet. It seemed marvelous to me, as exciting as any silver cup or blue ribbon. But the hunt was moving on, looking for another fox, and so I put it in my pocket. Later, I wrapped it in plastic and put it in the family freezer. Over the next two and a half years, while it stayed, untaxidermied, in the freezer, my mother would unwrap it from time to time, wondering what sort of meat was in the small package. I would unwrap it from time to time, too, and stare at its wonderfulness. I considered it very important that the freezer was close to the back door, because, should the house catch fire, the last thing I would do after saving our dogs would be to snatch my fox pad from the inferno.

Education interfered with later foxhunting in the most literal 32 way—when I got to college, I found I had neither the time nor the money to keep riding, and I hated the dangers of hitchhiking to the stable. My mother had pressed me to go to Vassar instead of one of those horse colleges in Virginia that had been my original inclination. She beat the lure of the horses and set my walking feet on the path of learning and art. Pretty soon I was too well educated for either blood sports or Anglophilia, and so I remain. The equestrian activity that interests me now is dressage, which is to foxhunting rather what ice dancing is to hockey. Horses rarely if ever break their necks or their legs at dressage, and dressage, like all the arts (trout fishing, ballet, novel writing) is full of theorists and intellectuals, as well as practitioners, both human and equine, who are advanced in years.

My present horse is also a Thoroughbred, though, and I sometimes sense beneath his self-restraint that inbred urge to GO, to join the galloping herd, to be caught up in headlong forward motion. And I sometimes sense that inborn urge in myself, too.   33

MEANINGS AND VALUES

1. Why does Smiley weave the thread of education level throughout her essay (pars. 1, 27, and 32)?

2. Smiley says, "The horses are impeccably clean and fitted out—in any equestrian endeavor there is a high premium placed on making a pristine appearance that I see now is a sort of conspicuous consumption rooted in the days of grooms and servants—and they are fresh and eager too . . . giving off their horsey scent to the accompaniment of the happy chatter of many riders who know one another and are secure in sharing social rituals of long standing" (par. 1). Explain the significance of this sentence. What argument is Smiley trying to make here about the attitude of the people involved in the hunt?

3. What is Smiley's attitude toward her horse in paragraph 23? Why does she compare her feelings to those of her friend Dorothy (par. 22)?

4. The author implies in the last section of the essay (pars. 32 and 33) that she is educated beyond being "Anglophile." What does Smiley mean by this? Why is she no longer interested in fox hunting?

5. Does the reader get the feeling that the young Smiley often confuses the thrill of galloping with the hunters with the actual killing of the fox? Does this attitude explain paragraph 16's comparison of American and British foxhunting? Why, or why not?

ARGUMENTATIVE TECHNIQUES

1. Identify as many descriptive passages as you can in this essay. How does her use of description help Smiley's essay succeed?

2. Does Smiley have a clear thesis statement? If so, identify it. If not, where in the essay does she make her outlook clear, and how? In paragraph 28 is Smiley attempting to justify behavior? How does this fit with her argument?

3. Why in paragraph 1 does Smiley define words that are specific jargon of foxhunting yet applied to everyday objects? What might have been the purpose of this collection of synonyms? Does language choice create camaraderie for people who have similar interests? Please explain your answer.

DICTION AND VOCABULARY

1. If you do not know their meaning, look up the following words in a dictionary: abdication (par. 4); verminous (8); apotheosis (12); dank (15); and unalloyed (29).

2. What is Smiley's tone throughout this essay? (See "Guide to Terms": *Tone*.) How do her language choices reflect her attitude toward foxhunting? Please explain. (Guide: *Diction*.)

READ TO WRITE

1. **Collaborating:** Working in a group, list activities or events that are usually engaged in by the wealthy. Choose one, research it as a group, and plan an essay similar to Smiley's in which you subtly argue for or against the practice.

2. **Considering Audience:** How do you think most readers will react to Smiley's tone in this essay? What position does she take in her conclusion? Is she believable when she condemns the society rituals of foxhunting in the same paragraph where she speaks of her own elevated education? Write an analysis of a working class reader's possible response to this essay.

3. **Developing an Essay:** Think of an activity that gave you pleasure in your youth, but which you feel you have moved beyond. Write an essay similar to Smiley's which incorporates description to help create an argument for or against the activity.

(NOTE: Suggestions for activities requiring development by ARGUMENT are on pp. 635–636 at the end of this chapter.)

ARGUMENT THROUGH DEFINITION

BARBARA LAWRENCE

> BARBARA LAWRENCE was born in Hanover, New Hampshire. After re-
> ceiving a B.A. in French literature from Connecticut College, she
> worked as an editor on *McCall's, Redbook, Harper's Bazaar,* and the
> *New Yorker.* During this period she also took an M.A. in philosophy
> from New York University. Currently a professor of humanities at
> the State University of New York's College at Old Westbury,
> Lawrence has published criticism, poetry, and fiction in *Choice,
> Commonweal, Columbia Poetry, The New York Times,* and the *New
> Yorker.*

Four-Letter Words Can Hurt You

> "Four-Letter Words Can Hurt You" first appeared in *The New York
> Times* and was later published in *Redbook.* In arguing against the
> "earthy, gut-honest" language often preferred by her students,
> Lawrence also provides a thoughtful, even scholarly, extended de-
> finition of *obscenity* itself. To accomplish her purpose, the author
> makes use of several other patterns as well.

Why should any words be called obscene? Don't they all describe   1
natural human functions? Am I trying to tell them, my students
demand, that the "strong, earthy, gut-honest"—or, if they are fans of
Norman Mailer, the "rich, liberating, existential"—language they use
to describe sexual activity isn't preferable to "phony-sounding, middle-class words like 'intercourse' and 'copulate'?" "Cop You Late!"
they say with fancy inflections and gagging grimaces. "Now, what
is *that* supposed to mean?"

Well, what is it supposed to mean? And why indeed should one   2
group of words describing human functions and human organs be
acceptable in ordinary conversation and another, describing presumably the same organs and functions, be tabooed—so much so, in
fact, that some of these words still cannot appear in print in many
parts of the English-speaking world?

The argument that these taboos exist only because of "sexual hangups" (middle-class, middle-age, feminist), or even that they are a result of class oppression (the contempt of the Norman conquerors for the language of their Anglo-Saxon serfs), ignores a much more likely explanation, it seems to me, and that is the sources and functions of the words themselves.

The best known of the tabooed sexual words, for example, comes from the German *ficken,* meaning "to strike"; combined, according to Partridge's etymological dictionary *Origins,* with the Latin sexual verb *futuere:* associated in turn with the Latin *fustis,* "a staff or cudgel"; the Celtic *buc,* "a point, hence to pierce"; the Irish *bot,* "the male member"; the Latin *battuere,* "to beat"; the Gaelic *batair,* "a cudgeller"; the Early Irish *bualaim,* "I strike"; and so forth. It is one of what etymologists sometimes called "the sadistic group of words for the man's part in copulation."

The brutality of this word, then, and its equivalents ("screw," "bang," etc.) is not an illusion of the middle class or a crotchet of Women's Liberation. In their origins and imagery these words carry undeniably painful, if not sadistic, implications, the object of which is almost always female. Consider, for example, what a "screw" actually does to the wood it penetrates; what a painful, even mutilating, activity this kind of analogy suggests. "Screw" is particularly interesting in this context, since the noun, according to Partridge, comes from words meaning "groove," "nut," "ditch," "breeding sow," "scrofula" and "swelling," while the verb, besides its explicit imagery, has antecedent associations to "write on," "scratch," "scarify," and so forth—a revealing fusion of a mechanical or painful action with an obviously denigrated object.

Not all obscene words, of course, are as implicitly sadistic or denigrating to women as these, but all that I know seem to serve a similar purpose: to reduce the human organism (especially the female organism) and human functions (especially sexual and procreative) to their least organic, most mechanical dimension; to substitute a trivializing or deforming resemblance for the complex human reality of what is being described.

Tabooed male descriptives, when they are not openly denigrating to women, often serve to divorce a male organ or function from any significant interaction with the female. Take the word "*testes,*" for example, suggesting "witnesses" (from the Latin *testis*) to the sexual and procreative strengths of the male organ; and the obscene counterpart of this word, which suggests little more than a mechanical shape. Or compare almost any of the "rich," "liberating" sexual verbs, so fashionable today among male writers, with that much-derived

Latin word "copulate" ("to bind or join together") or even that Anglo-Saxon phrase (which seems to have had no trouble surviving the Norman Conquest) "make love."

How arrogantly self-involved the tabooed words seem in comparison to either of the other terms, and how contemptuous of the female partner. Understandably so, of course, if she is only a "skirt," a "broad," a "chick," a "pussycat" or a "piece." If she is, in other words no more than her skirt, or what her skirt conceals; no more than a breeder, or the broadest part of her; no more than a piece of a human being or a "piece of tail." 8

The most severely tabooed of all the female descriptives, incidentally, are those like a "piece of tail," which suggests (either explicitly or through antecedents) that there is no significant difference between the female channel through which we are all conceived and born and the anal outlet common to both sexes—a distinction that pornographers have always enjoyed obscuring. 9

This effort to deny women their biological identity, their individuality, their humanness, is such an important aspect of obscene language that one can only marvel at how seldom, in an era preoccupied with definitions of obscenity, this fact is brought to our attention. One problem, of course, is that many of the people in the best position to do this (critics, teachers, writers) are so reluctant today to admit that they are angered or shocked by obscenity. Bored, maybe, unimpressed, aesthetically displeased, but—no matter how brutal or denigrating the material—never angered, never shocked. 10

And yet how eloquently angered, how piously shocked many of these same people become if denigrating language is used about any minority group other than women; if the obscenities are racial or ethnic, that is, rather than sexual. Words like "coon," "kike," "spic," "wop," after all, deform identity, deny individuality and humanness in almost exactly the same way that sexual vulgarisms and obscenities do. 11

No one that I know, least of all my students, would fail to question the values of a society whose literature and entertainment rested heavily on racial or ethnic pejoratives. Are the values of a society whose literature and entertainment rest as heavily as ours on sexual pejoratives any less questionable? 12

MEANINGS AND VALUES

1. Explain the meaning of *irony* by use of at least one illustration from the latter part of this essay. (See "Guide to Terms": *Irony*.)

2. Inasmuch as the selection itself includes many of the so-called "strong, earthy, gut-honest" words, could anyone logically call it obscene? Why or why not? To what extent, if at all, does the author's point of view help determine your answer? (Guide: *Point of View.*)

3. Compose, in your own words, a compact statement of Lawrence's thesis. (Guide: *Thesis.*) Are all parts of the essay completely relevant to this thesis? Justify your answer.

4. Evaluate this composition by use of our three-question system. (Guide: *Evaluation.*)

ARGUMENTATIVE TECHNIQUES

1. What is the purpose of this essay? (Guide: *Purpose.*)

2. What objection to her opinion does the author refute in paragraph 3, and how does she refute it? (Guide: *Refutation.*) Where else in the essay does she refute opposing arguments?

3. Are the evidence and supporting arguments in this essay arranged in a refutation-proof pattern? If not, describe the arrangement of the essay.

4. Which of the methods "peculiar to definition alone" (see the introduction to Chapter 9) does the author employ in developing this essay? What other patterns of exposition does she also use?

5. Which of the standard techniques of introduction are used? (Guide: *Introductions.*) Which methods are used to close the essay? (Guide: *Closing.*)

DICTION AND VOCABULARY

1. How, if at all, is this discussion of words related to *connotation?* (Guide: *Connotation/Denotation.*) To what extent would connotations in this matter depend on the setting and circumstances in which the words are used? Cite illustrations to clarify your answer.

2. In view of the fact that the author uses frankly many of the "gut-honest" words, why do you suppose she plainly avoids others, such as in paragraphs 4 and 7?

3. The author says that a "kind of analogy" is suggested by some of the words discussed (par. 5). If you have studied Chapter 6 of this book, does her use of the term *analogy* seem in conflict with what you believed it to mean? Explain.

4. Study the author's uses of the following words, consulting the dictionary as needed: existential, grimaces (par. 1); etymological, cudgel (4); sadistic (4–6); crotchet, scrofula, explicit, antecedent, scarify (5); denigrated (5–7, 10–11); aesthetically (10); pejoratives (12).

READ TO WRITE

1. **Collaborating:** Why do people use obscene language? Are these reasons satisfactory enough to keep from stigmatizing it or considering

it impolite? Have our views of obscene language undergone any recent changes? Should we discourage the use of obscene language in
more social situations than we currently do? Working in a group,
continue this list of questions until you have identified several possible topics for an essay. Words characterizing ethnic groups are likely
to get strong reponse from readers.

2. **Considering Audience.** Does the author make a justifiable compari-
    son between obscene words and ethnic pejoratives? Using illustra-
    tions for specificity, carry the comparison further to show why it is
    sound, or explain why you consider it a weak comparison.

3. **Developing an Essay:** Following Lawrence's lead, discuss some
    other closely related group of terms and their significance, and sug-
    gest ways we should alter the way we use them.

(NOTE: Suggestions for topics requiring development by ARGUMENT are on pp. 635–636
at the end of this chapter.)

ARGUMENT THROUGH NARRATIVE

SARAH MIN

Sᴀʀᴀʜ Mɪɴ works at *Glamour* magazine.

Language Lessons

Issues of bilingualism and bilingual education along with proposals for "English Only" in government and schools have drawn
much interest over the past decade. Sarah Min takes a somewhat
different, and personal, approach to bilingualism, arguing for its
importance through her own story.

Even though I could understand only snippets of their conversation, I comprehended enough to know that the manicurists at
the nail salon were talking about me.

What a shame! Another Korean who cannot speak the language, the
woman filing my fingernails said to her colleague, both of them
shaking their heads in disapproval. Her remark hit me, and I stumbled for the right words to defend myself.

The fact is, I traded my own Korean voice to give my parents
their English ones: My mom and dad came to this country 27 years
ago with an English vocabulary dominated by brand names like
Tropicana and Samsonite. But they were determined to master the
language of their new home. When I was in grade school, my dad
read my English textbooks and asked me to give him the same lessons
I had learned that day. On long car trips, my parents spent the confined hours in our Impala station wagon practicing their pronunciation aloud. My brother and I, captive tutors, led them in oral exercises,
repeating the difficult distinction between *ear* and *year*, *war* and *wore*.

As my parents' fluency increased, their use of Korean dwin-
dled. Though they spoke to each other in their native tongue, with
my brother and me they used only one language: English. They
didn't want us to speak Korean, they said, because they didn't want
even a trace of an accent to infect our American-style speech.

Still, I absorbed bits and pieces of Korean, important phrases
like "Oh-mo-mo" and "Whey-goo-deh?"—the equivalent of "Oh
no!" and "What's your problem?"—subtleties that can't be precisely
translated but are understood as readily as "oy vey" or "cool." In

private, I'd practice the sound effects—the gasps and clucks that are a part of the Korean language.

In public, though, I was reluctant to speak. My words sounded   6
clunky, choppy, unlike the rhythmic cadences of my mother's voice. Once when I attempted conversation with a Korean-speaking woman in my neighborhood, my efforts were clearly unimpressive: She snickered at my accent and answered me in English. By the time I was in college, I had stopped trying to speak Korean, a decision only I noticed. No one expected me to speak the language anyway.

Yet I always felt that a part of me had been silenced. As I got   7
older and moved to a city where I met more Koreans, I began to feel as the women in the nail salon did: That those of us who didn't speak Korean had something to be ashamed of, that we were distancing ourselves from our cultural heritage. Language, after all, involves much more than the ability to communicate. It conveys a desire to understand and participate in a culture, to make it one's own. Could I ever fully understand and appreciate my heritage if I couldn't speak the language of my ancestors?

So I registered for a course in Korean at an adult education   8
school. I expected my classmates to be Americans who were going abroad, but I discovered most of the students had come for the same reason that I had: to find their Korean voices.

To my surprise, I picked up the language quickly. Even though   9
my vocabulary was limited and my grammar was rough, I realized I knew quite a bit, as if the Korean words had been lurking somewhere in a quiet corner of my brain. The teacher taught phrases that sounded familiar and came to me effortlessly; I practiced the new tongue placements and inflections to hide my American accent. The first time I called my parents and said, in flawless Korean, "Hello, we haven't spoken in such a long time," I was 24 years old, but they reacted as proudly as if I were a toddler who had just uttered her first words. And when I walked into a Korean restaurant and casually greeted the waiter, who responded in Korean that I could sit anywhere I liked, I knew he took me for the genuine article.

Now whenever I visit my parents, I ask them to speak Korean   10
with me at least some of the time. Although I'm still struggling, still studying so I can become more fluent, I know enough now that my parents can tell me stories, jokes and proverbs that would otherwise have gotten garbled in the static of translation. Eagerly, I listen, laugh and nod in full understanding.

Being able to speak Korean has some surprising bonuses: In   11
American restaurants, my dad and I figure the tip right in front of

the waiter. And among Koreans, knowing the language forges an almost instant camaraderie.

That day at the nail salon, when I finally worked up the courage   12
to respond to the manicurist, I spoke slowly, but confidently: *I understand you and yes, it is shameful that I can only speak a little.*

The young woman polishing my fingernails paused. She looked   13
up at me and smiled, as if she were seeing me for the first time. And, for the first time, I too was seeing a new part of myself: a proud Korean American who could finally hear her own voice.

MEANINGS AND VALUES

1. Min devotes much of paragraphs 3 and 4 in her essay to a discussion of her parent's efforts to learn English and to encourage their children to speak English. Explain why her parents may have felt they needed to do this. As a young girl, how does Min react to her parents' effort?

2. What feelings inspired Min to take adult education courses in Korean (par. 8)? Is she justified in her concerns about heritage? How important are these cultural issues in the contemporary America?

ARGUMENTATIVE TECHNIQUES

1. The anecdote in Min's introduction (pars. 1 and 2) is readdressed in her conclusion. What element of surprise does she incorporate into this story? Does she convince her reader of the importance of her conversation with the manicurists?

2. Much of Min's argument is in the form of narrative. How effective is this technique? Why do you think she chose a first person narrative for this topic?

DICTION AND VOCABULARY

1. Are there any words in this essay with which you are unfamiliar? Why might Min have used a basic vocabulary for this piece? Who might her target audience include?

2. Min writes this as an autobiographical narrative. Point to specific uses of transitions, dialogue, and other techniques that help the narrative have a storylike quality.

READ TO WRITE

1. **Collaborating:** Working in a group, list the native languages of your ancestors. How many of you still speak that language? Discuss with

your teammates the reasons why you feel that your family no longer speaks in the native tongue, or if your family still does, why the members have chosen to continue. Compare your reasons and look for underlying cultural connections regarding the maintenance of native tongues. Keeping in mind your group discussions, write an individual paper in a style similar to Min's discussing your use or lack of use of your family's native tongue. If your ancestry is of English speaking people, write about a friend or someone you know who has had this issue arise in his/her family.

2.   **Considering Audience:** Min says, "And among Koreans, knowing the language forges an almost instant camaraderie" (par. 11). Would non-Korean readers identify with this statement? Does her point apply to others besides Koreans? Write a short analysis explaining your response.

3.   **Developing an Essay:** Min's essay clearly encourages the maintaining of a native tongue, but not at the sacrifice of learning English when living in the United States. This is one facet of a debate on language. Research the question of whether or not the United States should have a unified language and the impact of maintaining a native tongue in some capacity. Consider the unifying qualities of language both inside and outside of the cultural boundaries. Write an argumentative essay employing multiple patterns of development in which you address the issue of either the adoption of a national language, the use of native languages in the household, or the acceptance of bi- or multi-lingualism in society.

(NOTE: Suggestions for essays requiring development by use of ARGUMENT are on pp. 635–636 at the end of this chapter.)

ARGUMENT THROUGH INDUCTION AND DEDUCTION

BARBARA EHRENREICH

BARBARA EHRENREICH received a B.A. from Reed College and a Ph.D.
from Rockefeller University in biology. She has been active in the
women's movement and other movements for social change and
she has taught women's issues at several universities, including New
York University and the State University of New York—Old Westbury.
She is a fellow of the Institute for Policy Studies in Washington,
D.C., and is active in the Democratic Socialist of America. A prolific
author, Ehrenreich had published articles in a wide range of magazines, among them *Esquire,* the *Atlantic, Vogue, New Republic,* the
*Wall Street Journal, TV Guide, Ms., The New York Times Magazine,
Social Policy,* and *The Nation.* Her books include *For Her Own Good:
150 Years of the Experts' Advice to Women* (with Deirdre English)
(1978); *The Hearts of Men: American Dreams and the Flight from
Commitment* (1983); *Fear of Falling: The Inner Life of the Middle Class*
(1989); *The Worst Years of Our Lives: Irreverent Notes from a Decade
of Greed* (1990); and *The Snarling Citizen: Essays* (1995).

Making Sense of *La Différence*

An argument over gender differences might seem a good occasion
for comparison, and Ehrenreich uses this strategy to present much
of her evidence. Her overall strategy, however, is inductive: she reviews evidence and counterarguments on the way to presenting
her own thesis. This strategy is particularly appropriate for hotly
contested issues; in such settings, stating a thesis early in an essay
can polarize readers and make them less likely to consider carefully the evidence and ideas you present.

Few areas of science are as littered with intellectual rubbish as the   1
study of innate mental differences between the sexes. In the nineteenth century, biologists held that woman's brain was too small for
intellect, but just large enough for household chores. When the tiny-
brain theory bit the dust (elephants, after all, have bigger brains than
men), scientists began a long, fruitless attempt to locate the biological basis of male superiority in various brain lobes and chromo-
somes. By the 1960s sociobiologists were asserting that natural
selection, operating throughout the long human prehistory of hunting and gathering, had predisposed males to leadership and exploration and females to crouching around the campfire with the kids.

Recent studies suggest that there may be some real differences   2
after all. And why not? We have different hormones and body parts;
it would be odd if our brains were a hundred percent unisex. The
question, as ever, is, What do these differences augur for our social
roles?—meaning, in particular, the division of power and opportunity between the sexes.

Don't look to the Flintstones for an answer. However human be-   3
ings whiled away their first 100,000 or so years of existence, few of us
today make a living by tracking down mammoths or digging up tasty
roots. In fact, much of our genetic legacy of sex differences has already been rendered moot by that uniquely human invention: technology. Military prowess no longer depends on superior musculature
or those bursts of aggressive fury that prime the body for combat at
ax range. As for exploration, women—with their lower body weight
and oxygen consumption—may be the more "natural" astronauts.

But suppose that the feminists' worst-case scenario turns out to   4
be true, and that males really are better, on average, at certain mathematical tasks. If this tempts you to shunt the girls all back to Home
Ec—the only acceptable realm for would-be female scientists eighty
years ago—you probably need remedial work in the statistics of "av-
erages" yourself. Just as some women are taller and stronger than
some men, some are swifter at solid geometry and abstract algebra.
Many of the pioneers in the field of X-ray crystallography—which
involves three-dimensional visualization and heavy doses of
math—were female, including biophysicist Rosalyn Franklin, whose
work was indispensable to the discovery of the double-helical structure of DNA.

Then there is the problem that haunts all studies of "innate" sex   5
differences: the possibility that the observed differences are really
the result of lingering cultural factors—pushing females, for example, to "succeed" by dummying up. Girls' academic achievement,
for example, usually takes a nosedive at puberty. Unless nature has
selected for smart girls and dumb women, something is going very
wrong at about the middle-school level. Part of the problem may be
that males, having been the dominant sex for a few millennia, still
tend to prefer females who make them feel stronger and smarter.
Any girl who is bright enough to solve a quadratic equation is also
smart enough to bat her eyelashes and pretend that she can't.

Teachers too may play a larger role than nature in differentiat-   6
ing the sexes. Studies show that they tend to favor boys by calling on
them more often, making eye contact with them more frequently,
and pushing them harder to perform. Myra and David Sadker, pro-

fessors of education at American University, have found that girls do better when teachers are sensitized to gender bias and refrain from sexist language such as the use of "man" to mean all of us. Single-sex classes in math and science also boost female performance, presumably by eliminating favoritism and male disapproval of female achievement.

The success, so far, of such simple educational reforms only underscores the basic social issue: given that there may be real innate mental differences between the sexes, what are we going to do about them? A female advantage in reading emotions could be interpreted to mean that males should be barred from psychiatry—or that they need more coaching. A male advantage in math could be used to confine girls to essays and sonnets—or the decision could be made to compensate by putting more effort into girls' math education. In effect, we already compensate for boys' apparent handicap in verbal skills by making reading the centerpiece of grade-school education. 7

We are cultural animals, and these are cultural decisions of the kind that our genes can't make for us. In fact, the whole discussion of innate sex differences is itself heavily shaped by cultural factors. Why, for example, is the study of innate differences such a sexy, well-funded topic right now, which happens to be a time of organized feminist challenge to the ancient sexual division of power? Why do the media tend to get excited when scientists find an area of difference, and ignore the many reputable studies that come up with no differences at all? 8

Whatever science eventually defines it as, *la différence* can be amplified or minimized by human cultural arrangements: the choice is up to us, not our genes. 9

Meanings and Values

1. What is the "intellectual rubbish" (par. 1) that Ehrenreich describes in her introduction? Why do you think she included this phrase in her opening statement?

2. Does Ehrenreich believe that the sexes are different? Does she say so clearly and directly? Identify examples in the essay to support your response.

3. Do you agree with Ehrenreich's conclusion (par. 9)? How much of a role do you think that genes play? Can we culturally overcome the genetic differences? Be ready to explain your answer.

ARGUMENTATIVE TECHNIQUES

1.   Ehrenreich uses many patterns of development. Identify as many as you can. Which are the most and least effective? Why? (See "Guide to Terms": *Evaluation.*)

2.   In paragraph 6 Ehrenreich claims that teachers are partly to blame for differentiating between the sexes. How does she support this opinion? What types of evidence does she use? Is her evidence convincing enough for you to agree with her? Why, or why not?

3.   Does Ehrenreich consider opposing viewpoints to the notion of biological difference? If so, where in the essay does she mention them? Does she disagree with the notion that men and women are biologically different or with differing notions of how we should deal with biological differences? Be ready to explain your answer.

DICTION AND VOCABULARY

1.   Are there any words in the essay with which you are unfamiliar? Why might Ehrenreich have chosen a generally easy to understand vocabulary for her essay?

2.   Why does Ehrenreich use the French "la différence" as part of her title and as part of her conclusion?

READ TO WRITE

1.   **Collaborating:** Working in a group, list as many differences as you can think of between men and women or boys and girls. How many of these seem purely stereotypical with little basis in actual behavior? How many seem to be accurate, at least according to your experience? Write an essay of your own, drawing on the group's ideas about differences in behavior and the examples they provided.

2.   **Considering Audience:** Does Ehrenreich use enough evidence to make a skeptical reader believe her premise about the role of culture in the system of differences? Does she "take a side" in this essay, favoring either men or women? Consider especially paragraph 7, where Ehrenreich begins with discussing the negative effects of difference for men and for women but ends by arguing that women suffer more negative consequences. Write a paragraph in a similar style in which you begin by exploring some other effects of gender difference, but conclude by favoring one group or the other.

3.   **Developing an Essay:** Think back to your elementary and secondary education. In what ways were the boys and girls treated differently? Were these differences somehow detrimental to you and your peers, or did they help you better celebrate yourself or your gender? Prepare an essay addressing this question. Use specific examples and draw on some research on the role of gender in education.

(NOTE: Suggestions for topics to be developed by means of ARGUMENT follow.)

Writing Suggestions for Chapter 13

ARGUMENT

Choose one of the following topic areas, identify an issue (a conflict or problem) within it, and prepare an essay that tries to convince readers to share your opinion about the issue and to take any appropriate action. Use a variety of evidence in your essay, and choose any pattern of development you consider proper for the topic, for your thesis, and for the intended audience.

1. Gun control.
2. The quality of education in American elementary and secondary schools.
3. Treatment of critically ill newborn babies.
4. Hunting.
5. Euthanasia.
6. Censorship in public schools and libraries.
7. College athletics.
8. The problem of toxic waste or a similar environmental problem.
9. Careers versus family responsibilities.
10. The separation of church and state.
11. Law on the drinking age or on drunk driving.
12. Evolution versus creationism.
13. Medical ethics.
14. Government spending on social programs.
15. The quality of television programming.
16. The impact of divorce.
17. The effects of television viewing on children.
18. Professional sports.
19. Violence in service of an ideal or belief.
20. Scholarship and student loan policies.
21. Low pay for public service and the "helping" professions.
22. Cheating in college courses.
23. Drug and alcohol abuse.
24. Product safety and reliability.
25. Government economic or social policy.

COLLABORATIVE ACTIVITIES

As you prepare an essay on one of the given topics (1–25) or on some other topic, make a list of the evidence for your opinion. Share the list with one or more readers. Ask the reader to rank each piece of evidence for persuasiveness, using a scale of 1 (unpersuasive) to 5 (very persuasive).

14

Further Readings: Combining Patterns

MARGARET ATWOOD

MARGARET ATWOOD was born in Ottawa, Ontario, in 1939. After attending college in Canada, she went to graduate school at Harvard University. She has had a distinguished career as a novelist, poet, and essayist, and is generally considered to be one of the central figures in contemporary Canadian literature and culture. Atwood's international reputation as a writer rests on her novels, including *The Edible Woman* (1960), *Surfacing* (1972), *Life Before Man* (1979), *Bodily Harm* (1982), *The Handmaid's Tale* (1986), *Cat's Eye* (1989); *The Robber Bride* (1993) and her short stories, including *Bluebeard's Egg and Other Stories* (1986), though she has written poetry, television plays, and children's books as well. Her essays were collected in the volume *Second Words* (1982) and have continued to appear in magazines such as *Ms., Harper's, The Humanist, The New Republic,* and *Architectural Digest.* As an essayist, Atwood frequently writes about issues in contemporary culture and society, including the nature of Canadian culture and relationships between Canada and the United States.

Pornography

In the following essay, Atwood addresses the question of pornography with a directness and originality that are characteristic of her work. This essay originally appeared in *Chatelaine Magazine,* a mass-circulation women's magazine. As you read the selection, consider how well it addresses both the concerns of its original audience and the concerns about pornography a somewhat wider audience might have. Note also how she makes use of definition and a number of other expository patterns.

When I was in Finland a few years ago for an international writ-   1
ers' conference, I had occasion to say a few paragraphs in public on the subject of pornography. The context was a discussion of political repression, and I was suggesting the possibility of a link between the two. The immediate result was that a male journalist took several large bites out of me. Prudery and pornography are two halves of the same coin, said he, and I was clearly a prude. What

could you expect from an Anglo-Canadian? Afterward, a couple of pleasant Scandinavian men asked me what I had been so worked up about. All "pornography" means, they said, is graphic depictions of whores, and what was the harm in that?

Not until then did it strike me that the male journalist and I had   2
two entirely different things in mind. By "pornography," he meant naked bodies and sex. I, on the other hand, had recently been doing the research for my novel *Bodily Harm,* and was still in a state of shock from some of the material I had seen, including the Ontario Board of Film Censors' "outtakes." By "pornography," I meant women getting their nipples snipped off with garden shears, having meat hooks stuck into their vaginas, being disemboweled; little girls being raped; men (yes, there are some men) being smashed to a pulp and forcibly sodomized. The cutting edge of pornography, as far as I could see, was no longer simple old copulation, hanging from the chandelier or otherwise: it was death, messy, explicit and highly sadistic. I explained this to the nice Scandinavian men. "Oh, but that's just the United States," they said. "Everyone knows they're sick." In their country, they said, violent "pornography" of that kind was not permitted on television or in movies; indeed, excessive violence of any kind was not permitted. They had drawn a clear line between erotica, which earlier studies had shown did not incite men to more aggressive and brutal behavior toward women, and violence, which later studies indicated did.

Some time after that I was in Saskatchewan, where, because of the   3
scenes in *Bodily Harm,* I found myself on an open-line radio show answering questions about "pornography." Almost no one who phoned in was in favor of it, but again they weren't talking about the same stuff I was, because they hadn't seen it. Some of them were all set to stamp out bathing suits and negligees, and, if possible, any depictions of the female body whatsoever. God, it was implied, did not approve of female bodies, and sex of any kind, including that practiced by bumblebees, should be shoved back into the dark, where it belonged. I had more than a suspicion that *Lady Chatterley's Lover,* Margaret Laurence's *The Diviners,* and indeed most books by most serious modern authors would have ended up as confetti if left in the hands of these callers.

For me, these two experiences illustrate the two poles of the   4
emotionally heated debate that is now thundering around this issue. They also underline the desirability and even the necessity of defining the terms. "Pornography" is now one of those catchalls, like "Marxism" and "feminism," that have become so broad they can

mean almost anything, ranging from certain verses in the Bible, ads for skin lotion and sex tests for children to the contents of Penthouse, Naughty '90s postcards and films with titles containing the word *Nazi* that show vicious scenes of torture and killing. It's easy to say that sensible people can tell the difference. Unfortunately, opinions on what constitutes a sensible person vary.

But even sensible people tend to lose their cool when they start   5
talking about this subject. They soon stop talking and start yelling, and the name-calling begins. Those in favor of censorship (which may include groups not noticeably in agreement on other issues, such as some feminists and religious fundamentalists) accuse the others of exploiting women through the use of degrading images, contributing to the corruption of children, and adding to the general climate of violence and threat in which both women and children live in this society; or, though they may not give much of a hoot about actual women and children, they invoke moral standards and God's supposed aversion to "filth," "smut" and deviated *perversion,* which may mean ankles.

The camp in favor of total "freedom of expression" often comes   6
out howling as loud as the Romans would have if told they could no longer have innocent fun watching the lions eat up Christians. It too may include segments of the population who are not natural bedfel-lows: those who proclaim their God-given right to freedom, includ-ing the freedom to tote guns, drive when drunk, drool over chicken porn and get off on videotapes of women being raped and beaten, may be waving the same anticensorship banner as responsible liber-als who fear the return of Mrs. Grundy, or gay groups for whom sexual emancipation involves the concept of "sexual theater." *Whatever turns you on* is a handy motto, as is *A man's home is his castle* (and if it includes a dungeon with beautiful maidens strung up in chains and bleeding from every pore, that's his business).

Meanwhile, theoreticians theorize and speculators speculate. Is   7
today's pornography yet another indication of the hatred of the body, the deep mind-body split, which is supposed to pervade Western Christian society? Is it a backlash against the women's movement by men who are threatened by uppity female behavior in real life, so like to fantasize about women done up like outsize parcels, being turned into hamburger, kneeling at their feet in slave-like adoration or sucking off guns? Is it a sign of collective impotence, of a generation of men who can't relate to real women at all but have to make do with bits of celluloid and paper? Is the current flood just a result of smart marketing and aggressive promotion by the money men in

what has now become a multibillion-dollar industry? If they were selling movies about men getting their testicles stuck full of knitting needles by women with swastikas on their sleeves, would they do as well, or is this penchant somehow peculiarly male? If so, why? Is pornography a power trip rather than a sex one? Some say that those ropes, chains, muzzles and other restraining devices are an argument for the immense power female sexuality still wields in the male imagination: you don't put these things on dogs unless you're afraid of them. Others, more literary, wonder about the shift from the 19th-century Magic Woman or Femme Fatale image to the lollipop-licker, airhead or turkey-carcass treatment of women in porn today. The proporners don't care much about theory; they merely demand product. The antiporners don't care about it in the final analysis either; there's dirt on the street, and they want it cleaned up, now.

It seems to me that this conversation, with its *You're-a-prude/You're-a-pervert* dialectic, will never get anywhere as long as we continue to think of this material as just "entertainment." Possibly we're deluded by the packaging, the format: magazine, book, movie, theatrical presentation. We're used to thinking of these things as part of the "entertainment industry," and we're used to thinking of ourselves as free adult people who ought to be able to see any kind of "entertainment" we want to. That was what the First Choice pay-TV debate was all about. After all, it's only entertainment, right? Entertainment means fun, and only a killjoy would be antifun. What's the harm?   8

This is obviously the central question: *What's the harm?* If there isn't any real harm to any real people, then the antiporners can tsk-tsk and/or throw up as much as they like, but they can't rightfully expect more legal controls or sanctions. However, the no-harm position is far from being proven.   9

(For instance, there's a clear-cut case for banning—as the federal government has proposed—movies, photos and videos that depict children engaging in sex with adults: real children are used to make the movies, and hardly anybody thinks this is ethical. The possibilities for coercion are too great.)   10

To shift the viewpoint, I'd like to suggest three other models for looking at "pornography"—and here I mean the violent kind.   11

Those who find the idea of regulating pornographic materials repugnant because they think it's Fascist or Communist or otherwise not in accordance with the principles of an open democratic society should consider that Canada has made it illegal to disseminate   12 material that may lead to hatred toward any group because of race or religion. I suggest that if pornography of the violent kind depicted these acts being done predominantly to Chinese, to blacks, to Catholics, it would be off the market immediately, under the present laws. Why is hate literature illegal? Because whoever made the law thought that such material might incite real people to do real awful things to other real people. The human brain is to a certain extent a computer: garbage in, garbage out. We only hear about the extreme cases (like that of American multimurderer Ted Bundy) in which pornography has contributed to the death and/or mutilation of women and/or men. Although pornography is not the only factor involved in the creation of such deviance, it certainly has upped the ante by suggesting both a variety of techniques and the social acceptability of such actions. Nobody knows yet what effect this stuff is having on the less psychotic.

Studies have shown that a large part of the market for all kinds 13 of porn, soft and hard, is drawn from the 16-to-21-year-old population of young men. Boys used to learn about sex on the street, or (in Italy, according to Fellini movies) from friendly whores, or, in more genteel surroundings, from girls, their parents, or, once upon a time, in school, more or less. Now porn has been added, and sex education in the schools is rapidly being phased out. The buck has been passed, and boys are being taught that all women secretly like to be raped and that real men get high on scooping out women's digestive tracts.

Boys learn their concept of masculinity from other men: is this 14 what most men want them to be learning? If word gets around that rapists are "normal" and even admirable men, will boys feel that in order to be normal, admirable and masculine they will have to be rapists? Human beings are enormously flexible, and how they turn out depends a lot on how they're educated, by the society in which they're immersed as well as by their teachers. In a society that advertises and glorifies rape or even implicitly condones it, more women get raped. It becomes socially acceptable. And at a time when men and the traditional male role have taken a lot of flak and men are confused and casting around for an acceptable way of being male (and, in some cases, not getting much comfort from women on that score), this must be at times a pleasing thought.

It would be naïve to think of violent pornography as just harm- 15 less entertainment. It's also an educational tool and a powerful propaganda device. What happens when boy educated on porn meets girl brought up on Harlequin romances? The clash of expectations can be heard around the block. She wants him to get down on his knees with a ring, he wants her to get down on all fours with a ring in her nose. Can this marriage be saved?

Pornography has certain things in common with such addictive substances as alcohol and drugs: for some, though by no means for all, it induces chemical changes in the body, which the user finds exciting and pleasurable. It also appears to attract a "hard core" of habitual users and a penumbra of those who use it occasionally but aren't dependent on it in any way. There are also significant numbers of men who aren't much interested in it, not because they're undersexed but because real life is satisfying their needs, which may not require as many appliances as those of users.

16

For the "hard core," pornography may function as alcohol does for the alcoholic: tolerance develops, and a little is no longer enough. This may account for the short viewing time and fast turnover in porn theaters. Mary Brown, chairwoman of the Ontario Board of Film Censors, estimates that for every one mainstream movie requesting entrance to Ontario, there is one porno flick. Not only the quantity consumed but the quality of explicitness must escalate, which may account for the growing violence: once the big deal was breasts, then it was genitals, then copulation, then that was no longer enough and the hard users had to have more. The ultimate kick is death, and after that, as the Marquis de Sade so boringly demonstrated, multiple death.

17

The existence of alcoholism has not led us to ban social drinking. On the other hand, we do have laws about drinking and driving, excessive drunkenness and other abuses of alcohol that may result in injury or death to others.

18

This leads us back to the key question: what's the harm? Nobody knows, but this society should find out fast, before the saturation point is reached. The Scandinavian studies that showed a connection between depictions of sexual violence and increased impulse toward it on the part of male viewers would be a starting point, but many more questions remain to be raised as well as answered. What, for instance, is the crucial difference between men who are users and men who are not? Does using affect a man's relationship with actual women, and, if so, adversely? Is there a clear line between erotica and violent pornography, or are they on an escalating continuum? Is this a "men versus women" issue, with all men secretly siding with the proporners and all women secretly siding against? (I think not; there *are* lots of men who don't think that running their true love through the Cuisinart is the best way they can think of to spend a Saturday night, and they're just as

19

nauseated by films of someone else doing it as women are.) Is pornography merely an expression of the sexual confusion of this age or an active contributor to it?

Nobody wants to go back to the age of official repression, when   20 even piano legs were referred to as "limbs" and had to wear pantaloons to be decent. Neither do we want to end up in George Orwell's *1984*, in which pornography is turned out by the State to keep the proles in a state of torpor, sex itself is considered dirty and the approved practice it only for reproduction. But Rome under the emperors isn't such a good model either.

If all men and women respected each other, if sex were consid-   21 ered joyful and life-enhancing instead of a wallow in germ-filled glop, if everyone were in love all the time, if, in other words, many people's lives were more satisfactory for them than they appear to be now, pornography might just go away on its own. But since this is obviously not happening, we as a society are going to have to make some informed and responsible decisions about how to deal with it.

LESLIE MARMON SILKO

LESLIE MARMON SILKO was born in 1948 in Albuquerque, New Mexico. She was raised on the Laguna Pueblo Reservation and attended the University of New Mexico (B.A., 1969). Formerly on the English faculty of the University of Arizona, Silko now focuses full time on her writing, for which she has received many awards, including a MacArthur Foundation grant. Much of Silko's writing draws on Native American traditions and myths and on the interactions of Native American cultures and perspectives with the contemporary world. Her novels include the much-praised *Ceremony* (1977) and *Almanac of the Dead* (1991). She has also published a volume of poetry, *Laguna Woman* (1974); a collection of short stories, *Storyteller* (1981); an autobiography, *Sacred Water* (1993); and a collection of essays, *Yellow Woman and a Beauty of the Spirit* (1996).

Yellow Woman and a Beauty of the Spirit

"Yellow Woman and a Beauty of the Spirit," comes from the book with the same title. In this essay, Silko recalls her differences in appearance from other Laguna Pueblo children, the result of her mixed ancestry, and uses this memory as a springboard to an explanation of the traditional Pueblo disregard of physical appearance and emphasis instead on individual qualities of spirit as the basis of true beauty. She also discusses the Pueblo disregard of fixed gender, work, and family roles, but a correspondingly strong emphasis is on the quality of relationships among people, animals, and the land. As in much of her work, Silko's perspective lies at the center of the intersection between cultures.

From the time I was a small child, I was aware that I was different. 1 I looked different from my playmates. My two sisters looked different too. We didn't look quite like the other Laguna Pueblo children, but we didn't look quite white either. In the 1880s, my great-grandfather had followed his older brother west from Ohio to the New Mexico Territory to survey the land for the U.S. government. The two Marmon brothers came to the Laguna Pueblo reservation because they had an Ohio cousin who already lived there. The Ohio cousin was involved in sending Indian children thousands of miles

away from their families to the War Department's big Indian boarding school in Carlisle, Pennsylvania. Both brothers married full-blood
Laguna Pueblo women. My great-grandfather had first married my
great-grandmother's older sister, but she died in childbirth and left
two small children. My great-grandmother was fifteen or twenty
years younger than my great-grandfather. She had attended Carlisle
Indian School and spoke and wrote English beautifully.

I called her Grandma A'mooh because that's what I heard her   2
say whenever she saw me. *A'mooh* means "granddaughter" in the
Laguna language. I remember this word because her love and her
acceptance of me as a small child were so important. I had sensed
immediately that something about my appearance was not acceptable to some people, white and Indian. But I did not see any signs of
that strain or anxiety in the face of my beloved Grandma A'mooh.

Younger people, people my parents' age, seemed to look at the   3
world in a more modern way. The modern way included racism. My
physical appearance seemed not to matter to the old-time people.
They looked at the world very differently; a person's appearance
and possessions did not matter nearly as much as a person's behavior. For them, a person's value lies in how that person interacts with
other people, how that person behaves toward the animals and the
earth. That is what matters most to the old-time people. The Pueblo
people believed this long before the Puritans arrived with their notions of sin and damnation, and racism. The old-time beliefs persist
today; thus I will refer to the old-time people in the present tense as
well as the past. Many worlds may coexist here.

I spent a great deal of time with my great-grandmother. Her   4
house was next to our house, and I used to wake up at dawn, hours
before my parents or younger sisters, and I'd go wait on the porch
swing or on the back steps by her kitchen door. She got up at dawn,
but she was more than eighty years old, so she needed a little while
to get dressed and to get the fire going in the cookstove. I had been
carefully instructed by my parents not to bother her and to behave,
and to try to help her any way I could. I always loved the early mornings when the air was so cool with a hint of rain smell in the breeze.
In the dry New Mexico air, the least hint of dampness smells sweet.

My great-grandmother's yard was planted with lilac bushes   5
and iris; there were four o'clocks, cosmos, morning glories, and hol-
lyhocks, and old-fashioned rosebushes that I helped her water. If the
garden hose got stuck on one of the big rocks that lined the path in
the yard, I ran and pulled it free. That's what I came to do early
every morning: to help Grandma water the plants before the heat of
the day arrived.

Grandma A'mooh would tell about the old days, family stories   6
about relatives who had been killed by Apache raiders who stole the
sheep our relatives had been herding near Swahnee. Sometimes she
read Bible stories that we kids liked because of the illustrations of
Jonah in the mouth of a whale and Daniel surrounded by lions.
Grandma A'mooh would send me home when she took her nap, but
when the sun got low and the afternoon began to cool off, I would be
back on the porch swing, waiting for her to come out to water the
plants and to haul in firewood for the evening. When Grandma was
eighty-five, she still chopped her own kindling. She used to let me
carry in the coal bucket for her, but she would not allow me to use
the ax. I carried armloads of kindling too, and I learned to be proud
of my strength.

I was allowed to listen quietly when Aunt Susie or Aunt Alice   7
came to visit Grandma. When I got old enough to cross the road
alone, I went and visited them almost daily. They were vigorous
women who valued books and writing. They were usually busy
chopping wood or cooking but never hesitated to take time to answer my questions. Best of all they told me the *hummah-hah* stories,
about an earlier time when animals and humans shared a common
language. In the old days, the Pueblo people had educated their children in this manner; adults took time out to talk to and teach young
people. Everyone was a teacher, and every activity had the potential
to teach the child.

But as soon as I started kindergarten at the Bureau of Indian   8
Affairs day school, I began to learn more about the differences between the Laguna Pueblo world and the outside world. It was at
school that I learned just how different I looked from my classmates.
Sometimes tourists driving past on Route 66 would stop by Laguna
Day School at recess time to take photographs of us kids. One day,
when I was in the first grade, we all crowded around the smiling
white tourists, who peered at our faces. We all wanted to be in the
picture because afterward the tourists sometimes gave us each a
penny. Just as we were all posed and ready to have our picture
taken, the tourist man looked at me. "Not you," he said and mo-
tioned for me to step away from my classmates. I felt so embarrassed that I wanted to disappear. My classmates were puzzled by
the tourists' behavior, but I knew the tourists didn't want me in their
snapshot because I looked different, because I was part white.

IN THE VIEW of the old-time people, we are all sisters and broth-   9
ers because the Mother Creator made all of us—all colors and all
sizes. We are sisters and brothers, clanspeople of all the living beings around us. The plants, the birds, fish, clouds, water, even the

clay—they all are related to us. The old-time people believe that all things, even rocks and water, have spirit and being. They understood that all things want only to continue being as they are; they need only to be left as they are. Thus the old folks used to tell us kids not to disturb the earth unnecessarily. All things as they were created exist already in harmony with one another as long as we do not disturb them.

As the old story tells us, Tse'itsi'nako, Thought Woman, the   10
Spider, thought of her three sisters, and as she thought of them, they came into being. Together with Thought Woman, they thought of the sun and the stars and the moon. The Mother Creators imagined the earth and the oceans, the animals and the people, and the *ka'tsina* spirits that reside in the mountains. The Mother Creators imagined all the plants that flower and the trees that bear fruit. As Thought Woman and her sisters thought of it, the whole universe came into being. In this universe, there is no absolute good or absolute bad; they are only balances and harmonies that ebb and flow. Some years the desert receives abundant rain, other years there is too little rain, and sometimes there is so much rain that floods cause destruction. But rain itself is neither innocent nor guilty. The rain is simply itself.

My great-grandmother was dark and handsome. Her expres-   11
sion in photographs is one of confidence and strength. I do not know if white people then or now would consider her beautiful. I do not know if the old-time Laguna Pueblo people considered her beautiful or if the old-time people even thought in those terms. To the Pueblo way of thinking, the act of comparing one living being with another was silly, because each being or thing is unique and therefore incomparably valuable because it is the only one of its kind. The old-time people thought it was crazy to attach such importance to a person's appearance. I understood very early that there were two distinct ways of interpreting the world. There was the white people's way and there was the Laguna way. In the Laguna way, it was bad manners to make comparisons that might hurt another person's feelings.

In everyday Pueblo life, not much attention was paid to one's   12
physical appearance or clothing. Ceremonial clothing was quite elaborate but was used only for the sacred dances. The traditional Pueblo societies were communal and strictly egalitarian, which means that no matter how well or how poorly one might have dressed, there was no social ladder to fall from. All food and other resources were strictly shared so that no one person or group had more than another. I mention social status because it seems to me that most of the definitions of beauty in contemporary Western cul-

ture are really codes for determining social status. People no longer hide their face-lifts and they discuss their liposuctions because the point of the procedures isn't just cosmetic, it is social. It says to the world, "I have enough spare cash that I can afford surgery for cosmetic purposes."

In the old-time Pueblo world, beauty was manifested in behavior and in one's relationships with other living beings. Beauty was as much a feeling of harmony as it was a visual, aural, or sensual effect. The whole person had to be beautiful, not just the face or the body; faces and bodies could not be separated from hearts and souls. Health was foremost in achieving this sense of well-being and harmony; in the old-time Pueblo world, a person who did not look healthy inspired feelings of worry and anxiety, not feelings of well-being. A healthy person, of course, is in harmony with the world around her; she is at peace with herself too. Thus an unhappy person or spiteful person would not be considered beautiful.   13

In the old days, strong, sturdy women were most admired. One of my most vivid preschool memories is of the crew of Laguna women, in their forties and fifties, who came to cover our house with adobe plaster. They handled the ladders with great ease, and while two women ground the adobe mud on stones and added straw, another woman loaded the hod with mud and passed it up to the two women on ladders, who were smoothing the plaster on the wall with their hands. Since women owned the houses, they did the plastering. At Laguna, men did the basket making and the weaving of fine textiles; men helped a great deal with the child care too. Because the Creator is female, there is no stigma on being female; gender is not used to control behavior. No job was a man's job or a woman's job; the most able person did the work.   14

My Grandma Lily had been a Ford Model A mechanic when she was a teenager. I remember when I was young, she was always fixing broken lamps and appliances. She was small and wiry, but she could lift her weight in rolled roofing or boxes of nails. When she was seventy-five, she was still repairing washing machines in my uncle's coin-operated laundry.   15

The old-time people paid no attention to birthdays. When a person was ready to do something, she did it. When she no longer was able, she stopped. Thus the traditional Pueblo people did not worry about aging or about looking old because there were no social boundaries drawn by the passage of years. It was not remarkable for young men to marry women as old as their mothers. I never heard anyone talk about "women's work" until after I left Laguna for college.   16

Work was there to be done by any able-bodied person who wanted
to do it. At the same time, in the old-time Pueblo world, identity was
acknowledged to be always in a flux; in the old stories, one minute
Spider Woman is a little spider under a yucca plant, and the next instant she is a sprightly grandmother walking down the road.

When I was growing up, there was a young man from a nearby   17
village who wore nail polish and women's blouses and permed his
hair. People paid little attention to his appearance; he was always
part of a group of other young men from his village. No one ever
made fun of him. Pueblo communities were and still are very inter-
dependent, but they also have to be tolerant of individual eccentricities because survival of the group means everyone has to cooperate.

In the old Pueblo world, differences were celebrated as signs of   18
the Mother Creator's grace. Persons born with exceptional physical
or sexual differences were highly respected and honored because
their physical differences gave them special positions as mediators
between this world and the spirit world. The great Navajo medicine
man of the 1920s, the Crawler, had a hunchback and could not walk
upright, but he was able to heal even the most difficult cases.

Before the arrival of Christian missionaries, a man could dress   19
as a woman and work with the women and even marry a man without any fanfare. Likewise, a woman was free to dress like a man, to
hunt and go to war with the men, and to marry a woman. In the old
Pueblo worldview, we are all a mixture of male and female, and this
sexual identity is changing constantly. Sexual inhibition did not begin until the Christian missionaries arrived. For the old-time people,
marriage was about teamwork and social relationships, not about
sexual excitement. In the days before the Puritans came, marriage
did not mean an end to sex with people other than your spouse.
Women were just as likely as men to have a *si'ash*, or lover.

New life was so precious that pregnancy was always appropri-   20
ate, and pregnancy before marriage was celebrated as a good sign.
Since the children belonged to the mother and her clan, and women
owned and bequeathed the houses and farmland, the exact determination of paternity wasn't critical. Although fertility was prized,
infertility was no problem because mothers with unplanned preg-
nancies gave their babies to childless couples within the clan in
open adoption arrangements. Children called their mother's sisters
"mother" as well, and a child became attached to a number of parent figures.

In the sacred kiva ceremonies, men mask and dress as women   21
to pay homage and to be possessed by the female energies of the

spirit beings. Because differences in physical appearance were so highly valued, surgery to change one's face and body to resemble a model's face and body would be unimaginable. To be different, to be unique was blessed and was best of all.

THE TRADITIONAL CLOTHING of Pueblo women emphasized a 22 woman's sturdiness. Buckskin leggings wrapped around the legs protected her from scratches and injuries while she worked. The more layers of buckskin, the better. All those layers gave her legs the appearance of strength, like sturdy tree trunks. To demonstrate sisterhood and brotherhood with the plants and animals, the old-time people make masks and costumes that transform the human figures of the dancers into the animal beings they portray. Dancers paint their exposed skin; their postures and motions are adapted from their observations. But the motions are stylized. The observer sees not an actual eagle or actual deer dancing, but witnesses a human being, a dancer, gradually changing into a woman/buffalo or a man/deer. Every impulse is to reaffirm the urgent relationships that human beings have with the plant and animal world.

In the high desert plateau country, all vegetation, even weeds 23 and thorns, becomes special, and all life is precious and beautiful because without the plants, the insects, and the animals, human beings living here cannot survive. Perhaps human beings long ago noticed the devastating impact human activity can have on the plants and animals; maybe this is why tribal cultures devised the stories about humans and animals intermarrying, and the clans that bind humans to animals and plants through a whole complex of duties.

We children were always warned not to harm frogs or toads, 24 the beloved children of the rain clouds, because terrible floods would occur. I remember in the summer the old folks used to stick big bolls of cotton on the outside of their screen doors as bait to keep the flies from going in the house when the door was opened. The old folks staunchly resisted the killing of flies because once, long, long ago, when human beings were in a great deal of trouble, a Green Bottle Fly carried the desperate messages of human beings to the Mother Creator in the Fourth World, below this one. Human beings had outraged the Mother Creator by neglecting the Mother Corn altar while they dabbled with sorcery and magic. The Mother Creator disappeared, and with her disappeared the rain clouds, and the plants and the animals too. The people began to starve, and they had no way of reaching the Mother Creator down below. Green Bottle Fly took the message to the Mother Creator, and the people were saved. To show their gratitude, the old folks refused to kill any flies.

THE OLD STORIES demonstrate the interrelationships that the   25
Pueblo people have maintained with their plant and animal clanspeople. Kochininako, Yellow Woman, represents all women in the
old stories. Her deeds span the spectrum of human behavior and are
mostly heroic acts, though in at least one story, she chooses to join
the secret Destroyer Clan, which worships destruction and death.
Because Laguna Pueblo cosmology features a female Creator, the
status of women is equal with the status of men, and women appear
as often as men in the old stories as hero figures. Yellow Woman is
my favorite because she dares to cross traditional boundaries of ordinary behavior during times of crisis in order to save the Pueblo;
her power lies in her courage and in her uninhibited sexuality,
which the old-time Pueblo stories celebrate again and again because
fertility was so highly valued.

The old stories always say that Yellow Woman was beautiful,   26
but remember that the old-time people were not so much thinking
about physical appearances. In each story, the beauty that Yellow
Woman possesses is the beauty of her passion, her daring, and her
sheer strength to act when catastrophe is imminent.

In one story, the people are suffering during a great drought   27
and accompanying famine. Each day, Kochininako has to walk farther and farther from the village to find fresh water for her husband
and children. One day she travels far, far to the east, to the plains,
and she finally locates a freshwater spring. But when she reaches the
pool, the water is churning violently as if something large had just
gotten out of the pool. Kochininako does not want to see what huge
creature had been at the pool, but just as she fills her water jar and
turns to hurry away, a strong, sexy man in buffalo skin leggings appears by the pool. Little drops of water glisten on his chest. She cannot help but look at him because he is so strong and so good to look
at. Able to transform himself from human to buffalo in the wink of
an eye, Buffalo Man gallops away with her on his back. Kochininako
falls in love with Buffalo Man, and because of this liaison, the
Buffalo People agree to give their bodies to the hunters to feed the
starving Pueblo. Thus Kochininako's fearless sensuality results in
the salvation of the people of her village, who are saved by the meat
the Buffalo People "give" to them.

My father taught me and my sisters to shoot .22 rifles when we   28
were seven; I went hunting with my father when I was eight, and
I killed my first mule deer buck when I was thirteen. The Kochininako
stories were always my favorite because Yellow Woman had so many
adventures. In one story, as she hunts rabbits to feed her family, a giant

monster pursues her, but she has the courage and presence of mind to outwit it.

In another story, Kochininako has a fling with Whirlwind Man and returns to her husband ten months later with twin baby boys. The twin boys grow up to be great heroes of the people. Once again, Kochininako's vibrant sexuality benefits her people.   29

The stories about Kochininako made me aware that sometimes an individual must act despite disapproval, or concern for appearances or what others may say. From Yellow Woman's adventures, I learned to be comfortable with my differences. I even imagined that Yellow Woman had yellow skin, brown hair, and green eyes like mine, although her name does not refer to her color, but rather to the ritual color of the east.   30

There have been many other moments like the one with the camera-toting tourist in the schoolyard. But the old-time people always say, remember the stories, the stories will help you be strong. So all these years I have depended on Kochininako and the stories of her adventures.   31

Kochininako is beautiful because she has the courage to act in times of great peril, and her triumph is achieved by her sensuality, not through violence and destruction. For these qualities of the spirit, Yellow Woman and all women are beautiful.   32

MARTIN LUTHER KING, JR.

Martin Luther King, Jr. (1929–1968), was a Baptist minister, the president of the Southern Christian Leadership Conference, and a respected leader in the nationwide movement for equal rights for blacks. He was born in Atlanta, Georgia, and earned degrees from Morehouse College (A.B., 1948), Crozer Theological Seminary (B.D., 1951), Boston University (Ph.D., 1955), and Chicago Theological Seminary (D.D., 1957). He held honorary degrees from numerous other colleges and universities and was awarded the Nobel Peace Prize in 1964. Some of his books are *Stride Toward Freedom* (1958), *Strength to Love* (1963), and *Why We Can't Wait* (1964). King was assassinated April 4, 1968, in Memphis, Tennessee.

Letter from Birmingham Jail[1]

This letter, written to King's colleagues in the ministry, is a reasoned explanation for his actions during the civil rights protests in Birmingham. It is a good example of both persuasion and logical argument. Here the two are completely compatible, balancing each other in rather intricate but convincing and effective patterns.

My Dear Fellow Clergymen:

While confined here in the Birmingham city jail, I came across   1
your recent statement calling my present activities "unwise and un-timely." Seldom do I pause to answer criticism of my work and ideas. If I sought to answer all the criticisms that cross my desk, my secretaries would have little time for anything other than such correspon-

---

[1]This response to a published statement by eight fellow clergymen from Alabama (Bishop C. C. J. Carpenter, Bishop Joseph A. Durick, Rabbi Hilton L. Grafman, Bishop Paul Hardin, Bishop Holan B. Harmon, the Reverend George M. Murray, the Reverend Edward V. Ramage, and the Reverend Earl Stallings) was composed under somewhat constricting circumstances. Begun on the margins of the newspaper in which the statement appeared while I was in jail, the letter was continued on scraps of writing paper supplied by a friendly Negro trusty, and concluded on a pad my attorneys were eventually permitted to leave me. Although the text remains in substance unaltered, I have indulged in the author's prerogative of polishing it for publication.—King's note.

dence in the course of the day, and I would have no time for constructive work. But since I feel that you are men of genuine good will and that your criticisms are sincerely set forth, I want to try to answer your statement in what I hope will be patient and reasonable terms.

I think I should indicate why I am here in Birmingham, since 2
you have been influenced by the view which argues against "outsiders coming in." I have the honor of serving as president of the Southern Christian Leadership Conference, an organization operating in every southern state, with headquarters in Atlanta, Georgia. We have some eighty-five affiliated organizations across the South, and one of them is the Alabama Christian Movement for Human Rights. Frequently we share staff, educational, and financial resources with our affiliates. Several months ago the affiliate here in Birmingham asked us to be on call to engage in a nonviolent direct-action program if such were deemed necessary. We readily consented, and when the hour came, we lived up to our promise. So I, along with several members of my staff, am here because I was invited here. I am here because I have organizational ties here.

But more basically, I am in Birmingham because injustice is 3
here. Just as the prophets of the eighth century B.C. left their villages and carried their "thus saith the Lord" far beyond the boundaries of their home towns, and just as the Apostle Paul left his village of Tarsus and carried the gospel of Jesus Christ to the far corners of the Greco-Roman world, so am I compelled to carry the gospel of freedom beyond my own home town. Like Paul, I must constantly respond to the Macedonian call for aid.

Moreover, I am cognizant of the interrelatedness of all communi- 4
ties and states. I cannot sit idly by in Atlanta and not be concerned about what happens in Birmingham. Injustice anywhere is a threat to justice everywhere. We are caught in an inescapable network of mutuality, tied in a single garment of destiny. Whatever affects one directly, affects all indirectly. Never again can we afford to live with the narrow, provincial "outside agitator" idea. Anyone who lives inside the United States can never be considered an outsider within its bounds.

You deplore the demonstrations taking place in Birmingham. 5
But your statement, I am sorry to say, fails to express a similar concern for the conditions that brought about the demonstrations. I am sure that none of you would want to rest content with the superficial kind of social analysis that deals merely with effects and does not grapple with underlying causes. It is unfortunate that demonstrations are taking place in Birmingham, but it is even more unfortunate

that the city's white power structure left the Negro community with no alternative.

In any nonviolent campaign there are four basic steps: collection of the facts to determine whether injustices exist; negotiation; self-purification; and direct action. We have gone through all these steps in Birmingham. There can be no gainsaying the fact that racial injustice engulfs this community. Birmingham is probably the most thoroughly segregated city in the United States. Its ugly record of brutality is widely known. Negroes have experienced grossly unjust treatment in the courts. There have been more unsolved bombings of Negro homes and churches in Birmingham than in any other city in the nation. These are the hard, brutal facts of the case. On the basis of these conditions, Negro leaders sought to negotiate with the city fathers. But the latter consistently refused to engage in good-faith negotiation.

Then, last September, came the opportunity to talk with leaders of Birmingham's economic community. In the course of the negotiations, certain promises were made by the merchants—for example, to remove the stores' humiliating racial signs. On the basis of these promises, the Reverend Fred Shuttlesworth and the leaders of the Alabama Christian Movement for Human Rights agreed to a moratorium on all demonstrations. As the weeks and months went by, we realized that we were the victims of a broken promise. A few signs, briefly removed, returned; the others remained.

As in so many past experiences, our hopes had been blasted, and the shadow of deep disappointment settled upon us. We had no alternative except to prepare for direct action, whereby we would present our very bodies as a means of laying our case before the conscience of the local and the national community. Mindful of the difficulties involved, we decided to undertake a process of self-purification. We began a series of workshops on nonviolence, and we repeatedly asked ourselves: "Are you able to accept blows without retaliating?" "Are you able to endure the ordeal of jail?" We decided to schedule our direct-action program for the Easter season, realizing that except for Christmas, this is the main shopping period of the year. Knowing that a strong economic-withdrawal program would be the by-product of direct action, we felt that this would be the best time to bring pressure to bear on the merchants for the needed change.

Then it occurred to us that Birmingham's mayoral election was coming up in March, and we speedily decided to postpone action until after election day. When we discovered that the Commissioner of Public Safety, Eugene "Bull" Connor, had piled up enough votes to be in the run-off, we decided again to postpone action until the day after the run-off so that the demonstrations could not be used to cloud the issues. Like many others, we waited to see Mr. Connor defeated, and to this end we endured postponement after postponement. Having aided in this community need, we felt that our direct-action program could be delayed no longer.

You may well ask, "Why direct action? Why sit-ins, marches, 10 and so forth? Isn't negotiation a better path?" You are quite right in calling for negotiation. Indeed, this is the very purpose of direct action. Nonviolent direct action seeks to create such a crisis and foster such a tension that a community which has constantly refused to negotiate is forced to confront the issue. It seeks so to dramatize the issue that it can no longer be ignored. My citing the creation of tension as part of the work of the nonviolent-resister may sound rather shocking. But I must confess that I am not afraid of the word "tension." I have earnestly opposed violent tension, but there is a type of constructive, nonviolent tension which is necessary for growth. Just as Socrates felt that it was necessary to create a tension in the mind so that individuals could rise from the bondage of myths and half-truths to the unfettered realm of creative analysis and objective appraisal, so must we see the need for nonviolent gadflies to create the kind of tension in society that will help men rise from the dark depths of prejudice and racism to the majestic heights of understanding and brotherhood.

The purpose of our direct-action program is to create a situation 11 so crisis-packed that it will inevitably open the door to negotiation. I therefore concur with you in your call for negotiation. Too long has our beloved Southland been bogged down in a tragic effort to live in monologue rather than dialogue.

One of the basic points in your statement is that the action that I 12 and my associates have taken in Birmingham is untimely. Some have asked: "Why didn't you give the new city administration time to act?" The only answer that I can give to this query is that the new Birmingham administration must be prodded about as much as the outgoing one, before it will act. We are sadly mistaken if we feel that the election of Albert Boutwell as mayor will bring the millennium to Birmingham. While Mr. Boutwell is a much more gentle person that Mr. Connor, they are both segregationists, dedicated to maintenance of the status quo. I have hoped that Mr. Boutwell will be reasonable enough to see the futility of massive resistance to desegregation. But he will not see this without pressure from devotees of civil rights. My

friends, I must say to you that we have not made a single gain in civil
rights without determined legal and nonviolent pressure. Lamentably,
it is an historical fact that privileged groups seldom give up their privileges voluntarily. Individuals may see the moral light and voluntarily
give up their unjust posture; but, as Reinhold Niebuhr has reminded
us, groups tend to be more immoral than individuals.

We know through painful experience that freedom is never voluntarily given by the oppressor; it must be demanded by the op-   13
pressed. Frankly, I have yet to engage in a direct-action campaign that
was "well timed" in the view of those who have not suffered unduly
from the disease of segregation. For years now I have heard the word
"Wait!" It rings in the ear of every Negro with peircing familiarity.
This "Wait" has almost always meant "Never." We must come to see,
with one of our distinguished jurists, that "justice too long delayed is
justice denied."

We have waited for more than 340 years for our constitutional
and God-given rights. The nations of Asia and Africa are moving   14
with jetlike speed toward gaining political independence, but we still
creep at horse-and-buggy pace toward gaining a cup of coffee at a
lunch counter. Perhaps it is easy for those who have never felt the
stinging darts of segregation to say, "Wait." But when you have seen
vicious mobs lynch your mothers and fathers at will and drown your
sisters and brothers at whim; when you have seen hate-filled policemen curse, kick, and even kill your black brothers and sisters; when
you see the vast majority of your twenty million Negro brothers
smothering in an airtight cage of poverty in the midst of an affluent
society; when you suddenly find your tongue twisted and your
speech stammering as you seek to explain to your six-year-old daughter why she can't go to the public amusement park that has just been
advertised on television, and see tears welling up in her eyes when
she is told that Funtown is closed to colored children, and see ominous clouds of inferiority beginning to form in her little mental sky,
and see her beginning to distort her personality by developing an un-
conscious bitterness toward white people; when you have to concoct
an answer for a five-year-old son who is asking, "Daddy, why do
white people treat colored people so mean?"; when you take a cross-
country drive and find it necessary to sleep night after night in the uncomfortable corners of your automobile because no motel will accept
you; when you are humiliated day in and day out by nagging signs
reading "white" and "colored"; when your first name becomes "nigger," your middle name becomes "boy" (however old you are) and

your last name becomes "John," and your wife and mother are never given the respected title "Mrs."; when you are harried by day and haunted by night by the fact that you are a Negro, living constantly at tiptoe stance, never quite knowing what to expect next, and are plagued with inner fears and outer resentments; when you are forever fighting a degenerating sense of "nobodiness"—then you will understand why we find it difficult to wait. There comes a time when the cup of endurance runs over, and men are no longer willing to be plunged into the abyss of despair. I hope, sirs, you can understand our legitimate and unavoidable impatience.

You express a great deal of anxiety over our willingness to break   15
laws. This is certainly a legitimate concern. Since we so diligently urge people to obey the Supreme Court's decision of 1954 outlawing segregation in the public schools, at first glance it may seem rather paradoxical for us consciously to break laws. One may well ask: "How can you advocate breaking some laws and obeying others?" The answer lies in the fact that there are two types of laws: just and unjust. I would be the first to advocate obeying just laws. One has not only a legal but a moral responsibility to obey just laws. Conversely, one has a moral responsibility to disobey unjust laws. I would agree with St. Augustine that "an unjust law is no law at all."

Now, what is the difference between the two? How does one   16
determine whether a law is just or unjust? A just law is a man-made code that squares with the moral law or the law of God. An unjust law is a code that is out of harmony with the moral law. To put it in the terms of St. Thomas Aquinas: An unjust law is a human law that is not rooted in eternal law and natural law. Any law that uplifts human personality is just. Any law that degrades human personality is unjust. All segregation statutes are unjust because segregation distorts the soul and damages the personality. It gives the segregator a false sense of superiority and the segregated a false sense of inferiority. Segregation, to use the terminology of the Jewish philosopher Martin Buber, substitutes an "I-it" relationship for an "I-thou" relationship and ends up relegating persons to the status of things. Hence segregation is not only politically, economically, and sociologically unsound, it is morally wrong and sinful. Paul Tillich has said that sin is separation. It not segregation an existential expression of man's tragic separation, his awful estrangement, his terrible sinfulness? Thus it is that I can urge men to obey the 1954 decision of the Supreme Court, for it is morally right; and I can urge them to disobey segregation ordinances, for they are morally wrong.

Let us consider a more concrete example of just and unjust laws. An unjust law is a code that a numerical or power majority group compels a minority group to obey but does not make binding on itself. This is *difference* made legal. By the same token, a just law is a code that a majority compels a minority to follow and that it is willing to follow itself. This is *sameness* made legal.   17

Let me give another explanation. A law is unjust if it is inflicted on a minority that, as a result of being denied the right to vote, had no part in enacting or devising the law. Who can say that the legislature of Alabama which set up that state's segregation laws was democratically elected? Throughout Alabama all sorts of devious methods are used to prevent Negroes from becoming registered voters, and there are some counties in which, even though Negroes constitute a majority of the population, not a single Negro is registered. Can any law enacted under such circumstances be considered democratically structured?   18

Sometimes a law is just on its face and unjust in its application. For instance, I have been arrested on a charge of parading without a permit. Now, there is nothing wrong in having an ordinance which requires a permit for a parade. But such an ordinance becomes unjust when it is used to maintain segregation and to deny citizens the First Amendment privilege of peaceful assembly and protest.   19

I hope you are able to see the distinction I am trying to point out. In no sense do I advocate evading or defying the law, as would the rabid segregationist. That would lead to anarchy. One who breaks an unjust law must do so openly, lovingly, and with a willingness to accept the penalty. I submit that an individual who breaks a law that conscience tells him is unjust, and who willingly accepts the penalty of imprisonment in order to arouse the conscience of the community over its injustice, is in reality expressing the highest respect for the law.   20

Of course, there is nothing new about this kind of civil disobedience. It was evidenced sublimely in the refusal of Shadrach, Meshach, and Abednego to obey the laws of Nebuchadnezzar, on the ground that a higher moral law was at stake. It was practiced superbly by the early Christians, who were willing to face hungry lions and the excruciating pain of chopping blocks rather than submit to certain unjust laws of the Roman Empire. To a degree, academic freedom is a reality today because Socrates practiced civil disobedience. In our own nation, the Boston Tea Party represented a massive act of civil disobedience.   21

We should never forget that everything Adolf Hitler did in
Germany was "legal" and everything the Hungarian freedom fighters did in Hungary was "illegal." It was "illegal" to aid and comfort
a Jew in Hitler's Germany. Even so, I am sure that, had I lived in
Germany at the time, I would have aided and comforted my Jewish
brothers. If today I lived in a Communist country where certain
principles dear to the Christian faith are suppressed, I would openly
advocate disobeying that country's anti-religious laws.

I must make two honest confessions to you, my Christian and
Jewish brothers. First, I must confess that over the past few years I
have been gravely disappointed with the white moderate. I have almost reached the regrettable conclusion that the Negro's great stum-
bling block in his stride toward freedom is not the White Citizen's
Counciler or the Ku Klux Klanner, but the white moderate, who is
more devoted to "order" than to justice; who prefers a negative
peace which is the absence of tension to a positive peace which is the
presence of justice; who constantly says, "I agree with you in the goal
you seek, but I cannot agree with your methods of direct action";
who paternalistically believes he can set the timetable for another
man's freedom; who lives by a mythical concept of time and who
constantly advises the Negro to wait for a "more convenient season."
Shallow understanding from people of good will is more frustrating
than absolute misunderstanding from people of ill will. Lukewarm
acceptance is much more bewildering than outright rejection.

I had hoped that the white moderate would understand that
law and order exist for the purpose of establishing justice and that
when they fail in this purpose they become the dangerously structured dams that block the flow of social progress. I had hoped that
the white moderate would understand that the present tension in
the South is a necessary phase of the transition from an obnoxious
negative peace, in which the Negro passively accepted his unjust
plight, to a substantive and positive peace, in which all men will respect the dignity and worth of human personality. Actually, we who
engage in nonviolent direct action are not the creators of tension. We
merely bring to the surface the hidden tension that is already alive.
We bring it out in the open, where it can be seen and dealt with. Like
a boil that can never be cured so long as it is covered up but must be
opened with all its ugliness to the natural medicines of air and light,
injustice must be exposed, with all the tension its exposure creates,
to the light of human conscience and the air of national opinion, before it can be cured.

22

23

24

In your statement you assert that our actions, even though peaceful, must be condemned because they precipitate violence. But is this a logical assertion? Isn't this like condemning a robbed man because his possession of money precipitated the evil act of robbery? Isn't this like condemning Socrates because his unswerving commitment to truth and his philosophical inquiries precipitated the act by the misguided populace in which they made him drink hemlock? Isn't this like condemning Jesus because his unique God-consciousness and never-ceasing devotion to God's will precipitated the evil act of crucifixion? We must come to see that, as the federal courts have consistently affirmed, it is wrong to urge an individual to cease his efforts to gain his basic constitutional rights because the quest may precipitate violence. Society must protect the robbed and punish the robber.   25

I had also hoped that the white moderate would reject the myth concerning time in relation to the struggle for freedom. I have just received a letter from a white brother in Texas. He writes: "All Christians know that the colored people will receive equal rights eventually, but it is possible that you are in too great a religious hurry. It has taken Christianity almost two thousand years to accomplish what it has. The teachings of Christ take time to come to earth." Such an attitude stems from a tragic misconception of time, from the strangely irrational notion that there is something in the very flow of time that will inevitably cure all ills. Actually, time itself is neutral; it can be used either destructively or constructively. More and more I feel that the people of ill will have used time much more effectively than have the people of good will. We will have to repent in this generation not merely for the hateful words and actions of the bad people, but for the appalling silence of the good people. Human progress never rolls in on wheels of inevitability; it comes through the tireless efforts of men willing to be co-workers with God, and without this hard work, time itself becomes an ally of the forces of social stagnation. We must use time creatively, in the knowledge that the time is always ripe to do right. Now is the time to make real the promise of democracy and transform our pending national elegy into a creative psalm of brotherhood. Now is the time to lift our national policy from the quicksand of racial injustice to the solid rock of human dignity.   26

You speak of our activity in Birmingham as extreme. At first I was rather disappointed that fellow clergymen would see my nonviolent efforts as those of an extremist. I began thinking about the fact that I stand in the middle of two opposing forces in the Negro com-   27 munity. One is a force of complacency, made up in part of Negroes who, as a result of long years of oppression, are so drained of self-respect and a sense of "somebodiness" that they have adjusted to segregation; and in part of a few middle-class Negroes who, because of a degree of academic and economic security and because in some ways they profit by segregation, have become insensitive to the problems of the masses. The other force is one of bitterness and hatred, and it comes perilously close to advocating violence. It is expressed in the various black nationalist groups that are springing up across the nation, the largest and best-known being Elijah Muhammad's Muslim movement. Nourished by the Negro's frustration over the continued existence of racial discrimination, this movement is made up of people who have lost faith in America, who have absolutely repudiated Christianity, and who have concluded that the white man is an incorrigible "devil."

I have tried to stand between these two forces, saying that we   28
need emulate neither the "do-nothingism" of the complacent nor the hatred and despair of the black nationalist. For there is the more excellent way of love and nonviolent protest. I am grateful to God that, through the influence of the Negro church, the way of nonviolence became an integral part of our struggle.

If this philosophy had not emerged, by now many streets of the   29
South would, I am convinced, be flowing with blood. And I am further convinced that if our white brothers dismiss as "rabble-rousers" and "outside agitators" those of us who employ nonviolent direct action, and if they refuse to support our nonviolent efforts, millions of Negroes will, out of frustration and despair, seek solace and security in black-nationalist ideologies—a development that would inevitably lead to a frightening racial nightmare.

Oppressed people cannot remain oppressed forever. The yearn-   30
ing for freedom eventually manifests itself, and that is what has happened to the American Negro. Something within has reminded him of his birthright of freedom, and something without has reminded him that it can be gained. Consciously or unconsciously, he has been caught up by the *Zeitgeist*, and with his black brothers of Africa and his brown and yellow brothers of Asia, South America, and the Caribbean, the United States Negro is moving with a sense of great urgency toward the promised land of racial justice. If one recognizes this vital urge that has engulfed the Negro community, one should readily understand why public demonstrations are taking place. The Negro has many pent-up resentments and latent frustrations, and he must release them. So let him march; let him make prayer

pilgrimages to the city hall; let him go on freedom rides—and try to understand why he must do so. If his repressed emotions are not released in nonviolent ways, they will seek expression through violence; this is not a threat but a fact of history. So I have not said to my people, "Get rid of your discontent." Rather, I have tried to say that this normal and healthy discontent can be channeled into the creative outlet of nonviolent direct action. And now this approach is being termed extremist.

But though I was initially disappointed at being categorized as   31
an extremist, as I continued to think about the matter I gradually gained a measure of satisfaction from the label. Was not Jesus an extremist for love: "Love your enemies, bless them that curse you, do good to them that hate you, and pray for them which despitefully use you, and persecute you." Was not Amos an extremist for justice: "Let justice roll down like waters and righteousness like an everflowing stream." Was not Paul an extremist for the Christian gospel: "I bear in my body the marks of the Lord Jesus." Was not Martin Luther an extremist: "Here I stand; I cannot do otherwise, so help me God." And John Bunyan: "I will stay in jail to the end of my days before I make a butchery of my conscience." And Abraham Lincoln: "This nation cannot survive half slave and half free." And Thomas Jefferson: "We hold these truths to be self-evident, that all men are created equal . . ." So the question is not whether we will be extremists, but what kind of extremists we will be. Will we be extremists for hate or for love? Will we be extremists for the preservation of injustice or for the extension of justice? In that dramatic scene on Calvary's hill three men were crucified. We must never forget that all three were crucified for the same crime—the crime of extremism. Two were extremists for immorality, and thus fell below their environment. The other, Jesus Christ, was an extremist for love, truth, and goodness, and thereby rose above his environment. Perhaps the South, the nation, and the world are in dire need of creative extremists.

I had hoped that the white moderate would see this need.   32
Perhaps I was too optimistic; perhaps I expected too much. I suppose I should have realized that few members of the oppressor race can understand the deep groans and passionate yearnings of the oppressed race, and still fewer have the vision to see that injustice must be rooted out by strong, persistent, and determined action. I am thankful, however, that some of our white brothers in the South have grasped the meaning of this social revolution and committed themselves to it. They are still all too few in quantity, but they are

big in quality. Some—such as Ralph McGill, Lillian Smith, Harry Golden, James McBride Dabbs, Anne Braden, and Sarah Patton Boyle—have written about our struggle in eloquent and prophetic terms. Others have marched with us down nameless streets of the South. They have languished in filthy, roach-infested jails, suffering the abuse and brutality of policemen who view them as "dirty nigger-lovers." Unlike so many of their moderate brothers and sisters, they have recognized the urgency of the moment and sensed the need for powerful "action" antidotes to combat the disease of segregation.

Let me take note of my other major disappointment. I have been 33
so greatly disappointed with the white church and its leadership. Of course, there are some notable exceptions. I am not unmindful of the fact that each of you have taken some significant stands on this issue. I commend you, Reverend Stallings, for your Christian stand on this past Sunday, in welcoming Negroes to your worship service on a nonsegregated basis. I commend the Catholic leaders of this state for integrating Spring Hill College several years ago.

But despite these notable exceptions, I must honestly reiterate 34
that I have been disappointed with the church. I do not say this as one of those negative critics who can always find something wrong with the church. I say this as a minister of the gospel, who loves the church; who has nurtured in its bosom; who has been sustained by its spiritual blessings and who will remain true to it as long as the cord of life shall lengthen.

When I was suddenly catapulted into the leadership of the bus 35
protest in Montgomery, Alabama, a few years ago, I felt we would be supported by the white church. I felt that the white ministers, priests, and rabbis of the South would be among our strongest allies. Instead, some have been outright opponents, refusing to understand the freedom movement and misrepresenting its leaders; all too many others have been more cautious than courageous and have remained silent behind the anesthetizing security of stained glass windows.

In spite of my shattered dreams, I came to Birmingham with the 36
hope that the white religious leadership of this community would see the justice of our cause and, with deep moral concern, would serve as the channel through which our just grievances could reach the power structure. I had hoped that each of you would understand. But again I have been disappointed.

I have heard numerous southern religious leaders admonish 37
their worshipers to comply with a desegregation decision because it is the law, but I have longed to hear white ministers declare: "Follow

this decree because integration is morally right and because the Negro is your brother." In the midst of blatant injustices inflicted upon the Negro, I have watched white churchmen stand on the side-line and mouth pious relevancies and sanctimonious trivialities. In the midst of a mighty struggle to rid our nation of racial and eco-nomic injustice I have heard many ministers say: "Those are social issues, with which the gospel has no real concern." And I have watched many churches commit themselves to a completely other-worldly religion which makes a strange, un-Biblical distinction be-tween body and soul, between the sacred and the secular.

I have traveled the length and breadth of Alabama, Mississippi, and all the other southern states. On sweltering summer days and crisp autumn mornings I have looked at the South's beautiful churches with their lofty spires pointing heavenward. I have beheld the impressive outlines of her massive religious-education build-ings. Over and over I have found myself asking: "What kind of peo-ple worship here? Who is their God? Where were their voices when the lips of Governor Barnett dripped with words of interposition and nullification? Where were they when Governor Wallace gave a clarion call for defiance and hatred? Where were their voices of sup-port when bruised and weary Negro men and women decided to rise from the dark dungeons of complacency to the bright hills of creative protest?"   38

Yes, these questions are still in my mind. In deep disappoint-ment I have wept over the laxity of the church. But be assured that my tears have been tears of love. There can be no deep disappoint-ment where there is not deep love. Yes, I love the church. How could I do otherwise? I am in the rather unique position of being the son, the grandson, and the great-grandson of preachers. Yes, I see the church as the body of Christ. But, oh! How we have blemished and scarred that body through social neglect and through fear of being nonconformists.   39

There was a time when the church was very powerful—in the time when the early Christians rejoiced at being deemed worthy to suffer for what they believed. In those days the church was not merely a thermometer that recorded the ideas and principles of popu-lar opinion; it was a thermostat that transformed the mores of society. Whenever the early Christians entered a town, the people in power became disturbed and immediately sought to convict the Christians for being "disturbers of the peace" and "outside agitators." But the Christians pressed on, in the conviction that they were "a colony of heaven," called to obey God rather than man. Small in number, they   40

were big in commitment. They were too God-intoxicated to be "astro-
nomically intimidated." By their effort and example they brought an
end to such ancient evils as infanticide and gladiatorial contests.

Things are different now. So often the contemporary church is a   41
weak, ineffectual voice with an uncertain sound. So often it is an
archdefender of the status quo. Far from being disturbed by the presence of the church, the power structure of the average community is
consoled by the church's silent—and often even vocal—sanction of
things as they are.

But the judgment of God is upon the church as never before. If   42
today's church does not recapture the sacrificial spirit of the early
church, it will lose its authenticity, forfeit the loyalty of millions, and
be dismissed as an irrelevant social club with no meaning for the
twentieth century. Every day I meet young people whose disappointment with the church has turned into outright disgust.

Perhaps I have once again been too optimistic. Is organized reli-   43
gion too inextricably bound to the status quo to save our nation and
the world? Perhaps I must turn my faith to the inner spiritual
church, the church within the church, as the true *ekklesia*[2] and the
hope of the world. But again I am thankful to God that some noble
souls from the ranks of organized religion have broken loose from
the paralyzing chains of conformity and joined us as active partners
in the struggle for freedom. They have left their secure congrega-
tions and walked the streets of Albany, Georgia, with us. They have
gone down the highways of the South on tortuous rides for freedom.
Yes, they have gone to jail with us. Some have been dismissed from
their churches, have lost the support of their bishops and fellow
ministers. But they have acted in the faith that right defeated is
stronger than evil triumphant. Their witness has been the spiritual
salt that has preserved the true meaning of the gospel in these troubled times. They have carved a tunnel of hope through the dark
mountain of disappointment.

I hope the church as a whole will meet the challenge of this de-   44
cisive hour. But even if the church does not come to the aid of justice,
I have no despair about the future. I have no fear about the outcome
of our struggle in Birmingham, even if our motives are at present
misunderstood. We will reach the goal of freedom in Birmingham
and all over the nation, because the goal of America is freedom.
Abused and scorned though we may be, our destiny is tied up with
America's destiny. Before the pilgrims landed at Plymouth, we were

[2]The Greek New Testament word for the early Christian church. (Editors' note.)

here. Before the pen of Jefferson etched the majestic words of the Declaration of Independence across the pages of history, we were here. For more than two centuries, our forbears labored in this country without wages; they made cotton king; they built the homes of their masters while suffering gross injustice and shameful humiliation— and yet out of a bottomless vitality they continued to thrive and develop. If the inexpressible cruelties of slavery could not stop us, the opposition we now face will surely fail. We will win our freedom because the sacred heritage of our nation and the eternal will of God are embodied in our echoing demands.

Before closing I feel impelled to mention one other point in your   45
statement that has troubled me profoundly. You warmly commended the Birmingham police force for keeping "order" and "preventing violence." I doubt that you would have so warmly commended the police force if you had seen its dogs sinking their teeth into unarmed, nonviolent Negroes. I doubt that you would so quickly commend the policemen if you were to observe their ugly and inhumane treatment of Negroes here in the city jail; if you were to watch them push and curse old Negro women and young Negro girls; if you were to see them slap and kick old Negro men and young boys; if you were to observe them, as they did on two occasions, refuse to give us food because we wanted to sing our grace together. I cannot join you in your praise of the Birmingham police department.

It is true that the police have exercised a degree of discipline in handling the demonstrators. In this sense they have conducted them-   46
selves rather "nonviolently" in public. But for what purpose? To preserve the evil system of segregation. Over the past few years I have consistently preached that nonviolence demands that the means we use must be as pure as the ends we seek. I have tried to make clear that it is wrong to use immoral means to attain moral ends. But now I must affirm that it is just as wrong, or perhaps even more so, to use moral means to preserve immoral ends. Perhaps Mr. Connor and his policemen have been rather nonviolent in public, as was Chief Pritchett in Albany, Georgia, but they have used the moral means of nonviolence to maintain the immoral end of racial injustice. As T.S. Eliot has said, "The last temptation is the greatest treason: To do the right deed for the wrong reason."

I wish you had commended the Negro sit-inners and demonstrators of Birmingham for their sublime courage, their willingness   47
to suffer, and their amazing discipline in the midst of great provocation. One day the South will recognize its real heroes. They will be the James Merediths, with the noble sense of purpose that enables

them to face jeering and hostile mobs, and with the agonizing loneliness that characterizes the life of the pioneer. They will be old, oppressed, battered Negro women, symbolized in a seventy-two-year-old woman in Montgomery, Alabama, who rose up with a sense of dignity and with her people decided not to ride segregated buses, and who responded with ungrammatical profundity to one who inquired about her weariness: "My feets is tired, but my soul is at rest." They will be the young high school and college students, and young ministers of the gospel and a host of their elders, courageously and nonviolently sitting in at lunch counters and willingly going to jail for conscience' sake. One day the South will know that when these disinherited children of God sat down at lunch counters, they were in reality standing up for what is best in the American dream and for the most sacred values in our Judaeo-Christian heritage, thereby bringing our nation back to those great wells of democracy which were dug deep by the founding fathers in their formulation of the Constitution and the Declaration of Independence.

48 Never before have I written so long a letter. I'm afraid it is much too long to take your precious time. I can assure you that it would have been much shorter if I had been writing from a comfortable desk, but what else can one do when he is alone in a narrow jail cell, other than write long letters, think long thoughts, and pray long prayers?

49 If I have said anything in this letter that overstates the truth and indicates an unreasonable impatience, I beg you to forgive me. If I have said anything that understates the truth and indicates my having a patience that allows me to settle for anything less than brotherhood, I beg God to forgive me.

50 I hope this letter finds you strong in the faith. I also hope that circumstances will soon make it possible for me to meet each of you, not as an integrationist or a civil-rights leader but as a fellow clergyman and a Christian brother. Let us all hope that the dark clouds of racial prejudice will soon pass away and the deep fog of misunderstanding will be lifted from our fear-drenched communities, and in some not too distant tomorrow the radiant stars of love and brotherhood will shine over our great nation with all their scintillating beauty.

Yours for the cause of Peace and Brotherhood,
Martin Luther King, Jr.

A Guide to Terms

Abstract (See *Concrete/Abstract.*)

Allusion (See *Figures of Speech.*)

Analogy (See Chapter 6.)

Argument is writing that uses factual evidence and supporting ideas to convince readers to share the author's opinion on an issue or to take some action the writer considers appropriate or necessary. Like exposition, argument conveys information; however, it does so not to explain but to induce readers to favor one side in a conflict or to choose a particular course of action.

Some arguments appeal primarily to reason, others primarily to emotion. Most, however, mix reason and emotion in whatever way is appropriate for the issue and the audience. (See Chapter 13.)

Support for an argument can take a number of forms:

1. *Examples*—Real-life examples or hypothetical examples (used sparingly) can be convincing evidence if they are typical and if the author provides enough of them to illustrate all the major points in the argument or combines them with other kinds of evidence. (See Daly, Freeman, Lynn.) Some examples are *specific,* referring to particular people or events. (See Daly.) Others are *general,* referring to kinds of events or people, usually corresponding in some way to the reader's experiences. (See Lynn.)

2. *Facts and figures*—Detailed information about a subject; particularly if presented in statistical form, can help convince readers by showing that the author's perspective on an issue is consistent with what is known about the subject. (See Lynn, Ehrenreich.) But facts whose accuracy is questionable or statistics that are confusing can undermine an argument.

3. *Authority*—Supporting an argument with the ideas or the actual words of someone who is recognized as an expert can be an effective strategy as long as the author can show that the expert is a reliable witness and can combine the expert's opinion with other kinds of evidence that point in the same direction.

4. *Personal experience*—Examples drawn from personal experience or the experience of friends can be more detailed and vivid (and hence

more convincing) than other kinds of evidence, but a writer should use this kind of evidence sparingly because readers may sometimes suspect that it represents no more than one person's way of looking at events. When combined with other kinds of evidence, however, examples drawn from personal experience can be an effective technique for persuasion. (See Daly.)

In addition, all the basic expository patterns can be used to support an argument. (See Chapter 13.)

Cause (See Chapter 8.)

Central Theme (See *Unity.*)

Classification (See Chapter 4.)

Clichés are tired expressions, perhaps once fresh and colorful, that have been overused until they have lost most of their effectiveness and become trite or hackneyed. The term is also applied, less commonly, to trite ideas or attitudes.

We may need to use clichés in conversation, of course, where the quick and economical phrase is an important and useful tool of expression—and where no one expects us to be constantly original. We are fortunate, in a way, to have a large accumulation of clichés from which to draw. To describe someone, without straining our originality very much, we can always declare that he is *as innocent as a lamb, as thin as a rail,* or *as fat as a pig;* that she is *as dumb as an ox, as sly as a fox,* or *as wise as an owl;* that he is *financially embarrassed* or *has a fly in the ointment* or *her ship has come in;* or that, *last but not least, in this day and age,* the *Grim Reaper* has taken him to *his eternal reward.* There is indeed *a large stockpile* from which we can draw for ordinary conversation. But the trite expression, written down on paper, is a permanent reminder that the writer is either lazy or not aware of the dullness of stereotypes—or, even more damaging, it is a clue that the ideas themselves may be threadbare, and therefore can be adequately expressed in threadbare language.

Occasionally, of course, a writer can use obvious clichés deliberately (see Lawrence, par. 1; Ehrenreich, and Stone). But usually to be fully effective, writing must be fresh, and should seem to have been written specifically for the occasion. Clichés, however fresh and appropriate at one time, have lost these qualities.

Closings are almost as much of a problem as introductions, and they are equally important. The function of a closing is simply "to close," of course, but this implies somehow tying the entire writing into a neat package, giving the final sense of unity to the whole endeavor, and thus leaving the reader with a sense of satisfaction instead of an uneasy feeling that there ought to be another page. There is no standard length for closings. A short composition may be effectively completed with one sentence—or even without any real closing at all, if the last point discussed is a strong or climactic one. A longer piece of writing, however, may end more slowly, perhaps through several paragraphs.

A few types of weak endings are so common that warnings are in order here. Careful writers will avoid these faults: (1) giving the effect of suddenly tiring and quitting; (2) ending on a minor detail or an apparent afterthought; (3) bringing up a new point in the closing; (4) using any new qualifying remark in the closing (if writers want their opinions to seem less dogmatic or generalized, they should go back to do their qualifying where the damage was done); (5) ending with an apology of any kind (authors who are not interested enough to become at least minor experts in their subject should not be wasting the reader's time).

Of the several acceptable ways of giving the sense of finality to a paper, the easiest is the *summary,* but it is also the least desirable for most short papers. Readers who have read and understood something only a page or two before probably do not need to have it reviewed for them. Such a review is apt to seem merely repetitious. Longer writings, of course, such as research or term papers, may require thorough summaries.

Several other closing techniques are available to writers. The following, which do not represent all the possibilities, are useful in many situations, and they can frequently be employed in combination:

1. *Using word signals*—e.g., *finally, at last, thus, and so, in conclusion,* as well as more original devices suggested by the subject itself. (See Simpson.)

2. *Changing the tempo*—usually a matter of sentence length or pace. This is a very subtle indication of finality, and it is difficult to achieve. (For examples of modified use, see Simpson, Walker, Dorris.)

3. *Restating the central idea of the writing*—sometimes a "statement" so fully developed that it practically becomes a summary itself. (See Catton, Carter, Buczynski.)

4. *Using climax*—a natural culmination of preceding points or, in some cases, the last major point itself. This is suitable, however, only if the materials have been so arranged that the last point is outstanding. (See Catton, Lawrence, Walker, Szalavitz.)

5. *Making suggestions,* perhaps mentioning a possible solution to the problem being discussed—a useful technique for exposition as well as for argument, and a natural signal of the end. (See Lynn.)

6. *Showing the topic's significance,* its effects, or the universality of its meaning—a commonly used technique that, if carefully handled, is an excellent indication of closing. (See Buckley, Lawrence, Noda.)

7. *Echoing the introduction*—a technique that has the virtue of improving the effect of unity by bringing the development around full circle, so to speak. The echo may be a reference to a problem posed or a significant expression, quotation, analogy, or symbol used in the introduction or elsewhere early in the composition. (See Buckley, Min, Berendt.)

8. *Using some rhetorical device*—a sort of catchall category, but a good supply source that includes several very effective techniques; pertinent quotations, anecdotes and brief dialogues, metaphors, allusions, ironic comments, and various kinds of witty or memorable remarks. All, however, run the risk of seeming forced and hence amateurish; but properly handled, they make for an effective closing. (See White, Lopate, Lawrence, Simpson, King.)

Coherence is a quality of good writing that results from the presentation of all parts in logical and clear relations.

Coherence and unity are usually studied together and, indeed, are almost inseparable. But whereas unity refers to the relation of parts to the central theme (see *Unity*), coherence refers to their relations with each other. In a coherent piece of writing, each sentence, each paragraph, each major division seems to grow out of those preceding it.

Several transitional devices (see *Transition*) help to make these relations clear, but far more fundamental to coherence is the sound organization of materials. From the first moment of visualizing the subject materials in pattern, the writer's goal must be clear and logical development. If it is, coherence is almost ensured.

Colloquial Expressions are characteristic of conversation and informal writing, and they are normally perfectly appropriate in those contexts. However, most writing done for college, business, or professional purposes is considered "formal" writing; and for such usage, colloquialisms are too informal, too *folksy* (itself a word most dictionaries would label "colloq.").

Some of the expressions appropriate only for informal usage are *kid* (for child), *boss* (for employer), *flunk, buddy, snooze, gym, a lot of, phone, skin flicks,* and *porn*. In addition, contractions such as *can't* and *I'd* are usually regarded as colloquialisms and are never permissible in, for instance, a research or term paper.

Slang is defined as a low level of colloquialism, but it is sometimes placed "below" colloquialism in respectability; even standard dictionaries differ as to just what the distinction is. (Some of the examples in the preceding paragraph, if included in dictionaries at all, are identified both ways.) At any rate, slang generally comprises words either coined or given novel meanings in an attempt at colorful or humorous expression. Slang often becomes limp with overuse, however, losing whatever vigor it first had. In time, slang expressions either disappear completely or graduate to more acceptable colloquial status and thence, possibly, into standard usage. (This is one way in which our language is constantly changing.) But until their "graduations," slang and colloquialism have an appropriate place in formal writing only if used sparingly and for special effect. Because dictionaries frequently differ in matters of usage, the student should be sure to use a standard edition approved by the instructor. (For further examples, see Viorst; Wolfe; Simpson, pars. 8, 16, 17.)

Comparison (See Chapter 5.)

Conclusions (See *Closings.*)

Concrete and **Abstract** words are both indispensable to the language, but a good rule in most writing is to use the concrete whenever possible. This policy also applies, of course, to sentences that express only abstract ideas, which concrete examples can often make clearer and more effective. Many expository and argumentative paragraphs are constructed with an abstract topic sentence and its concrete support. (See *Unity.*)

A concrete word names something that exists as an entity in itself, something that can be perceived by the human senses. We can see, touch, hear, and smell a horse—hence *horse* is a concrete word. But a horse's *strength* is not. We have no reason to doubt that strength exists, but it does not have an independent existence: something else must *be* strong or there is no strength. Hence *strength* is an abstract word.

Purely abstract reading is difficult for average readers; with no concrete images provided, they are constantly forced to make their own. Concrete writing helps readers to visualize and is therefore easier and faster to read. (See *Specific/General* for further discussion.)

Connotation and **Denotation** both refer to the meanings of words. Denotation is the direct, literal meaning as it would be found in a dictionary, whereas connotation refers to the response a word *really* arouses in the reader or listener. (See Wolfe, par. 14; Daly, Lawrence.)

There are two types of connotation: personal and general. Personal connotations vary widely, depending on the experiences and moods that an individual associates with the word. (This corresponds with personal symbolism; see *Symbol.*) *Waterfall* is not apt to have the same meaning for the happy young honeymooners at Yosemite as it has for the grieving mother whose child has just drowned in a waterfall. General connotations are those shared by many people. *Fireside,* far beyond its obvious dictionary definition, generally connotes warmth and security and good companionship. *Mother,* which denotatively means simply "female parent," means much more connotatively.

A word or phrase considered less distasteful or offensive than a more direct expression is called a *euphemism,* and this is also a matter of connotation. (See Mitford.) The various expressions used instead of the more direct "four-letter words" referring to daily bathroom events are examples of euphemisms. (See Wolfe's "mounting," pars. 16 and 17.) *Remains* is often used instead of *corpse,* and a few newspapers still have people *passing away* and being *laid to rest,* rather than *dying* and being *buried.*

But a serious respect for the importance of connotations goes far beyond euphemistic practices. Young writers can hardly expect to know all the different meanings of words for all their potential readers, but they can at least be aware that words do *have* different meanings. Of course, this is most important in persuasive writing—in political speeches, in advertising copywriting, and in any endeavor where some sort of public image is being created. When President Franklin Roosevelt began his series of informal radio talks, he called them "fireside chats," thus putting connotation to work. An advertising copywriter trying to evoke the feeling of love and tenderness associated with motherhood is not seriously tempted to use *female parent* instead of *mother.*

In exposition, where the primary purpose is to explain, the writer ordinarily tries to avoid words that may have emotional overtones, unless these can somehow be used to increase understanding. In argument, however, a writer may on occasion wish to appeal to the emotions.

Contrast (See Chapter 5.)

Deduction (See Chapter 12.)

Denotation (See *Connotation/Denotation.*)

Description (See Chapter 10.)

Diction refers simply to "choice of words," but, not so simply, it involves many problems of usage, some of which are explained under several other headings in this guide, e.g., *Clichés, Colloquial Expressions, Connotation/Denotation, Concrete/Abstract*—anything, in fact, that pertains primarily to word choices. But the characteristics of good diction may be more generally classified as follows:

1. *Accuracy*—the choice of words that mean exactly what the author intends.

2. *Economy*—the choice of the simplest and fewest words that will convey the exact meaning intended.

3. *Emphasis*—the choice of fresh, strong words, avoiding clichés and unnecessarily vague or general terms.

4. *Appropriateness*—the choice of words that suit the subject matter, the prospective reader-audience, and the purpose of the writing.

(For contrasts of diction see Stone, Welsch, Walker, King, Twitchell, Murphy, Carter.)

Division (See Chapter 4.)

Effect (See Chapter 8.)

Emphasis is almost certain to fall *somewhere,* and the author should be the one to decide where. A major point, not some minor detail, should be emphasized.

Following are the most common ways of achieving emphasis. Most of them apply to the sentence, the paragraph, or the overall writing—all of which can be seriously weakened by emphasis in the wrong places.

1. By *position*—The most emphatic position is usually at the end, the second most emphatic at the beginning. (There are a few exceptions, including news stories and certain kinds of scientific reports.) The middle, therefore, should be used for materials that do not deserve

special emphasis. (See Buckley, for saving the most significant example until last; Catton, par. 16; Raybon, for gradually increasing emphasis; and Dorris, for the long-withheld revelation of the real central theme.)

A sentence in which the main point is held until the last is called a *periodic sentence*, e.g., "After a long night of suspense and horror, the cavalry arrived." In a *loose sentence*, the main point is disposed of earlier and followed by dependencies, e.g., "The cavalry arrived after a long night of suspense and horror."

2. By *proportion*—Ordinarily, but not necessarily, important elements are given the most attention and thus automatically achieve a certain emphasis.

3. By *repetition*—Words and ideas may sometimes be given emphasis by reuse, usually in a different manner. If not cautiously handled, however, this method can seem merely repetitious, not emphatic. (See Atwood, who repeats words to give them varied meanings and highlight their importance.)

4. By *flat statement*—Although an obvious way to achieve emphasis is simply to *tell* the reader what is most important, it is often least effective, at least when used as the only method. Readers have a way of ignoring such pointers as "most important" and "especially true." (See Catton, par. 16.)

5. By *mechanical devices*—Emphasis can be achieved by using italics (underlining), capital letters, or exclamation points. But too often these devices are used, however unintentionally, to cover deficiencies of content or style. Their employment can quickly be overdone and their impact lost.

6. By *distinctiveness of style*—The author can emphasize subtly with fresh and concrete words or figures of speech, crisp or unusual structures, and careful control of paragraph or sentence lengths. (These methods are used in many essays in this book: see Buckley; Twain, who changes style radically for the second half of his essay; Catton; Stone, who uses numerous puns; Wolfe; Curtin, pars. 7–15.) *Verbal irony* (see *Irony*), including *sarcasm* (see Buckley, Atwood.) and the rather specialized form known as *understatement,* is another valuable means of achieving distinctiveness of style and increasing emphasis. (See Wolfe; Mitford; Ehrenreich.)

Essay refers to a brief prose composition on a single topic, usually, but not always, communicating the author's personal ideas and impressions. Beyond this, because of the wide and loose application of the term, no satisfactory definition has been universally accepted.

Classifications of essay types have also been widely varied and sometimes not very meaningful. One basic and useful distinction, however, is between *formal* and *informal* essays, although many defy classification even in such broad categories as these. It is best to regard the two types as opposite ends of a continuum, along which most essays may be placed.

The formal essay usually develops an important theme through a logical progression of ideas, with full attention to unity and coherence, and in a serious tone. Although the style is seldom completely impersonal, it is literary rather than colloquial. (For examples of essays that are somewhere near the "formal" end of the continuum, see Buckley, Lynn, Eiseley, Catton, Kilbourne, Negroponte, Lawrence.)

The informal, or personal, essay is less elaborately organized and more chatty in style. First-person pronouns, contractions, and other colloquial or even slang expressions are often freely used. Informal essays are less serious in apparent purpose than formal essays. Although most do contain a worthwhile message or observation of some kind, an important purpose of many is to entertain. (See Stone, Wolf.)

The more personal and intimate informal essays may be classifiable as *familiar* essays, although, again, there is no well-established boundary. Familiar essays pertain to the author's own experience, ideas, or prejudices, frequently in a light and humorous style. (See Buczynski, Viorst, Curtin, White, Murphy.)

Evaluation of a literary piece, as for any other creative endeavor, is meaningful only when based on the answers to three questions: (1) What was the author's purpose? (2) How successfully was it fulfilled? (3) How worthwhile was it?

An architect could hardly be blamed for designing a poor gymnasium if the commission had been to design a library. Similarly, an author who is trying to explain for us why women are paid less than men cannot be faulted for failing to make the reader laugh. An author whose purpose is simply to amuse (a worthy goal) should not be condemned for teaching little about trichobothria. (Nothing prevents the author from trying to explain pornography through the use of humor, or trying to amuse by comparing two Civil War generals, but in these situations the purpose has changed—and grown almost unbearably harder to achieve.)

An architect who was commissioned to design a gymnasium, and who, in fact, designed one, however, could be justifiably criticized on whether the building is successful and attractive *as a gymnasium*. If an author is examining matters of cognition and personality, the reader has a right to expect sound reasoning and clear expository prose; and varied, detailed support ought to be expected in an essay that looks at the physical basis of human behavior (Perry and Dawson) or at the attitudes of people toward work and careers (Rothenberg).

Many things are written and published that succeed very well in carrying out the author's intent—but simply are not worthwhile. Although this is certainly justifiable grounds for unfavorable criticism, readers should first make full allowance for their own limitations and perhaps their narrow range of interests, evaluating the work as nearly as possible from the standpoint of the average reader for whom the writing was intended.

Figures of Speech are short, vivid comparisons, either stated or implied; but they are not literal comparisons (e.g., "Your car is like my car," which is presumably a plain statement of fact). Figures of speech are more imaginative. They imply analogy but, unlike analogy, are used less to inform than to make quick and forceful impressions. All figurative language is a comparison of unlikes, but the unlikes do have some interesting point of likeness, perhaps one never noticed before.

A *metaphor* merely suggests the comparison and is worded as if the two unlikes are the same thing—e.g., "the language of the river" and "was turned to blood" (Twain, par. 1) and "a great chapter in American life" (Catton, par. 1). (For another example in this book, see King.)

A *simile* (which is sometimes classified as a special kind of metaphor) expresses a similarity directly, usually with the word *like* or *as* (Lopate, par. 12).

A *personification,* which is actually a special type of either metaphor or simile, is usually classified as a "figure" in its own right. In personification, inanimate things are treated as if they had the qualities or powers of a person. Some people would also label as personification any characterization of inanimate objects as animals, or of animals as humans.

An *allusion* is literally any casual reference, any alluding, to something, but rhetorically it is limited to a figurative reference to a famous or literary person, event, or quotation, and it should be distinguished from the casual reference that has a literal function in the subject matter. Hence casual mention of Judas Iscariot's betrayal of Jesus is merely a reference, but calling a modern traitor a "Judas" is an allusion. A rooster might be referred to as "the Hitler of the barnyard," or a lover as a "Romeo." Many allusions refer to mythological or biblical persons or places. (See Buckley, par, 11; Wolfe, title and par. 1; and Simpson, par. 2, for a discussion of some commonly employed allusions.)

Irony and paradox (both discussed under their own headings) and analogy (see Chapter 6) are also frequently classed as figures of speech, and there are several other less common types that are really subclassifications of those already discussed.

General (See *Specific/General.*)

Illustration (See Chapter 3.)

Impressionistic Description (See Chapter 10.)

Induction (See Chapter 12.)

Introductions give readers their first impressions, which often turn out to be the lasting ones. In fact, unless an introduction succeeds in somehow attracting a reader's interest, he or she probably will read no further. The importance of the introduction is one reason that writing it is nearly always difficult.

When the writer remains at a loss for how to begin, it may be a good idea to forget about the introduction for a while and go ahead with the main body of the writing. Later the writer may find that a suitable introduction has suggested itself or even that the way the piece begins is actually introduction enough.

Introductions may vary in length from one sentence in a short composition to several paragraphs or even several pages in longer and more complex expositions and arguments, such as research papers and reports of various kinds.

Good introductions in expository writing have at least three and sometimes four functions.

1. *To identify the subject and set its limitations,* thus building as solid foundation for unity. This function usually includes some indication of the central theme, letting the reader know what point is to be made about the subject. Unlike the other forms of prose, which can often benefit by some degree of mystery, exposition has the primary purpose of explaining, so the reader has a right to know from the beginning just *what* is being explained.

2. *To interest the readers,* and thus ensure their attention. To be sure of doing this, writers must analyze their prospective readers and the readers' interest in their subject. The account of a new X-ray technique would need an entirely different kind of introduction if written for doctors than if written for the campus newspaper.

3. *To set the tone* of the rest of the writing. (See *Style/Tone.*) Tone varies greatly in writing, just as the tone of a person's voice varies with the person's mood. One function of the introduction is to let the reader know the author's attitude since it may have a subtle but important bearing on the communication.

4. *Frequently,* but not always, *to indicate the plan of organization.* Although seldom important in short, relatively simple compositions and essay examinations, this function of introductions can be especially valuable in more complex papers.

These are the necessary functions of an introduction. For best results, keep these guidelines in mind: (1) Avoid referring to the title, or even assuming that the reader has seen it. Make the introduction do all the introducing. (2) Avoid crude and uninteresting beginnings, such as "This paper is about . . . ." (3) Avoid going too abruptly into the main body—smooth transition is at least as important here as anywhere else. (4) Avoid overdoing the introduction, either in length or in extremes of style.

Fortunately, there are many good ways to introduce expository writing (and argumentative writing), and several of the most useful are illustrated by the selections in this book. Many writings, of course, combine two or more of the following techniques for interesting introductions.

1. *Stating the central theme,* which is sometimes fully enough explained in the introduction to become almost a preview summary of the exposition or argument to come. (See Tajima, Noda, Viorst.)

2. *Showing the significance of the subject,* or stressing its importance. (See Catton, Wolfe, Simpson.)

3. *Giving the background of the subject,* usually in brief form, in order to bring the reader up to date as early as possible for a better understanding of the matter at hand. (See Stone, Lynn.)

4. *"Focusing down" to one aspect of the subject,* a technique similar to that used in some movies, showing first a broad scope (of subject area, such as a landscape) and then progressively narrowing views until the focus is on one specific thing (perhaps the name "O'Grady O'Connor" on a mailbox by a gate—or the silent sufferers on Buckley's train). (See also Rooney.)

5. *Using a pertinent rhetorical device* that will attract interest as it leads into the main exposition—e.g., an anecdote, analogy, allusion, quotation, or paradox. (See Welsch, Simpson.)

6. *Using a short but vivid comparison or contrast* to emphasize the central idea. (See Lynn.)

7. *Posing a challenging question,* the answering of which the reader will assume to be the purpose of the writing. (See Lawrence, Buczynski.)

8. *Referring to the writer's experience with the subject,* perhaps even giving a detailed account of that experience. Some writings are simply continuations of experience so introduced, perhaps with the expository purpose of making the telling entirely evident only at the end or slowly unfolding it as the account progresses. (See White, Daly.)

9. *Presenting a startling statistic or other fact* that will indicate the nature of the subject to be discussed.

10. *Making an unusual statement* that can intrigue as well as introduce. (See Wolfe, Gansberg.)

11. *Making a commonplace remark* that can draw interest because of its very commonness in sound or meaning.

Irony, in its verbal form sometimes classed as a figure of speech, consists of saying one thing on the surface but meaning exactly (or nearly) the opposite—e.g., "this beautiful neighborhood of ours" may mean that it is a dump. (For other illustrations, see Stone, Wolfe, Mitford, Walker.)

Verbal irony has a wide range of tones, from the gentle, gay, or affectionate to the sharpness of outright *sarcasm* (see Buckley), which is always intended to cut. It may consist of only a word or phrase, it may be a simple *understatement* (see Mitford), or it may be sustained as one of the major components of satire.

Irony can be an effective tool of exposition if its tone is consistent with the overall tone and if the writer is sure that the audience is bright enough to recognize it. In speech, a person usually indicates by voice or eye-expression that he is not to be taken literally; in writing, the words on the page have to speak for themselves. (See Stone for the use of parentheses to indicate ironic or humorous statements.)

In addition to verbal irony, there is also an *irony of situation,* in which there is a sharp contradiction between what is logically expected to happen and what does happen—e.g., a man sets a trap for an obnoxious neighbor and then gets caught in it himself. Or the ironic situation may simply be some discrepancy that an outsider can see while those involved cannot. (See Lawrence, pars. 11–12.)

Logical Argument (See Chapter 13.)

Loose Sentences (See *Emphasis.*)

Metaphor (See *Figures of Speech.*)

Narration (See Chapter 11.)

Objective writing and **Subjective** writing are distinguishable by the extent to which they reflect the author's personal attitudes or emotions. The difference is usually one of degree, as few writing endeavors can be completely objective or subjective.

Objective writing, seldom used in its pure form except in business or scientific reports, is impersonal and concerned almost entirely with straight narration, with logical analysis, or with the description of external appearances. (For somewhat objective writing, see Simpson; Staples, par. 1)

Subjective writing (in description called "impressionistic"—see Chapter 10) is more personalized, more expressive of the beliefs, ideals, or impressions of the author. Whereas in objective writing the emphasis is on the object being written about, in subjective writing the emphasis is on the way the author sees and interprets the object. (For some of the many examples in this book, see Twain; Lopate; Wolfe; Mitford; Welsch; Lawrence; Staples, after par. 1.)

Paradox is a statement or remark that, although seeming to be contradictory or absurd, actually contains some truth. Many paradoxical statements are also ironic.

Paragraph Unity (See *Unity.*)

Parallel Structure refers in principle to the same kind of "parallelism" that is studied in grammar: the principle that coordinate elements should have coordinate presentation, as in a pair or a series of verbs, prepositional phrases, gerunds. It is often as much a matter of "balance" as it is of parallelism.

But the principle of parallel structure, far from being just a negative "don't mix" set of rules, is also a positive rhetorical device. Many writers use it as an effective means of stressing variety of profusion in a group of nouns or modifiers, or of emphasizing parallel ideas in sentence parts, in two or more sentences, or even in two or more paragraphs. At times it can also be useful stylistically, to give a subtle poetic quality to the prose.

(For illustrations of parallel parts within a sentence, see Wolfe, pars. 1, 4; of parallel sentences themselves, see Catton, par. 14; of both parallel parts and parallel sentences, see Twain, Maynard, Viorst.)

Periodic Sentence (See *Emphasis.*)

Persona refers to a character created as the speaker in an essay or the narrator of a story. The attitudes and character of a persona often differ from those of the author, and their persona may be created as a way of submitting certain values or perspectives to examination and criticism. The speaker in Ehrenreich's "Star Dreck" is clearly a persona and advocates actions that the author would consider abhorrent if put into practice.

Personification (See *Figures of Speech.*)

Point of View in *argument* means the author's opinion on an issue or the thesis being advanced in an essay. In *exposition,* however, point of view is simply the position of the author in relation to the subject matter. Rhetorical point of view in exposition has little in common with the grammatical sort and differs somewhat from point of view in fiction.

A ranch in a mountain valley is seen differently by the ranch hand working at the corral, by the gardener deciding where to plant the petunias, by the artist or poet viewing the ranch from the mountainside, and by the geographer in a plane above, map-sketching the valley in relation to the entire range. It is the same ranch but the positions and attitudes of the viewers are different.

So it is with expository prose. The position and attitude of the author are the important lens through which the reader sees the subject. Consistency is important, because if the lens is changed without sufficient cause and explanation, the reader will become disconcerted, if not annoyed.

Obviously, since the point of view is partially a matter of attitude, the tone and often the style of writing are closely linked to it. (See *Style/Tone.*)

The expository selections in this book provide examples of numerous points of view. Twain's are those of an authority in his own fields of experience; Mitford's is as the debunking prober; Ehrenreich's is that of the angry observer of human behavior. In each of these (and the list could be extended to include all the selections in the book), the subject would seem vastly different if seen from some other point of view.

Process Analysis (See Chapter 7.)

Purpose that is clearly understood by the author before beginning to write is essential to both unity and coherence. A worthwhile practice, certainly in the training stages, is to write down the controlling purpose before even beginning to outline. Some instructors require both a statement of purpose and a statement of central theme or thesis. (See *Unity; Thesis.*)

The most basic element of a statement of purpose is the commitment to "explain" or, in some assignments, to "convince" (argument). But the statement of purpose, whether written down or only decided upon, goes further—e.g., "to argue that 'dirty words' are logically offensive because of the sources and connotations of the words themselves" (Lawrence).

Qualification is the tempering of broad statements to make them more valid and acceptable, the authors themselves admitting the probability of exceptions. This qualifying can be done inconspicuously, to whatever degree needed, by the use of *possibly, nearly always* or *most often, usually* or *frequently, sometimes* or *occasionally.* Instead of saying, "Chemistry is the most valuable field of study," it would probably be more accurate and defensible to say that it is for *some* people, or that it *can* be the most valuable.

Refutation of opposing arguments is an important element in most argumentative essays, especially where the opposition is strong enough or reasonable enough to provide a real alternative to the author's opinion. A refutation consists of a brief summary of the opposing point of view along with a discussion of its inadequacies, a discussion which often helps support the author's own thesis.

Here are three commonly used strategies for refutation:

1. *Pointing out weaknesses in evidence*—If an opposing argument is based on inaccurate, incomplete, or misleading evidence, or if the argument does not take into account some new evidence that contradicts it, then the refutation should point out these weaknesses.

2. *Pointing out errors in logic*—If an opposing argument is loosely reasoned or contains major flaws in logic, then the refutation should point these problems out to the reader.

3. *Questioning the relevance of an argument*—If an opposing argument does not directly address the issue under consideration, then the refutation should point out that even though the argument may well be correct, it is not worth considering because it is not relevant.

Refutations should always be moderate in tone and accurate in representing opposing arguments; otherwise, readers may feel that the writer has treated the opposition unfairly and as a result judge the author's own argument more harshly.

Rhetorical Questions are posed with no expectation of receiving an answer; they are merely structural devices for launching or furthering a discussion or for achieving emphasis (See Lawrence.)

Sarcasm (See *Irony.*)

Satire, sometimes called "extended irony," is a literary form that brings wit and humor to the serious task of pointing out frailties or evils of human institutions. It has thrived in Western literature since the time of the ancient Greeks, and English literature of the eighteenth century was particularly noteworthy for the extent and quality of its satire. Broadly, two types are recognized: *Horatian satire,* which is gentle, smiling, and aims to correct by invoking laughter and sympathy, and *Juvenalian* *satire,* which is sharper and points with anger, contempt, and/or moral indignation to corruption and evil.

Sentimentality, also called *sentimentalism,* is an exaggerated show of emotion, whether intentional or caused by lack of restraint. An author can sentimentalize almost any situation, but the trap is most dangerous when writing of timeworn emotional symbols or scenes—e.g., a broken heart, mother love, a lonely death, the conversion of a sinner. However sincere the author may be, if readers are not fully oriented to the worth and uniqueness of the situation described, they may be either resentful or amused at any attempt to play on their emotions. Sentimentality is, of course, one of the chief characteristics of melodrama. (For examples of writing that, less adeptly handled, could easily have slipped into sentimentality, see Buczynski, Twain, Catton, Raybon, Staples, Curtin, Simpson, Gansberg.)

Simile (See *Figures of Speech.*)

Slang (See *Colloquial Expressions.*)

Specific and **General** terms, and the distinctions between the two, are similar to concrete and abstract terms (as discussed under their own heading), and for our purpose there is no real need to keep the two sets of categories separated. Whether *corporation* is thought of as "abstract" and *Ajax Motor Company* as "concrete," or whether they are assigned to "general" and "specific" categories, the principle is the same: in most writing, *Ajax Motor Company* is better.

But "specific" and "general" are relative terms. For instance, the word *apple* is more specific than *fruit* but less so than *Winesap.* And *fruit,* as general as it certainly is in one respect, is still more specific than *food.* Such relationships are shown more clearly in a series, progressing from general to specific: *food, fruit, apple, Winesap;* or *vehicle, automobile, Ford, Mustang.* Modifiers and verbs can also have degrees of specificity: *bright, red, scarlet;* or *moved, sped, careened.* It is not difficult to see the advantages to the reader—and, of course, to the writer who needs to communicate an idea clearly—in "the scarlet Mustang careened through the pass," instead of "the bright-colored vehicle moved through the pass."

Obviously, however, there are times when the general or the abstract term or statement is essential—e.g., "A balanced diet includes some fruit," or "There was no vehicle in sight." But the use of specific language whenever possible is one of the best ways to improve diction and thus clarity and forcefulness in writing.

(Another important way of strengthening general, abstract writing is, of course, to use examples or other illustrations. See Chapter 3.)

Style and **Tone** are so closely linked and so often even elements of each other that it is best to consider them together.

But there is a difference. Think of two young men, each with his girlfriend on separate moonlit dates, whispering in nearly identical tender and loving tones of voice. One young man says, "Your eyes, dearest, reflect a thousand sparkling candles of heaven," and the other says, "Them eyes of yours—in this light—they sure do turn me on." Their *tones* were the same; their *styles* considerably different.

The same distinction exists in writing. But, naturally, with more complex subjects than the effect of moonlight on a lover's eyes, there are more complications in separating the two qualities, even for the purpose of study.

The tone is determined by the *attitude* of writers toward their subject and toward their audience. Writers, too, may be tender and loving, but they may be indignant, solemn, playful, enthusiastic, belligerent, contemptuous—the list could be as long as a list of the many "tones of voice." (In fact, wide ranges of tone may be illustrated by essays in this book. Compare, for example, those of the two parts of Twain; Viorst and Lynn; Staples and Ehrenreich.)

Style, on the other hand, expresses the author's individuality through choices of words (see *Diction*), sentence patterns (see *Syntax*), and selection and arrangement of details and basic materials. (All these elements of style are illustrated in the contrasting statements of the moonstruck lads.) These matters of style are partially prescribed, of course, by the adopted tone, but they are still bound to reflect the writer's personality and mood, education and general background.

(Some of the more distinctive styles—partially affected by and affecting tone—represented by selections in this book are those of Viorst, Wolfe, Buckley, White, Noda, Stone, Silko, Murphy, Staples, and Walker.)

Subjective Writing (See *Objective/Subjective.*)

Symbol refers to anything that although real itself also suggests something broader or more significant—not just in greater numbers, however. A person would not symbolize a group or even humankind itself, although a person might be typical or representative in one or more abstract qualities. On the most elementary level, even words are symbols—e.g., *bear* brings to mind the furry beast itself. But more important is that things, persons, or even acts may also be symbolic, if they invoke abstract concepts, values, or qualities apart from themselves or their own kind. Such symbols, in everyday life as well as in literature and the other arts, are generally classifiable according to three types, which, although terminology differs, we may label *natural, personal,* and *conventional.*

In a natural symbol, the symbolic meaning is inherent in the thing itself. The sunrise naturally suggests new beginnings to most people, an island is almost synonymous with isolation, a cannon automatically suggests war; hence these are natural symbols. It does not matter that some things, by their nature, can suggest more than one concept. Although a valley may symbolize security to one person and captivity to another, both meanings, contradictory as they might seem, are inherent, and in both respects the valley is a natural symbol.

The personal symbol, depending as it does on private experience or perception, is meaningless to others unless they are told about it or allowed to see its significance in context (as in literature). Although the color green may symbolize the outdoor life to the farm boy trapped in the gray city (in this respect perhaps a natural symbol), it can also symbolize romance to the young woman proposed to while wearing her green blouse, or dismal poverty to the woman who grew up in a weathered green shanty; neither of these meanings is suggested by something *inherent* in the color green, so they are personal symbols. Anything at all could take on private symbolic meaning, even the odor of marigolds or the sound of a lawnmower. The sunrise itself could mean utter despair, instead of fresh opportunities, to the man who has long despised his daily job and cannot find another.

Conventional symbols usually started as personal symbols, but continued usage in life or art permits them to be generally recognized for their broader meanings, which depend on custom rather than any inherent quality—e.g., the olive branch for peace, the flag for love of country, the cross for Christianity, the raised fist for revolutionary power.

Symbols are used less in expository and argumentative writing than in fiction and poetry, but a few authors represented in this book have either referred to the subtle symbolism of others or made use of it in developing their own ideas.

Syntax is a very broad term—too broad, perhaps, to be very useful—referring to the arrangement of words in a sentence. Good syntax implies the use not only of correct grammar but also of effective patterns. These patterns depend on sentences with good unity, coherence, and emphasis, on the use of subordination and parallel construction as appropriate, on economy, and on a consistent and interesting point of view. A pleasing variety of sentence patterns is also important in achieving effective syntax.

Theme (See *Unity.*)

Thesis In an argumentative essay, the central theme is often referred to as the thesis, and to make sure that readers recognize it, the thesis is often summed up briefly in a *thesis statement.* In a very important sense, the thesis is the center of an argument because the whole essay is designed to make the reader agree with it and, hence, with the author's opinion. (See *Unity.*)

Tone (See *Style/Tone.*)

Transition is the relating of one topic to the next, and smooth transition is an important aid to the coherence of a sentence, a paragraph, or an entire piece of writing. (See *Coherence.*)

The most effective coherence, of course, comes about naturally with sound development of ideas, one growing logically into the next—and that depends on sound organization. But sometimes beneficial even in this situation, particularly in going from one paragraph to the next, is the use of appropriate transitional devices.

Readers are apt to be sensitive creatures, easy to lose. (And, of course, the writers are the real losers since they are the ones who presumably have something they want to communicate.) If the readers get into a new paragraph and the territory seems familiar, chances are that they will continue. But if there are no identifying landmarks, they will often begin to feel uneasy and will either start worrying about their slow comprehension or take a dislike to the author and the subject matter. Either way, a communication block arises, and very likely the author will soon have fewer readers.

A good policy, then, unless the progression of ideas is exceptionally smooth and obvious, is to provide some kind of familiar identification early in the new paragraph, to keep the reader feeling at ease with the different ideas. The effect is subtle but important. These familiar landmarks or transitional devices are sometimes applied deliberately but more often come naturally, especially when the prospective reader is kept constantly in mind at the time of writing.

An equally important reason for using some kinds of transitional devices, however, is a logical one: while functioning as bridges between ideas, they also assist the basic organization by pointing out the *relationship* of the ideas—and thus contributing still further to readability.

Transitional devices useful for bridging paragraph changes (and, some of them, to improve transitional flow within paragraphs) may be roughly classified as follows:

1. *Providing an "echo"* from the preceding paragraph. This may be the repetition of a key phrase or word, or a pronoun referring back to such a word, or a casual reference to an idea. (See Lopate, last two paragraphs; Wolfe, especially from pars. 1 to 2 and 4 to 5; Mitford.) Such an echo cannot be superimposed on new ideas, but must, by careful planning, be made an organic part of them.

2. *Devising a whole sentence or paragraph* to bridge other important paragraphs or major divisions. (See Lynn, pars. 11, 20, and 21.)

3. *Using parallel structure* in an important sentence of one paragraph and the first sentence of the next. This is a subtle means of making the reader feel at ease in the new surroundings, but it is seldom used because it is much more limited in its potential than the other methods of transition. (See Lawrence, pars. 1 to 2.)

4. *Using standard transitional expressions,* most of which have the additional advantage of indicating relationship of ideas. Only a few of those available are classified below, but nearly all the selections in this book amply illustrate such transitional expressions:

Time—soon, immediately, afterward, later, meanwhile, after a while.
Place—nearby, here, beyond, opposite.
Result—as a result, therefore, thus, consequently, hence.
Comparison—likewise, similarly, in such a manner.
Contrast—however, nevertheless, still, but, yet, on the other hand, after all, otherwise.
Addition—also, too, and, and then, furthermore, moreover, finally, first, second, third.
Miscellaneous—for example, for instance, in fact, indeed, on the whole, in other words.

Trite (See *Clichés.*)

Unity in writing is the same as unity in anything else—in a picture, a musical arrangement, a campus organization—and that is a *one*-ness, in which all parts contribute to an overall effect.

Many elements of good writing contribute in varying degrees to the effect of unity. Some of these are properly designed introductions and closings; consistency in point of view, tone, and style; sometimes the recurring use of analogy or thread of symbolism; occasionally the natural time boundaries of an experience or event, as in the selections of Mitford, Simpson, Gansberg, Orwell, and Williams.

But in most expository and argumentative writing the only dependable unifying force is the *central theme,* which every sentence, every word, must somehow help to support. (The central theme is also called the *central idea* or the *thesis* when pertaining to the entire writing and is almost always called the *thesis* in argument. In an expository or argumentative paragraph it is the same as the *topic sentence,* which may be implied or, if stated, may be located anywhere in the paragraph, but is usually placed first.) As soon as anything appears that is not related to the central idea, there are *two* units instead of one. Hence unity is basic to all other virtues of good writing, even to coherence and emphasis, the other two organic essentials. (See *Coherence; Emphasis.*)

An example of unity may be found in a single river system (for a practical use of analogy), with all its tributaries, big or little, meandering or straight, flowing into the main stream and making it bigger—or at least flowing into another tributary that finds its way to the main stream. This is *one* river system, an example of unity. Now picture another stream nearby that does not empty into the river but goes off in some other direction. There are now two systems, not one, and there is no longer unity.

It is the same way with writing. The central theme is the main river, flowing along from the first capital letter to the last period. Every drop of information or evidence must find its way into this theme-river, or it is not a part of the system. It matters not even slightly if the water is good, the idea-stream perhaps deeper and finer than any of the others: if it is not a tributary, it has no business pretending to be relevant to *this* theme of writing.

And that is why most students are required to state their central idea or thesis, usually in solid sentence form, before even starting to organize their ideas. If the writer can use only tributaries, it is very important to know from the start just what the river is.

Credits

Margaret Atwood, "Pornography" from *Chatelaine Magazine*. Copyright (c) 1983 by Margaret Atwood. Reprinted by permission of Phoebe Larmore, Literary Agent.

Amy Bell, "Perception of Truth" from *A Student's Guide to First-Year Composition*, 20th Edition. Reprinted by permission of the author.

John Berendt, "The Hoax" from *Esquire*, April,1994. Reprinted by permission of International Creative Management, Inc. Copyright (c) 1994.

Adrian Boykin, "Overcoming an Impediment: A Rite of Passage" from *A Student's Guide to First-Year English*, 10th edition. Reprinted by permission.

William F. Buckley, Jr, "Why Don't We Complain?" Copyright (c) 1960 by William F. Buckley, Jr. Reprinted by permission of The Wallace Literary Agency, Inc.

Mark Buczynski, "About Men: Iron Bonding" from *The New York Times*, 7/19/92. Copyright (c) 1992 by *The New York Times*. Reprinted by permission.

Joe Buhler and Ron Graham, "Give Juggling a Hand" from *The Sciences*, January/February 1984. Reprinted by permission of *The Sciences*.

Stephen Carter, "The Insufficiency of Honesty" from *The Atlantic Monthly*, February 1996. Copyright (c) 1996 by Stephen Carter. Reprinted by permission of the author.

Bruce Catton, "Grant and Lee: A Study in Contrasts" from *The American Story*, Earl Schenck Miers, editor. Copyright (c) 1956 by Broadcast Music, Inc. Copyright Renewed, 1984. Reprinted by permission of the U.S. Capitol Historical Society.

Veronica Chambers, "A Mother's Day Present" from *Mama's Girl*. Copyright (c) 1996 by Veronica Chambers. Reprinted by permission of Riverhead Books, a division of Penguin Putnam Inc.

Edie Clark, "Ice Flowers" from *Yankee Magazine*. Reprinted by permission of *Yankee Magazine*.

691

Index